Bhaktivinoda Vāṇī Vaibhava

That day is not far distant when the priceless volumes penned by Ṭhākura Bhaktivinoda will be reverently translated, by the recipients of his grace, into all the languages of the world.

-(Śrīla Bhaktisiddhānta Sarasvatī Ṭhākura)

Other Publications by Touchstone Media:

Gītā Mahātmya and Śrīmad-Bhāgavatam Mahātmya
Prārthanā
Śrī Prema Bhakti-candrika
Sārvabhauma Śataka
Hari Bhakti Kalpa Latika
Śrī Nityānanda-caritāmṛta
Pada Sevana
Sweet Pastimes of Damodara
The Dog and the Wolf
Great Heroes of the Mahabharata Series
Krishna Pocket Guide
Amṛta Vāṇī
Śrī Prema Vilasa
Uddhava Gītā
Adventures of India Series
Śrī Krishna Vijaya
Mahābharata
Bhagavad-gītā at a Glance
Vrindāvana, the Playground of God

If you are interested in the purchasing or the distribution of this book or any of the above publications, you may contact:

Touchstone Media
Block EC 178Sector 1, Salt Lake, Kolkata 700064, INDIA

www.touchstonemedia.com
e-mail : info@touchstonemedia.com

TOUCHSTONE
MEDIA
Matter for the Soul

ŚRĪ ŚRĪ GURU-GAURĀṄGAU JAYATĀḤ

Śrī Bhaktivinoda Vāṇī Vaibhava

Divine Opulence of the Teachings of Śrīla Bhaktivinoda Ṭhākura

Complete Edition Featuring Sambandha, Abhidheya and Prayojana

Compiled under the direct order of
His Divine Grace
Bhaktisiddhānta Sarasvatī Ṭhākura Prabhupāda

by
Śrīpāda Sundarānanda Vidyāvinoda

Produced and Published by Īśvara dāsa
Translated by Bhumipati dāsa

Śrī Bhaktivinoda Vāṇī Vaibhava

Compiled under the direct order of His Divine Grace
Bhaktisiddhānta Sarasvatī Ṭhākura Prabhupāda
by Śrīpāda Sundarānanda Vidyāvinoda
Produced and published by Īśvara dāsa
Translated by Bhumipati dāsa
Edited by Īśodyānā devī dāsī
Typed by Caitanya devī dāsī
Proofreading by Krishna-kṛpa dāsa
Design and layout by Īśvara dāsa
Cover painting by Saccitānanda dāsa

Dedicated to
His Divine Grace
A. C. Bhaktivedānta Swami Prabhupāda
Founder - *Ācārya* International Society for Krishna Consciousness,
who fulfilled the predictions of Śrīla Bhaktivinoda Ṭhākura
by making Krishna consciousness available to the entire world.

Foreword

Once upon a time – or in a moment that transcends time – The great Gaudiya Vaiṣṇava teacher Śrīla Bhaktisiddhānta Sarasvati Ṭhākura instructed one of his more academically gifted disciples to write a book that would sum up the vast and profound teachings of Krishna Consciousness. The disciple was Sundarānanda Vidyāvinoda, who was specifically asked to accomplish this task by quoting only from the work of Śrīla Bhaktivinoda Ṭhākura, Bhaktisiddhānta's father and intimate spiritual advisor. Bhaktivinoda, in many ways, was the first to express the rich Gaudiya theological system in modern language, both in his native Bengali and in English. He is also renowned as the systematizer of the tradition for the contemporary world. Moreover, he is revered in his lineage as a singularly empowered individual, whose writings are on an equal footing with sacred scripture. The eager Sundarānanda thus took his Master's mandate to heart, and the result is the book you now hold in your hands, *Bhaktivinoda Vāṇī Vaibhava*.

Many words and precious time have been wasted on detailing Sundarānanda's strained relationship with the Gaudiya Math, and this is not the place to belabor the issue. Suffice it to say that Sundarānanda's books speak for themselves, and their analysis of Gaudiya philosophy is deep and penetrating. A few of his titles should be known: *Śrī Kṣetra*, *Acintya Bhedābheda*, *Gaudiyera Tin Ṭhākura*, *Gaudiya Vaiṣṇava Siddhāntera Itihasa*, *Harināma-cintamani-kiraṇa-lesh*, among other's. While there may be points of detail in some of these works that differ from the common understanding of Gaudiya Math devotees, overall they bear the same message of Krishna-*bhakti*, and they explain the science of love of God with exacting detail. And we must consider Sundarānanda's other services: For many years he was Śrīla Bhaktisiddhānta's chief editor and a respected intellectual in his movement. He was trusted enough to be given Bhaktivinoda's autobiography for editing purposes, which is something Bhaktisiddhānta would not allow anyone else to do.

Sundarānanda was clearly not an ordinary personality. Further proof of this can be found in a thorough reading of *Bhaktivinoda Vaṇi Vaibhava*, which systematically conveys"the power of Bhaktivinoda's teachings," as the title suggests. Originally written in Bengali, the work is a veritable encyclopedia of knowledge, revealing both general information about spiritual life and intimate details of Gaudiya *siddhānta*. Sundarānanda draws on works ranging from Bhaktivinoda's autobiography to the Ṭhākura's novels and more *saṣtra*-like literature. What's more, he adopts Bhaktivinoda's frequent style of presenting detailed information in the easy-to-read format of questions and answers: Sundarānanda composed the questions and then allowed Bhaktivinoda himself to answer by quoting the Ṭhākura's various books.

Sundarānanda also divides the book into *sambandha* (the path), *abhidheya* (the means), and *prayojana* (the goal), which are themes Bhaktivinoda uses in many of his own works, such as *Jaiva Dharma*, *Kalyāna Kalpa-taru*, and so on. In doing this, both authors follow much of the traditional literature of their lineage. For example, Jīva Goswami's *Sat-sandarbha* is expressed in terms of *sambandha*, *abhidheya* and *prayojana*, and, in fact, the entire gamut of Vedic literature subscribes to this format, either directly or indirectly. As Kavirāja Goswami says in his *Caitanya Caritāmṛta*:"The Vedic literature gives information about the living entity's eternal relationship with Krishna, which is called *sambandha*. The living entity's understanding of this relationship and acting accordingly is called *abhidheya*. Returning home, back to Godhead, is the ultimate goal of life and is called *prayojana*. These are the three subject-matters of these books of knowledge."

His Grace Bhumipati dāsa, the translator, and Īśvara dāsa, the publisher and organizer of this great effort, have done an invaluable service to the modern world by presenting this book in English – in the spirit of Bhaktivinoda Ṭhākura. The first volume (*Sambandha*), presumably one of three, covers such subjects as the Vedic literature, spiritual lineage, the spiritual master, sacred space, God, His associates, and so on. The volume is made even more precious by including a brief life of the Ṭhākura, and a list of his literary accomplishments. In conclusion, then, we find that Bhaktivinoda, Bhaktisiddhānta, Sundarānanda, Bhumipati, and Īśvara have, in a sense, worked together to produce an ocean of transcendental nectar. If one plies this ocean properly, one will emerge in Vṛndāvana, the holy land of Krishna, where Bhaktivinoda now serves as Kamala Mañjarī, a maidservant of Śrī Rādhā. And by giving keen attention to the teachings of this book, one can begin to assist him in his service to that best of *gopīs*.

*Satyarāja dāsa (Steven J. Rosen) is the author of twenty books on Vaiṣṇavism and related subjects. He is also the senior editor of the *Journal of Vaiṣṇava Studies*, an academic quarterly esteemed by scholars around the world.

Contents

ABHIDHEYA

PRAYOJANA

Introduction

Vasudeva Ghosa, one of the associates of Śrī Caitanya, composed the following prayer:

yadi gaura na hoito, tabe ki hoito,
kemone dharitam de
rādhār mahima, prema-rāsa-sima,
jagate janato ke

"If Lord Gaura had not appeared as the yuga avatar in this age of Kali, then what would have become of us? How could we have tolerated living? Who in this universe would have learned about the topmost limits of loving mellows that comprise the glory of Śrī Rādhā?"

madhura vṛnda, vipina-madhuri,
praveṣa caturi sar
baraja-yuvati, bhaver bhakati,
sakati hoito kar

"Who would have had the power to render ecstatic devotional service that follows in the footsteps of the damsels of Vraja? Indeed, the clever expertise of the Vraja-gopis is a prerequisite for entering the supremely sweet forest of Vṛnda-devī."

The above verses could rightly be applied to Śrīla Bhaktivinoda Ṭhākura. If he had not appeared and mercifully made the teachings of Śrī Gaurāṅga Mahāprabhu available to the world, Vaisnavism or the true worship of Lord Kṛṣna, as enunciated in the *Bhagavad-gītā* and *Śrīmad-Bhāgavatam* would not be present today.

Śrīla Bhkativinoda Ṭhākura was the seventh Goswami. The famous six Goswamis of Vṛndāvana were directly ordered by Lord Caitanya

Mahāprabhu to spread Lord Krishna's teachings for the benefit of the conditioned souls were bereft of the loving devotional service unto the Supreme Lord.

Sisira Kumara Ghoṣa, an intellectual and a contemporary of Śrīla Bhaktivinoda Ṭhākura wrote in one of his letters to the Ṭhākura, "I have not seen the six Goswamis of Vṛndāvana, but I considered you the seventh Goswami." Śrīla Bhaktivinoda Ṭhākura's literary contribution to the Gaudiya Vaiṣṇavas' philosophy and practice can only be compared to the works of the famed six Goswamis. Śrīla Bhaktivinoda Ṭhākura was single-handedly responsible for re-establishing Lord Chaitanya's *sankīrtana* movement, which had almost been lost by the mid-nineteenth century due to the unscrupulous practices of pseudo Vaiṣṇavas (*sahajiyas*). The sahajiya movement had perverted the purity of the mission, the mission thus became degenerated as a result. This degeneration continued up till the British rule of India. However Śrīla Bhaktivinoda Ṭhākura worked tirelessly to restore the Vaiṣṇava creed's purity, dignity, and respectabiliy among the cultured elite of his day. He also sowed the seed for the future worldwide propagation of Lord Caitanya's movement.

In 1896, he sent a copy of his small book, "*Caitanya Mahāprabhu, His Life and Precepts*," to the library of the Royal Asiatic Society in London and to McGill University of Canada, as well as several foreign institutions. That same glorious year, His Divine Grace A.C. Bhaktivedanta Swami Prabhupāda, the greatest exponent of the modern day Krishna consciousness movement, was born.

Much has been written on Śrīla Bhaktivinoda Ṭhākura's unique contribution. Today, in every continent of the world, the holy name of Kṛṣna is being chanted due to the seed of *Kṛṣna-bhakti* planted by him.

Śrīla Bhaktivinoda Ṭhākura, the divine potency of Śrī Gaurāṅga Mahāprabhu (gaura-śakti), graciously came to this material world. He was attracted by the sufferings of the conditioned living entities, who were bereft of the nectar obtained by rendering devotional service unto Śrī Śrī Rādhā-Kṛṣna. Due to his magnanimity, he gave his mercy to the world by personally revealing his own supereminence as the personification of the mercy-potency of Śrī Gaurāṅga.

Śrīla Bhaktisiddhanta Śarasvatī Ṭhākura wrote:

"We avail of the opportunity offered by the Anniversary Celebrations of the advent of Ṭhākura Bhaktivinoda to reflect on the right method of obtaining those benefits that have been made accessible to humanity by the grace of this great devotee of Krishna. Ṭhākura Bhaktivinoda has been specifically kind to those unfortunate persons who are engrossed in mental speculation of all kinds. This is the prevalent malady of the present age. The other *ācāryas* who appeared before Ṭhākura Bhaktivinoda did not address their discourses so directly to the empiric thinkers. They had been more merciful to those who are naturally disposed to listen to discourses on the Absolute without being dissuaded by the spurious arguments of avowed opponents of Godhead.

"Śrīla Ṭhākura Bhaktivinoda has taken the trouble of meeting the perverse arguments of mental speculators by the superior transcendental logic of the Absolute Truth. It is thus possible for the average modern readers to profit by the perusal of his writings. That day is not far distant when the priceless volumes penned by Ṭhākura Bhaktivinoda will be reverently translated, by the recipients of his grace, into all the languages of the world.

"The writings of Ṭhākura Bhaktivinoda provide the golden bridge by which the mental speculators can safely cross the raging waters of fruitless empiric controversies that trouble the peace of those who choose to trust in their guidance for finding the Truth. As soon as the sympathetic reader is in a position to appreciate the sterling quality of Ṭhākura Bhaktivinoda's philosophy the entire vista of the revealed literatures of the world will automatically open out to his reclaimed vision."

This book has been collected from many wonderful jewels of the literary ocean of Oṁ Viṣṇupāda Śrīla Bhaktivinoda Ṭhākura Mahaṣaya, and includes his essays, stories, novels, books, songs, and poems. Śrīla Bhaktisiddhānta Sarasvati Ṭhākura Prabhupāda ordered one of his foremost disciples, Śrīpāda Sundarānanda Vidyavinoda Prabhu, a staunch follower of Śrīla Bhaktivinoda's instructions, to compile this book.

This book is in three sections: one's relationship with the Lord, the process for achieving the goal of life, and the ultimate goal of life. It contains one hundred and eight chapters and has become more attractive, because the teachings and conclusions of Śrīla Bhaktivinoda Ṭhākura are presented in the form of questions and answers. The perfect answers for all questions of the practioners of *bhakti* are thus provided in this book.

Śrīla Ṭhākura Bhaktivinoda is always manifest to the unduplicitous devotees in the form of his teachings. Sincere readers can find Śrī Gaurasundara in *Siksaṣṭaka*, Śrī Rupa Goswami in *Bhakti-rasāmṛta-sindhu*, Śrī Sanatana Goswami in *Bṛhād-bhāgavatāmṛta* and *Vaiṣṇava-toṣani*, Śrī Raghunatha dāsa Goswami in *Stavavali*, Śrī Jīva Goswami in *Sat-sandarbha*, Śrī Kṛṣnadasa Kavirāja Goswami in *Śrī Caitanya-caritāmṛta* and *Śrī Govinda-lilāmṛta*, Śrī Narottama dāsa Ṭhākura in *Pra-*

rthana and *Prema-bhakti-chandrika*, Śrī Visvanātha Cakravārtī Ṭhākura in his commentary on *Śrīmad-Bhāgavatam* and *Bhāgavad-gītā*. Similarly surrendered and sincere persons can find Śrīla Ṭhākura Bhaktivinoda within his books. The transcendental teachings of Śrīla Ṭhākura Bhaktivinoda are the teachings of Śrī Caitanya, Śrī Śvārūpa Damodara, Śrī Sanātana, Śrī Raghunātha, Śrī Jīva, Śrī Kavirāja, and Śrī Narottama dāsa Ṭhākura.

What is *Bhaktivinoda Vaṇi Vaibhava*? The word *vaibhava* is derived from the word *vibhu*. The meanings of the word *vaibhava* are divinity, extraordinary ability, incarnation, and might. Since the teachings of Śrīla Bhaktivinoda are fully in accordance with the teachings of Śrī Gaura, Rūpa, and Raghunātha, they are automatically divinely powerful and glorious. The teachings of Śrīla Bhaktivinoda are scientific, all-pervading, and full of bliss, glories, wealth, potencies, and unlimited energies. Another meaning of the word vibhu is self-satisfied. Śrīla Bhaktivinoda was fully self-satisfied and a *rasika* devotee.

The opulence of Śrīla Bhaktivinoda is the teachings and knowledge of Śrī Caitanyadeva, which gave him immense pleasure. This book has been compiled with a desire to guide the hearts of the surrendered souls toward the holy names, abode, and activities of Śrī Gaurāṅga. The opulence and glories of Śrī Bhaktivinoda's teachings are not temporary like material opulence. Śrīla Bhaktisiddhanta Sarasvati Prabhupāda said:"The Vaiṣṇavas also possess fame, but it is never temporary material fame."

If one worships a Vaiṣṇava's activities, glories, and opulence, one will achieve auspiciousness. However, if one becomes envious of a Vaiṣṇava's activities, glories, and opulence, one can never achieve any auspiciousness. Śrīla Bhaktisiddhanta Sarasvati Prabhupāda therefore sang:"The tree of material fame is illusory just like water in a desert. Although Ravana fought with Rama, he could not accomplish anything."

Śrī Bhaktivinoda Vaṇi Vaibhava has manifested in this world to attract faithful and surrendered souls toward the *sankīrtana* movement of Śrī Gaurasundara. If one relishes even a single drop from the ocean of these divine teachings, one's dormant propensity to cultivate of Kṛṣna consciousness will certainly awaken.

We should not simply become satisfied by praising or buying this book as a matter of formality, like proud, foolish, ordinary people. Rather, our only duty is to express our gratitude and pray at the feet of Śrī *Bhaktivinoda Vaṇi Vaibhava* without any duplicity so that the divine teachings will be established within our hearts under the subordination of Śrī Guru and the Vaiṣṇavas.

Śrīla Bhaktivinoda Ṭhākura took pleasure in preaching, and he was unique in feeling distress on seeing other's' distress. Out of his causeless mercy, he generously distributed many invaluable jewels with his vast range of literature for the benefit of the fallen conditioned souls.

Krishna conciousness is a dynamic process. Understanding and applying it guarantees that we will one day develop love of God. Thus Vaiṣṇava masters have written tremendous amount of literature to explainthe Krishna conscious process. They have divided Krishna conscious practice into three levels; *sambandha, abhidheya,* and *prayojana.* Sambandha refers to understanding one's eternal relationship with the Supreme Lord and His creations, abhidheya refers to the practical aspects of developing that relationship, and *prayojana* refers to the achievement of the goal of life, love of God. All *Gaudiya* teachers recognize these three conceptions and have based their teachings upon them. Thus this book, *Śrī Bhaktivinoda Vaṇi Vaibhava* is divided into three sections following the same.

Śrīla Bhaktivinoda Ṭhākura wrote more than one hundred volumes of devotional literature during his life. His books are as good as Vedic scriptures, and one can develop pure devotion to the Lord by absorbing and applying his teachings. But in this age, we seem to have little time to study religious texts, and so little capacity to understand the vast teachings of the scriptures. Therefore great personality, Sundarananda Vidyavinoda Prabhu, one of Śrīla Bhaktisiddhanta Sarasvati Ṭhākura's prominent disciples, made a deep study of all the writings of Śrīla Bhaktivinoda Ṭhākura, and on the order of his spiritual master, composed questions related to sambandha, abhidheya, and *prayojana.* He then answered those questions by drawing directly from the writings of Śrīla Bhaktivinoda Ṭhākura.

We are eternally grateful to Śrīpada Sundarananda Vidyavinoda Prabhu for his great effort in studying and mastering the writings and teachings of Śrīla Bhaktivinoda Ṭhākura and presenting them in this format.

Śrīpada Sundarananda Vidyavinoda Prabhu himself wrote as follows:

"I had the good fortune to hear from a few constant associates of Śrīla Bhaktivinoda Ṭhākura that he ordered his instructions to be spread all over the world in various languages. A number of times Śrīla Bhaktisiddhanta Sarasvati Goswami Prabhupāda, who was not different from Śrīla Bhaktivinoda Ṭhākura, directly ordered me, an insignificant creature, to carefully collect all the jewel-like instructions of Śrīla Bhaktivinoda Ṭhākura and distribute them to the people of the world. To purify myself, I took up his order, and under the subordination of the Vaiṣṇavas, I have endeavored to compile this book."

In conclusion, we pray at the lotus feet of Śrī Bhaktivinoda Ṭhākura that his instructions may uproot the weeds around the creeper of devotional service and allow us to enter into the *sankīrtana* movement of Śrī Gaurāṅga Mahāprabhu.

Praying to be the servant of the servant of the servant of those who are trying to serve the Lord,

Revision completed June, 2011

Īśvara dāsa

Mayapura, India.

A Glimpse into the Life of Śrīla Bhaktivinoda Ṭhākura

Much had been written on the life and teachings of Śrīla Saccidananda Bhaktivinoda Ṭhākura. Just as less intelligent, mundane persons cannot understand the birth and activities of Lord Kṛṣna, similarly the life and activities of a pure devotee of the Lord cannot be understood by mundane intelligence. Sometimes the account of the life and activities of great devotees are bewildering for the nondevotees, because they cannot comprehend how a devotee of Kṛṣna could seem to be an ordinary person. But such are the ways of the Lord. He makes His activities and the activities of His pure devotees bewildering for those who are not devoted to Him.

Śrīla Bhaktivinoda Ṭhākura was responsible for re-establishing Śrī Caitanya Mahāprabhu's san*kīrtana* movement, which had become almost extinct by the mid-nineteenth century. The mission had deteriorated greatly, due to the influence of the sahajiyas and later the British rule in India. Through his tireless efforts, however, the Ṭhākura restored the purity, prestige, and respect of the Vaisnavism amongst the cultured people of his day. He also sowed the seeds for future worldwide propagation of the mission.

Śrīla Bhaktivinoda Ṭhākura was born on Sunday, September 2, 1838 in the wealthy Datta family in the ancient village of Ulanagara and was given the name Kedaranath. From early childhood, he was attracted to hearing about Rāma and Krishna. He loved to hear the recitation of Rāmayana and Mahābharata at festival times. The village Ulanagara, was very prosperous in those days.

At the age of seven, he excelled in reading Bengali and studying mathematics. That year, his elder brother and his maternal uncle both passed away. The following year, his two younger brothers also met their death, and he was obliged to experience the pain of this temporary material world. At nine, he studied astrology. The family fortunes, however, began to decline, and at the age of eleven, his father died. Young Kedaranath began to question,"What is this world? Who are we?"

At twelve, his mother arranged his marriage to a five-year-old girl. His mother hoped to improve the family finances by this arrangement. At fourteen, his uncle brought him to Calcutta to further his education. In his first year at the Hindu Charitable Institution School, he took top honors in the examinations and received a medal. He began to contribute articles to the Literary Gazette, and at eighteen he completed an epic poem called *The Poriade* in two volumes.

He spent his college years studying world religions and the works of western philosophers. He read the Bible and the Koran. He soon became known as a great debater and logician, and gave lectures in Calcutta.

In 1856, he returned to Ulanagara. There had been an outbreak of cholera. The village was empty and hundreds of people he knew had died, including his sister. His wife had also been ill, but she recovered and lived with her father. Kedarnatha took his mother and grandmother to live with him in Calcutta. At nineteen, his first job was teaching second grade at the Hindu Charitable Institution School for fifteen rupees a month, but he could not meet expenses. His mother had to sell a gold necklace to pay the back rent.

In 1858, a letter arrived with word that his paternal grandfather was about to leave this world and wished to see him before dying. He set out with his wife and mother. The old man appeared healthy on arrival. He was sitting on a bed in the courtyard of his house, leaning against a bolster pillow, and chanting the holy name continuously. Śrīla Bhaktivinoda described the incident in his autobiography, which he wrote as a letter in 1896.

"He called for me and said, 'After my death, do not tarry many days in this place. Whatever work you do by the age of twenty-seven will be your principal occupation. You will become a great Vaiṣṇava. I give you all my blessings.' Immediately after saying this, his life left him, bursting out from the top of his head. Such an amazing death is rarely seen."

Thereafter, he took his wife and mother to Cuttack and lived comfortably on a sixth grade teacher's salary of twenty rupees a month. In 1860, he moved his family to Bhadrak taking the position of headmaster for forty-five rupees a month. A year later, he took another position in Midnapur. There, he developed a desire to read *Caitanya Caritāmṛta.*

"I developed a feeling for pure *bhakti*, but I did not begin to practice it. While I was at the school in Midnapur I decided that I would obtain and read books on the Vaiṣṇava *dharma*. There was a Jati Vaiṣṇava pandita at the school. I learned from talking to him how Caitanya Mahāprabhu preached the Vaiṣṇava *dharma* in Bengal, and that the history and teachings of Caitanya were recorded in the book known as Caitanya Caritāmṛta. I began to search, but I could not secure a copy of the Caitanya Caritāmṛta. I had faith that by reading that book I would achieve happiness, but Vaiṣṇava books were not in print then."

Toward the end of 1861, his wife became ill and died, leaving him with a ten-month-old son."I endured this grief like a warrior according to the Psalm of Life." His mother tried to raise the child, but she was too old and found it difficult. Two months later, he married Śrīmati Bhagavati Devī, a sincere Vaisnavi of noble character, peaceful, and accomplished in all she did.

In 1863, he wrote two poems that were published in the prestigious Calcutta Review, volume 39. He was highly praised for this work. He was then the Head Clerk at the Judge's Court in Chuadanga on a salary of 150 rupees a month, and passed the law examination. In 1866, he accepted the position of Special Deputy Registrar of Assurances with powers of a Deputy Magistrate and Deputy Collector. He was twenty-seven years old!

He took his first tour of Vṛndāvana later that year and visited other holy places including Mathura, Prayaga, and Kasi. In March of 1868, he finally obtained a copy of *Caitanya Caritāmṛta* at Dinajpur, where he was appointed Deputy Magistrate.

"On my first reading of *Caitanya Caritāmṛta* I developed some faith in Śrī Caitanya. On the second reading, I understood that there was no pandita equal to Śrī Caitanya. Then I had a doubt. Being such a learned scholar, and having manifested the reality of love of Godhead to such an extent, how is it that He recommends the worship of the improper character of Kṛṣna? I was initially amazed at this, and I thought about it deeply. Afterwards, I prayed to the Lord with great humility. 'O Lord! Please let me understand the mystery of this matter.' The mercy of God is without limit. Seeing my eagerness and humbleness, within a few days He bestowed his mercy upon me and supplied the intelligence by which I could understand. I then understood that the truth of Kṛṣna is very deep and confidential and the highest principle of the science of Godhead. From this time on, I knew God as Śrī Caitanya Mahāprabhu. I made an effort to always speak with renounced Vaiṣṇava *panditas*, and I came to understand many aspects of the *Vaiṣṇava dharma*. In my very childhood, the seed of faith in the Vaiṣṇava religion was planted in my heart, and now it had sprouted. From the beginning, I experienced anuraga, and it was very wonderful. Day and night I liked to read about *kṛṣna-tattva*."

Shortly thereafter, out of ecstatic feeling for Lord Caitanya, Bhaktivinoda wrote a short poem, called "*Sac-cid-ananda-premalankara*." From that time, he became known as *Sac-cid-ananda* — one who embodies eternity, knowledge, and bliss.

Here we see Lord Caitanya reawakening the feelings of devotion in Śrīla Bhaktivinoda; they had been kept hidden to allow the Ṭhākura to establish himself within the British Raja. At this time, his spiritual mission began to manifest. Like Arjuna, it was for the benefit of all that came after him.

In 1869, he gave a lecture in Dinajpur to many learned gentlemen of religion and culture, who had come from all over India. Some interested Englishmen also attended. This speech later took the form of a book: *The Bhagavat: Its Philosophy, Its Ethics and Its Theology*. In this talk, he criticized the sectarianism that characterizes the religious strife between men. He also recounted his own history as a sectarian thinker who ignored the beauty of the *Bhāgavatam* due to early prejudices imbibed from the English. He presented himself as a sectarian thinker who had his eyes opened by Śrī Caitanya. He glorified the *Bhāgavatam*, and finally he explained the mysterious nature of Krishna's dalliances with the gopis, enlightening the audience with its profound universal meaning.

What better person could Lord Caitanya choose to preach to the intelligentsia of his day than the Ṭhākura? He was fully conversant with the burning issues of the times, well studied in the major philosophies and religions of the world, and was a highly respectable figure in both Hindu and English circles. His opinions were seriously heard by both camps.

In 1871 he moved to Purī and took up the study of the Goswami's literature while serving there as Chief Magistrate. Inspired by the holy dhama, he composed two English poems. The first, on Śrīla Haridasa Ṭhākura's *samadhi*, contains one of his most famous verses:

He reasons ill who tells that Vaiṣṇavas die
When thou art living still in sound.
The Vaiṣṇavas die to live, and living try
To spread holy name around.

The Ṭhākura's heart was overflowing with deep spiritual emotions as he visited the holy sites of Mahāprabhu's pastimes. In his second poem, *Saragrahi Vaiṣṇava*, Verse twenty-two, he described the futility of material aspirations for sense pleasures, and the soul's journey to the eternal spiritual realm.

There rests my Soul from matter free
Upon my Lover's arms,

Eternal peace and Spirit's love
Are all my chanting charms!

The same year he wrote an essay To Love God, wherein he gave a deep purport to the commandment of Jesus Christ;"Love the Lord thy God with all thy heart, with all thy mind, with all thy soul, and with all thy strength, and love thy neighbor as thy self." He compared this commandment to the teachings of Vaisnavism, demonstrating how Śrī Caitanya further broadcast the teachings of Jesus Christ.

Within the first year of the Ṭhākura's stay in Purī, the British asked him to watch over the affairs of the Jagannātha Temple on behalf of the government. Due to his untiring work, many bad practices at the temple were curbed, and the offerings to the Lord were punctual.

As the magistrate for Purī, he arrested a scoundrel yogi called Bisakisen, who possessed mystic powers and proclaimed himself the incarnation of Mahā-Viṣṇu. Fearing his mystic powers, the foolish people of the locality had succumbed to him. The people of nearby villages were outraged by the yogi's affairs with married women and were anxious that this fever might spread to the women of their own villages, resulting in scandal and humiliation.

Bhaktivinoda apprehended the yogi and held him in jail for trial. Fasting from food and drink, the yogi increased his mystic potency to inflict hardship on the Ṭhākura's family.

"All over Purī there were disturbances. At that time, the Purī School had a fire, and all of the people suspected him. Also at this time, Kadur [a pet name for Ṭhākura's daughter, Kadambini] came down with fever. Bisakisen, by his practice of yoga, had by some means attained yogic powers, and I obtained a lot of evidence against him. For twenty-one days he did not eat or drink even a drop of water, but he did not show any weakness and gave unfailing cures to many people."

At last, he was brought to trial and sentenced. Thousands of the yogi's followers were outside the courtroom chanting"Injustice." A young British officer, who had been reading about mystic powers, rushed up behind the yogi as he was being taken from the courtroom and cut off his matted locks with a huge pair of scissors. The yogi immediately fell down on the floor unable to walk. When his followers saw that he had been overcome simply by having his hair removed, they deserted him. The Ṭhākura continued to prosecute other self-proclaimed incarnations and thwarted their attempts to exploit the innocent public.

During this period, Śrīla Bhaktivinoda carefully studied the twelve cantos of Bhāgavatam, and began writing the *Kṛṣna-samhita*, one of his most famous works. In great happiness, he toured the holy places of Purī and constantly associated with the most elevated Vaiṣṇavas in the area.

"While in Purī I made much advancement in devotional service. I became more detached from worldly life. The idea that worldly progress produces anything of lasting value was gone forever. Almost every evening I would go to the temple to see the Lord, to hear and chant the Holy Name and associate with the devotees. Just as the Jagannātha Temple is very lofty and beautiful, so also the service to the Deity was wonderful. To see it was charming to the mind. Daily, from five to seven hundred people were present to see the routine festivals like the evening *arati*, etc. What bliss! Many kinds of pilgrims came from all over India to attend the religious festivals. Seeing that, one's eyes are soothed."

On a Friday afternoon, 6 February 1874, at Jagannātha Purī, Śrīmati Bhagavatī Devī and Ṭhākura Bhaktivinoda were delighted with the appearance of a son. He was born with the umbilical cord wrapped around his neck, resembling the sacred thread. Everyone was astonished. They took it as an auspicious sign. As Śrī Bimala Devī represents the *para śakti*, spiritual energy, of Lord Jagannātha, he was given the name Bimala Prasada. Śrīla Bhaktivinoda had prayed for a ray of Viṣṇu to help him with his preaching, and this son, Śrīla Bhaktisiddhanta Sarasvatī Prabhupāda, would fulfill that mission.

Six months later in July, the annual *Ratha-yatra* festival was in progress. Inexplicably, the three chariots stopped at the gate in front of Bhaktivinoda Ṭhākura's residence and remained there for three days. Mother Bhagavatī Devī took advantage of the situation to benefit her six-month-old son. She was allowed to ascend the chariot since her husband was the manager of the Purī Temple. As she approached Lord Jagannātha, the baby extended his arms to touch the feet of Śrī Jagannātha Deva and was blessed with a garland from the Lord. His *anna-prasana*, first feeding of rice, was celebrated with the *mahāprasada* of Lord Jagannātha on the chariot.

In the temple, Bhaktivinoda Ṭhākura began regular lectures on *Śrīmad-Bhāgavatam*. Due to his association, many Mayavadi brahmins became devout Vaiṣṇavas. One day, the King of Purī burst noisily into the temple, disturbing the Ṭhākura's discourses. Unable to tolerate this disrespectful behavior, the Ṭhākura voiced his displeasure.

"You have the right to hold the position of kingship over your small kingdom, but the Supreme Lord, Jagannātha Puruṣottama, is the King of all kings. Therefore it is mandatory that you show respect to His Bhakti Mandapa, where His glories are daily sung."

The king, immediately realizing his offense, bowed before the assembled Vaiṣṇavas, begging for their forgiveness. Later that year, the King misappropriated eighty thousand rupees from the Jagannātha Temple. Subsequently Bhaktivinoda punished the king by obliging him to make fifty-two offerings daily to Lord Jagannātha.

Seeing his treasury depleting rapidly, the king sought revenge and made an attempt on the Ṭhākura's life. A secret *yajna* was performed within the confines of the palace with fifty brahmins chanting *mantras* in order to kill the Ṭhākura by mystic power. At the end of the thirty-day *yajna*, when the Ṭhākura was supposed to die, the king's only son died.

"The king and other persons connected with the temple used to commit many illegal acts. I would go there to prevent all such things, and thus I made enemies of the king and the king's men. Because I was helped by Lord Jagannātha, no one was able to harm me in any way."

After five years of service in Purī, Ṭhākura Bhaktivinoda was posted at different locations in Bengal and finally settled in Narail in August 1878. While residing in 1880, he published his *Kṛṣna-samhita*. Immediately he received high acclaim for this work. The following year he published *Kalyāna-kalpataru*, a collection of songs describing the various stages of spiritual life, from the earliest to the highest stage of *prema-bhakti*. It was also highly acclaimed and was accepted as an immortal work equal to the songs of Narottama dāsa Ṭhākura. In Narail, he also started to publish the monthly Vaiṣṇava journal, *Sajjana Tosani*. Its aim was to educate influential and learned people about the divine mission of Śrī Caitanya Mahāprabhu.

The Ṭhākura now felt a great need to accept Vaiṣṇava initiation.

"I had been searching for a suitable guru for a long time, but I did not obtain one. I was very unhappy. I was feeling very anxious, and in a dream Mahāprabhu diminished my unhappiness. In that dream, I received a little hint. That very day I became happy. One or two days later Gurudeva wrote a letter to me saying, 'I will soon come and give you *dikṣa*.'"

Subsequently, he received Bipin Bihari Goswami as his guest and became his disciple. In his commentary to *Śrī Caitanya-caritāmṛta* written fourteen years later, he concluded with this prayer:

"The eminent Bipin Bihari Prabhu, who is the manifestation of the transcendental energy of Lord Hari, who sports in the forests of Vraja, has descended in the form of the spiritual preceptor. Seeing me in the dark well of worldly existence, he has delivered this humble servant of his."

Towards the end of 1881, the Ṭhākura again desired to visit Vṛndāvana, after an absence of fifteen years. He set out with his wife, his youngest son, and two servants. Upon arrival, he came down with fever, and prayed to the Lord to relieve him for the duration of his pilgrimage. The illness disappeared. While in Vṛndāvana, he met Jagannātha dāsa Babaji Mahārāja, an exalted Vaiṣṇava coming in disciplic succession from Baladeva Vidyabhusana. Babaji Mahārāja was a constant source of inspiration and guidance for the Ṭhākura, who became increasingly absorbed in the mission of Lord Caitanya.

Upon his return, he was transferred to Jessore where he suffered from a heavy fever in accordance with his prayer in Vṛndāvana. Receiving medical leave, he returned to Calcutta, purchased a house -- the Bhakti Bhavan -- and held many meetings there to discuss spiritual topics. He expressed his realizations in an article printed in the *Sajjana Tosani*.

"Lord Caitanya did not advent Himself to liberate only a few men of India. Rather, His main objective was to emancipate all living entities of all countries throughout the entire universe and preach the Eternal Religion. Lord Caitanya says in the *Caitanya Bhagavat*: 'In every town, country and village, My name will be sung.' There is no doubt that this unquestionable order will come to pass. Very soon the unparalleled path of *harināma sankīrtana* will be propagated all over the world. Oh! For that day when the fortunate English, French, Russian, German and American people will take up banners, drums and cymbals, amid raised arms and perform congregational *kīrtana* through their streets and towns. When will that day come? Oh for that day when the fair-skinned men from their side will raise up the chanting of Jai Sacinandana, Jai Sacinandana ki jai, and join with the Bengali devotees." (*Sajjana Tosani* 1885, pp. 4-5)

The article was a powerful prayer to bring the people of the world together under the banner of the Holy Name. Next, he made a bold prophecy.

"A personality will soon appear to preach the teachings of Lord Caitanya and move unrestrictedly over the whole world with His message."

As Advaita Acarya invoked the descent of Lord Caitanya through his prayer, so Ṭhākura Bhaktivinoda invoked the descent of the person who would fulfill the ancient prophecy.

In 1887, at the age of forty-nine, he discovered *Śrī Caitanyopanisad*, which could only be found in very old manuscripts of the *Atharva Veda*. He wrote a Sanskrit commentary on the work. In 1886 and 1887, he produced ten books and was awarded the title Bhaktivinoda for his outstanding work of preaching and writing. He became known as Saccidānanda Bhaktivinoda Ṭhākura.

At this point in his life, he considered retiring from government duties to concentrate on his *bhajana*. One night Lord Caitanya appeared to him in a dream: "You will certainly go to Vṛndāvana, but first there is some service you must perform in Navadvipa. What will you do about that?"

He requested a transfer to Navadvipa, and on 15 November 1887, his transfer to nearby Krishnanagar was granted. He was jubilant on receiving the news, but experienced high fevers at that time.

"How shall I speak of my misfortune? Returning home in joy, I became anxious because a horrible fever came on. It did not subside. Collector Toynbee arrived and expressed a desire to postpone my substitution. But then I thought, 'I'll live or I'll die, but I will go to Krishnanagar.'"

Every Saturday he went to Navadvipa to search out the holy birthsite of Lord Caitanya. Most of the locals had no interest in the project and he became a little discouraged. They believed that due to the shifting course of the Ganga, the actual site was lost. Others claimed the site was on the opposite bank of the river. The Ṭhākura was neither satisfied nor convinced by these assertions. He continued his research and discovered that the present town of Navadvipa was less than a hundred years old. On an old map, he found the town Śrī Mayapura on the opposite bank, situated at the same site as the current village of Ballaldighi. Some elderly locals of the village pointed to a mound covered with tulasi, saying that it was the actual place of Lord Caitanya's birth.

One day he found this verse: "In the center of Navadvipa there is a special place called Mayapura. At this place the Supreme Lord, Śrī Gauracandra, took His birth." (*Bhakti Ratnakara* 12.83)

To confirm his discovery, the Ṭhākura requested the elderly Śrīla Jagannātha dāsa Babaji, who at the time was crippled and carried in basket, to come. When he was brought to the site, Babaji Mahārāja became overwhelmed with ecstasy, jumped up, and exclaimed,"This is indeed the birthplace of Nimai!" The discovery lead to further research and the publication in 1890 of *Śrī Navadvipa Dhama Mahātmyam* describing the holy places of Lord Caitanya's pastimes.

The Ṭhākura then established his own place of *bhajana*, Surabhikunja. From there, he could look out across the Jalangi River towards Mayapura. One day he had a fantastic vision; he saw a large golden city rising beyond the Ganges at the place of Śrī Mayapura. He understood he was getting a glimpse of the fulfillment of Lord Caitanya's prophecy.

In August 1891, Ṭhākura Bhaktivinoda received a two-year furlough from government service and began preaching from Godrumadvipa. He called this preaching *nāma-haṭṭa*, the marketplace of the holy name. He traveled with three close friends to chant and lecture in many places. Altogether, the Ṭhākura established over five hundred *nāma-haṭṭa* associations, and in this period, he also wrote profusely, producing eighteen books!

"We performed *nama-sankīrtana* everywhere. After coming to my house in Calcutta, I proceeded to Surabhikunja and we performed a great deal of san*kīrtana* there too."

Government service had now become a hindrance to his real work of *sankīrtana*, preaching the glories of the holy name. He retired to Surabhikunja at the age of fifty-six. Determined to build a temple in Mayapura, he went door to door in Calcutta begging donations. As the foundation for the temple was being dug, a Deity of Adhoksaja Viṣṇu was found. Referring to the Vaiṣṇava scriptures, the Ṭhākura discovered that this was the family Deity worshipped by Jagannātha Misra, Mahāprabhu's father. The archeological evidence further confirmed the authenticity of the birthsite of the Lord.

On Gaura Purnima, 21 March 1895, the temple was opened with an enormous installation ceremony and *sankīrtana* festival. The occasion was compared to the Kheturi festival, which was organized by Narottama dāsa Ṭhākura to unite the followers of Śrī Caitanya Mahāprabhu. Śrīla Bhaktivinoda Ṭhākura installed deities of Lord Caitanya and His eternal consort Visnupriya Devī as thousands of Vaiṣṇavas at the celebration chanted, danced and feasted.

The following year, 1896, was one of the momentous moments in Vaiṣṇava history. A small book entitled Caitanya Mahāprabhu — *His Life and Precepts* was written in English by the Ṭhākura, and was sent to major university libraries around the world. On 1 September of that year in Calcutta, a son was born to Gaura Mohan De and his wife. Their son, Śrīla A.C. Bhaktivedanta Swami Prabhupāda, was destined to fulfill the Ṭhākura's prediction.

With natural humility, Śrīla A.C. Bhaktivedanta Swami Prabhupāda gave the credit to his Guru Mahārāja as follows:

"Ṭhākura Bhaktivinoda also wanted to beget a son who could preach the philosophy and teachings of Lord Caitanya to the fullest extent. By his prayers to the Lord, he had as his child Bhaktisiddhanta Sarasvati Goswami Mahārāja, who at the present moment is preaching the philosophy of Lord Caitanya throughout the entire world through his bona fide disciples." (*Śrīmad-Bhāgavatam* lecture, Iran, August 8, 1976)

The prediction also applied to Śrīla Bhaktisiddhanta Sarasvati Ṭhākura, but the personality moving"unrestrictedly over the whole world with the message of Mahāprabhu" was certainly Śrīla A.C. Bhaktivedanta Swami Prabhupāda. Therefore, we can say that both of these great personalities fulfilled Lord Caitanya's prophecy, because the sincere disciple was never separated from the instructions of his Guru Mahārāja.

Returning to Purī in 1900, Ṭhākura Bhaktivinoda established a place for his *bhajana*, called Bhakti Kutir, which was near the *samadhi* of Śrīla Haridasa Ṭhākura. In the same year, one of his most important books, *Śrī Harināma Cintamani*, was published.

In 1908, he gave up his household life and accepted initiation into the Babaji order of life from Gaura Kisora dāsa Babaji Mahārāja, a renowned saint. He put on the outer cloth and kaupina previously worn by Śrīla Jagannātha dāsa Babaji Mahārāja, which he had saved since the Babaji entered samadhi. After a brilliant life in which he had single-handedly re-established the *Vaiṣṇava dharma* according to the teachings of Śrī Caitanya Mahāprabhu, Śrīla Ṭhākura Bhaktivinoda retired from public life and spent his final years in solitude, ecstatically tasting the nectar of pure *kṛṣṇa-prema*.

On 23 June 1914, on the disappearance day of Śrī Gadadhara Pandita, Śrīla Bhaktisiddhanta Sarasvati Ṭhākura mourned the passing of his father, Śrīla Saccidananda Bhaktivinoda Ṭhākura. Immediately, Śrīla Bhaktisiddhanta began printing the various books that his father had left unpublished, and he also continued to publish *Sajjana Tosani*.

Sambandha

1

Relationship with the Lord

1. What is the science or knowledge of one's relationship with the Supreme Lord?

There are three truths regarding one's relationship with the Lord. These are knowledge about the material world, knowledge about the living entities, and knowledge about the Supreme Lord.

The Supreme Lord is one without a second, omnipotent, all-attractive, the source of all opulence and sweetness, and the only shelter of the living entities and material nature. Although He is the shelter of the living entities and material nature, He is always fully independent. His bodily effulgence is known as the impersonal Brahman. He created the living entities and the material world by His spiritual potency, and then as Paramātmā, a plenary portion, He entered into the universes. In His form of opulence or *aiśvarya*, He is Lord Nārāyaṇa in the spiritual sky. In His form of sweetness or *mādhurya*, He is Śrī Kṛṣṇacandra, the beloved Lord of the *gopīs*, in Goloka Vṛndāvana. His manifestations and pastimes are unlimited. There is nothing greater than or equal to Him. All His forms and pastimes manifest through His internal spiritual energy.

The living entities are aware of the three energies among the many potencies of the Lord. One is His spiritual energy, by which all His pastimes take place. Another is His marginal energy, the living entities, by which unlimited living entities are produced and sustained. The other is His external energy, Māyā, by which all material objects, time, and activities are created.

Sambandha-tattva refers to the following relationships: the living entities toward the Supreme Lord, the Supreme Lord toward the living entities and the material world, and the material world toward the Supreme Lord and the living entities. If one properly understands *sambandha-tattva*, one becomes acquainted with knowledge of one's relationship with the

Supreme Lord. Persons who are devoid of knowledge of their relationship with the Supreme Lord can never become pure Vaiṣṇavas.

(*Jaiva Dharma*, Chapter 4)

2. Is the feeling of "I" and "mine" in relationship with the Lord abominable?

The feeling of"I" and"mine" in connection with one's relationship with Krishna is not born of material pride. Rather it is born from one's service attitude.

(*Yāmuna-bhāvāvalī, Gītamālā*)

2

Vedic Knowledge

1. What is āmnāya?

Āmnāya is Vedic literature consisting of spiritual knowledge received through disciplic succession coming from Lord Brahmā, the creator of the universe.

(*Manaḥ-śikṣā*, Verse 2)

2. What are the basic teachings of Śrī Caitanyadeva?

Śrī Hari is the Supreme Absolute Truth. He is Omniscient. He is the nectarean ocean of transcendental mellows. The living entities are His separated parts and parcels. The conditioned souls are controlled by Māyā, whereas the liberated souls are free from Māyā. Both the spiritual and material worlds are simultaneously one with and different from Śrī Hari. Devotional service is the only way to obtain the goal of life, and love of God is the ultimate goal of life.

(*Sajjana-toṣaṇī* 9/9)

3. What are the ten principal teachings?

(1) Vedic statements are the only evidence.

(2) Lord Hari is the Supreme Personality of Godhead.

(3) He is omnipotent.

(4) He is the reservoir of transcendental mellows, and His abode is the spiritual sky.

(5) Living entities are unlimited spiritual sparks, parts and parcels of Krishna, and they are of two kinds: eternally conditioned and eternally liberated.

(6) Māyā conditions living entities who are averse to Krishna.

(7) Pure devotees of the Lord are free from Māyā.

(8) The living entities and the material world are produced from the Lord's inconceivable potency, and they are simultaneously one with and different from the Lord.

(9) The nine types of devotional service to Krishna are the only processes to achieve the goal of life.

(10) Love of Krishna is the ultimate goal of life.

(*Harināma-cintāmaṇi*)

4. Is the Absolute Truth one or many?

The Absolute Truth is one without a second, *tattvam ekam evādvitīyam.*

(*Āmnāya Sūtra* 2)

5. Where do we find the teachings of Śrī Caitanya?

The teachings of Śrī Mahāprabhu are properly described in two books. The teachings regarding the Absolute Truth are described in *Śrī Brahma Saṁhitā*, and the teachings regarding *bhajana* are described in *Krishna Karṇāmṛta.*

(*Krishna Karṇāmṛta*, Introduction)

6. What is the purpose of the Vedas?

Vedic literature teaches one to engage in pure devotional service. According to the nature and qualification of its so-called followers, Vedic literature has recommended various processes such as karma and *jñāna.* Due to the faults of these followers, various opinions have cropped up. Actually, the Vedas are the only evidence and the instructing spiritual master of mankind. On account of misinterpretation, various opinions other than pure devotional service have been preached.

(*Bhāgavatārka Marīcī Mālā* 1–6)

7. What is transcendental literature?

If a blind person guides another person, both of them fall into a ditch; similarly the mundane authors and their blind followers are misguided and regrettable. The Vedas and literature in pursuance of the Vedas are to be understood as transcendental literature.

(*Caitanya-śikṣāmṛta* 1/2

8. What are the Vedas?

It is not that if one gets a book of Vedas from anywhere, it should be accepted everywhere. Whatever the *ācāryas* of the authorized *sampradāyas* have accepted as Vedas, we should accept, and whatever they have rejected as false, we should reject.

(*Jaiva Dharma*, Chapter 13)

9. What is the difference between the teachings of Śrī Caitanya and the teachings of Bhagavad-gītā, Śrīmad-Bhāgavatam, Pañcarātras, and Vedas?

Bhagavad-gītā, known as *Gītopaniṣad*, was spoken by the Lord and is therefore Veda. The ten principal truths taught and spoken by Śrī Gaurāṅga are also Vedas. *Śrīmad-Bhāgavatam*, the essence of all Vedic literature, is the crest jewel among all evidence. If the statements of other revealed scriptures follow the teachings of the Vedas, they are also evidence. The Tantras are of three types: *sāttvika*, *rājasika*, and *tāmasika*. Since the *sāttvika-tantras*, such as the *Pañcarātra*, preach the confidential purport of the Vedas, they are also evidence.

(*Jaiva Dharma*, Chapter 13)

10. What is the necessity of a perpetual disciplic succession?

No book is without errors. God's revelation is Absolute Truth, but it is rarely received and preserved in its original purity. Truth that has been revealed is absolute, but over the course of time, it becomes tainted by the nature of the receivers, and from age to age, it is transformed by the continual change of hands. New revelations, therefore, are continuously necessary to keep truth in its original purity.

(*The Bhagavat*: *Its Philosophy, Its Ethics & Its Theology*)

3

Spiritual Master or Ācārya

1. What is the symptom of a bona fide spiritual master? Can a person who has accepted a family preceptor take shelter of a bona fide spiritual master?

Due to the influence of time, people's conception regarding the spiritual master has been greatly polluted. Nowadays, people take instructions either from a family preceptor or from anyone else, and as a result they are bereft of the shelter of the most worshipable bona fide spiritual master. It is stated in the scriptures that a person who is inquisitive about his own self and the Supreme Lord should approach and surrender to a spiritual master who is firmly fixed both in the service of the Supreme Brahman and in the transcendental sound vibration.

(*Sajjana-toṣaṇī* 2/1)

2. Who is a qualified spiritual master?

One who is fully acquainted with and successful in spiritual life is qualified to become a spiritual master.

(*Harināma-cintāmaṇi*)

3. Should a person accept a spiritual master who is born in a high family? Why is it stated in Hari-bhakti-vilāsa that a person should accept a spiritual master who is born in a brāhmaṇa family or who is a gṛhastha?

Knowledge about Krishna is most essential for all living entities. A person who knows the science of Krishna, whether that person is a *brāhmaṇa*, *śūdra*, *gṛhastha*, or *sannyāsī*, is qualified to become a spiritual master. *Śrī Hari Bhakti Vilāsa* instructs one not to take initiation from a person of the lower caste when a qualified person from a higher caste is available. This instruction is meant for Vaiṣṇavas who are dependent on social custom; it is for those who wish to progress on the path of spiritual life according to worldly rules and regulations. But those who wish to obtain pure devotional service to Krishna, by carefully understanding the purport of *vaidhī* and *rāgānuga-bhakti*, should accept a spiritual master who fully knows the science of Krishna, regardless of his *varṇa* or *āśrama*.

(*Amṛta-pravāha-bhāṣya, Caitanya Caritāmṛta* Madhya 8/127)

4. Are the principal qualifications of a spiritual master that he is a brāhmaṇa and a householder?

Caitanya Caritāmṛta states that whether one is a *brāhmaṇa*, a *sannyāsī*, or a *śūdra*, if he knows the science of Krishna, he is qualified to become a spiritual master. One who possesses the internal or primary quality (he knows the science of Krishna) is qualified to become a spiritual master, even though he does not possess one or two of the external qualities (being a *brāhmaṇa* and a householder). It is good if a spiritual master possesses the primary and the two external qualities. But those who lack the primary quality, even though they possess the external qualities, cannot become qualified spiritual masters.

(*Sajjana-toṣaṇī* 11/6)

5. What is the difference between taking shelter of the lotus feet of a bona fide spiritual master and taking shelter of a bogus spiritual master?

There are two types of gurus: *antaraṅgā* or internal, and *bahiraṅgā* or external. The living entity who is situated in *samādhi* is his own internal spiritual master. One who accepts argument as his spiritual master and who learns the process of worship from such a spiritual master is said to have accepted the shelter of a bogus spiritual master. Then argument poses as nourishment for the living entities constitutional duties; this may be compared to Putana's falsely posing as a nurse. Worshipers on the path of attachment must immerse all arguments in spiritual subjects and take shelter of *samādhi*. The external spiritual master is he from whom the science of worship is learned. One who knows the proper path of attachment and who instructs his disciples according to their qualification is a *sad-guru*, or eternal spiritual master.

(*Śrī Krishna-saṁhitā* 8/14)

6. According to Vaiṣṇava literature, who is qualified to become jagat-guru?

Vaiṣṇava literature accepts that one who has understood the difference between material and spiritual subject matters, and thus learned about transcendental devotional service to Krishna is *jagat-guru*. He is qualified to instruct all living entities, and he is completely aloof from the consideration of *varṇa* and *āśrama*.

(*Amṛta-pravāha-bhāṣya, Caitanya Caritāmṛta* Antya 5/84-85)

7. What is the basic qualification of a bona fide spiritual master?

The qualification of a bonafide spiritual master is that he knows the science of Krishna and lives outside the consideration of *varṇāśrama*.

(*Jaiva Dharma*, Chapter 20)

8. What does a bona fide spiritual master instruct his disciple?

Pure spiritual knowledge is glorified everywhere in Vaiṣṇava literature. In the teachings of Mahāprabhu, three topics are prominently discussed; they are knowledge of one's relationship with the Supreme Lord, the process of achieving the goal of life, and the goal of life. *Sambandha* is understanding the Supreme Lord, the living entity, the material world, and the relationships between them. Anyone who properly instructs his disciple about *sambandha* and trains him in the process of achieving the goal of life is a bona fide spiritual master. After receiving this knowledge, a living entity needs no other knowledge. All kinds of scientific and theoretical knowledge of this world are automatically known to him.

(*Sajjana-toṣaṇī* 11/10)

9. What is the difference between the spiritual master who gives initiation mantra and the spiritual master who gives Harināma?

The *nāma-guru*, the spiritual master who gives *harināma*, teaches his disciples about the supremacy of the holy names and gives *mantras*, consisting of the holy names. The *dīkṣā-guru* is nondifferent from the *nama-guru* because the *mantras* are nondifferent from the holy names. If *mantras* are separated from the holy names, they are no longer *mantras*. By simply uttering the holy names, one automatically utters the *mantras*.

(*Harināma-cintāmaṇi*)

10. How should a disciple treat his spiritual master?

A disciple should accept his spiritual master as the manifestation of the Supreme Personality of Godhead and should never consider him an ordinary human being.

(*Amṛta-pravāha-bhāṣya, Caitanya Caritāmṛta* Ādi 1/46)

11. Do the spiritual masters, after they disappear, bestow their mercy upon the living entities?

The souls of great thinkers of bygone ages, who now live spiritually, often approach an inquiring spirit and assist him in his development.

(*The Bhagavat*: *Its Philosophy*, *Its Ethics & Its Theology*)

12. Who is an ācārya? What are the duties of the Gauḍīya Vaiṣṇava ācāryas?

One who follows religious principles and teaches other's is an *ācārya.* One cannot become an *ācārya* by simply creating arguments and thereby making worldly advancement. Those who have been entrusted with the responsibility of being *ācāryas* in the Gauḍīya Vaiṣṇava-sampradāya should try to remove all *anarthas* from their *sampradāya.*

(*Sajjana-toṣaṇī* 4/1)

13. What is the primary duty of the sons of the ācāryas?

Various types of *anarthas* have surfaced in the Gauḍīya-sampradāya in the last four hundred years. The primary duty of all the sons of the *ācāryas* is to totally uproot those *anarthas.*

(*Sajjana-toṣaṇī* 4/1)

14. How do living entities gain faith in an ācārya?

Those who act as *ācāryas* must first follow the religious path. Then, by exhibiting their own behavior, they attract the attention and faith of other living entities. Only by proper conduct are the *ācāryas* respectfully accepted by one and all.

(*Sajjana-toṣaṇī* 8/9)

15. Is it proper to call cheaters or persons opposed to Krishna the sons of Vaiṣṇava ācāryas?

Every Vaiṣṇava is our master. Wherever there is devotional service, there is Lordship, but family prestige is not a limb of devotional service.

Some time ago, a person told us that Advaita Ācārya, the husband of Sītā, rejected all his sons, except Acyutānanda, because they were averse to Gaura. Therefore, only Acyutānanda was qualified to be addressed as Goswami. Another time a person said that since Śrī Vīracandra Prabhu, the son of Nityānanda, had no sons, nobody should be addressed as the descendant of Nityānanda, and the Goswamis of Khaḍadaha cannot be addressed as Prabhus. We are also hearing that the Goswamis of Baghnapada should not be called Prabhus either because they are disciples of Śrī Jāhnavā Mātā.

We do not wish to hear such false arguments. We worship all Vaiṣṇavas as nondifferent from Krishna, and we show due respect to the descendants of the *ācāryas*. However, we can never show respect to the descendants of the *ācāryas* who are either opposed to Krishna or have been converted into another religion. Can we show respect to a *brāhmaṇa* who has changed his religion and become a Christian? Similarly if a descendant of an *ācārya* gives up his occupational duties, then he can no longer expect any family prestige.

(*Sajjana-toṣaṇī* 2/12)

16. Can a learned person who does not know the conclusion of devotional service be called an ācārya?

Before the birth of Śrīmān Mahāprabhu, Devānanda Paṇḍita was famous as an *ācārya* because of his explanations on *Śrīmad-Bhāgavatam*. Being a teacher and preacher of devotional service Himself, Mahāprabhu became extremely displeased upon hearing the nondevotional explanation of Devānanda Paṇḍita. Later, Devānanda Paṇḍita realized the science of pure devotional service by the mercy of Vakreśvara Paṇḍita.

(*Sajjana-toṣaṇī* 9/12)

17. What harm is caused if one acts against the conclusion of devotional service?

A Vaiṣṇava who acts against the conclusion of devotional service is the root cause of *anarthas* within the *sampradāya*.

(*Sajjana-toṣaṇī* 4/1)

18. If an ācārya or a spiritual master criticizes the improper conclusions of devotional service, will he be considered a prajalpi or gossiper?

Śukadeva Goswami did not become a *prajalpi* even though he discussed the materialists to instruct his disciples. Therefore, such activities should be accepted as beneficial. Moreover, to instruct His disciples, Śrīmān Mahāprabhu discussed the false renunciates.

(*Sajjana-toṣaṇī* 10/10)

19. Are there any differences of opinion among the ācāryas?

Whatever a self-realized soul in India will speak, a self-realized soul in another part of the world will speak. A devotee in Vaikuṇṭha will also speak the same thing, because there are no material qualities in the conclusions of pure, liberated souls. Therefore the conclusions cannot be different.

(*Tattva Viveka*, Chapter 1/2)

20. Does an ācārya give initiation without any consideration?

The worshipable, qualified *ācāryas* should give initiation to the qualified candidates. Although in *Śrī Hari-bhakti-vilāsa* the method for testing each other is recommended, it is often not practiced. That is why the fall of both the spiritual master and the disciple, as well as pollution of the *sampradāya*, become inevitable.

(*Sajjana-toṣaṇī* 4/1)

21. Can a householder become an ācārya?

Among the householder devotees, only those who are expert in executing the nine types of devotional service are qualified to take the position of an *ācārya*.

(*Sajjana-toṣaṇī* 4/2)

22. Should a household set the example of awarding sannyāsa?

When the devotee householders act as *ācārya* and award *mantras* and symbols of *sannyāsa*, great inauspiciousness is created for the recipient of the *sannyāsa*.

(*Sajjana-toṣaṇī* 4/2)

23. Do the ācāryas have any faults?

There are no faults in the activities of the *mahājanas*.

(*Sajjana-toṣaṇī* 10/10)

24. Why do people criticize even an extremely qualified ācārya?

Even though Śrī Nityānanda Prabhu, the *ācārya* of all *ācāryas*, was an *avadhūta*, He never displayed any sinful behavior. Those who say that the Lord was sinful are abominable. Sinful persons attribute false faults in the character of the *ācārya* and try to prove their own faults as qualifications. Alas! O Kali! Whatever you have promised you have done! Some artificial Vaiṣṇavas say that Śrī Nityānanda Prabhu was a meat and fish eater, and accuse Śrī Mahāprabhu, the personification of religious principles, of associating with women, and thus call Him a paramour. They also cheat the people of the world by falsely accusing pure devotees, such as Śrī Rūpa Goswami and Śrī Rāmānanda Rāya, of associating with women.

(*Sajjana-toṣaṇī* 8/9)

4

Previous Ācāryas

1. Why are the four-authorized sampradāya ācāryas distinguished from each other?

Śrī Rāmānuja, Śrī Madhva, Śrī Viṣṇusvāmī, and Śrī Nimbāditya are the four Vaiṣṇava *ācāryas*. Many other's also became Vaiṣṇava *ācāryas*, and they are certainly followers of one of the four above-mentioned *ācāryas*. Śrī Rāmānuja is the propounder of *viśiṣṭādvaita* philosophy, Śrī Madhva is the profounder of *śuddha-dvaita* philosophy, Śrī Viṣṇusvāmī is the propounder of *śuddhādvaita* philosophy, and Śrī Nimbāditya is the propounder of *dvaitādvaita* philosophy.

(*Sajjana-toṣaṇī* 7-7)

2. What preaching responsibility did Śrī Gaurasundara entrust upon Śrī Nityānanda, Śrī Advaita, Śrī Rūpa, Śrī Sanātana, Śrī Jīva Goswami, and other's?

Śrīmān Mahāprabhu empowered and ordered Śrī Nityānanda Prabhu and Śrī Advaita Prabhu to preach the glories of the Lord's holy name. He empowered and ordered Śrī Rūpa Goswami to reveal the science of the mellows of devotional service. He ordered Śrī Sanātana Goswami to preach about *vaidhī-bhakti* and its relationship with *rāgānuga-bhakti*. He also ordered Śrī Sanātana Goswami to reveal the relationship between the manifest and unmanifest pastimes of Gokula. He empowered Śrī Jīva Goswami through Śrī Nityānanda Prabhu and Śrī Sanātana to reveal the science of *sambandha*, *abhidheya*, and *prayojana*.

(*Jaiva Dharma*, Chapter 39)

3. What responsibility was entrusted to Śrī Svarūpa Dāmodara Goswami?

Śrīmān Mahāprabhu ordered Śrī Svarūpa Dāmodara to teach worship of the Lord through loving devotional service. According to the Lord's order, Śrī Svarūpa Dāmodara composed his kaḍacā or writings in two parts. He described worshiping the Lord in the mood of transcendental mellows: by the internal path in the first part and by the external path in the second part. He imparted the internal path to Śrī Raghunātha dāsa Goswami, who revealed it in his books, and he imparted the external path to Śrīmad Vakreśvara Goswami.

(*Jaiva Dharma*, Chapter 39)

4. Rāya Rāmānanda was entrusted to spread the science of the mellows of devotional service. Who completed that responsibility?

The responsibility of preaching the science of the mellows of devotional service, which Śrīmān Mahāprabhu entrusted to Rāya Rāmānanda, was completed by Śrī Rūpa Goswami.

(*Jaiva Dharma*, Chapter 39)

5. Who was the commander-in-chief of the Gauḍīya ācāryas?

Śrī Sanātana Goswami was the commander-in-chief of our Gauḍīya *ācāryas*.

(Tātparya vaidhī-bhakti-anuvāda, *Bṛhad-bhāgavatāmṛta* 2/1/14)

6. Why are all the Vaiṣṇavas eternally indebted to Śrī Sanātana?

After fully empowering Śrī Sanātana, Śrī Caitanya Mahāprabhu sent him from Kāśī to Śrī Vṛndāvana to rediscover the lost holy places. Being fully ecstatic on receiving the mercy of Mahāprabhu, Śrī Sanātana went to Vṛndāvana and met his brother Śrī Rūpa and other devotees. Thereafter he discovered many holy places in Vṛndāvana, inaugurated deity worship, and compiled much literature glorifying devotional service to the Lord. O Readers! The entire Vaiṣṇava society is indeed eternally indebted to the Goswamis, headed by Śrī Sanātana.

(*Sajjana-toṣaṇī* 2/7)

7. What are the activities and preaching of Śrī Rūpa?

Śrī Rūpa heard the name Mahāprabhu, the son of Śacī and the moonlike personality of Navadvīpa, and from that day, Śrī Rūpa felt pain in his heart because of his intense desire to see Mahāprabhu. On his way to Śrī Vṛndāvana, Śrī Caitanyadeva, who is fully acquainted with the heart of

His devotees, and who is the Supersoul of everyone, came to the village Rāmakeli and gave *darśana* to Śrī Rūpa. After seeing Mahāprabhu, Śrī Rūpa considered his life successful and became merged in the ocean of transcendental bliss. The illusory energy of the Lord can never bind the eternally liberated devotees of Krishna. Within a few days of their meeting, Śrī Rūpa gave up the desire for material happiness, and being fully detached, he went to the holy place Prayāga and fell at the lotus feet of Mahāprabhu. Mahāprabhu empowered Śrī Rūpa by bestowing mercy on him, and after instructing him on the subject of transcendental mellows, Mahāprabhu sent him to Śrī Vṛndāvana to discover the lost holy places. Taking the instructions of Mahāprabhu as his life and soul, Śrī Rūpa went to Vraja. In Vraja, after meeting with all the devotees, he discovered the lost holy places and inaugurated the deity worship of the Lord.

Thereafter, with a desire to benefit the living entities of this age of Kali, who are bewildered by their sinful activities and the threefold material miseries, he composed many books based on the teachings of Śrīmān Mahāprabhu. Some of his books are *Bhakti-rasāmṛta-sindhu, Laghu-bhāgavatāmṛta, Haṁsadūta, Uddhava-sandeśa, Krishna-janma-tithi-vidhi, Laghu* and *Bṛhat Gaṇoddeśa-dīpikā, Stavamālā, Vidagdha-mādhava, Lalita-mādhava, Dāna-keli-kaumudi, Ujjvala-nīlamaṇi, Prayuktākhya Candrikā, Mathurā-māhātmya, Padyāvalī*, and *Nāṭaka-candrikā*.

Śrī Gaurāṅgadeva, the deliverer of the fallen souls, preached humility through Rūpa and Sanātana, detachment through Svarūpa Dāmodara, tolerance through Haridāsa Ṭhākura, and self-control through Rāmānanda Rāya. According to the statements of some devotees, Mahāprabhu preached about His pastimes through Śrī Rūpa, devotional service through Śrī Sanātana, the glories of holy names through Haridāsa Ṭhākura, and love of God through Rāya Rāmānanda. We have no argument in this regard.

However, the sad part is that many mundane *sahajiyās*, such as *neḍās, bāulas, karttābhajās*, and *rasika-śekharas*, unlawfully claim that those great souls are *ācāryas* of their respective line, and therefore many civilized persons do not have faith in the most sanctified philosophy of Vaiṣṇavism preached by Mahāprabhu.

(*Sajjana-toṣaṇī* 2/8)

8. Are the conclusions of Śrī Rūpa acceptable to all?

Śrī Rūpa has always established his conclusions with reason and scriptural evidence. Followers of different *sampradāyas* do not like to accept many of his conclusions, but those who follow the path of worship to attain the platform of pure goodness certainly respect the conclusions of Śrī Rūpa.

(*Sajjana-toṣaṇī* 11/3)

9. Is Raghunātha dāsa Goswami a follower of Śrī Rūpa?

Śrī Krishna Caitanya, the Lord of the *sannyāsīs*, lived at Nīlācala in the guise of a *sannyāsī*. He enjoyed spiritual bliss in the association of Svarūpa Dāmodara and Rāmānanda Rāya, and revealed to them the most confidential subject matter. He taught this same spiritual truth to Raghunātha and sent him to Śrī Rūpa. Śrī Raghunātha dāsa Goswami worshiped Krishna in Vraja in the association of Śrī Rūpa and composed the famous book *Manaḥ-śikṣā*.

(*Manaḥ-śikṣā*, Verse 5)

10. What responsibility did Mahāprabhu entrust to Śrī Raghunātha Bhaṭṭa Goswami?

Śrī Raghunātha Bhaṭṭa Goswami was entrusted to preach the glories of *Śrīmad-Bhāgavatam*.

(*Jaiva Dharma*, Chapter 39)

11. What was the responsibility of Śrī Gopāla Bhaṭṭa Goswami?

His responsibility was to prevent anyone disregarding the process of *vaidhī-bhakti* and distorting the truth of the mellows of pure devotional service.

(*Jaiva Dharma*, Chapter 39)

12. What responsibility was entrusted to Śrīla Prabhodānanda Sarasvatī?

His responsibility was to preach to the world that worship on the path of *rāga* according to the moods of the Vrajavāsīs is the highest of all.

(*Jaiva Dharma*, Chapter 39)

13. What was Sārvabhauma's responsibility?

Lord Caitanya entrusted Sārvabhauma Bhaṭṭācārya to spread knowledge of the Absolute Truth. Sārvabhauma Bhaṭṭācārya passed on this knowledge through one of his disciples to Śrī Jīva.

(*Jaiva Dharma*, Chapter 39)

14. What was the responsibility entrusted to the Gauḍīya Vaiṣṇavas?

The Gauḍīya Vaiṣṇavas were instructed to reveal to the living entities the truth about Śrī Gaura and to awaken their faith in Krishna. The Lord also ordered some great devotees to perform and engage other's in performing ecstatic *kīrtana*, glorifying the pastimes of the Lord.

(*Jaiva Dharma*, Chapter 39)

15. Who is the ācārya or the authority on the science of the Absolute Truth in the Gauḍīya Vaiṣṇava-sampradāya?

Śrī Jīva Gosvāmīpāda is our *ācārya* or authority on the science of the Absolute Truth. He was always situated under the care and guidance of Śrī Rūpa and Śrī Sanātana.

(*Brahma-saṁhitā* 5/37)

16. What are the characteristics of Śrī Jīva Goswami?

Just by hearing the name Śrī Jīva Goswami, the hearts of the Vaiṣṇavas begin to dance in ecstasy. Śrī Jīva Goswami studied all the devotional literature from Śrī Rūpa. Within a short time, Śrī Jīva Goswami was accepted as the only *ācārya* or authority on literature regarding the Absolute Truth in the Gauḍīya-sampradāya. Śrī Jīva Goswami did not leave Śrī Vṛndāvana-dhāma. During his stay in Vṛndāvana, Śrī Jīva Goswami composed twenty-five books. In the *Vedānta* philosophy, there was no one equal to Śrī Jīva at that time. It is said that once Śrī Vallabhācārya, who belongs to the Viṣṇusvāmī-sampradāya, showed his book, *Tattva-dīpa*, to Śrī Jīva. Śrī Jīva pointed out many impersonal thoughts in his book and exposed Śrī Vallabhācārya's disgraceful opinion. Later, Śrī Vallabhācārya amended the major portion of his book according to the guidance of Śrī Jīva. The *ṣaṭ-sandarbha* written by Śrī Jīva is a jewel in this world. If someone properly understands the *ṣaṭ-sandarbha*, no Vedic conclusions remain unknown to him.

(*Sajjana-toṣaṇī* 2/12)

17. What are the characteristics of Śrī Gopāla Bhaṭṭa Goswami?

From his childhood, Gopāla Bhaṭṭa was a staunch follower of the Vaiṣṇava religion. He properly studied the Vedas and other Vedic literature from his uncle, Śrī Prabhodānanda Sarasvatī, who was a wandering mendicant. When Śrī Caitanya Mahāprabhu traveled to South India to bestow His mercy on the residents there, He met Gopāla Bhaṭṭa. When they met, Gopāla Bhaṭṭa took shelter at Śrī Mahāprabhu's lotus feet. The most merciful Mahāprabhu empowered him by showering special mercy upon him. On the strength of this empowerment, Gopāla Bhaṭṭa left home, went to Śrī Vṛndāvana and in the association of Śrī Rūpa, discovered many lost holy places of Śrī Vṛndāvana and compiled many books on devotional service and *Vaiṣṇava-smṛti*. By the order of Śrī Rūpa, he manifested the service of Śrī Rādhā-ramaṇa in Vṛndāvana.

(*Sajjana-toṣaṇī* 2/7)

18. Who is Śrī Jāhnavā-devī? How did she benefit the Vaiṣṇava society?

The appearance festival of Śrīmatī Jāhnavā-devī is very auspicious for the pure devotees, who are attached to the lotus feet of Śrī Caitanya. In the year 1409 or 1410 of the Śaka Era, Śrī Jāhnavā-devī appeared at Ambikā-kālanā from the womb of Bhadrāvatī, the fortunate wife of Śrī Sūryadāsa Paṇḍita, who was a dear associate of Mahāprabhu. In due course of time, Śrī Nityānanda Prabhu married Śrī Jāhnavā and her elder sister, Śrīmatī Vasudhā-devī, who were adorned with all divine qualities. In approximately 1465 Śaka, Jāhnavā-devī adopted as her son Rāmacandra, the grandson of Śrī Vaṁśīvadanānanda and the son of Śrī Caitanya, and thereafter she gave him initiation. The many wonderful activities performed by Śrī Jāhnavā-devī, who was the energy of Śrī Nityānanda Prabhu and who was nondifferent from Anaṅga-mañjarī, are almost unknown to the Vaiṣṇava society.

(*Sajjana-toṣaṇī* 2/4)

19. Who is the original emperor of the empire of pure devotional literature?

Ṭhākura Vṛndāvana dāsa was not only a jewel in the Vaiṣṇava society but was also an ornament in the society of Bengali literature. Just as the poet Chaucer is highly regarded among the English-speaking people, similarly Ṭhākura Vṛndāvana dāsa should be highly regarded among the Bengali-speaking people. Actually, before Ṭhākura Vṛndāvana dāsa, no one composed any book of poems regarding pure devotional service in Bengali. His chaste mother, Nārāyaṇī, was worshipable by all the Vaiṣṇavas, and there is no doubt that Vṛndāvana dāsa Ṭhākura was an incarnation of Vyāsadeva.

(*Sajjana-toṣaṇī* 2/2)

20. What beneficial activity did Śrīla Kṛṣṇadāsa Kavirāja Goswami perform for the world?

Kavirāja Goswami was a learned scholar of all the scriptures. This is easily realized by reading his books *Śrī Caitanya Caritāmṛta*, *Govinda-līlāmṛta*, and his *Sāraṅga Raṅgada* commentary on *Śrī Krishna Karṇāmṛta*. Śrīla Kavirāja Goswami was a great devotee and one of the principal scholars in the *sampradāya* of Śrī Caitanyadeva. We do not need to prove this statement. The books written by Kavirāja Goswami are proof of this. One becomes struck with wonder by seeing the unlimited glories of Kavirāja. *Śrī Caitanya-caritāmṛta* is an extremely wonderful book, compiled out of compassion for persons who have no knowledge of Sanskrit. In our opinion, if Kavirāja Goswami did not exhibit such compassion, then persons who are ignorant of scriptural knowledge and philosophy would never know the eternal Vaiṣṇava religion instructed by Śrī Caitanya Mahāprabhu. Who knows what would have been their fate. Kavirāja! You are glorious! Learned and ignorant devotees of the Vaiṣṇava *sampradāya* are indebted to you. How much can we sing about your glories with one mouth? The pure Vaiṣṇavas are always singing your qualities. O Kavirāja! Which atheist will not like to take shelter of your lotus feet if he remembers your perfect words? You have said in *Caitanya Caritāmṛta*, Madhya 2.87:

yebā nāhi bujhe keha śunite śunite seha
ki adbhuta caitanya-carita
kṛṣṇe upajibe prīti jānibe rasera rīti
śunilei baḍa haya hita

"If one does not understand in the beginning but continues to hear again and again, the wonderful effects of Lord Caitanya's pastimes will bring love for Krishna. Gradually one will come to understand the loving affairs between Krishna and the gopīs and other associates of Vṛndāvana. Everyone is advised to continue to hear over and over again in order to greatly benefit." (BBT Translation©)

On the strength of such perfect words, many foolish persons in the Vaiṣṇava *sampradāya* are becoming greatly qualified to understand *Śrī Caitanya Caritāmṛta*. O Kavirāja! We offer innumerable obeisances at your lotus feet.

(*Sajjana-toṣaṇī* 2/10—11)

21. What benefit did Śrīnivāsa Ācārya Prabhu do for the society of Gauḍīya Vaiṣṇavas?

In his childhood, Śrīnivāsa heard about the transcendental qualities of Mahāprabhu from the mouth of his own father, who was a surrendered soul at the feet of Śrī Caitanya Mahāprabhu, and who took shelter of Him. As soon as Śrīnivāsa reached boyhood, he took permission from his parents and accepted the renounced order of life.

Thereafter, he went to Śrī Navadvīpa-dhāma with a desire to see Śrīmatī Viṣṇuprīya Ṭhākurani, the consort of Mahāprabhu, and Śrī Vaṁśīvadanānanda Prabhu, who was her guard and a favorite of Mahāprabhu. Śrīnivāsa also wanted to visit all the places of Mahāprabhu's pastimes. After arriving in Navadvīpa, he stayed at the house of Śrī Viṣṇuprīya-mātā for a few days and heard topics about Mahāprabhu. Then he visited the places of Mahāprabhu's pastimes in the company of Vaṁśīvadanānanda Prabhu. Thereafter he took leave of Viṣṇuprīya and Vaṁśīvadanānanda. He visited twelve birth sites of renowned Vaiṣṇavas and other places where the devotees of Caitanya were residing. After meeting and associating with devotees for some time, he went to Śrī Puruṣottama-dhāma. Śrīnivāsa returned from Puruṣottama to Gaura-maṇḍala and stayed there for some time.

Then he departed for Śrī Vṛndāvana-dhāma for *darśana*. After arriving in Vraja, Śrīnivāsa met with the Goswamis. He visited all the holy places in Vraja in their association and began to relish newer and newer sentiments. After residing in Vraja for a long time, he returned to the spiritual abode of Gaura-maṇḍala and delivered all the sinful people.

(*Sajjana-toṣaṇī* 2/10/11)

22. What favor did Śrī Śyāmānanda Prabhu do for the Vaiṣṇava world?

Śyāmānanda was born in the Karana family on the full moon day in the month of April in a village called Dandakeśvara in Orissa. He spent his childhood at home and as soon as he became a youth he left home and accepted the renounced order of life. On seeing his renunciation, the devotees of Śrī Gaurāṅga Mahāprabhu, awarded him the name Dukhī Kṛṣṇadāsa. Realizing that it was useless to perform *bhajana* without first taking initiation, he took initiation from Śrī Hṛdaya-caitanya, who was the dear disciple of Śrī Gaurīdāsa Paṇḍita, an associate of the Lord. After taking initiation and understanding that it is a disciple's duty to serve his spiritual master, he stayed with his spiritual master and served him. After some time, he took permission from his spiritual master and went to visit the holy places of Vṛndāvana. After arriving in Vṛndāvana, he soon received the mercy of the Goswamis, headed by Śrī Raghunātha dāsa.

The high standard of his renunciation was simply wonderful. Everyone was struck with wonder by seeing his renunciation. He joined Śrīnivāsa Ācārya and Narottama Ṭhākura in Bengal and lived there for a long time, delivering many foolish atheists by preaching devotional service to Krishna. These topics are elaborately described in many Vaiṣṇava books. We have a great desire to publish the glories of the great personalities in detail.

(*Sajjana-toṣaṇī* 2/6)

23. Why were Śrīnivāsācārya, Śrī Narottama, and Śrī Śyāmānanda Prabhu called "Gītācāryas"?

The three great souls, Śrīnivāsācārya, Śrī Narottama, and Śrī Śyāmānanda lived in Vṛndāvana for some time as the students of Śrī Jīva Goswami. With the approval of Śrī Jīva Goswami, they arranged the method of performing *kīrtana*. All three of them were expert in the art of music and proficient in Indian classical music. Their lives were one, their goal was one, and they were the most intimate friends. Being encouraged by Śrī Jīva Goswami, the three expert and melodious singers went to their respective provinces. These three great souls were the ornaments of the land of Gauḍa, Bengal. It does not appear that they were as learned in Sanskrit as the Goswamis, because we do not find any Sanskrit books written by them. They were fully mature in knowledge of the mellows of Vraja, expert in Vaiṣṇava conclusions, and proficient in the art of music and singing.

After the disappearance of Śrīmān Mahāprabhu, there was some commotion within the Vaiṣṇava society. Since there was no qualified candidate in the line of Mahāprabhu at that time and since various ideologies entered the philosophy of Vaiṣṇavism, the land of Gauḍadeśa became bereft of the administration of an *ācārya*. Due to His independent nature, Śrī Vīracandra Prabhu could not bring all of Gauḍa-maṇḍala-bhūmi under His control. At the same time, there was great confusion among the sons of Śrī Advaita Prabhu. Gradually the associates and devotees of Mahāprabhu began to disappear. Taking this opportunity, many preachers of unauthorized sects, such as *bāula*, *sahajiyā*, *daraveśa*, and *sāṅi*, began to spread their ideologies at different places. Taking advantage of the faith that the people had in the names of Śrī Caitanya and Nityānanda, these preachers of unauthorized cults began to spread their evil teachings to the unfortunate living entities.

Śrī Jīva Goswami was the only undisputed Vaiṣṇava *ācārya* at that time. Although he was a resident of Vraja, on hearing the pathetic condition of Gauḍa-maṇḍala, he became extremely distressed and immediately sent Śrīnivāsācārya Prabhu, Śrī Narottama dāsa Ṭhākura, and Śrī Śyāmānanda Prabhu to Bengal as ācāryas to teach religious principles. He also arranged to send many conclusive writings of the Lord's associates. By the will of Mahāprabhu, all these books were stolen on the way. Having no books with them, they began to preach the pure principles of Vaiṣṇava religion on the strength of their own *bhajana*.

(*Sajjana-toṣaṇī* 6/2)

24. Who was Śrīla Baladeva Vidyābhū ṣaṇa? What is the difference between Śrīla Jīva Goswami and Śrīla Baladeva Vidyābhūṣaṇa?

Vidyābhūṣaṇa Mahāśaya was a special star in the Gauḍīya Vaiṣṇava-sampradāya. Nobody after the six Goswamis has done the amount of service that he did for this *sampradāya*. From this, we can clearly understand that he was one of the eternal associates of Śrīmān Mahāprabhu. One Vaiṣṇava book mentions that Śrī Gopīnātha Miśra, an associate of Śrī Caitanya, was an incarnation of Brahmā. Gopīnātha Miśra directly heard Mahāprabhu explain the Absolute Truth to Sārvabhauma Bhaṭṭācārya. Later, Śrī Gopīnātha Miśra appeared as Baladeva Vidyābhūṣaṇa, the commentator of Brahma-sampradāya. The words of the Vaiṣṇavas are always true and this fact appears to be correct.

Some foolish people say that the philosophy of Vidyābhūṣaṇa is more modern than the philosophy of the Goswamis. We have carefully checked this and found that there is no difference whatsoever between the philosophy of Śrī Baladeva and Śrī Jīva Goswami. The only difference is that (to protect the gravity of the commentaries of Śrī Jīva Goswami) Śrī Baladeva has used more sophisticated and intellectual words. Still he did not change the philosophy at all. Both of them stated the same conclusion regarding the Absolute Truth and the processes of worship.

(*Sajjana-toṣaṇī* 9/10)

25. What did Śrī Bhaktivinoda say about Śrīla Jagannātha dāsa Goswami?

O dear devotees of Gaurāṅga, like Śrī Jagannātha dāsa, we offer our respectful obeisances at your feet and pray with folded hands that all of you may take the position of Śrī Sanātana Goswami and point out the exact land of Śrī Māyāpura. Now all of you are our authorities and spiritual masters. Who else should we approach?

(*Śrī Viṣṇuprīya Magazine*)

26. How have the present ācāryas carried out the mission of the previous ācāryas?

The great reformers will always assert that they have come, not to destroy the old law, but to fulfill it. Vālmīki, Vyāsa, and Caitanya Mahāprabhu assert the fact either directly or by their conduct.

(*The Bhagavat*: *Its Philosophy, Its Ethics & Its Theology*)

5

Unauthorized Instructor or So-Called Ācārya

1. What is the behavior and opinion of learned godless instructors of fruitive activities?

They will say to themselves:

"O my brother, don't stay away from sense pleasures. Enjoy sense pleasures as you like, as long as other's do not know of them. Why not? I do not think the world will collapse because of them. There is no God, an all-seeing God who gives to us the results of our actions. What have you to fear? Just be a little careful, so no one will know. If they learn of it, then you will lose your good reputation, and perhaps the government or bad people will make trouble for you. If that happens, neither you nor other's will be happy."

Know for certain that if the hearts of the preachers of atheistic morality were examined, these thoughts would be found.

(*Tattva Viveka* 1/9 –12 commentary)

2. Is it proper for a bona fide spiritual master to give hari-nāma or mantra initiation to a faithless person?

One who gives *hari-nāma* to a faithless person with a desire to receive some dakṣiṇā is a seller or trader of *hari-nāma.* By exchanging an invaluable jewel for an insignificant object, a person falls down from the spiritual life of worshiping Hari.

(*Caitanya-śikṣāmṛta*)

3. Can an imposter become a spiritual master?

O my mind! Your definition of a saintly person is he who is expert in juggling words, and you become fully influenced by his association. If you see a cruel person, you show respect to him and fall down at his feet with devotion.

(*Kalyāṇa-kalpataru*, song 16)

4. Can a sannyāsī who has given up the shelter of his spiritual master become an ācārya?

Even though Rāmacandra Purī was a disciple of Mādhavendra Purī, he accepted polluted conclusions from the society of dry speculators and preached irreligious principles. As a result, Mādhavendra Purī Goswami rejected him and considered him an offender. Then, Rāmacandra Purī blasphemed and found fault with other's. He gave instructions on dry knowledge and thus became neglected by the Vaiṣṇavas.

(*Amṛta-pravāha-bhāṣya, Caitanya Caritāmṛta* Antya, Chapter 8)

5. Are the conclusions of a bonafide ācārya and an unauthorized ācārya the same?

After carefully discussing the Vedas and the *Vedānta-sūtras*, the *ācāryas* have drawn two kinds of conclusions. Śrīmat Śaṅkarācārya preached the philosophy of monism based on the conclusions put forth by the sages like Dattātreya, Aṣṭāvakra, and Durvāsā. This is one kind of conclusion. The Vaiṣṇava *ācāryas* preach the science of pure devotional service based on the conclusion put forth by the great souls like Nārada, Prahlāda, Dhruva, and Manu. This is the other kind of conclusion.

(*Manaḥ-śikṣā*, Chapter 9)

6

Sampradāya

1. Is the process of authorized sampradāya eternal or modern?

The system of *sampradāya* is extremely necessary. Therefore the system of authorized *sampradāya* has been coming down from time immemorial among saintly persons.

(*Jaiva Dharma*, Chapter 13)

2. Who accepts pure religious principles?

Only those who have received pure spiritual knowledge of the Vedas coming from Brahmā through disciplic succession accept the path of pure religious principles. Others become servants of atheistic philosophy due to differences of opinion.

(*Manaḥ-śikṣā*, Chapter 2)

3. What is the disciplic succession of the servants of Śrī Caitanya? Who are their enemies?

Śrī Brahma-sampradāya is the disciplic succession of the servants of Śrī Caitanya. Śrī Kavikarṇapūra Goswami has written the gradual order of this disciplic succession in his book, *Gaura-gaṇoddeśa-dīpikā*. Śrī Baladeva Vidyābhūṣaṇa, who wrote a commentary on *Vedānta-sūtra*, also accepted this disciplic succession. Those who do not accept this line of disciplic succession are the main enemies of the servants of Śrī Krishna Caitanya.

(*Manaḥ-śikṣā*, Chapter 2)

4. Who are Kali's spies?

Those who accept the disciplic succession of Śrī Krishna Caitanya but secretly do not follow the rules and regulations laid down by the disciplic succession are the spies of Kali.

(*Manaḥ-śikṣā*, Chapter 2)

5. In the future, which authorized sampradāya will exist?

Within a short time, there will be only one *sampradāya* left and that is the Śrī Brahma-sampradāya. All other *sampradāyas* will be merged into it.

(*Manaḥ-śikṣā*, Chapter 2)

6. Why are there differences of opinion in the philosophy of the Vaiṣṇava sampradāyas?

Vaiṣṇavas from all *sampradāyas* have one philosophy. There are only some differences in some insignificant matters. All the Vaiṣṇavas accept that the living entity is a separate truth from the Supreme Lord. All of them have accepted the path of devotional service.

(*Prema-pradīpa*, Chapter 6)

7. Is accepting a disciplic succession harmful for the living entity?

The process of accepting a *sampradāya* is extremely beneficial for the living entity. If one takes shelter of a bona fide *sampradāya*, one can easily take shelter of the lotus feet of a saintly person, learn religious principles, discuss spiritual topics, and gradually become detached from worldly affairs. As long as one has a tendency to mingle with persons from unauthorized *sampradāyas* and engage in argument and counter argument for one's whole life, one can never achieve perfection. Useless people, occasionally seeing some selfish persons from a bona fide *sampradāya* indulge in sinful activities, condemn the process of bona fide *sampradāya*. The duty of an intelligent person is to try to purify the *sampradāya* after joining it. When good items are not available in the market and various artificial items are abundant, it is sensible to reform the market; if someone tries to stop the process of selling, you can never praise his intelligence. The founder-*ācāryas* of the *sampradāyas* created the system of *sampradāya* for the benefit of the people of the world.

(*Sajjana-toṣaṇī* 4/4)

8. When did the philosophy of opposing the system of sampradāya start?

By discussing the history, we understand that there was never any opinion against the system of *sampradāya* in this holy land of India. Only since India came in contact with scholars from Western countries have some people become opposed to the system of *sampradāya*.

(*Sajjana-toṣaṇī* 4/4)

9. Are there more faults or more good qualities in the system of sampradāya?

If one considers the system of *sampradāya*, naturally one will find that there are more good qualities than faults. If the major portion of an object is good, even though there are some bad elements, learned people eagerly accept it.

(*Sajjana-toṣaṇī* 4/4)

10. Do those outside the sampradāya belong to their own concocted sampradāya?

Persons who present opinions opposed to the system of the authorized *sampradāya* consider themselves outsiders. Actually, using their concocted theory, they create a new *sampradāya*.

(*Sajjana-toṣaṇī* 4/4)

11. What is the evidence that the philosophy of Vaiṣṇavism is eternal?

The constitutional duties of the Vaiṣṇavas existed from the time of creation of the living entities. Lord Brahmā was the first Vaiṣṇava. Śrī Mahādeva is also a Vaiṣṇava. The original prajāpatis, or progenitors, are all Vaiṣṇavas. Śrī Nārada Goswami, who was born from the mind of Brahmā, is also a Vaiṣṇava. The names of those who are especially renowned have been mentioned in history. Actually, we can not estimate how many hundreds of more Vaiṣṇavas there were during the time of Prahlāda and Dhruva. Later, the kings from the sun and moon dynasties, and many great sages and ascetics became devotees of Lord Viṣṇu. In the age of Kali, these things are mentioned about Satya-yuga, Tretā-yuga, and Dvāpara-yuga. Śrī Rāmānuja, Śrī Madhvācārya, Śrī Viṣṇusvāmī, and Śrī Nimbāditya Svāmī of South India brought many thousands of people to pure Vaiṣṇavism.

(*Jaiva Dharma*, Chapter 10)

12. What is the history of the fully-blossomed Vaiṣṇava religion?

The Vaiṣṇava religion is just like a lotus flower. It gradually blossomed with the help of time. At first, it was in the form of a bud; later, it blossomed a little, and ultimately, it became a fully-blossomed flower. At the time of Brahmā, this Vaiṣṇava religion, which consists of knowledge of the Absolute Truth, devotional service to the Lord, *sādhana*, and love of God, manifested in the hearts of the living entities in the form of seeds. During the period of Prahlāda, these seeds appeared as buds. Gradually during the time of Bādarāyaṇa Ṛṣi [Vyāsadeva], these buds began to blossom and during the time of the *ācāryas* of Vaiṣṇava religion, they became flowers. When Śrīmān Mahāprabhu appeared, these flowers of love of God became fully blossomed and began to spread wonderful fragrance to the people of the world. Śrīmān Mahāprabhu has revealed to the people that chanting the holy names of the Lord with love is the most confidential goal of Vaiṣṇava religion.

(*Jaiva Dharma*, Chapter 10)

13. How has knowledge of the Absolute Truth gradually become clear and mature?

Spiritual science gradually evolved from ancient times and became simpler, clearer, and more condensed. The more the impurities (arising from time and place) are removed, the more the beauty of spiritual science shines brightly before us. This spiritual science took birth in the land of kuśa grass on the banks of the Sarasvatī River in Brahmāvarta. As it gradually gained strength, this spiritual science spent its childhood in the abode of Badarikāśrama, which is covered with snow. It spent its boyhood in Naimiṣāraṇya on the banks of the Gomatī River, and its youth on the beautiful banks of the Kāverī River in the province of Draviḍa. This spiritual science attained maturity in Navadvīpa, on the banks of the Ganges, which purifies the universe.

(*Śrī Krishna-saṁhitā*, Introduction)

14. How were the authorized sampradāyas established?

The flower of devotion in the hearts of the devotees became unsteady as it floated in the current of Śaṅkarācārya's arguments. Based on the strength of Śaṅkarācārya's philosophy, Rāmānujācārya, by the mercy of the Lord, wrote a commentary on *Vedānta* that differed from *Śārīraka-bhāṣya*. Thus, the strength and prosperity of Vaiṣṇavism again increased. Within a short time, Viṣnusvāmī, Nimbārka, and Madhvācārya all introduced slight variations of the Vaiṣṇava principles by presenting their own commentaries on *Vedānta*. They followed in the footsteps of Śaṅkarācārya; they all wrote commentaries on the *Bhagavad-gītā*, *Viṣṇu-sahasra-nāma*, and the *Upaniṣads*. At that time, people thought that in order to establish a *sampradāya*, one must have commentaries on the four above-mentioned works. From these four Vaiṣṇavas, the four Vaiṣṇava *sampradāyas*, such as the Śrī-sampradāya, were introduced.

(*Śrī Krishna-saṁhitā*, Introduction)

15. Where does spiritual science reach its peak?

By studying the history of the world, it is found that spiritual science reached its peak in Navadvīpa. The Supreme Absolute Truth is the only object of love for the living entities. Unless one worships Him with attachment, the living entity can never attain Him. Even if a person gives up all affection for this world and thinks of the Supreme Lord, still the Lord is not easily achieved.

(*Śrī Krishna-saṁhitā*, Introduction)

7

Unauthorized Sampradāyas

1. Which philosophies and beliefs from foreign countries are equal to Indian philosophy that is opposed to the Vedas?

People in our country accept subordination to the Vedas and *Vedānta-sūtra*, which are the source of perfect spiritual knowledge. Even so, various philosophies (such as that of Cārvāka and Buddha), and various writings (such as Sāṅkhya, Patañjala, and Vaiśeṣika) which oppose the philosophy of the Vedas, have come about. Various"isms" such as materialism, positivism, secularism, pessimism, skepticism, pantheism, and atheism have been preached in countries like China, Greece, Iraq, France, England, Germany, and Italy. A few philosophies have been invented by establishing God with the help of arguments. A philosophy that one should faithfully worship God has also been preached in many places in the world. In some places, this philosophy is accepted only as a faith; in some other countries, it is preached as the God-given religion. Wherever it is accepted only as a faith, it has been known as theism, and wherever it is accepted as a God-given religion, it has been accepted as Christianity and Mohammedanism.
(*Tattva Viveka* 1/3)

2. Which religions are called irreligion, cheating religion, reflection of religion, or nonreligion?

Religion in which various *anarthas* such as atheism, skepticism, materialism, and impersonalism are present, the devotees do not accept as religion. In fact, such religions are to be accepted as irreligion, cheating religion, reflection of religion, or nonreligion.
(*Caitanya-śikṣāmṛta* 1/1)

3. What is the religious principle of the materialists?

Religious principles that are propagated by the materialists are baseless and fallible like a house.
(*Tattva Viveka* 1/9/12)

4. What are the characteristics of selfish and selfless materialists of India and other countries?

The philosophy of attaining material pleasures is of two kinds: the philosophy of selfish material pleasures, *svārtha-jaḍānanda-vādī*, and the philosophy of unselfish material pleasures, *niḥsvārtha-jaḍānanda-vādī*.

Those who follow the philosophy of selfish material pleasures think:"Neither God, nor soul, nor afterlife, nor karmic reactions exist. Therefore, concerned only for results visible in this world, let us spend our time in sense pleasures. We don't need to waste our time performing useless religious activities." Because of bad association and sinful deeds, this atheistic philosophy has existed in human society from ancient times. However, this philosophy has never become prominent among faithful, respectable people. Still, in different countries some people have taken shelter of this idea and even written books propounding it. In India the *brāhmaṇa* Cārvāka, in China the atheist Yangchoo, in Greece the atheist Leucippus, in Central Asia Sardanaplus, in Rome Lucretious, and many other's in many countries all wrote books propounding these ideas. Von Holback says that one should perform philanthropic deeds to increase one's personal happiness. By working to make other's happy, one increases one's own happiness, and that is good.

Trying to persuade the people in general, the authors of modern books propounding the philosophy of material pleasure often talk about unselfish material pleasure or doing good materially for other's. In India, atheism existed even in ancient days. With great erudition, one philosopher wrote a great distortion of the Vedic teaching. A distortion called the *Mīmāṁsā-sūtra*, beginning with the words *codanā-lakṣaṇo dharmaḥ*, replaces God with an abstract origin, before which nothing existed (*apūrva*). In Greece, a philosopher named Democritus preached this philosophy also. He said that matter and void exist eternally. When these two meet, there is creation, and when they are separated, there is destruction. Material elements are different only because their atoms are of different sizes. Otherwise the elements are not different. Knowledge is a sensation that comes when something within touches something without. His philosophy holds that all existence is composed of atoms.

In our country also, Kaṇāda in his Vaiśeṣika philosophy taught that the material elements are composed of eternal atoms. However, the Vaiśeṣika philosophy is different from Democritus' atomic theory, for the Vaiśeṣika philosophy accepts the eternal existence of both God and soul. In Greece, Plato and Aristotle refused to accept an eternal God as the only creator of the material world. Kaṇāda's errors are also seen in their views. Gassendi accepted the existence of atoms, but concluded that God created the atoms.

In France, Diderot and Lamettrie preached the theory of unselfish material pleasure. The theory of unselfish material pleasure reached its high point in France's philosopher Compte, who was born in 1795 and died in 1857. His impure philosophy is called positivism. It is inappropriately named, for it accepts the existence of matter only, and nothing else. It claims that aside from sense knowledge there is no true knowledge. The mind is only a special arrangement of material elements. In the final conclusion, no origin of all existence can be described. Furthermore, there is no need to discover any origin of the material world. There is no sign that any conscious creator of the material world exists. The thinking mind should categorize things according to their relationships, results, similarities, and dissimilarities. One should not accept the existence of anything beyond matter. Belief in God is for children. Adults know God is a myth. Discriminating between good and evil, one should act righteously. One should try to do good to all human beings.

That is the philosophy of unselfish material pleasure. Thinking in this way, one should act for the benefit of all human beings. One should imagine a female form and worship it. That form is, of course, unreal. Still, by worshiping it one attains good character. The earth, or the totality of material existence, is called the Supreme Fetish, the land is called the Supreme Medium, and the primordial human nature is called the Supreme Being. A female form with an infant in her hands should be worshiped morning, noon, and night. This imaginary female form, which is an amalgam of one's mother, wife, and daughter, should be meditated and worshiped in the past, present, and future. One should not seek any selfish benefit from these actions.

In England, a philosopher named Mill taught a philosophy of sentimentalism that is largely like Compte's philosophy of unselfish material pleasure. In this way atheism, or secularism, attracted the minds of many youths in England. Mill, Lewis, Paine, Carlyle, Bentham, Combe, and other philosophers preached these ideas. This philosophy is of two kinds. One kind was taught by Holyoake, who kindly accepted God's existence to some extent. Bradlaugh, who was a thorough atheist, taught the other kind.

(*Tattva Viveka* 1/5/8)

5. What is the real nature of the selfless materialists?

The selfish materialists are understood by their name, but actually the selfless materialists are also selfish.

(*Tattva Viveka* 1/9/12)

6. Is the philosophy of the selfless materialist devoid of selfishness?

The philosophy of godless secularism was vigorously preached in India by the learned smārtas, who cleverly tried to connect God with their philosophy. The self-interest of one person created obstacles for the self-interest of another person. As soon as less intelligent people heard the word selfless, they immediately respected the philosophy of the selfless materialist, with a desire to achieve their own self-interest.

(*Tattva Viveka* 1/9/12)

7. How much fundamental knowledge do the learned scholars of the Western countries possess?

In the Western countries very few people are civilized and intelligent. In those countries people like Tindale, Haxli, and Darwin are considered very learned. They are supposed to be learned because they can present old topics in a new language. In *Bhagavad-gītā*, which appeared five thousand years ago, the demoniac propensities are described. It is stated therein that the theory of evolution and the theory of gradual advancement are born from a demoniac nature.

("Religion and Science", *Sajjana-toṣaṇī* 7/7)

8. Is the atonement prescribed by mundane smārtas without duplicity?

Once a *smārta-paṇḍita* prescribed the *candrāyaṇa-vrata* and other harsh penances to a person who had asked him about the atonement for a particular sin. Hearing this, the person said,"O Bhaṭṭācārya Mahāśaya, if I must perform a *candrāyaṇa-vrata* for killing that spider, then your son, who was also implicated in that act, must also perform that penance." Seeing this would be a great calamity for his son, the Bhaṭṭācārya Mahāśaya turned two or three pages in his big book and said,"Aha! I made a mistake. Now I see. The books state that a dead spider is only a piece of rag. So you need not perform any atonement at all." The atheist *smārta-paṇḍitas* are like that.

(*Tattva Viveka* 1/9/12)

9. What is the fate of persons who follow the philosophy of skepticism?

The philosophy of skepticism ruins its followers, because they are always doubtful of the Absolute Truth.

(*Tattva Viveka* 1/16)

10. What is the position of the modern atheists?

Modern atheists preach philosophies that are illusory and establish themselves as new propounders. They only change the name and form of an old philosophy.

(*Tattva Viveka* 1/17)

11. What is the conception of mundane transcendentalists?

We meet many so-called *paṇḍitas* who think that they have understood *bhakti* by their knowledge and intelligence. Some conclude that devotional service mixed with *jñāna* is pure *bhakti*, and other's conclude that devotional service mixed with karma is pure *bhakti*. They are so proud that if they hear the teachings of *Śrī Caitanya Caritāmṛta*, they say,"Everyone can make their own conclusion. What is the need to take the conclusion of *Caitanya Caritāmṛta*?" These people never come in touch with sad-*dharma* because they have no desire to know it. The result of performing their own concocted process of devotional service is that they can never relish pure devotion.

("Tat-tat-karma-pravārtana", *Sajjana-toṣaṇī* 11/6)

12. Does morality without faith in God have any value?

Some people accept worldly morality, but they do not accept God. To protect themselves, they say that morality without faith in God is always fearless and dutiful. If one does not accept God, all his worldly morality is useless.

(*Caitanya-śikṣāmṛta* 3/3)

13. Have the mundane psychologists or scientists done any good for the world?

Those who have written volumes of books on the subject of psychology, with the help of arguments but without understanding the real form of psychology, have simply poured ghee onto ashes. They labored uselessly and became intoxicated with pride while accumulating name and fame.

What to speak of doing good for the people of this world, they have created inauspiciousness.

(*Sajjana-toṣaṇī* 8/9)

14. How did Śaṅkarācārya convert fruitive workers and Buddhists to his own philosophy?

Śaṅkarācārya was not satisfied with his *brāhmaṇa* followers, so he introduced ten types of *sannyāsīs*, such as Giri, Purī, and Bhāratī. With the help of the physical and mental strength of these *sannyāsīs*, Śaṅkarācārya converted the *brāhmaṇa*s who were attached to fruitive activities, and he prepared himself to vanquish the Buddhists. Wherever he failed to convert the Buddhists to his philosophy, he engaged nāgās, naked *sannyāsīs*, who used weapons such as spears. Ultimately, he wrote a commentary on *Vedānta* and thus combined the karma-*kāṇḍa* of the *brāhmaṇa*s with the *jñāna*-kāṇḍa of the Buddhists. In this way, he united both groups. The Buddhist temples were converted into Vedic temples. Out of fear of being beaten, as well as by realizing the insignificance of their own religious practices, the Buddhists helplessly accepted the authority of the *brāhmaṇa*s. The Buddhists who hated being converted took the remnants of their cult and fled to Śrī Lanka and Brahmādeśa (Myanmar or Burma). The old Buddhists took Lord Buddha's tooth and went to Śrī Laṇkā from Jagannātha Purī.

(*Śrī Krishna-saṁhitā*, Introduction)

15. Is it proper to accept a living entity or a sannyāsī as Lord Nārāyaṇa?

The Māyāvādī *sannyāsīs* consider themselves Brahman and address each other Nārāyaṇa. It is the custom of the smārtas that if the *brāhmaṇa*s and the householders see a *sannyāsī*, they should offer him obeisances, thinking him to be Nārāyaṇa. To stop this wrong belief, Śrīmān Mahāprabhu said that any living entity, including a *sannyāsī*, can never become Krishna, who is full of six opulences. The living entity is only a spiritual spark; therefore he is like a particle of the rays of the sun Krishna. It is improper to offer obeisances to a living entity because one considers him to be Nārāyaṇa.

(*Amṛta-pravāha-bhāṣya, Caitanya Caritāmṛta* Madhya 18/112 to 116)

16. Do the demigods accept the worship offered by the Māyāvādīs?

The demigods do not accept the worshipable ingredients and foods offered to them by the Māyāvādīs because the Māyāvādīs are infected with the faults of Māyāvāda philosophy.

(*Jaiva Dharma*, Chapter 10)

17. Do the Māyāvādīs hear, chant, and offer prayers that are pleasing to Krishna?

Māyāvādīs consider the glories of devotional service, the object of worship, and the Lord's servants as temporary. Their hearing, chanting, serving, and offering prayers, therefore, are felt by Krishna as blows of thunderbolts.

(A song from *Śaraṇāgati*)

18. Is the philosophy of accepting an animal as God pure religion?

A person or a community who worships an animal as God is understood to be following the philosophy of monism.

(*Caitanya-śikṣāmṛta* 5/3)

19. To whom alone should one worship?

Māyāvādīs engage in the worship of five gods: Durgā, the sungod, Gaṇapati, Śiva, and Viṣṇu. At first, there is the material energy (under the control of Durgā), then appears the sun, which induces action in the material energy, then appears Ganeśa (Gaṇapati), who confirms the existence of consciousness. Then appears Lord Śiva, who is perceived as all-pervading, and finally, Lord Viṣṇu is served. He is the Supersoul, sac-cid-ānanda, incomparable, and beyond the reach of ordinary living entities. From a doubtful person to a learned scholar of spiritual topics, all are eligible to worship the Supreme Brahman. The symptom of actual worship is to make advancement on the path of *rāga*. One should therefore worship the Supreme Lord, who is sac-cid-ānanda and the controller of all living entities. However, if one remains entangled in other processes of worship, one will never achieve the goal of life.

(*Tattva-sūtra* 47)

20. How do less intelligent people define the role of material nature?

Less intelligent people accept material energy as the doer of everything. However, the learned scholars attribute the killing of Mahiṣāsura, Chandamunda, Śumbha, and Niśumbha to material nature as follows: The word"doer" is attributed to a male or female who performs a particular activity in the material world. For example, the water of the Ganges is the purifier, Calcutta is the giver of happiness, Kali is the destroyer of religious principles, and education is the giver of wealth. In the same way as the Ganges, Calcutta, Kali, and education are the doer, material energy is also the doer.

(*Tattva-sūtra* 22)

21. Is the worship of Viṣṇu among the worship of the five gods, not pure Vaiṣṇava religion?

The worship of Viṣṇu that exists in the worship of the five gods, is not pure Vaiṣṇava religion, even though it consists of taking initiation, worshiping Viṣṇu, or even worshiping Rādhā and Krishna.

(*Jaiva Dharma*, Chapter 4)

22. Are the impersonalist sannyāsīs of Kāśī the only Māyāvādīs?

The *sannyāsīs* of Vārāṇasī are famous Māyāvādīs. The householders who worship five gods and who belong to their cult are also Māyāvādīs. Although they are initiated into Viṣṇu *mantras*, they are still called Māyāvādīs. Even many of those who identify themselves as close to Śrī Caitanya Mahāprabhu are Māyāvādīs. Many cults such as bāula and daraveśa also fall into the category of Māyāvāda.

(*Sajjana-toṣaṇī* 5—12)

23. What did Śaṅkarācārya say regarding the living entities destination after liberation?

Śrī Śaṅkara is totally silent about the wonderful destination a living entity achieves after his liberation. Those who pass their lives accepting only the external portion of his teachings become distracted from the path of Vaiṣṇava religion.

(*Jaiva Dharma*, Chapter 2)

24. What are the principles of Brahmo-dharma propounded by Ram Mohan Raya?

Brahmo-dharma propounded by Ram Mohan Raya is a mixture of Christianity and Hinduism. One can never expect the truth to be established in such a religion. The followers of Brahmo-*dharma* learned the superiority of *śanta-rāsa* from the Christian religion and foreign logicians, and thus they dare to disregard the other superior *rāsas* such as *dāsya*, *sākhya*, *vātsalya*, and *mādhura*. The pathetic condition of a person who tries to consider the superiority and inferiority of the *rāsas* without understanding the difference between matter and spirit is the same as the pathetic condition of a person who tries to learn geometry without understanding the difference between an axiom and a postulate.

(*Sajjana-toṣaṇī* 8/4)

25. What is the basis of the philosophy of Ram Mohan Raya?

Raja Ram Mohan Raya crossed the gate of the *Vedānta*, which was a Māyāvāda construction designed by Śaṅkarācārya, the chosen enemy of the Buddhists and Jains, and chalked his way to the Unitarian form of the Christian faith converted into an Indian appearance.

(*The Bhagavat*: *Its Philosophy*, *Its Ethics & Its Theology*)

26. What did Śrī Bhaktivinoda Ṭhākura say about the ascending process of Ram Mohan Raya's philosophy?

Ram Mohan Raya was an able man. He could not be satisfied with the theory of illusion contained in the Māyāvāda philosophy of Śaṅkara. His heart was full of love of nature. Through the eye of his mind, he saw that he could not believe in Śaṅkara's identity with God. He ran furiously from the bounds of Śaṅkara to those of the Koran. Even then, he was not satisfied. Next, he studied the pre-eminently beautiful precepts and history of Jesus, first in the English translations and then in the original Greek, and took shelter under the holy banner of the Jewish Reformer. But Ram Mohan Raya was also a patriot. He wanted to reform his country in the same way as he reformed himself. He knew that truth does not belong exclusively to any individual, nation, or race. Truth belongs to God, and whether at the poles or the equator, man has a right to claim it as the property of his father. On these grounds, Ram Mohan Raya claimed the truths inculcated by the Western Savior as the property of himself and his fellow citizens, and thus he established the Brahmo-samāja independently of what was in his own country in the beautiful Bhāgavatam. His noble deeds will certainly secure him a high position in the history of reformers. But then, to speak the truth, he would have done more if he had commenced his work of reformation from the point where the last reformer of India left off.

(*The Bhagavat*: *Its Philosophy*, *Its Ethics & Its Theology*)

27. What is the principal reason of Ram Mohan Raya's opposition to the teachings of Śrīmad-Bhāgavatam?

The Bhāgavatam did not attract Ram Mohan Raya. His thought, mighty though it was, unfortunately branched like the Ranigunj line of the railway. From the barren station of Śaṅkarācārya, he did not attempt to go beyond the Delhi Terminus to the great Bhāgavatam expounder of Nadia.

(*The Bhagavat: Its Philosophy, Its Ethics & Its Theology*)

28. What is the worship of matter?

"The sky that exists within the cosmic creation is all-pervading and formless; this is also true of its controller." This is called the worship of matter.

(*Tattva Viveka* 1/28)

29. Why are the followers of Brahmo-dharma against accepting the lotus feet of a spiritual master?

Fearing that they will be misguided by taking shelter at the lotus feet of a spiritual master, they do not endeavor to obtain his shelter, and even if they happen to meet a bona fide spiritual master, they do not respect him. They give up the shelter of a bona fide spiritual master, because unauthorized gurus misguide their disciples.

(*Tattva Viveka* 1/28)

30. What is the difference between metaphysical truth and transcendental truth?

Until one realizes the subtle scientific difference between metaphysical truth and transcendental truth, one does not distinguish them when using these terms. Dry speculators find it very difficult to awaken transcendental love of God. Due to an immense amount of piety, one develops attachment for transcendental subject matters; one cannot see the transcendental variegatedness by staying on the other side of the wall in the form of metaphysical arguments.

(*Sajjana-toṣaṇī* 6/2)

31. When did the philosophy of Trinity come into being?

Zarathustra is a very ancient philosopher. When his philosophy found no honor in India, Zarathustra preached in Iran. It was by the influence of Zarathustra ideas that Satan, an equally powerful rival to God, made his imaginary appearance first in the religion of the Jews and then in the religion based on the Koran. Then, influenced by Zarathustra's idea of two Gods, the idea of three gods, or a"Trinity" made its appearance in the religion that had come from the Jewish religion.

(*Tattva Viveka* 1/21)

32. How did the philosophy of Trinity spread?

At first, three separate gods were concocted in the philosophy of Trinity. Later, learned scholars were no longer satisfied with this, so they made a compromise, stating that these three concocted gods were God, the Holy Ghost, and Christ. Also in India, because of an *anartha,* Lord Brahmā, Lord Viṣṇu, and Lord Śiva were imagined as separate gods by a particular sect of people. However, scholars of the scriptures have defined these three demigods are one in truth, and thus, they have often instructed not to differentiate between them.

(*Tattva Viveka* 1/21)

33. Is the blasphemy of sanātana-dharma by the Christians reasonable?

One who is at heart a follower of Mohammed will certainly find the doctrines of the New Testament to be a forgery created by a fallen angel. A Trinitarian Christian on the other hand will denounce the precepts of Mohammed as those of an ambitious reformer. The simple reason they criticize each other is that they are of a different disposition of mind. Thoughts have different ways. One trained in the thoughts of the Unitarian Society or of the *Vedānta* at the Benares School will scarcely find piety in those who beg from door to door in the name of Nityānanda, and the followers of Nityānanda will find no piety in the Christian. The Vaiṣṇava does not think the way the Christian thinks about the Vaiṣṇava religion. It may be that both the Christian and the Vaiṣṇava will utter the same sentiment, but they will never stop fighting with each other, because they have arrived at their common conclusion by different thoughts. Thus a great deal of unkindness enters into the arguments of pious Christians when they pass their imperfect opinion on the religion of the Vaiṣṇavas.

(*The Bhagavat*: *Its Philosophy*, *Its Ethics & Its Theology*)

34. From which philosophy has the tantric philosophy appeared?

There are various opinions regarding the tantras: it cannot be said that they have arisen from a particular philosophy. That which is accepted in one place is rejected in another place. In different places, the Supreme Brahman, material nature, or the living entity are accepted as the doer of everything. In this philosophy, the living entities are sometimes accepted as false and sometimes as truth.

(*Tattva Viveka* 1/14)

35. What is the real form of the philosophy of tantric power?

The various *sādhana*s that are described in the tantras—such as lāta-*sādhana*, the ritual of performing illicit sex, pañca-makāra-*sādhana*, the ritual activities of sex and the consumption of wine, flesh, and fish, and surā-*sādhana*, the ritual of drinking wine, certainly do not appear to be taken from any religious philosophy. They are nothing more than the philosophy of secularism and Comte's concocted philosophy of worshiping women.

(*Tattva Viveka* 1/14)

36. What is the brief history of the birth of Māyāvāda philosophy?

The philosophy of Buddhism gradually turned into tantric philosophy, and at that time, the Māyāvāda philosophy was created. This philosophy remained within Buddhism along with the philosophy of Buddhism. But as the philosophy of Māyāvāda or impersonalism spread, the followers of Buddhism called it covered Buddhism.

(*Tattva Viveka* 1/14)

37. Are the Māyāvādīs religious?

The Māyāvādīs are atheists.

(Kathasara, *Caitanya Caritāmṛta* Madhya, Chapter 6)

38. From where did the philosophy of Śaivite come?

In our opinion, the philosophy of Śaivite emanated from the Sāṅkhya philosophy of pseudo Kapila. However, there is a great deal of respect for material nature in this philosophy, and therefore ignorant people mistakenly think it is the same as tantric philosophy. In the tantric philosophy, two seeds have been compared to the enjoyer and material nature, but in conclusion, material nature has been accepted as the creator of spiritual variegatedness.

(*Tattva Viveka* 1/14)

39. Why did Buddhism and Jainism spread?

When the *kṣatriyas* and vaiśyas of India were extremely disturbed by the supreme rule of the *brāhmaṇa*s and the propagation of godless secularism, the *kṣatriyas* made a group and preached the philosophy of Buddhism, and vaiśyas made a group and preached the philosophy of Jainism.

(*Tattva Viveka* 1/13)

40. What is the brief history of Buddhism and Jainism?

According to Buddhism, after many births of practicing kindness and renunciation, one becomes first a *bodhisattva* and finally a Buddha. In this philosophy by practicing humbleness, peacefulness, tolerance, kindness, selflessness, meditation, renunciation, and friendliness, the soul eventually attains parinirvāṇa. In *parinirvāṇa* the soul no longer exists. In ordinary *nirvāṇa* the soul continues to exist in a form of mercy.

The followers of Jainism say that by practicing kindness and renunciation, and by cultivating all virtues, the soul gradually passes through the stages of *Nāradatva, Mahādevatva, Vāsudevatva, Paravāsudevatva, Cakravartitva,* and, at the end, attains *nirvāṇa, Bhagavattva.*

Buddhism and Jainism both accept the following ideas: The material world is eternal. Karma has no beginning, but it does have an end. Existence is suffering, and cessation of existence (*parinirvāṇa*) is happiness. Jaimini's karma-*mīmāṁsā* philosophy, which claims to accept the authority of the Vedas, is inauspicious for the living entities. Cessation of existence (*parinirvāṇa*) is auspicious for the living entities. Although they are masters of the followers of karma-*mīmāṁsā,* Indra and the demigods are servants of the sages who seek *nirvāṇa.*

(*Tattva Viveka* 1/13)

41. Is there any philosophy of nirvāṇa like Buddhism and Jainism in the Western countries?

A philosophy of ultimate emancipation or *nirvāṇa* similar to that of Buddhism and Jainism has been preached in Europe. The people of Europe call this religion Pessimism. There is no difference between Pessimism and Buddhism except that in Buddhism, the living entities are suffering birth after birth and in some lifetime they will accept the process of *nirvāṇa*, gradually attain *nirvāṇa*, and then the ultimate *nirvāṇa*. But the philosophy of Pessimism does not accept reincarnation.

(*Tattva Viveka* 1/13)

42. Did Śrī Bhaktivinoda Ṭhākura support any imitator incarnation?

In different places, some people, mostly Māyāvādīs, were trying to become new Gaurāṅgas. They created an illusion in people's minds by performing *hari-kīrtana* in disguise. One was Gaurāṅga, one Nityānanda, and another Advaita, and thus they made a group and began to perform *hari-kīrtana*. Their main purpose was to create illusion in the minds of ordinary people. The surprising fact was that many people actually thought Śrī Gaurāṅga had manifested again because of the way the group displayed symptoms of ecstatic love during the *kīrtana*. Many of the people were educated in English and were very expert in Western literature like Theosophy. Some of them came to us and said"When Gauracandra has personally appeared, why are you, His associate, sitting quietly?"

(*Sajjana-toṣaṇī* 8/1)

43. Are the Khadajathiyas or the followers of the Synthesis philosophy, pure devotees?

As soon as these people see the devotees, tears flow down from their eyes and hairs of their body stand on end. Sometimes, when they discuss the topics of the Lord, they fall unconscious. In a religious assembly, they support religious sentiments. Sometimes, they become fully absorbed in material enjoyment and act like madmen. They are not only committing offenses at the feet of Bhakti-devī by teaching such behavior to other people, but they are also ruining their own lives.

(*Sajjana-toṣaṇī* 8/10)

44. Who are self-deceivers?

Those who call themselves Vaiṣṇavas and make a show of performing *kīrtana* but do not accept initiation are certainly self-deceivers.

(*Sajjana-toṣaṇī* 11/6)

45. Who are hypocrites?

Hypocrites are those who do not accept that devotional service is eternal, but they always display external signs of devotional service. Their goal is to accomplish some remote purpose.

(*Caitanya-śikṣāmṛta* 3/3)

46. Who are sinful and cheating on the pretext of being an ācārya?

Pseudo ascetics and hypocrites give other's *mantras* and pretend to be *ācāryas*, but they engage in various sinful activities. Detached Vaiṣṇavas must develop extremely pure characteristics.
(*Sajjana-toṣaṇī* 5/10)

47. Who are imposters?

Those who put on external signs of religion but do not follow the religious principles are imposters. There are two types of imposters: cheaters and fools, and cheaters and cheated.
(*Sajjana-toṣaṇī* 10/11)

48. What are the characteristics of cheaters who imitate successful yogīs?

Some cheaters dress themselves as successful yogīs and thus cheat the world. They search after sensual happiness and try to increase their own glories by living their lives as yogīs. Because chanting the holy names of Hari is the constitutional duty of the devotees of Krishna, the cheaters artificially preach the principles of *kīrtana*, and they act whimsically in regard to the fruitive and religious activities of real yogīs. They engage in various material enjoyments and create illusion in the minds of ordinary people, but these material activities cause their own downfall. They artificially cry and fall unconscious during *kīrtana*, and they become more materialistic than ordinary people. They become proud of being devotees, on account of accepting the dress of a Vaiṣṇava and the signs of the renounced order of life. They can therefore never approach the pure Vaiṣṇavas, and they take shelter of and associate with worldly abominable people. Even though they are averse to glorifying the qualities of Krishna, they sometimes manifest artificial symptoms of ecstatic love, such as shivering while dancing in the *kīrtana*. Day by day, these activities become the object of their enjoyment.
(*Bhajanāmṛtam*)

49. What is the most harmful association in the world?

There is no worse association in the whole world than that of a dharmadvāji. One should rather associate with sense enjoyers. Being deceitful, the dharmadvājis take on the appearance of devotees with a desire to cheat everyone, and to fulfill their crooked desires, they cheat the foolish by helping them in their rascaldom. Some of the *dharmadvājis* become gurus and other's become disciples, and by trickery, they accumulate wealth, women, false prestige, and material assets. If one gives up the association of crooked hypocrites, one can honestly engage in devotional service.

(*Sajjana-toṣaṇī* 10/11))

50. Is the endeavor of the sinful living entities against the system of varṇāśrama beneficial?

To preach religious principles without respecting the *varṇāśrama* system or the *sannyāsīs* engaged in devotional service is extremely harmful. The endeavors against the *varṇāśrama* system by impersonalists, whimsical devotees, and various unauthorized *sampradāyas*, such as neḍā, bāula, karttābhajā, daraveśa, kumbhapaiya, ativāḍī, are also extremely harmful.

(*Caitanya-śikṣāmṛta*)

51. What is the harm if persons who follow pseudo religion identify themselves as brahmacārīs, sannyāsīs, and paramahaṁsas?

Nowadays, being involved in various pseudo religions, many people identify themselves as brahmacārīs, *sannyāsīs*, and paramahaṁsas, and thus they destroy the religious principles of the Āryans.

(*Sajjana-toṣaṇī* 10/7)

52. By accepting any philosophy as Mahāprabhu's philosophy can one obtain the teachings of the Lord?

Many times, because of bad karma, miscreants of various unauthorized cults, such as pseudo religion and irreligion, say that they preach the teachings of Śrī Caitanyadeva. Being absorbed in material enjoyment and not having the ability to discriminate, many people accept those unauthorized cults as the line of Mahāprabhu, and thus they are cheated from receiving the actual instructions of the Lord.

(*Caitanya-śikṣāmṛta*)

53. Is the bāula philosophy similar to the Vaiṣṇava philosophy?

The philosophies of the bāulas, sāṅis, neḍās, daraveśas, karttābhajās, and ativāḍīs are those of nondevotees. Their instructions and activities are most incoherent. Many people lose respect in Vaiṣṇavism by discussing these philosophies.

(*Prema-pradīpa*, Chapter 6)

54. Was the bāula philosophy propounded by Śrī Sanātana Goswami or Śrī Vīracandra Goswami?

The form in which the bāula philosophy is seen at present is totally opposed to the scriptures. There are two types of instructions on devotional service that are found in the *śāstras*: *vaidhī* and *rāgānuga*. The *bāulas* do not follow any limbs of *vaidhī-bhakti*; they engage in various improper activities on the pretext of *rāgānuga-bhakti*. It is very hard to say who started the *bāula* philosophy. Sometimes the bāulas claim Śrī Sanātana Goswami and sometimes Śrī Vīracandra Goswami as their propounder. Actually neither Śrī Sanātana Goswami nor Vīracandra Goswami ever thought of the sinful path of the *bāulas*.

(*Sajjana-toṣaṇī* 4/4)

55. Is dressing in an uncivilized way approved by Śrīmān Mahāprabhu?

With a desire to receive Mahāprabhu's mercy, Śrī Sanātana saw the Lord's sweet form. At that time, Śrī Sanātana had a moustache and beard. Bāulas use this as a reason for their keeping a moustache and beard. But, after seeing Śrī Sanātana, Mahāprabhu embraced him and immediately instructed him to shave. At that time, therefore, the bāulas' reason for keeping a beard and moustache was cut by the sharp razor of the barber.

(*Sajjana-toṣaṇī* 2/7)

56. Do the bāulas belong to the disciplic succession of Śrī Caitanya's followers?

The *bāulas* can never be identified as Vaiṣṇavas belonging to the line of Śrī Caitanya's followers.

(*Sajjana-toṣaṇī* 2/7)

57. Do the groups, like sāṅi and daraveśa, belong to the line of Śrī Caitanya's followers? If not, then who are they?

Since Sanātana was addressed as a fakir, persons who belong to various unauthorized groups, such as *sāṅi*, *daraveśa*, *caranapali*, and *dulalcandi*, dress themselves as Mohammedan mendicants and often act like them. In this way, they claim to be Vaiṣṇavas belonging to the line of Śrī Caitanya.

If someone asks them, "Why do you dress and almost behave like Mohammedan mendicants but identify yourselves as Vaiṣṇavas belonging to Śrī Caitanya-sampradāya?"

In answer, they say, "Sanātana Goswami was a Mohammedan mendicant."

But when Mahāprabhu had Sanātana shave his moustache and beard, and ordered him to dress as a Vaiṣṇava, the authenticity of the sāṅi, daraveśa, caranapali, and dulalcandi was put to an end. For this reason the followers of *sāṅi* and *daraveśa* can never become Vaiṣṇava followers of Śrī Caitanya; rather they should be known as belonging to the Mohammedan religion.

(*Sajjana-toṣaṇī* 2/7)

58. Are the following terms right and prestigious for the Vaiṣṇava religion: Vaiṣṇava-vaṁśa (Vaiṣṇava dynasty), Vaiṣṇava-jāti (Vaiṣṇava caste), and Vaiṣṇava-ācārya-vaṁśa (dynasty of the Vaiṣṇava ācārya)?

There cannot be a Vaiṣṇava-vaṁśa. There is no guarantee that every descendant of a particular dynasty will become a Vaiṣṇava. We are seeing many rogues take birth in various Vaiṣṇava families, and they are acting like demons. Whereas many great people have taken birth in the family of dog-eaters and Mohammedans, and have become Vaiṣṇavas on the strength of pure devotional service. Many non-Vaiṣṇavas are found in the families of Vaiṣṇava *ācāryas*. On the other hand, many Vaiṣṇavas have taken birth in the family of gross nondevotees. The prestige that is given to the caste Vaiṣṇavas and descendants of Vaiṣṇava *ācāryas* does not increase the glories of the Vaiṣṇava religion; rather the audacity of non-Vaiṣṇavism is increasing.

(*Sajjana-toṣaṇī* 9/9)

59. Is the sahajiyā religion a Vaiṣṇava religion?

An abominable sect known as *sahajiyā* is secretly being followed in many parts of Bengal. The activities of this cult are extremely sinful. They do not follow *sahajiyā-dharma* or spontaneous duties that are mentioned in the *śāstras*. The spontaneous duties of the pure spirit soul are to engage in the transcendental service of Krishna. These duties are spontaneous for the soul, and they manifested at the same time as the soul, but they are not spontaneous when the soul is materially conditioned.

The cheaters and the cheated have turned their pure love of Krishna into mundane spontaneous activities by the meeting of man and woman. Actually pure love is not like that. For a soul in its constitutional position, the contact of a material male and female body is extremely abominable and improper. The cult that is being advertised at present as *sahajiyā-dharma* is against all the scriptures.

(*Sajjana-toṣaṇī* 4/6)

60. For what purpose was the process of begging alms introduced? What is the present condition of this process?

Begging alms was first introduced for the benefit of pure Vaiṣṇavas. But now it has become a business. The hypocrite Vaiṣṇavas and Vaiṣṇavīs, deciding not to earn their food by any work in the world, have taken to begging alms.

(*Sajjana-toṣaṇī* 6/3)

61. How did the process of begging alms become spoiled?

Seeing that the Vaiṣṇavas did not agree to accept alms, useless men and women took advantage of the profession of begging alms.

(*Sajjana-toṣaṇī* 6/3)

62. Do pure Vaiṣṇavas approve of hearing hari-kīrtana from the mouths of professional singers?

Professional singers have neither associated with real *sādhus* nor properly understood the Vaiṣṇava conclusion. Their words therefore strike the ears of Vaiṣṇavas like thunderbolts.

(*Sajjana-toṣaṇī* 6/2)

63. Is illicit association with women approved by Śrīmān Mahāprabhu or Vaiṣṇava religious principles?

The temples of Navadvīpa-maṇḍala became polluted by persons like Govinda dāsa Bābājī. Fearing such faults, our beloved Lord Śrī Gaurāṅgadeva rejected Junior Haridāsa from the Vaiṣṇava society. Even after seeing His action, do the hypocrites not become afraid?

(*Śrī Viṣṇuprīya Magazine*, Vol. 1)

64. What was the condition of Gaura-maṇḍala during the time of Śrī Bhaktivinoda?

Conclusions against Vaiṣṇava philosophy have spread everywhere. Some people promote Māyāvāda philosophy as Vaiṣṇava philosophy. Some people mix impersonalism and secularism with a portion of pure religious principles and present a perverted Vaiṣṇava religion. Those who are sober Vaiṣṇavas remain as *kaniṣṭha-adhikārīs* as defined in the *Śrīmad-Bhāgavatam*, beginning with the words arcāyām eva haraye. There is a definite absence of intelligent pure Vaiṣṇavas. The same condition that a living entity is put in if he does not have a teacher is being faced by Gaura-maṇḍala.

(*Sajjana-toṣaṇī* 6/2)

65. How was the Vaiṣṇava religion accepted during the time of Śrī Bhaktivinoda Ṭhākura?

The age of Kali is so formidable that it does not allow pious activities to go on for long. When the three *ācāryas* (Śrī Śrīnivāsa Ācārya, Śrī Śyāmānanda Prabhu, and Śrī Narottama dāsa Ṭhākura) and their followers (such as Śrī Govinda dāsa) disappeared from this world, immediately the supreme religious principles began to vanish again. Gradually pure devotional service began to disappear from the land of Gauḍa. The descendants of the *ācārya* families began to act like authorized preachers of various religions, no matter whether they were Vaiṣṇavas, *śāktas*, or *karma-kāṇḍīs*. As a result, the pure Vaiṣṇava religion inaugurated by Śrī Gaurāṅga, Śrī Nityānanda, and Śrī Advaita gradually disappeared from sight. On one side, the revolution of the *ācāryas* was going on, and on the other, disturbances created by *bāulas, sahajiyās*, and other's gradually increased. That is why a pathetic condition of Vaiṣṇava religion is found even today.

(*Sajjana-toṣaṇī* 6/2)

66. After the disappearance of Śrīmān Mahāprabhu what revolution took place in the world of the Vaiṣṇavas?

After the disappearance of Śrīmān Mahāprabhu, there was some commotion within the Vaiṣṇava society. Since there was no qualified candidate in the line of Mahāprabhu at that time and since various ideologies entered the philosophy of Vaiṣṇavism, the land of Gauḍadeśa became bereft of the administration of an *ācārya*. Due to His independent nature, Śrī Vīracandra Prabhu could not bring all of Gauḍa-maṇḍala-bhūmi under His control. At the same time, there was great confusion among the sons of Śrī Advaita Prabhu. Gradually the associates and devotees of Mahāprabhu began to disappear. Taking this opportunity, many preachers of unauthorized sects, such as *bāula, sahajiyā, daraveśa*, and *sāṅi*, began to spread their ideologies at different places. Taking advantage of the faith that the people had in the names of Śrī Caitanya and Nityānanda, these preachers of unauthorized cults began to spread their evil teachings to the unfortunate living entities.

Śrī Jīva Goswami was the only and undisputed Vaiṣṇava *ācārya* at that time. Although he was a resident of Vraja, on hearing the pathetic condition of Gauḍa-maṇḍala, he became extremely distressed and immediately sent Śrī Śrīnivāsa Ācārya, Śrī Narottama dāsa Ṭhākura, and Śrī Śyāmānanda Prabhu to Bengal as *ācāryas* to teach religious principles. He also arranged to send many conclusive writings of the Lord's associates. By the will of

Mahāprabhu, all these books were stolen on the way. Having no books with them, they began to preach the pure principles of Vaiṣṇava religion on the strength of their own *bhajana*.

(*Sajjana-toṣaṇī* 6/2)

67. Which persons tried to eliminate pure devotional service after the disappearance of Śrīmān Mahāprabhu?

After the disappearance of the transcendental pastimes of Śrī Gaurāṅgadeva, various unauthorized *sampradāyas* such as *bāula*, *karttābhajā*, and *sahajiyā* as well as the *smārta-brāhmaṇa*s and impersonalists tried their best to pollute the Vaiṣṇava religion on the pretext of supporting it. Even today there is no lack of such people. Gradually the number of these classes of people is increasing. It is extremely unreasonable and nondevotional to say that Haridāsa Ṭhākura was a mercy *brāhmaṇa*, that Śrī Īśvara Purī belonged to a *brāhmaṇa* or *śūdra* family, and that nobody except a *brāhmaṇa* is qualified to teach the philosophy of Vaiṣṇavism. These activities have not enhanced devotional service. Therefore these activities are not respected by the devotees.

(*Sajjana-toṣaṇī* 11/10)

68. What is the duty of a devotee during a crisis, especially when an incarnation of the Lord disappears from the world?

A practitioner is prone to falldown when various deceptions surface after the disappearance of an incarnation of the Lord. It is a limb of devotional service for a practitioner to remain careful of these deceptions.

(*Bhajanāmṛtam* commentary)

69. Who is the servant of Kali?

One can worship Krishna with the Gaura *mantra* and Gaura with the Krishna *mantra*. They are all one. Anyone who differentiates between Them is extremely ignorant and a servant of Kali.

(*Jaiva Dharma*, Chapter 14)

70. Why do many people call pseudo-Vaiṣṇavism pure Vaiṣṇavism?

Due to the influence of Kali many people, not understanding the principle of pure Vaiṣṇavism, call pseudo-Vaiṣṇavism pure Vaiṣṇavism.

(*Jaiva Dharma*, Chapter 4)

71. Is there any approval of associating with women in the religion of Mahāprabhu?

All living entities are female by nature; still junior Haridāsa was rejected by the Lord for his offense of conversing with a woman. Distorting the real meaning of the above phrase that"all living entities are female," cunning people create various methods for gratifying their senses. Saintly persons and Vaiṣṇavas should ignore them. A householder associating with his wife is not a limb of devotional service. Such association is accepted only for the sake of maintaining family life.

(*Sajjana-toṣaṇī* 5/6)

8

Śrī Gaurasundara

1. What is the difference between Śrī Caitanya and other ordinary teachers?

If one very carefully and impartially discusses the characteristics, instructions, and scriptural conclusion of Śrī Mahāprabhu Caitanyadeva, one will be compelled to accept Him as sarvācārya or the supreme authority of everything. All the *ācāryas* who belong to the authorized *sampradāyas* are subordinate to Him. Although Śrī Caitanyadeva is the indwelling Supersoul of all living entities, He has personally manifested before them. Therefore all living entities should become free from material bondages and drink the nectar of freedom from the lotus feet of Śrī Caitanyadeva.

(*Tattva-sūtra* 49)

2. Who came first, Śrī Krishna or Śrī Caitanya?

Śrī Krishna and Śrī Caitanya are eternally manifested. It is hard to say who manifest first and who manifest second. First Caitanya was there, then He became Rādhā and Krishna, and again this combination of Rādhā and Krishna manifested as Caitanya. The conclusion of this statement is not that one manifested before and the other manifested later, but both manifestations are eternal.

(*Jaiva Dharma*, Chapter 14)

3. Are Krishna and Gaura, separate truths? What are the differences between Them?

Krishna and Gaura Kiśora are not separate truths; both of Them are the shelter of *mādhurya-rāsa*. The only difference is that in *mādhurya-rāsa* there are two divisions: *mādhurya* (sweetness) and *audārya* (magnanimity). When the presence of *mādhurya* is prominent, the Lord

manifests as Krishna, and when the presence of *audārya* is prominent, the Lord manifests as Śrī Gaurāṅga.
(*Jaiva Dharma*, Chapter 17)

4. Why is Gaurāṅga known as a covered incarnation?

In the age of Kali, the incarnation of the Lord distributes the rarest love of God through the process of *kīrtana*. Because love of God is rare, Lord Gaurāṅga, the best among the Lord's incarnations, is unknown to ordinary living entities.
(*Rasika Ranjana* commentary on the *Bhagavad-gītā* 4/8)

5. What are the combined forms of Gaurāṅga on the path of arcanā and bhajana?

On the path of arcanā, Śrī Gaurāṅga is worshiped with Viṣṇupriyā, and on the path of *bhajana*, Śrī Gaurāṅga is worshiped with Gadādhara.
(*Jaiva Dharma*, Chapter 14)

6. Is Śrī Gaura a paramour?

Know for certain that Śrī Nimāi is directly the son of Mahārāja Nanda. Do not consider Him separate from Krishna. Do not think that because He incarnated in Navadvīpa and exhibited separate pastimes to demonstrate the process of *bhajana* that He is therefore Navadvīpa-nagara or the paramour of Navadvīpa. If you think in that way, you will ruin your *bhajana*; your *bhajana* should be in the mood of Vraja.
(*Jaiva Dharma*, Chapter 39)

7. What is the difference in worshiping Krishna by following or by not following in the footsteps of Gaurāṅga?

Anyone who worships Krishna without first chanting the holy names of Gaura, attains Krishna after a long, long time. Whereas a person who chants the holy names of Gaura, immediately attains Krishna because such a person is free from all offenses.
(*Navadvīpa-māhātmya*, Chapter 7)

8. Unless one takes shelter of Gaura, one cannot worship Śrī Rādhā Govinda properly. Does this mean that the worship performed by previous ācāryas was incomplete?

Unless one worships Krishna by taking shelter of the lotus feet of Śrī Gaurāṅgadeva, one cannot achieve the ultimate goal of life. Before the advent of Śrī Gaurāṅga, many great personalities like Śrīmān Mādhavendra

Purī performed their *bhajana*, which was full of love of God. Although Śrī Gaurāṅgadeva had not externally manifested at that time, nevertheless, their hearts were filled with His sentiments.
(*Sajjana-toṣaṇī* 11/6)

9. Why is it a disturbance to worship Gaura but neglect Krishna, or to worship Krishna but neglect Gaura?

The unfortunate situation is that those who have resolved to give up the worship of Krishna to worship Śrī Gaurāṅga do not follow the order of Śrī Gaurāṅga. There is no difference between Gaura and Krishna. Some people think that by taking shelter of Gaurāṅga's lotus feet they do not need to remember Krishna. We can understand that such persons think Gaura and Krishna are different. There is no difference between the pastimes of Krishna and Gaura; they are the same. In the pastimes of Krishna, the object of worship is exhibited, whereas in the pastimes of Gaura, the process of that worship is exhibited. Worshiping without the object and simply following the process can never become complete. The more one studies the characteristics of Śrī Gaurāṅga, the more one develops love for the pastimes of Krishna. And the more one studies the pastimes of Krishna, the more one remembers the pastimes of Gaura. One can never relish Krishna without Gaura, and one can never relish Gaura without Krishna. When someone firmly believes that Śrī Gaurāṅga is the supreme worshipable Lord, the Krishna pastimes of Śrī Gaurāṅga fully manifest to such a person. Although these topics are most confidential, I have to disclose them with great distress. Some wicked people propose,"We will worship Gaura but we will not remember Krishna" or"We will worship Krishna but we will not remember Gaura." This is most unfortunate.
(*Sajjana-toṣaṇī* 11/6)

9

Energies of Śrī Gaura

1. In what manner does Śrī Lakṣmīpriyā love Śrī Gaurasundara?

Lakṣmī is the eternal consort of the Supreme Lord, and the Supreme Lord is the eternal husband of Lakṣmī. Therefore the eternal love that exists between Them is natural.

(*Amṛta-pravāha-bhāṣya, Caitanya Caritāmṛta* Ādi 14/64)

2. Who is Śrī Viṣṇupriyā?

Śrī Viṣṇupriyā is the Lord's combined energies of *hlādinī* and *saṁvit*. In other words, she is the personification of devotional service. She appeared during the advent of Śrī Gaura to assist Him in preaching the holy names of the Lord. Just as Śrī Navadvīpa, which consists of nine islands, is the personification of the nine types of devotional service, similarly, Śrīmatī Viṣṇupriyā is also the personification of the nine types of devotional service.

(*Jaiva Dharma*, Chapter 14)

3. What is the harm if one does not worship Śrī Viṣṇupriyā?

If one gives up the worship of Viṣṇupriyā, one cannot claim to be a devotee of the Lord.

(*Sajjana-toṣaṇī* 4/4)

4. What are the symptoms of persons who disrespect Śrī Viṣṇupriyā-devī?

Those who separate themselves from Śrī Viṣṇupriyā certainly separate themselves from devotional service. As ignorant bhaṭṭācāryas make a partition between themselves and the goddess of learning, similarly so-called Vaiṣṇavas, who are devoid of devotional service, also make a partition between themselves and Śrī Viṣṇupriyā.

(*Sajjana-toṣaṇī* 4/4)

5. Does Śrī Bhaktivinoda view Śrī Gaura-Gadādhara as Śrī Rādhā-Mādhava?

O my dear fresh youth Gaurāṅga! O enchanter of my mind! When will You mercifully appear before me in the forest of Godruma? When will You appear inside Ānanga-sukhadā-kuñja with Gadādhara on Your left? Your bodily hue will be golden, Your hair will be curly, and You will be dressed as an expert dancer. Thereafter You and Gadādhara will transform into the beautiful forms of Rādhā-Mādhava. Wearing an attractive flower garland around Your neck, You will dance with the *gopīs*. Then Anaṅga-mañjarī will catch hold of the hands of this maidservant and offer her at Your lotus feet. I will see the sweet beauty of the divine couple to the satisfaction of my eyes.

(*Kalyāṇa-kalpataru*)

6. What is the identity and service of Śrī Svarūpa, who is the energy of Śrī Gaura, and Śrī Raghunātha, who is very dear to Śrī Svarūpa?

Śrī Svarūpa Goswami is Lalitā-devī. Śrī Raghunātha dāsa Goswami entered into her group and offered confidential service to the Lord of Vraja.

(*Amṛta-pravāha-bhāṣya, Caitanya Caritāmṛta* Antya 6/241)

7. What confidential service did Śrī Svarūpa offer to Śrī Gaura?

Svarūpa Goswami was very expert in the scriptures and proficient in the art of music and singing. Realizing Svarūpa Goswami's expertise in singing, Śrīmān Mahāprabhu gave him the name Dāmodara. When the name Svarūpa, which was given to him by his *sannyāsa* guru, was added, he became famous as Dāmodara Svarūpa. He composed a book of music called *Saṅgīta-dāmodara*.

(*Amṛta-pravāha-bhāṣya, Caitanya Caritāmṛta* Madhya 10/116)

8. The unalloyed devotees of mādhurya-rāsa have taken shelter of the holy names of the Lord. Who is their spiritual master?

O Hari! Śrī Rūpa Goswami, in the form of my spiritual master, instructed me through my ears,"Take my words and pray at the feet of the holy name. By singing the Lord's holy name you will achieve love of God."

(*Śaraṇāgati*)

9. What is the truth of Śrī Rūpa, the energy of Śrī Gaura?

When will I approach Śrī Rūpa-mañjarī to learn the mellows of devotional service? I will happily reside on the bank of Rādhā-kuṇḍa under her subordination.

(*Gītāvalī*)

10. Where do the associates in gaura-līlā and kṛṣṇa-līlā reside?

There are two divisions in the original abode of Vṛndāvana. They are called Krishna-pīṭha and Gaura-pīṭha. In Krishna-pīṭha, eternally-perfect and eternally-liberated associates, who enjoy the mood of *mādhurya* with a little audārya, associate with Krishna. The same eternally-perfect and eternally-liberated associates, who enjoy the mood of audārya with a little *mādhurya*, are found in Gaura-pīṭha. Sometimes these associates expand to enjoy pastimes with the Lord in both pīṭhas and sometimes they remain at one pīṭha in their original form and do not stay at the other pīṭha. While executing *sādhana*, those who worship only Gaura will serve only at Gaura-pīṭha after they achieve perfection; those who worship only Krishna will live at Krishna-pīṭha; and those who worship Krishna and Gaura will assume two bodies and simultaneously reside at both the pīṭhas. This is the supreme mystery of Gaura Krishna's philosophy of acintya-bhedābheda.

(*Jaiva Dharma*, Chapter 17)

11. How did Mahāprabhu propagate His teachings?

The specialty of Śrīmān Mahāprabhu's pastime is that He preached His different teachings through His different devotees, who were expert in their respective types of devotional service.

(*Harināma-cintāmaṇi*)

12. What services did Śrī Gaurasundara entrust upon His different associates?

Śrīmān Mahāprabhu ordered Śrī Svarūpa Dāmodara to preach about the worship of the Lord through loving devotional service. According to the Lord's order, Śrī Svarūpa Dāmodara composed his kaḍacā, writing, in two parts. He described worshiping the Lord in the mood of transcendental mellows. In the first part, he described the internal path and in the second, the external path. He taught the internal path to Śrī Raghunātha dāsa Goswami, who revealed it in his own books, and the external path to Śrīmad Vakreśvara Goswami. Śrīmān Mahāprabhu empowered and ordered Śrī Nityānanda Prabhu and Śrī Advaita Prabhu to preach the glories of the Lord's holy name. He empowered and ordered Śrī Rūpa Goswami to reveal the science of the mellows of devotional service. He ordered Śrī Sanātana Goswami to preach about *vaidhī-bhakti* and its relationship with *rāgānuga-bhakti*. He also ordered Śrī Sanātana Goswami to establish the relationship between the manifest and the unmanifest pastimes of Gokula. Through Śrī Nityānanda Prabhu and Śrī Sanātana, Śrīmān Mahāprabhu empowered Śrī Jīva Goswami to establish the science of *sambandha*, *abhidheya*, and *prayojana*.

(*Jaiva Dharma*, Chapter 39)

13. Do the devotees of Śrī Gaura know the difference between aiśvarya and mādhurya-rāsa?

The servants of Śrīmān Mahāprabhu know very well about the subtle differences between the mood of servitorship to Nārāyaṇa that is mixed with aiśvarya (opulence) and the mood of servitorship to Krishna that is mixed with *mādhurya* (sweetness).

(*Sajjana-toṣaṇī* 7/3)

10

Abode of Śrī Gaura

1. Is there any difference between Śrī Gauḍa-maṇḍala and Vraja-maṇḍala?

I will not differentiate between the residents of Gauḍa and Vraja. In this way, I will always reside in Vraja, see the actual form of the *dhāma*, and become a maidservant of Rādhārāṇī.

(*Śaraṇāgati*)

2. Why have Navadvīpa, Vraja, and Goloka manifest differently even though they are one in truth?

Navadvīpa-maṇḍala, Vraja-maṇḍala, and Goloka are one indivisible truth. They have manifest differently because of their unlimited different loving sentiments.

(*Brahma-saṁhitā* 5/5)

3. What pastimes does Lord Krishna perform in Goloka, in Vraja, and in Śvetadvīpa?

Goloka, Vṛndāvana, and Śvetadvīpa are the interior of the spiritual sky. In Goloka, Krishna performs His *svakīya* pastimes, in Vṛndāvana His *parakīya* pastimes, and in Śvetadvīpa the remainder of His pastimes. In truth, there is no difference between Goloka, Vṛndāvana, and Śvetadvīpa. Śrī Navadvīpa is nondifferent from Śvetadvīpa, and it is also nondifferent from Vṛndāvana.

(*Jaiva Dharma*, Chapter 14)

4. Why is Navadvīpa called the abode of audārya?

Because Śrī Gauracandra appeared in Navadvīpa, it is the crest jewel of all holy places. Offenders are punished at other holy pilgrimage places, but they are purified in Navadvīpa-*dhāma*. Examples of this are the two brothers Jagai and Madhai, who committed great offenses yet still received Nitāi-Gaura.

(*Navadvīpa Mahatmya*, Chapter 1)

5. When can one see the nature of the spiritual abode?

Through eyes affected by material illusion, one will see only a small house, some earth, water, and a few articles. Nevertheless, if Māyā becomes merciful and lifts her covering, one will see a vast spiritual dwelling.

(*Navadvīpa-bhāva-taraṅga*, Verse 11)

6. Why is Godruṁa nondifferent from Nandagrāma?

Godruṁa is nondifferent from Nandīśvara, the home of Nanda Mahārāja and the cowherd men. Gaurāṅga performs various pastimes there. Having eaten some milk products at a cowherd's house, Nimāi goes with His gopa friends and herds the cows.

(*Navadvīpa-bhāva-taraṅga*, Verse 44)

7. How do the devotees of Gaura hanker to reside at Godruṁa?

I do not want to reside at Kāśī or offer obeisances to the forefathers at Gayā. I reject liberation and the four objectives of life. I am not afraid of going to hell or suffering in the material world if, by the mercy of the Lord, I get an opportunity to live in Śrī Godruṁa.

(*Navadvīpa-śataka*, Verse 100)

8. What prayer do the devotees of Gaura make to Koladvīpa?

O Koladvīpa, please be merciful to this worthless person. Kindly allow me to reside in Navadvīpa among the devotees, and give me the right to the wealth of the pastimes of Gaurāṅga. He is my Lord in life and in death.

(*Navadvīpa-bhāva-taraṅga*, Verse 75)

9. Where is the place where offenses are nullified?

The present city of Navadvīpa, formerly known as the village of Kuliyā, is situated on the western bank of ancient Navadvīpa. This is the place where the offenses of Devānanda Paṇḍita and Gopāla Cāpāla were nullified. In those days, one had to cross a branch of the Ganges to go from Vidyānagara to Kuliyā, and to go from Kuliyā to Navadvīpa, one had to cross the main river of Bhāgīrathī [another name of the Ganges]. Even today, one can see the ruins of those places, such as Cināḍāṅga, which was formerly situated in Kuliyā and is now known as Kolera Gañja.

(*Amṛta-pravāha-bhāṣya, Caitanya Caritāmṛta* Madhya 1/151)

10. At which forest of Vraja did Śrī Bhaktivinoda Ṭhākura see the village of Campahaṭṭa?

In Campahaṭṭa village is a campaka forest from which the *gopī* Campakalatā gathers flowers to make garlands for Rādhā and Krishna. This place is nondifferent from Khadiravana in Vraja, where Krishna and Balarāma take rest.

(*Navadvīpa-bhāva-taraṅga*, Verse 78)

11. At which forest did Śrī Bhaktivinoda Ṭhākura see the island of Modadruma?

The forest of Modadruma is nondifferent from Śrī Bhāṇḍīravana in Vraja, where the birds and beasts are all spiritual entities.

(*Navadvīpa-bhāva-taraṅga*, Verse 110)

12. What blessings did Śrī Bhaktivinoda Ṭhākura bestow upon the residents of"the world of Kali," Calcutta?

O brothers of Calcutta! You are glorious because you are living in a place that used to be the village called Varāhanagara. Because Śrī Gaurāṅga performed His pastimes there, that place is nondifferent from Śrī Vṛndāvana. Because Bhāgavata Ācārya, a most intimate associate of Śrī Gaurāṅga, performed his devotional service there, it is an auspicious place. O devotees who live in Calcutta! When will we become absorbed in chanting the holy names of Krishna together in the transcendental grooves of Śyāma-mañjarī? It is most unfortunate that we abandon gold in our own yard and search for gold in other countries.

(*Sajjana-toṣaṇī* 9/12)

11

Śrī Māyāpura

1. What is the nature of Śrī Māyāpura?

The great holy place of Māyāpura is a manifestation of Śrī Gokula in this age of Kali, and it is extremely potent. As Paurṇamāsī is in charge of Vṛndāvana, so Śrī Prauḍāmāyā (popularly known as Poḍāmā) is in charge of Māyāpura. Among the seven great holy places, such as Ayodhyā, Haridwāra, and Māya, there is a holy place known as Māyātīrtha situated at Haridwāra and Gauḍadesa. The influence of Māyātirtha is such that even some sinless Muslims who live there proudly consider our beloved Lord Gaurāṅga as their own Lord and treat the devotees of Gaurāṅga as their friends.

(*Viṣṇupriyā Pallī Magazine*, Vol. 1)

2. How eager was Śrī Bhaktivinoda Ṭhākura to discover the land of Gaurāṅga's birth?

Poor sinful persons like us have become extremely eager to see the places of the pastimes of the Lord and His associates. When the devotees of Vraja became very eager to see the places of Śrī Krishna's pastimes, Śrī Caitanyadeva, who is the ocean of mercy, empowered Śrī Sanātana Prabhu and showed him the two paddy fields of Śrī Rādhā-kuṇḍa and Śrī Śyāma-kuṇḍa. Now, by the mercy of Śrī Sanātana Goswami, everyone is relishing the glories of these two holy places. O dear devotees of Gaurāṅga who are present today, such as Śrī Jagannātha dāsa, we fall at your lotus feet and pray with folded hands that you take the position of Śrī Sanātana Goswami and ascertain the places of Śrī Māyāpura. You are our spiritual master; to whom else will we pray?

(*Viṣṇupriyā Pallī Magazine*, Vol. 1)

3. What instructions did Śrī Bhaktivinoda Ṭhākura receive in this regard?

I felt that I was spending my days uselessly. I did not accomplish anything. I thought, "I will build a cottage in a secluded place in the forest on the banks of the Yamunā in Mathurā and Vṛndāvana, and then I will worship Krishna."

Once, in the course of my work, I went to Tārakeśvara. When I slept at night, the Lord appeared and said to me,"Are you planning to go to Vṛndāvana? What did you do about the work that is pending near your house in Navadvīpa?"

(*Autobiography of Ṭhākura Bhaktivinoda*)

4. How did Śrī Māyāpura manifest?

Every Saturday I went to Navadvīpa and searched for the places of the Lord's pastimes, but I did not find anything so I felt great distress. At that time, the people of Navadvīpa were simply interested in filling their bellies, and they did not make any endeavor to find the places of the Lord's pastimes. One evening, myself, Kamal, and a clerk went up on the roof and were looking around. I saw a brightly shining building on the other side of the Ganges, on the northern side. The next morning, I went up to the roof of the queen's house and carefully looked at that place, and I noticed that there was a palm tree on that very site. When I inquired from some people, they said that place was known as Ballāladighi where the remains of Lakṣmaṇa Sena's palace were still present.

The following Monday, I went back to Kṛṣṇanagara and then returned to see Ballāladighi on Saturday. Again I saw that wonderful vision. That night and the next morning I walked to see that place. After inquiring from the old people who lived there, I understood that it was the birthplace of Śrīmān Mahāprabhu. I gradually visited all the nearby villages, which are described in *Bhakti-ratnākara* of Śrī Narahari Ṭhākura and *Śrī Caitanya-bhāgavata* of Śrī Vṛndāvana dāsa Ṭhākura. Thereafter, at Kṛṣṇanagara, I composed the book *Śrī Navadvīpa-dhāma-māhātmya* and sent it to Calcutta for printing. When I explained all these things in detail to Dvarika Bābu, an engineer from Kṛṣṇanagara, he understood my desire and drew a map of Navadvīpa-maṇḍala. This map was printed inside the book *Śrī Navadvīpa-dhāma-māhātmya* in a simplified form.

(*Autobiography of Ṭhākura Bhaktivinoda*)

5. What was Śrī Bhaktivinoda's desire regarding Śrī Māyāpura?

There is a beautiful place on the southern corner of Ballāladighi, where a beautiful temple can be built, and the worship of the Deities of Śrī

Gaurāṅga, Viṣṇupriyā, and Śacīmātā can be performed. As well as Deity worship, various other activities can be performed, such as providing a guesthouse for pilgrims. A huge festival in March-April and the protection of the Lord's birthplace can easily be carried out.

(*Viṣṇupriyā Pallī Magazine*, Vol. 1)

6. In whose heart did the desire to revive Śrī Navadvīpa-parikramā first appear?

It is the custom that Navadvīpa-parikramā should begin from Śrī Māyāpura. At present there is no place in Māyāpura where pilgrims can spend the night. The duty of rich householder Vaiṣṇavas is to build a huge column at the birthplace of Śrīmān Mahāprabhu immediately. A huge flag and a bright light should be placed on top of this column to mark Śrī Jagannātha Misra's house.

(*Viṣṇupriyā Pallī Magazine*, Vol. 1)

7. What is the history of Śrī Māyāpura?

The small villages of Śrī Gaṅgānagara and Bharadvāja Tilā belong to Antardvīpa. The school of Śrī Gaṅgādāsa Paṇḍita was situated in Gaṅgānagara. The tract of land that is found on the northeastern side of Māyāpura has been there since the time of Śrīnivāsa Ācārya Prabhu, as described in *Bhakti-ratnākara*. From there one can see the place Suvarṇa Vihāra. It is stated in the tantra that this is where Lord Brahmā, the creator of the universe, performed austerity. Long ago, a small river called Bāgdevi flowed through Antardvīpa and the eastern portion of Māyāpura, down to the Ganges. At that time, the temple of Prauḍhā Māyā was situated on the bank of the Bāgdevi. Students used to first take bath in the river, and after presenting their credentials in the Prauḍhā Māyā temple, they received their academic degrees. A little southeast of Śivadobā, the dry riverbed of the Bāgdevi can still be found.

(*Viṣṇupriyā Pallī Magazine*, Vol. 1)

8. Did Śrī Bhaktivinoda exhibit intense eagerness to discover the lost places of Śrī Gaura's pastimes?

O devotees! Give up other desires and thoughts for now and try to discover the lost places of this great *tīrtha*. Your research will not be as difficult as the research undertaken by astrologers like Bhāskarācārya and Āryabhaṭṭa. They were mundane scholars. Therefore, while researching material subjects, they were forced to undergo various difficulties, such as inventing many material machines. O devotees who are mad after Nityānanda! You do not belong to this world. If you wish, you can easily do everything. If you only once fall at the lotus feet of Lord Nityānanda and pray, you can obtain the transcendental abode of Śvetadvīpa, just as you can get a myrobalan fruit in your hand. If you cry while rolling on the surface of Pañca-tattva's spiritual abode and exclaim, "O Gaurāṅga! O Viṣṇupriyā! O Lord Nityānanda! O Lord Advaita! O Gadādhara! O Śrīnivāsa!" then Śrī Pañca-tattva will mercifully show you all the places. O Vaiṣṇavas! Do not wait any longer.

(*Viṣṇupriyā Pallī Magazine*, Vol. 1)

9. When the birthplace of Śrī Gaura was discovered, how envious were the professional traders of religion?

When ancient Navadvīpa was discovered, the people of modern Kuliyā, Navadvīpa, became very envious. They began to say so many things and showered various abusive words on the devotees of Gaurāṅga. But those who have surrendered their body and mind at the feet of Gaurāṅga will not retreat because of the devilish words of such people. Without paying attention to greedy godless people, Gaurāṅga's devotees endeavor to establish temples and worship the deity.

(*Autobiography of Ṭhākura Bhaktivinoda*)

10. Why can the first Śrī Gaura appearance festival at Śrī Māyāpura be compared to the festival at Kheturi?

The festival at Śrī Māyāpura was so great that, except for the festival at Kheturi, such a festival had never taken place anywhere. About fifty thousand people came to Māyāpura from various distant places to see this great festival. Only a few selfish people, fearing that the prestige of modern Navadvīpa would be diminished, acted against the improvement of Navadvīpa. But since the Lord's devotees are well aware of the glories of Navadvīpa, they disregarded the impediments put forth by such people and expressed great pleasure in visiting Śrī Māyāpura.

(*Sajjana-toṣaṇī* 6/1)

11. Does Mahāprabhu desire to observe the festivals in pomp?

Mahāprabhu does not wish to spend lavishly on the festivals in Śrī Māyāpura.

(*Sajjana-toṣaṇī* 12/1)

12. What was Śrī Bhaktivinoda's prediction regarding a future temple of Śrī Mahāprabhu at Yoga-pīṭha?

A huge and wonderful temple will be constructed at the birthplace of Mahāprabhu, and the eternal service to Gaurāṅga will manifest.

(*Navadvīpa-māhātmya*, Chapter 5)

13. Who are the great benefactors of the Vaiṣṇavas of the future?

Those who are trying their best to keep intact the flow of service to Śrī Māyāpura will be considered the benefactors of the future world of Vaiṣṇavas.

(*Sajjana-toṣaṇī* 12/1)

14. What was Śrī Bhaktivinoda's prediction regarding Śrī Māyāpura becoming world famous?

Those who take birth as devotees in various races and in many distant countries will one day desire to come and see the birthplace of Śrī Mahāprabhu.

(*Sajjana-toṣaṇī* 12/1)

15. What concept did Śrī Bhaktivinoda, a follower of Śrī Rūpa, have to take Śrī Gaurasundara to Śrī Māyāpura?

I long to take the Lord back to Māyāpura where, shining in the dress of a young boy with long curly hair and His dhotī folded thrice, He performs pastimes with His young friends in Īśodyāna (His own garden). Of course, this *sannyāsī* is my Lord and I am His servant. The different appearances the Lord assumes are just part of His unlimited pastimes, but still, my heart longs to take the Lord back to Śrīvasa Pandita's temple on the bank of Pṛthu-kuṇḍa!

(*Navadvīpa-bhāva-taraṅga*, Verse 70/71)

12

Abode of Śrī Krishna

1. What is the order of places from Devīdhāma to Haridhāma?

First there is Devīdhāma, this material world, which consists of fourteen worlds, such as Satyaloka. Above that is Śivadhāma. A portion of this *dhāma* is dark and known as Mahākāla. Beyond this darkness is the great illuminating abode of Sadāśiva. Above that is Harīdhāma, the spiritual abode of Vaikuṇṭha.

(*Brahma-saṁhitā* 5/43)

2. Has the Vedas described that there is no variegatedness in Vaikuṇṭha?

In some places, the *Upaniṣads* say that the Supreme Brahman is impersonal. It should be understood that in the material world atomic particles of water, air, and fire are distinct because of their respective material characteristics. Such material distinctions do not exist in the spiritual world. The Vedic literature, however, never says that there is no variety in the spiritual world. Existence and variety are simultaneously present everywhere.

(*Prema-pradīpa*, Chapter 9)

3. What is the difference between the variegated nature of the material and the spiritual worlds?

To understand the variegated nature of the spiritual world requires deep meditation. The variegated nature of the material world is temporary happiness and distress. The variegated nature of the spiritual world is vast and full of spiritual bliss.

(Brahmā-saṁhitā 5/56)

4. Do the four objectives of life found in the material world exist in Gokula?

Liberation to Vaikuṇṭha, religiosity, economic development, and sense gratification are situated in Gokula in their appropriate place in the form of seeds.

(Brahmā-saṁhitā 5/5)

5. What is the difference between Goloka and Gokula?

There is no difference between Goloka and Gokula. The only difference is that Goloka, which is the highest platform in the spiritual world and the place of Krishna's pastimes, is known as Gokula in the material world.

(Brahmā-saṁhitā 5/2)

6. What is the difference between Mathurā-maṇḍala and Goloka?

Goloka, where the Lord's unmanifest pastimes take place, is Mathurā in the material world, where the Lord's manifest pastimes take place.

(*Jaiva Dharma*, Chapter 31)

7. How can we understand the Lord's manifest and unmanifest pastimes of Vraja?

The most confidential interior of the eternal spiritual abode of Goloka is called Vraja. Just as the pastimes of Krishna are manifest in the material world, similarly pastimes are also eternally manifest in Vraja. There, the pastimes in the mood of *parakiyā-rāsa* eternally exist. In the third chapter of *Śrī Caitanya Caritāmṛta*, Śrī Kṛṣṇadasa Kavirāja Goswami wrote,"At the end of Dvāpara-yuga of the twenty-eighth cycle of four yugas, Lord Krishna appears in this world with His Vraja-*dhāma*. "By the words *vrajera sahit*e, with Vraja," it is clearly understood that there is an inconceivable spiritual abode called Vraja. Krishna, through His spiritual potency, appeared in the material world with His abode of Vraja. *Parakīya-rāsa* exists only in the eternal Vraja, which is the internal part of Goloka. In the manifest Vraja, the variegatedness of the unmanifest Vraja have been perceived by the living entities.

(*Amṛta-pravāha-bhāṣya, Caitanya Caritāmṛta* Ādi 4/46–50)

8. How can one perceive Goloka in Gokula?

The Lord's transcendental pastimes are eternal. One who is qualified to see pure spirit can see Goloka. What to speak of this, one can even see

Goloka in Gokula. One whose intelligence is conditioned by the illusory energy can never see Goloka. Such a person sees Gokula as the material world, although Gokula is nondifferent from Goloka.

(*Jaiva Dharma*, Chapter 31)

9. What is the nature of the abode of Krishna?

The abode of Krishna is full of bliss. Although opulence is present there in full form, it has no influence. Everything there is full of sweetness and eternal bliss. Flowers, fruits, and trees are the assets of the abode of Krishna. The cow are His subjects, the cowherd boys His friends, and the *gopīs* His girlfriends. Butter, yogurt, and milk are the food. The forests and gardens are full of love for Krishna. The River Yamunā engages in the service of Krishna. The females are the maidservants of Krishna. The personality, who in His various expansions accepts the worship and respect of everyone, is the only life and soul of that abode. Sometimes He is respected as much as the worshipers, and sometimes He is even treated inferior to them.

(*Caitanya-śikṣāmṛta* 1/1)

10. What is the nature of the pastimes in Goloka?

Goloka is the eternally perfect transcendental abode; therefore the sentiments of the pastimes make perfect the flow of *rāsa.*

(Brahmā-saṁhitā 5/37)

11. Who is qualified to see the abode of the Lord?

Both Vraja and Navadvīpa appear mundane in the eyes of materialistic persons. Fortunate souls who are endowed with spiritual vision are able to see the Lord's abode.

(*Jaiva Dharma*, Chapter 14)

13

Abode of Śrī Puruṣottama

1. How did Śrī Bhaktivinoda cultivate his Krishna consciousness at Puruṣottama?

I engaged Gopīnātha Paṇḍita to help me study the scriptures at Jagannātha Purī. At first, I studied from him the entire Twelfth Canto of *Śrīmad-Bhāgavatam* with Śrīdhara Svāmī's commentary. At the same time, Harihara dāsa Mahāpātra and Mārkaṇḍeya Mahāpātra began to study with me, but after five or seven days, they were so much behind that they began to take lessons from me. Before that they had studied logic and *Vedānta* in Nadia and Kāśī. I scrutinizingly studied the scriptures at Purī. After completing the study of *Śrīmad-Bhāgavatam*, I copied and studied the *Ṣaṭ-sandarbhas*. Thereafter I copied the *Govinda-bhāṣya* commentary of Baladeva Vidyābhūṣaṇa on *Śrīmad-Bhāgavatam* and studied it. Then I thoroughly studied *Bhakti-rasāmṛta-sindhu* and copied the book *Hari Bhakti Kalpa Latikā*. I began to compose something of my own. At Purī, I compiled the Sanskrit book *Dutta Kaustubha*. I also composed most of the verses of *Śrī Krishna-saṁhitā*. A few persons like Paramānanda and Nityānanda used to study *Śrīmad-Bhāgavatam* from me.

At that time, the assembly of devotees met at our house near Śrī Jagannātha-vallabha garden. Many learned scholars such as Nārāyaṇa dāsa, Mohan dāsa, and Harihara dāsa from the northern side of Purī began to attend the assembly. A bābājī, Raghunātha dāsa, was against our assembly and stopped some people from participating in it. He was living at Hāti Ākhaḍā. Raghunātha dāsa Bābājī was a self-realized soul, and therefore he knew everything. Soon he made friends with me and he said, "Seeing you without *tilaka* and neckbeads, I have disrespected you. Please forgive me."

I said, "Bābājī Mahāśaya! Where is my fault? The initiating spiritual master gives *tilaka* and beads. The Lord has not given me an initiating spiritual master yet. I only chant the holy names of Hari on beads. In such a situation is it proper for me to put on *tilaka* and neckbeads on my own?"

Bābājī Mahāśaya understood everything and praised me. He began to bestow mercy on me, and I remained under his guidance.

In between the Ṭoṭā-gopīnātha temple and Haridāsa Ṭhākura's *samādhi* was the *sat-saṅga bhajana-kuṭīra*, where many detached bābājīs used to constantly do their *bhajana*. Svarūpa dāsa Bābājī was also doing his *bhajana* there. He was a wonderful Vaiṣṇava. He would do his *bhajana* the whole day inside the *kuṭīra*. In the evening, he would come out into the courtyard, and after offering obeisances to *tulasī*, he would dance and cry while singing the holy names of Krishna. That was when Vaiṣṇavas would go to see him and someone would take a handful of *mahāprasāda* for him. He would not take more than required to satisfy his hunger. At that time, someone would recite *Caitanya-bhāgavata* for him. At ten o'clock at night, Bābājī Mahāśaya would return to his *kuṭīra* and engage in his *bhajana*. When it was dark, he would go alone to the seashore, wash his hands and mouth, and take a bath. The reason he did so was that he feared some Vaiṣṇava might help him. He was very blind; only Mahāprabhu knew how he went at night to take bath in the sea. There was no doubt that he was a self-realized soul. He was completely aloof from worldly thoughts. Sometimes I used to go and see him in the evening. He would speak sweetly to any stranger that came to see him. He gave me this instruction,"You should never forget Krishna."

(*Autobiography of Ṭhākura Bhaktivinoda*)

2. How did Śrī Bhaktivinoda Ṭhākura performed his bhajana at Jagannātha Purī?

During my stay at Jagannātha Purī, I used to regularly visit the temple of Lord Jagannātha, chant the holy names of Krishna, and hear the topics of Krishna in the association of saintly persons. I was not satisfied if I did not eat the arahar dhal *mahāprasāda* of Jagannātha. Every day, as soon as I used to enter the temple, someone would appear from nowhere to give me arahar dhal. On one side of the temple was a courtyard called Mukti-maṇḍapa where only the administrative *brāhmaṇa*s were eligible to sit. They were all Māyāvādīs. I did not feel happy going to that side. Therefore, I usually remained within the temple of Śrī Lakṣmīdevī or sat down near the lotus feet of Śrī Mahāprabhu. When I used to sit there, many learned scholars from Mukti-maṇḍapa would regularly come and join me. I named our place"the courtyard of the devotees." Gradually it became an assembly of learned Vaiṣṇava scholars.

Just as the temple of Śrī Jagannātha-deva is huge and enchanting, similarly His service is also wonderful. All His pastimes overwhelm the hearts of everyone. Between five and seven hundred people would be present in the temple to see the daily festivals such as *sandhyā-ārati*. What a blissful event! In the course of their traveling to the holy places, many pilgrims from all over India would come there. One's eyes became satiated by seeing such a sight. Many people came there to participate in the festivals of Holi and Rathayātrā. I was entrusted with the responsibility of looking after them. What can I write about the amount of trouble and hard labor that I faced to guide the pilgrims at Purī in those days? I became the object of many people's anger while trying to arrange for the pilgrims' *darśana* and *prasāda*. Many temple administrators including the king sometimes acted unlawfully to fulfill their own self-interest. I made enmity with the king and his men while trying to stop their unlawful activities, but since Lord Jagannātha-deva supported me, no one could cause me any harm. I spent five years in the service of Śrī Jagannātha-deva.

I shifted my residents a few times at Śrī Puruṣottama-kṣetra. In 1280 Bengali Era in the month of February, Bimala and Rāmacandra were born. Their auspicious grain-giving ceremonies were performed with the *mahāprasāda* of Śrī Jagannātha-deva. We gave up all fruitive activities and became attached to *mahāprasāda*.

(*Autobiography of Ṭhākura Bhaktivinoda*)

3. What are the characteristics of Śrī Jagannātha, Śrī Baladeva, and Śrī Subhadrā?

Jagannātha, the emblem of God, has no other form than eyes and hands, which show that God sees, knows, and creates. Balarāma is the source of *jīva-śakti*, Subhadrā is Māyā-*śakti*, and Sudarśana is the energy of will.

(*The Temple of Jagannātha at Purī*)

4. Why did Śrī Bhaktivinoda Ṭhākura take shelter in a bhajana-kuṭīra at Puruṣottama?

Today we are sitting inside a *bhajana-kuṭīra* at Śrī Puruṣottama-kṣetra. Why are we living in this faraway place, leaving the great city of Calcutta, which is full of people and learned communities? A long time ago, when we published this magazine *Sajjana-toṣaṇī*, I had a desire in my heart. I thought that the more this pure Vaiṣṇava religion is spread through this magazine, the more the people of the world would benefit. We began to work with a free mind. Many educated gosvāmīs and bābājīs of Bengal came and pledged to help us. Some learned impersonalists joined us, and being overwhelmed by the beauty of devotional service, they began to help spread pure Vaiṣṇavism. After hearing nice instructions regarding Vaiṣṇavism, materialists also became attracted. Professional singers and players floated in the waves of pure *hari-kīrtana* and considered themselves fully satisfied. Gradually many assemblies for chanting the holy names of Hari were established in villages and cities. In this way, the glories of pure Vaiṣṇavism filled the hearts of the inhabitants of Bengal and overwhelmed everyone by their beauty and sweetness. On seeing such an unexpected response from the people of Bengal, we began to preach pure Vaiṣṇavism with more and more enthusiasm.

Then, by the influence of time, a sudden change took place. The glowwormlike superstitions that were hidden in the scorching heat of the sun of Vaiṣṇavism suddenly took various forms and came from four directions. The demoniac religious principle in the form of Māyāvāda, which was immersed within the deep water of forgetfulness for some time, again surfaced in the form of discourses, taking shelter of the boat of the smārta teachers. At the same time, some Indian and foreign yogīs appeared as supporters of the smārtas and created a revolution in the world of religion. Moreover, some useless people, who were fond of sense gratification, took shelter of unauthorized religious practices and began to create disturbance in society, identifying themselves as sahajiyās and bāulas. Displaying the limit of their sinful propensity, a few wormlike people, who take pleasure in the stool of fame, began to advertise themselves as"the incarnation of the Lord" in the society of fools. Some other people even accepted names befitting a Vaiṣṇava, acted as *ācāryas*, and began to spread ideas that were opposed to Vaiṣṇavism as if they were the religious principles of Vaiṣṇavas.

After seeing all such unimaginable activities, our hearts began to shatter. When we try to search for the cause of such a change, we suddenly remember the following verse written by Śrīla Prabodhānanda Sarasvatīpada, "The age of Kali is formidable and the senses of the human beings are very powerful. Now the path of devotional service is full of millions of thorns. Where shall I go? What shall I do? I am completely helpless without the mercy of Gauracandra."

While crying and speaking in this way, I went to the birthplace of the Lord at Śrī Māyāpura. Still my mind did not become peaceful. Thereafter I left my place in search of the Lord and after arriving at Purī, I began to roll on the goldlike sand. At that time, the Lord informed me in my heart, "O well-wisher of the devotees. May you obtain peace! The nature that the living entities have developed, according to their respective karma from birth after birth in this world, influences them to engage in fruitive activities. Until desires opposed to devotional service are destroyed from the heart, no amount of good instruction can bring any auspiciousness. Such instructions will simply come out of the ear-holes and will not enter into the heart. No amount of preaching to them or discussing devotional service will produce a good result because of their bad karma. Your discourses and discussions will therefore not yield any result. My order to you is that you should live at the place where I kept my dear Haridāsa and where I loudly chanted the holy names of the Lord. You should constantly sing the glories of the holy names for the benefit of the fallen souls. As a result of the piety that people will achieve by hearing from you, and the faith they will develop, they will attain unduplicitious faith in pure devotional service in a future lifetime."

Following these instructions of our beloved Lord Śrī Krishna Caitanya, we built our *bhajana-kuṭīra* in the tract of land surrounded by huge waves.

(*Sajjana-toṣaṇī* 15/1)

14

Mahāprasāda

1. Is mahāprasāda, material?

Mahāprasāda, Krishna, the names of Krishna, and the pure Vaiṣṇavas—these four items, present in the material world, are spiritual.

(*Jaiva Dharma*, Chapter 6)

2. Why has mahāprasāda incarnated in this world?

Krishna is very merciful; to help us conquer our tongue He has given us His remnants. Please honor His nectarean remnants of food and sing the qualities of Rādhā Krishna and in ecstasy chant the names of Caitanya and Nityānanda.

(*Gītāvalī*)

3. What is the result of honoring prasāda?

By accepting foodstuffs that have been offered to the Lord, all one's material desires are conquered.

(*Śaraṇāgati*)

4. What does one obtain by the mercy of mahāprasāda?

Any living entity who is favored by *mahāprasāda* will certainly obtain pure devotional service to Krishna.

(*Navadvīpa-bhāva-taraṅga* 131)

5. What is the consequence of thinking prasāda is mundane?

When we were residing at Śrī Puruṣottama-kṣetra, we heard many learned smārtas make false arguments regarding *mahāprasāda*. Some said that *mahāprasāda* should be honored within the temple premises; other's said that *mahāprasāda* should be honored within 10 miles of the temple; yet other's said that *mahāprasāda* touched by śūdras should not be accepted; and still other's said that one should not accept *mahāprasāda* inside the temple or outside the temple. We have also seen the kind of superior punishment these learned classes of people received.

(*Sajjana-toṣaṇī* 10/8)

6. What is the need for offering foodstuffs to the Lord? What is the purpose of honoring mahāprasāda?

Honoring *mahāprasāda* is not only symbolic of the superior life of the Vaiṣṇavas, but it is part of worship, which ordinary theists cannot fully understand. Ordinary men are very much inclined to preserve the superiority of reason over the intuitive feelings of man toward the God of love. We must now proceed to show with healthy arguments that our intuitive feelings want us to offer everything we eat to the Lord of our heart. We must first examine the arguments of the antagonists.

The rationalist states that God is infinite and without wants, and consequently it is foolish to offer eatables to such a being. It is a sacrilege to offer created things to the creator and thereby degrade the divinity of God, treating Him as a human being. These are reasonable arguments indeed, and one who has heard them will certainly be inclined to declare to other's,"Down with *mahāprasāda.*" These conclusions, which may appear reasonable, are dry and destructive. They tend to separate us from all connection in worshiping God. When you say that the Infinite wants nothing, you forbid all contemplation and prayer. The Infinite does not want your grateful expressions or flattery. Utter a word to the unconditioned Lord and you are sure to degrade Him into a conditioned being. Hymns, prayers, and sermons are all over! Shut your temple door and church gates because our rationalist has advised you to do so. Believe a creative principle and you have done your duty! Oh! What a shame! What a dreadful fall! Theists, beware of these degrading principles!

Now the rationalist appears in another form and allows prayers, sermons, psalms, and church going, saying that these things are wanted for the improvement of the soul, but God does not want them at all. We are glad that the rationalist has come toward us and will make further approaches in the course of time.

Yes, the progressive rationalist has admitted a very broad principle in theology: whatever we do toward God is for our own benefit and not for the benefit of God, who is not in want of anything. However, the rationalist is a rationalist still and will continue to be so as long as he seeks self-interest. We know for certain that religion promises to give eternal happiness to man and it is impossible to conceive of any religion, which is not based on self-interest. This view, however, smells of utilitarianism and can never be theism. We must love God for God's sake even if our actions appear unreasonable. Our love must be without any goal concerning ourselves. This love must be a natural emotion to the deity, as our well-wisher, without inference or experience. Salvation, dear as it is, should not be the object of this love. What then about other forms of happiness? Love of God is its own reward. Salvation, as a concomitant consequence, must be a servant of love, but we must not look on it as the main goal. If a rationalist is prepared to believe this, he becomes a theist of the Vaiṣṇava class, but the mere assuming of a name is of no consequence.

Though fully aware that the Lord is completely unconditioned, our holy and sweet principle of love takes a different view to that of the rationalist. Reason says one thing but love prescribes the opposite. Reason tells me that God has no sorrow, but love sees God in tears for His sons who are misled to evil. Reason tells me that the strict laws of God reward and punish me in a cold manner, but love reveals that God slackens His laws to the repentant soul. Reason tells me that, with all his improvements, man will never touch God, but love preaches that on the conversion of the soul into a state of spiritual womanhood, God, unconditioned as He is, accepts an eternal marriage with the liberated soul. Reason tells me that God is in infinite space and time, but love describes that the all-beautiful Lord is sitting before us like a respected relative and enjoying the pleasures of society. As a father in his amusements with his young children, God is spreading all sorts of delicious food all over the earth and expecting His sons to gather them for their own benefit. But the loving children, out of their holy and unmixed love, gather all the scattered blessings and with strong feelings of love, regardless of reason, offer all the blessings to the Father whom they love more than their lives.

The Father again, in reply to their kind feelings, gives back the offering to the children and kindly tells them, "O My children! These blessings are intended for you! Out of your natural love, you bring them to Me for My enjoyment, but naturally I have no wants for you to supply. I have, however, accepted that part of your offering which is for Me: your unmixed love and unbiased affections, for which I am exceedingly anxious. Take back these sweet things and enjoy them."

This process of unbiased love, which dry reason can never approach, sanctifies the food we take and brings us harmless enjoyment every day of our natural life! This is a system of sincere worship, which theists of a higher class alone can act upon. We cannot express the joy we often felt when we took the *mahāprasāda* in the temple! The holiness we attach to it is its sweetness and often we pray that all men may enjoy it.

(*The Temple of Jagannātha at Purī*)

15

Śrī Krishna

1. Why is pure love most applicable to Śrī Krishna?

Among all the features of the Absolute Truth that are found in this world, the form of Krishna is most suitable for pure love. The conception of"Allah" established in the Islamic scripture cannot be the object of pure love. Even the dearmost prophet could not meet Him because, even though the worshipable is achievable through friendship, He remains far away from His worshipers due to their conception of His opulence. The conception of God in Christianity is a faraway object. What then can be said about Brahman? Even Lord Nārāyaṇa does not become an object of the living entities' spontaneous love. Rather Lord Krishna eternally resides in the spiritual abode of Vraja as the only object of pure love.

(*Caitanya-śikṣāmṛta* 1/1)

2. Is there any object other than Krishna for pure love?

Even though words like Krishna, Vṛndāvana, gopas, *gopīs*, Yamunā, and kadamba are not found elsewhere due to linguistic differences, still the name, form, abode, paraphernalia, and pastimes are revealed by the words and moods of exalted devotees. There is no object for pure love other than Krishna.

(*Caitanya-śikṣāmṛta* 1/1)

3. What is the highest manifestation of Viṣṇu?

Śrī Krishna alone is the highest manifestation of Viṣṇu. When a living entity transcends the three material modes and becomes situated in pure goodness, he achieves the service of Krishna.

(*Sajjana-toṣaṇī* 11/6)

4. Are Brahman, Paramātmā, and Bhagavān separate truths?

Brahman, Paramātmā, and Bhagavān are one object. According to one's qualification, one sees a particular feature of the Supreme Lord and accepts Him as the highest.

(*Caitanya-śikṣāmṛta* 1/3)

5. How is Krishna different from Brahman and Paramātmā?

Śrī Krishna is eternal, full of knowledge and bliss. He is the source of Brahman and Paramātmā.

(*Manaḥ-śikṣā*, Chapter 3)

6. What is the difference between Brahman and Bhagavān, and the result of Their worship?

Brahman and Bhagavān, the Personality of Godhead, are not separate truths. Brahman refers to indirect qualities or unmanifest energies of the Lord. Bhagavān refers to the possessor of manifest, inconceivable, wonderful variegated energies. That is why contradictory qualities are perfectly present in Him. A living entity in Brahman realization, possessing dry knowledge, only attains a token of the happiness of liberation. But one in Bhagavān realization can relish unlimited happiness in the form of mellows of pure devotional service.

(Purport of *Bṛhad-bhāgavatāmṛta*)

7. What is the difference between Brahman and form of the Supreme Lord?

The lotus feet of Krishna are the only source of happiness and can be compared to a piece of sugar candy. Brahman gives that happiness, but it is not the source of happiness. Such differences between Bhagavān and Brahman are made possible only by Bhagavān's energy of inconceivable oneness and difference.

(Purport of *Bṛhad-bhāgavatāmṛta*)

8. Is there any difference between Lord Krishna's body and soul?

The body of Śrī Krishna is eternal, full of knowledge and bliss. There is no difference between His body and His soul, unlike ordinary embodied beings. On the platform of *advaya-jñāna* or nondual knowledge, the body is the self and the self is the body. Although the form of Krishna is situated in one place, it is all-pervading.

(*Manaḥ-śikṣā*)

9. Why is it unreasonable to say that the Supreme Brahman is without variegatedness?

Whatever exists has a distinct characteristic by which it can be differentiated from other objects. If there is no distinction, an object may be said to have no existence. If the Supreme Brahman is without variety, how could it be differentiated from the material creation? If we cannot say that the Supreme Brahman is different from creation, then the creator and creation become one. Then hope, faith, fear, reasoning, and all kinds of knowledge become nonexistent.

(*Prema-pradīpa*, Chapter 9)

10. Why can there not be any competitor to the Supreme Lord?

The Supreme Lord is one without a second; no one is equal to or superior to Him. He controls everything. There is nothing that can arouse enviousness in Him. He awards the results of one's activities according to the firm determination in one's heart to attain devotion to Him.

(*Prema-pradīpa*, Chapter 5)

11. Why is Brahman called the bodily effulgence of the Supreme Lord?

The Supreme Personality of Godhead is the complete whole; He is the noun, not the adjective. Both Brahman and Paramātmā are His qualities. Before creation, there was only the Supreme Lord and no one else, not even Brahman. When the material world was created, a concept of the Supreme Lord came into being—"the whole universe is Brahman." There are two concepts regarding Brahman. The first is that everything is Brahman, and the second is that Brahman is beyond the created or materially conditioned world. Both these concepts are applicable to the material world. Brahman, the bodily effulgence of the Supreme Lord, pervades the universe. It is most correct to refer to Brahman as the Supreme Lord's bodily effulgence.

(*Sajjana-toṣaṇī* 2/6)

12. What is Brahman? Is it a manifestation of Krishna, who is fully sac-cid-ānanda?

The glories of Śrī Krishna are reflected everywhere in the form of His effulgence, which is known as Brahman.

(*Manaḥ-śikṣā*, Chapter 3)

13. In Bhagavad-gītā, what evidence is there that Śrī Krishna is the shelter of Brahman?

Śrī Krishna, transcendental and full of variegatedness, is the source of Brahman, the goal of the impersonalists. Eternity, inexhaustibility, deathlessness, pure eternal love, and the unalloyed happiness of *vraja-rāsa* are the characteristics of Krishna.

(Commentary on *Bhagavad-gītā* 14/27)

14. What is the difference between Brahman and the Supreme Brahman?

Brahman that is full of spiritual energies is called the Supreme Brahman. Brahman without variegatedness and energy is a partial manifestation of the Supreme Brahman.

(*Tattva Viveka* 1/32)

15. What are the two manifestations of Paramātmā?

Paramātmā has two manifestations: collective and localized. In His collective manifestation, He is the universal form. In His localized manifestation, He is the constant companion of the living entities, the indwelling Supersoul and the Supreme Person, who measures the height of the thumb.

(*Caitanya-śikṣāmṛta* 5/3)

16. What is the difference between Brahman realization, Paramātmā realization, and Bhagavān realization?

Brahman and Paramātmā realizations have designations. Brahman realization is the opposite of material designations, and Paramātmā realization is in agreement with material designations. Only when one sees through spiritual eyes and without mundane vision can one see the spiritual form of the Supreme Lord.

(*Manaḥ-śikṣā*, Chapter 4)

17. What are the characteristics of Brahman, Paramātmā, and Bhagavān?

The feature of the Lord that is devoid of energy and variegatedness is called Brahman, and the same Brahman that is full of energies and variegatedness is called Bhagavān. Therefore, the feature of Bhagavān is the ultimate realization of the Supreme Lord. Brahman is only His bodily effulgence, which is devoid of variegatedness. Paramātmā is His plenary portion who enters into the universes.

(*Manaḥ-śikṣā*, Chapter 4)

18. When does the conception of impersonal Brahman come about?

Krishna, who is full of unlimited opulence, is one without a second. In the cultivation of knowledge, as soon as one separates power and energy from Krishna, one sees the nondual truth as impersonal Brahman.

(*Harināma-cintāmaṇi*)

19. What are the characteristics of Krishna's pastimes?

Krishna alone is the supreme enjoyer and the living entities are enjoyed by Him in the eternal abode of Vṛndāvana. These pastimes are blissful and unlimited. They are eternal and uninterrupted.

(*Kalyāṇa-kalpataru*)

20. What are the considerations of Krishna's pastimes?

Although the quality of being self-satisfied is eternally present in Krishna, the quality of enjoying pastimes is also eternally present in Him. For the Supreme Lord to possess contradictory characteristics in perfect harmony is natural. In one aspect, Krishna has the quality of self-satisfaction, and in another aspect, He manifests His opposite quality of enjoying pastimes with other's.

(*Caitanya-śikṣāmṛta* Part 2, 7/7)

21. What are the limits of āśraya, worshiper, and viṣaya, the object of worship?

The limit of *āśraya-tattva* is Śrī Rādhikā, the personification of attachment, and the limit of *viṣaya-tattva* is Śrī Krishna, the personification of conjugal pastimes.

(*Caitanya-śikṣāmṛta* Part 2, 7/7)

22. What is the truth of Krishna's manifest and unmanifest pastimes?

The pastimes of Krishna are of two types: manifest and unmanifest. The Vṛndāvana pastimes which are visible to the eyes of ordinary people are called manifest pastimes, and those pastimes that are not seen through material eyes are called Krishna's unmanifest pastimes. The unmanifest pastimes are always manifest in Goloka, and by the will of Krishna, they become visible to the material eyes.

(*Brahma-saṁhitā* 5/3)

23. What are these terms in truth: Mathurā, Vasudeva, Devakī, and Kaṁsa?

In the pious land of Bhārata-varṣa is Mathurā, the manifestation of absolute knowledge, where King Vasudeva, the personification of pure goodness, took birth. Vasudeva appeared in a family of devotees and married Devakī, the so-called sister of Kaṁsa, the personification of atheism. Fearing the Lord's advent from this couple, the wretched Kaṁsa of the Bhoja dynasty arrested them and put them in the jail of remembrance.

(*Śrī Krishna-saṁhitā*, Chapter 4)

24. What is the truth of the six sons of Devakī and the seventh son, Baladeva? What is the mystery of Vasudeva bringing the son of Devakī to Vraja out of fear of Kaṁsa?

The couple Vasudeva and Devakī gradually begot six sons, such as Yaśā and Kīrti, but Kaṁsa, who was against the Lord, killed them in their childhood. Śrī Baladeva was decorated with service to the Lord and was the transcendental reservoir of all living entities. He was their seventh son. He appeared in the womb of Devakī, who represents a heart filled with knowledge, but out of fear of His maternal uncle Kaṁsa, He was taken to His home in Vraja.

(*Śrī Krishna-saṁhitā*, Chapter 4)

25. Are the pastimes of Krishna imagined from human behavior?

The pure activities of Krishna have been perceived through the *samādhi* of swanlike persons like Vyāsadeva. Krishna's activities are not exactly historical like those of people under the clutches of Māyā, because Krishna's activities are not limited to any time or place. Nor are His activities comparable with the activities of ordinary people.

(*Śrī Krishna-saṁhitā*, Chapter 3)

26. Why are all the pastimes of Krishna eternal?

Krishna performs different pastimes in the hearts of different devotees depending on their qualification at a particular time. Krishna takes birth in one devotee's heart, He steals the *gopīs*' clothes in another's, and He performs the rāsa dance in another's. He kills Pūtanā in one other devotee's heart, He kills Kaṁsa in another's, He has an affair with Kubjā in yet another's, and He enacts His disappearance in the heart of a devotee who is leaving his body. The planets, like the living entities, are innumerable.

As one pastime takes place on one planet, another pastime takes place on another planet. In this way, each pastime continually takes place. Therefore, all of the Lord's pastimes are eternal; there is no break, because the Lord's energies are always active.

(*Śrī Krishna-saṁhitā*, Chapter 7)

27. What is the purport behind Krishna's stealing the garments of the gopīs?

Those who have an intense desire to serve Krishna have no secrets amongst themselves or with other's. To teach this principle to the devotees, Krishna stole the clothes of the *gopīs*.

(*Śrī Krishna-saṁhitā*, Chapter 5)

28. Are the rāsa-līlā pastimes not obscene?

In the transcendental rāsa-līlā pastimes, Śrī Krishna is the only enjoyer and all other's are enjoyed. The conclusion is that the sunlike personality of the spiritual world, Lord Śrī Krishna, is the only male and the living entities are all female. All the relationships of the spiritual world are based on pure love. One, therefore, finds the enjoyer is male and the enjoyed are female. The males and females of the material world are perverted reflections of the enjoyer and enjoyed of the spiritual world. If one searches through every dictionary, one will not find the words to properly describe the spiritual pastimes of the supremely conscious Lord and His associates. Hence, the descriptions of man and woman of the material world are used here as an appropriate indication. There is no necessity or suggestion of obscene thoughts concerning Krishna.

(*Śrī Krishna-saṁhitā*, Chapter 5)

29. Who are Ugrasena, Kaṁsa, the wives of Kaṁsa, and Jarāsandha?

After the atheist Kaṁsa was killed, his father—Ugrasena, the personification of freedom—was installed on the throne by Krishna. The two wives of Kaṁsa, Asti and Prāpti, described the killing of their husband to Jarāsandha, the personification of fruitive activities.

(*Śrī Krishna-saṁhitā*, Chapter 5)

30. Are the pastimes of Krishna concocted by human beings?

Krishna's pastimes are neither human concoction nor the blind faith of cheated people. Only persons conversant with spiritual science can understand this truth. Arguments and moralities cannot touch the glories of Krishna's pastimes. Argument, morality, knowledge, mystic yoga, religiosity, and irreligiosity lay to one side and the great illumination of the science of Vraja manifests in the hearts of the pure devotees and thus enlightens them.

(*Manaḥ-śikṣā*, Chapter 5)

31. Are the pastimes of Krishna metaphysical or fantasy tales?

We consider Rādhā Krishna's pastimes as transcendental, not metaphysical. The endeavors to establish the philosophy of dry impersonalism through fantasy tales are metaphysical, because the impersonal philosophy accepts material variegatedness and then rejects it. The impersonal philosophy is described in this way, but the descriptions of Vraja pastimes are different. The transcendental spiritual variegatedness, which is the ideal for material variegatedness, is very much present in Vraja. The transcendental descriptions are realized through transcendental variegatedness.

(*Sajjana-toṣaṇī* 6/2)

32. Why are the pastimes of Krishna not metaphysical?

The pastimes of Krishna are not metaphysical. When all truths are seen in relation to Brahman, metaphysical activities begin. The philosophy of impersonalism is a metaphysical subject matter.

Wherever the metaphysical mood is prominent, the transcendental pastimes of Krishna in Vṛndāvana are vanquished. Krishna's pastimes are full of variegatedness. The metaphysical mood and the mood of variegatedness are totally opposite to each other. In the metaphysical realm, Brahman, whose energies are dormant, is the goal of life. In the realm of variegatedness, only the eternal pastimes of Kṛṣna are manifest. Although these two features are contradictory, in the Absolute Truth they do not contradict each other. While the nondual Brahman realization remains present on the path of *jñāna*, the Supreme Absolute Truth, who is full of variegatedness, continues to manifest transcendental pastimes in His eternal abode of Vṛndāvana. Such simultaneous considerations of metaphysical and transcendental truths cannot take place in the human thought. Only one who is favored by the Absolute Truth can see such contradictory characteristics present in the Lord in perfect harmony. This simultaneous oneness and difference has been made possible due to the inconceivable potency of the Lord.

(*Sajjana-toṣaṇī* 8/7)

33. Are the pastimes of Krishna mundane?

The descriptions of the Lord's transcendental pastimes are factual and eternal. They are never imaginary. Mundane activities are totally material and under the control of time and place, and are therefore temporary. Transcendental pastimes may appear like mundane activities, but they have no tinge of materialism; they are fully spiritual. Just because transcendental pastimes can be seen with material eyes, no part of them should be considered a product of matter. The pastimes of Krishna are beyond the reach of material perception and material senses. They are the object for the spiritual senses of the spirit souls.

(*Sajjana-toṣaṇī* 5/7)

34. How are Krishna's pastimes transcendental? What are the ingredients of such pastimes?

The material world is the perverted reflection of the spiritual world. Here everything is polluted by Māyā. In the spiritual world, Māyā and the three modes of material nature do not exist. There everything is impeccable and made of pure goodness including time, place, and all other objects. The pastimes of Krishna are transcendental to material nature, and therefore they are fully spiritual. Krishna's pastimes are nourished by faultless time, place, sky, water, and so on. Within spiritual time, which is unlike material time, the pastimes of Krishna are eightfold. They take place at dawn, morning, pre-noon, noon, afternoon, evening, night, and late at night. In this way Krishna's pastimes are divided into eight, according to the different times of the day and night, and thus they are nourishing the eternal uninterrupted *rāsa*.

(*Caitanya-śikṣāmṛta* 6/5)

35. How many types of manifest Vraja pastimes are there?

The manifest pastimes of Vraja are of two types: eternal and occasional. The *aṣṭa-kālīya* (eightfold) pastimes of Vraja are eternal, whereas other pastimes, such as the killing of Pūtanā and leaving to go to a faraway place, are occasional.

(*Jaiva Dharma*, Chapter 38)

36. What can one learn from the killing of the demons?

Through the pastimes of killing the demons, one indirectly learns about Krishna.

(*Caitanya-śikṣāmṛta* Part 2, 7/7)

37. Does the Supreme Lord have a form or no form?

Because of His inconceivable potency, the Supreme Lord is formless and simultaneously He has a spiritual form. If we say that the Lord cannot have a spiritual form, we are denying His inconceivable potency.

(*Jaiva Dharma*, Chapter 11)

38. Why do the Vedas declare that the Supreme Lord is formless?

A material object has a gross form, but the Supreme Lord does not have such a form. That is why we cannot see Him with our material senses. Therefore, the Vedas have sometimes described the Supreme Lord as formless.

(*Caitanya-śikṣāmṛta* 1/1)

39. Should one consider the Supreme Lord has no form or He has a form?

The Supreme Lord has no form and He has a form. We can understood that those who accept one of these truths and neglect the other do not see with both their eyes.

(*Tattva-sūtra* 4)

40. What is the definition of the Lord's form?

According to Vedic literature the Supreme Lord's form is eternal, full of knowledge and bliss. The spiritual form exists beyond the material creation and is transcendental.

(*Caitanya Caritāmṛta* Madhya 6/166 —167 commentary)

41. How is it appropriate that the Supreme Lord simultaneously has no form and has a form?

It is useless to argue over whether the Supreme Lord has no form or has a form. The Supreme Lord does not have a material form; He possesses a form that is transcendental, spiritual, eternal, full of knowledge and bliss, and beyond material perception. This form can only be approached by His devotees. The conclusion is that for material eyes the Supreme Lord is formless, and for spiritual eyes He has a form. Therefore, we accept that He has no form and He has a form.

(*Tattva-sūtra* 4)

42. How is it possible for the Lord to simultaneously be an individual and be all-pervading?

Because of His inconceivable potency, the Supreme Lord can simultaneously be all-pervading and be an individual. This understanding is impossible for those who are not on the level of Brahman.

(*Tattva-sūtra* 4)

43. Is the Supreme Lord compelled to follow the rules and regulations that have been created either by Him or by the living entities?

The physical rule is that if you add a foot of rope to another foot of rope, it will be two feet of rope, never three feet of rope. However, the Supreme Lord is not bound by such rules. He is the creator of the rules; therefore, He is not forced to follow His own rules.

(*Tattva-sūtra* 4)

44. Is the Supreme Lord constrained by time and space?

Our ideas are constrained by the idea of time and space, but God is above that constraint.

(*The Bhagavat*: *Its Philosophy*, *Its Ethics & Its Theology*)

45. When does the concept of formlessness and having a form vanquish?

The Absolute Truth is beyond all *sampradāyas*. Therefore, the swanlike devotees should not argue whether the Lord has no form or has a form. As soon as devotional service is awakened in one's heart, one will automatically realize both features of the Lord.

(*Tattva-sūtra* 4)

46. Why is no one equal to or greater than Krishna?

Sixty-four transcendental qualities are fully manifest in Śrī Krishna, who is eternal, full of knowledge and bliss. The last four qualities are present only in Śrī Krishna. Even His opulent forms do not possess them. Not having these four qualities, Nārāyaṇa, who is the Lord of the spiritual sky and whose form is fully spiritual, possesses the other sixty qualities in full. Demigods like Lord Śiva possess fifty-five qualities in small quantities. The living entities possess the first fifty qualities in minute quantities. Śiva, Brahmā, Sūrya, Gaṇeśa, and Indra are all part and parcel of the Supreme Lord. They are qualitative incarnations of the Lord. They are empowered by the Lord and are awarded the responsibility of managing the material creation. Actually they are all servants of the Supreme Lord. By their mercy, many persons have attained pure devotional service.

(*Jaiva Dharma*, Chapter 13)

47. How does Śrī Krishna behave toward a surrendered soul?

Śrī Krishna is always pure, self-satisfied, and an affectionate master to His devotees. If Krishna wants to save someone, who can kill him? Krishna is the creator of all the rules and regulations.

(*Śaraṇāgati*)

48. Why is Śrī Krishna the reservoir of all transcendental pastimes?

Śrī Krishna is the Supreme Absolute Truth and His pastimes are pure. The illusory energy, Māyā, is His distant maidservant. To benefit the living entities, the most merciful Lord Hari manifested His transcendental pastimes.

(*Gītāmālā* 28)

49. What do the Vedas say regarding the transcendental form of the Supreme Brahman?

The *Chāndogya Upaniṣad* states *bahu syām*, the Supreme Lord desired to become many, and the *Aitareya Upaniṣad* states *sa aikṣata*, He glanced at material nature. At that time, there was no existence of material mind or eyes. This means that the mind by which the Lord thought and the eyes by which He glanced were existing before material creation. The Vedas therefore give evidence that the Supreme Brahman has transcendental mind and eyes.

(*Caitanya Caritāmṛta* Madhya 6/143-148 commentary)

50. What considerations are there regarding the six opulences of the Supreme Lord? Is the impersonal Brahman dependent or independent?

The Supreme Lord is the inconceivable Absolute Truth. He is full of six opulences: wealth, fame, beauty, knowledge, power, and renunciation. These qualities are always present in the Lord. A question may arise: among them which is the possessor and which is the possessed?

The possessor is He in whom these qualities are found. For example, the tree is the possessor and the branches are possessed, the body is the possessor and the hands and legs are possessed. The beauty of the Lord's transcendental body is the possessor and other qualities are possessed. Wealth, power, and fame are possessed. Knowledge and renunciation have emanated from the vast effulgence of fame; they are qualities of fame; they themselves are not separate qualities. Knowledge of changeless spirit and renunciation of matter are the parts of the body of the impersonal Brahman. The impersonal Brahman is the effulgence emanating from the spiritual worlds. The unchanging, inactive, formless, qualityless Brahman is not the independent highest truth. It is the form of the Supreme Personality of Godhead, who is the independent highest truth. The light of fire is not independent; it is a quality of fire.

(*Jaiva Dharma*, Chapter 13)

16

The Lord's Incarnation

1. What is the science of the Lord's incarnation? Why does the Supreme Lord appear in this world?

When the conditioned souls receive a body according to their nature, the Supreme Lord Krishna, by His inconceivable potency, agrees to accompany them by incarnating and enjoying pastimes with them. When the living entities accept the body of a fish, the Lord accepted His fish incarnation, Matsya. Matsya is without a daṇḍa or spine. When the living entities accept the body of vajradaṇda or half-grown spine, the Lord incarnates as Kūrma. When vajradaṇda gradually becomes meru-daṇda or fully-grown spine, the Lord incarnates as Varāha. When the living entities accept the combined position of human and animal, the Lord accepts His incarnation of Nṛsiṁha. When the living entities are short, He appears as Vāmana. When the living entities are uncivilized, He comes as Paraśurāma. When they are civilized, He appears as Rāmacandra. When the living entities possess the wealth of practical knowledge, Lord Krishna Himself appears. When the living entities develop the tendency for argument, the Lord appears as Buddha. Moreover, when they are atheistic, the Lord comes as Kalki. These are well-known facts.

During the gradual development in the hearts of the living entities, the Lord incarnates in a form corresponding to the mood of the devotees. The source and activities of His forms are untouched by material contamination. After due consideration, the sages have divided the history of the living entities' advancement into ten divisions. Each one has different symptoms: each successive mood is superior to the previous one. The Lord's ten incarnations correspond to these ten moods. Some learned scholars have divided the living entities' advancement into twenty-four divisions and have stated that there are twenty-four incarnations. Yet other's have divided it into eighteen and have stated eighteen incarnations.

(*Śrī Krishna-saṁhitā*, Chapter 3)

2. What is the scientific consideration about the truth of the Lord's incarnations?

From an invertebrate living entity up to a fully developed vertebrate human being, some sages have defined eight, eighteen, or twenty-four corresponding incarnations of the Lord. Most authentic sages agree that there are ten principle incarnations. From the conditional state up to the end of a living entities progress, the sages have defined ten stages. The first stage is life as an invertebrate, second a thin vertebrate, third a vertebrate, fourth a raised vertebrate or animalistic human being, fifth a small human being, sixth an uncivilized human being, seventh a civilized human being, eighth a knowledgeable human being, ninth a most knowledgeable human being. And the tenth stage is devastation. According to these stages of development of the living entities, the ten incarnations of the Supreme Lord appear and enjoy transcendental pastimes. The ten incarnations are Matsya, Kurma, Varāha, Nṛsimha, Vāmana, Parasurāma, Rāma, Krishna, Buddha, and Kalki.

(*Tattva-sūtra* 6)

3. Who is the original incarnation?

With a desire to create the material worlds, Saṅkarṣaṇa, who is a plenary portion of Krishna, lies in the causal ocean as the original puruṣa and glances over Māyā. This act of glancing is the original cause of material creation.

(*Brahma-saṁhitā* 5/8 purport)

4. Why does the Supreme Lord incarnate?

The Supreme Lord has two kinds of pastimes. The first is to create the material world and to maintain it by establishing stringent laws. The dry speculators can understand these pastimes to some extent. The second is the Lord's pastimes within this material world, where the living entities are His companions. Because of their desire for material enjoyment, some living entities fall from their constitutional position. Whatever situation they go through in the association of matter, the Supreme Lord responds accordingly. The principle cause for the Lord's appearance is His causeless mercy toward the living entities.

(*Tattva-sūtra* 6)

5. What is the necessity for worshiping the deity form of the Lord?

All formless truths have some representation. A representation, although different from the object it represents, symbolizes the mood of the object. Watches represent formless time, essays represent subtle knowledge, and pictures represent acts of mercy. In the same way, there is no doubt that one gets benefit in performing devotional service to the deity.

(*Prema Pradipa*, Chapter 5)

6. Is deity worship of the Vaiṣṇavas idol worship?

The deity worshiped by the Vaiṣṇavas is not an idol, which is separate from the Lord. The deity is a representation that invokes devotion to the Lord.

7. Is the deity the direct manifestation of the Lord?

The deity of the Lord cannot be anything other than the direct manifestation of the Lord. Just as in industry or in science, every unseen object has a gross image, the Lord, unseen by material eyes, has an image in the form of the deity. Because of their devotional propensity, the pure devotees constantly experience that the deity is truly the Supreme Lord. The connection between an electric light and a generator is understood only by seeing the result when the electric light is switched on. What will those who are ignorant of electricity understand when they see a generator? Similarly, what will those who have no devotion in their hearts say about the deity except"idol"?

(*Caitanya-śikṣāmṛta* 5/3)

8. What is the difference between the deity worshiped by the devotees and the symbols of the mental speculators?

At first, the Lord's form manifests in the spiritual consciousness of the living entities and thus He appears in their hearts. Then the devotees see no difference between the spiritual form within their hearts and the external deity form. However, the mental speculators do not worship the deity in this way. According to their opinion, Brahman is imagined within a deity made of material elements, and that image is there as long as the worship continues. Thereafter the form remains a material object and nothing else.

(*Jaiva Dharma*, Chapter 5)

9. Is everyone qualified to worship the deity?

Worship of the Lord's deity is the foundation of religious principles for human beings. Great devotees have seen the form of the Supreme Lord by pure knowledge and they meditate on this pure spiritual form. When the hearts of the devotees spread toward the material world, a reflection of that spiritual form is illustrated in the material world. The form of the Supreme Lord has thus manifest as a deity by the mercy of the *mahājanas*. For *uttama-adhikārīs*, the deity is always the spiritual form of the Lord. For *madhyama-adhikārīs*, the deity is the spiritual form in their heart. For *kaniṣṭha-adhikārīs*, the deity at first appears material, but by gradual purification of their intelligence, they accept the deity as the spiritual form of the Lord. Therefore, it is the duty of all kinds of devotees to engage in the worship of the Lord's deity. There is no need to worship any concocted God. The worship of the eternal form of the Lord is auspicious.

(*Jaiva Dharma*, Chapter 11)

10. How do mental speculators, who do not accept the deity, worship the deity?

Some people establish with devotion the Supreme Lord's deity within their self, their mind, or the material world. They then worship that form considering it nondifferent from the Supreme Lord. The followers of some religions, due to attachment to argument, imagine the Lord's form within their mind and worship that form, but they do not accept the external deity form of the Lord. Actually, all these forms are His deities.

(*Caitanya-śikṣāmṛta* 1/1)

11. How do the swanlike Vaiṣṇavas see Śrī Jagannātha Deva?

The worship of Jagannātha is viewed in two ways. Superstitious and ignorant people think it is idolatry to worship God Almighty, who has appeared in the shape of carved wood for the salvation of the people of Orissa. However, the Sāragrāhī Vaiṣṇavas accept the deities as eternal truth, as Vyāsa has explained in *Vedānta-sūtra*.

(*The Temple of Jagannātha at Purī*)

12. How did Śrī Bhaktivinoda refute the atheistic philosophy that is opposed to deity worship?

Some are startled at the idea of worshiping the deity (*śrī-mūrti*). They say,"It is idolatry to worship the deity, which is an idol made by an artist and introduced by Beelzebub himself. Worshiping such an object would arouse the jealousy of God and limit His omnipotence, omniscience, and omnipresence."

We reply to them in the following way."Brothers! Candidly understand the subject and do not allow yourselves to be misled by sectarian dogma.

God is not jealous—He is without a second. Beelzebub or Satan is only an imaginary figure or a being used in an allegory. An allegorical or imaginary person should not be allowed to act as an obstacle to *bhakti.* Those who believe God is impersonal simply identify Him with some power or quality of nature. In fact He is above nature, her laws, and her rules. His holy wish is law, and it is sacrilege to confine His unlimited excellence by identifying Him with such attributes as omnipotence, omnipresence, and omniscience—attributes which may exist in created objects, such as time and space. His excellence is such that He has mutually contradicting powers and qualities, which are ruled by His supernatural Self. He is identical with His all-beautiful person, and His powers of omnipresence, omniscience, and omnipotence cannot be found elsewhere. His holy and perfect person exists eternally in the spiritual world and is simultaneously existing in every created object and place in full. This understanding excels all other ideas about the deity.

"Mahāprabhu also rejected idolatry, but considered deity worship to be the only unexceptionable means of spiritual culture. It has been shown that God is personal and all-beautiful. Vyāsa and other sages have seen God's beauty with their souls' eyes. They have left us descriptions. Of course, words carry the grossness of matter, but truth is perceivable in those descriptions. According to those descriptions one delineates a deity and sees the Supreme Lord of one's heart with intense pleasure. Brothers! Is that wrong or sinful? Those who say that God has no form either material or spiritual, and then imagine a false form of worship are idolatrous. But those who see the spiritual form of the deity in their souls' eyes carry that impression as far as possible to the mind and then frame an emblem for the satisfaction of the material eye and for the continual study of higher feelings. They are by no means idolatrous.

"When you see a deity, do not even see the image itself; see the spiritual form of the image. Then you are a pure theist. Idolatry and deity worship are two different things. But my brothers, you simply confound one with the other in hastiness. To tell you the truth, deity worship is the only true form of worship of the Lord, without which you cannot sufficiently cultivate your religious feelings. The world attracts you through your senses and as long as you do not see God in the objects of your senses, you live in an awkward position, which scarcely helps you secure your spiritual elevation.

"Place a deity in your house. Consider God the guardian of the house and the food that you take His *prasāda.* The flowers and scents are also His *prasāda.* The eyes, the ears, the nose, the tongue, and the sense of touch can be spiritually satisfied. Worship God with a holy heart. God will know and judge you by your sincerity. In this way, Satan and Beelzebub will have nothing to do with you.

"All sorts of worship are based on the principle of deity worship. Look into the history of religion and you will understand this noble truth. The Semitic idea of a patriarchal God, both in the pre-Christian period of Judaism and post-Christian period of Christianity and Mohammedanism, is nothing but a limited idea of deity worship. The monarchic idea of Jupiter among the Romans and Indra among the Āryan karma-kāṇḍīs is also based on the same principle. The idea of a force and Jyotirmaya Brahma of the meditators and a formless energy of the Śaktas is also a very faint view of the deity. In fact, the deity is the Truth differently exhibited by different people according to their beliefs. Even Jaimini and Compte, who were not prepared to accept a creating God, have prescribed certain forms of deity worship, simply because they were impelled by the soul. And we meet people who have adopted the cross, the śālagrāma-śilā, the liṅgam, and such emblems as indicators of the Lord within.

"Furthermore, if divine love, justice, and compassion can be portrayed by the pencil and expressed by the chisel, why shouldn't the personal beauty of the deity (embracing all other qualities) be portrayed in poetry and in pictures, and carved by the chisel for the benefit of man? If a word provokes thought, a watch indicates time, and a sign tells us of history, why shouldn't a picture or deity bring higher thoughts of and feelings for the transcendental beauty of the Divine Person?"

(*Caitanya Mahāprabhu, His Life and Precepts*)

17

Transcendental Mellows

1. Why is Śrī Krishna the personification of all nectarean rāsas? Why is He unique in this regard?

Śrī Krishna is the object of the highest transcendental mellows. If one considers impartially and becomes free from the clutches of prejudice, one will conclude that in *rāsa* the form of Śrī Krishna is the most suitable and the best. His other forms are eternal, spiritual, transcendental, and full of divine qualities. They are the master of Māyā. Krishna also possesses all these transcendental qualities. The special characteristic of Krishna is that He displays His spiritual pastimes in this material world through His spiritual energy and allows the material senses to perceive them. When the Lord descends to this world, His behavior appears mundane, but actually He is always full of all opulences. He reciprocated with the cowherd boys as their beloved friend, with His parents as their dependent child, and with His devotees who are absorbed in *mādhurya-rāsa* as their beloved Lord, yet He never failed to display His supremacy. Even while performing His pastimes as a human being, He surprised the learned community by exhibiting His superiority over the demigods, who are dependent on Him. If Krishna had not mercifully displayed His most enchanting pastimes as a cowherd boy, could anyone realize the Supreme Lord as the object of *mādhurya-rāsa*?

(*Manaḥ-śikṣā* 5)

2. Are Śrī Krishna's pastimes as a paramour abominable?

When Śrī Krishna Himself is the only enjoyer, there is no question of His pastimes as a paramour being abominable. Whenever an ordinary living entity claims to be the enjoyer, immediately the question of religiosity or irreligiosity arises.

(*Jaiva Dharma*, Chapter 31)

3. What is the science of Śrī Rādhā Krishna?

According to the teachings of Śrīmān Mahāprabhu, worship of the Lord in the mood of *mādhurya-rāsa* is the highest. In this mood one cannot relish the transcendental mellows of devotional service unless one becomes subordinate to Śrī Rādhikā. The Supreme Brahman is eternal *(sat)*, full of knowledge (*cit*), and full of bliss (*ānanda*). Śrī Krishna is the personification of *sat-cit* and Śrī Rādhā is the manifestation of *ānanda*. Rādhā and Krishna are one truth, but for the expansion of *rāsa*, They have appeared as two.

(*Caitanya-śikṣāmṛta* 6/5)

4. What are the symptoms of ecstatic love for Krishna?

After honoring prasād, Vijay Kumar, taking the road by the ocean, immediately departed for the house of Kāśī Miśra. On seeing the waves and billows of the ocean, the mood of the ocean of transcendental mellows began to appear in his mind.

He thought,"Oh! This ocean is awakening my sentiments. Although it is a material object, it is arousing my internal spiritual mood. The topic of the ocean of mellows, which the Lord always explains to me, are as follows. When my gross and subtle bodies are thrown away, I sit on the shore of the ocean of mellows in my own form as a mañjarī and relish transcendental mellows. Krishna alone, whose complexion is like a new cloud, is my beloved Lord. On His side stands the daughter of King Vṛṣabhānu. She is our controller. In other words, She is the controller of all living entities. The ocean is the transformation of Rādhā Krishna's ecstatic love. Transcendental mellows of ecstatic love are the waves. Whenever a particular mood arises, it drowns me, a sakhī, in the mellows of ecstatic love, as I stand on the shore. Krishna is the ocean of mellows and therefore the ocean has adopted the complexion of Krishna. The current of the ocean is Śrī Rādhā and therefore it appears golden. The big waves are the sakhīs and the small waves are their maidservants. I am one of the maidservants thrown away from the ocean to the shore."

Thinking in this way, Vijay became overwhelmed. Coming back to external consciousness after some time, he went before his spiritual master, offered his respectful obeisances, and sat down.

(*Jaiva Dharma*, Chapter 32)

18

Holy Names of Śrī Krishna

1. What is the holy name of Krishna?

The holy name of Lord Krishna is the bud of the flower of *rāsa*. *Rāsa* is pure and unbroken, and by the mercy of Krishna, it has been spread in the world as the holy name.

(*Harināma-cintāmaṇi*)

2. Which instruction in the Vedas is the best?

Of all the instructions in the Vedas, the best is to chant the holy names of Hari.

(*Jaiva Dharma*, Chapter 24)

3. How is the chanting of the holy names simultaneously the goal of life and the process of achieving that goal?

The mercy of the Supreme Lord is the highest goal of all living entities. The principal method for achieving that goal is not fruitive activities and mental speculation, because they vanish as one comes closer to the goal. The process of chanting is not like that. The holy name is nondifferent from the Supreme Lord and, therefore, He always remains present as both the goal and the process.

(*Harināma-cintāmaṇi*)

4. How many types of names does the Supreme Lord have? Is it proper to consider the Lord's names as inferior or superior?

The holy names of the Lord are of two types: primary and secondary. The names given to Him because He created the material world through Māyā (such as creator of the universe, maintainer of the universe, controller of the universe, sustainer of the universe, and Paramātmā) are His secondary names. Some names, such as Brahman, that are beyond the jurisdiction of the three modes of material nature are also counted among His secondary names. Although these holy names award various results, they seldom award the supreme spiritual goal. The Lord's holy names that are transcendental to material time and space, and are eternally present in the spiritual world are the Lord's primary and spiritual names. They are names such as Nārāyaṇa, Vāsudeva, Janārdana, Hṛṣīkeśa, Hari, Acyuta, Govinda, Gopāla, and Rāma. These principal names are eternally present in the spiritual realm and are inseparably connected with the Supreme Lord.

(*Jaiva Dharma*, Chapter 23)

5. What is special about the name Krishna?

The holy name Krishna is the Lord's eternal name that attracts everyone toward His ecstatic love and reveals His supreme existence.

(*Brahma-saṁhitā* 5/3)

6. What is Krishna's first identification?

Krishna's first identification is the holy name Krishna. The living entity should chant Krishna's holy name, and resolve to achieve His shelter.

(*Caitanya-śikṣāmṛta* 6/4)

7. Is the holy name a material sound vibration? Can a material tongue chant the holy name?

The holy name of Hari is not a product of the material world. A pure spirit soul situated in his constitutional position is qualified to chant the holy name of Hari in his spiritual body.

A materially conditioned living entity cannot chant the holy name through his material senses. However, when one's constitutional propensities are awakened by the mercy of the *hlādinī* potency, one is eligible to chant the holy name of the Lord. At that time, the pure name mercifully appears in the devotee's heart and then dances on his devotion-filled tongue. The mystery of the holy name is that it is not a combination of letters but manifests as a combination of letters when it dances on a material tongue.

(*Jaiva Dharma*, Chapter 23)

8. Why are there different holy names for deliverance in different yugas?

After analyzing people's level of advancement, the compilers of the scriptures established the appropriate holy names to deliver people in the different ages.
(*Śrī Krishna-saṁhitā*, Introduction)

9. What are the prescribed holy names for Satya-yuga and what is their significance?

nārāyaṇa-para vedā
nārāyaṇa-parākṣarā
ḥ nārāyaṇa-parā muktir
nārāyaṇa-parā gatiḥ

The meaning of this verse is that Lord Nārāyaṇa is the goal of all science, language, and liberation, and He is the supreme destination. The Supreme Lord is fully realized in the form of Nārāyaṇa, surrounded by His associates in Vaikuṇṭha. The name of the Absolute Truth for devotees who admire His opulence is Nārāyaṇa. Such devotees have a relationship with the Lord in *śānta-rāsa* and a little *dāsya-rāsa.*
(*Śrī Krishna-saṁhitā*, Introduction)

10. What are the prescribed holy names for Tretā-yuga and what is their significance?

rāma, nārāyaṇa, ananta, mukunda, madhusūdana
kṛṣṇa, keśava, kaṁsāre, hare, vaikuṇṭha, vāmana

These are the holy names to deliver one in Tretā-yuga. These names indicate Nārāyaṇa's prowess. Devotees who worship the Lord with these names have a relationship in *dāsya-rāsa* and a reflection of *sakhya-rāsa.*
(*Śrī Krishna-saṁhitā*, Introduction)

12. What are the prescribed holy names for Dvāpara-yuga and what is their significance?

hare, murāre, madhu-kaitabhāre,
gopāla, govinda, mukunda, saure yajñeśa,
nārāyaṇa, kṛṣṇa, viṣṇo,
virāśrayaṁ māṁ, jagadīśa rakṣa

These are the holy names to deliver one in Dvāpara-yuga. These names aim toward Krishna, who is the shelter of unsheltered persons. Devotees who worship the Lord with these names have a relationship in *śānta, dāsya, sakhya,* or *vātsalya-rāsa.*

(*Śrī Krishna-saṁhitā,* Introduction)

13. What are the prescribed holy names for Kali-yuga and what is their purport?

hare kṛṣṇa hare kṛṣṇa kṛṣṇa kṛṣṇa hare hare
hare rāma hare rāma rāma rāma hare hare

These are the topmost sweet names of the Lord. There is no prayer in this *mantra.* Provocation for all *rāsas* mixed with intimate attachment is found in this *mantra.* There is no mention of the Lord's prowess or giving liberation. This *mantra* reveals only that a soul has an indescribable attraction for the Supersoul by a thread of love. These names are the *mantra* for those who are on the path of *mādhurya-rāsa.* Constant deliberation on these names is the best form of worshiping the Lord. All spiritual activities of swanlike people, such as worshiping the deity, following vows, and studying the scriptures, are included in these holy names. There is no consideration of time, place, or candidate for chanting this *mantra.* The chanting of this *mantra* does not depend on the instructions of a guru or worshiping a deity for some reward. Swanlike people are duty-bound to take shelter of these names while accepting the previously mentioned twelve truths. Swanlike people of foreign countries, whose language and social positions are different, should accept these holy names in their own language by taking a hint from this *mantra.* This means that in chanting this *mantra,* there should be no complex scientific consideration, useless argument, or any type of direct or indirect prayer. If there is any prayer at all, it should be to increase one's love for God.

(*Śrī Krishna-saṁhitā,* Introduction)

14. Does a liberated person need to chant Hari's holy names? How does one chant the holy names to develop unalloyed devotional service?

For the living entities, there is no other wealth or goal than chanting Krishna's holy names. In the liberated stage, pure living entities in Vaikuṇṭha always sing the holy names of Hari. Unless one chants the holy names offenselessly, one can never take shelter of the holy name without deviation.

(*Sajjana-toṣaṇī* 8/9)

15. What is the instruction of Mahāprabhu?

Mahāprabhu instructs us to fill our lives with chanting Krishna's holy names. There is nothing permanent and real in this material world except the holy names of Krishna.

(*Sajjana-toṣaṇī* 11/5)

16. How did Śrīmān Mahāprabhu deliver the fallen souls?

Śrīmān Mahāprabhu delivered the fallen souls simply by distributing the holy names of Krishna to the living entities and inducing them to chant these names.

(*Sajjana-toṣaṇī* 11/5)

17. How can one achieve all perfection?

If, by the mercy of the spiritual master, one can chant the holy names of Krishna while keeping firm faith in the words of the Lord, one is sure to achieve all perfection. There is no doubt about it.

(*Sajjana-toṣaṇī* 11/5)

18. How can one counteract offenses committed in deity worship?

If one commits offenses while performing service to the deity of Krishna, one can be delivered from one's offenses by taking shelter of the Lord's holy names.

(*Bhajana-rahasya*, Chapter 2)

19. Are the names, forms, qualities, and pastimes of Śrī Krishna approachable by the material body and senses of the living entity?

The material body and senses of the living entity do not realize the pure transcendental names, forms, qualities, and pastimes of the Lord. Out of His causeless mercy, Śrī Krishna has directly manifest truth in this world for the benefit of the living entity. The self-manifest spiritual science appears directly.

(*Harināma-cintāmaṇi*)

20. How does the holy name manifest His form?

As soon as the budlike holy name begins to blossom, enchanting spiritual forms, such as Krishna's form, begin to manifest.

(*Harināma-cintāmaṇi*)

21. How does the holy name manifest His qualities?

When the bud of the holy name blossoms, one appreciates the fragrance of the sixty-four transcendental qualities of Krishna just like one appreciates the fragrance of a flower.

(*Harināma-cintāmaṇi*)

22. How does the holy name manifest His pastimes?

When the flowerlike holy name is fully blossomed, the eternal transcendental pastimes of Krishna manifest in this world even though they are beyond material nature.

(*Harināma-cintāmaṇi*)

23. Can one relish the chanting of the holy names of Hari in both separation and meeting?

In both separation and meeting the chanting of the holy names are eternally relishable.

(*Harināma-cintāmaṇi*)

24. What is the difference between the kāma-bīja mantra of Goloka and of the material world?

The kāma-bīja of Goloka is purely spiritual whereas the kāma-bīja of the material world is under the subordination of time and the shadow energy [Māyā] of the Supreme Lord.

(*Brahma-saṁhitā* 5/8)

25. What is the sound of Krishna's flute?

The sound of Krishna's flute is transcendental sound vibration. It is eternal, full of knowledge, and full of bliss. Therefore all the truths of the Vedas are present in it.

(*Brahma-saṁhitā* 5/27)

26. Following the directions of the eight verses of Śikṣāṣṭaka, how should one cultivate chanting the sixteen names of the mahā-mantra?

The sixteen names of the Hare Krishna *mahā-mantra* are called *aṣṭa-yugas* or eight verses. This is the verdict of the Lord.

The first verse,"Hare Krishna," destroys one's nescience. One is advised to congregationally chant the holy names of Krishna with faith.

The second verse,"Hare Krishna," means that the Supreme Lord Krishna is omnipotent. One is advised to take shelter of the holy names in the association of the devotees. This process will vanquish all one's unwanted desires. When one's unwanted desires are destroyed, one develops fixed faith.

While chanting the third verse,"Krishna Krishna," one is advised to constantly chant the holy names with determination in the association of pure devotees.

Chanting the fourth verse,"Hare Hare," awakens one's unalloyed devotion to the Lord. One is advised to congregationally chant the holy names with taste.

While chanting the fifth verse,"Hare Rāma," one is advised to become attached to the pure service and to remember the holy names of the Lord.

The sixth verse,"Hare Rāma," is chanted to develop *bhāva*. This results in detachment for material life, and taste for Krishna's lotus feet.

By chanting the seventh verse,"Rāma Rāma," one becomes attached to *mādhurya-rāsa* and takes shelter of the lotus feet of Rādhā. This also awakens one's mood of separation.

The eighth verse,"Hare Hare," refers to the devotees who are in the mood of the *gopīs* and who constantly engage in loving devotional service to Rādhā-Krishna in Vraja and thus achieve the ultimate goal of life.

(*Bhajana-rahasya*, Chapter 1)

27. Why is the most attractive holy name"Krishna" supremely unique?

Keeping a great quality of the Lord in mind, the devotees have awarded a name to the Lord. Names such as Brahman, Paramātmā, and Nārāyaṇa indicate the Lord's great qualities, but these qualities do not establish the relationship between the Supreme Lord and the living entities. A transcendental rope in the form of relationship connects the Lord and His devotees. Through this rope the Supreme Lord attracts all living entities. The highest manifestation of the Lord is this attraction. Krishna is all-attractive. As far as worship of the Lord is concerned, there is an eternal relationship between Krishna and the living entities.

(*Tattva-sūtra* 40)

19

Associates of Śrī Krishna

1. What are the characteristics of the devotees in Vaikuṇṭha?

Five kinds of devotees are eternally present in Vaikuṇṭha. They are *jñāna-bhakta*s, *śuddha-bhaktas*, *prema-bhakta*s, *premapara-bhaktas*, and *premātura-bhaktas*. *Jñāna-bhakta*s such as Bharata engage in nine types of devotional service to the Lord's lotus feet with awe and reverence; they disregard liberation, and their devotion is mixed with *jñāna*. *Śuddha-bhaktas* such as Ambarīṣa are free of the desire for karma, *jñana*, and *vairāgya*; they only desire devotional service. *Prema-bhakta*s such as Hanumān only desire to serve the Lord with love. *Premapara-bhaktas* such as Arjuna are bound by pure love, are well-wishers of the Lord, are friends of the Lord, and always hanker to see the Lord. *Premātura-bhaktas* such as Uddhava are always overwhelmed by their wealth of love and are attracted to the Lord in various wonderful loving relationships.

(*Bṛhad-bhāgavatāmṛta* Purport)

2. Does Lord Nārāyaṇa have a father and a mother in Vaikuṇṭha?

Because of the principle of opulence in Vaikuṇṭha, there is no possibility of an eternal father or mother there. Yet, if the devotees remember the loving feelings of Nanda and Yaśodā, they feel shivering in their bodies.

(*Bṛhad-bhāgavatāmṛta* Purport)

3. Where do the pure devotees of Vraja and Navadvīpa live?

By the inconceivable potency of Krishna, devotees of various *rāsas* live in Goloka. Pure devotees who worship the Lord in the mood of Vraja live in Kṛṣṇaloka, and devotees who worship the Lord in the mood of Navadvīpa live in Gauraloka. Devotees who worship the Lord in both the moods of Vraja and Navadvīpa live simultaneously in Kṛṣṇaloka and Gauraloka.

(*Brahma-saṁhitā* 5/5)

4. Do the devotees who are attached to the Lord's spiritual pastimes become overwhelmed by His opulence?

The transcendental devotees are so much overwhelmed by the Lord's sweetness that they cannot accept the Lord's opulence in spite of its presence. This nescience, however, is not material.

(*Śrī Krishna-saṁhitā*, Chapter 4)

20

Energy of the Lord

1. Are the energy and the energetic separate?

The energy and the energetic are simultaneously one and different; therefore, by nature, the object and its energy are inconceivably one and different.

(*Manaḥ-śikṣā* 4)

2. How is the Lord's energy nondual and unlimited?

The mood one adopts while building a boat certainly differs from the mood while building a house. The ability to build different things comes from the same energy, but different moods are adopted. Therefore there is no contradiction regarding the Lord's energy being nondual and unlimited.

(*Tattva-sūtra* 6)

3. Why is the Lord's energy female?

Energy is dependent; so energy is imagined as a female and thus she has become qualified to be embraced by the supreme energetic. To make the truth more easily understood great sages have added ornamental language to their descriptions. Actually, Rādhā-Krishna is one Absolute Truth.

(*Tattva-sūtra* 7)

4. What are the characteristics and activities of the internal, external, and marginal energies of the Lord?

The living entities are the fragmental parts and the marginal energy of the spiritual internal energy of the Supreme Lord. The external energy or Māyā is the illusory energy or shadow energy of the Lord. From marginal potency, the living entities have been created. From external potency, this material world has been created. Because of the living entities' misconception of thinking the body to be the self, they come in contact with the material world.

(*Śrī Bhāgavatārka-marīci-mālā* 1/1, Introduction)

5. What are the special characteristics of the Lord's energy?

The Lord's energy is of three kinds: *sandhinī*, *saṁvit*, and *hlādinī*. Existence—such as the existence of the body, death, time, association, and ingredients—manifests from the *sandhinī* potency. Relationships and feelings manifest from *saṁvit*. *Rāsa* manifests from *hlādinī*. Existence and also relationships and feelings culminate in *rāsa*. Those who don't accept variety, the impersonalists, are dry. Variety is the life of enjoyment.

(*Prema-pradīpa*, Chapter 5)

6. What is the internal potency of the Lord called in the Vedas?

The wonderful variegated internal spiritual potency of Śrī Krishna is called *śabala*.

(*Manaḥ-śikṣā*, Verse 3)

7. What is the function of the sandhinī aspect of the Lord's spiritual potency?

sā śaktiḥs sandhinī bhūtvā sattājātaṁ vitanyate pīṭha-sattā svarūpā sā vaikuṇṭha-rūpiṇī satī kṛṣṇādyākhyābhidhā-sattā rūpa-sattā kale-varam rādhādyā-saṅginī-sattā sarva-sattā tu sandhinī sandhinī-śakti-sambhūtāḥ sambandhā vividhā matāḥ sarvādhāra svarūpeyaṁ sarvākārā sad aṁsakā

The superior energy of the Absolute Truth is realized in three aspects—*sandhinī*, *saṁvit*, and *hlādinī*. The first manifestation of the Absolute Truth is *sat* (*sandhinī*), *cit* (*saṁvit*), and *ānanda* (*hlādinī*)."In the beginning there was only the Supreme Brahman, and then, after manifesting His energies, He became known as *sac-cid-ānanda*"; this kind of misconception arises due to consideration of material time and should not be applied to the Absolute Truth. Swanlike people understand that the *sac-cid-ānanda* form of the Lord is beginningless, endless, and eternal. The *sandhinī* energy manifests the existence of the eternal abode, name, form, associates, relationships, features, and foundation of the Absolute Truth. The superior energy of the Lord has three potencies: cit or spiritual, *jīva* or marginal, and acit or material. The spiritual potency, cit, is His internal potency.

The marginal and material potencies are separated. These potencies are considered according to the proportion of the energy manifest. Vaikuṇṭha is the abode of spiritual potency of the *sandhinī* aspect of the superior energy. The names of Krishna manifest from the *abhidhā-sattā*, the body of Krishna manifests from the *rūpa-sattā*, and the lovers of Krishna like Rādhā manifest from a mixture of the *rūpa-sattā* and *saṅginī-sattā*. All kinds of relationships manifest from the *sandhinī* aspect. The *sandhinī* aspect of the Lord is the source of all spiritual manifestations and features.
(*Śrī Krishna-saṁhitā*, Chapter 2)

8. What is the function of the saṁvit aspect of the Lord's spiritual potency?

samvid bhūtā parā śaktir jñāna-vijñāna rūpiṇī sandhinī-nirmite sat-tve bhāva-saṁyojinī satī bhāvābhāve ca sattāyāṁ na kiñcid apy lakṣyate tasmāt tu sarva-bhāvānāṁ samvid eva prakāsinī sandhini-kṛta-sattveṣu sambandha-bhāva-yojikā samvid-rūpā mahā-devī kāryākārya vidhāyinī viśeṣābhāvataḥ samvid brahmā-jñānaṁ prakāśayet viśeṣa-saṁyutā sā tu bhagavad bhakti-dāyinī

The *saṁvit* aspect of the superior energy consists of knowledge (*jñāna*) and its practical application (*vijñāna*). When *saṁvit* interacts with the manifestations of the *sandhinī* aspect, emotions appear. Without the presence of emotions, existence would be unknown. Therefore all truths are illuminated by *saṁvit*. The *saṁvit* aspect of the spiritual potency creates all the emotions of Vaikuṇṭha. All relationships in Vaikuṇṭha have been established by Saṁvit-devī, who is the director of action and inaction. The different *rāsas*, such as *śānta* and *dāsya*, and the respective activities in those *rāsas* have been established by *saṁvit*. If one does not accept the quality of variegatedness, then Saṁvit-devī manifests the impersonal feature of the Absolute Truth. The living entity then takes shelter of the impersonal knowledge of Brahman. Therefore, impersonal knowledge of Brahman is only the impersonal consideration of Vaikuṇṭha. For one who accepts the quality of variegatedness, Saṁvit-devī manifests the Supreme Personality of Godhead. The living entity then accepts the devotional service of the Lord.
(*Śrī Krishna-saṁhitā*, Chapter 2)

9. What is the function of the hlādinī aspect of the Lord's spiritual potency?

hlādinī-nāma samprāptā saiva śaktiḥ parākhyikā mahābhāvādiṣu sthitvā paramānanda-dāyinī sarvorddha-bhāva-sampannā kṛṣṇārddha-rūpa-dhāriṇī rādhikā sattva-rūpeṇa kṛṣṇānanda-mayī kila mahā-bhāva-svarūpeyaṁ rādhā-kṛṣṇa-vinodinī sakhya aṣṭa-vidhā bhāva hlādinyā rāsa-poṣikāḥ tat tad bhāva-gatā jīvā nityānanda-parāyaṇāḥ sarvadā jiva-sattāyāṁ bhāvānāṁ vimalā sthitiḥ

When the spiritual potency of the superior energy interacts with the *hlādinī* aspect, it creates attachment up to the state of *mahābhāva*, in which She (*hlādinī*) bestows the topmost ecstasy. This *hlādinī* is Śrī Rādhikā. She is the energy of the energetic, possesses the topmost loving sentiments, and is half of the Supreme Lord's form. She expands into the indescribable forms of Krishna's inconceivable happiness. Rādhā gives pleasure to Krishna. She is the embodiment of *mahābhāva*. There are eight varieties of emotions that nourish the *rāsa* of *hlādinī*. They are known as Rādhā's eight *sakhīs*. By the association of devotees and the mercy of the Lord, the *hlādinī* energy of the living entities realizes a portion of the spiritual *hlādinī*. Then the living entities become eternally happy and attain the stage of pure eternal sentiments while remaining individual entities.
(*Śrī Krishna-saṁhitā*, Chapter 2)

10. What is the characteristic of hlādinī?

The *hlādinī* energy is the greatest among all the energies of the Lord. Śrī Rādhikā is the personification of this energy.
(*Jaiva Dharma*, Chapter 33)

11. What is the importance of the Lord's hlādinī energy?

Without the mercy of the *hlādinī* energy, the living entities cannot obtain love of God, which is the ultimate goal of life. Having received strength from the *hlādinī* energy, the living entities can penetrate the abode of Brahman and reach the spiritual sky.
(*Manaḥ-śikṣā*, Verse 11)

12. What are the activities of sandhinī, saṁvit, and hlādinī in the spiritual energy and in the material energy?

By the influence of the Lord's three energies (spiritual, marginal, and material), the spiritual world, the living entities, and the material world have been created. Within each of the three energies, we find three separate propensities called *sandhinī*, *saṁvit*, and *hlādinī*.

By the interaction of the spiritual potency and the *sandhinī* propensity, all kinds of spiritual opulences such as the spiritual abode, spiritual forms, and spiritual paraphernalia manifest. The names, forms, qualities, and pastimes of Krishna are the work of *sandhinī*. By the interaction of the spiritual potency with the *saṁvit* propensity, all spiritual sentiments manifest. By the interaction of the spiritual potency with the *hlādinī* propensity, the cultivation of ecstatic love manifests.

By the interaction of the marginal potency and the *sandhinī* propensity, spiritual existence and the names and abode of the living entities manifest. By the interaction of the marginal potency with the *saṁvit* propensity, impersonal knowledge manifests. By the interaction of the marginal potency with the *hlādinī* propensity, happiness derived from merging into Brahman manifests as well as the happiness of trance attained through aṣṭāṅga yoga or the happiness of being one with the Lord.

By the interaction of the material potency with the *sandhinī* propensity, the material universe (consisting of fourteen worlds, the gross and subtle bodies of the conditioned souls, their attainment of the heavenly planets and their material senses) has been created. The material name, form, qualities, and activities of the conditioned soul are also the result of this interaction. By the interaction of the material potency with the *saṁvit* propensity, the conditioned souls' thought, desire, imagination, and concepts are manifest. By the interaction of the material potency with the *hlādinī* propensity, gross material pleasure and subtle heavenly pleasure manifest.

(*Manaḥ-śikṣā*, Verse 4)

13. How has the spiritual world manifest?

The Lord's inconceivable energy displays its power through variety in the Lord's body, the living entity's body, the situation of both, and the spiritual realm.

(*Prema-pradīpa*, Ray 9)

14. What is the marginal energy?

The energy suitable for both the material and spiritual worlds is called the marginal energy.

(*Manaḥ-śikṣā*, Verse 6)

15. What is yoga-nidrā?

The Supreme Lord's ecstatic trance in the intrinsic joy of His own self is called *yoga-nidrā*.

(*Brahma-saṁhitā* 5/12)

16. What is yogamāyā? What is her work?

Another name of spiritual energy is *yogamāyā*. She manifests the pastimes of Krishna in such a way that they appear ordinary to the eyes of the materialists.

(*Jaiva Dharma*, Chapter 32)

17. Which Gāyatrī mantra and other mantra are used in the worship of Krishna?

The *kāma-gāyatrī mantra*, consisting of twenty-four and a half syllables, is derived from Vedic tantras. This and the *mūla-mantra*, also known as the *kāma-bīja*, are used for the worship of Krishna.

(*Caitanya Caritāmṛta* Madhya 8/137—138, commentary)

18. What is Kāma-gāyatrī?

Gāyatrī, the mother of the Vedas, became a *gopī*, attained the shelter of Krishna, and thus became known as *kāma-gāyatrī*. By the will of Krishna, *yogamāyā*, the Lord's spiritual potency, has arranged the Vraja pastimes. These pastimes are totally faultless, because they are arranged by *yogamāyā*, not the Lord's illusory energy. In these pastimes Krishna's eternally perfect maidservants enjoy with Him. Demigoddesses and the personifications of the *Upaniṣads* and *Gāyatrī*, after attaining the association of Krishna's eternally liberated maidservants, serve Krishna in *parakīyā-bhāva* (paramour relationship).

(*Caitanya-śikṣāmṛta* 7/7)

19. What is the duty of Durgā, who is worshiped in the material world?

The material world, where Brahmā is situated and singing the glories of the Lord of Goloka, is the world of fourteen planetary systems. It is called Devī-*dhāma*, and Durgā is the presiding goddess. She has ten arms, representing the ten karmas, fruitive activities. Her prowess as a heroine is indicated by her riding on a lion. She is the subduer of vice, represented in her punishing Mahiṣāsura, the buffalo-demon. She is the mother of two sons, Kārttikeya and Gaṇeśa, indicating her beauty and success. She is positioned between Lakṣmī and Sarasvatī, who are the companions of worldly opulence and knowledge. To suppress vice, she is the bearer of twenty weapons, representing the manifold Vedic religious duties. She holds a snake, representing the beauty of time, the vanquisher. Durgā possesses all these features, and she also possesses a *durga*, which means a prison. When the *jīvas*, who have their origin in the marginal potency, become opposed to Krishna, they are interned in Durgā's *durga*. The instrument of punishment in that prison is the wheel of karma. Her duty, by the wish of Govinda, is to fulfill the task of reforming these *jīvas* by corrective measures; a task that she executes perpetually. When the *jīvas* have the fortune of attaining *sādhu-saṅga*, the holy association of pure devotees and they turn toward the Lord, the very same Durgā, by the wish of Govinda, becomes the cause of their liberation.

It is conducive to show the prison warden, Durgā, one's reformed favorable attitude, and to satisfy her and gain her undeceiving grace. Wealth, successful, agriculture, assurance of the health of one's family members, and so on—all such benedictions are the deceptive grace of Durgā. To delude souls opposed to Krishna, Durgā manifests her ten forms known as *daśa-mahā-vidyā* in the mundane world. These forms display psychic pastimes.

(*Brahma-saṁhitā* 5/44)

20. Are Mahāmāyā, Durgā, or Kālī spiritual energies? What are their duties?

Māyādevī is known and worshiped in the forms of Durgā, Kālī, and so on. Spiritual energy is Lord Krishna's original and primeval energy; Māyā is its shadow. Māyā's intention is to rectify the erring *jīvas* who have fallen away and bring them back to Krishna consciousness; this is her prime duty to the Lord. Māyā showers two kinds of graces—niskapata (honest and unrestricted) and sakapaṭa (capricious and illusory). By her niskapata mercy, she gives the science of devotional service to Lord Krishna subtly mixed with material knowledge. By her sakapaṭa mercy, she offers temporary material favors and comforts, and thus controls the *jīva*. When she is dissatisfied with a *jīva*'s behavior, she casts him into the brahmajyoti through sāyujya liberation; thus the *jīva* is doomed.

(*Harināma-cintāmaṇi*)

21. What is the difference between Durgā who belongs to the covering of Krishna's abode and Durgā who is worshiped in the material world?

The spiritual Durgā is the outer covering of the spiritual realm of the Supreme Lord. She is the eternal maidservant of Krishna and is, therefore, the transcendental reality. Her shadow, the Durgā of this world, functions in this mundane world as her maidservant.

(*Brahma-saṁhitā* 5/44)

22. What is the function of Yogamāya in Gokula and Navadvīpa in the material world?

Just as Śrī Krishna had His birth in the mundane Gokula through the agency of Yogamāyā who is the primal energy of the Supreme Lord, so with her help He manifests the līlā of His birth in the womb of Śacīdevī in Navadvīpa on this mundane plane. These are the absolute truths of spiritual science and not the outcome of imaginary speculation under the thralldom of the deluding energy of Godhead.

(*Brahma-saṁhitā* 5/5)

23. What are the activities of Durgā in Goloka?

Durgā, the spiritual energy of Krishna, maintains and arranges the Lord's pastimes.

(*Jaiva Dharma*, Chapter 14)

24. What is the difference between a pure follower of Durgā and a pure follower of Lord Viṣṇu?

We find a difference between the followers of Durgā and the followers of Viṣṇu. Those who are attached only to the Lord's illusory energy and do not take shelter of the Lord's spiritual energy are followers of Durgā but they are not Vaiṣṇavas. They are materialists. The energy is not twofold. Rādhikā represents the same energy in the spiritual form, and in the material form, Durgā represents it. On the transcendental platform, the energy of Viṣṇu is the spiritual potency, and in the material world, it is the illusory energy.

(*Jaiva Dharma*, Chapter 9)

25. Why should we accept the Supreme Lord or His energy?

The rules of material nature are possible by the glance of the Supreme Lord. Such rules are the formation of clouds and then rain, according to the different seasons; earthquakes and the breaking of mountains, caused by heat; and the ebb and flow of the tide, caused by attraction. The heat or attraction can never be independent qualities. Consciousness is like the creator, and qualities such as attraction are only rules. Therefore, it is not reasonable to deny the creator but accept the rules.

(*Tattva-sūtra* 22)

26. How do the contradictory qualities of the Supreme Lord exist in perfect harmony?

Viruddha dharma sāmanjasyaṁ tat acintya śaktvāt means that through His inconceivable potency the Absolute Truth possesses contradictory qualities of variegatedness and nonvariegatedness in perfect harmony.

(*Āmnāya Sūtra* 6)

27. How is it possible for Śrī Krishna to simultaneously possess contradictory qualities?

Śrī Krishna, who is eternal, full of knowledge and bliss, possesses an inconceivable energy that removes contradictions. On the strength of this energy, various contradictory qualities are simultaneously and undisputedly present in Him. Some of His contradictory qualities are having a form and being formlessness, being all-pervading and having the deity form, being unattached and being compassionate to the devotees, being unborn and taking birth, being the worshipable Supreme Person and being a cowherd boy, being omniscient and having a humanlike form, being full of variety and being without variety. Unlimited contradictory qualities are perfectly present in Śrī Krishna, and they are constantly assisting in the service of Śrī Rādhā, the personification of *hlādinī mahābhāva.*

(*Manaḥ-śikṣā*, Verse 4)

21

Illusory Energy of the Lord

1. Is the mode of goodness the cause of material bondage?

The shackles of Māyā are of three kinds. They are shackles made of the mode of goodness, shackles made of the mode of passion, and shackles made of the mode of ignorance. The illusory energy or Māyā binds the punishable living entities accordingly. The living entities are entangled by the shackles of Māyā, regardless of whether they are situated in the mode of goodness, passion, or ignorance. Although golden shackles, silver shackles, and iron shackles are made of different metals, nevertheless they are shackles and nothing else.

(*Jaiva Dharma*, Chapter 16)

2. Which sense enjoys which material object?

Form by the eyes, sound by the ears, smell by the nose, taste by the tongue, feeling heat and cold, soft and hard by the sense of touch—in this way, the five senses enjoy.

(*Sajjana-toṣaṇī* 10/9)

3. What is the definition of happiness for conditioned souls?

The attached householders, who are absorbed in various material miseries in family life, constantly search after the remedy of their miseries. In this way they think that they are happy. Happiness in this world is not actually happiness, only a remedy for some distress.

(*Śrī Bhāgavatārka-marīci-mālā* 8-13)

4. What is the position of the conditioned souls?

Because of their misdeeds, the conditioned souls fall into the ocean of material existence and suffer perpetually. They continue swimming, trying to reach the shore, but they can't, because the material ocean is unlimited and insurmountable.

(*Gītāmālā* 10/1)

5. What result do the conditioned souls achieve after being disturbed in the happiness and distress of repeated birth and death?

Conditioned souls think that material life is the source of happiness and separation from this life is the source of distress. Thus they give up the shelter of the Lord's lotus feet. Being asslike servants of Māyā, they become fully absorbed in material life.

(*Gītāmālā* 8/6)

6. Why is it wrong to have attachment for one's material belongings, opulence, wife, children, and relatives?

Material wealth is of no value. Supreme wealth is spiritual knowledge. Just once consider this in your heart. You have no real relationship with your wife, sons, and friends. After your death, they will immerse your body in water and return to their homes. If one cannot claim anything as one's own, why hold onto the false hope and desire of material relationships, and why hold onto the thirst for material belongings; material belongings are like a drop of water, unable to quench one's thirst.

(*Navadvīpa Mahātmya*, Chapter 7)

7. Why are the living entities entangled in the cycle of birth and death?

O Lord! You are the personification of complete spiritual bliss. I am a fragmental spiritual spark. Therefore, by nature I am Your servant. You are supremely independent and I am dependent on You. I have brought about my ruination by rejecting Your lotus feet. When I misused my independence and turned to Māyā, my original nature left me. Conditioned by Māyā, I came into the material world and fell into the wheel of karma. By Your sweet will, Māyā binds me with the iron chain of misfortune. By this unseen power of Yours, I have been put into the womb of Mālinī as her son in the house of Śrīvāsa.

(*Gītāmālā* 8/1—3)

8. Does Krishna associate with māyā?

As the sun cannot enjoy its shadow, Krishna cannot enjoy Māyā. What to speak of Krishna enjoying Māyā, He is not even seen by persons who are under the shelter of Māyā. Yet simply by the mercy of Krishna one can easily see Him through *samādhi*.

(*Śrī Krishna-saṁhitā*, Chapter 3/15)

22

Living Entities

1. What is the history of the living entities falling from their constitutional position into the material world and their attaining their eternal service?

The living entity is like a minute spiritual spark. As soon as he forgets Krishna, he is attracted by the illusory energy of the Lord and is thrown into the material world. As soon as he falls down, Durgā gives him a gross body made of five gross elements, their five attributes, and eleven senses, and then puts him into the wheel of karma. He is just like a prisoner and experiences happiness and distress, heaven and hell. Durgā also gives him a subtle body made of mind, intelligence, and false ego within the gross body. By means of the subtle body, the living entity forsakes one gross body and takes on another. The living entity cannot get rid of the subtle body, full of nescience and evil desires, unless and until he is liberated. On getting rid of the subtle body, he bathes in the Virajā and goes up to the abode of Hari. Such are the duties performed by Durgā in accordance with the will of Govinda.

(*Brahmā-saṁhitā* 5/44)

2. What are the different stages of consciousness of the living entities?

The conditioned souls are situated in five different stages of consciousness: covered consciousness, diminished consciousness, budding consciousness, blossomed consciousness, and fully blossomed consciousness.

(*Jaiva Dharma*, Chapter 16)

3. What are the constitutional and conditional states of the living entities?

The living entity has two states of existence. In the pure state, he is fully spiritual and untouched by matter. Because he is a minute part and parcel, there is the possibility of his changing his position. By nature, Krishna, the supreme consciousness, never changes His position. He is truly great, complete, pure, and eternal. The living entity is a tiny part and parcel of Krishna, and is able to become impure and unwise. But constitutionally the living entity is great, complete, pure, and eternal. As long as the living entity is pure, he is in his constitutional position. Only when the living entity becomes contaminated due to his contact with Māyā does he fall from his original constitutional position. Then he becomes impure, shelterless, and afflicted by happiness and distress. As soon as the living entity forgets his position as an eternal servant of Krishna, he falls into material existence.

As long as the living entity remains pure, he is proud of his constitutional position. He proudly considers himself a servant of Krishna. As soon as he becomes contaminated due to contact with Māyā, his pride as a servant of Krishna becomes diminished and his pride takes different forms. The pure state of the living entity becomes covered with gross and subtle bodies when he is in contact with Māyā.

Cultivation of pure love of God is the constitutional duty of the living entity. This love pervertedly appears in the subtle body in the form of happiness, distress, attachment, and detachment. When it is further condensed, this perverted form of pure love appears in the gross body in the form of eating, drinking, and enjoying sex pleasure. You can therefore understand that the eternal constitutional duties of a living entity are manifest only when he is situated in the pure state. The characteristics that appear in the conditional state of a living entity are temporary. Constitutional duties are eternal, complete, and pure.

(*Jaiva Dharma*, Chapter 2/14 —15)

4. What is the meaning of eternally forgetful?

Service to Krishna is the eternal constitutional duty of the living entity. Forgetting his position, the living entity becomes controlled by Māyā and forgets Krishna. Because he is forgetful of Krishna ever since he came to the material world, there is no history of the living entity's fallen condition within material time. Therefore, the words"eternally forgetful" have been used. From the time of the living entity's forgetfulness of the Lord and entrance into the material world, his constitutional duty has become perverted.

(*Jaiva Dharma*, Chapter 1/11—12)

5. Which souls have covered consciousness?

Trees, grass, and stones have covered consciousness. The symptoms of consciousness are almost nonexistent in them.

(*Jaiva Dharma*, Chapter 16)

6. Which living entities have diminished consciousness?

Animals, birds, insects, reptiles, and aquatics like fish have diminished consciousness.

(*Jaiva Dharma*, Chapter 16)

7. What are the stages of consciousness for the conditioned souls?

The consciousness of the embodied conditioned souls can be divided into three: seedling consciousness, blossomed conscious and fully blossomed consciousness.

(*Jaiva Dharma*, Chapter 16)

8. Who has seedling consciousness? Who has blossomed consciousness? In addition, who has fully blossomed consciousness?

People without morality and atheists possessing morality have seedling consciousness. Theists who possess morality and practitioners of devotional service have blossomed consciousness. Devotees who have attained the stage of *bhāva* have fully blossomed consciousness.

(*Jaiva Dharma*, Chapter 16)

9. How are living entities entangled in the three modes of material nature?

Living entities who reside in the upper planetary systems and who are in the mode of goodness are called demigods. Their feet are bound by the rope of goodness or gold. Living entities that are in the mode of passion have a nature like both the demigods and human beings. Their feet are bound by the rope of passion or silver. Living entities who are intoxicated by material pleasure are in the mode of ignorance. Their feet are bound by the rope of ignorance or iron.

(*Jaiva Dharma*, Chapter 16)

10. Do living entities go through birth and death in their spiritual existence?

Birth is an act in the mode of passion, and death is an act in the mode of ignorance. The eternally existing spiritual essence, śuddha-sattva, has never been touched by birth nor by death.

(*Harināma-cintāmaṇi*, Chapter 1)

11. Does a spirit soul suffer in his conditional stage?

The material body is a prison for the living entity. The spirit soul is never a limited object, but due to accepting a material body, he suffers distress and inertia.

(*Tattva-sūtra* 23)

12. In what category are demigods like Lord Brahmā and Lord Śiva?

Lord Śiva and Lord Brahmā did not take birth from the womb. They are not counted among the living entities who possess fifty qualities in minute quantity, but Lord Brahmā and Lord Śiva are separated parts of the Supreme Lord. Since they possess not only the fifty qualities in a greater quantity but also five other qualities, they are known as the principal demigods. Gaṇeśa and Sūrya, the sun-god, are also principal demigods and they are worshiped on the same level as Lord Brahmā. The other demigods are considered ordinary living entities. All the demigods are separated parts of Krishna. Their wives are also separated parts of the spiritual potency. Before the advent of Krishna, Lord Brahmā ordered the demigoddesses to take birth in this world for Krishna's pleasure.

(*Jaiva Dharma*, Chapter 32)

13. What are the activities of Lord Śiva?

Śrīmad-Bhāgavatam verses such as *vaiṣṇavānāṁ yathā śambhuḥ* glorify Śambhu as a Vaiṣṇava. The purport of such statements is that Śambhu unites with Durgā-devī according to his own time potency and the will of Govinda. Thus, he accomplishes his tasks. In many scriptures headed by the tantras, he teaches religious duties that are a ladder for the *jīvas* of various qualifications to come to *bhakti*, devotion. By Govinda's sweet will, Śambhu (indirectly) protects and sustains *śuddha-bhakti* or pure devotion by preaching the doctrine of Māyāvāda (illusionism) and intellectual or imaginary fabrications of the scriptures.

The fifty qualities of the *jīva* are present within Śambhu in copious proportion, and five more great qualities unattainable by the ordinary *jīva* are also found in him in partial proportion. So Śambhu cannot be

categorized as a *jīva*; he is the lord of *jīvas* (īśvara) although he partakes of the nature of a separated part (vibhinnāṁśa) of the Supreme Lord.
(*Brahma-saṁhitā* 5/45)

14. Is Lord Śiva a separate truth from Krishna? What is the difference between Sadāśiva and Rudra?

Śambhu is not another God separate from Krishna. Those who hold such a biased view are blasphemers of the Supreme Lord. Śambhu's control is subject to the control of Govinda, and so they are not really different from each other. Their nondifference is illustrated by the example of milk transformed into yoghurt by the addition of an agent; similarly, the Lord becomes transformed into another form. That form is dependent.

Tamoguṇa or the material quality of inertia, the quality of minuteness of the marginal potency, and a minute degree of a mixture of divine cognizance (*saṁvit*) and ecstasy (*hlādinī*)—all these elements combined constitute a particular transformation. The plenary portion of the Supreme Lord that is amalgamated with this transformation constitutes the halo of the divinity of Sadāśiva, the masculine generative organ of Lord Śambhu, and from Śambhu, Rudradeva is manifest.
(*Brahma-saṁhitā* 5/45)

15. Why do Lord Brahmā and Lord Śambhu have delegated functions?

The progenitor (Brahmā) and Śambhu are the dislocated portions of Mahā-Viṣṇu. Hence they are gods with delegated functions.
(*Brahma-saṁhitā* 5/15)

16. What is the meaning of the Śiva Liṅgam?

Efficiency is Māyā or the productive feminine organ. The material principle is Śambhu or the procreative masculine organ.
(*Brahma-saṁhitā* 5/8)

17. Who are Rudra (Bhava or Bhairava) and Rudrānī (Bhavānī or Bhairavī)?

Śambhu, the symbol of masculine mundane procreation, is the dim halo of this reflected effulgence. It is this symbol, which is applied to the organ of generation of Māyā, the shadow of Ramā or the divine potency. The first phase of the appearance of the mundane desire created by Mahā-Viṣṇu is called the seminal principle of mahat or the perverted cognitive faculty.
(*Brahma-saṁhitā* 5/8)

18. Why do Lord Brahmā and Lord Rudra enjoy pastimes with the inferior energies of the Lord?

The dislocated portions of the Supreme Lord, Prajāpati and Śambhu, both identifying themselves as entities who are separate from the divine essence. They sport with their respective nonspiritual (acit) consorts, Sāvitrī-devī and Umā-devī, the perverted reflections of the spiritual (cit) potency.

(*Brahma-saṁhitā* 5/17)

19. Who is Śambhu? What is the purport behind the combination of Lord Śiva and Goddess Durgā?

The original unadulterated entity is the Supreme Personality of Godhead, the All-Truth, free from any concept of separate egoism. The separate masculine organic egoism—that is, the separate symbolic existence that appears in the mundane world—is only an illusory reflection of that pure existence, and represented by the original Śambhu. That existence unites with the distorted representation of Ramādevī, the *māyic* or mundane female womb receptacle principle. At that point, Śambhu is represented as the efficient cause only in terms of elementary matter. Again, when in the course of evolution all the universes are manifest, the evolved conception of Rudra also appears within the entity of Śambhu who is, as previously explained, born from the brow of Mahā-Viṣṇu. However, the entity of Śambhu is constitutionally egoistic in all circumstances.

When the innumerable *jīvas*—who are sparks of cit or transcendental consciousness emanating from the *cit*-rays of the Paramātma—identify themselves in the (pure) ego of exclusive servitors of the Supreme Lord, their relationship with the *māyic* world no longer endures; they become members of Vaikuṇṭha. When they forget that ego and want to become enjoyers of Māyā, the egoistic principle of Śambhu enters their existence and gives them the frame of reference of being separate enjoyers. Thus, Śambhu is the basic truth underlying the egoistic world and the mundane bodily ego of the *jīvas*.

(*Brahma-saṁhitā* 5/16)

20. What is the description of Lord Brahmā and Lord Rudra?

Brahmā is the dislocated portion of the Divinity, manifested in the principle of mundane action, endowed with the functional nature of His subjective portion; and Śambhu is the dislocated portion of the Divinity manifested in the principle of mundane inertia possessing similarly the functional nature of His subjective portion.

(*Brahma-saṁhitā* 5/46)

21. Is Brahmā or Śambhu the Supreme Lord?

By principle Brahmā is superior to ordinary *jīvas* but is not the direct Divinity. The divine nature is present in a greater measure in Śambhu than in Brahmā.

(*Brahma-saṁhitā* 5/49)

22. What is the description of Gaṇeśa?

The self-same Gaṇeśa is a god in possession of delegated power by infusion of the divine power. All his glory rests entirely on the grace of Govinda.

(*Brahma-saṁhitā* 5/50)

23. Is Sūrya, the sun-god, the supreme controller?

The sun is after all, the presiding deity of a sphere of the sum total of all mundane heat, and hence, a demigod exercising delegated authority. The sun performs his specific function of service certainly by the command of Govinda.

(*Brahma-saṁhitā* 5/52)

24. What are the special characteristics of Lord Viṣṇu that distinguish Him from other delegated demigods such as Lord Śiva?

Although the Supreme Lord's separated parts and parcels, the *jīvas*, belong to the category of *śuddha-sattva* (pure goodness), because of their contact with nescience or material nature, they have come under the sway of the material modes of passion and ignorance, and are now in the *miśra-śattva* (mixed) category. Even demigods like Lord Śiva, though far superior in many ways to the ordinary *jīvas*, are nevertheless captivated by the material glare due to false identification, and so they fall in the category of *miśra-śattva*. The Supreme Lord is always in pure goodness. He descends to the material world by His inconceivable spiritual potency and is always the controller of the material nature, Māyā, who is ever ready to act as His maidservant.

(*Harināma-cintāmaṇi*, Chapter 1)

25. How are the living entities superior to material nature?

Living entities are spiritual sparks, and therefore, spiritual qualities are present in them. Spiritual sparks possess free will, because they cannot be separated from spiritual qualities. Free will is certainly present in the living entities according to the proportion of their constitutional size. Because of possessing free will, the living entities are superior to material nature.

(*Jaiva Dharma*, Chapter 16)

26. If free will is a disadvantage, why did the Supreme Lord give free will to the living entities?

Free will is like a special jewel. If the living entities were not given free will, they would be very lowly and insignificant like matter.

(*Jaiva Dharma*, Chapter 16)

27. Is the Supreme Lord responsible for the living entities misuse of free will?

It cannot be said that God gives the distress the living entities suffer due to misuse of free will. The Supreme Lord is not to be blamed in anyway. He is not responsible for the distress the living entities suffer due to their transgressing rules and regulations. If the Supreme Creator forced the living entities to accept *anartha*s, He would be at fault for discrimination. However, if the living entities had used their free will to strengthen their spiritual attachment, they would have increased their own glories. If they did not have free will, they would not have an opportunity to increase their own glories. We should know that by giving such wonderful free will to the living entities, the Supreme Lord has displayed His mercy upon them and degradation caused by misuse of free will is meant to rectify and deliver the living entities.

(*Tattva-sūtra* 20)

28. What is the meaning of marginal nature?

Sometimes a riverbank is washed away by the force of the water and becomes part of the river, and again, when soil accumulates at the riverside, it becomes the riverbank. If he looks to Krishna, the living entity comes under the shelter of Krishna's spiritual potency. If he looks to Māyā, he becomes opposed to Krishna and is entangled in Māyā's trap. This nature of the living entity is called the marginal nature.

(*Jaiva Dharma*, Chapter 15)

29. Can a living entity and the Supreme Lord ever be equal?

The Supreme Lord has created the material world through His external energy, Māyā. In the material world, a separate truth from the Supreme Lord, called the living entities, have been conditioned by Māyā. Māyā is the energy of the Supreme Lord, and the Supreme Lord is the master of Māyā. The living entities are always different from the Supreme Lord.

(*Manaḥ-śikṣā*, Verse 6)

30. How many types of parts does the Supreme Lord have?

The Supreme Lord has two parts: His own expansions and His separate parts. The quadruple plenary portions are His own expansions, and the living entities are His separate parts. We can compare the differences between them. The plenary portions are nondifferent from Krishna; they are always omnipotent, their will is dependent on the will of Krishna, and they have no independence. The separate parts are eternally separate from Krishna; they are less potent because of their finite nature, and their desire is completely different from Krishna's desire.

(*Manaḥ-śikṣā*, Verse 6)

33. Are the living entities eternal or temporary?

The living entities can be eternal, and they can also be temporary. The source of the living entities is the energy of the Supreme Lord, and this energy is eternal, beginningless, and unlimited. Therefore, the living entities are eternal.

The living entities, who come from the eternal unlimited energy are eternal, but the will of the Supreme Lord is most powerful. If the Supreme Lord wishes to destroy the living entities, He can certainly destroy them. For this reason, the living entities can also be temporary.

34. Can the living entity become the Supreme Brahman?

Although the living entities are called Brahman, they cannot become the Supreme Brahman, because the Supreme Brahman is complete and unchangeable. The living entities emanate from the marginal potency of the Supreme Brahman. There is therefore a specific distinction between the living entities and the Supreme Brahman.

(*Tattva-sūtra* 13)

35. When can a living entity attain peace of mind?

As long as a living entity enjoys the fruits of his own karma, he can never attain peace, because he is weak, unable, and incomplete. However, when he surrenders to the Supreme Lord, he no longer laments.

(*Tattva-sūtra* 13)

36. Who is opposed to the Supreme Lord?

Those who have not had loving devotion to Krishna awakened in their heart are always proud of remaining under the shelter of *jñāna* and karma. They are called *bhagavad-bahirmukha*, opposed to Krishna. Those who worship many gods, those who are Māyāvādīs and thirsty for impersonal *jñāna*, and those atheists who defy Vedic literature are all *bhagavad-bahirmukha*, opposed to Krishna.

(*Sajjana-toṣaṇī* 11/6)

37. What is the difference between the endeavors of the fruitive workers and the mental speculators? When do the living entities become introspective?

The gross materialist endeavors for sensual delights and aspires for ephemeral heavenly bliss in his next life. The mental speculator is wholly concerned with how to mitigate his existential suffering. After surpassing these stages, the *jīva* becomes introspective.

(*Harināma-cintāmaṇi*, Chapter 15)

38. What concept do mundane people have?

They take credit for the so-called advancement of scientific technology and the material comfort it brings. But everything happens by the Lord's will; they conveniently forget this fact.

(*Harināma-cintāmaṇi*, Chapter 13)

39. Who does not accept the existence of God? Can atheism harm God?

Those who learn to make arguments in their childhood due to bad association gradually become controlled by prejudice and deny the existence of God. This attitude only harms them, not God.

(*Caitanya-śikṣāmṛta* 1/1)

40. Can one realize the existence of God materially?

Some unfortunate people do not believe in the existence of God. Their eyes of knowledge are shut. Since they cannot see God with their material eyes, they think that there is no God. Just as blind people cannot see the light of the sun, spiritually blind people cannot believe in the existence of God.

(*Caitanya-śikṣāmṛta* 1/1)

41. When can the living entity realize his constitutional position?

A fire that is covered by ash is not identified as ash, and when the ash is removed, the fire displays its heat and light; similarly, when the gross and subtle bodies of a living entity are destroyed, the constitutional position of the living entity is realized at once. The ash of the gross and subtle bodies covers the fire of the living entity. Does the living entity not have an identity until these two coverings are removed? Yes, he does. As one can feel some heat if one sits in front of a fire covered with ash, similarly the living entity covered with the gross and subtle bodies can also identify himself to a certain extent.

(*Sajjana-toṣaṇī* 8/7)

42. What is the definition of the living entity's material existence?

Considering the subtle body to be the self, the living entity has concocted a new body made of mind, intelligence, and false ego. Considering the psychological and physical factors, the embodied soul is mistakenly thinking these items are his assets. Being proud of his gross body, made of five material elements, he thinks"I am such and such Bhaṭṭācārya" and"I am such and such Saheb." Sometimes he dies, sometimes he takes birth, sometimes he is puffed up with happiness, and sometimes he is overwhelmed with distress. How glorious these changes are! How glorious are the tricks of Māyā!

Accepting a male body, sometimes the living entity marries a female, and sometimes accepting a female body, he marries a male and establishes family life. In this material existence, he serves his respectable elders, maintains his dependence, fears the king, and hates his enemies. Becoming a chaste woman, he feels very shy and is afraid of people's criticism. In this way, being entangled in temporary relationships in this magical material existence, the living entity has fallen far away from his original constitutional position. The condition of the living entity situated in material existence is pathetic! Considering some rules and regulations of material existence as his master, he has totally forgotten Krishna, his eternal master.

(*Sajjana-toṣaṇī* 8/9)

43. Who are non-Vaiṣṇavas?

Learned scholars, rich people, powerful people, *brāhmaṇa*s, kings and their subjects who are devoid of devotional service are non-Vaiṣṇavas.

(*Sajjana-toṣaṇī* 10/2)

44. What is the result of proper thought?

The only difference between the animals and the human beings is that the animals are devoid of proper thought and the human beings are capable of such thought. Self-realization is the result of proper thought.

(*Caitanya-śikṣāmṛta* 2/2)

45. Is a Godless civilization better than animal life?

Even though human beings are civilized and advanced in material science and morality, they can never become superior to animals unless they accept God.

(*Caitanya-śikṣāmṛta* 1/1)

46. Who is not fit to be called a human being?

A person who does not know what this world is, who he is, who the world was created by, what his duty is, or what he will gain or lose by performing his duty can not be counted as a human being.

(*Caitanya-śikṣāmṛta* 2/2)

47. What is the destination of a person who believes his life is in the hands of fate?

Those who immerse their existence in the current of their fortune are like dead fish; while floating in the ocean of material existence, they are sometimes tossed up and sometimes tossed down by the tide. They can never reach their desired destination.

(*Caitanya-śikṣāmṛta* 3/1)

48. What is the symptom of a conditioned soul?

Even after degrading to hell, a condition soul does not wish to give up his body. After getting respite from hell, be becomes bewildered by the Lord's illusory energy.

(*Śrī Bhāgavatārka-marīci-mālā* 8/10)

49. What is the nature of the materialists?

Materialists do not have time to hear or speak about Krishna. Whether they engage in pious activities or in sinful activities, they are always far away from the science of self-realization.

(*Sajjana-toṣaṇī* 10/11)

50. What is the nature of the conditioned soul?

Though a cloud impedes the eyes of an observer when he gazes at the sun, with his cloudy vision he sees that the tiny cloud is covering the sun, not himself. In the same way, the conditioned souls with their material intelligence, senses, and decisions accept Gokula as a piece of measurable land.

(*Brahma-saṁhitā* 5/2)

51. Is the mind spiritual?

An element that does not remain with the living entity in all circumstances is not eternal. The mind is a temporary faculty. In its constitutional position, the soul does not accept a material faculty. The mind is therefore a product of matter. However, since the mind is very subtle, it is superior to many material objects.

(*Tattva-sūtra* 30)

52. What is material time?

In the liberated state, a living entity is not influenced by material time. In the conditioned state, the living entities come under the control of time in the form of meeting, separation, existence, and activity. The conditioned souls contact with the material world is therefore called material time.

(*Tattva-sūtra* 25)

53. Who attains which destination in the fourteen worlds?

Gṛhasthas who engage in pious activities and who desire to enjoy the fruits of their karma attain the three planetary systems, Bhūloka, Bhuvarloka, and Svarloka. Above these are four planets, Maharloka, Janaloka, Tapoloka, and Satyaloka, which are the destination of the *brahmacārīs*, *vānaprasthas*, and *sannyāsīs*. *Gṛhasthas* who have no material desires and who engage in their occupational duties also attain these four planets.

(*Bṛhad-bhāgavatāmṛta*)

54. What questions arise when contemplating the Absolute Truth?

In spite of drawing conclusions on various topics, I have drawn none regarding the Absolute Truth. While contemplating on the Absolute Truth, a few questions arose in my mind: Who am I? What is my relationship with this world? What is my relationship with God? What is my ultimate goal of life?

(*Caitanya-śikṣāmṛta*, Chapter 8)

55. What are the four principal questions of inquisitive living entities?

If a person develops such a mentality out of good fortune, he detaches himself from material enjoyment and becomes inquisitive. Then, to obtain knowledge, such a person asks himself these four questions: Who am I? Who is the enjoyer of the material world? What is this vast universe? What is my actual relationship with this universe?

(*Tattva Viveka* 1/2)

56. When does an embodied soul becomes liberated?

By nature, an embodied soul is a materialist. When he obtains the shelter of a bona fide spiritual master and desires to become free from material enjoyment, he gradually endeavors to free his mind from material contamination. When he achieves success in this attempt, he becomes liberated.

(*Sajjana-toṣaṇī* 4/2)

57. When can the living entities, who are parts and parcels of the Supreme Lord, arouse their love of God?

As sparks emanate from a complete fire, the living entities emanate from Krishna, who is the supreme complete consciousness. Just as a spark possesses the same quality as the fire, each living entity can manifest the qualities of the supreme consciousness. As a spark, possessing the power to burn, can reveal itself by the help of air and burn the entire world, a living entity after obtaining Kṛṣṇacandra, the object of love, can arouse the flood of his love of God.

(*Jaiva Dharma*, Chapter 2)

58. What is the fate of a fortunate and an unfortunate person?

Amongst the introspective *jīvas*, those who are more fortunate and pious get the association of *sādhus*. In such association, those pious *jīvas* take to chanting the Lord's holy name, which eventually transports them to the doorways of the spiritual sky. The less fortunate introspective *jīvas* are attracted to the paths of karma and *jñāna*, by which they worship many demigods or try to merge into the impersonal Brahman.

(*Harināma-cintāmaṇi*, Chapter 15)

59. What is material bondage for the living entity?

The spirit soul is pure. He does not have any bondage. Material bondage means that a living entity is bewildered by Māyā and proudly considers his subtle body, which he received from Māyā, as himself. Therefore, material bondage of the living entity is not factual. Forgetting one's constitutional position is like the illusion of seeing wealth where there is none or seeing a person without a head.

(*Śrī Bhāgavatārka-marīci-mālā* 7/22)

60. How did the spirit soul develop material propensities?

According to his own nature, every spirit soul has a pure identity as the eternal servant of the Supreme Lord. This identity is based on the pure ego of the spirit soul. Under the shelter of the pure ego, the spirit soul also possesses the power of discrimination and feelings of happiness. He knows other objects and other living entities as well as the Supreme Lord, who is the object of his worship. He also has full knowledge and a mind suitable for meditation. When a spirit soul becomes materially conditioned, his spiritual qualities transform into a gross and a subtle body, and manifests mundane propensities because of association with matter.

(*Caitanya-śikṣāmṛta* Part 2, 7/1)

61. What is the difference between the liberated state and the conditioned state?

A living entity who is a pure devotee of Krishna is not conditioned by Māyā. By the mercy of Krishna such a soul is liberated from the material world. He is a liberated soul and is in the liberated state. Then again, a living entity who avoids Krishna falls into the clutches of Māyā. He is a conditioned soul and is in the conditioned state.

(*Jaiva Dharma*, Chapter 7)

62. Who is superior, a brāhmaṇa or a Vaiṣṇava?

A *brāhmaṇa* is the highest among human beings whose intelligence is not fully developed. A person whose intelligence is fully developed is a Vaiṣṇava.

(*Jaiva Dharma*, Chapter 3)

63. What is the purpose and result of the dry speculators' questions?

Questions are of two types: one type is under the shelter of dry speculation and the other is with faith in devotional service. The second type is such that the faith of the inquirer is satisfied. One should never answer the questions of the dry speculators, because they will never believe the truth. Their arguments are influenced by Māyā and they cannot progress on the path of inconceivable spiritual truth. Even if one tries hard to convince them, they will not make any spiritual progress. Their goal is to give up trust in God.

(*Jaiva Dharma*, Chapter 34)

64. What is the difference between the jñānī and the Vaiṣṇava?

There are many differences between the liberated souls who are on the path of impersonal knowledge, and those who are devotees. The *jñānī* hates his material body and always endeavors to not receive another body. The devotee becomes detached from his body because of separation from Krishna and on seeing Krishna considers his body successful. The *jñānī* exhausts his sinful reactions by enjoying them, but the devotee simply depends on the will of Krishna.

(*Bhāgavatārka-marīci-mālā* 17/22)

65. Can one see the spiritual world in one's mind?

As long as the mind of a living entity remains absorbed in material thoughts and wanders in the material world, it cannot see the spiritual world, which lies beyond the material sky and is full of knowledge.

(*Gītāmālā* 7/1)

66. Who is an intelligent person and who is an unfortunate person?

One who understands material existence is an intelligent person, and one who remains in the wheel of material existence is an unfortunate person.

(*Jaiva Dharma*, Chapter 7)

67. Is the life of a devotee and the life of a conditioned soul the same?

There is a gulf of difference between the life of the devotees and that of persons bewildered by Māyā. Although they appear the same on the outside, on the inside the difference is vast.

(*Jaiva Dharma*, Chapter 7)

68. What is the difference between a materialist and a spiritualist?

Externally there is no difference between a materialist and a spiritualist, but their internal moods are different.

(*Sajjana-toṣaṇī* 4/1)

69. Who is the enjoyer? Is the living entity not an enjoyer?

A living entity can never be the enjoyer of another living entity. All living entities are enjoyed and Lord Krishna is the only enjoyer.

(*Caitanya-śikṣāmṛta* Part 2, 7/7)

70. Is the life of a person who possesses good qualities useless?

Even though a person possesses good qualities, his life is useless if he is without devotional service to Krishna.

(*Sajjana-toṣaṇī* 5/1)

71. What is the difference between liberated and conditioned states?

In the liberated state, we have a spiritual form. In the conditioned state, we have a form of indistinct matter and spirit. In the liberated state *vaikuṇṭha-rāsa* is enjoyed, and in the conditioned state it should be sought after.

(*Prema-pradīpa*, Chapter 9)

72. What is the understanding of"I" and"mine" in the liberated state?

In the liberated state, the idea of"I" and"mine" is fully spiritual and faultless.

(*Jaiva Dharma*, Chapter 7)

73. How does a living entity develop his spiritual body and realize his spiritual identity?

The *jīva* is pure spirit soul, part and parcel of the Absolute Whole. He has a transcendental original form that is all-perfect. He has forgotten his perfect spiritual state and come under the clutches of Māyā. He is offensive to Lord Krishna and is inebriated with the false mundane designations of his gross body. If, by the mercy of a pure devotee spiritual master, he regains knowledge of his origin, the rediscovery of his original identity can quickly be accomplished.

(*Harināma-cintāmaṇi*, Chapter 15)

74. What is the meaning of spiritual male body and spiritual female body?

Because of the power of Māyā, a soul residing in the material world imagines that she is male. In the understanding of pure spirit, Krishna is the only male and all other's are female. In spirit, there is no sign of material male or female. If one intently meditates on this *rāsa*, one can become qualified to become a *gopī* in Vraja. A person who yearns to attain *mādhurya-rāsa* will become qualified to become a *gopī* in Vraja. By repeatedly desiring in this way, one attains that perfection.

(*Jaiva Dharma*, Chapter 32)

75. What is the difference between Krishna, māyā, and the living entity? Why does a living entity becomes entangled in matter?

Krishna is compared to the sun and is full of knowledge and bliss. Māyā is His shadow or perverted reflection. The living entity is an infinitesimal particle of Krishna's effulgence. When the living entity contacts Māyā, he is captured and bound by Māyā, because of his marginal nature (taṭasthā).

(*Navadvīpa Mahātmya*, Chapter 7)

76. Why is the difference between the Supreme Brahman and the living entity an eternal one?

If water is mixed with milk no one can detect it, but a swan can immediately separate the milk from the water. Similarly, following the words of their spiritual master, the devotees can at once tell the difference between the Supreme Brahman and the living entities, even though the Māyāvādīs claim that the living entities merge into Brahman at the time of annihilation.

(*Tattva-sūtra* 82)

77. Why can the living entities and the Supreme Lord not merge together?

If milk is added to milk or water is added to water, they mix, but they do not become one in all respects, because the quantity of the two objects does not diminish. In the same way, despite merging into the Supreme Lord through meditation, the living entities do not attain oneness. This is the verdict of the pure-hearted learned scholars.

(*Tattva-sūtra* 83)

78. Can a living entity become God?

Although the waves are part of the ocean, they are never the ocean. Although the living entities are parts and parcels of God, they can never become God.

(*Tattva-sūtra* 10)

79. What are the symptoms of an unfortunate soul?

Everyone should know that an unfortunate living entity is overconfident in the power of his own intelligence. Such a person rejects the mercy of the Lord, and by the force of false logic, falls repeatedly into the pit of illusion.

(*Navadvīpa Mahātmya*, Chapter 1)

80. Why should one give up attachment for his body?

The flesh is not our own alas!
The mortal frame a chain;
The soul confined for former wrongs
Should try to rise again!

(*Sāragrāhī Vaiṣṇava*)

23

Material World

1. What is the material world?

The material world is the perverted reflection of the spiritual world; that which is best in the ideal world is worst in its reflection and that which is lowest in the ideal is highest in its reflection. One can easily understand this by watching one's bodily limbs reflected in a mirror.

(*Jaiva Dharma*, Chapter 31)

2. Does the material world have an independent existence?

The material world has no independent existence. It is simply a perverted reflection of the spiritual world. The existence, mood, and process, which are pure and auspicious in their ideal position, become inauspicious when reflected here. The qualities that directly create eternal auspiciousness there become pious activities when reflected here. The qualities that indirectly produce auspiciousness there create inauspiciousness here and are considered sinful activities.

(*Caitanya-śikṣāmṛta* Part 2 7/1)

3. Is the material world false?

The material world is not false; it is real, because of the will of Krishna. However, the material concept of"I and mine," which we are maintaining in the material world, is false. Those who say that the material world is false are Māyāvādīs—they are offenders.

(*Jaiva Dharma*, Chapter 7)

4. Why is the material world not false?

If you say that this visible world is false, how can you possibly fulfill your purpose? If you bring water in a pitcher, you can use it for many purposes. You cannot say that the pitcher is false, but you can say it is temporary. Similarly, since this visible world helps you fulfill your purpose, you cannot say it is false.

(*Tattva-sūtra* 10)

5. How is the material world temporary even though it is not false?

To say that the material world is eternal and real because it has emanated from the eternal cognizant Absolute Truth is unreasonable. Such a statement is an outright lie. To say that the material world is the transformation of God is also unreasonable. The truth is that this material world is real but temporary. As a touchstone produces gold, the energy of the Supreme Lord has produced the temporary material world.

(*Bhāgavatārka-marīci-mālā* 1/15)

6. Is attachment to the material world auspicious?

I have wasted my time uselessly in trying to become happy in the material world. I have not gained anything; rather I have created havoc. What kind of material existence is this? It is just like a magic show. I am wasting my days uselessly by becoming attached to it.

(*Kalyāṇa-kalpataru*, Song 4)

7. What is the value of enjoyment in the material world?

There is no happiness in material enjoyment. We simply gratify our senses. Even if there is any happiness, it is only the absence of distress. Happiness that is full of fear is not actual happiness. Learned scholars call it distress.

(*Kalyāṇa-kalpataru*, Song 3)

8. How is the total material ingredients (ego, five gross elements, their attributes, and the senses of the living entities) created? What are the living entities?

In the transcendental atmosphere (*paravyoma*), where spiritual majesty preponderates, there is present Śrī Nārāyaṇa who is not different from Krishna. Mahā-Saṅkarṣaṇa, subjective plenary facsimile of the extended personality of Śrī Nārāyaṇa, is also the divine plenary portion of the propagatory embodiment of Śrī Krishna.

By the power of His spiritual energy a plenary subjective portion of Him, eternally reposing in the neutral stream of Virajā forming the boundary between the spiritual and mundane realms, casts His glance, at creation, unto the limited shadow potency, Māyā, who is located far away from Himself.

Thereupon Śambhu, lord of *pradhāna* embodying the substantive principle of all material entities, who is the same as Rudra, the dim reflection of the Supreme Lord's own divine glance, consummates his intercourse with Māyā, the efficient mundane causal principle. But he can do nothing independently of the energy of Mahā-Viṣṇu representing the direct spiritual power of Krishna.

Therefore, the principle of mahāt, or the perverted cognitive faculty, is produced only when the subjective plenary portion of Krishna, viz., the prime divine avatāra Mahā-Viṣṇu who is the subjective portion of Saṅkarṣaṇa, Himself the subjective portion of Krishna, is propitious towards the active mutual endeavors of Māyā, Śiva's consort (*śakti*), and pradhāna or the principle of substantive mundane causality.

Agreeably to the initiative of Mahā-Viṣṇu, the consort of Śiva creates successively the mundane ego (*ahaṅkāra*), the five mundane elements (*bhūtas*) viz., space etc., their attributes (tanmātras) and the limited senses of the conditioned soul (*jīva*). The constituent particles, in the form of effulgence of Mahā-Viṣṇu, are manifest as the individual souls (*jīvas*).

(Brahmā-saṁhitā 5/10, purport)

24

Spiritual World

1. Is the spiritual world incomplete?

The storehouse of Vaikuṇṭha is always complete. Lord Śrī Kṛṣṇacandra, the lovable object of all, constantly invites the living entities to come through the open door of that storehouse.

(*Śrī Krishna-saṁhitā*, Chapter 9)

2. What is Vraja? What does"Vraja" mean?

The appearance of the truth of Vaikuṇṭha in the pure consciousness of the living entities of this world is called Vraja. The word vraja means"to go."

(*Śrī Krishna-saṁhitā*, Chapter 5)

3. Is Vaikuṇṭha incomplete and limited?

sad bhāve 'pi viśeṣasya sarvaṁ tan nitya-dhāmani. The splendor of the spiritual abode is established by the quality of variegatedness. Although that splendor is eternal, Vaikuṇṭha is nevertheless nondual and constitutionally eternal, full of knowledge and bliss. The material world consists of dualities arising from time, place, and circumstance, yet because Vaikuṇṭha is transcendental to the material creation, it is without duality and fault.

(*Śrī Krishna-saṁhitā*, Chapter 1)

4. Are the descriptions about the spiritual world taken and concocted from matter?

cic-chakti-nirmitaṁ sarvaṁ yad vaikuṇṭhe sanātanam
pratibhātaṁ prapañce 'smin jaḍa-rūpa malānvitam

Some people try to impose their material ideas on the nature of Vaikuṇṭha and thus they become overwhelmed by prejudices. Later they try to establish their prejudices by shrewd arguments. Their descriptions of Vaikuṇṭha and the pastimes of the Lord are material. These types of conclusions arise only due to improper knowledge of the Absolute Truth. Only those who have not deeply discussed spiritual topics will have the propensity to rationalize in this way.

The doubtful hearts of the *madhyama-adhikārīs* are always swinging between the material and the spiritual due to their being unable to cross into the realm of the Absolute Truth. Actually, the variegatedness seen in the material world is only a perverted reflection of the spiritual world. The difference between the material and spiritual worlds is this: In the spiritual world, everything is blissful and faultless, whereas in the material world everything is a temporary mixture of happiness and distress, and full of impurities arising from time and place. Therefore, the descriptions of the spiritual world are not imitations of those of the material world; rather they are most coveted ideals.

(*Śrī Krishna-saṁhitā*, Chapter 1)

5. Are the pastimes, abode, and form of Krishna in the spiritual world imaginary or transcendental?

Actual truth is spiritual truth. Variegatedness is eternally present in it. By this feature the spiritual abode, spiritual form, spiritual name, qualities, and pastimes of Krishna are established. Only those who are self-realized and who have no relationship with Māyā relish His pastimes. The transcendental world, the abode for performing pastimes, is made of touchstone, and the forms of Krishna are all spiritual.

(*Brahmā-saṁhitā* 5/27)

6. What is the spiritual world made of? What do the desire trees and kāmadhenu give?

Just as Māyā builds this mundane universe with the five material elements, so the spiritual (cit) potency has built the spiritual world of transcendental gems. The cintāmaṇi, which serves as material in the building of the abode of the Supreme Lord of Goloka, is a far rarer and more agreeable entity than the philosopher's stone. The purpose tree yields only the fruits of piety, wealth, fulfillment of desire and liberation; but the purpose trees in the abode of Krishna bestow innumerable fruits in the shape of checkered divine love. Kāmadhenus (cows yielding the fulfillment of desire) give milk when they are milked; but the kāmadhenus of Goloka pour forth oceans of milk in the shape of the fountain of love showering transcendental bliss that does away with the hunger and thirst of all pure devotes.

(*Brahma-saṁhitā* 5/29)

7. Can the living entity understand that the spiritual world exists within the material world but remains untouched by matter?

Poor human understanding cannot possibly make out how the extensive triquadrantal, which is beyond human comprehension, can be accommodated in the limited material universe of a uniquadrantal disclosure. Gokula is a spiritual plane, hence its condescended position in the region of material space, time, etc., is in no way restricted but unlimitedly manifested with its full boundless propriety.

(*Brahma-saṁhitā* 5/2)

8. Are all the ingredients of Gokula present in Goloka?

The distinction of paramourship and concubinage, the variegatedness of the respective *rāsas* of all different persons, the soil, water, river, hill, portico, bower, cows, etc., all the features of Gokula exist in Goloka and disposed in an appropriate manner.

(*Brahma-saṁhitā* 5/37)

9. What is the difference between the nature of the spiritual world and the material world?

In the transcendental realm there is no past and future but only the unalloyed and immutable present time. In the transcendental sphere there is no distinction between the object and its qualities and no such identity as is found in the limited mundane region. Hence, those qualities that seem to be apparently contradictory in the light of mundane conception limited by time and space, exist in agreeable and dainty concordance in the spiritual realm.

(*Brahma-saṁhitā* 5/33)

10. How does Krishna enjoy His pastimes in the spiritual world of opulence?

Krishna manifests His internal energy in the form of Lakṣmīs in the spiritual world of opulence and enjoys with them in the mood of *svakīya-rāsa*.

(*Brahma-saṁhitā* 5/37)

11. How and with whom does Krishna enjoy His pastimes in Goloka?

In Goloka, Krishna separates His internal energy into hundreds and thousands of *gopīs* and eternally enjoys pastimes by causing them to forget *svakīya-rāsa.*

(Brahmā-saṁhitā 5/37)

12. What position do the devotees of different rāsas attain in the spiritual world?

In discussing *rāsa*, we meet with five kinds of devotion or service. *Śānta* or unattached, *dāsya* or pertaining to reverential willing service, *sakhya* or friendship, *vātsalya* or parental love, and śṛṅgāra or conjugal love.

The devotees surcharged with the ideas of their respective service serve Krishna eternally and ultimately reach the goal of their respective ideals. They attain the real nature of their self-befitting their respective *rāsas*, their glories, conveyances, seats befitting their sacred service, and transcendental qualities of ornaments enhancing the beauty of their real nature. Those who are advocates of *śānta-rāsa* attain the region of Brahma-Paramātmā, the seat of eternal peace; those of *dāsya-rāsa* get to Vaikuṇṭha, the spiritual majestic abode of Śrī Nārāyaṇa; those of *sakhya*, *vātsalya* and *mādhurya-rāsa* (conjugal love) attain Goloka-*dhāma*, Krishna's abode, above Vaikuṇṭha.

(Brahmā-saṁhitā 5/36)

25

Vaiṣṇavism

1. How does one recognize a Vaiṣṇava?

A Vaiṣṇava is not recognized by his acceptance or rejection of *varṇāśrama*, or by his appearance. Devotional service of Krishna is the only indication of a Vaiṣṇava. One should carefully see that a person possesses the required amount of devotion to Krishna before one accepts him as a Vaiṣṇava.

(*Sajjana-toṣaṇī* 2/12)

2. What is Vaiṣṇavism?

The truth of Vaiṣṇavism cannot be realized by philosophical discussions, intellectual language, or proper description. By taking words from the dictionary and putting them together does not make Vaiṣṇavism wonderful. Vaiṣṇavism is the awakening of one's *rāsa* through the process of *bhajana* by taking shelter at the lotus feet of the spiritual master.

(*Sajjana-toṣaṇī* 6/2)

3. Who is a Vaiṣṇava? Who is a better Vaiṣṇava? Who is the best Vaiṣṇava?

As long as a person commits offenses against the chanting of the Lord's holy name, the pure name does not appear to him. When he seldom commits offenses against the holy name, the reflection of the pure name appears to him. This is the *nāmābhāsa* stage, wherein all his sinful reactions are destroyed. When sinful reactions are destroyed, his heart becomes pure. Then, he does not get a chance to commit offenses against the holy name. When a person chants the holy name and is rarely offensive, he is a Vaiṣṇava. When a person chants without offense, he is a better Vaiṣṇava. When the *hlādinī* potency arises in a person, he becomes the best Vaiṣṇava.

(*Sajjana-toṣaṇī* 6/1)

4. What is the difference between a Vaiṣṇava, a better Vaiṣṇava, and the best Vaiṣṇava?

A Vaiṣṇava who is attached to the chanting of the Lord's holy names offenselessly is a Vaiṣṇava follower of Śrī Caitanya's lotus feet. Occasional cultivation of the holy names is the role of a Vaiṣṇava. Constant cultivation of the holy names is the role of a better Vaiṣṇava. The best Vaiṣṇava is he by whose association one is induced to chant the pure names of the Lord. Everyone's duty is to associate with these saintly persons.

(*Manaḥ-śikṣā*, Chapter 10)

5. How great is a Vaiṣṇava?

The greatness of a Vaiṣṇava depends on the amount of attachment he has for chanting the holy names of Krishna.

(*Harināma-cintāmaṇi*)

6. Among the introspective persons what is the difference between a kaniṣṭha-adhikārī, a madhyama-adhikārī, and an uttama-adhikārī?

The introspective *jīva* is divided into three categories: kaniṣṭha, madhyama, and uttama (neophyte, intermediate, and advanced). The introspective neophyte, the *kaniṣṭha-adhikārī*, rejects demigod worship and worships only Krishna but with material motivations. He is inexperienced in understanding the spiritual identities of himself, Lord Krishna, and the pure devotee of the Lord. Though simple and naive, he is not offensive; he is just preoccupied with himself. Therefore, the neophytes are not considered pure Vaiṣṇavas, though they are certainly to be seen as *Vaiṣṇava-prāya* or resembling Vaiṣṇavas. The intermediate introspective *jīva*, the *madhyama-adhikārī*, is a pure devotee and is very firmly situated in devotion. The advanced introspective *jīva*, the *uttama-adhikārī*—so much can be said about him; he has reached a state of perfect equanimity. One cannot be truly introspective unless one knows the equal position of the holy name and Krishna Himself. The introspective *jīva* automatically has single-minded faith in the Supreme Lord.

(*Harināma-cintāmaṇi*, Chapter 15

7. What is the position of a madhyama-adhikārī?

A *madhyama-adhikārī* is subordinate to the *uttama-adhikārī* and a benefactor of the *kaniṣṭha-adhikārī.*

(*Sajjana-toṣaṇī* 10/12)

8. To which category does a person who chants the holy names belongs?

A person who chants the holy names of the Lord belongs immediately to the *madhyama* platform.

(*Caitanya-śikṣāmṛta* 6/4)

9. By which qualities is the status of a Vaiṣṇava ascertained?

In the teachings of Śrīmān Mahāprabhu, there are two principal instructions: developing a taste for the chanting of the Lord's holy names and displaying compassion to the fallen souls. The greatness of a Vaiṣṇava depends on the extent he possesses these qualities. There is no need to endeavor for other good qualities. All good qualities of a Vaiṣṇava automatically manifest in a Vaiṣṇava who endeavors for these two qualities.

(*Caitanya-śikṣāmṛta* 1/7)

10. When does a person become qualified to be called a Vaiṣṇava?

When a person graduates from the kaniṣṭha platform by the mercy of the Vaiṣṇavas, he is fit to be called a Vaiṣṇava. At that time his compassion toward the fallen souls arises.

(*Sajjana-toṣaṇī* 4/8)

11. How does one measure the different levels of the Vaiṣṇavas?

The renunciate Vaiṣṇavas should not think that they are more respectable than the *gṛhastha* Vaiṣṇavas. One should know that the difference in respect among the Vaiṣṇavas lies only between *uttama-adhikārī* and *madhyama-adhikārī*. Both *uttama-adhikārīs* and *madhyama-adhikārīs* are found among the gṛhasthas. This rule also applies to the renunciate Vaiṣṇavas. The glories of the renunciate Vaiṣṇavas are that they have given up the association of women, greed for money, and bodily pleasure. The *gṛhastha* Vaiṣṇavas have special glories. Many of them work hard to earn money, and after serving Krishna, they serve *gṛhastha* and *sannyāsī* Vaiṣṇavas. Whether one is a *gṛhastha* or a *sannyāsī*, the principal cause for respect is the attainment of devotional service. One should be respected as a Vaiṣṇava according to one's advancement in devotional service. There is no other cause to distinguish the level of a Vaiṣṇava.

(*Sajjana-toṣaṇī* 5/11)

12. Does one's position as a Vaiṣṇava depend on varṇāśrama, high birth, opulence, scriptural knowledge, or beauty?

One who has devotion is a Vaiṣṇava whether he is *gṛhastha*, *sannyāsī*, rich, poor, learned, foolish, weak, or strong.

(*Sajjana-toṣaṇī* 10/2)

13. How many special qualities determine a Vaiṣṇava? Among them, which is the primary symptom?

A Vaiṣṇava is recognized by twenty-six qualities. Among these, the quality of full surrender to Krishna is the primary symptom of a Vaiṣṇava.

(*Sajjana-toṣaṇī* 4/1)

14. If a Vaiṣṇava possesses the primary symptom, does he possess the secondary symptoms? If a person who is fully surrendered to Krishna has discrepancies, how should he be treated?

Undeviating surrender to Lord Krishna is the svarūpa-lakṣaṇa, natural characteristic, of devotional service. Whoever possesses this quality will soon find that the other symptoms come to him unfailingly. If the marginal symptoms have not reached full maturity in a surrendered *sādhu* and some serious discrepancies in his character are visible, he is still to be respected as a *sādhu* or saintly soul.

(*Harināma-cintāmaṇi*, Chapter 4)

15. What symptom distinguishes the quality of a Vaiṣṇava?

The twenty-five kinds of secondary qualities certainly manifest in proportion to the attainment of devotional service. The more devotional service increases, the more these qualities increase. Where these secondary qualities are absent, it should be understood that the devotional service is less. This is the only symptom by which one can distinguish the quality of a Vaiṣṇava.

(*Sajjana-toṣaṇī* 4/1)

16. What are the different kinds of devotees according to their moods?

According to their moods, the devotees are divided into three categories: the devotees who mainly preach, the devotees who mainly practice, and the devotees who practice and preach. If one considers the *uttama-adhikārīs*, *madhyama-adhikārīs*, and *kaniṣṭha-adhikārīs*, one can understand that the devotees who practice and preach are the best. The devotees who only practice are kaniṣṭha-adhikārīs, and the devotees who only preach are madhyama-adhikārīs.

(*Sajjana-toṣaṇī* 4 /1)

17. What differences exist between a kaniṣṭha-adhikārī, a madhyama-adhikārī, and an uttama-adhikārī?

One who is expert in scriptural reasoning and is always firmly determined, having mature faith is an *uttama-adhikārī* in devotional service. One who is not particularly expert in scriptural reasoning yet possesses firm faith is a *madhyama-adhikārī* in devotional service. One who somehow or other developed some faith but has not taken shelter of scriptural reasoning is a *kaniṣṭha-adhikārī*. If *kaniṣṭha-adhikārīs* associate with devotees and keep faith in the words of the scriptures, they can also gradually become mature Vaiṣṇavas.

(*Sajjana-toṣaṇī* 4/9)

18. What is the symptom of a mundane devotee?

Before the eyes of the people, *kaniṣṭha-adhikārīs* accept a traditional family guru or worship the Lord's deity after taking initiation into Viṣṇu *mantras* with worldly faith. In other words, they are mundane devotees, not pure devotees.

(*Jaiva Dharma*, Chapter 8)

19. Should a madhyama-adhikārī discriminate between superior and inferior Vaiṣṇavas?

One should not discriminate, thinking,"This Vaiṣṇava is good or a *madhyama*." Only an *uttama-adhikārī* can do so. If a *madhyama-adhikārī* discriminates like this, he will become an offender.

(*Jaiva Dharma*, Chapter 8)

20. What is the danger for kaniṣṭha-adhikārīs?

Because *kaniṣṭha-adhikārīs* cannot discriminate between the different classes of Vaiṣṇavas, they often become unfortunate.

(*Caitanya-śikṣāmṛta* 6/4)

21. When does a kaniṣṭha-adhikārī become qualified to serve the Vaiṣṇavas and purely chant the holy name of the Lord?

In the neophyte stage, a kaniṣṭha-adhikārī engages in *nāmābhāsa* or chanting a reflection of the holy name. By this chanting, his *anarthas* are destroyed and he becomes qualified to serve the Vaiṣṇavas and purely chant the Lord's holy name.

(*Harināma-cintāmaṇi*)

22. Who is qualified to serve the Vaiṣṇavas? Is one being partial if one discriminates in one's service to the Vaiṣṇavas?

Only a *madhyama-adhikārī* is qualified to respect and serve the Vaiṣṇavas. A *madhyama-adhikārī* should serve three kinds of Vaiṣṇavas: those who chant Krishna's holy names once, those who chant Krishna's holy names constantly, and those who cause one to chant Krishna's holy names just by seeing them. According to the different classes of Vaiṣṇavas—a Vaiṣṇava, a superior Vaiṣṇava, and a topmost Vaiṣṇava—one should serve them accordingly.

(*Jaiva Dharma*, Chapter 8)

23. Should one discriminate while making friendship with the Vaiṣṇavas, bestowing mercy on the Vaiṣṇavas, and neglecting the nondevotees?

It is the duty of pure devotees, who are situated on the platform of madhyama-adhikārī, to love God, to make friendship with pure devotees, to bestow mercy on subordinates, and to neglect envious people. They behave in this way according to scripture. To discriminate while making a friendship, according to the degree of the friend's devotional service, is proper. To discriminate while bestowing mercy, according to the degree of the ignorant people's simplicity, is proper. To discriminate while neglecting an envious person, according to the degree of his envy, is proper.

(*Jaiva Dharma*, Chapter 8)

24. When does the spiritual ego of a living entity arise?

When a living entity realizes that he is a pure spiritual particle, his spiritual ego naturally arises. He identifies himself as the servant of Krishna. At that time, the intelligence in its pure form rejects materialism and accepts spiritualism. Then the living entity has no other desire than the service of Krishna.

(*Sajjana-toṣaṇī* 10/11)

25. What is the duty and symptom of a Vaiṣṇava?

To give up the association with nondevotees is the duty of a Vaiṣṇava, and to fully surrender to the holy names of Krishna is the symptom of a Vaiṣṇava.

(*Sajjana-toṣaṇī* 11/6)

26. Who is a Vaiṣṇava? Who is almost a Vaiṣṇava?

If a conditioned soul purely chants the holy names of the Lord with faith, he is a Vaiṣṇava. A person who practices *nāmābhāsa* is almost a Vaiṣṇava and by the mercy of the holy names, he will gradually become purified.

(*Harināma-cintāmaṇi*)

27. Are the Vaiṣṇavas followers of the Lord's energy?

The Vaiṣṇavas are followers of the Lord's energy. They are under the subordination of Śrī Rādhikā, who is the personification of the Lord's spiritual potency.

(*Jaiva Dharma*, Chapter 9)

28. Who are engaged in welfare activities?

Although a living entity does not specifically gain anything from the advancement of the world, if one examines the lives of devotees, one will find that devotees only do welfare activities.

(*Caitanya-śikṣāmṛta*, Chapter 8)

29. Which qualities manifest in a devotee as the companions of devotional service?

When one's devotional service is awakened, the following qualities are automatically and simultaneously manifest: purity, gravity, peacefulness, truthfulness, friendliness, humility, simplicity, equanimity, indifference to sin, compassion for all living entities, refraining from sinful activities, and abandoning insignificant material desires.

(*Sajjana-toṣaṇī* 5/1)

30. What is the complete and auspicious human form of life?

The life of a devotee is the perfection of the human form of life. It is complete and all auspicious. It is the only spiritual truth found in the material world.

(*Caitanya-śikṣāmṛta*, Chapter 8 Conclusion)

31. Can a devotee conceal himself?

No matter how much a devotee hates name and fame, and gives up bad association, he can never remain hidden from anyone because of his devotional effulgence.

(*Harināma-cintāmaṇi*)

32. What is the nature of a Vaiṣṇava?

As long as his family life remains favorable to devotional service, a Vaiṣṇava remains soft-hearted toward his wife and children; when his family life becomes unfavorable to devotional service, his heart becomes hard and he leaves his crying wife and children forever.

(*Sajjana-toṣaṇī* 4/11)

33. When there is friction between karma and jñāna, which side does the Vaiṣṇava take?

The Vaiṣṇava remains a neutral spectator during a fight between karma-*kāṇḍa* and *jñāna-kāṇḍa.*

(*Sajjana-toṣaṇī* 7/1)

34. When is a brāhmaṇa qualified to accept Vaiṣṇava initiation and when has he fallen from his position as a Vaiṣṇava?

When a *brāhmaṇa* receives Vaiṣṇava *Gāyatrī mantra,* which is the mother of the Vedas, he becomes an initiated Vaiṣṇava. If he later takes non-Vedic initiation, he falls from his position as a Vaiṣṇava.

(*Jaiva Dharma,* Chapter 10)

35. What is the scale for measuring love for Śrī Gaura?

The more one has love for Śrīmān Mahāprabhu, the more one will try to follow His order.

(*Sajjana-toṣaṇī* 11/5)

36. Who is a real devotee?

If one is internally a Vaiṣṇava and externally a materialist, one is counted among the devotees.

(*Sajjana-toṣaṇī* 11/12)

37. Who is a real sādhu?

A real *sādhu* is he who by good fortune has awakened his own nature by associating with another *sādhu.*

(*Sajjana-toṣaṇī* 9/9)

38. Are the birth and activities of the Vaiṣṇavas similar to those of the living entities who are forced to enjoy the fruits of their karma?

The appearance and activities of the Vaiṣṇavas appear like that of the mundane fruitive workers, but they are completely different.

(*Sajjana-toṣaṇī* 11/10)

39. What is the difference between a Vaiṣṇava, a karmī, and a jñānī?

The difference between a Vaiṣṇava and a *karmī* or *jñānī* is huge. The *karmīs* engage in fruitive activities and attain self-satisfaction. The *jñānīs* cultivate impersonal knowledge and attain liberation. Devotees who engage in pure devotional service as their *sādhana* are *rasika-bhakta*s. When these great devotees, who know the science of devotional service, attain perfection, their devotional service becomes nectarean love of God, emanating from the lotus feet of Krishna.

(*Bṛhad-bhāgavatāmṛta*, purport)

40. Can a Vaiṣṇava be bound or destroyed?

No one can destroy one whom Krishna wants to protect. The strength of regulations cannot influence the devotees. What to speak of the bondage of regulations, nothing other than the bondage of love for the Lord can bind the devotees.

(*Śrī Krishna-saṁhitā*, Chapter 5)

41. How should one pray to go to Vṛndāvana, following in the footsteps of the Vaiṣṇavas?

O Sāragrāhī Vaiṣṇava soul!
Thou art an angel fair;
Lead, lead me on to Vṛndāvana
And spirit's power declare!
There rests my soul from matter free
Upon my Lover's arms,
Eternal peace and spirit's love
Are all my chanting charms!

(*Sāragrāhī Vaiṣṇava*)

42. What are the characteristics of a perfect soul and a practitioner?

Those who have attained the mood of the *gopīs* are perfect beings, and those who follow them are practitioners. Therefore the learned, who know the Absolute Truth, accept two types of *sādhus*: perfect beings and practitioners.

(*Śrī Krishna-saṁhitā*, Chapter 9)

26

Pure Vaiṣṇavas

1. What is the nature of a pure devotee?

Simplicity, determination, and exclusiveness are the characteristics of a pure devotee. He never approves of any topic that is opposed to devotional service just to keep people happy; the pure devotees are always neutral.

(*Sajjana-toṣaṇī* 8/10)

2. What is the character of a Vaiṣṇava? Who is qualified to be called a Vaiṣṇava?

The character of a Vaiṣṇava is sinless and no part of his character is fit for hiding. Simplicity is the life of a Vaiṣṇava. He always teaches other's by setting his own examples. Unless his character is pure, he is not fit to be called a Vaiṣṇava.

(*Sajjana-toṣaṇī* 5/10)

3. Does a great personality, who worships Krishna in his spiritual body, give up the rules and regulations?

Do swanlike persons engage only in spiritual activities and neglect material activities? No. Swanlike persons worship Krishna in the mood of one who is enjoyed, and they boldly take care of the external body. Eating, sleeping, enjoying, traveling, exercising, protecting society, protecting the body, riding in vehicles, engaging in industrial enterprises, and walking in the open air are seen in the lives of swanlike persons.

(*Śrī Krishna-saṁhitā*, Chapter 10/12)

4. During his life, can a swanlike Vaiṣṇava work rather than worship Hari?

The swanlike Vaiṣṇavas valiantly remain and work among men. They are the shelter of women and are respected by them. They take part in social activities and gain much experience. They teach their children artha-*śāstra* and thus become known as headmasters.

(*Śrī Krishna-saṁhitā,* Chapter 10/13)

5. Why is dry renunciation not pleasing to Krishna? How does Śrī Hari bestow His mercy on one who favorably cultivates devotional service to Krishna, and who is devoid of material enjoyment, fruitive activities, and mental speculation?

The role of *sannyāsa* is a sort of karma befitting an *āśrama* and is not pleasing to Krishna when it aims at liberation. *Sannyāsīs* receive the fruits of their karma and even if they are unmotivated, their karma ends in *ātma-mamatā,* self-pleasure. Pure devotees always serve Krishna by gratifying His senses. They forsake all attempts of karma and *jñāna,* being free from all desires except to serve Krishna. Krishna has fully destroyed the karma, its desires, and nescience of those devotees.

(*Brahma-saṁhitā* 5/54)

6. Who is best among those who follow the principles of varṇāśrama-dharma? Does an unalloyed devotee of Viṣṇu accept the rules and regulations of karma-kāṇḍa?

It has been said that among those who follow *varṇāśrama-dharma,* a devotee of Lord Viṣṇu is the best. A devotee gives up eternal and occasional activities that are in the mode of passion and ignorance, such as offering oblations to the forefathers and worshiping the demigods. On the other hand, if an unalloyed devotee's behavior and activities are like those of śūdras and outcastes, still it is to be understood that he will give up all activities that cause his material bondage.

(Sat-kriyā-sāra-dīpikā)

7. Can a pure Vaiṣṇava born in any caste become a qualified brāhmaṇa?

It does not matter in which family one is born; if one becomes a pure Vaiṣṇava, one automatically becomes a qualified *brāhmaṇa.*

(*Jaiva Dharma,* Chapter 6)

8. Does a Vaiṣṇava born from any family have a right to teach the Vedas?

A person who has developed unflinching devotion to Krishna is eligible to become a teacher of the Vedas, which reveal the truth.
(*Jaiva Dharma*, Chapter 6)

9. Without the mercy of Krishna, can one attain liberation simply by cultivating knowledge? Does a pure devotee pray for liberation?

Despite following various methods, such as performing fruitive activities, cultivating knowledge, practicing yoga, and undergoing austerities, no one can attain liberation. That is why persons who are on the path of knowledge take shelter of the reflection of devotional service to Krishna. The authorities of pure devotional service do not pray for liberation, but liberation herself humbly tries to serve the pure devotees.
(*Manaḥ-śikṣā*, Verse 8)

10. Should a Vaiṣṇava pray for worldly opulence or heavenly pleasures?

The kingdom on earth, the beauty of heaven, and the sovereignty over the material world are never the subject of Vaiṣṇava prayer.
(*The Bhagavat*: *Its Philosophy, Its Ethics & Its Theology*)

11. How does a self-realized surrendered soul worship Hari? Does he have any pride for his material possessions?

A self-realized person, having no material assets, knows that attachment to Krishna is the essence of life. Therefore he gives up the desire for material enjoyment and liberation. He maintains his family in a simple way and constantly serves Hari through his eternal spiritual body. Such a person abandons pride of his beauty, high birth, and physical strength, and always engages in devotional service.
(*Kalyāṇa-kalpataru*, Song 1)

12. Who are the highest type of practitioners?

The highest type of practitioners are those who believe that, of all the processes of *sādhana-bhakti*, taking shelter of the Lord's holy name awards one all perfection.
(*Harināma-cintāmaṇi*)

13. Are the arguments or loving quarrels among the pure Vaiṣṇavas comprehensible to mundane intelligence?

What the unalloyed devotee of the Supreme Lord says is all-true and is independent of any consideration of unwholesome pros and cons. There is, however, the element of mystery in their verbal controversies. Those, whose judgment is made of mundane stuff, being unable to enter into the spirit of the all loving controversies among pure devotees, due to their own want of unalloyed devotion, are apt to impute to the devotees their own defects of partisanship and opposing views.

(*Brahma-saṁhitā* 5/37)

14. Do the pure Vaiṣṇavas ever endeavor to protect their independence? What kind of service to Krishna have they achieved?

A Vaiṣṇava should always carefully remember that he is a servant of the servant of the lover of the *gopīs*. He is always dependent and never independent. He cannot have independence, because he has sold his nature of independence in the form of being a servant of the Lord and in this way, he has obtained service to Krishna.

(*Sajjana-toṣaṇī* 11/10)

15. Do pure devotees, who are intoxicated by drinking the honey from the lotus feet of Krishna, feel the pangs of the threefold material miseries?

Pure devotees are immersed in an ocean of happiness by drinking the intoxicating beverage of service to Krishna. They do not know the pains of this world, nor do they have trouble of any want, because they are situated in their pure bodies and have pure desires.

(*Navadvīpa-bhāva-taraṅga* 102)

16. What is the character of a Vaiṣṇava?

A Vaiṣṇava is always transcendental, faultless, and blissful. He is fond of chanting the Krishna's holy name, indifferent to material enjoyments, and very kind to all living entities. He is devoid of pride, expert in worshiping the Lord, and detached from material objects. He is always without duplicity and is attached to relishing the eternal pastimes of the Lord.

(*Kalyāṇa-kalpataru*)

17. By whose appeal does Krishna bestow mercy?

By the appeal of the Vaiṣṇavas, the most merciful Krishna becomes compassionate toward a sinful person like me.

(*Kalyāṇa-kalpataru*)

18. What does a pure Vaiṣṇava pray to the Lord? Through which relationship does he appeal to the Lord to engage in His service?

The Vaiṣṇava meekly and humbly says,"Father, Master, God, Friend and Husband of my soul! Hallowed be Thy name. I do not approach You for anything that You have already given me. I have sinned against You and I now repent and solicit Your pardon. Let Thy Holiness touch my soul and make me free from grossness. Let my spirit be devoted meekly to Your holy service in absolute love towards Thee. I have called You my God, and let my soul be wrapped up in admiration at Your Greatness! I have addressed You as my Master and let my soul be strongly devoted to Your service. I have called You my Friend and let my soul be in reverential love toward You and not in dread or fear! I have called You my Husband and let my spiritual nature be in eternal union with You, forever loving and never dreading, or feeling disgust. My love! Let me have strength enough to go up to You as the consort of my soul, so that we may be one in eternal love! Peace to the world!"

(*The Bhagavat*: *Its Philosophy*, *Its Ethics & Its Theology*)

27

Impure Vaiṣṇavas

1. Are offenders to the holy name pure Vaiṣṇavas?

Persons who commit offense against the holy name are never pure Vaiṣṇavas; thus, Śrīmān Mahāprabhu has distinguished them by saying that they are not pure Vaiṣṇavas but are like Vaiṣṇavas.

(*Sajjana-toṣaṇī* 8/9)

2. If a person is sinful, in spite of externally displaying the transformation of love of God, is he a Vaiṣṇava?

Those who are sinful have not taken shelter of the holy names with undivided faith. Even if they exhibit all other symptoms, still we will never accept that they have taken shelter of the holy names without deviation. Sinful persons who shed tears of love while chanting the holy name will be counted among the cheating Vaiṣṇavas, because they are offenders at the feet of the holy names.

(*Sajjana-toṣaṇī* 8/9)

3. If external transformations of love of God are found in a Māyāvādī, can he be called a Vaiṣṇava?

The Māyāvādīs are pseudo *nāmābhāsīs*; therefore, they are offenders. It is very difficult for them to become pure Vaiṣṇavas. They can never be called Vaiṣṇavas—no matter how much reflection of love of God they manifest.

(*Sajjana-toṣaṇī* 5/12)

4. If a person who worships five gods worships Śrī Rādhā-Krishna, can he be called a pure Vaiṣṇava?

There are two types of impure Vaiṣṇava religions; one is contaminated by karma and the other by *jñāna*. The Vaiṣṇava religion found among the smārtas is contaminated by karma. Although in this religion the followers accept initiation into Vaiṣṇava *mantras*, nevertheless they establish the universal Lord Viṣṇu as a limb of karma. According to their opinion, Lord Viṣṇu is the controller of all demigods and He is personally a part of karma and under the control of karma. Karma is not dependent on the wheel of Viṣṇu, rather Viṣṇu is dependent on the wheel of karma. In their opinion, worshiping, offering service, and following rules and regulations are limbs of karma, because there is no truth higher than karma. For a long time, such Vaiṣṇava principles of the fruitive workers have been going on. In India, many followers of this philosophy proudly consider themselves Vaiṣṇavas, but they do not want to accept the pure Vaiṣṇavas as Vaiṣṇavas. It is simply their misfortune.

The Vaiṣṇava religion contaminated by *jñāna* is also vigorously followed in India. According to the philosophy of the *jñānīs*, the unknown Brahman is the highest truth. In their opinion, to attain the impersonal Brahman, one needs to worship the personal forms of Sūrya, Gaṇeśa, Durgā, Śiva, and Viṣṇu. When one attains perfection, the worship of these personal forms is no longer required; one ultimately merges into the existence of the impersonal Brahman. Followers of this philosophy disregard the pure Vaiṣṇavas. Although the worship of Viṣṇu among the worship of five gods appears to be related to Viṣṇu or even Rādhā-Krishna, it is not pure Vaiṣṇava religion.

If we separate such impure Vaiṣṇava religions, the actual Vaiṣṇava religion will manifest. Because of the influence of Kali, many people do not understand pure Vaiṣṇava religious principles and consider impure Vaiṣṇava religion as pure Vaiṣṇava religion.

(*Jaiva Dharma*, Chapter 4)

5. Are the Rāmānandīs pure Vaiṣṇavas?

One who desires to attain liberation can never be considered a pure Vaiṣṇava. Since Rāmadāsa of the Rāmānandī-sampradāya was a worshiper of Lord Rāma, he was Vaiṣṇava prāya or almost a Vaiṣṇava. In those days, no one could distinguish between a pure Vaiṣṇava and a pseudo Vaiṣṇava. However, Śrī Rāmadāsa who was born in a kāyastha family, was known as a Vaiṣṇava because he worshiped Lord Rāmacandra.

(*Caitanya Caritāmṛta* Antya 13/92, commentary)

28

Householder Vaiṣṇava

1. Who is a real householder? In whose house should a pure Vaiṣṇava accept prasāda?

One who chants one million holy names of the Lord every day is a real householder; a pure Vaiṣṇava should take *prasāda* in his house.

(*Sajjana-toṣaṇī* 11/12)

2. What are the general characteristics of the renunciates and the householders?

Persons who are filled with attachment for material enjoyment can never tolerate the urges of the genitals. Many of them engage in illicit activities. Those who thirst for devotional service are divided into two groups. Those whose attraction has been purified by the strength of *sādhu-saṅga* give up the association of women altogether and continuously engage in devotional service. Persons in this group are known as renounced Vaiṣṇavas. Those whose propensity for associating with women has not been destroyed accept the code of marriage and remain as householders while engaging in devotional service.

(*Sajjana-toṣaṇī* 11/5)

3. How should a Vaiṣṇava householder behave with his wife and children?

A Vaiṣṇava householder should get his wife initiated into the Vaiṣṇava religion and, as far as possible, teach her the science of Vaiṣṇavism. If one enhances the world of Vaiṣṇavas by the assistance of one's Vaiṣṇava wife, one no longer indulges in discussing material topics. A Vaiṣṇava householder should consider his children servants of the Supreme Lord.

(*Caitanya-śikṣāmṛta* 3/2)

4. Is the instruction to control the six urges meant for householders?

A self-realized person who is able to conquer the six urges can conquer the entire world. The instructions to tolerate the urges are only meant for the householder devotees, because the renunciates have already achieved perfection in this regard before they left their house.

(*Upadeśāmṛta* 1, commentary)

5. How should the householder Vaiṣṇavas maintain their life?

The householder Vaiṣṇavas should always refrain from sinful activities, and after earning money through proper means, they should maintain their family, which belongs to Krishna. The character of the renunciate Vaiṣṇavas should particularly become pure.

(*Sajjana-toṣaṇī* 5/90)

6. How can the householders best use their earnings?

Those who earn a healthy amount of money can spend some of it to pay tax to the government and some of it to maintain their families. In this way, they can save whatever surplus money they have. They should spend the accumulated money for religious activities. There are various types of improper spending, such as using money to eat meat, drink wine, engage in useless court cases, give charity to unqualified persons, and go to the cinema and theater. Those who wish to become the servants of Śrīmān Mahāprabhu should not use their surplus money in sinful activities; they should use it for a good cause. Apart from serving a guest, educating a student, giving medicine to a sick person, feeding a poor or a distressed person, and relieving a poor person from the responsibility of his daughter's marriage, there is a more important way to properly use one's accumulated money. One should spend one's money in the service of the Supreme Lord and His devotees. The duty of householder Vaiṣṇavas is to donate some portion of their surplus money for the smooth running of the daily service of the Lord.

(*Sajjana-toṣaṇī* 7/2)

7. Why should the householders serve guests?

Serving guests is the principal duty of the householders. Any country where this principle is absent is as good as a desert and should be rejected. The lives of householders who do not entertain guests are useless and are in the lead among sinful people. Serving guests is a must for householders.

The inevitable sinful activities that a householder commits are destroyed simply by serving guests.
(*Sajjana-toṣaṇī* 8/12)

8. Should a Vaiṣṇava householder discriminate between an ordinary guest and a Vaiṣṇava guest?
Whenever a devotee householder receives a guest, he examines whether the guest is an ordinary guest or a Vaiṣṇava guest. If he has a Vaiṣṇava guest, then he exhibits more affection to his guest than to his own brother. He serves his guest properly and tries to enhance his own devotional service by associating with such a guest. If he receives an ordinary guest, he serves him to the best of his ability, according to worldly etiquettes. Such is the behavior of a Vaiṣṇava householder.
(*Sajjana-toṣaṇī* 8/12)

9. What is the principal activity of a householder?
The principal activity of a householder is to serve the devotees of the Lord.
(*Sajjana-toṣaṇī* 11/12)

10. When should a householder become attentive?
A Vaiṣṇava householder should take special care in associating with saintly persons.
(*Sajjana-toṣaṇī* 11/12)

11. What ideal example should a Vaiṣṇava householder follow?
Why should they give up the desire for material enjoyment? The Vaiṣṇava householders should build their character following in the footsteps of Mahāprabhu and His associates. The behavior that the Lord and His devotees personally displayed in earning their livelihood and maintaining their lives should be totally imitated by the householder devotees. To engage in activities with a desire to please Krishna is always good. On the other hand, if they engage in activities with a desire for sense gratification and to obtain irrelevant results, they become materialists.
(*Sajjana-toṣaṇī* 11/12)

12. What are the other activities of a Vaiṣṇava householder?
A Vaiṣṇava householder should offer respect to Tulasī.
(*Sajjana-toṣaṇī* 11/12)

13. Should a Vaiṣṇava householder collect more than necessary?

The Vaiṣṇava householders should accumulate as much wealth as they require to maintain their devotional life. If they accumulate more than that, they will be at fault for accumulating too much. Persons who endeavor to worship the Lord should give up this habit of the materialists.

(*Upadeśāmṛta* Verse 2, commentary)

14. Should a Vaiṣṇava householder endeavor hard for his food and clothes?

A Vaiṣṇava householder should feel happy with whatever food and clothing he easily gets.

(*Sajjana-toṣaṇī* 11/12)

15. With what kind of Vaiṣṇavas should a Vaiṣṇava householder hold a festival?

A Vaiṣṇava householder should respect other Vaiṣṇavas, and he should take shelter of the lotus feet of the superior as well as the topmost Vaiṣṇavas. He should hold festivals in the company of such Vaiṣṇavas.

(*Manaḥ-śikṣā*, Verse 10)

16. In which subject should a householder remain particularly careful?

A householder should remain extremely careful not to commit offenses against the Vaiṣṇavas.

(*Sajjana-toṣaṇī* 11/12)

17. Should a devotee become a sannyāsī or a householder?

For a devotee to remain a householder or to become a *sannyāsī* is the same thing.

(*Sajjana-toṣaṇī* 11/12)

18. What is the position of a householder? Should one remain a householder forever?

The position of the householder is like a school for the living entity to learn and awaken the science of the self.

(*Jaiva Dharma*, Chapter 7)

19. Can a householder award one sannyāsa?

One should take *sannyāsa* only from a renounced Vaiṣṇava. Since a devotee householder has not relished the behavior of a renunciate, he should not give *sannyāsa* to anyone.

(*Jaiva Dharma*, Chapter 7)

29

Who is a Paramahaṁsa?

1. Who is a paramahaṁsa?

The self-realized devotee is a real *paramahaṁsa*.

(*Caitanya-śikṣāmṛta* 6/4)

2. Who were the real paramahaṁsas in the pastimes of Śrī Gaura and in ancient times?

Pure exalted devotees such as Śrīvāsa Paṇḍita, Śrī Puṇḍarīka Vidyānidhi, and Śrī Rāmānanda Rāya were real *paramahaṁsas*. In ancient times, many personalities, like Ribhu, were real *paramahaṁsas*, even though they were householders.

(*Caitanya-śikṣāmṛta* 6/4)

3. What is the definition of a paramahaṁsa? Which literature do paramahaṁsas study?

Those who have divine eyes consider a *paramahaṁsa* to be an equipoised yogī, and those who are less intelligent or third-class consider a paramahaṁsa to be attached to material enjoyment. Some people may occasionally even consider a *paramahaṁsa* to be opposed to the Lord. A swanlike person can identify another swanlike brother who possesses all the appropriate symptoms, whether they are from the same country or not. Although their dress, language, worship, deity, and behavior may appear different, they freely address each other as brother. These type of people are called *paramahaṁsas*, and *Śrīmad-Bhāgavatam* is the scripture for these *paramahaṁsas*.

(*Śrī Krishna-saṁhitā*, introduction)

4. Are the paramahaṁsas bound by the rules and regulations of the scriptures?

Whatever rules and regulations people of a lower level follow, the great personalities of the higher level follow, simply as their independent pastimes.

(*Sajjana-toṣaṇī* 10/10)

5. Whose association do the paramahaṁsas reject?

There is so much difference between the fruitive workers and the devotees who engage in pious religious activities; what to speak of *karmīs* who are devoid of devotional service to Krishna. Taking shelter of pure devotional service, the devotees who engage in pious religious activities spend their lives in serving the Vaiṣṇavas and chanting the Lord's holy names. Within their hearts, they are indifferent to fruitive activities and they follow the principles of *varṇāśrama-dharma*, because they know that it is favorable to devotional service. Although temporary and causal activities are often obstacles on the path of devotional service, devotees engage in them only as much as they need to maintain their livelihood without committing any sin; therefore they are always indifferent to such activities.

Fruitive workers think that action is the cause of their deliverance and they have no interest in activities in relationship with Krishna. They remain neutral both in happiness and distress in relation with Krishna and teach the people of the world about mundane fruitive activities. Even though they follow the Vedas, they blaspheme the impartial mature yogīs and misguide people by claiming their own conclusion is the Vaiṣṇava conclusion. Foolish people are bewildered by such propaganda, and thus, they are ruined because of narrow-mindedness, and they make arguments with the impartial mature yogīs. The followers of the Vedas do not understand the hearts of the perfect yogīs, but they accept the mundane fruitive workers as great personalities and deal with them accordingly. The swanlike pure devotees know that the mundane followers of the Vedas are nondevotees and do not associate with them.

(*Bhajanāmṛtaṁ*, commentary)

6. Who is the most glorious person in the world?

The swanlike devotees who are expert in discriminating between matter and spirit are glorious persons in the world. Only the devotees are learned, because they have surpassed the ocean of illusion in the material world. Only the devotees are full of good qualities, because they have attained the platform of pure goodness, surpassing the three modes of material nature: goodness, passion, and ignorance. Only the devotees are happy, because they have attained the transcendental happiness of Vraja, surpassing the happiness and distress of the material world. Only the devotees are fearless, because they have become the inhabitants of Goloka, surpassing material time, which consists of past and future. May the devotees live forever and benefit unfortunate persons, who are tortured by Māyā, which gives them her audience, associates with them, and converses with them.

(*Bhajanāmṛtaṁ*, commentary)

30

Preacher

1. Who is more beneficial to the world, those who perform bhajana in a solitary place or those who preach the holy name of Hari?

A preacher of the holy name, following the example of saintly persons, is more beneficial to the world than devotees who neglect the preaching work by becoming absorbed in the bliss of their own *bhajana* according to their inclination.

(*Sajjana-toṣaṇī* 4/2)

2. Who is qualified to preach?

Only devotees who possess full knowledge of pure devotional service and who relish the mellows of offenseless chanting of the Lord's holy names are qualified to preach.

(*Sajjana-toṣaṇī* 10/11)

3. Can anyone become a preacher if he is an expert speaker?

The responsibility of preaching is better entrusted to those who are engaged in performing *bhajana*. Simply being an expert speaker does not qualify one to preach the teachings of Gaurāṅga.

(*Sajjana-toṣaṇī* 10/11)

4. Is it necessary for a preacher to know the science of offenses against the chanting of the holy name?

The preacher should certainly know the offenses against the chanting of the Lord's holy name. If they know this, they will become qualified preachers of the holy name. In the course of preaching the holy names, they should instruct everyone to always remain careful to avoid committing offenses against the chanting of the holy name. Otherwise, the preachers will themselves become offenders to the holy name.

(*Sajjana-toṣaṇī* 10/11)

5. What does one require for pure preaching work?

To preach purely, one should first chant the Lord's holy name in a pure systematic way; second, one should maintain one's purity; and third, the audience should be pure. To chant the Lord's holy name in a pure systematic way means that the holy names should be indicative of the Lord's pastimes and free from fruitive activities and mental speculation.

(*Viṣṇupriyā Pallī Magazine*, Vol. 1)

6. Why does a preacher need to be exemplary?

When saintly people follow religious principles, this is called *ācāra*, proper code of conduct. To preach those religious principles to other living entities in the world is called *pracāra*, preaching. If one wants to engage in the activities of *ācāra* or *pracāra*, one should first learn the saintly person's code of conduct. Some people, after learning, begin to preach even before they themselves follow. Hence, they yield insufficient results. If one does not personally follow the religious principles but preaches to other's, he creates a great deal of disturbance in the world.

(*Sajjana-toṣaṇī* 4/2)

7. Can the smārtas become preachers of devotional service?

Some people do not practice pure devotional service themselves; rather they follow the doctrine of the *smārtas*, which is based on karma-*kāṇḍa*. The science of devotional service that they instruct is totally opposed to all the scriptures. To preach, first one should follow.

(*Sajjana-toṣaṇī* 4/2)

8. Why is it necessary for a preacher to become pure?

For preachers to become pure is extremely necessary. Singing the holy names is found everywhere, but when we go to hear them, we feel extremely sorry to see the impurity of the singers. Either they are chanting the holy names to stop the spread of disease in the village or they are chanting the holy names out of fear of Yamarāja. Such chanting, which comes from a heart that is polluted by thirst for liberation and material enjoyment, is the perverted reflection of the holy names. To achieve eternal auspiciousness by such chanting is impossible. If the shopkeepers and vendors give up such desires, they can preach the pure holy names. If, however, they chant the holy names with a desire to either accumulate money, or name and fame, the very purpose of opening the marketplace for distributing the Lord's holy names will not be fulfilled.

(*Viṣṇupriyā Pallī Magazine*, Vol. 2)

9. Are pure preachers responsible for the result of their preaching when their preaching is pervertedly reflected in the living entities who are inclined toward material enjoyment?

The reformers, out of their universal love and anxiety for good work, endeavor by some means or other to make the thoughtless drink the cup of salvation, but the latter drink it with wine and fall to the ground under the influence of intoxication, for imagination has the power of making a thing what it never was. Thus, it is that the evils of nunneries and the corruptions to Akharas proceeded. No, we are not to scandalize the Savior of Jerusalem or the Savior of Nadia for these subsequent evils. Luthers, instead of critics, are what we want for the correction of those evils by the true interpretation of the original precepts.

(*The Bhagavat*: *Its Philosophy*, *Its Ethics & Its Theology*)

31

Science

1. What is the principal cause of heat?

By mixing metals like iron and sulphur, mountains are broken, the earth shakes, and ammunition is released from guns to create havoc in the world. Where is the inspiration of the consciousness in these activities? Although heat is seen as the principal cause of all movement, yet without the inspiration of the spirit nothing can happen. If we scrutinizingly study what is this heat, we come to know that heat is a quality. When a particular propensity becomes active within one's body, heat manifests in the body. It is well known that if one is excessively lusty, his bodily temperature increases. It is to be known that heat, which is experienced in all kinds of material objects, is the result of the interaction of spirit.

(*Tattva-sūtra* 22)

2. Are reason and argument the cause of scientific discoveries? Is human nature satisfied by remaining entangled in sensual knowledge?

All mental and material science is discovered through reasoning. Material science is of many kinds: science of matter and motion, magnetism, electricity, medicine, physiology, optics, music, logic, and mental philosophy. Art and manufacture are part of the science of the quality and the energy of objects. Science and art together create huge enterprises in the world. Ships, railways, buildings, and electrical items are the products of sensual knowledge. Geography, chronology, and astronomy are products of sensual knowledge. Zoology, mineralogy, and surgery are also products of sensual knowledge. Those who wish to remain entangled in this knowledge call it positive knowledge. Since human nature does not want to remain confined only to sensual positive knowledge, people try to attain higher and higher knowledge.

(*Caitanya-śikṣāmṛta* 5/3)

3. What is science according to swanlike personalities?

According to the Vaiṣṇavas, proper use of material knowledge is science. Those who are engaged in advancing in material knowledge, being induced by mundane desires, indirectly help the spiritual advancement of the Vaiṣṇavas to some extent.

(*Jaiva Dharma*, Chapter 9)

4. In which religion is the full cultivation of spiritual science available?

The science of *bhakti* is not found in modern religions. *Sanātana-dharma* is evolved from Āryan culture, and Vaiṣṇavism is the best part of sanātana-*dharma*. Therefore, the science of *bhakti* is only possible in Vaiṣṇavism. In Jīva Goswami's *Ṣaṭ-sandarbha* and Rūpa Goswami's *Bhakti-rasāmṛta-sindhu*, the science of *bhakti* is particularly expounded.

(*Prema-pradīpa*, Chapter 6)

5. In whose service should science be used to benefit the world?

The duty of the artist and the scientist is to serve the knower of the Absolute Truth with their advanced art and science. The science of the self is extremely confidential. Those people who are engaged in discussing such topics have no time to entangle themselves in ordinary art and science. Others should therefore try to help maintain those people. O brothers! O believers of gradual advancement! O believers of gradual discovery! Please mind your own business and, as a result, you and the whole world will be benefited. Do not cause unauthorized interference and try to find faults and qualities in the science of the self. If you act like gentlemen, we will constantly bless you.

(Sajjana Toṣanī 7/7)

6. When do science, society, and art reach their highest stage?

When karma works under the subordination of *bhakti*, it is no longer identified as karma but as *bhakti*. As long as karma is identified by its own name, it tries to become equal to *bhakti*. The advancement of science, society, and art are the acts of karma. But, when karma is transformed into *bhakti*, then science, society, and art become bright and advanced.

(*Tattva Viveka* 1/9/12)

7. In which scientific knowledge is the swanlike Vaiṣṇavas expert?

Books on physical and mental science, books on industry, books on languages, books on grammar, and books on poetry are known as *artha-śāstra*. Some physical, mental, familial, and social benefits are obtained from these writings. The name of these benefits is artha. The advantage of these books is that by studying medicine, one can get the benefit of a cure; by studying music, one can get the benefit of happiness to the mind and ears; by material scientific knowledge, various wonderful machines are created; by astrology, one can get the benefit of understanding subjects like proper and improper times. Those who study such *artha-śāstras* are known as artha-vit scholars. The *smṛti-śāstra* establishes *varṇāśrama-dharma* and are also known as *artha-śāstra*. The *smārta* scholars are also known as *artha-vit* scholars, because the main purpose of their occupational duties is to protect society. Spiritual scholars practice spiritual life with these arthas. Swanlike Vaiṣṇavas are never opposed to discussing these scriptures. They extract the supreme goal of spiritual life from these *artha-śāstras* and become worshipable among *artha-vit* scholars. The *artha-vit* scholars are happy to assist them in ascertaining the Absolute Truth. The swanlike Vaiṣṇavas are present in the battlefield as negotiators. They do not hate or reject various sinful persons. Swanlike Vaiṣṇavas are always engaged in purifying the hearts of sinful people by giving public lectures, friendly advice, and confidential instructions, and by rebuking, setting an example, and sometimes punishing sinners.

(*Śrī Krishna-saṁhitā* 10/14)

32

Philosophy

1. How is the material, metaphysical, and spiritual science divided?

According to their qualifications, living entities in the world are divided into three categories: mundane, metaphysical, and spiritual. People say that philosophy is of six kinds, but we have divided it into three categories. Material philosophy consists of Nyāya, Vaiśeṣika, and Pūrva-mīmāṁsā. Metaphysical philosophy consists of Sāṅkhya, Pātañjala, and the Māyāvāda commentary on *Vedānta-sūtra*. Spiritual philosophy consists of the *Vedānta* itself.

(*Krishna Karṇāmṛta*, Introduction)

2. Where is the synthesis of various philosophies preached by different ācāryas?

The philosophies such as *kevalādvaita-vāda* (exclusive monism), *kevaladvaita-vāda* (exclusive dualism), *dvaitādvaita-vāda* (monism and dualism), *viśiṣṭādvaita-vāda* (specific monism), and *śuddhādvaita-vāda* (purified monism) quarrel for the sake of name only. The supreme truth, which remains after the isms of different philosophies, is the philosophy of *acintya-bhedābheda* (inconceivable oneness and difference). The Vedas and the great authorities approve this supreme philosophy.

(*Śrī Bhāgavatārka-marīci-mālā* 10/4)

3. Why is the philosophy of acintya-bhedābheda complete?

In his book *Sarvasambādinī*, Śrī Jīva Goswami has established this philosophy of *acintya-bhedābheda* as the ultimate conclusion. The *dvaitādvaita* philosophy propounded by Śrī Nimbārka was not complete. However, the Vaiṣṇava world accepted this philosophy as perfect through the teachings of Śrīmān Mahāprabhu. Since the acceptance of the Lord's eternal *sac-cid-ānanda* form found in Śrī Madhva-sampradāya is the main principle of the acintya-bhedābheda philosophy, Śrīmān Mahāprabhu has accepted the Madhva-sampradāya. Since there are some little scientific differences in the conclusions of the previous Vaiṣṇava *ācāryas*, different *sampradāyas* have come into being. By the strength of His omniscience, the Supreme Personality of Godhead, Śrī Caitanya Mahāprabhu has fulfilled the deficiencies of the different philosophies. He made the philosophies and conclusions of Śrī Madhva, Śrī Rāmānuja, Śrī Viṣṇusvāmī, and Śrī Nimbārka faultless and perfect, and mercifully gave everyone in the world His pure conclusion of *acintya-bhedābheda.*

(*Manaḥ-śikṣā*, Verse 9)

4. Is the conclusion of acintyā-bhedābheda based on the Vedas and on universal philosophical conclusions?

Since the philosophies of *kevala-vāda*, *kevalā-vāda*, *śuddhādvaita*, and *viśiṣṭādvaita* consist of partial statements of the Vedic literature, they are opposed to the remaining parts. The philosophy of *acintya-bhedābheda* is universal and it is the actual purport of the Vedas. It is the object of the living entities constitutional faith, and saintly persons accept it.

(*Manaḥ-śikṣā*, Verse 9)

5. Why is the philosophy of acintya-bhedābheda accepted by everyone?

The conclusion of acintya-bhedābheda is based on devotional scriptures. The more one discusses it with reasoning the more one will find it pure and perfect. Arguments are of two kinds: argument to support one's own side and arguments to defeat one's opposition. The Vedas, the *Purāṇas*, and the conclusions of the *mahājanas* nourish the acintya-bhedābheda philosophy; they are arguments to support this philosophy. Śrī Śaṅkarācārya and other dry speculators are opposed to this philosophy. Śrī Śaṅkara has said,"O Lord! When the difference between You and me is removed, I will remain Yours, but I cannot say that You are mine." Such opposing arguments also nourish the acintya-bhedābheda philosophy. Everyone therefore accepts this conclusion.

(*Bṛhad-bhāgavatāmṛta* purport)

6. Why is the word"acintya," inconceivable, used in the conclusion of acintya-bhedābheda?

The truth has been established; the living entities are simultaneously one with and different from Krishna, and the material world is also simultaneously one with and different from Krishna. Since limited human reasoning cannot comprehend it, this eternal truth of simultaneously oneness and difference has been called *acintya.*

(*Caitanya-śikṣāmṛta* 1/5)

7. Is the philosophy of kevalādvaita-vāda nondual knowledge, and is it approved by the Vedas?

Many people think that the philosophy of *advaita-vāda* is *advaya-jñāna* or nondual knowledge. But this is not a fact. The philosophy of *kevalādvaita-vāda* is opposed to the Vedas. The philosophy of oneness is established in many places in the Vedas and the philosophy of eternal separation is also established in many places in the Vedas. Vedic literature is perfect knowledge; therefore, there is no possibility of any contradiction. The Vedas conclude that simultaneous oneness and difference are eternal and perfect, because of the inconceivable potency of the Supreme Brahman. Thus, the material world and the living entities are simultaneously one with and different from the Supreme Brahman. Dvaita and advaita are simultaneously a fact; therefore in the science of oneness, there is a difference between matter and spirit, and in the science of the self, the minute spirit souls are eternally different from the Supreme Lord. One who knows the truth of oneness and difference has nothing more to know. When one realizes the conclusion of *acintya-bhedābheda*, one automatically achieves *advaya-jñāna* or nondual knowledge. The living entity who is the seer cannot see anything separate from the Absolute Truth. When he is under the control of material vision, he only sees a difference in them. Since matter is an eternally perfect element, it appears separate from consciousness. This is called *dvaita-jñāna.*

(*Sajjana-toṣaṇī* 2/6) Bhajanāmṛtaṁ

8. Who perfected the philosophical conclusions preached by the authorized Vaiṣṇava ācāryas?

Śrī Rāmānujācārya preached devotional service according to the philosophy of *viśiṣṭādvaita-vāda.* Śrī Madhvācārya preached devotional service according to the philosophy of *śuddhādvaita-vāda.* Śrī Nimbādityācārya preached devotional service according to the philosophy of *dvaitādvaita-vāda.* Śrī Viṣṇusvāmī preached devotional service according to the philosophy of *śuddhādvaita-vāda.* All four are preachers of pure devotional service. In the opinion of Rāmānuja, the Supreme Lord is one, and matter and spirit are His qualities. In the opinion of Madhva, the living entities are separate from the Supreme Lord, and devotional service to the Lord is the nature of the living entities. In the opinion of Nimbāditya, the living entities are simultaneously one with and different from the Supreme Lord; thereby the eternity of difference is accepted. In the opinion of Viṣṇusvāmī, the object is one but the Supreme Brahman and the living entities are eternally different. Even though there are differences in their opinions, all of them have accepted that devotional service is eternal, the living entities are eternal servants of the Supreme Lord, and love of God is the ultimate goal of life. Therefore, all of them were Vaiṣṇavas. Although they were authorized Vaiṣṇavas, their philosophies were incomplete and there were differences between them. Śrī Caitanyadeva, who is directly the Supreme Personality of Godhead, appeared in the world and, after removing those scientific imperfections, taught the people of the world scientific pure devotional service.

(*Manaḥ-śikṣā*, Verse 9)

9. Is the conclusion of Śrī Rāmānujācārya opposed to the conclusion of the Gauḍīyas?

The conclusions of Śrīmad Rāmānuja Svāmī are like the foundation of our Gauḍīya temple of love.

(*Sajjana-toṣaṇī* 7/3)

10. Are the philosophy of Śrī Nimbāditya and the conclusion of acintya-bhedābheda the same?

Many people say that the philosophy of the Gauḍīya Vaiṣṇavas is identical to that of Śrī Nimbāditya, but that is not true. The philosophy of Nimbāditya is dvaitādvaita and the Gauḍīya philosophy is acintya-bhedābheda.

(*Sajjana-toṣaṇī* Volume 7)

11. When was philosophical literature composed?

The *Darśana-śāstra*, philosophical scriptures, was compiled a short time after the compilation of the *Mahābhārata*. There are six prominent philosophical systems current in India—*Nyāya* (logic), *Sāṅkhya*, *Pātañjala* (yoga), *Kaṇāda* or *Vaiśeṣika*, *Pūrva-mīmāṁsā* or *Karma-mīmāṁsā*, and *Uttara-mīmāṁsā* or *Vedānta*. All these philosophical systems were introduced after Buddhism. The ṛṣis who propounded these systems first composed their philosophies in *sūtras*. The Vedic *sūtras* were compiled to facilitate easy remembrance, but this was not the case with the *sūtras* of these philosophical systems. When the *brāhmaṇa*s were attacked by the mighty Buddhist philosophy, they first compiled the *Upaniṣads*, which are the pinnacle of Vedic literature, and thus they strengthened their doctrine with logic and argument. The Buddhists gradually presented many philosophical systems such as *Saugata*, *Mādhyamika*, and *Yogācāra*. Soon afterwards, the Buddhists entered into intense debate with the *brāhmaṇa*s. The *brāhmaṇa*s then introduced their six philosophical systems, beginning with *Nyāya* and *Sāṅkhya*. They kept their teachings in the form of *sūtras* and passed them on only to their disciples. During the time of Rāmacandra, Gautama Ṛṣi composed *Ānvīkṣikī*, Vedic logic, which was accepted at that time. According to their needs, the *brāhmaṇa*s composed the present system of *Nyāya* under Gautama's name and substituted it for the previous system. In Gautama's *śāstra*, there are statements that could be used against the *Saugata* philosophy. The scriptures of *Kaṇāda* come under the category of *Nyāya* scriptures. In the system of *Sāṅkhya*, there are also many statements against Buddhism. The system of *Pātañjala* falls under the category of *Sāṅkhya*. The *Pūrva-mīmāṁsā* propounded by Jaimini supports the karma-*kāṇḍa* system that was rejected by the Buddhists. Although *Vedānta* scriptures are the most recent, they have been accepted as another form of *Ānvīkṣikī*, since they are based on the *Upaniṣads*. Therefore all philosophical scriptures were written during the 800 years between 400 B.C. and A.D. 400.

(*Śrī Krishna-saṁhitā*, Introduction)

12. What are the nine conclusions found in the philosophy of Buddhism?

In the opinion of the Buddhists, there are two ways of understanding philosophy: *Hīnāyāna* and *Mahāyāna*. There are nine conclusions for those who travel through these paths. (1) The universe is beginningless therefore godless. (2) The world is false. (3) The sense of"I" is the only truth. (4) Reincarnation and the next life are real. (5) Lord Buddha is the means of achieving the truth. (6) *Nirvāṇa* is the supreme truth. (7) Buddhism is the only philosophical path. (8) The Vedas are composed by human beings. (9) Following religious principles such as compassion is the way of the Buddhists.

(*Caitanya Caritāmṛta* Madhya 9/49 commentary)

13. Which well-known foreigners followed the six Indian philosophies?

There is no doubt that philosophical literature originated in India. Although there are many kinds of philosophies, they are grossly divided into six categories. These six categories of philosophy are known in India as *ṣaḍ-darśana*. These six philosophies are also widely respected in Greece. Through intensive research, Garbe, who was a professor in Greece, has recently ascertained that Aristotle was the disciple of Gautama's philosophy of *Nyāya*, Thelis was the disciple of *Kaṇāda*'s philosophy of Vaiśeṣika, Sacretis was the disciple of Jaimini's Mīmāṁsā, Pluto was the disciple of Vyāsadeva's *Vedānta*, Pythagoras was the disciple of Kapila's *Sāṅkhya*, and Zino was the disciple of Patañjali's yoga.

(*Sajjana-toṣaṇī* 7/1)

14. Is there any pure spiritual truth in the philosophy of Patañjali?

The state of liberation that was described in the philosophy of Patañjali is a mood of gross and subtle existence, but there is no discussion about spiritual science found in it.

(*Tattva Viveka* 1/23)

15. What is the position of the Yoga-śāstras?

The *yoga-śāstra* is one of the irrelevant positions found among all irrelevant positions between gross matter and pure spiritual truth.

(*Tattva Viveka* 1/23)

16. What is the devotional explanation of the Vedic statement tat tvam asi?

The Māyāvādī commentators say that the Vedic statement *tat tvam asi* concludes that the Supreme Brahman and the living entities are nondifferent. The word *tat* means"He," the word *tvam* means"you," and the word *asi* means"are"; so the words *tat tvam asi* means"you are the Supreme Brahman." There is no difference between you and Him. But the Vaiṣṇava commentators have given different meanings of the word *tat tvam asi*. According to them, the word tat means"He who is infallible" and this word has been derived from the word *tasya* meaning"His." Therefore, the word *tat tvam asi* means"you belong to Him." The word *tasya* makes the distinction between the Supreme Brahman and the living entities. From this, it is concluded that you are not the Supreme Brahman.

(*Tattva-sūtra* 6)

17. Do the compilers of the six philosophies accept Lord Viṣṇu as the Supreme Personality of Godhead? Is Lord Viṣṇu in the mode of material goodness?

Jaimini rejected devotional service, which is the purport of the Vedas, and made the Supreme Lord subordinate to karma. Kapila rejected the true purport of the Vedas and declared that material nature is the cause of the material world. Gautama and *Kaṇāda* stated that the atom is the cause of the material world. In the same way, Māyāvādīs, such as Astavakra, said that the impersonal Brahman is the cause of the material world. The *raja-yogīs*, headed by Patañjali, established their imaginary God to be the Absolute Truth, based on their *Yoga-śāstras*. All these *ācāryas* rejected the Supreme Lord, who is supported by the Vedas, and they established their own idea of God. After carefully discussing and refuting the opinion of these six philosophers, Śrī Vyāsadeva compiled *Vedānta-sūtra*, which establishes the supremacy of the Lord. In the opinion of *Vedānta*, the Supreme Brahman has a *sac-cid-ānanda* form. The impersonalists say that the Supreme Brahman is without qualities and sometimes with material qualities. But actually the Absolute Truth is not only transcendental to the modes of the material nature but He is also the source of unlimited spiritual qualities. His body is purely spiritual. According to other philosophers, no one can achieve Viṣṇu, the supreme cause. In other words, they do not accept Viṣṇu as the cause of all causes. Yet they endeavored to establish their own opinion by refuting the true authorized conclusion.

(*Caitanya Caritāmṛta* Madhya 25/45 — 55, commentary)

33

Cultural Heritage

1. What is the need of history and knowledge of time?

History and knowledge of time are part of *artha-śāstra,* literature that gives material prosperity. If the people of India discuss history and time with reason and argument, they will be greatly benefited. By this process, they can also make spiritual advancement. By mixing the waves of reasoning in the river of ancient belief, moss in the form of illusion will be destroyed and in due course of time, when the bad smell of infamy is removed, the knowledge of the residents of India will become healthy.

(*Śrī Krishna-saṁhitā*)

2. Who built the temple of Śrī Jagannātha? Why Purī is called Nilācala? How old is Purī?

Rāja Anaṅga-bhīma erected the temple about 800 years ago in place of the old temple, which was in a state of dilapidation. In old accounts, we find the former temple was called Nīlādri, the blue hill. It appears that the former temple, which was probably built by the eminent Rāja Indradyumna was blue or a dark color. Otherwise, we cannot account for the name Nilācala, unless the name was taken from the Nīlagiri Hills, which is a small range running through the province from one end to the other. The Utkāla-khaṇḍa in the *Purāṇas*, the Nīlādri Mahodaodhi, and the Matla Panjee (an account regularly kept by the temple officers) declare that Jagannātha is a very ancient Deity among the Hindus. Whatever may be the value of the authorities quoted, we are inclined to believe that Purī was considered sacred even at the time when the *Purāṇas* were written, because we find in Wilson's copy of the *Viṣṇu Purāṇa* that Kaṇḍu Ṛṣi resorted to a place called Puruṣottama for the purpose of divine contemplation. In any case, Rāja Indradyumna, to whom the whole affair is generally ascribed, lived a long time before Raja Vikramāditya, the contemporary of Augustus Caesar of Rome. We are sure that Purī is not as old as Benares and Gayā, which are repeatedly mentioned in all the *Purāṇas* and the *Mahābhārata*, but it is not a place of recent origin, created after the commencement of the Christian era.

(*The Temple of Jagannātha at Purī*, September 15, 1871)

3. According to modern scholars, how many reigns is the history of India divided into?

The modern scholars have divided the history of India into eight periods, as illustrated in the following chart:

	Ruling dynasty's name	Meaning of the name	Years duration of rule	Beginning date
	Prajāpatis	Rule of the sages	50	4463 B.C.
	Manus	Rule of Svāyambhuva Manu and descendants	50	4413
	Demigods	Rule of Indra and other's	100	4363
	Vaivasvata	Rule of Vaivasvata and descendants	3465	4263

(*Śrī Krishna-saṁhitā*, Introduction)

4. When was the Veda written?

During the rule of the *Prajāpatis*, no scriptures were written; there were only a few pleasing words. In the very beginning, *praṇava* was manifested. Written script had not yet been introduced. There was only one syllable with *anusvāra* added to it to produce *oṁ*. When the Manus rule began, other syllables like *tat sat* were introduced. During the rule of the demigods, ancient *mantras* were composed by joining small words together. The performance of sacrifices began at this time. Gradually ancient poetic meters like *Gāyatrī* appeared. Cākṣuṣa Manu was the eighth generation after Svāyambhuva Manu. It is said that Lord Matsya appeared during his reign and delivered the Veda. Perhaps during this time many poetic meters and verses of the Veda were composed, but they were only in sound vibration, not written. They were passed on by hearing. After the Veda had remained in this unwritten state for a long time and the number of verses gradually increased, it became difficult to grasp. Then the sages, headed by Kātyāyana and Āśvalāyana, composed the *sūtras* of the Veda after careful consideration to make memorizing them easier. Still, many other *mantras* were composed after this.

When the one Veda became greatly expanded, then Vyāsadeva, after duly considering the subjects, divided the Veda into four and wrote them in book form. This took place a few years before King Yudhiṣṭhira's reign. Vyāsadeva's disciples then divided those works amongst themselves. Those ṛṣis, who were disciples of Vyāsadeva, divided the four Vedas into different branches so that people could easily study them.

(*Śrī Krishna-saṁhitā*, Introduction)

5. When was the Rāmāyaṇa composed?

Although the *Rāmāyaṇa* is considered poetry, it is also history. Vālmīki Ṛṣi, who was a contemporary of Rāmacandra, wrote it. We do not feel that Vālmīki alone wrote the current *Rāmāyaṇa*. By considering the conversation between Nārada and Vālmīki, and the recitation of the *Rāmāyaṇa* in Rāmacandra's assembly by Lava and Kuśa, it is understood that Vālmīki composed many of the verses glorifying the character of Rāmacandra in the *Rāmāyaṇa*, but after some time another scholar elaborated on Vālmīki's work. I think that the present day *Rāmāyaṇa* was completed after the composition of the *Mahābhārata*, because, while chastising Jābāli, Rāmacandra accuses him of being polluted by the Śakya philosophy. I believe that the present day *Rāmāyaṇa* was written around 500 B.C.

(*Śrī Krishna-saṁhitā*, Introduction)

6. What is the truth concerning the Mahābhārata?

It is said that Vyāsadeva composed the *Mahābhārata*, and there is no objection to this, but it cannot be said that the author of the *Mahābhārata* was the same Vyāsa who divided the Vedas and received the title Vedavyāsa at the time of Yudhiṣṭhira. The reason for this is that in the *Mahābhārata* there are descriptions of kings such as Janamejaya, who ruled after Yudhiṣṭhira. There are specific references about the Manu scriptures in the *Mahābhārata*. Therefore, the present-day *Mahābhārata* must have been written some time after 1000 B.C. It appears that Vedavyāsa first made a draft of the *Mahābhārata*, and later another Vyāsa elaborated on it and presented it under the name *Mahābhārata*.

(*Śrī Krishna-saṁhitā*, Introduction)

7. When was the present Manu-saṁhitā composed?

Manu-saṁhitā is the first and foremost of all *smṛtis*. There is no evidence that the *Manu-saṁhitā* was written during the time of Manu. When Manu became a prominent ruler, the *Prajāpatis* had him establish and live in a city named Barhiṣmatī, just outside Brahmāvarta, so that his sons would be a separate class. From that time, the *Prajāpatis* called themselves *brāhmaṇa*s and accepted the Manus as *kṣatriyas*. In this way, castes other than *brāhmaṇa*s were introduced. Manu also gave due respect to the *brāhmaṇa*s and arranged for the different occupational duties of the different castes with the help of ṛṣis such as Bhṛgu. The ṛṣis approved of Manu's arrangement. At the time, however, the various occupational duties were not written down.

Later, when the *brāhmaṇa*s and *kṣatriyas* fought, Paraśurāma appointed someone from the Bhṛgu dynasty who knew those arrangements, to write everything down inverse. The duties of vaiśyas and śūdras were also included. About 600 years after the battle of Kurukṣetra, the present Manu scriptures were written, with the assistance of another Paraśurāma, whose position was similar to the original Paraśurāma.

(*Śrī Krishna-saṁhitā*, Introduction)

8. What is the history of Buddhism and Jainism?

When the philosophy of Godless secularism was very prominent in India; when the Vedic literature, which is full of transcendental truths, was accepted only as religious literature; when the mundane *brāhmaṇa*s promoted secularism as the path of the Vedas; and when such *brāhmaṇa*s tried to attain sense gratification by performing sacrifices and searching after perpetual happiness and the association of the Apsarās in heaven after their death, at that time Śākyasiṁha established Buddhism. Becoming dissatisfied with material happiness, Śākyasiṁha, who was born in the family of a *kṣatriya*, established the philosophy of Buddhism, whose ultimate goal is the happiness of *nirvāṇa*. There is much evidence that even before Śākyasiṁha, other's preached the philosophy of attaining the happiness of *nirvāṇa*. However, since the time of Śākyasiṁha, this philosophy has been widely accepted, the followers of Buddha have accepted Him as the original preacher of this philosophy.

Before and at the same time as Śākyasiṁha, a scholar named Jin, born in a *vaiśya* family, preached a similar philosophy to that of Buddhism. The name of this philosophy was Jainism. Jainism was confined in India. The philosophy of Buddhism, however, crossed the rivers, mountains, and oceans and spread to countries like China, Tātāra, Shyama, Japan, Burma, and Śrī Lanka.

(*Tattva Viveka*)

9. During whose reign were various texts preached?

Name of scripture	Time when preached
Praṇava [oṁ] Hearing first codes of śrutis	During the reign of the *Prajāpatis*
Hearing the complete śruti and Gāyatrī	During the reign of the Manus, the demigods, and Vaivasvata
Sautra's śrutis	At the beginning of the reign of Vaivasvata
Manu's *smṛtis*	During the second half of the reign of Vaivasvata

(*Śrī Krishna-saṁhitā*, Introduction)

10. When did Śaṅkarācārya appear?

The holy places of the Āryans were converted into holy places for Buddhists. All signs of brahminical culture practically disappeared. In the seventh century, when this tragedy was no longer tolerable, the *brāhmaṇas* became very angry and conspired to destroy Buddhism. At that time, by providence, the most learned and intelligent Śaṅkarācārya became the commander-in-chief of the *brāhmaṇas* in Kāśī. By discussing his activities, it appears that he was an incarnation of Paraśurāma.

(*Śrī Krishna-saṁhitā*, Introduction)

11. How did India benefit from the appearance of Śaṅkarācārya?

Śaṅkarācārya has, to some extent, done a favor to India by evicting Buddhism. He helped stop the gradual deterioration of the ancient Āryan community. In particular, he changed the course of the Āryans' mentality by introducing a new method of thought in their scriptures. He even inspired in them an urge to consider new subjects with their intelligence.

(*Śrī Krishna-saṁhitā*, Introduction)

12. When did other civilizations of the world worship the Indians as the king, as the giver of punishment, and as the spiritual master?

When real culture was present at that time, the fame of India was brightly shining like the midday sun. All castes and civilizations worshiped the Indians as the king, as the giver of the punishment, and as the spiritual master. The people of Egypt, China, and other countries accepted instructions from Indians with awe and reverence.

(*Caitanya-śikṣāmṛta* 2/3)

13. Which is the most ancient country? Which is the oldest civilization? Which is the most ancient religion? And when was that religion at its peak?

India is the oldest civilized country. The followers of all accept this fact. Even though proud people of the Western countries believe that theirs is a civilization older than the Āryan civilization, the fact will remain true forever. The Āryans first lived in India. This has been proven during the time of the *Prajāpatis*, who were the sons of Brahmā. Kaśyapa was a *Prajāpati*. His grandson was Prahlāda,"the crest jewel among all the Vaiṣṇavas." Dhruva Mahārāja, the grandson of Manu, was also mentioned as a topmost Vaiṣṇava. Among the first sons of Brahmā, the four Kumāras and Nārada Muni were also great Vaiṣṇavas. Therefore, there is no religion older than Vaiṣṇava *dharma* in the world. While increasing gradually, this Vaiṣṇava religion reached its peak and perfection during the time of Mahāprabhu Caitanyadeva.

(*Sajjana Toṣanī* 2/9)

14. Who taught the process of preserving dead bodies? Why was this process followed?

In the *Chāndogya Upaniṣad* is the story of Indra and Virocana learning spiritual truth from *Prajāpati*. It clearly states that due to his gross mentality, like that of a *mleccha*, Virocana considered his material body to be himself and he taught his students how to preserve the body after death. Perhaps, according to his teachings, his Egyptian disciples taught the custom of mummifying or preserving dead bodies in their own country. Based on this custom, the system of burying dead bodies was spread to other *mleccha* countries.

(*Sajjana-toṣaṇī* 7/1)

15. When did keen and powerful intelligence exist in South India?

From the seventh century, keen and powerful intelligence was found among the people of South India—and nowhere else. From that time, Śaṅkarācārya, Śaṭhakopa, Yāmunācārya, Rāmānuja, Viṣṇusvāmī, Madhvācārya, and many other great learned scholars appeared like shining stars in the southern sky.

(*Śrī Krishna-saṁhitā*, Introduction)

16. In which philosophy did Viṣṇusvāmī, Nimbāditya, and Madhvācārya write their Vedānta-sūtra commentaries?

Viṣṇusvāmī, Nimbārka, and Madhvācārya wrote their own commentaries on *Vedānta*, following in the footsteps of Śaṅkarācārya. In this way, they introduced slight variations of the Vaiṣṇava principles.

(*Śrī Krishna-saṁhitā*, Introduction)

17. When did the authorized Vaiṣṇava ācāryas begin to write commentaries on the four writings such as Vedānta?

Like Śaṅkarācārya, they also wrote commentaries on the *Bhagavad-gītā*, *Viṣṇu-sahasra-nāma*, and *Upaniṣads*. At that time, a thought arose in the hearts of people that one must have commentaries on the four above-mentioned works to establish a *sampradāya*. From these four Vaiṣṇavas[Madhva, Rāmānuja, Viṣṇusvāmī, Nimbārka], the four Vaiṣṇava *sampradāyas*, such as the Śrī-sampradāya, were introduced.

(*Śrī Krishna-saṁhitā*, Introduction)

18. Which contemporary and later associates of Śrīmān Mahāprabhu preached His philosophy?

Śrī Caitanya Mahāprabhu, with the help of Nityānanda and Advaita, clearly explained the truth regarding one's relationship with the Lord. Through Rūpa, Sanātana, Jīva, Gopāla Bhaṭṭa, the two Raghunāthas, Rāmānanda Rāya, Svarūpa Dāmodara, and Sārvabhauma Bhaṭṭācārya, He clearly explained the truth of the living entity's relationship with the Lord. He strengthened the process of acting in that relationship by establishing the supremacy of performing *kīrtana*. Regarding the goal of life, He ascertained the simple means of relishing the mellows of Vraja.

(*Śrī Krishna-saṁhitā*, Introduction)

19. What is the history of the three methods of singing: Manohara Sāhī, Garāṇhāty, and Regeti?

Śrīnivāsācārya Prabhu made Katwa and its adjoining places glorious. His place was under the subdivision of Manohara Sāhī. Therefore, the method of singing inaugurated by him was known as Manohara Sāhī. Śrī Narottama dāsa was a resident of the village Kheturi, which is in Gaḍerhāta or Garāṇhāty in the district of Rājasāhī. Therefore, the method of singing his songs is known as Garāṇhāty. Śrī Śyāmānanda Prabhu was from Midnapur District. The method of singing his songs is called Regeti. To encourage these great singers, Śrī Jīva Goswami awarded Śrīnivāsācarya the title "Prabhu," Śrī Narottama the title "Ṭhākura," and Śrī Śyāmānanda the title "Prabhu." Śrī Jīva Goswami was very magnanimous and saw only good qualities in other's. Śrīnivāsācārya Prabhu was a *brāhmaṇa* and therefore Śrī Jīva Goswami had no hesitation in awarding him the title "Prabhu."

(*Sajjana-toṣaṇī* 6/2)

20. What is the history of Guṇarāja Khān (Mālādhara Vasu)?

The poet Guṇarāja Khān began to write his book *Śrī Krishna Vijaya* in 1395 Śaka Era and completed it in 1402 Śaka Era. Although Chandi dāsa and Vidyāpati Ṭhākura composed something in Bengali before this, they did not compose any poetry. We can only see a few songs composed by them. We have not seen any poetry written in Bengali before 1400 Śaka Era. As the people of Britain show great respect to Chaucer, similarly we show respect to Guṇarāja Khān for his poetry. Any Bengali library is incomplete without the book *Śrī Krishna Vijaya*. Moreover, this book is extremely respected by the devotees. Śrī Guṇarāja Khān, a most respected Vaiṣṇava, compiled this book as the translation of the Tenth and the Eleventh Cantos of *Śrīmad-Bhāgavatam*, the crest jewel among all literature. Therefore, we are unable to describe the wonderful glories of this book here. This book is worshipable by all Vaiṣṇavas. After studying this book, Śrī Mahāprabhu glorified it in such a way that it will draw much respect from the Gauḍīya Vaiṣṇava society.

Not finding any qualified *brāhmaṇa*s in Bengal, which was polluted by Buddhism, the King of Bengal, Ādiśūra, arranged to bring five qualified *brāhmaṇa*s and five qualified kāyasthas from Kānyakubja. Among those five *kāyasthas*, Daśaratha Vasu, a civilized and simple-minded person, came to Gauḍa-deśa. Śrī Guṇarāja Khān appeared in that dynasty as the thirteenth descendent from Daśaratha Vasu. Guṇarāja Khān's actual name was Mālādhara Basu. The King of Bengal awarded the title"Guṇarāja Khān" to him. He had fourteen sons; among them the second son, Lakṣmīnātha, was awarded the title "Satyarāja Khān." His son, Śrī Rāmānanda Vasu was an associate of Śrīmān Mahāprabhu. Rāmānanda Vasu was thus the fifteenth descendent from Daśaratha Vasu. After extensive research at the village of Kulīna-grāma, we have collected this information from the house of the Vasu's during the winter of 1885. There we discovered that Śrī Mālādhara Vasu Mahāśaya was a rich and famous person. By seeing his palace and temple room, it appears that his kingdom was very prosperous.

(*Śrī Krishna Vijaya*, Introduction)

21. What is the history of the ativāḍī-sampradāya and Viṣa Kiṣana?

Jagannātha dāsa had a group of followers in Orissa. They were known as *ativāḍīs*. By the order of Mahāprabhu, Jagannātha dāsa became a follower of Haridāsa Ṭhākura. Later, when he gave up pure devotional service and took shelter of Māyāvāda philosophy, Mahāprabhu rejected him, saying he was an ativāḍī. The sect of *ativāḍī* was expanded like the *bāulas* of Bengal. The *ativāḍīs* have some false literature, which states that Lord Caitanya will manifest again. On this pretext, a few wicked persons began to pose themselves as Caitanya, Brahmā, Baladeva, Krishna, and so on.

Having obtained some mystic power, an imposter named Viṣa Kiṣana began to promote himself as Mahā-Viṣṇu. He and his followers constructed a temple in the jungle, two miles from Sardāipur. It was written on the beads of the followers of *ativāḍī* that Mahā-Viṣṇu Viṣa Kiṣana remains incognito and on 14 March, he will manifest himself and display his four arms of Mahā-Viṣṇu. As soon as this news spread, many *brāhmaṇa* women began to serve him, neglecting the prohibition of their husbands.

When some illicit affairs between Viṣa Kiṣana and the wives of the Choudhary's of Bhrangārapura surfaced, then the people of Bhrangārapura reported this to the Revered Walten Sahib, who was the commissioner of Bhrangārapura. He advised me to go to the jungle and investigate the matter. I went there at night and after a long conversation with that "Mahā-Viṣṇu," I concluded that he was determined to destroy the British Rule. After returning to Purī, the trial of "Mahā-Viṣṇu" began in my court. After a long trial and hearing, I awarded him the punishment of one and half years in prison. When his matted hair was cut, his worshipers and followers abandoned him as a cheater.

(*Autobiography of Śrī Bhaktivinoda Ṭhākura*)

22. What brief information did Śrī Bhaktivinoda Ṭhākura give regarding Śrī Māyāpura, the birth place of Śrī Gaurasundara?

After carefully researching and going through various authentic books, such as *Śrī Caitanya Bhāgavata*, we have discovered many places of the Lord's pastimes. We have resolved to gradually find all the places of the Lord's pastimes for the pleasure of the devotees. First, we are locating the exact place of Mahāprabhu's village. Śrī Kavi-karṇapūra has written that the land of Navadvīpa is surrounded by the Ganges. This is also mentioned in the tantras. The actual name of the River Khaḍiyā which flows by Goyāḍi and mixes with the Ganges near Svarupaganj is Bāgdevī or Jalangi. Long, long ago, the River Bāgdevī flowed by the village Hariśpura and after mixing with the River Mandākinī, it flowed near Devapallī. Thereafter, touching the city of Bhālukā, this river mixed with the Ganges near Goyālpāḍā. When the Mandākinī portion of the Ganges dried up, the Bāgdevi reached the Ganges, while flowing by the side of Māyāpura. Because of the confluence of Bāgdevī and the Ganges, many parts of Śrī Māyāpura were destroyed. At that time, the homeless learned *brāhmaṇa*s of Māyāpura took Śrī Prouḍhā Māyā and Vriddha Śiva across the Ganges to the village Kuliyā, which is the present-day city of Navadvīpa.

In this village, there are no places of Mahāprabhu's pastimes. However, this place is the forest of Vṛndāvana within Navadvīpa. The map that we have provided in the book *Śrī Navadvīpa-dhāma-māhātmya* shows that there is a *cakra* in the middle. The entire tract of land, which covers this cakra, is called Antardvīpa. Only two tiny portions of land have extended to the other side of the Ganges. During the time of Śrī Mahāprabhu, Māyāpura village was certainly the home of learned *brāhmaṇa*s, but because of the movement of the River Bāgdevī, it has almost become ruined. Only one portion of Māyāpura is inhabited by human beings. This portion is situated in the southern corner of Ballāladhīgi.

After intensive research and according to some confidential hint, we have been able to locate the exact stream of the Ganges. A long stream called Śivera Dobā or the pond of Śiva near Khaḍvana, which lies to the south of Māyāpura, is still present. If one stands on the bank of this stream and looks towards Gaṅganagāra, one can see that a tract of land resembling the bank of a river is by the side of Māyāpura. Let us consider the exact location that we find in the description of Śrī Vṛndāvana dāsa Ṭhākura. "In Nadia, Lord Gaurāṅga first went through the road that led to the Ganges, while He danced. He came to His own bathing ghāṭa and after dancing there for a long time, He went to Mādhāi's *ghāṭa*. From there, Gaura Hari went to Bārakoṇā-ghāṭa and then He went to Nāgariyā-ghāṭa. From there, the Lord went to Simuliyā through Ganganagara."

Now the point is, if one walks to the bank of the Ganges, Bārakoṇā-ghāṭa and Nāgariyā-ghāṭa are not very far. The Nāgariyā-ghāṭa was situated near the main market in ancient Nadia. In addition, this market was situated on the western side of Ballāladhīgi. There is no doubt that if the devotees search for Śrī Māyāpura, the birthplace of Mahāprabhu and His places of pastimes, after carefully considering all these topics, they will certainly find those places. The Vaiṣṇavas who live in the cottages on the alluvial land of Kuliyā do not endeavor to know anything in this regard. Hence, the visiting devotees face so much difficulty.

(*Viṣṇupriyā Pallī Magazine*)

23. What is the proof that the present municipal city of Navadvīpa was previously Koladvīpa?

There are quite a few villages called Kuliyā situated in different parts of Bengal. However, the village of Kuliyā that we are discussing right now is a matchless place in the whole world; history has described this Kuliyā with great respect. The name of this Kuliyā is Śrīpāta Kuliyā. At this place, Śrīmad Gaurāṅga Prabhu, who incarnated to purify the age of Kali, resided for seven days, punished a great offender named Gopāla Cāpāla, and thereby forgave the offenses of a teacher who lived at Śrī

Navadvīpa. Here, the Lord pardoned the offenses committed against the devotees by a learned *Śrīmad-Bhāgavatam* reciter, Devānanda Paṇḍita, who was a resident of Maheśvara Viśārada's mound. At this place, Śrīmān Mahāprabhu mercifully delivered Kṛṣṇānanda, who was expert in tantras, from his offenses against the Vaiṣṇavas and cured him of his disease. What better method can there be in determining the exact location of the holy place Kuliyā, than discussing the literature composed by the learned scholars who were contemporaries of Mahāprabhu?

In a small village, three miles east of Kumārahaṭṭa, the Kuliyā-pātera-melā was set up a few years ago. Many people from Calcutta participate in the melā every year during January. For this reason when we speak of Kuliyā in front of ordinary people, they think that Kuliyā is the place where the melā is held. Actually, Kuliyā, the place where the Lord forgave the offenses of Devānanda is mentioned in *Śrī Caitanya Bhāgavata*, *Śrī Caitanya Caritāmṛta*, *Śrī Caitanya Maṅgala*, *Śrī Caitanya-candrodaya-nāṭaka*, *Śrī Caitanya-carita-mahākāvya*, and in the commentary on *Candrodaya* by Premadāsa Bābājī. This Kuliyā must be present within the thirty-two-mile circle of Śrī Navadvīpa. *Śrī Caitanya Bhāgavata* Antya-khaṇḍa, Chapter Three states: "As soon as the Lord, the crest jewel among the *sannyāsīs* came to Kuliyā, a tumultuous sound vibrated on all directions. Only the Ganges divides Nadia and Kuliyā. On hearing of the Lord's arrival, everyone came running. The people from Vācaspati's village were soon multiplied by millions. Soon after, Vācaspati also came there."

Elsewhere in the same book is the description:"Sometimes, during His stay at Navadvīpa, Nityānanda Prabhu went to Khālāchaḍā, Baḍagāchi, and Dogāchiyā, and sometimes the Lord went to Kuliyā, which is situated on the other side of the Ganges."

Caitanya Caritāmṛta Madhya-līlā, Chapter One Text 153—154 describes:

kuliyā-grāme kaila devānandere
prasāda gopāla-viprere kṣamāila
śrīvāsāparādha pāṣaṇḍī nindaka āsi 'paḍilā
caraṇe aparādha kṣami 'tāre dila kṛṣṇa-preme

"The Lord bestowed mercy on Devānanda in the village of Kuliyā. He also forgave the offenses of the *brāhmaṇa* Gopāla, which he committed against Śrīvasa Paṇḍita. When Gopāla came and fell at the Lord's feet, the Lord forgave his offenses and bestowed upon him love of Krishna."

In his *Caitanya Caritāmṛta*, Śrī Kavirāja Goswami did not elaborate on Mahāprabhu's arrival at Kuliyā. Therefore, to understand the exact location of Kuliyā from his descriptions is difficult unless one is thoughtful. In Madhya-līlā, Chapter Sixteen, he wrote that the Lord went to Kumārahaṭṭa from the house of Rāghava Paṇḍita at Pānihāṭi and after giving *darśana* to Śrīvāsa Paṇḍita, He went to Kāñcanapallī. There He visited the houses of Śivānanda Sena and Vāsudeva Datta and then went to the house of Vācaspati. We will show later that Vācaspati's house is in Vidyānagara. To avoid the huge crowd, the Lord left the house of Vācaspati, went to the house of Mādhava dāsa in Kuliyā, and stayed there for seven days. Then the Lord went to Śāntipura and from there to Rāmakeli. In his description, Śrī Kavirāja Goswami has not given the proper order of the places; he wrote:"The Lord stayed at Śāntipura for ten days. This has been elaborately described by Vṛndāvana dāsa Ṭhākura. Therefore I am not describing this elaborately, because it would be redundant and the book would be voluminous." Thus, we can clearly understand that Kavirāja Goswami has not described all the topics in the proper order. He fully depended on the description of Vṛndāvana dāsa Ṭhākura.

Śrī Caitanya Maṅgala states:

gaṅga snāna kari prabhu rāḍadeśa
diyā krame krame uṭṭarilā nagara
kuliyā purvāśrama dekhivena sannyāsera
dharma navadvīpa āilā prabhu ei tāra
marma māyera bacane punaḥ gelā
navadvīpa bārakonā ghāṭa nija bāḍīra samīpa

"After taking bath in the western side of the Ganges, the Lord gradually arrived at Kuliyā. The duty of a *sannyāsī* is to visit his birthplace after taking *sannyāsa*. With this in mind and on the order of His mother, the Lord again went to Navadvīpa. He went through Bārakoṇā-ghāṭa and arrived at His house."

From this description, we can clearly understand that the Kuliyā village is situated within Navadvīpa-maṇḍala and on the opposite side of the Ganges is Māyāpura, where the Lord took birth. The Lord's house is situated near Bārakoṇā-ghāṭa.

Moreover, the village Sātakuliyā is also situated on the eastern side of the Ganges about seven or eight miles away from ancient Navadvīpa. This village is also not the place where the offenses where nullified; there is no hearsay that Sātakuliyā was ever a city or that influential people ever lived there. We have to accept therefore that Kuliyā is a village situated on the western bank of the Ganges opposite Navadvīpa. Perhaps due to the changes of the Ganges flow, the major portion of Kuliyā has been destroyed; still there is no doubt that some hearsay identify it.

We can see that the house of Vidyā Vācaspati was not far from Kuliyā, because as soon as Vācaspati heard that Mahāprabhu had arrived at the village of Kuliyā, he reached there immediately and did not have to cross the Ganges. Therefore, we can understand that Kuliyā and Vidyānagara are situated on the same side of the Ganges and are one or two miles apart. Now we should find out where Vidyā Vācaspati's house is. *Śrī Caitanya Bhāgavata* says that Vidyā Vācaspati was Sārvabhauma's brother. *Śrī Caitanya Bhāgavata* Madhya-khaṇḍa, Chapter 21 states:"In this way, Lord Viśvambhara constantly enjoyed His pastimes in the association of Nityānanda Prabhu and Gadādhara. One day the Lord went out to visit the city accompanied by his devotees. Lord Viśvambhara went to the mound of Maheśvara Viśārada, the father of Sārvabhauma. At that place lived Devānanda Paṇḍita who was a most peaceful *brāhmaṇa*, desiring liberation."

From this description we can understand that Maheśvara Viśārada was the father of Sārvabhauma and Vidyā Vācaspati. Near the mound on which the house and school of Maheśvara Viśārada stood was the house and *Bhāgavata* school of Devānanda Paṇḍita. At that time, the Ganges flowed near Mahātpur or Mātāpur. From there she touched villages like Maugāchi and Jānnangar and went toward Gaṅgānagara, keeping Viśārada's mound on her western bank. From there she flowed southwest near Śrī Māyāpura and after keeping Kuliyā on her western bank she flowed south.

Long before the advent of Śrīmān Mahāprabhu, the Ganges used to flow by the western side of Kuliyā toward the south. During the time of Maheśvara Viśārada, this flow of the Ganges dried up. Although that part of the river dried up, still that piece of land is filled with water, kuśa grass, and thorns even today. Since it was impossible to reside there during the rainy reason, a few learned *brāhmaṇa*s built a raised platform of mud, which they brought from the other side of Navadvīpa. Thereafter they established a village on the mound and named it Vidyānagara. To go to Viśārada's mound from ancient Navadvīpa, one had to walk by the bank of the Ganges via Gaṅgānagara, Ātapapur, and Deowan Bazār ghāṭa. After crossing the ghāṭa, one had to walk through thorny bushes to reach the mound. There is much evidence that Vidyā Vācaspati's house was situated at Vidyānagara. To go to Viśārada's mound from Navadvīpa people had to walk through forests, bushes, water, and thorns, but this was not the case to get to Kuliyā. To go to Kuliyā from ancient Navadvīpa, one had to simply cross the Ganges. Although the village of Vidyānagara was previously known as"the mound of Viśārada," still we assume that it became known as Vidyānagara because of the glories of Vidyā Vācaspati.

Even today, there is a place called Kuliyā-grāma situated on the western bank of the Ganges. Some people call this place Kolera Gañja. Many parts of the village have been destroyed. Because of the change in the flow of the Ganges, the western part of ancient Navadvīpa has merged with Kuliyā. As a result, a major portion of Kuliyā has merged with Navadvīpa and become one. We have many more things to say regarding this change, which we will discuss later. There were two villages, Kuliyā and Pāhāḍapura, situated next to each other. There is no doubt that this village of Kuliyā is the present-day Navadvīpa, and we do not hesitate to declare Navadvīpa is the ancient place of Kuliyā, the place of Devānanda Paṇḍita, and the place where the Lord pardoned his offenses.

(*Sajjana-toṣaṇī* 7/2)

24. When and where was the Viśva-vaiṣṇava Rāja-sabhā first established? What is the goal of this sabhā?

The Viśva-vaiṣṇava Rāja-sabhā was established in Calcutta in 399 Śrī Caitanya Era in April. The goal of the society is to improve the Vaiṣṇava religion in various ways. The goal and rules of this society were written in a *Viśva-vaiṣṇava* brochure. Under the guidance of this *sabhā*, various pictures of the pastimes of the Lord have been painted. A Vaiṣṇava trust has also been established. Because of a lack of funds, we have yet to establish an assembly hall, a temple of Lord Caitanya, and a printing press, but we have no doubt that soon Mahāprabhu will arrange for all these.

(*Sajjana-toṣaṇī* 2/1)

25. When were the Viśva-vaiṣṇava Rāja-sabhā and the Vaiṣṇava-sabhā merged?

A centre for the Viśva-vaiṣṇava Rāja-sabhā has been constructed in Sarkār Lane, Kāṇsāripārā, and Calcutta. A huge conference for this *sabhā* was held on the last Saturday in July, and the resolutions of the *sabhā* were published in the daily newspaper after a few days. Under the care of the General Secretary, Śrī Lāl Mohan Dutta, the activities of the *sabhā* went on smoothly. It was written that the Bhāratvarṣiya Hari *sādhana* Samāj and the Vaiṣṇava-sabhā have merged with the Viśva-vaiṣṇava Rāja-sabhā. But as far as we know, the Vaiṣṇava-sabhā has not merged completely. Although the Vaiṣṇava-sabhā is very eager to benefit the *sabhā*, it will not merge fully with the Viśva-vaiṣṇava Rāja-sabhā unless it approves of the activities of that *sabhā* for some time. Moreover the Vaiṣṇava-sabhā has been established for one year and it will continue to maintain its separate identity until the Viśva-vaiṣṇava Rāja-sabhā is established. Because the goal and activities of both *sabhās* are the same, the Viśva-vaiṣṇava Rāja-sabhā will soon merge with its parent *sabhā*, the Vaiṣṇava-sabhā.

(*Sajjana-toṣaṇī* 2/3)

34

Vedic Literature

1. Which are the principal śāstras?

The eleven *Upaniṣads*: *Īśa*, *Kena*, *Kaṭha*, *Praśna*, *Muṇḍaka*, *Māṇḍūkya*, *Taittirīya*, *Aitareya*, *Chāndogya*, *Bṛhad-āraṇyaka*, and *Śvetāśvatara*, which are the crest jewel of the Vedas, as well as the *Brahma-sūtra* [*Vedānta-sūtra*], which consists of four chapters and sixteen divisions, are the principal *śāstras* among all *śāstras*.

(*Caitanya Caritāmṛta* Ādi 7/108)

2. Is the purpose of the Vedas to attain Brahman?

The *Upaniṣads*, the *Brahma-sūtra*, and the *Bhagavad-gītā* are pure devotional literature. According to necessity, discussions about karma, *jñāna*, *mukti*, and Brahman are found at particular places, but in the conclusion, nothing other than pure devotional service has been instructed.

(*Bhagavad-gītā*, Introduction)

3. Are the Atharva-veda and Bṛhad-āraṇyaka Upaniṣad modern? What is Jaimini's conclusion?

The *Ṛg*, *Sāma*, and *Yajur* Vedas are the most widely respected. The *Muṇḍaka Upaniṣad* states: *tasmād ṛcaḥ sāma yajūṁṣi,*"The *mantras* of the *Ṛg*, *Sāma*, and *Yajur Vedas* emanated from the Supreme Lord." It seems that all the ancient verses were compiled in these three Vedas. However, we cannot neglect the *Atharva Veda* or consider it modern. In the *Bṛhad-āraṇyaka Upaniṣad* (4.5.11) the following verse is found:

asya mahato bhūtasya niśvasitam etad yad ṛg-vedo yajur-vedaḥ
sāma-vedo 'tharvāṅgirasa itihāsaḥ purāṇaṁ vidyā upaniṣadaḥ ślokāḥ
sūtrānyānuvyākhyānānyasyai vaitāni sarvāṇi niśvasitāni

"The Ṛg, Yajur, Sāma, and Atharva Vedas, the Itihāsas or histories, the Purāṇas, the Upaniṣads, the ślokas or mantras chanted by the brāhmaṇas, the sūtras or Vedic statements, vidyā or transcendental knowledge, and the explanations of the sūtras and mantras are all emanations from the breathing of the great Personality of Godhead."

The *Bṛhad-āraṇyaka* cannot be considered modern, because it was composed before the writings of Vyāsadeva. The above-mentioned verse describes that the Itihāsas and *Purāṇas*, which are both Vedic literature, contain ancient topics similar to those found in the Vedas.

Jaimini Ṛṣi presented arguments to establish that the Vedas are for the eternal benefit of the neophytes. Swanlike personalities should accept the purport of swanlike Jaimini's teachings. The purport of his teachings is as follows: All truths discovered are related to the Supreme Lord and are therefore eternal. Those who describe the Vedic truths as temporary by citing the examples of kikaṭa (low-class residents of the province of Gaya, Bihar, mentioned in the *Ṛg Veda* 3.53.14), *naicasaka* (low-class persons, mentioned in the same verse), and *pramaṅgada* (low-class sons of money lenders, also mentioned in the same verse) are not aspiring to understand the truth. This is Jaimini's conclusion.

(*Śrī Krishna-saṁhitā*, Introduction)

4. What have the ācāryas accepted as Vedic literature?

The *ācāryas* have accepted the following as Vedic literature: eleven *Upaniṣads* (*Īśa, Kena, Kaṭha, Praśna, Muṇḍaka, Māṇḍūkya, Taittirīya, Aitareya, Chāndogya, Bṛhad-āraṇyaka,* and *Śvetāśvatara*), which are full of spiritual knowledge; a few *tāpanīs* (such as *Gopāla-tāpanī* and *Nṛsiṁha-tāpanī*), which help one to worship the Lord; and the four Vedas (*Ṛg, Sāma, Yajur, and Atharva*), which are divided into *brāhmaṇa*s and *maṅgalas*. Since these scriptures have been received through disciplic succession, they are authentic Vedic literature.

(*Jaiva Dharma*, Chapter 13)

35

Vedānta-sūtra

1. What is the characteristic of Vedānta-sūtra?

Greatly learned scholars, who have appeared in India just like the stars and illuminated the entire world, have praised the *Brahma-sūtra* profusely. The *ācāryas* of the *jñānī* community headed by Śrīmat Śaṅkarācārya and the *ācāryas* of the devotee community headed by Śrīmat Rāmānujācārya have established their respective philosophy based on the *Brahma-sūtra*. What to speak of this, any community which has not composed a commentary on the *Brahma-sūtra* is not highly regarded in India. The definition of the *Brahma-sūtra* is as follows;"Although the statements of the *Upaniṣads* consist of all knowledge, they are incomprehensible." To understand the meaning of one statement in relation to another statement is difficult. For a student to understand truth by studying the *Upaniṣads* is extremely hard. One can never understand the actual meaning of the *Upaniṣads* without the guidance of a bona fide spiritual master. The *Upaniṣads* are the head of Vedic literature. They consist of knowledge regarding the soul and the duty of the living entities.

One cannot become successful in human life if one does not realize the meaning of the *Upaniṣads*. After contemplating on this point, Lord Vyāsadeva wrote the *Brahma-sūtra* by dividing the statements of the *Upaniṣads*. The *Brahma-sūtra* is not simply a philosophy like *Sāṅkhya*, *Patañjala*, *Nyāya*, *Vaiśeṣika*, and *Pūrva-mīmāṁsā*, but it is spiritual literature that properly establishes the purport of the *Upaniṣads*, which are the head of the Vedas. Hence, everyone worships it. Those who desire to accumulate spiritual knowledge should study *Brahma-sūtra* and not labor hard to study other scriptures.

It is not easy for a person to understand the true meaning of the *Brahma-sūtra*. It is not that simply by studying the *sūtras* one will understand the meaning. Without the help of the commentary on the *sūtras*, the meaning cannot be understood. Therefore, one will achieve spiritual knowledge if one learns the meaning of the *sūtras* from a bona fide spiritual master. Now the difficult question is where can we get a proper commentary on the *sūtras* or where can we find a bona fide spiritual master who is expert in explaining the meaning of the *sūtras*.

The commentary on *Brahma-sūtra* written by the sage Baudhāyana is almost extinct. With utmost care, Śrī Rāmānuja Svāmī collected that commentary from Sāradā-pīṭha and thereafter wrote his own commentary on *Brahma-sūtra* known as *Śrī-bhāṣya*. This description is found in a Sanskrit book, *Prapannāmṛta*. Sāradā-pīṭha was the place of Śrī Śaṅkarācārya. There is no doubt that Śaṅkara Svāmī kept the commentary of Baudhāyana with great care in his *maṭha*. Śaṅkara Svāmī, the direct incarnation of Rudra, composed the *Śārīraka-bhāṣya* on *Brahma-sūtra* to carry out his own work. It is said that to spread his own commentary Śaṅkarācārya hid the commentary of Baudhāyana.

(*Sajjana-toṣaṇī* 8/1)

2. Which is the genuine commentary on Brahma-sūtra? What is the main reason behind Śaṅkarācārya's hiding the Śrīmad-Bhāgavatam and the commentary of Baudhāyana?

Vedavyāsa is the compiler of the *Brahma-sūtra*. After composing the *sūtras*, he thought,"The purpose for which I composed these *sūtras*, by extracting the meaning of the *Upaniṣads*, has not become successful. Unless I personally compose a commentary, the *sūtras* will not be understood." When he was contemplating in this way, Nārada Muni appeared and instructed him to compose a commentary. Thus, Vyāsadeva wrote a commentary on *Brahma-sūtra* called the *Śrīmad-Bhāgavatam*. These events are described in many *Purāṇas*.

Although *Śrīmad-Bhāgavata Mahāpurāṇa* is the genuine commentary of *Brahma-sūtra*, still by the order of his spiritual master, the great sage Baudhāyana compiled a commentary on *Brahma-sūtra*. Therefore, there were two commentaries on the *Brahma-sūtra* available in the world. To carry on with his work in following the order of the Lord, Śrī Śaṅkara Svāmi wrote a commentary on *Brahma-sūtra* called Māyāvāda-bhāṣya and tried his best to conceal both the commentaries as explained above.

(*Sajjana-toṣaṇī* 8/1)

3. How many divisions does the Brahma-sūtra have and what do they establish?

The *Brahma-sūtra* is divided into four chapters. Each chapter is further divided into four parts. The first chapter of *Brahma-sūtra* describes that all the Vedas are in perfect harmony with the Supreme Brahman, the second chapter describes that the scriptures do not contradict each other, the third chapter describes the process for attaining Brahman, and fourth chapter describes that attaining Brahman is the ultimate goal of life.

Living entities who are faithful, peaceful, pure-hearted, self-controlled, free from material desires, and greedy to associate with saintly persons are qualified to study this scripture. This scripture gives knowledge, and that knowledge is about the Supreme Brahman; therefore, this scripture and the Supreme Brahman are related to each other. This scripture establishes that Śrī Krishna is the Supreme Personality of Godhead; He is pure, eternal, flawless, and full of bliss, knowledge, unlimited qualities, and inconceivable potencies. The goal of this scripture is to remove the unlimited faults of the living entities and help them meet the Supreme Lord.

There are five branches of knowledge in this scripture: *viṣaya*, *saṁśaya*, *pūrva-pakṣa*, *siddhānta* or *sangati*, and *nyāya*. *Nyāya* is a particular portion of each chapter, *viṣaya* are statements for consideration, *saṁśaya* discuss doubts, *pūrva-pakṣa* discusses opposing arguments, and *siddhānta* is the authentic conclusion.

(*Sajjana-toṣaṇī* 8/1)

4. What philosophical conclusions have the ācāryas preached based on the Brahma-sūtra?

The statements of the *Upaniṣads* are called *Vedānta*. To properly explain the *Vedānta*, Śrī Vedavyāsa divided it into four chapters and composed *sūtras* called the *Brahma-sūtra* or the *Vedānta-sūtra*. The *Vedānta-sūtra* has been widely respected by the intellectual people of the world. The simple conclusion is that the instructions found in the *Vedānta-sūtra* are the true purport of the Vedas. Different *ācāryas* have extracted different conclusions from the *Vedānta-sūtra*, which nourish their own philosophies.

Śrī Śaṅkarācārya preached the philosophy of *vivarta-vāda* from these *sūtras*. He said that Brahman becomes transformed and is no longer Brahman, and so the philosophy of *pariṇāma-vāda* [the theory of transformation] is not proper, but the philosophy of *vivarta-vāda* is certainly proper. Another name of *vivarta-vāda* is Māyāvāda. He gathered necessary Vedic *mantras* and nourished his philosophy of *vivarta-vāda*. From this, it appears that the philosophy of *pariṇāma-vāda* was current a long time ago. By establishing the philosophy of *vivarta-vāda*, Śrī Śaṅkara suppressed the philosophy of *pariṇāma-vāda*.

Vivarta-vāda is a theory; not being satisfied with this theory, Śrīmān Madhvācārya established *dvaita-vāda* with the support of Vedic *mantras*.

In the same way, with the support of Vedic *mantras*, Śrīmad Rāmānujācārya established the philosophy of *viśiṣṭādvaita-vāda*, Śrī Nimbādityācārya established the philosophy of *dvaitādvaita-vāda*, and Śrī Viṣṇu Svāmī established the philosophy of *suddhādvaita-vāda.*

The Māyāvāda philosophy preached by Śrī Śaṅkarācārya is totally opposed to the science of devotional service. In spite of establishing and propagating separate philosophies, the conclusions of the four Vaiṣṇava *ācāryas* are in accordance with devotional service. Śrīmān Mahāprabhu extracted the conclusion of all Vedic statements while respecting the philosophies of the four Vaiṣṇava *ācāryas* and taught that philosophy to His followers. The name of His philosophy is *acintya-bhedābheda-tattva.* Even though He accepted the *sampradāya* of Śrīmān Madhvācārya, He only accepted the essence of Madhavācārya's philosophy.

(*Jaiva Dharma*, Chapter 18)

5. Is Vedānta, impersonal knowledge?

In all respects *Vedānta* is philosophy that aims at devotional service to the Lord.

(*Tattva Vīveka*)

6. How did the commentaries on Vedānta develop and who discovered the science of mādhurya-rāsa?

After collecting Baudhāyana's commentary on the *Vedānta-sūtra*, Śrī Rāmānuja, who was an incarnation of Saṅkarṣaṇa, wrote his own commentary on *Vedānta-sūtra* known as *Śrī-bhāṣya.* The science of *mādhurya-rāsa* was not revealed in that commentary, and therefore Śrīmad Govindadeva ordered Śrī Baladeva Vidyābhūṣaṇa to reveal that science for the inquisitive devotees. At a place near Jaipur, Baladeva Vidyābhūṣaṇa, a surrendered devotee of Śrī Caitanyadeva, engaged in studying Vedic literature and wrote a commentary on the *Brahma-sūtra* known as *Govinda-bhāṣya.*

(*Sajjana-toṣaṇī* 8/1)

7. Do the Vaiṣṇavas need to study Govinda-bhāṣya?

Many people think"I am a Vaiṣṇava," but one should study *Śrī Govinda-bhāṣya* to know exactly what one must do and understand to become a Vaiṣṇava. For the Vaiṣṇavas, this *Govinda-bhāṣya* is invaluable treasure.

(*Sajjana-toṣaṇī* 8/1)

36

Revealed Scripture

1. If everyone has a right to study the Purāṇas, are they not inferior to the Vedas?

Just as everyone has a right to chant the holy names of Krishna, the essence of all Vedic literature, everyone has a right to study the *Purāṇas* and histories, which are as good as the Vedas. The same Vyāsadeva who divided the Vedas compiled the *Purāṇas* and histories; therefore, the glories of the *Purāṇas* and histories are equal to the Vedas.

(*Sajjana-toṣaṇī* 11/10)

2. What is the purport of Bhagavad-gītā? Why was devotional service kept in the middle of the book?

Bhagavad-gītā consists of eighteen chapters. Among them, the first six chapters deal with karma, the second six deal with *bhakti*, and the last six deal with *jñāna*. The supremacy of devotional service has been established in this book. Devotional service is most confidential, but it is the life of *jñāna* and karma. Since it awards one the goal of life, devotional service has been placed in the middle six chapters.

(*Bhagavad-gītā*, Introduction)

3. According to Bhagavad-gītā, what is the ultimate goal of the living entities?

Bhagavad-gītā instructs that the ultimate goal for the living entities is pure devotional service alone. Surrendering to the Supreme Lord, the most confidential instruction, is found in the concluding verses of *Bhagavad-gītā*, beginning with *sarva-dharmān parityajya.*

(*Bhagavad-gītā*, Introduction)

4. Does Bhagavad-gītā recommend fighting?

Arjuna's fighting is an example of attachment to one's occupational duties. Fighting is not the conclusion of *Bhagavad-gītā*.
(*Bhagavad-gītā*, Introduction)

5. What is the confidential meaning of Bhagavad-gītā?
The confidential purport of *Bhagavad-gītā* is that according to a person's nature his qualification is determined. He should only engage in activities that are necessary to maintain his livelihood and that are prescribed according to his qualification, and he should search after the Absolute Truth. His perfection lies in doing so.
(*Bhagavad-gītā*, Introduction)

6. What is devotional literature?
Śrīmad-Bhāgavatam is devotional literature.
(*Sajjana-toṣaṇī* 11/10)

7. By studying which literature can one achieve auspiciousness?
One should study all the Vedas, *smṛtis*, *purāṇas*, *pañcarātras*, and conclusive writings of the *mahājanas* wherein the topics of pure devotional service are instructed and discussed. By studying literature containing other opinions, one simply learns useless arguments.
(*Sajjana-toṣaṇī* 11/6)

8. Which scripture is the essence of all scriptures?
Śrīmad *Bhagavad-gītā* is the essence of all scriptures. For one who has not received the nectarean instructions of *Bhagavad-gītā*, studying other scriptures is like an ass carrying a big burden.
(*Sajjana-toṣaṇī* 12/2)

9. Which scripture reveals the true meaning of the Vedas?
The *Purāṇas* reveal the true meaning of the Vedas. The Vaiṣṇava community believes that the Absolute Truth, which is ascertained in Vedic literature like the *Upaniṣads*, is explained in the *Purāṇas* in simple language by personalities like Parāśara Muni and Vedavyāsa.
(*Tattva-sūtra* 2)

10. Where can one find the real purport of the Vedas?

The meanings of the Vedic statements are extremely confidential. To help the people of the world understand the purport of the Vedic statements, the great sages have put those purports in the *Purāṇas*.

(*Caitanya Caritāmṛta* Madhya 6/143 —148)

11. What is the difference between Sat-kriya-sāra-dīpikā and the smṛti composed by the karmīs?

To protect the constitutional duties of the devotees, Śrīmad Gopāla Bhaṭṭa Goswami composed the book *Sat-kriya-sāra-dīpikā*. According to Vedic injunctions, Aniruddha Bhaṭṭa, Bhīma Bhaṭṭa, and Śrīmad Govindānanda Bhaṭṭa wrote separate *smṛtis* for the *karmīs*. Śrī Nārāyaṇa Bhaṭṭa also wrote a book about the injunctions of the *smṛtis* for the *karmīs*, and Śrī Bhāvadeva Bhaṭṭa wrote a similar book for persons who are fond of Vedic rituals. The *Sat-kriya-sāra-dīpikā* was composed from authentic statements of the Vedas, *Purāṇas*, and *dharma-śāstras*, headed by the *Manu-saṁhitā*. After carefully considering the subject of *nāma-aparādha*, and rejecting the process of worshiping the forefathers and the demigods, Śrīmad Gopāla Bhaṭṭa Goswami wrote *Sat-kriya-sāra-dīpikā* for the benefit of the devotees of Govinda who are either outcastes or situated on the platform of *varṇāśrama*.

(*Sat-kriya-sāra-dīpikā* translation)

37

Mahājanas

1. Why are the books written by the mahājanas honorable?

The pure devotees know that the books written by the *mahājanas* are beehives. The newer the beehives, the more the *rāsas* are awakened.

(*Sajjana-toṣaṇī* 10/5)

2. Did the mahājanas compose books using imagination born of mental speculation?

vākyānāṁ jaḍa-janyatvān na śaktā me sarasvatī
varṇane vimalānanda vilasasya cid-ātmanaḥ

"To describe the pure ecstatic pastimes of the living entities is beyond my power of speech, because the words I would use in such descriptions are products of the material world."

tathāpi sārajuṭa vṛtyā samādhim avalambya vai
varṇitā bhagavad vārtā mayā bodhyā samādhinā

"Although I am unable to clearly describe the Lord by words, *samādhi*, and the process of *sārajuṭ*, I have described the topics of the Lord to the best of my ability."

If one simply takes the insignificant literal meanings of the words, one will not properly realize the described subject. I therefore request the reader to try to realize the truth through *samādhi*. One should try to understand subtle points from gross statements, as in *Arundhatī-nyāya* [when one points out a faint star with the help of a bright star]. The process of argument is useless, because it cannot lead one to the Absolute Truth. The subtle process of directly perceiving the soul is called *samādhi*. I have given these descriptions based on this process. The reader should also follow this process to realize the truth.

(*Śrī Krishna-saṁhitā* 1/32–33)

3. Why are the nectarean instructions of Śrī Caitanya, the essence of all scriptures?

By careful analysis, one will find that the nectarean instructions of Śrī Caitanya are the essence of all scriptures. The essence of the unfathomable truth that has been discovered in the *Ṛg*, *Sāma*, *Yajur*, and *Atharva* Vedas and in the *Vedānta-sūtra* is available in the nectarean teachings of Śrī Caitanya. The beneficial instructions that are found in the eighteen *Purāṇas*, twenty *dharma-śāstras*, *Rāmāyaṇa*, *Mahābhārata*, *ṣaḍ-darśana*, and *tantra-śāstras* are truly found in the nectarean teachings of Śrī Caitanya. Anything essential that is found in the religious teachings in foreign countries and in the religious teachings in our own country is available in *Śrī Caitanya-śikṣāmṛta*. Whatever is not found in Indian or foreign literature is found in this most relishable book.

(*Śrī Caitanya-śikṣāmṛta*, Introduction)

4. By whose inspiration did Śrī Bhaktivinoda Ṭhākura compile the book Śrī Bhāgavatārka-marīci-mālā?

I offer my respectful obeisances unto Svarūpa Dāmodara, who was an associate of Gaurāṅga. By his mercy I am compiling this book.

(*Maṅgalācaraṇa* of *Śrī Bhāgavatārka-marīci-mālā*)

5. What was Śrī Mahāprabhu's order regarding the compilation of Śrī Bhāgavatārka-marīci-mālā?

When I was preparing to write this book, Svarūpa Dāmodara appeared in my heart and told me,"By the order of Mahāprabhu, arrange *Śrīmad-Bhāgavatam* ślokas in gradual sequence to show *sambandha*, *abhidheya*, and *prayojana*. By the mercy of the Lord, the Vaiṣṇavas will daily read this book, which consists of verses from *Śrīmad-Bhāgavatam*." Thereafter, Svarūpa Dāmodara explained to me the purport of the verse beginning *janmādy asya*. He also disclosed the process for explaining the meaning in terms of Gauḍīya philosophy. By his inspiration, this fallen servant, Bhaktivinoda, wrote this book. Without duplicity I fall down at the feet of both the speakers and the listeners and beg their mercy.

(*Śrī Bhāgavatārka-marīci-mālā*, Conclusion)

6. What is the result of relishing Śrī Bhāgavatārka-marīci-mālā?

In conclusion, with great humility the compiler says:"The garland of verses from *Śrīmad-Bhāgavatam* sewn by Bhaktivinoda Ṭhākura, who is always absorbed in ecstatic love for Śrī Gaura and Gadādhara, is now complete. Those devotees who blissfully relish this book daily will certainly obtain the mercy of Śrī Rādhā-Mādhava. Śrī Rādhā-Mādhava have appeared in Śrī Navadvīpa in Gauḍa-maṇḍala along with Their abode Vraja, as Śrī Gadādhara-Gaurāṅga, and They have performed Their eternal pastimes in a different manner.

"O mind, your duration of life is short and whatever time is left is full of obstacles. Therefore O brother, keep on drinking the nectar of *Śrīmad-Bhāgavatam* with special care."

(*Śrī Bhāgavatārka-marīci-mālā*, Verses 1–3, Conclusion)

7. How did the book Śrī Krishna-saṁhitā appear?

śrī kṛṣṇa-tattva -nirdeśe kṛpā yasya prayojanam
vande taṁ jñānadaṁ kṛṣṇaṁ caitanyaṁ rāsa-vigraham

"I offer my respectful obeisances unto Śrī Krishna Caitanya, who is full of transcendental mellows and the giver of spiritual knowledge. Without His mercy, no one can understand the truth of Krishna."

samudra-śoṣaṇaṁ reṇor yathā na ghaṭate kvacit
tathā me tattva -nirdeśo mūḍhasya kṣudra-cetasaḥ

"Just as a particle of dust cannot absorb the ocean, foolish people like me have extreme difficulty in understanding the truth."

kintu me hṛdaye ko 'pi puruṣaḥ śyāmasundaraḥ
sphuran samādiśat kāryam etat tattva -nirūpaṇam

"Although a living entity can never understand the truth with his small intelligence, a blackish personality with a form of pure consciousness has appeared in my heart and engaged me in the work of establishing the truth. For this reason I have boldly taken up this work."

(*Śrī Krishna-saṁhitā* 1/1–3)

8. Is there a commentary on Bhagavad-gītā based on the conclusion of acintya-bhedābheda philosophy?

Unfortunately, the commentaries and Bengali translations of *Śrīmad Bhagavad-gītā* that have been published to date are mostly composed by monists. Commentaries or translations based on pure devotional service are rarely published. The commentaries of Śaṅkarācārya and Ānandagiri are full of monistic conclusions. Śrīdhara Svāmī's commentary is not based on the philosophy of monism, but it has a scent of the sectarian philosophy of *śuddhādvaita-vāda*. Śrī Madhusudana Sarasvatī's commentary is full of statements nourishing devotional service, but the conclusion is not beneficial. Śrī Rāmānuja Svāmī's commentary is fully based on devotional service, but unless a commentary on *Bhagavad-gītā* that is full of the teachings of Śrī Gaurāṅga Mahāprabhu's *acintya-bhedābheda* philosophy is published in our country, the happiness of those who relish pure devotional service does not increase.

We have therefore carefully published the *Bhagavad-gītā* with the Bengali translation called *Rasika-rañjana* according to the commentary written by Śrī Viśvanātha Cakravartī Ṭhākura. He was a follower of Śrī Gaurāṅga, a great teacher, and the crest jewel among all devotees. Śrī Baladeva Vidyābhūṣaṇa also wrote a commentary on *Bhagavad-gītā* based on the teachings of Śrīmān Mahāprabhu. Although Baladeva's commentary is philosophical, Cakravartī Mahāśaya's commentary is not only philosophical, but also full of the mellows of love of God. Particularly, Cakravartī Mahāśaya's commentary on *Śrīmad-Bhāgavatam* is particularly well known and respected. Cakravartī Mahāśaya's philosophy is simple and his Sanskrit language is sublime.

(*Bhagavad-gītā* translation)

9. What is the purpose of and inspiration behind composing the Vidvad-rañjana commentary on Śrīmad Bhagavad-gītā?

Śrī Baladeva Vidyābhūṣaṇa wrote a commentary on *Bhagavad-gītā* and removed the cloud of Māyāvāda, which covered the moonlike nectarean truth of *Bhagavad-gītā*. By the mercy of the Pañca-tattva, he wrote his commentary and made everyone happy. According to his commentary, I, the most insignificant Bhaktivinoda, wrote a nectarean commentary on *Bhagavad-gītā*. After offering my respectful obeisances at the feet of the pure devotees, I wrote and named this commentary *Vidvad-rañjana*. Śrī Advaita Prabhu is an authority on *Bhagavad-gītā*, so I offer my respectful obeisances unto Him. May He place His lotus feet on the head of this servant and fulfill my desire by empowering me. Out of compassion for the living entities of the world, Śrī Advaita Prabhu brought Gaura Hari here and taught everyone the essence of *Bhagavad-gītā*. There is no doubt that if I receive Śrī Advaita Prabhu's mercy, I will cross beyond the ocean of spiritual truth. O Śrī Gaura! O Nityānanda! O Advaita, the abode of love of God! O Lakṣmī! O Viṣṇupriyā! O Gadhādara! O Jāhnavā! O Vaṁśīvadanānanda! O Rūpa! O Sanātana! O Svarūpa! O Rāmānanda! O Śrīvāsa! O Śrīdhara! I am most poor and fallen; therefore, by your mercy alone this foolish person can achieve perfection. Please destroy all obstacles, reveal all truths to me, and give me the strength to write this commentary.

(*Maṅgalācaraṇa* of *Vidvad-rañjana-bhāṣya*)

10. What is the purpose of and introduction to the Prakāśinī commentary on Brahma-saṁhitā?

After carefully collecting many jewels of conclusions, Brahmā offered prayers to Lord Krishna. Those conclusive prayers were included in the fifth chapter of the book *Brahma-saṁhitā* for the benefit of human beings. While traveling throughout South India, Śrī Gaurāṅga, the ocean of mercy and the only friend of the living entities in this age of Kali, discovered the treasure *Brahma-saṁhitā* to deliver the people of Gauḍa-deśa. After considering various scriptures, Śrī Jīva Goswami Prabhu wrote a commentary on this book. Out of compassion, he presented it to the devotees of Bengal.

My spiritual master, Śrī Bipin Bihārī, ordered me to write according to Śrī Jīva Goswami's commentary and to add more. Thus, this poor servant wrote a commentary with great pleasure. If the devotees study this commentary with pure intelligence, carefully considering the difference between matter and spirit, then this servant will be satisfied, his desire will be fulfilled, and pure devotional service will be propagated.

O Rūpa! O Jīva and Sanātana! You are the life and the wealth of the devotees and your mercy is as great as the ocean. Please give me strength so that I can understand the confidential purport of Śrī Jīva Goswami's commentary for I am the most foolish person. The words of Śrī Jīva are as beautiful as the buds; I have simply tried to help them blossom. Offering my respectful obeisances to my spiritual master and to Krishna, I wrote this commentary for the pleasure of the pure devotees.

(*Maṅgalācaraṇa* of *Brahma-saṁhitā Prakāśinī*)

11. What is the aim and who is the author of the Prakāśinī commentary?

jīvābhayapradā vṛttir jīvāśaya prakāśinī
kṛtā bhaktivinodena surabhī kuñjavāsinā

"This *prakāśinī* commentary presented by Śrī Bhaktivinoda, who lives at Surabhi-kuñja, is meant to award fearlessness and the goal of life to the living entities."

12. What is the purpose of writing Amṛta-pravāha-bhāṣya on Caitanya Caritāmṛta?

I offer my humble obeisances unto the lotus feet of Śrī Caitanya, Śrī Nityānanda, Śrī Advaita (the storekeeper of love of God), Haridāsa, Svarūpa Gosāi, Śrī Vaṁśīvadanānanda, Sārvabhauma Bhaṭṭācārya, Rāmānanda Rāya, Śrī Rūpa, Śrī Sanātana, Śrī Jīva, Gopāla Bhaṭṭa, Raghunātha dāsa, Raghunātha Bhaṭṭa, Śivānanda, Kavi-karṇapūra, Narottama, Śrīnivāsa, Rāmacandra, Kṛṣṇadāsa, Baladeva Vidyābhūṣaṇa and Viśvanātha Cakravartī. By the mercy of these great devotees of the Lord, I wrote an elaborate commentary called *Amṛta-pravāha-bhāṣya* on *Śrī Caitanya-caritāmṛta* for the devotees to study. The descriptions of Śrī Gaura are just like the ocean of nectar. Out of compassion, Kṛṣṇadāsa Kavirāja, who is floating in the nectar, has delivered that flow of nectar. The Vaiṣṇavas want to sooth their lives by drinking the nectarean descriptions in his book. The devotees ordered me, who has nothing to give materially, to write a commentary on *Śrī Caitanya Caritāmṛta*. Taking the orders of the devotees on my head, I carefully composed this commentary and offered it to the devotees for their pleasure.

(of *Amṛta-pravāha-bhāṣya*)

13. By whose mercy did Śrī Bhaktivinoda Ṭhākura compose the book Tattva Viveka?

jayati saccidānanda rasānubhava vigraḥ
procyate saccidānandā nubhūtir yat prasādataḥ

"May Śrī Krishna Caitanya become glorious. He is the personification of *sac-cid-ānanda-rāsa*, and by His mercy, this book called *Sac-cid-ānandānubhūti* has been composed."

(*Tattva Viveka* 1/1)

14. What is the Maṅgalācaraṇa of the book Tattva-sūtra?

praṇamya kṛṣṇa caitanyaṁ bhāradvāja sanātanam
tattva-sūtraṁ sa vyākhyānāṁ bhāṣāyāṁ vivṛtaṁ mayā

The author of *Tattva-sūtra,* Śrīla Bhaktivinoda Ṭhākura said,"I offer my humble obeisances to the Primeval Lord, Śrī Krishna Caitanya, by whose mercy I am writing a Bengali commentary on the book *Tattva-sūtra.*"
(*Maṅgalācaraṇa* of *Tattva-sūtra*)

15. What is the introduction of the book Vyāsasūtrādhikaraṇamālā?

nityaṁ cinmā kuṅja vṛndāsubhage vṛndāvane saṅgataṁ rādhā kṛṣṇa iti dvayaṁ rāsamayaṁ brahmāvirāste param tadbhāvāpti makaranda pāna tarala ca iti ali asti ahaṁ kedārābhidha utsūkāḥ prabhuvaraṁ yāche nibadhāṅjaliḥ

"With folded hands and intense eagerness, I, Śrī Kedārnātha Dutta, pray at the lotus feet of Śrī Rādhā Krishna, who enjoy eternal transcendental pastimes within the divine groves of Vṛndāvana, and who are the Supreme Absolute Truth, to allow me to drink the nectar emanating from Their lotus feet."
(*Vyāsasūtrādhikaraṇamāla,*Introduction)

16. Who wrote the commentary Bedārkadīdhiti, and where was it written?

vedārkadīdhitir ayaṁ bhajana pradī
aḥ gaurāṅga bhaktaprada bhaktivinodena
śrī godrūma dvijapatescaraṇa prasādāt prajvālitaḥ
surabhī kuṅjavanāntarāle

"By the mercy of the Lord of Godruma and the *brāhmaṇa*s, I, Śrī Bhaktivinoda Ṭhākura, sitting in a forest called Surabhi-kuñja, write a commentary called *Vedārkadīdhiti* for the pleasure of the devotees of Lord Gaurāṅga."
(*Vedārkadīdhiti*)

17. What is the Maṅgalācaraṇa of the book Āmnāya Sūtra?

After offering obeisances to Śrī Krishna Caitanyacandra, the original *ācārya* in the world, a person named Bhaktivinoda composed one hundred and thirty *sūtras*, by the mercy of the Vaiṣṇavas. Following the eight kinds of *pramāṇas* (evidences) and six kinds of signs required to understand the Vedic statement and accepting the direct meaning of Vedic statements, he has composed these *sūtras*, on the order of the great Vaiṣṇavas. May all the Vaiṣṇavas who have taken shelter of the lotus feet of Śrī Caitanya read this book.

(*Maṅgalācaraṇa* of *Āmnāya Sūtra*)

18. Which mahājana composed the book Āmnāya Sūtra and when was it composed?

caitanyaṁ devasya catuḥ śatābde netrādhike bhaktivinodakena
amnāyamālā prabhu bhakta kaṇṭhe gauḍe pradattā harijannaghasre

"Four hundred and two years after the appearance of Lord Śrī Caitanyadeva, Śrī Bhaktivinoda Ṭhākura composed this garland of *āmnāya-sūtra* and offered it to the devotees of the Lord."

(*Āmnāya Sūtra,* Conclusion)

19. Śrī Caitanyopaniṣad-bhāṣya is a commentary on Śrī Caitanya-caraṇāmṛtaṁ. What is the Maṅgalācaraṇa of this commentary?

pañcatattvāmṛtaṁ natvā caitanya rāsa vigraha
caitanyopaniṣad bhāsyaṁ karomi ātma viśuddhye

"After offering my obeisances to the most blissful Personality, Śrī Caitanya, who is nondifferent from the Pañca-tattva, I write this commentary on *Śrī Caitanya Upaniṣad* for my own purification."

(*Maṅgalācaraṇa* of *Caitanya-caraṇāmṛtaṁ* commentary)

20. Who has been glorified in the Maṅgalācaraṇa verse of the book Śrī ***Caitanya-śikṣāmṛta*****?**

Śrī Krishna Caitanya is the giver of devotional service to Krishna, in which all erroneous, incomplete, and contradictory conclusions are merged. After offering my respectful obeisances unto Him, I prepare to write the book *Śrī Caitanya-śikṣāmṛta.*

(*Maṅgalācaraṇa* of *Śrī Caitanya-śikṣāmṛta* 1/1)

21. Is the sweetness of the writing of the mahājanas extraordinary?

No writing is sweeter than the writing of the *mahājanas*. Oh! Which book is more instructive on *rāsa* than *Bhakti-rasāmṛta-sindhu*? All glories to Śrī Rūpa Goswami! All glories to Śrī Sanātana Goswami! We do not find any composition sweeter than theirs. O readers, every day please relish the essence of *Brahma-saṁhitā*, *Śrī Krishna Karṇāmṛta*, and *Śrī Bhāgavatāmṛta*.

(*Sajjana-toṣaṇī* 10/5)

22. Why is Śrī Mahābhārata widely respected by the Āryans? What is the special feature of Baladeva Vidyābhūṣaṇa's commentary on Viṣṇu-sahasra-nāma?

If the sages put all Vedic literature in one side of the weighing scale and *Śrī Mahābhārata* on the other side, the *Mahābhārata* will be heavier. We can therefore understand that the Aryans find no book as worshipable as the *Mahābhārata*. Two precious jewels are within the *Mahābhārata*. One of them is *Śrīmad Bhagavad-gītā* and the other is *Śrī Viṣṇu-sahasranāma*. If the *ācāryas* of the authorized *sampradāyas* cannot support their doctrine from these two books, they cannot establish their *sampradāya* as authentic. Therefore *ācāryas* such as Śrī Śaṅkarācārya have written commentaries on the Vedas, *Vedānta-sūtra*, *Gītā*, and *Sahasranāma* and thus propagated them. In the line instructed by Śrīmān Mahāprabhu, Śrī Baladeva Vidyābhūṣaṇa Prabhu is the *vedāntācārya*. Therefore I am publishing his commentary on *Viṣṇu-sahasranāma*.

(An article written in 400 Caitanya Era about *Śrī Viṣṇu-sahasranāma*)

23. Is Śrīmat Cakravartī's verse on the teachings of Śrī Caitanya about bhajana or truth?

Śrīmat Cakravartī Ṭhākura has revealed Śrīmān Mahāprabhu's teachings regarding *bhajana* in his own *śloka*. But he has not included all the Lord's teachings regarding the Absolute Truth in that *śloka*. He did not mention various subject matters such as the living entities, the material world, the energies of the Lord, and regulative devotional service. Regarding truth, this *śloka* is incomplete.

If one wants to enumerate the complete teachings of the Lord, one must follow the description given in the six *sandarbhas*. The nine separate truths are Krishna, the energy of Krishna, the pastimes of Krishna, the science of the Absolute Truth, the two kinds of living entities (eternally conditioned and eternally liberated), the illusory external energy, the process of *sādhana* and the ultimate goal of life. These nine truths are *prameya*, knowledge of an object. The perfect Vedic literature, *Śrīmad-Bhāgavatam*, and the revealed scriptures are the *pramāṇa*, evidence. An idea that is without these ten conclusions cannot be accepted by the Vaiṣṇavas as complete.

(*Sajjana-toṣaṇī* 4/3)

38

Śrīmad-Bhāgavatam

1. What is the mystery of the four original verses of Śrīmad-Bhāgavatam? According to which original principle was Śrī Krishna-saṁhitā written?

Oṁ tat sat satyaṁ paraṁ dhimahi

The mystery behind four original *Bhāgavatam* verses [Canto 2, Chapter 9, Verses 33–36]:

jñānaṁ parama-guhyaṁ me—Knowledge about Me as described in the scriptures is very confidential:— Direct perception of the Absolute Truth.

yad vijñāna-samanvitam—It has to be realized:—Indirect perception of the Absolute Truth.

sarahasyaṁ—With devotional service:—The activities of the living entities and the Supreme Lord, known as the science of love.

tad-aṅgaṁ ca—The necessary paraphernalia for that process:—The confidential science of devotional service.

gṛhāṇa gaditaṁ mayā—You may take it up carefully.

yāvān ahaṁ—I Myself in My eternal form

yathā-bhāvo—My transcendental existence.

yad-rūpa-guṇa-karmakaḥ—My color, qualities, and activities.

tathaiva tattva -vijñānam—By factual realization.

astu te mad-anugrahāt—Let it be awakened within you out of My causeless mercy.

(*Śrī Krishna-saṁhitā*, First Edition, 1880)

2. How has Śrī Bhaktivinoda Ṭhākura translated the four original verses of Śrīmad-Bhāgavatam?

aham evāsam evāgre nānyad yat sad-asat param
paścād ahaṁ yad etac ca yo 'vaśiṣyeta so 'smy aham

(1) O Brahmā! I, the Personality of Godhead, was existing before creation, when there was nothing but Myself. There was no material nature, the cause of this creation. That which you see now is also I, the Personality of Godhead, and after annihilation what remains will also be I, the Personality of Godhead.

ṛte 'rthaṁ yat pratiyeta na pratīyeta cātmani
tad vidyād ātmano māyāṁ yathābhāso yathā tamaḥ

(2) O Brahmā! That which appears to be of value, but has no relation to Me, has no reality. Know that it is My illusory energy, a reflection, which appears in darkness.

(For detailed explanation of the above two verses, please refer to *Śrī Krishna-saṁhitā*, Chapters One and Two.)

yathā mahānti bhūtāni bhūteṣūccāvaceṣv anu
praviṣṭāny apraviṣṭāni tathā teṣu na teṣv aham

(3) O Brahmā! Please know that the universal elements enter into the cosmos; similarly, I Myself also exist within everything created, and at the same time I am outside of everything.

(For detailed explanation of this verse please refer to *Śrī Krishna-saṁhitā*, Chapters Three, Four, Five, Six, and Nine)

etāvad eva jijñāsyaṁ tattva -jijñāsunātmanah
anvaya-vyatirekābhyāṁ yat syāt sarvatra sarvada

(4) A person searching after the Supreme Absolute Truth, the Personality of Godhead, must certainly search in all circumstances, in all space and time, and both directly and indirectly.

(For detailed explanation of this verse please refer to *Śrī Krishna-saṁhitā*, Chapters Seven, Eight, and Ten.)

(*Śrī Krishna-saṁhitā*, First Edition 1880)

3. Is Śrīmad-Bhāgavatam a man-written, modern book?

Śrīmad-Bhāgavatam is not a recent book. It is eternal and ancient like the Vedas. Respected Śrīdhara Svāmī has confirmed the eternality of the *Bhāgavatam* by using the words *tārāṅkuraḥ sajjaniḥ*. *Śrīmad-Bhāgavatam* has been accepted as the supreme fruit of the Vedic desire tree.

nigama-kalpa-taror galitaṁ phalaṁ
śuka-mukhād amṛta-drava-saṁyutam
pibata bhāgavataṁ rāsam ālayaṁ
muhur aho rasikā bhuvi bhāvukāḥ

"O expert and thoughtful men, relish *Śrīmad-Bhāgavatam*, the mature fruit of the desire tree of Vedic literatures. It emanated from the lips of Śrī Śukadeva Goswami. Therefore this fruit has become even more tasteful, although its nectarean juice was already relishable for all, including liberated souls."

(*Śrīmad-Bhāgavatam*, 1.1.3)

From *praṇava* (*oṁ*) came *Gāyatrī*, from *Gāyatrī* came the Vedas, from the Vedas came the *Brahma-sūtra*, and from the *Brahma-sūtra* came *Śrīmad-Bhāgavatam*, which is known as *Paramahaṁsa-saṁhitā*. *Śrīmad-Bhāgavatam*, which has brightly risen like a *sac-cid-ānanda* sun after being reflected through the *samādhi* of the author, consists of inconceivable topics related to the Supreme Truth. Those who have eyes should see, those who have ears should hear, and those who have minds should meditate on the topics of *Śrīmad-Bhāgavatam*. People infected by the blindness of prejudice are deprived of the sweet taste of *Śrīmad-Bhāgavatam*.

(*Śrī Krishna-saṁhitā*, Introduction)

4. What is the true statement and commentary on Vedānta?

Śrīmad-Bhāgavatam, composed by Vyāsadeva, is the only commentary on *Vedānta-sūtra*. All the conclusions of *Śrīmad-Bhāgavatam* are the true conclusions of *Vedānta*. Śrīmān Mahāprabhu said that when the author himself writes the commentary the true meaning is derived. Therefore the commentary *Śrīmad-Bhāgavatam* should be accepted by everyone as the statements of *Vedānta*.

(*Sajjana-toṣaṇī* 2/6)

5. What kind of writing is Śrīmad-Bhāgavatam?

The *Bhāgavata* does not allow its followers to ask anything from God except eternal love for Him.

(*The Bhagavat: Its Philosophy, Its Ethics & Its Theology*)

6. By whose character the identification of Śrīmad-Bhāgavatam is illustrated?

When we were in the college, reading philosophical works of the West, and exchanging thoughts with the thinkers of the day, we had a real hatred toward the *Bhagavat*. The great work looked like a collection of wicked and stupid ideas, scarcely adapted to the nineteenth century, and we hated to hear any arguments in its favor. Then, the volumes of Channing, Parker, Emerson, and Newman had more weight than all the Vaiṣṇava books. Greedily we poured over the various commentaries of the Bible and of the labors of the *Tattva Bodhini Sabha*, which contained extracts from the *Upaniṣads* and the *Vedānta*, but no work of the Vaiṣṇavas had any favor with us.

When we advanced in age and our religious sentiment developed, we turned to our own belief and prayed, as Jesus prayed in the garden. Accidentally, we came across a book about the great Caitanya and on reading it with some attention to settle the historical position of that Mighty Genius of Nadia, we had the opportunity of gathering His explanation of *Bhāgavat*, given to the wrangling Vedantists of the Benares school. The accidental study created within us a love for all the works that we find about our Eastern Savior. With difficulty, we gathered the famous *Karchas* (diaries) in Saṅskrit, written by the disciple of Caitanya. The explanations of the *Bhāgavat* that we got from these sources were of such a charming character that we secured a copy of the complete *Bhāgavat*. We studied its texts (difficult of course for those not trained in philosophical thoughts) with the assistance of the famous commentaries of Śrīdhara Swami. From such study, we have gathered the real doctrines of the Vaiṣṇavas. Oh! What a trouble to get rid of prejudices gathered in unripe years.

(*The Bhagavat*: *Its Philosophy*, *Its Ethics & Its Theology*)

7. Why are the identity and glories of Śrīmad-Bhāgavatam hidden from the materialists and the foreigners?

"What sort of thing is the *Bhagavat*?" asks a European gentleman newly arrived in India.

With a serene look, his companion tells him, "The *Bhagavat* is a book, which an Oriya-bearer reads daily in the evening to a number of hearers. It contains jargon of unintelligible and savage writing of those men who paint their noses with some sort of clay or sandalwood, and wear beads all over their bodies to secure salvation for themselves."

Another of his companions, who has traveled a little in the interior, would immediately contradict him and say, "The *Bhagavat* is a Sanskrit work claimed by a sect of men, the Goswamis, who give *mantras* to the common people, like the popes of Italy, and pardon their sins on payment of enough gold to pay their social expenses."

A third gentleman will give a third explanation. A young Bengali, chained up in English thoughts and ideas, and wholly ignorant of the pre-Mohammedan history of his own country will add one more explanation. He says, "The *Bhagavat* is a book containing an account of the life of Krishna, who was an ambitious and immoral man!" This is all that he could gather from his grandmother before he went to school.

Thus, the great *Bhagavat* remains unknown to the foreigners, like the elephant of the six blind men who caught hold of different parts of the body of the beast! But truth is eternal and is never injured but for awhile by ignorance.

(*The Bhagavat: Its Philosophy, Its Ethics & Its Theology*)

8. What did Śrī Bhaktivinoda say regarding the Śrīmad-Bhāgavatam being the only book that is beneficial for all?

We can say that if all the religious scriptures of the Hindus are thrown into the ocean and only the *Śrīmad-Bhāgavatam* is kept aside, there will be no harm for the Āryans or the ordinary living entities.

(*Sajjana-toṣaṇī* 8/12)

9. Why is Śrīmad-Bhāgavatam not accepted by everyone?

Because of great fortune, a living entity develops a taste for *Śrīmad-Bhāgavatam*, which is the crest jewel among all religious literature that is available in the world.

(*Sajjana-toṣaṇī* 9/12)

10. In which kingdom does Śrīmad-Bhāgavatam have its followers? Who is qualified to study Śrīmad-Bhāgavatam and under whose shelter can one realize its truth?

The *Bhāgavata* is pre-eminently the book in India. Once you enter into it and you are transplanted, as it were, into the spiritual world where gross matter has no existence. The true follower of the *Bhāgavata* is a spiritual man who has already cut his temporary connection with phenomenal nature and has made himself the inhabitant of that region where God eternally exists and loves. This mighty work is founded upon inspiration and its superstructure is upon reflection. To the common reader it has no charms and is full of difficulty. We are, therefore, obliged to study it deeply with the assistance of such great commentators as Śrīdhara Svāmī and the Divine Caitanya and His contemporary followers.

(*The Bhagavat*: *Its Philosophy*, *Its Ethics & Its Theology*)

11. What does Śrīmad-Bhāgavatam teach? What did Śrī Caitanyadeva teach about the essence of Śrīmad-Bhāgavatam through His own behavior and preaching?

The whole of this incomparable work teaches us, according to our great Caitanya, the three great truths which compose the absolute religion of man. Our Nadia preacher calls them *sambandha*, *abhidheya*, and *prayojana*, i.e. the relationship between the creator and the created, the duty of man to God, and the aim of humanity. These three words include the ocean of human knowledge as far as it has been explored to this era of human progress. These are the cardinal points of religion and the whole *Bhagavat* is, as we are taught by Caitanya, an explanation both by precept and example of these three great points.

(*The Bhagavat*: *Its Philosophy*, *Its Ethics & Its Theology*)

12. Does Śrīmad-Bhāgavatam recommend worshiping many gods?

In all its twelve *skandhas* or divisions, the *Bhāgavata* teaches us that there is only one God, without a second. He was complete in Himself in the past, He is complete now, and will remain complete in the future. Time and space, which prescribe conditions to created objects, are much below His supreme spiritual nature, which is unconditioned and absolute.

(*The Bhagavat*: *Its Philosophy*, *Its Ethics & Its Theology*)

13. What is the definition of devotional service? How many kinds of bhāgavatas are there?

Those who worship God as the all in all with all their heart, body, and strength approach Him as Bhagavān. This principle is *bhakti*. The book that prescribes the relationship and worship of Bhagavān is called *Bhāgavata* and the worshiper is called by the same name.

(*The Bhagavat*: *Its Philosophy*, *Its Ethics & Its Theology*)

14. Why is bhāgavata-dharma supreme?

The superiority of the *Bhagavat* consists in uniting all sorts of theistical worship into one excellent principle in human nature, which is called *bhakti*. This word has no equivalent in the English language. Piety, devotion, resignation, and spiritual love, unalloyed with any sort of petition except repentance—compose the highest principle of *bhakti*. The *Bhagavata* tells us to worship God in that great and invaluable principle, which is infinitely superior to human knowledge and the principle of yoga.

(*The Bhagavat*: *Its Philosophy*, *Its Ethics & Its Theology*)

15. Has Śrīmad-Bhāgavatam preached the process of constant spiritual cultivation and the gradual progress of the soul?

The voluminous *Bhagavat* is nothing more than a full illustration of the principle of continual development and progress of the soul from gross matter to the all-perfect universal spirit, which is distinguished as personal, eternal, absolutely free, all-powerful, and all-intelligent. There is nothing gross or material in that spirit. The whole affair is spiritual.

(*The Bhagavat*: *Its Philosophy*, *Its Ethics & Its Theology*)

16. What is the definition of the worshipable object as indicated by Śrīmad-Bhāgavatam? What is the ultimate goal of the Vaiṣṇavas?

Bhagavān is holy, good, just, active, personal, merciful, omnipresent, all-intelligent, all-powerful, and absolutely free. He is the supremely spiritual deity, without a second, who creates and preserves all that is in the universe. The highest aim of the Vaiṣṇava is to spiritually serve that infinite being forever in the activity of absolute love.

(*The Bhagavat*: *Its Philosophy*, *Its Ethics & Its Theology*)

17. Can an impartial critic refrain from glorifying the conclusions of Vyāsadeva's Śrīmad-Bhāgavatam?

The critic should first read deeply the pages of the *Bhagavat* and train his mind in the best eclectic philosophy that the world has ever obtained, and then, we are sure, he will publicly praise the college of theology at Badrikāśrama, which existed about 4000 years ago.

(*The Bhagavat*: *Its Philosophy*, *Its Ethics & Its Theology*)

18. When does the Absolute Truth, discussed in Śrīmad-Bhāgavatam, reveal Himself?

The *Bhagavat* teaches us that God gave the truth to Vyāsa, and He gives it to us when we earnestly seek it. Truth is eternal and unexhausted.

(*The Bhagavat*: *Its Philosophy*, *Its Ethics & Its Theology*)

19. Is bhāgavata-dharma universal?

See how universal is the religion of *Bhagavat*. It is not intended for a certain class of Hindus alone, but it is a gift to all men in every country and every society.

(*The Bhagavat*: *Its Philosophy*, *Its Ethics & Its Theology*)

20. What does Śrīmad-Bhāgavatam say about the independence and progress of the spirit soul?

Two more principles characterize the *Bhagavat*: liberty and progress of the soul throughout eternity.

(*The Bhagavat*: *Its Philosophy*, *Its Ethics & Its Theology*)

39

Spiritual Literature

1. What kind of poetry is Śrī Gīta-govinda? Who is qualified to study it?

Gīta-govinda is a special poetry book, full of transcendental mellows of devotional service, and it describes the exalted pastimes of the Supreme Brahman. There is no other such book in the world. Since the ordinary readers cannot realize the conjugal mellows of the Supreme Lord and since they are fond of material enjoyment, their study of *Śrī Gīta-govinda* is not perfect. The poet Jayadeva Goswami has not offered his book to such readers; rather he forbade them to study this book. For persons who are inexperienced in the transcendental mellows of Vraja, discussing Jayadeva Goswami and his work is proof of their shamelessness.

(*Sajjana-toṣaṇī* 7/2)

2. What is the purport of Śrī Ujjvala-nīlamaṇi? Is the science of Krishna consciousness under the jurisdiction of material nature?

The purport of *Śrī Ujjvala-nīlamaṇi* is very confidential. The pastimes of Śrī Krishna are always transcendental. Although they appear in the material world, there is no tinge of matter in them. The supremely exalted pure pastimes of Śrī Krishna have appeared in the material world along with Vraja from Goloka by the energy of the Lord for the benefit of the living entities. The association between male and female in this world is most abominable. A living entity attaining Krishna's association and a *gopī* form in a spiritual body is beyond the twenty-four material elements.

(*Sajjana-toṣaṇī* 10/6)

3. Why is the Ṣaṭ-sandarbha very dear to the Vaiṣṇavas?

Śrī Rūpa and Sanātana are adorned by the members of the Viśva-vaiṣṇava Rāja-sabhā and are followers of Śrī Krishna Caitanyadeva, who incarnated to purify the people of Kali-yuga and award them the ultimate goal of life. Under the guidance of Śrī Rūpa and Sanātana, Śrī Jīva Goswami composed this great work, the Sandarbhas. We do not have the ability to describe the glories of this work, which is divided into six parts. The first part is called *Tattva-sandarbha*, the second part *Bhagavat-sandarbha*, third part *Paramātma-sandarbha*, fourth part *Kṛṣṇa-sandarbha*, fifth part *Bhakti-sandarbha*, and the sixth part *Prīti-sandarbha*. All the conclusions and thoughts of the Vaiṣṇava *sampradāya* are found in this work.

(*Sajjana-toṣaṇī* 10/12)

4. Is the book Prema-taraṅgiṇī available nowadays?

The Sanskrit book *Prema-taraṅgiṇī* written by Śrīmad Bhāgavatācārya is extremely rare nowadays. We have a photocopy of the book, but it is full of printing mistakes and in many places things do not make sense. If any devotee has a copy of the book in good condition, kindly give to us so that we can do something with it. We are appealing to the Vaiṣṇavas with folded hands to please glance mercifully on us in this regard.

(*Sajjana-toṣaṇī* 9/12)

5. What is the difference between an ordinary worldly newspaper and a spiritual newspaper? Which reflects the writings of the mahājanas?

Newspapers that make the readers happy by daily writing of new topics only write about varieties of the material world, but the topics of Lord Hari are different. They never become old. The more one hears or speaks of the Lord, the more one relishes these topics. O readers! If you have any attachment for the topics of Hari, then relish the descriptions written by the *mahājanas* again and again. Although this newspaper is very small, nevertheless in each edition the conclusive descriptions of the mellows of devotional service written by the previous *mahājanas* are published part by part.

Since there is no question of worldly stories in this paper, we must publish some compositions of the previous great learned scholars. The material world is full of nonsense talks; therefore do not avoid relishing the pastimes and the science of devotional service available in this small newspaper *Śrī Sajjana-toṣaṇī*. There is no doubt that the compositions of the previous great saintly persons will be more covered than our own writings.

Another point of consideration is that those who are fond of reading should certainly read the devotional works of the previous saintly persons.

If such readers gradually enter into and relish these writings, they will obtain immense pleasure. Unfortunately, we love to read our own writing or the writing of some new modern authors. But when we deeply absorb ourselves in the compositions of the *mahājanas*, we no longer like the modern compositions. The point is that, we think we can compose better than the *mahājanas*, but when this illusion is destroyed, we no longer like the modern compositions. Great personalities and poets do not always come to the material world. They are rare. Therefore it is very difficult to find great poets after Jayadeva Goswami and Śrī Rūpa Goswami. Only when some recipients of Śrī Krishna's mercy appear in this world, we will again see books like *Śrī Gīta-govinda* and *Śrī Bhāgavatāmṛta*. To feel happy by reading the work of modern authors and poets is like imagining one is relishing milk by drinking buttermilk because there is an absence of milk.

We do not find any writing sweeter than the writing of the *mahājanas*. Oh! What can be a more instructive book about *rāsa* than *Bhakti-rasāmṛta-sindhu*? All glories to Śrī Rūpa Goswami! All glories to Śrī Sanātana Goswami! We do not find any sweet and conclusive composition other than their compositions. O readers! Please daily relish the essence of *Brahma-saṁhitā*, *Śrī Krishna Karṇāmṛta*, and *Śrī Bhāgavatāmṛta*.

(*Sajjana-toṣaṇī* 10/5)

6. Is Śrīla Vṛndāvana dāsa Ṭhākura the original Bengali poet?

Śrī Vṛndāvana dāsa Ṭhākura is certainly the original Bengali poet. Although there were other devotees, like Caṇḍīdāsa, who also composed songs, none of them composed poems. The book *Krishna-maṅgala* or *Krishna-vijaya* written by Mālādhara Vasu contains songs.

(From the article"Śrīla Ṭhākura Vṛndāvana dāsa" written by Śrī Bhaktivinoda Ṭhākura, found in *Śrī Caitanya Bhāgavata*, published by Śrī Atul Kṛṣna Goswami)

7. In which books are the teachings of Śrīmān Mahāprabhu available? Why should Śrī Caitanya-caritāmṛta be accepted in all respects?

The Goswamis have composed many books. Although the teachings of Mahāprabhu are found in them, there is nothing mentioned about Mahāprabhu's own writing. *Śrī Caitanya-caritāmṛta* is an authentic book. It is fully enriched with the characteristics and instructions of the Lord. These instructions of the Lord are fully confirmed by the statements of the Goswamis. *Śrī Caitanya-caritāmṛta* is therefore found to be the most respected book. Just after the disappearance of Mahāprabhu, Śrī Kṛṣṇadāsa Kavirāja Goswami composed this book. Many direct disciples of Śrīmān Mahāprabhu, such as Śrī Rūpa Goswami and Śrī Raghunātha dāsa Goswami helped Śrī Kavirāja Goswami in composing *Śrī Caitanya Caritāmṛta*. Prior to that, Śrī Kavi-karṇapūra helped Śrī Kavirāja Goswami in many ways by writing *Śrī Caitanya-candrodaya-nāṭaka* and Śrī Vṛndāvana dāsa Ṭhākura helped Śrī Kavirāja Goswami in many ways by writing *Śrī Caitanya Bhāgavata*. By considering all aspects, we are compelled to accept *Śrī Caitanya Caritāmṛta*.

(*Caitanya-śikṣāmṛta*)

8. Can a living entity be benefited by reading the topics of Harī written in the form of novels?

Nowadays people love to read novels. Our duty is to teach the science of devotional service little by little through novels, like administering a dose of homeopathic medicine. By injecting small amounts of spiritual knowledge into the hearts of the materialists, their hearts will become faithful to devotional service.

(*Sajjana-toṣaṇī* 10/12)

9. Should we offer any respect to the books of the sahajiyās?

Amṛta-rasāvalī is purely a *sahajiyā* book. In that book, it is written:"The life of one who cannot understand the meaning of *sahaja* or spontaneous and who does not become *sahaja* or spontaneous is useless." Many such books are found among the *bāulas* and *sahajiyās*. While searching for some books we came across a few of those books. After reading them, we felt disgusted; we threw them into the Ganges and became purified.

(*Sajjana-toṣaṇī* 10/12)

40

Sajjana-toṣaṇī

1. What are the principal precepts of Śrī Sajjana-toṣaṇī magazine?

aśeṣa kleśa viśleṣa pareśāveśa sādhini
jīyād eśa parā patrī sarva sajjana toṣanī

This spiritual magazine, *Sajjana-toṣaṇī*, is meant to destroy unlimited miseries of the living entities, to award transcendental feelings toward the Absolute Truth, and to please all the devotees of the Lord.

(*Sajjana-toṣaṇī*, Vol. 4)

2. What is the meaning of Sajjana-toṣaṇī?

The pure state of the living entity's constitutional propensity is"love of God." That is the ultimate goal of the living entity. The lives of those who can revive that propensity even while remaining in the conditional state are glorious. Those who have not awakened pure love of God but are aiming to do so in their life are also glorious, because within a short time they will also become glorious. These great personalities are called sajjana. The purpose of this newspaper is to satisfy such personalities. Therefore the name of this newspaper is *Sajjana-toṣaṇī*.

(*Sajjana-toṣaṇī* 2/4)

3. What subject does Sajjana-toṣaṇī discuss?

Sajjana-toṣaṇī will not discuss temporary news of the material world. Such news is published daily in various newspapers. The aim of this newspaper is to discuss the eternal constitutional duties of the living entities.

(*Sajjana-toṣaṇī* 2/4)

4. Is Sajjana-toṣaṇī the supplier of mundane news?

I am a poor Vaiṣṇava. I have no interest in big, big mundane topics such as the battle between Britain and Russia, the demarcation of Afghanistan's border, and the qualification or incompetence of the Governor Generals. I do not need to waste my time in this way. My only duty is to award spiritual benefit to the Indians, particularly the Bengalis. While carrying out that duty, whatever topics I need to discuss I must do it.

I do not have any special connection with mundane newspapers. Still, to see how much the hearts of the Indians are turning toward devotional service to Krishna, I read almost all the newspapers. When I read some articles regarding the fight between the British and the Bengalis in those newspapers, I feel hurt in my heart.

(*Sajjana-toṣaṇī* 2/5)

5. What has been the good result of circulating the newspaper Sajjana-toṣaṇī?

In the beginning, the Vaiṣṇava society did not have a newspaper. Now we can see that being encouraged by the success of *Sajjana-toṣaṇī*, a newspaper called *Ratnākara,* which preaches Vaiṣṇavism is being published in Dhaka; a newspaper called *Śrī Hari Bhakti Pradāyinī* is being published in Bālesvara; and a newspaper called *Vaiṣṇava* is being published in Calcutta.

Sajjana-toṣaṇī also aims to preach Vaiṣṇavism among modern societies. The supremely pure Vaiṣṇava religion is gradually entering into the hearts of the members of modern societies. We hope that these members soon achieve devotional service to Hari. *Sajjana-toṣaṇī* has also become quite effective among the pure householder Vaiṣṇavas. Seeing the good result, the publisher of this humble newspaper, who is an unalloyed maidservant of Śrīmān Mahāprabhu, is feeling great pleasure.

(*Sajjana-toṣaṇī* 2/12)

6. Is Sajjana-toṣaṇī the first spiritual newspaper in Bengali? Did its preaching bring any success?

At one time, *Sajjana-toṣaṇī* was the only spiritual newspaper, but now the *Sajjana-toṣaṇī* has brought so much spiritual excitement in the minds of many people that many other spiritual newspapers are being published. This is indeed an auspicious symptom.

(*Sajjana-toṣaṇī* 12/1)

7. Is the editor of Sajjana-toṣaṇī interested to publish the biographies of the mahājanas?

We have a strong desire to elaborately publish the glories of the great personalities, but we cannot fulfill this desire, because the poor *Sajjana-toṣaṇī* is extremely thin. If pious people ever make *Sajjana-toṣaṇī* bigger and healthier, then our desire can be fulfilled.

(*Sajjana-toṣaṇī* 2/6)

8. What is the history of Sajjana-toṣaṇī?

Sajjana-toṣaṇī first was published at Naḍāla in April 1882. When some residents of Naḍāla established a new printing press and asked me for some work, I printed my first edition of *Sajjana-toṣaṇī* there. Later on, we kept moving place and could not publish the newspaper regularly. Finally, when I stayed at Barasat, I published in English the journal *Nityarupa-saṁsthāpanaṁ*, written by Śrī Upendra Goswami. When this English edition was published in 1883, the *Sajjana-toṣaṇī* was temporarily suspended. In 1885, a Vaiṣṇava fund was established at my house in Rāmbāgān. Thereafter I spent some time at Saptagrāma. Then, the *Sajjana-toṣaṇī* started coming out again. Later, *Sajjana-toṣaṇī* was again discontinued as an individual newspaper and merged into Śrī Viśva-vaiṣṇava Sabhā. From 1892, *Sajjana-toṣaṇī* again began to come out regularly.

(*Autobiography of Śrī Bhaktivinoda Ṭhākura*)

9. Why was Sajjana-toṣaṇī not published for two years? Who became her sister concern?

Sajjana-toṣaṇī was sleeping for almost two years. For various reasons we had no opportunity to break her sleep. Being encouraged by members of the Vaiṣṇava Sabhā, I have requested the sleeping girl to please wake up and again sing the glories of Hari and explain the science of Hari. Out of love, the ecstatic girl again took up her duty. Now the devotees can hear her words attentively. Previously, *Sajjana-toṣaṇī* was alone, now she will be together with her sister named *Premapracāriṇī* and will shower the nectarean science of Śrī Hari. We hope that the hearts of the devotees will be satisfied. The more the devotees express their eagerness, the more the two girls carry out their duties perfectly.

(*Sajjana-toṣaṇī* 2/1)

Abhidheya

41

The Science of Abhidheya

1. What is abhidheya?

"A human being should be inquisitive to know who he is, what the universe is, what God is, and what the relationship is between himself, God and the material world. Knowledge of these four items—namely oneself, the universe, God, and their internal relationship—is called *Sambandha-jñāna*, or the knowledge of one's relationship. When one's relationship with the Supreme Lord is established, the next program is to act in that relationship. This is called *abhidheya*, or activity in relationship with the Lord."

(Commentary on *Caitanya Caritāmṛta* Ādi 7/146)

2. What is the 'Science of Abhidheya?

"To cultivate Krishna consciousness with proper code of conduct is called the 'science of *abhidheya.*' Since this science has been prominently addressed in the Vedic literatures, Śrīman Mahāprabhu has called it the science of *abhidheya*."

(*Jaiva Dharma*, Chapter 4)

3. Is it possible for a conditioned soul to attain perfection without following Sādhana?

"A conditioned soul should not disregard, the process of *sādhanā*, rather he should follow carefully. The more one follows the process of *sādhanā* the more one comes closer to perfection."

(*Sajjana-toṣaṇī* 11/5)

4. How is the relationship between the living entities and the Supreme Lord revived?

"There is a confidential relationship between the living entity and the Supreme Lord. When one's spontaneous attachment for the Lord is awakened this relationship is revived. Although this relationship is eternal, it has been dormant for the conditioned souls. Just as fire is ignited by rubbing a matchstick or hitting two pieces of stones, similarly by following the process of *sādhanā* this relationship becomes manifest."

(*Caitanya-śikṣāmṛta* 1/1)

5. What is 'Sevā'?

"Cultivation of Krishna consciousness is the only function of a living entity. In the liberated stage it is called '*sevā*' or service."

(*Tattva-sutra* – 33)

6. How many kinds of devotional service are there?

"The processes of devotional service are divided into two. These are direct or primary devotional service in the form of hearing and chanting, and the indirect or secondary devotional service in the form of performing selfless activities for the pleasure of Krishna."

(Commentary on *Bhagavad-gitā* 2/41)

7. What is the indirect or secondary process of devotional service?

"The vow of satisfying Lord Hari by following the system of Varnāśrama is the indirect or secondary process of devotional service."

(*Harināma-cintāmani*)

8. What is the symptom of pure devotional service?

"Offering the result of one's Karma to the Lord is superior than following the principles of Varnāśrama, accepting the renounced order of life after giving up one's occupational duties is superior than offering the fruits of one's karma to the Lord, and execution of devotional service mixed with impersonal knowledge is superior than accepting *sanyassa*. Though all the above processes can be considered to be devotional service, they are all external because pure devotional service, which is the ultimate goal of life, is not found in the conclusion of these processes. Devotional service with material designations can never be called pure devotional service; it is totally separate truth. It is eternally independent of karma, *sanyassa*, and *jnana*. The symptom of pure devotional service is that it is free from desire for sense gratification, uncovered by fruitive activities and mental speculation, and executed favorably for the pleasure of Krishna. This is the ultimate goal of life; because even though it is seen at the time of *sādhana* it is clearly visible at the time of perfection."

(Commentary on *Caitanya Caritāmṛta* Madhya 8/68)

9. What is the path of the mahājanas?

"Our *mahājana*'s path is that which was shown by Śrīla Vyāsadeva, Śukadeva Goswami, Prahlāda Mahārāja, Śrī Caitanya Mahāprabhu, and His associates. We are not to leave aside that path to follow the instructions of new puffed-up devotees."

(*Sajjana-toṣaṇī* 10/10)

10. Can the path of spiritual life be freshly created?

"A path cannot be manufactured. Whatever path is there should be accepted by sadhus. Those who are proud and want fame, try vigorously to discover new paths. Those who have good fortune from past lives give up pride and respect the established path. Those who are unfortunate walk on a new path and thus cheat the world."

(*Sajjana-toṣaṇī* 11/6)

11. What is the previous mahājana's path of bhajana?

"The path of *bhajana* displayed by the previous mahajana's is to constantly chant the holy names of Hari with firm determination and show compassion to all living entities."

(*Sajjana-toṣaṇī* 11/6)

12. What is the identity of bhajana performed under the complete shelter of the holy names of Hari?

"There are many disciplines and processes of worship, but the process of chanting the holy name is paramount. All the saintly Vaiṣṇavas since Lord Caitanya have followed the same singular method of chanting as enunciated by Śrīla Haridāsa Ṭhākura. Even the ancient Vaiṣṇava sages residing in Vrajadhāma have chanted in this same manner. The elevated Vaiṣṇavas residing in Purī, whom we were fortunate to have seen with our own eyes and who were constantly relishing the divine nectar of the holy name, are following the same method of chanting. Both Sanātana Goswami and Gopal Gopāla Bhaṭṭa Goswami have unequivocally established in the *Hari-bhakti-vilasa* that the singular procedure for chanting the holy name is to do it free from offense, incessantly and in a secluded spot—away from the tumult of material activities."

(Introduction to *Harinām Cintāmani*)

13. What is Vaiṣṇava religion?

"Congregationally chanting the holy names of the Lord according to one's qualification is called Vaiṣṇava religion."

(*Harināma-cintāmani*)

14. At what point can the cultivation of knowledge be called regulative devotional service?

"The fruit of karma is material enjoyment; the fruit of *jñāna* is liberation. It is to be understood that devotional service is the ultimate fruit of both of them. Whenever cultivation of knowledge does not aim at devotional service it is materially designated and averse to the Lord, and whenever it aims at devotional service it is called regulative devotional service."

(Introduction to *Bhagavad-gitā*)

9. Which devotional service is the eternal constitutional duty of a living entity?

"The devotional service which remains before, during and after liberation is a separate eternal truth. That is the eternal constitutional duty of a living entity. Liberation is only an irrelevant fruit before devotional service."

(*Jaiva Dharma*, Chapter 6)

10. Which jñāna is desirable and which jñāna is abominable?

"The *jñāna* or cultivation of knowledge which awakens one devotional service and which is performed in order to achieve devotional service is the most desirable. The *jñāna* which rejects the supreme path of devotional service and simply imparts information about the gross external world is extremely abominable."

(*Sajjana-toṣaṇī* 11/10)

11. What is the matured stage of pure knowledge?

"The devotional service executed by the Vaiṣṇavas is the matured stage of pure knowledge."

(*Sajjana-toṣaṇī* 11/10)

12. When can one attain pure devotional service?

"When the 'distressed' living entities give up their desire for material enjoyment, when the 'inquisitive' living entities give up their desire for worldly morality, when the 'needy' living entities give up their desire for attaining heavenly pleasures, and when the 'impersonalists' give up their desire for merging into the existence of Brahman and think that the Absolute Truth is temporary, then these four types of living entities can become eligible to perform devotional service. As long as they maintain such desires their devotional service is impure and materially designated. When their desires are destroyed, then their devotional service is called pure unalloyed devotional service."

(Commentary on *Bhagavad-gītā* 7/16)

13. Is renunciation a limb of devotional service?

"Just as darkness follows behind light, similarly where there is devotional service renunciation automatically follows. But renunciation with adverse quality cannot be counted as a limb of devotional service. As shadow is not a limb of light but a concomitant, similarly renunciation is only a companion of devotional service. The conclusion is that knowledge and renunciation must accompany devotional service but they cannot be called limbs of devotional service."

(*Tattva-sutra* – 33)

14. What is the difference between karma and service to Hari?

"The constitutional duties of a pure spirit soul are called service to the Lord and the materially designated activity of a conditioned soul is called karma. When a living entity is freed from matter his activities are without material designations."

(Introduction to *Bhagavad-gītā*)

15. Is the performance of karma superior to chanting the holy names of Hari?

"Performance of karma is like a dark well compare to the ocean of mellows of the Lord's holy names. One should give up all kinds of worship and constantly chant the holy names of Hari in the association of the devotees who are attached to chanting the holy names. This is most desirable."

(*Sajjana-toṣaṇī* 11/6)

16. What are the two colors of devotional service?

"Devotional service has two colors – devotional service mixed with the knowledge of opulence and pure unalloyed devotional service. When one worships the Supreme Lord with gratitude, fear and reverence it is called devotional service mixed with opulence. Worship of Nārāyaṇa, the Lord of the spiritual sky and not is devotional service mixed with opulence. But worshiping the Supreme Lord Krishna who is eternal, full of knowledge and bliss is called pure unalloyed devotional service."

(*Tattva-sutra* – 40)

17. How can one become a Vaiṣṇava?

"One become a Vaiṣṇava by the mercy of a Vaiṣṇava."

(*Jaiva Dharma*, Chapter10)

18. What are the primary symptoms of devotional service?

"Full surrender and subordination to the Supreme Lord are the primary symptoms of devotional service."

(*Sajjana-toṣaṇī* 10/9)

19. Besides chanting the holy names how will the other limbs of devotional service be accepted?

"After accepting the chanting of the holy names of Hari as the best form of Sādhanā and taking shelter of the holy names without deviation, other limbs of devotional service can be accepted only as practitioners of the chanting."

(*Sajjana-toṣaṇī* 11/5)

20. Are other limbs of sādhanā helpful for original sādhanā?

"Chanting the holy names of Hari is the only *sādhanā*. Other limbs of *sādhanā* are only support of the chanting of the holy names of Hari."

(*Sajjana-toṣaṇī* 11/5)

21. Does one disregard the demigods by executing unalloyed devotional service to Hari?

mūlete siñcile jala śākhā-pallavera bala
śire bari nāhi kārjakara
hari-bhakti āche jaṅra sarva-deva bandhu tāṅra
bhakte sabe korena ādara

If one waters the root of a tree all the branches and twigs become nourished. But if one waters the top of a tree, however, it yields no result. Similarly, one who possesses devotion towards Lord Hari, all the demigods automatically becomes his friend as the devotees are respected by all."

(*Kalyāna Kalpataru*, Song 4)

22. Why only the Bhāgavat-dharma is eternal and other dharmas are temporary?

"Devotional service to Hari is Brahmān known as *suddha-vaiṣṇava-dharma, nityā-dharma, jaiva-dharma, bhāgavata-dharma, paramātma-dharma* and *para-dharma*. All religious principles that have arisen from the predisposition towards Brahman and Paramātmā are temporary. There is a motive behind searching after impersonal Brahman, therefore it is causal. In other words it is temporary. A conditioned soul trying to get freedom from material bondage takes shelter of temporary religious principles in the form of searching after impersonal Brahman. Therefore the predisposition towards Brahman is not eternal. A living entity who meditates on the Supersoul to achieve happiness derived from *samādhi* is also following temporary religious principles, keeping the subtle material enjoyment within his mind. Therefore the predisposition towards Paramātmā is also not eternal. Only pure *Bhāgavata-dharma* is eternal."

(*Jaiva Dharma*, Chapter 4)

23. What is the relationship of Vaiṣṇava-dharma with other religious systems?

"There is no religious principles other than *Vaiṣṇava-dharma*. All other religious principles that have been preached or will be preached are either supportive or a distorted form of *Vaiṣṇava-dharma*. Whenever they manifest as support one should respect them and whenever they appear as distorted form one should cultivate one's own devotional service without being envious."

(*Jaiva Dharma*, Chapter 8)

24. What is the only religion which is free from all cheating propensities?

"There is only one religion in this world, that is *Vaiṣṇava-dharma*. All other systems of religion are full of differences in opinion, arguments, counter arguments, envy and eagerness to prove their supremacy over other's. Those religious systems which did not specify the relationship between karma, *jñāna*, *bhakti* and *vairāgya*, are all cheating religion. Only *Vaiṣṇava-dharma* is pure and without cheating. The pure *Vaiṣṇava-dharma* cannot be polluted by the characteristics and conclusions of pseudo Vaiṣṇavas."

(*Sajjana-toṣaṇī* 11/10)

25. Are humility and compassion separate from devotional service?

"Humility and compassion are not separate qualities; they are included in devotional service."

(*Jaiva Dharma*, Chapter 8)

26. Is devotional service dependent?

"Devotional service is fully independent. Devotional service itself is beauty and ornaments; it does not depend on any other good qualities."

(*Jaiva Dharma*, Chapter 8)

27. Is cultivation of devotional service very hard or austere?

"This swanlike *dharma* is very simple; it is not very austere. There are two principles found in it namely attachment and good character. Attachment is applied to the Supreme Lord and the living entities. One should apply full attachment to the Supreme Lord and brotherly attachment to all living entity. Both attachment and good character can be found in their proper place."

(*Tattva-sutra* – 50)

28. Are there different stages of devotional service?

"There are unlimited stages in devotional service to Krishna. There are no end to the stages beginning from faith up to *mahābhāva*. In those stages one makes gradual advancement by cultivating Krishna consciousness and withdrawing the senses from their objects."

(*Tattva-sutra* – 47)

29. Is liberation the fruit of devotional service?

"The transcendentalists do not accept liberation to be the fruit of devotional service. As long as the desire for material enjoyment and liberation is present in the heart, pure devotional service does not manifest."

(*Caitanya-śikṣāmṛta* 5/3)

30. Should one pray to Krishna to be relieved from the three-fold miseries of material existence?

"Since getting freedom from material miseries, such as birth, death etc., depends on Krishna's desire and not a subject matter for living entities' endeavor, one should not pray for this."

(Commentary on *Śikṣāstakaṁ* 4)

31. Why is it that devotional service to Hari is a secret or confidential?

"Devotional service to Hari mostly awards liberation and keeps people happy, and unless it finds a qualified person it does not award pure devotional service."

(*Jaiva Dharma*, Chapter 19)

42

Vaidhi Bhakti

1. What is the path of regulative principles?

"The rules and regulations given by the self-realized physicians to remove the disease of the conditioned souls whose eternal constitutional propensities are either dormant or perversely reflected as attachment for material enjoyment, are called regulative principles. This is the main purport behind prescribing these regulative principles."

2. Which propensities are prominent in Vaidhi Bhakti and Rāgātmikā Bhakti?

"Awe and reverence, fearfulness and faith are prominent in *Vaidhi Bhakti* while intense greed for the pastimes of Krishna is prominent in *Rāgānugā Bhakti*."

(*Jaiva Dharma*, Chapter 21)

3. What is the duty of a living entity prior to attaining the platform of Rāga?

"It is one's main duty to take shelter of the regulative devotional service until one's *rāga* is awakened."

(*Caitanya-śikṣāmṛta* 1/1)

4. What is the difference between Smārta dharma and Sādhana bhakti?

"*Smārta dharma* is another name of worldly morality. The prescribed religious principles for spiritual advancement is called *sādhana-bhakti*."

(*Caitanya-śikṣāmṛta* 3/1)

5. What is the ultimate benefit for a conditioned soul?

"The conditioned souls are prone to material enjoyment and, as a result, suffering in the cycle of birth and death is inevitable for them. Serving Krishna by giving up material enjoyments brings about their soul's **bhajana** ultimate benefit."

(Commentary on *Śikṣāstaka*, Verse 1)

6. What is the duty of an embodied soul?

"As long as you have this material body, carefully remain fixed in the principles of *bhakti*. Always serve the devotees, chant the name of Krishna, worship Rādhā and Krishna, and remain indifferent to sense gratification.

"With the mercy of the devotees, the name, and the *dhāma*, keep undesirable association far away. Soon you will attain residence in the eternal *dhāma* where pure service to Rādhā and Krishna manifests."

(*Navadvīpa-bhāva-taranga*, Verses 107/108)

7. What is the difference between karma yoga, jñāna yoga, indirect devotional service and direct devotional service?

"When acts are performed for one's selfish enjoyment, they are called karma-*kāṇḍa*; when the desire for attainment of freedom from activity by knowledge underlies these actions, they are termed *jñāna-yoga* or karma-*yoga*. And when these activities are managed to be performed in this way that is conducive to endeavor for attainment of *bhakti* they are called *jñāna-bhakta-yoga*, i.e., the subsidiary devotional practices. But only those activities that are characterized by the principle of pure worship are called *bhakti* proper."

(*Brahma Saṁhitā* 5/61)

6. How many types of sukṛtis are there? How can one accumulate sukṛti born of devotional service?

"There are three types of *sukṛtis* – *sukṛti* born of Karma, *sukṛti* born of *jñāna* and *sukṛti* born of *bhakti*. In the first type of *sukṛti* one enjoys the fruits of one's karma, in the second type of *sukṛti* one attains liberation and in the third type of *sukṛti* one develops firm faith in unalloyed devotional service. Performance of the limbs of the devotional service without one's knowledge is called *sukṛti* born of devotional service ."

(*Harināma-cintāmani*, Chapter 1)

7. What is the difference between the real bhajana and as good as bhajana?

"'Even if one worships Krishna with various material desires still he attains perfection in devotional service. By worshiping Krishna to fulfill one's material desire one attains mellows of devotional service to Krishna. If an ambitious person worships Krishna then even though he does not desire still Krishna allows him to serve His lotus feet.' These statements are referred to those who are as good as Vaiṣṇavas among the neophytes who practice the chanting of *nāmābhāsa*. The word *bhajana* that has been used in these context is referring to the severe *sādhana* practiced by those who are almost Vaiṣṇavas. The real *bhajana* lies in the favorable cultivation of Krishna consciousness without any desire for sense gratification, fruitive activities, and mental speculation."

(*Sajjana-toṣaṇī* 4/12)

8. What is a householder's controlling the urge of genital?

"To have sex with one's legitimate wife is called controlling the urge of the genital."

(*Sajjana-toṣaṇī* 11/5)

9. Can the foodstuffs cooked by the nondevotees or pseudodevotees be offered to Krishna?

"Foodstuffs that are cooked only by pure devotees should be offered to Krishna. During the time of worshiping Krishna no nondevotee should stay there."

(*Harināma-cintāmani*)

10. Should one take the remnants of the demigods? What is the harm if one does so?

When can one take the remnants of the demigods and demigoddesses?

"Worshipers of the demigods are mostly Māyāvādīs. If one accepts *prasāda* from them one's devotional service is diminished, and it is an offense to Bhakti Devī. If a pure devotee offers the remnants of Krishna to the demigods and demigoddesses then they accept it with great pleasure and dance in ecstacy. Thereafter a devotee can take their *prasāda* and become joyful."

(*Jaiva Dharma*)

11. What is the resolution of those who desire their own benefit?

"One should maintain simplicity in all of one's activities. One should not keep one thing in the heart and display something else in one's behavior. One should not try to collect cheap adoration from persons who are averse to devotional service by displaying some artificial symptoms of ecstatic love. One should be partial to pure devotional service and should not support any other conclusion. One's intention and behavior should be one and the same."

(*Sajjana-toṣaṇī* 8/10)

12. Are the worshipers of Krishna immoral or attached to matter? When can one actually worship Krishna?

"In order to worship Krishna one must first become saintly. The women should not associate with men, and the men should not associate with women. If one can gradually give up mundane thoughts and activities and tries to make advancement on the path of spiritual advancement then one will attain the body of a *gopī* in Braja. Unless one becomes a *gopī* one will not be able to worship Krishna."

(*Sajjana-toṣaṇī* 10/6)

13. How should one respect the day of Ekādaśī?

"On the day before Ekādaśī one should strictly follow celibacy, on the day of Ekādaśī one should observe a total fast even from water, stay up all night and constantly chant the holy names of Krishna. On the day after Ekādaśī one should observe strict celibacy and break one's fast in the appropriate time. This is the way to respect the day of Ekādaśī."

(*Jaiva Dharma*, Chapter 20)

14. How should one observe the vows like Puruṣottama?

"There are three kinds of transcendentalists. They are *svanistha*, *parinisthita* and *nirapekṣa*. Observing vows like Śrī Puruṣottama Adhika Māsa are meant for *svanistha* transcendentalists. The *parinisthita* devotees are eligible to observe the vows of Puruṣottama, Kārttika and so on as instructed by their respective spiritual teachers. Through their unalloyed propensity the *nirapekṣa* devotees honor *prasādam* and engage in hearing and chanting the holy names of Hari day and night according to their ability throughout the year."

(*Sajjana-toṣaṇī* 10/6)

15. What kind of behavior should one follow?

"In which ever *āśrama* one stays one should give up the attachment for sense enjoyment and follows the principles of that *āśrama*. One should become enthusiastic about the execution of devotional service to Krishna and follow the behavior of the devotees."

(*Sajjana-toṣaṇī* 2/7)

18. What is the procedure for the conditional souls for attaining Krishna's mercy?

"A conditioned soul should gradually give up nature and activities of the modes of passion and ignorance, and accept only the mode of goodness in all dealings regarding the maintenance of his livelihood. He should make those activities fully transcendental to material modes of nature through the process of devotional service. The more one's practice of devotional service becomes purified the more one becomes eligible to receive Krishna's mercy."

(*Śrī Bhāgavatārka Maricīmālā*)

19. What is the duty of a renounced Vaiṣṇava?

"A renounced Vaiṣṇava should give up association with his wife, accumulating wealth, idle talk, palatable foodstuffs, opulent dress and great enterprises and should spend his days in a place where he can worship Lord Hari peacefully."

(*Sajjana-toṣaṇī* 5/11)

20. How should a renounced Vaiṣṇava maintain his livelihood? How will he attain knowledge about Krishna?

"A renunciate must not accumulate any wealth. He should maintain his life by begging alms everyday and practice devotional service. He should not get involved in any kind of enterprise. Involving into any enterprises will make him faulty. The more he worships the Lord with simplicity and humility, the more he will understand the science of Krishna by the Lord's mercy."

(*Sajjana-toṣaṇī* 10/9)

21. Should a renunciate associate with women?

"The Vaiṣṇava who has accepted the renounced order of life should maintain his livelihood by begging alms door to door, just like a bee who collects honey from one flower to another. He should never converse or associate with any woman. He should keep equal distance from the association of woman, king and the poisonous snake."

22. Is it possible to worship Hari in one's childhood?

"It is improper to think that it is not possible to worship Hari in one's childhood. We find in the history that Dhruva and Prahlāda achieved the Supreme Lord's mercy in their early childhood. If any person is able to do anything then every person is capable of doing that provided he tries to do so. As such whatever is practiced from one's childhood gradually becomes a habit when one grows up."

(*Caitanya-śikṣāmṛta* 1/1)

23. What are the primary and secondary differences in the process of bhajana? What harm can be caused by the secondary differences?

"As the situations of human beings throughout the world gradually change from uncivilized to civilized, then from civilized to scientific, from scientific to moral and from moral to devotional, the process for worshiping God also changes according to the differences in the language, dress, food and mental condition. If one considers from an impartial point of view, one can understand that these secondary differences do not actually cause any harm. As long as there is unanimity in the process of *bhajana* there will be no problem at the time of perfection."

(*Caitanya-śikṣāmṛta* 1/1)

24. What is the proof of advancement on the path of sādhana?

"There are mysteries in the practice of *sādhana.* Transcendental knowledge, devotional service and detachment for material objects simultaneously increase. Whenever a reversion is seen it is to be understood that there is a fault in the root of one's *sādhana.* Without the association of devotees and the mercy of the spiritual master one can not always get protection from the danger of misguidance."

(*Caitanya-śikṣāmṛta* 1/6)

25. What is gradual advancement?

"The gradual levels of advancement is proper and certainly effective. In the beginning one should lead a pious life by becoming fixed in the principles of varnāśrama. When one is advanced one can certainly lead a life of regulative devotee and finally one can achieve perfection by engaging in loving devotional service to Krishna."

(*Caitanya-śikṣāmṛta* 1/6)

26. What are the gradual levels of advancement beginning from animalistic life to the temple of love?

"After surpassing various levels of advancement from animal life to civilize life, Godless moral life, moral life with imaginary God, moral life with God at the centre and ultimately devotional life, a living entity has to reach the temple of love."

27. Is the life of a devotee on the path of rāga the same as the life of a devotee on the path of regulative devotional service?

"The structure of human life is full of various levels. The life of the outcastes is on the lowest grade, Godless moral life is the second grade, the theistic moral life is the third grade, the life of the regulative devotees is fourth grade, and the life of the devotees who are agitated by *rāga* is on the topmost grade."

28. What is the difference between the miseries of the devotees and the nondevotees?

"The nondevotees think that their perishable material body is all in all. Whatever distress they suffer is severe. Even though they try to remove these miseries in various ways they are unable to do so. The devotees, however, know their temporary material life as the life of guests. Therefore due to the influence of their pure spiritual bliss their temporary ordinary distresses are passed off most insignificantly."

(*Sajjana-toṣaṇī* 10/2)

28. What is the first limb of bhajana? What should be the first teaching of a spiritual master to his disciple?

"The first limb of *bhajana* is to serve the ten original principles. After teaching these ten essential instructions a spiritual master should teach his disciple about the five *samskāras* or purificatory processes. Unless one begins to worship the Lord after drinking the nectar of these ten principles, one's *anarthas* will not be destroyed."

(*Sajjana-toṣaṇī* 9/9)

29. How is the misconception regarding one's constitutional position destroyed and how does one revive one's constitutional position and cultivate Krishna consciousness?

"The misconception regarding one's constitutional position does not go away in one day. It gradually vanquishes as one cultivates Krishna consciousness. The constitutional position of a living entity is that he is an eternal servant of Krishna. Cultivation of Krishna consciousness with this conviction is the actual cultivation of Krishna consciousness. The science of self-realization is awakened by the mercy of the spiritual master. A disciple should try to realize his constitutional position with utmost care otherwise his first *anartha* in the path of spiritual life will not be destroyed."

(*Sajjana-toṣaṇī* 9/9)

30. How would material desires be removed from the heart?

"If one has got some material desires in the heart, then with all humility one should reluctantly accept them and continue to worship the Lord without any duplicity. Then within a short period of time the Lord will sit in one's heart, and thereafter remove all material desires except His loving service."

(*Caitanya-śikṣāmṛta* 1/7)

31. How is one's state of bhāva and prema awakened?

"While cultivating the holy names of Hari by the strength of the association of the saintly persons one's state of *bhāva* is awakened and then gradually one's state of *prema* is awakened. As *prema* manifests liberation personally appears as a secondary fruit before a devotee."

(*Sajjana-toṣaṇī* 9/9)

33. How can one get freedom from the influence of offenses against the holy names and how does the state of nāmābhāsa is destroyed?

"By the mercy of the spiritual master the state of *nāmābhāsa* is destroyed and one is protected from the offense against chanting of the holy names."

(*Caitanya-śikṣāmṛta* 6/4)

34. What is the essence of various methods of bhajana?

"Among all methods of *bhajana* the chanting of the holy names of Hari is the essence."

(*Caitanya-śikṣāmṛta* 3/3)

35. How does one develop a taste for chanting the holy names and how does one achieve unalloyed devotional service in the form of taking complete shelter of the holy names?

"Just by mere belief in the science of the holy names or studying about the holy names in the scriptures is not enough. If we practically apply them then will get the desired result. Those who do not chant the holy names even after understanding the glories of the holy names are not offenseless. Such people do not develop a taste for chanting the holy names because their hearts are weak due to bad association. Therefore they are offenders at the feet of the holy names. The auspicious symptom is that one should nullify all one's offenses by associating with the devotees and take shelter of the holy names without any duplicity. If one carefully chants the holy names offenselessly then in a very short time the holy names appears blissfully. Gradually this bliss increases in such a way that one does not wish to give up chanting the holy names and thus one takes complete shelter of the holy names."

(*Sajjana-toṣaṇī* 11/5)

36. How does one's offenses against the chanting of the holy names become exhausted? Can they be exhausted by the performance of pious activities or by undergoing atonement?

"Apart from the time of resting which are necessary for keeping the body and soul together one should always humbly chant the holy names. Then the offenses against the holy names will be nullified. No other pious activities of atonements can counteract the offenses against the holy names."

(*Harināma-cintāmani*)

37. How does one make advancement in the worship of the Lord?

"By eagerly contemplating the actual meaning of chanting of the holy names and by praying to Krishna with humility one gradually makes advancement on the path of *bhajana*. Unless one follows this process one will spend many births in *sādhana*, just like the *karmīs* and the *jñānis*."

(*Caitanya-śikṣāmṛta* 6/4)

38. How does one come to the platform of pure goodness?

"If there is some dirt on the body it can not be cleaned by any other dirt. The material activities are themselves dirt, therefore how can they

clean other dirt? Indirect knowledge is just like the fire, if it is applied to the contaminated state it will burn out the very contaminated state. So how can it give happiness that is derived due to the purification of the dirt? Therefore the state of pure goodness is awakened by the process of devotional service achieved by the mercy of the spiritual master, Krishna and the Vaiṣṇavas. This state of pure goodness illuminates one's heart."
(*Caitanya-śikṣāmṛta* 7/7)

39. Who are introspective? What is introspection?

"Those who know that the Supreme Lord is their life and soul and thus spend their lives by dovetailing their scientific knowledge, art, morality, religiousness, and thought into the devotional service to the supreme controller, though conditioned, are fully introspective. This life of introspection is called life of regulative devotional service."
(*Caitanya-śikṣāmṛta* 8, Conclusion)

40. Which process of sādhana determines which planet the devotees who have developed love of God attain?

"In this material creation there are fourteen worlds. They are progressively situated one after another. The ambitious and fruitive householders wander throughout Bhu, Bhuva and Sva *lokas*. By the performance of pious activities without expecting any thing in return the strict celibates, ascetics as well as truthful and peaceful persons wander throughout Maharloka, Janaloka, Tapoloka and Satyaloka. On the upper portion of Satyaloka is the abode of four-headed Brahmā and beyond that is the spiritual abode of Vaikuṇṭha where Kṣirodakaśāyī Vishnu resides. The *sannyāsi paramahaṁsas* and the demons who are killed by Lord Hari surpass the river Virajā, in other's words, the fourteen worlds, and after entering into the effulgent abode of Brahman attain *nirvāna* in the form of self-destruction. The devotees of the Lord who are attached to His opulent feature, the pure devotees, the loving devotees, the more loving devotees, and the most loving devotees attain the abode of transcendental Vaikunṭa or the spiritual sky. The devotees who worship the Lord in the mood of *mādhurya* of Braja attain the abode of Goloka."
(*Brahma Saṁhita*)

41. By which process is the perfection of Vaiṣṇavism attained?

"In that case, his life will follow whichever attachment is greater. A boat moves by the strength of oars, but when the water's current carries away the boat, the oars are defeated. In the same way, as the *sādhaka* tries to cross the ocean with the boat of the mind and various oars like *dhyāna*, *pratyāhāra*, and *dhāraṇā*, sometimes the current of attachment quickly carries him into sense gratification."Devotional service to Viṣṇu is executed with spontaneous love. The *sādhaka* certainly achieves spiritual attachment in no time through spontaneous devotional service."

(*Prema Pradeep*, Ray 4)

42. How can the attachment for material objects transform into the attachment to the Supreme Lord?

"When the cause of the mind's restlessness is sense gratification and this restlessness is the main obstacle in the practice of devotional service, then all sensual activities should be dovetailed in the service of the Lord and the attachment to sense gratification should be transformed into attachment for the Lord."

(*Sajjana-toṣaṇī* 10/11)

43. What is the cause for achieving the mercy of Krishna?

"Spontaneous worship of the Lord is the cause for achieving the mercy of Krishna."

(*Sajjana-toṣaṇī* 10/11)

44. How many platforms are there in sādhana-bhakti? What is the doorway of love of God?

"In *sādhana-bhakti* there are four platforms namely *śraddhā*, *nisthā*, *rūci* and *āsakti*. After crossing these four platforms one has to come the platform of *bhāva* which is the doorway of *prema*."

(*Sajjana-toṣaṇī* 10/10)

45. How is the supremacy of the sādhana-bhaktas proved? Who is the actual candidate for receiving the Lord's mercy?

"One should maintain one's life by following the principles of *varnāśrama*. By practicing Yoga one can regulate and improve the state of the mind. But by performance of *sādhana-bhakti* one makes advancement on the path of spiritual life. Although a practitioner of devotional service may not be an experienced farmer, an expert businessman or a clever warrior, nevertheless according to his qualification he has matured in the tactics of the highest human life. Even though an expert royal minister may not be able to operate a tank still he arranges the battle has the head of the army. In the same way a person who sees that a practitioner of devotional service is situated on the highest platform in all respects is actually intelligent and as such has achieved the mercy of the Lord."

(*Caitanya-śikṣāmṛta* 1/6)

46. Should the transcendentalists accept the conclusions of the Goswāmīs along with the conclusions of the sages who have compiled the scriptures?

"All processes of the cultivation of Krishna consciousness that the sages have written in their own literature are legitimate. Among them many processes have been quoted in '*Hari Bhakti Vilāsa*.' In his book '*Bhakti Rasāmṛta Sindhu*' Śrī Rūpa Goswāmī has picked up sixty-four famous processes from them and included in it."

(*Tattva-sutra* 35)

43

Śraddhā

1. What does one gain when one develops faith?

"*tayā deśika pādāśrayaḥ*—that due to faith one receives an opportunity to take shelter at the lotus feet of a bonafide spiritual master ."

(*Āmnāya-sutra* 59)

2. Can sraddhās of the karmīs and jñānis be called the actual śraddhā?

"*śraddhā* which the *karmīs* and *jñānis* repeatedly refer to cannot be called actual a *śraddhā*. They simply misinterpret it. If you call a piece of iron gold then it is very much annoying. Still the iron is iron, and it is never gold until it is touched by a touchstone. Devotional service to Krishna is touchstone and if fruitive activities and cultivation of knowledge which are like iron come in contact with it then they also transform into gold. This is the influence of the touchstone of devotional service."

(*Śrī Rūpānuga Bhajana Darpana*, Song 3)

3. What is śraddhā? What is the difference between śraddhā or faith and śaranāgati or surrender?

"The firm faith one develops after hearing the topics of Hari from the mouths of the saintly persons is called *śraddhā*. As soon as *śraddhā* is awakened, a little bit of *śaranāgati* also awakened. Both *śraddhā* and *śaranāgati* are almost the same."

(*Jaiva Dharma*, Chapter 20)

4. What is called śraddhā?

"Knowledge, opulence and pious activities are not the best processes for achieving perfection in the ultimate goal of life; devotional service alone is the pure process. When such a mentality towards unalloyed devotional service is developed it is called *śraddhā.*"

(*Sajjana-toṣaṇī* 4/9)

5. What is the symptom of the awakening of śraddhā?

"Having firm faith in the scriptures is called *śraddhā*. The purport of the scripture is that if one does not surrender to Krishna he is full of fear, and if he is surrendered to Krishna he has no fear. Therefore the development of *śraddhā* is evident by the presence of the symptoms of *śaranāgati*."

(*Sajjana-toṣaṇī* 4/9)

6. Who can actually please Krishna?

"It is not a fact that just by executing the limbs of devotional service after taking initiation, Krishna becomes pleased; only one who has unflinching faith in unalloyed devotional service can please the Lord."

(*Sajjana-toṣaṇī* 8/10)

7. What is the possibility of attaining devotional service?

"Until one develops faith in devotional service even though one has other good qualities apart from the quality of full surrender to Krishna, one will not achieve devotional service."

(*Sajjana-toṣaṇī* 5/1)

8. How many kinds of sraddhās are there? What qualifications do they award?

"*Vaidhi-śraddhā* awards one the qualification to engage in regulative devotional service. Staunch faith awards one the qualification to engage in *ragatmika* devotional service."

(*Jaiva Dharma*, Chapter 21)

9. Who are bereft of śraddhā?

"Those who have no pious activities have no *śraddhā*. Even if they are preached to heavily, still they will not understand anything."

(*Sajjana-toṣaṇī* 11/11)

10. Who can easily understand the purport of the ācaryas' instructions?

"Those who have developed faith according to their pious activities receive pure intelligence by the mercy of Krishna. Due to this intelligence they can easily understand the purport of the *ācaryas*' instructions."

(*Sajjana-toṣaṇī* 11/11)

11. What is the qualification for performing Kṛṣṅa-kīrtana?

"Faith is the only qualification for engaging in the performance of *Kṛṣṇa-kīrtana*. There is no other consideration."

(*Harināma Cintamani*)

12. Is śraddhā a limb of devotional service?

"*śraddhā* is not a limb of devotional service, it is an instrument to destroy an unalloyed devotee's attachment for fruitive activities."

(*Sajjana-toṣaṇī* 4/9)

13. What is the seed of devotional service which brings one to the platform of transcendence?

"Due to *sādhu-saṅga*, *śraddhā* gradually increases. The more one's *śraddhā* increases the more one becomes eager. At that time the only endeavor of a living entity is that he always searches for an opportunity to attain the lotus feet of the Lord. He sees that he is fully influenced by his *anarthas* and that his constitutional nature is dormant. He then engages in devotional service without deviation in the association of the saintly persons who are devoid of all *anarthas* and who are self-realized. This state of *śraddhā* is called the *śraddhā* which brings one to the platform of transcendence. This is the seed of devotional service."

(*Sajjana-toṣaṇī* 9/5)

14. Is śraddhā which renounces the service of the devotees, actual śraddhā?

"The word *śraddhā* which is found in theverse of *Śrīmad-Bhāgavatam* 11/2/47 is only *śraddhā-abhāsa*; because the development of *śraddhā* in the worship of Krishna by giving up the service of devotees is only a reflection of the real *śraddhā*, in other words it is only traditional worldly *śraddhā*. It is not the transcendental *śraddhā* for unalloyed devotional service. The *śraddhā* and worship of such persons is mundane."

(*Jaiva Dharma*, Chapter 25)

44

Sādhu Saṅga

1. How does a devotee worship Krishna?

"This material world is useless and only foolish people take pleasure in it. But a renounced person worships Rādhā and Krishna in Braja in the association of saintly persons and constantly takes shelter of the holy names of the Lord."

(Conclusion to the commentary on *Śrī Caitanya Caritāmṛta*)

2. When does a living entity develops desire for associating with saintly persons?

"As a result of heaps of pious activities and due to the mercy of the Lord a living entity's desire for material existence becomes weak. Then he automatically develops a desire for *sādhu-saṅga.* By discussing the topics of Krishna in the association of the devotees one develops faith, and when one gradually cultivates Krishna consciousness with more determination then one develops greedy for attaining Krishna. On such a platform one learns the art of performing *bhajana* by taking shelter at the lotus feet of a bonafide pure spiritual master."

(*Sajjana-toṣaṇī* 11/5)

3. What is the necessity for sādhu-saṅga?

"One should follow the characteristics of the *sādhus* and learn the scriptural conclusions from them."

(*Sajjana-toṣaṇī* 11/6)

4. What is taking shelter at the lotus feet of a spiritual master?

"Associating with an intimate devotee of the Lord is taking shelter at the lotus feet of a spiritual master."

(*Sajjana-toṣaṇī* 2/1)

5. What is the result of traveling to holy places? What does one gain from sādhu-saṅga?

jathā sādhu tathā tīrtha sthira kori' nija citta
sādhu-saṅga koro nirantara
yathāya vaiṣṇava-gaṇa sei sthāna vṛndāvana
sei sthāne ānanda aśeṣa

"Wherever the devotees reside is a holy place. Therefore pacify your mind and associate constantly with the devotees. Where the Vaiṣṇavas reside, that very place is Vṛndāvana. One experiences unlimited happiness at that place."

(*Kalyāna Kalpataru,* Song 4)

6. Do the sādhus ever become selfish?

"The demigods may become selfish but the devotees never become selfish. Therefore persons who desire their own benefit should eagerly hanker after wherever there is a desire for pure love, wherever there is a discussion of Krishna's topics, wherever there is *hari-sankīrtana,* wherever there is a desire for hearing the glories of Krishna, and wherever there is a glorification of Krishna and the Vaiṣṇavas."

(Commentary on *Bhajanāmṛtaṁ*)

7. How can the dormant constitutional nature of a living entity be revived?

"What can revive a living entity's dormant constitutional nature? Fruitive activities, mental speculation and renunciation can not revive it. Only by association of self-realized souls can the dormant nature of a living entity become revived. Two things are required in this connection. A person who desires to revive his dormant constitutional nature acquires a little faith due to his accumulated previous pious activities. This is one incident. On the strength of such a *sukṛti* a person receives an opportunity to associate with qualified *sādhus.* This is the second incident."

(*Sajjana-toṣaṇī* 9/9)

8. What is the root of a living entity's original nature?

"Nature is born from association. One's nature is determined according to one's association. The faith that a living entity develops by the performance of his karma of his previous life's association is changed by the association of his present life. Therefore association is the root cause of a living entity's nature."

(*Sajjana-toṣaṇī* 15/2)

9. What is the only cause of advancement for the mundane Vaiṣṇavas?

"The matured yogis who are expert in devotional service are the *uttama adhikāris*. The immature yogis who desire devotional service and who sometimes engage in fruitive activities, and follow religious principles are *madhyama adhikāris*. The neophyte devotees who are attached to karma are counted in the category of mundane Vaiṣṇavas or *kaniṣṭha adhikāris*. In the hearts of these last kinds of Vaiṣṇavas the reflection of devotional service is awakened. If a little bit of pure devotional service arises in their hearts they also give up attachment for karma and become *madhyama adhikaris*. Association with *sādhus* is the only criteria for all these types of advancements.

(Commentary on *Bhajanāmṛtaṁ*)

10. Whose association is desirable? By whose association can one make advancement on the path of spiritual life?

"One who has awakened pure devotional service in his heart is an unalloyed devotee of Krishna. His association is most desirable. The association of *madhyama adhikāris* is also suitable. A practitioner of devotional service should always take shelter of devotees who are superior to him. In this way he can make advancement on the path of spiritual advancement."

(Commentary on *Bhajanāmṛtaṁ*)

11. How should one associate with pure devotees even in ordinary dealings?

"One should behave with ordinary people as one externally behaves with a stranger while buying something in the market. The dealings with a pure devotee of the Lord should be done out of love."

(*Sajjana-toṣaṇī* 11/11)

12. Does one waste time by simply sits near a Vaiṣṇava?

"The foremost instruction of Śrī Rāmānujācārya is this: 'If you cannot purify yourself by any endeavor whatsoever, then just go sit with the Vaiṣṇavas and you will achieve all auspiciousness.'"

(*Sajjana-toṣaṇī* 11/11)

13. Is there any direct proof of auspiciousness attained due to the association with the Vaiṣṇavas?

"By observing the pure characteristics of a devotee, in a very short time a person's mind is changed, his attachment for sense enjoyment decreases, and the seedling of *bhakti* sprouts in the heart. One even gradually develops a taste for the Vaiṣṇavas' food and behavior. We have seen how by associating with Vaiṣṇavas, people have given up many *anartha*s—taste for associating with women, thirst for wealth, desire for sense enjoyment and liberation, inclination for karma and *jñāna*, eating meat and fish, drinking wine, smoking tobacco, and the desire to chew pan. By observing a Vaiṣṇava's quality of not uselessly wasting time, many people have easily given up *anarthas* such as laziness, oversleeping, useless talk, the urge of speech, etc. We have also seen that by associating with Vaiṣṇavas for sometime, someone's cheating propensity and desire for fame have been destroyed. We have seen with our own eyes that by associating with Vaiṣṇavas with a little affection, all other association, such as attachment for prejudices, has been vanquished. Those who are attached to winning fights, those who are expert at attaining dominion, those who are eager to accumulate great wealth—all such types of people have attained devotional service by being purified in the association of Vaiṣṇavas. Even the hearts of persons who think,"I will defeat the world by my arguments and attain supremacy," have been pacified. Without the association of Vaiṣṇavas there is no alternative for rectifying the attachment to prejudices.

(*Sajjana-toṣaṇī* 11/11)

14. What does a sādhu do?

"The *sādhus* award divine eyes to our hearts."

(*Bhāgavatārka Marici-mālā* 15/17)

15. What is the nature of a sādhu?

"A *sādhu* never find faults in other's. He respects whatever little qualities are there in other's."

16. Are the number of sādhus too many? Is it proper to ascertain a sādhu by seeing his external dress?

"In this age of Kali the consideration of a *sādhu* is being lost. The sad part is that we should always remember that we ourselves are gradually being cheated by associating with *sādhus* just by seeing their external dress. The *sādhus* are not too many. The number of *sādhus* are so few nowadays that it has become very rare to find a real *sādhu* even after searching for a long time and traveling to many countries."

(*Sajjana-toṣaṇī* 15/2)

17. Is it proper to manipulate while ascertaining the difference between a pure Vaiṣṇava and a cheater?

"In order to distinguish the pure devotional service and the pure devotees Śrī Kṛṣṇadas Kavirāja Goswami has displayed the method for ascertaining the branches of the devotees. According to that method even today we can distinguish between the pure Vaiṣṇavas and the cheaters. No compromise should be made in this regard. There is no possibility for the living entities to achieve auspiciousness without *sādhu-saṅga*. Therefore the pure Vaiṣṇavas should certainly be distinguished."

(*Sajjana-toṣaṇī* 10/5)

18. Is sādhu-saṅga a limb of devotional service in the conditional state?

"In the conditional state, association with devotees helps one to develop a taste regarding Hari. It is not a limb of devotional service."

(*Tattva-sutra* – 33)

19. What is the piety that awards one devotional service?

"Associating with the devotees is the only piety that awards one devotional service."

(*Jaiva Dharma*, Chapter 17)

20. What is the result of pretentious sādhu-saṅga?

"Many people think that by serving the lotus feet of a *sādhu*, by offering obeisances to him, by drinking the water that has washed his feet, by honoring his remnants and by giving him some donation they can get the advantage of *sādhu-saṅga*. Although by such activities one can respect a *sādhu* and gain something but this is not actual *sādhu-saṅga*. If one can carefully search out the pure characteristics and the nature of the pure devotees and emulate them without duplicity, then one can attain pure devotional service to Krishna. A materialist approaches a *sādhu*, offers obeisances, and prays as follows: 'Oh merciful one! Please be kind to me, I am very poor and fallen therefore how will my attachment for material existence be destroyed?' These words of the materialists are simply cheating. They certainly know that, for themselves, accumulating wealth is the goal of life and collecting material objects is the aim of life. Their hearts are always filled with pride due to opulence. They artificially make a show of humility and devotion with a fear that by the curse of the *sādhus* their desire for obtaining name, fame and sense gratification may be destroyed. If a *sādhu* blesses them by saying, 'O dear! May your material desires, wealth and followers be destroyed.' Then the materialists quickly say, 'O *sādhu* Mahārāja! Please do not give us such a benediction. Such a benediction is simply a curse and always yields inauspiciousness.' Such a behavior of the materialists towards the *sādhu* is only cheating. In the course of our life we meet with many *sādhus* but due to our artificial behavior we do not gain anything from their association. Therefore if we can always carefully emulate the pure characteristics of the saintly persons with spontaneous faith then we can certainly make advancement by their association. We should always remember this while approaching *sādhus* and try our level best to realize the pure nature and character of the *sādhus* and build our own character like theirs. This is the teaching of *Śrīmad-Bhāgavatam*."

(*Sajjana-toṣaṇī* 15/2)

21. Is it possible to give up bad association without sādhu-saṅga?

"Only giving up bad association is not enough. It is our duty to carefully associate with the devotees."

(*Sajjana-toṣaṇī* 15/2)

22. Is it proper to give up bad association of the unauthorized guru and accept the association of the bonafide gurus?

"One should take leave of one's unqualified family guru by giving him his desired wealth and respect, and search out a bonafide spiritual master." (*Harināma-cintāmani*)

23. What kind of Vaiṣṇava should one associate with?

"One should associate with a Vaiṣṇava who is superior to oneself."

(*Śrī Manaḥ Śiksā*, Verse 10)

24. Are the sādhus always present in this world? Why sādhu-saṅga is rarely achieved?

"The *sādhus* are always present in the world. Because the nondevotees can not recognize them, *sādhu-saṅga* has become very rare."

(*Jaiva Dharma*, Chapter 7)

25. Should one indulge in gossiping with a sādhu? What is actual sādhu-saṅga?

"If one approaches a *sādhu* and converses with him like a witch-haunted man like 'it is very hot in this country, I feel healthy in the other country, that man is very nice, this year we will make a profit from harvesting paddy and wheat' then he is not gaining any thing from such *sādhu-saṅga*. Being absorbed in his own ecstasy a *sādhu* may reply to one or two questions of an inquisitive person, but this does not award the person devotion to Krishna or the benefit of *sādhu-saṅga*. One should approach a *sādhu* with love and devotion and discuss with him the topics of the Supreme Lord. Then one can attain devotional service."

(*Sajjana-toṣaṇī* 10/4)

45

Bhajana Kriyā

1. What is the perfection of bhajana?

"*Sādhana yogena ācārya prasādena ca turnaṁ tadapa nayanam eva bhajana naipunyaṁ*" The perfection of *bhajana* is to destroy the four *anarthas* through *sādhana* by the mercy of an *ācārya*."

(*Āmnāya-sutra* 75)

2. What is bhajana kriyā?

"The seed of devotional service is present in the hearts of all spirit souls. In order to fructify that seed and gradually transform it into a tree, one must act as a gardener. Activities like discussing devotional literatures, worshiping the Supreme Lord, associating with saintly persons and residing in a place infested with devotees are required to be performed. When the seed of devotional service is fructified it is extremely necessary to clean the land of thorns and particles of stones. These activities can be executed perfectly if one perfectly knows the science of devotional service."

(*Prema Pradip*, Ray 6)

3. In whose association is a possibility of achieving the Supreme Lord?

"The only cause for attaining the Supreme Lord is to take shelter of a *mahā-bhāgavata*. Knowing this perfectly well, one should follow his order."

(*Sajjana-toṣaṇī* 7/3)

4. Does acceptance of a bonafide spiritual master depend on the acceptance of a family guru?

"Before a disciple accepts a spiritual master both the spiritual master and the disciple test each other. This is described in the scriptures. In this case there is no need for a family guru."

(*Harināma-cintāmani*)

5. What is 'upāya buddhi' in the service to the Vaiṣṇavas?

"After giving up '*upāya buddhi*' in the service to the Vaiṣṇavas, intelligent persons should always aspire for 'upeya buddhi'. The phrase 'upāya buddhi' means to think that one can achieve some other fruits by serving the Vaiṣṇavas. And the phrase 'upeya buddhi' means to think that as a result of many pious activities, service to the Vaiṣṇavas is attained."

6. What is the first duty of devotee upon waking up in the morning?

"A devotee should utter the names of the exalted Vaiṣṇavas of the disciplic succession upon getting up in the morning,

(*Sajjana-toṣaṇī* 7/3)

7. What is the daily routine of a devotee?

"A devotee should faithfully describe the transcendental qualities of his spiritual master for one hour everyday."

(*Sajjana-toṣaṇī* 7/4)

8. How should one display his service attitude towards the guru and the Vaiṣṇavas?

"One should always serve the spiritual master and the Vaiṣṇavas by respecting them equally. One should keep firm faith in the words of the previous *ācāryas*."

(*Sajjana-toṣaṇī* 7/3)

9. How should one accept the chastisement of a Vaiṣṇavas?

"If a Vaiṣṇavas chastises then one should simply remain silent and not think of his harm."

(*Sajjana-toṣaṇī* 7/4)

10. What should be the mentality and behavior of a practitioner of devotional service?

"A practitioner of devotional service should display humility before the Supreme Lord, appear like a fool before the spiritual master, give up his independence before the Vaiṣṇavas, and display detachment towards material existence."

(*Sajjana-toṣaṇī* 7/3)

11. What are the tactics for removing anarthas? What is the mystery behind worshiping the Lord in the mood of Braja?

"With a desire to remove from the kingdom of one's heart, the disturbances created by those demons whom Lord Krishna had killed, one should humbly pray to Hari. Then Lord Hari certainly removes those *anarthas*. And the *anarthas* which are created by those demons who were killed by Baladeva should be removed by the practitioner's own endeavor. This is the mystery of worshiping the Lord in the mood of Braja."

(*Caitanya-śikṣāmṛta* 6/6)

12. What is the gradual process of bhajana?

"Certain pious activities, which lead to *bhakti*, generate faith. One then becomes interested in associating with pure devotees. Thereafter, one is initiated by the spiritual master and executes the regulative principles of devotional service under his orders. Thus one is freed from all unwanted habits and becomes firmly fixed in devotional service. Thereafter, one develops taste and attachment. This is the way of sadhana-*bhakti*, the execution of devotional service according to regulative principles. Gradually emotions intensify, and finally there is an awakening of love. This is the gradual development of love of Godhead for the devotee interested in Krishna consciousness. While chanting at the stage of niṣṭhā, *anarthas* are destroyed and one attains taste for the holy name. Then as more *anarthas* are destroyed, one comes to the stage of attachment. Gradually as one attains stage of *bhāva*, or *rati*, almost all *anarthas* are destroyed. In this development, if the desire for fame arises due to the company of nondevotees, it leads to kuṭīnāṭī (diplomacy), which then results in one's fall-down. Therefore, one should carefully abandon the company of nondevotees and at the same time one should always chant the Lord's name in great ecstasy."

(*Bhajana-rahasya*, Chapter 1)

13. What is the harm if one gives up the gradual path of devotional service?

"If one thinks of his *siddha-deha* without achieving the *adhikara* his intellect gets bewildered. One should carefully accept the sequence as given in the *sikṣāṣṭakam* if he wants to attain perfection. By observing the activities of *sadhus* one can attain pure intellect."

(*Bhajana-rahasya*, Chapter 1)

46

Anartha Nivṛtti

1. What is anartha?

"Sense gratification is the materialist primary *anartha.*"

(*Śrī Krishna-saṁhitā* 9/15)

2. How many kinds of anarthas are there?

"There are four kinds of *anarthas*. They are 'svarūpa bhram' identifying the body as self, '*asatṛṣṇā*' thirst for material enjoyment, '*aparādha*' committing offenses and '*hṛdaya daulabam*' weakness in the heart."

(*Sajjana-toṣaṇī* 9/9)

2. What are definitions of the four types of anarthas? How is it possible to destroy anarthas?

"By forgetting 'I am pure spirit soul and a servant of Krishna'—the conditional souls have fallen down from their eternal constitutional position. Forgetfulness of this constitutional position is the living entity's principal *anartha.* Considering all material objects as 'I' and 'mine' and the thirst for temporary material happiness is the second *anartha.* Desire for good children, wealth and heavenly pleasures are the examples of this *anartha.* The third *anartha* has ten types[1]. These are lamentation etc,. See the answer to question 8 on page 334 for these ten types. which arise from the weaknesses of the heart which is the fourth *anartha.* These four types of *anarthas* are the results of the living entities conditioned state due to nescience. These *anarthas* are gradually destroyed by the cultivation of pure Krishna consciousness."

(*Jaiva Dharma* Chapter 17)

---

1 See the answer to question 8 on page 334 for these ten types.

4. Can anarthas cover the great sun of holy names?

"The cloudlike *anarthas* of the conditioned souls cover the sun-like holy names and bring about darkness. Actually the *anarthas* only cover the eyes of the conditioned souls. The sun-like holy name is great and can never be covered."

(*Harinām Cintāmani*)

5. Why are the living entities not inclined towards the Supreme Lord?

"Living entities are not inclined towards the Supreme Lord, due to their incessant desires for sense gratification."

(*Sajjana-toṣaṇī* 11/5)

6. When does the thirst for material enjoyment cease?

"The thirst for material enjoyment does not get totally destroyed until pure attachment for transcendental Absolute Truth is awakened.

(*Sajjana-toṣaṇī* 11/6)

7. What is the harm if one's heart is weak?

"It is often difficult to give up bad association and activities unfavorable to devotional service due to weaknesses in the heart. One commits offenses at the feet of Bhaktidevi due to bad association or sinful activities. This makes one's *bhajana* impure. Therefore one should give up weaknesses of the heart and engage in pure *bhajana* with enthusiasm.

(*Sajjana-toṣaṇī* 11/7)

8. Which anarthas are produced from the weakness of the heart?

"Following activities arise from the weakness of the heart: laziness and subordination to insignificant objects, bewilderment of the heart due to lamentation, distraction from pure devotional service due to false argument, display miserliness in offering of all one's energy in the cultivation of Krishna consciousness, rejection of the nature of humility due to the pride of caste, wealth, education, follower, beauty and strength, becoming misguided by irreligious propensity and instructions, disinterest in rectifying the prejudice, abandoning compassion due to anger, illusion, envy and intolerance, falsely identifying oneself as Vaiṣṇavas due to desire for name, fame and cheating propensity, and torturing other living entities with a desire to enjoy woman, wealth and sense gratification."

(*Sajjana-toṣaṇī* 9/9)

9. What is the thirst for sense gratification?

"Desire for sense gratification with one's material body is called thirst for sense gratification. Heavenly pleasures, sense enjoyments, wealth, followers are all examples of this. The more one's constitutional position is awakened, the more one will be detached to insignificant material objects. At the same time one should take special care in giving up offenses against the holy names. By chanting the holy names of the Lord while giving up the offenses, one will quickly attain the treasured love of God."

(*Sajjana-toṣaṇī* 9/9)

10. Is it possible to worship Hari by one's own independent consideration?

"Pure unalloyed devotional service will not be awakened in the heart if one depends on one's own independent consideration."

(*Sajjana-toṣaṇī* 11/6)

11. Which disturbances are created as a result of anarthas?

"Bad association, duplicity, and dependent on Godless people are created due to *anartha*s. This hinders one's progress on the path of devotional service. One certainly indulges in various worldly topics in the course of bad association. As a result, strong attachment for temporary material objects is developed and one's life of pure *bhajana* is greatly hampered."

(*Sajjana-toṣaṇī* 11/7)

12. Is long and healthy life without love of God condemnable?

"A long and healthy life becomes a source of *anarthas* if there is no loving relationship with God."

(*Prema Pradipa*, Ray 2)

13. Which symbol of anartha is Putanā?

"Putanā symbolizes a pseudo spiritual master who teaches material enjoyment and liberation. The pseudo *sādhus* who are fond of material enjoyment and liberation belong to this category of Putanā. Out of compassion for pure devotees, the child Krishna killed Putanā to protect His newly grown mood."

(*Caitanya-śikṣāmṛta* 6/6)

14. Which anarthas should a practitioner destroy by the teachings of 'Śakata Bhajana' or the pastime of breaking the cart?

"The burden of former and modern prejudices, laziness and pride are destroyed by killing Śakatāsura. The child Krishna destroys such *anarthas* by killing Śakata demon."

(*Caitanya-śikṣāmṛta* 6/6)

15. Which anartha does Tṛnāvarta represent?

"Tṛnāvarta is the symbol of pride of useless learning, false arguments, dry logic or reasoning, and associating with like minded persons. Atheism is also included in Tṛnāvarta. Being compassionate by the humility of the practitioner, child Krishna kills the demon Tṛnāvarta and destroys the thorns on the path of *bhajana*."

(*Caitanya-śikṣāmṛta* 6/6)

16. Which anarthas are eradicated in the pastimes of uprooting Yamalārjuna trees?

"The madness caused by violence to the living entities, association with woman, and drinking wine are produced from the pride due to opulence and aristocracy. This makes a living entities tongue unrestricted and makes him envious to other living entities out of mercilessness and shamelessness. Krishna destroys such faults by mercifully uprooting the Yamalārjuna trees."

(*Caitanya-śikṣāmṛta* 6/6)

17. Which symbols of anartha is Vatsāsura?

"Sinful activities and being controlled by other's intelligence born from greed, due to a childish nature, are the *anarthas* called Vatsāsura. Krishna mercifully destroys them."

(*Caitanya-śikṣāmṛta* 6/6)

18. What is the definition of anartha known as Bakāsura?

"Duplicity, cheating propensity, and false behavior due to deceitfulness are the symptoms of *anartha* known as Bakāsura. One cannot attain pure devotional service to Krishna without destroying these faults."

(*Caitanya-śikṣāmṛta* 6/6)

19. Which symbols of anartha is the killing of Aghāsura?

"Killing of the demon Aghāsura symbolizes removing the sinful activities of violence towards living entities, and torturing other's due to hatred."

(*Caitanya-śikṣāmṛta* 6/6)

20. Which representation of anartha is the bewilderment of Brahmā?

"Bewilderment of Brahmā represents accumulation of doubts that arise from the cultivation of karma and *jñāna*, and disregarding the mood of sweetness due to being absorbed in the mood of opulence.

Caitanya-śikṣāmṛta 6/6.

21. Which symbol of anartha is Dhenukāsura?

"The killing of Dhenukāsura deals with the removal of gross mentality, lack of spiritual knowledge, ignorance about the Absolute Truth, and the opposition of the knowledge of one's constitutional position."

(*Caitanya-śikṣāmṛta*)

22. Which ideal of anartha is serpent Kaliya?

"The chastisement of Kāliya removes pride, cheating, cruelty, harming other's and absence of compassion to other living entities."

(*Caitanya-śikṣāmṛta* 6/6)

23. The Forest fire is indicative of which anartha?

"Destroying the forest fire illustrates the destruction of quareling between each other, becoming envious of authorised *sampradayas* demigods and conflicts such as war."

(*Caitanya-śikṣāmṛta* 6/6)

24. Which symbol of anartha is Pralamba?

"Killing of Pralamba illustrates removal of desire for woman hunting, profit, adoration and distinction."

(*Caitanya-śikṣāmṛta* 6/6)

25. Forest fire is indicative of which anartha?

"Drinking of forest fire illustrates the removal of disturbances in the practice of religious principles, and the disturbances caused by the atheists."

(*Caitanya-śikṣāmṛta* 6/6)

26. Which ideal of anartha is Yajñic brahmanas' negligence of Krishna?

"The behavior of the *yajñic brahmanas* illustrates indifference towards Krishna and attachment to fruitive activities due to pride of following the system of *varnāśrama*."

(*Caitanya-śikṣāmṛta* 6/6)

27. Which ideal of anartha is the worship of Indra?

"The prohibition of the worship of Indra illustrates the rejection of godless mentality and self worship."

(*Caitanya-śikṣāmṛta* 6/6)

28. What is the teaching behind the pastimes of delivering Nanda from the clutches of Varuna?

"Deliverance of Nanda from Varuna teaches that by drinking wine etc., one's happiness in the worship of the Lord certainly diminishes."

(*Caitanya-śikṣāmṛta* 6/6)

29. What is the purport of the pastimes of King Nanda's deliverance from the clutches of the snake?

"Deliverance of Nanda Mahārāja from the grip of the snake illustrates rejection of the association of the impersonalists, and the deliverance of the science of devotional service which is swallowed by impersonalism."

(*Caitanya-śikṣāmṛta* 6/6)

30. Sankhachuda is a symbol of which anartha?

"The killing of Sankhachuda teaches the abandonment of desire for name and fame as well as desire for association with women."

(*Caitanya-śikṣāmṛta* 6/6)

31. The bull-shaped Aristāsura is a symbol of which anartha?

"Killing of Aristāsura teaches the destruction of disregard of devotional service which manifests from the pride of cheating religion, etc."

(*Caitanya-śikṣāmṛta* 6/6)

32. The Keśi demon is a symbol of which anartha?

"The mentality: 'I am a great devotee or an *acarya*,' as well as mundane false ego and opulence are destroyed by the killing of the demon Keśi."

(*Caitanya-śikṣāmṛta* 6/6)

33. The Vyomāsura demon is a symbol of which anartha?

"The killing of Vyomāsura illustrates the abandonment of the association of the thieves and the hypocrites."

(*Caitanya-śikṣāmṛta* 6/6)

34. What kind of anartha is the lack of determination? What harm does this anartha cause?

"'Let me indulge in sense gratification today — tomorrow I will give it up,' such a weakness of heart can never bring any auspiciousness. Whatever one's feels to be obstacles on the path of devotional service, one should immediately give it up by the strength of Caitanya Mahāprabhu's mercy. Determination is the root of *sādhanā*. In the absence of determination even a step in the path of spiritual life will not be advanced."

(*Sajjana-toṣaṇī* 11/5)

35. Is hypocrisy an anartha?

"One should never hear the advice of the hypocrites who are fond of sense gratification."

(*Caitanya-śikṣāmṛta* 7/1)

47

Nisthā

1. What is the life of prīti?

"*Nisthā* is the life of *prīti.*"

(*Sajjana-toṣaṇī* 2/6)

2. What is the resolution of a devotee who has developed nisthā?

"The devotees of Krishna are my mother and father—they are my friends and brothers. Only Krishna is my husband. Leaving life with Krishna, I won't go anywhere.

(*Prema-pradīpa*, Ray 7)

3. What is most desirable in Bhajan?

"The most desirable things in Bhajan are determination and simplicity."

(*Kṛṣṇa-karnāmṛta* 1/12)

4. Why is the desire for nisthā and association with devotees superior to the indifference and renunciation exhibited by the so-called philosophy of synthesis?

"In the course of glorifying Paramahamsa it is written that he was extremely hostile to the sectarian religious principles and despite living among the followers of such religion, he feels happy. From this we understand that Paramahamsa Mahasaya was an impersonalist; he is not particularly acquainted with devotional service. The nature of impersonalism is that it ultimately makes a practitioner indifferent and free from any association. The nature of devotional service is that it ultimately induces a practitioner to desire to associate with devotees and awards him *nisthā* in his worshipable Lord. Now if we ask which is better among the two? Then Śrīman Mahāprabhu Caitanyadeva instructs us that *nisthā* in the worshipable object and association with the devotees are unlimitedly superior to renunciation and indifference."

(*Sajjana-toṣaṇī* 2/6)

5. What are the resolutions of a devotee who is fixed?

"The six symptons of surrender of a devotee are: the acceptance of those things favorable to devotional service, the rejection of unfavorable things, the conviction that Krishna will give protection, the acceptance of the Lord as one's guardian or master, full self-surrender, and humility."

(*Bhajana-rahasya*, Chapter 3)

6. What is nisthā in one's worshipable object?

"My Lord, You are not very much satisfied by the worship of the demigods, who arrange for Your worship very pompously with various paraphernalia, but are full of material hankerings. You are situated in everyone's heart as the Supersoul just to show Your causeless mercy. You are the eternal well-wisher, but You are unavailable for the nondevotees."

(*Bhajana-rahasya*, Chapter 3)

7. How should one faithfully hear the glories of Krishna's names and qualities?

"If one hears glorification of Krishna's name, form and qualities from the mouth of a devotee, but one's hairs do not stand erect, nor do tears of ecstasy flow from the eyes, then what is the use of maintaining such a life?"

(*Bhajana-rahasya*, Chapter 3)

8. How should one keep faith in Krishna and in devotional service to Krishna?

"May the spiritual master of the three worlds, Śrī Krishna, protect us all! Krishna is also known as Viśvambhara. He manifests this world, maintains it, and, in time, destroys it. The entire creation is situated in Krishna, and we are therefore all His servants. The wealth of the world is distributed by Him. Let us offer our obeisances with full faith unto Śrī Krishna, who awards one the ultimate goal.

You have taken birth for the purpose of performing devotional service to Krishna. Indeed, everything in this world other than devotional service to Krishna is false.

(*Bhajana-rahasya*, Chapter 3)

9. How should one have faith in one's bhajana?

"My dear Lord Krishna, I pray that the swan of my mind may immediately sink down to the stems of the lotus feet of Your Lordship and be locked up in their network. Otherwise at the time of my final breath, when my throat is choked up with cough, how will it be possible to think of You? In such a condition, Your holy name will not manifest on my tongue. If I leave my body without remembering You, then how will I attain You?"

(*Bhajana-rahasya*, Chapter 3)

10. How should one faithfully pray to his worshipable Lord?

"O Hari! I have no faith in religious principles, and I have no knowledge of the soul. Furthermore, I have no devotion to Your lotus feet. I am utterly destitute, a rogue with no idea of the goal of life. In this way I always cheat myself. You, however, are the deliverer of the fallen, and I am an insignificant fallen soul. Therefore, You are the only goal of my life. Having achieved Your lotus feet I take shelter of You, for You are my eternal Lord, and I am Your servant."

(*Bhajana-rahasya*, Chapter 3)

11. What is the mood of one's surrender to the supreme will of Krishna?

"There is no sin in this world which I have not committed. The results of those sinful activities are now beginning to fructify, and they are churning me in this material ocean. O Mukunda! Seeing no other path, I am crying again and again before You. Punish me as You deem fit. You are the giver of punishment, and You are my Lord."

(*Bhajana-rahasya*, Chapter 3)

12. How should one pray to remain fixed in the service of Krishna by giving up material desires?

"O Hari, being evil-minded and seeing no other refuge, I have taken shelter of Your lotus feet. I have now come to know that You are my Lord. You are the Lord of the universe, and I am Your eternal servant. When will that day come when I will actually realize myself as Your eternal servant? When will my material desires be completely destroyed so that I will spontaneously serve You to Your satisfaction?"

(*Bhajana-rahasya*, Chapter 3)

13. How should one keep faith in full surrender to the Lord?

"O Hari! I am an offender, and therefore I am always punishable. I have all bad qualities, and I am guilty of committing thousands and thousands of offenses. I am drowning inside this terrible, turbulent ocean of material existence. I have lost my way, and I desire to find the right path. O Hari, I have taken shelter of Your lotus feet out of fear. Please accept me as Your own. O Lord, Your vow is that You will definitely liberate anyone from material bondage who takes shelter of You."

(*Bhajana-rahasya*, Chapter 3)

14. What is nisthā in regard to self humility?

"O Hari! Let me submit one humble request before You. Be merciful and kindly hear my words. This is not a meaningless request, but it is confidential, coming from my heart. I am wretched, and You are most merciful. Therefore, You are the most capable person to bestow mercy. As You confer Your mercy unto one who is very fallen, I am a suitable candidate for Your mercy. If You ignore me, then it will be very, very difficult to find a more suitable candidate for Your mercy."

(*Bhajana-rahasya*, Chapter 3)

15. What is nisthā in regard to the desire for serving the lotus feet of the Lord?

"I am always transgressing the injunctions of the Vedas. I am degraded, fickle-minded, always envious, ungrateful, proud and sinful. I am controlled by lust and always engaged in cheating. In this condition how will I cross this ocean of material suffering and engage in the service of Your lotus feet?"

(*Bhajana-rahasya*, Chapter 3)

16. What is nisthā in obtaining the association of most desirable devotees?

"I may also take birth again according to my past activities, or by Your will. O Purusottama, kindly hear this one request! I pray that if I again take birth, let it be in the house of Your servant even as a worm and I will be satisfied at heart. I have no desire to take birth even with the opulence of Lord Brahma in the house of one averse to You. With folded hands, I am offering You this humble prayer."

(*Bhajana-rahasya*, Chapter 3)

17. What is nisthā in regard to one's self surrender?

"In this world there are bodily distinctions such as man and woman, and there are four *varṇas* and four *āśramas* divided according to the three modes of nature of goodness, passion and ignorance. In this way there are countless varieties of bodies. O Lord of my life! Whatever body I must reside in whatever condition doesn't matter, for I now surrender myself at Your lotus feet. From now on I have nothing left that I consider mine."

(*Bhajana-rahasya*, Chapter 3.)

18. What is nisthā in regard to one's humility?

"With folded hands this rascal cries, and without hesitation, sincerely offers his prayers to You. In a sobbing voice I pray, O merciful Lord, please be kind to me! Just cast Your merciful glance once on me and thus save my life.

(*Bhajana-rahasya*, Chapter 3)

19. What is nisthā in regard to pleasing Krishna?

"O Lord, kindly bestow mercy upon me in the form of Your side-long glance, followed by the sweet sound of Your flute. If You are pleased with me, and other's are displeased, it doesn't matter. But if You are displeased with me, and other's are pleased, then what is the benefit for me?

(*Bhajana-rahasya*, Chapter 3)

48

Ruci

1. What result does one achieve by engaging in rāgātmikā sevā?

"By developing greed for Krishna's service, the Vaiṣṇavas' service, and chanting the holy names, there will be no greed for inferior things. One who becomes greedy by seeing the Vrajavāsī's service to Krishna is very fortunate. By the mercy of that greed, he attains the qualification for *rāga-bhakti*. One's material greed is vanquished in proportion to one's development of greed for *rāgātmikā* service."

(*Sajjana-toṣaṇī* 10/11)

2. What is ruci?

"The propensity born from two kinds of prejudices, namely ancient and modern, is called '*ruci*.' This *ruci* of the living entities is temporary. Those who have no taste or *ruci* for *śṛngāra rāsa* but have taste for *dāsya* or *sakhya rāsa*, should follow the instructions suitable for their respective *rāsas*, otherwise it will create unnecessary problem. The perfected original *ruci* of the great Vaiṣṇavas Śrī Shyāmānanda Prabhu was not manifest at first, that is why he was instructed to enter into *sakhya rāsa*; later by the mercy of Śrī Jīva Goswāmi Prabhu, he attained his original spontaneous *bhajana*. This is a well known fact. The principle of qualification and eligibility plays a prominent role in the incarnation of Śrī Caitanyadeva."

(*Harināma-cintāmani*)

3. Who develops ruci for his constitutional propensity?

"Those whose hearts are fully transcendental develop a taste for the subordination to the residents of Vraja. Therefore greed or *ruci* for *rāgānugā bhakti* is the only indication of one's constitutional propensity."

(*Jaiva Dharma*, Chapter 21)

4. When one develops ruci for pure devotional service, does he develop detachment for objects not related to Krishna?

"Home paraphernalia, disciples, wealth in the form of animals and grains, wife, sons, servants, maidservants, relatives, fruitive activities described in flowery words, and beautiful women are all considered important objects in the material world. I, however, have no desire to obtain these things. O Krishna, I aspire only for Your mercy in the form of pure devotion for You."

(*Bhajana-rahasya*, Chapter 4)

5. When one develops a taste for chanting the holy names of the Lord, does he still keep a taste for name, fame, and so on?

"A *sannyasi* must not present allurements of material benefits to gather many disciples, nor should he unnecessarily read many (nondevotional) books or give discourses as a means of livelihood. He must never attempt to increase material opulence unnecessarily. One who has a taste for the holy name does not want such things."

(*Bhajana-rahasya*, Chapter 4)

6. How should one perform bhajana with ruci?

"Engage in hearing and chanting Krishna's name, form, and attributes with undivided attention, and try to destroy your *anartha*s. Then the creeper of devotion will quickly bear fruit."

(*Bhajana-rahasya*, Chapter 4)

7. If one is full of lamentation and illusion for material objects, is there a chance that he will have taste for the service of the Lord?

"One whose heart is full of anger, pride, or lamentation for the state of his wife or children, there is no possibility of Krishna being manifest."

(*Bhajana-rahasya*, Chapter 4)

8. What kind of rūci should one have in serving the lotus feet of Krishna in the association of the devotees?

"O Lord, if I take birth in this land of Vṛndāvana or in any other universe, or if I take birth as a bird or animal anywhere within Your creation, my only desire is that I may be able to serve You in various ways in the association of Your devotees."

(*Bhajana-rahasya*, Chapter 4)

9. What type of ruci should one have in hearing the glories of Krishna's transcendental qualities?

"I want the benediction of at least one million ears, for thus I may be able to hear about the glories of Your lotus feet from the mouths of Your pure devotees."

(*Bhajana-rahasya*, Chapter 4)

49

Āsakti

1. What is āsakti?

"When the state of *ruci* matures, it is called *āsakti.*"

(*Caitanya-śikṣāmṛta* 5/2)

2. What is desirable in developing attachment to Krishna?

"O vanquisher of all distress, please shows us mercy. To approach Your lotus feet we abandoned our families and homes, and we have no desire other than to serve You. Our hearts are burning with intense desires generated by Your beautiful smiling glances. O jewel among men, please make us Your maidservants."

(*Bhajana-rahasya*, Chapter 5)

3. How is the life of persons who are attached to Krishna?

"O Lord! I spend my day by honoring Your remnants such as flowers, sandalwood paste, ornaments and garments. My identification is that I am a servant of You and I survive by eating Your remnants. In this way I conquer Your illusory energy and remain unattached."

(*Bhajana-rahasya*, Chapter 5)

4. How intense is the eagerness of those who are attached to Krishna?

"Expert transcendentalists always direct their affection toward You because they recognize You as their true Self and their eternally beloved. What use do we have for these husbands, children, and relatives of ours, who simply give us trouble? Therefore, O supreme controller, grant us Your mercy. O lotus-eyed one, please do not cut down our long-cherished hope to have Your association."

(*Bhajana-rahasya*, Chapter 5)

5. Is it possible to become attached to Krishna without being attached to the service of the devotees?

"How is it possible to immerse oneself in the ocean of *Śyāma-rāsa* (love for Krishna or the *mādhurya rāsa*) without worshiping the dust of the lotus feet of Śrīmatī Rādhārāṇī, or without taking shelter of Vṛndāvana, which is decorated with Her footprints, or without serving Her devotees, whose grave hearts are always absorbed in love for Her?"

(*Bhajana-rahasya*, Chapter 5)

6. In developing attachment for Krishna, in which rāsa does one develop an eagerness to worship the Lord?

"After giving up the pride of falsely identifying the material body with the self by the mercy of Krishna, I reside in Vraja as a *gopī*. As Śrīmatī Rādhārāṇī's maidservant, I always take pleasure serving Rādhā and Krishna in Their *parakīya-rāsa* pastimes."

(*Bhajana-rahasya*, Chapter 5)

7. Do those who are attached to Krishna hanker after the four objectives of life? What are their goals of life?

"Abandoning attachment for family, friends, material pleasures, wealth, and all other spiritual paths, finding them distasteful I take on my head and worship the dust of the lotus feet of Śrī Rādhikā, which is a shower of wonderful, transcendental bliss."

(*Bhajana-rahasya*, Chapter 5)

8. What is the heartiest desire of those who are attached to Krishna?

"O Rādhā, O Vṛṣabhānunandinī! When, by Your mercy, will I stay on the banks of the Yamunā, and wander on the paths within the groves of Vṛndāvana as I engage in Your service as a maidservant?

(*Bhajana-rahasya*, Chapter 5)

9. Which sādhana or process for achieving the goal of life, and sādhya or the goal of life, are to be constantly cherished by those who are attached to Krishna?

"I will relish the most amazing festival of attachment to Rādhā by always remembering Krishna, who wears a peacock feather in His crown, by performing *saṅkīrtana*, by engaging in the service of His lotus feet, by chanting the best of *mantras*, and by remembering the most cherished service of the lotus feet of Rādhā within my heart."

(*Bhajana-rahasya*, Chapter 5)

10. What is the sole desired goal of those who are attached to Krishna?

"May I attain the service of Vṛṣabhānunandinī birth after birth! She is the personification of the essence of the transcendental mellows of divine sports. She is the supreme goddess of fortune with a form of the most wonderful transcendental bliss. Her lotus feet are difficult to attain even for the demigods headed by Lord Brahmā."

(*Bhajana-rahasya*, Chapter 5)

11. What do the devotees, who are attached to Krishna, cultivate with all their senses?

"May my tongue be overwhelmed by relishing the nectar of Rādhā's name! May my feet be engaged in wandering the paths of Vṛndāvana, which are marked by Rādhā's footprints! May my hands be engaged in the loving service of Rādhārāṇī! May my mind be constantly engaged in meditation on the lotus feet of Rādhā! May I attain firm attachment for the lotus feet of Śrī Krishna by attaining the festival of ecstatic love for Rādhā!"

(*Bhajana-rahasya*, Chapter 5)

12. What is the devotee's prayer to Śrīmatī Rādhārāṇī?

"O Devī ! In great distress I fall to the ground offering You obeisances and prayers with a voice choked with emotion. O Gāndharvikā! Please bestow Your mercy on this pauper and count me amongst Your own associates."

(*Bhajana-rahasya*, Chapter 5)

13. Why are the devotees of Krishna partial or more attached to the service of Śrīmatī Rādhārāṇī?

"When will I be delighted in the service of Śrīmatī Rādhārāṇī? Struck by the arrow of Her side-long glance, Krishna faints, His flute falls from His hands, the peacock feathers on His head become loosened, and His yellow scarf slips from His neck."

(*Bhajana-rahasya*, Chapter 5)

50

Bhava

1. What is bhāva? Which stage of prema bhakti is this bhāva?

"*Prema bhakti* is the fruit of *sādhana bhakti*. There are two stages of *prema bhakti*: '*bhāva*' and '*prema.*' *Prema* is just like the Sun, *bhāva* is its rays. *Bhāva* is the form of pure goodness and when mixed with *ruci* it melts the heart. The stage of Krishna consciousness that is mentioned in regard to the description of the symptoms of devotional service, that resembles the form of pure goodness, and melts the heart with the help of *ruci*, is called *bhāva*. *Bhāva* manifests in the propensity of the mind and attains its nature. In fact, *bhāva* is self-manifest, but accepting the nature of the mind it appears as manifested.

(*Caitanya-śikṣāmṛta* 5/1)

2. What is the example of bhāva born from vaidhi sādhana bhakti and bhāva born from Rāgānugā sādhana bhakti?

"The life of Śrī Nārada is the example of *bhāva* born from *vaidhi sādhana bhakti*. The example of *bhāva* born from *rāgānugā bhakti* is the women devotees, mentioned in *Padma Purāṇa*, who were on the platform of *rāgānugā bhakti*."

(*Caitanya-śikṣāmṛta* 5/11)

3. Is there any illicit activity found in the life of a devotee who has attained bhāva?

"It is not that the life of *bhāva* changes the life of regulative devotional service all of a sudden; but the activities of a *bhāva-bhakta* appear to be independent of the regulative principles. All his activities are regulated by his strong spontaneous attachment. Although the nature of a person on the platform of *bhāva* is independent, there is no possibility of any disturbance from him. Such a person does not have any taste for any kinds of pious and sinful activities. He does not engage in any activities as his duty. Hs does not feel like imitating anyone. Maintenance of his body, mind, and the society are automatically carried out due to his previous habit. Since he is indifference to any activity then there is never any possibility for him to engage in sinful activities."

(*Caitanya-śikṣāmṛta* 5/11)

4. What is the fate of a devotee who is practicing regulative devotional service if he disregards a devotee who has attained bhāva?

"The lifestyle of a *bhāva-bhakta* is similar to the lifestyle of *sādhana bhakta*. A devotee who has attained *bhāva* is fully satisfied. If a devotee who is on the level of regulative devotional service disrespects such a *bhāva-bhakta*, then his accumulated wealth of devotional service will gradually diminish."

(*Caitanya-śikṣāmṛta* 5/11)

5. What are the external symptoms of the awakening of bhāva?

"The first stage of *prema* is known as *bhāva*, when the eight *sāttvika-vikāras* (bodily transformations), such as standing of the hairs on end and crying, are slightly manifest."

(*Bhajana-rahasya*, Chapter 6)

6. What are the anubhāvas that manifest when the seed of bhāva fructifies?

"If love of Krishna in a seedling state has fructified in one's heart, one is not agitated by material things. Not a moment is lost. Every moment is utilized for Krishna or things connected with Him. In the material field, people are interested in material enjoyment, mystic power and sense gratification. However, these things do not appeal to the devotee at all. Although a pure devotee's standard is above all, he still considers himself to be in the lowest stage of life. A fully surrendered devotee always hopes that Lord Krishna will be kind to him. This hope is very firm in him. This eagerness is chiefly characterized by an ardent desire to attain the mercy of the Lord. Due to having great relish for the holy name, one is inclined to chant the Hare Krishna *maha-mantra* constantly. At this stage of *bhāva*, a devotee has awakened the tendency to chant and describe the transcendental qualities of the Lord. He has attachment for this process. A devotee absorbed in ecstatic emotion for Krishna always has affection for residing in a place where Krishna's pastimes were performed.

(*Bhajana-rahasya*, Chapter 6)

7. Do the eight symptoms of ecstatic love appear in the devotees who have attained bhāva?

"The eight symptoms of *bhāva* are: being stunned, trembling, perspiring, standing of hairs on end, fading away of bodily color, weeping, choking, and devastation. These symptoms manifest in the devotees who have attained *bhāva*.

(*Bhajana-rahasya*, Chapter 6)

8. How do the devotees who have attained bhāva spend their lives?

"They constantly chant the holy name and fame of the Lord ignoring all the formalities of the material world. Such chanting and remembering of the transcendental pastimes of the Lord are benedictory. So doing, they travel all over the world, without envy, humble and fully satisfied.

(*Bhajana-rahasya*, Chapter 6)

9. How are the dealings of the devotees who have attained bhāva beyond the worldly and Vedic consideration?

"Having achieved love of Godhead, the devotees sometimes cry out loud, absorbed in thought of the infallible Lord. Sometimes they laugh, feel great pleasure, speak out loud to the Lord, dance or sing. Such devotees, having transcended conditioned life, sometimes imitate the unborn Supreme by acting out His pastimes. And sometimes, achieving His personal audience, they remain peaceful and silent.

(*Bhajana-rahasya*, Chapter 6)

10. What is devotees' darśana of Śri Śyamasundara?

"Śri Śyamasundara's complexion is dark blue, and His garment golden. He is dressed just like a dramatic dancer. He is wearing a peacock feather, colored minerals, sprigs of flower buds, and a garland of forest flowers and leaves. He rests one hand upon the shoulder of a friend, and with the other twirls a lotus. Lilies grace His ears, His hair hangs down over His cheeks, and His lotus-like face is smiling.

(*Bhajana-rahasya*, Chapter 6)

11. How do the qualities of the Supreme Lord manifest in the hearts of the devotees who have attained bhāva?

"O Lord, we do not know how the serpent Kāliya has attained this great opportunity of being touched by the dust of Your lotus feet. For this end, the goddess of fortune performed austerities for centuries, giving up all other desires and taking austere vows."

(*Bhajana-rahasya*, Chapter 6)

12. What kind of humility and desire for perfection do renunciate devotees who have attained bhāva display?

"The *gopīs* of Vṛndāvana have given up the association of their husbands, sons, and other family members, who are very difficult to give up, and they have forsaken the path of chastity to take shelter of the lotus feet of Mukunda, Krishna, who is searched for by Vedic knowledge. Oh, let me be fortunate enough to be one of the bushes, creepers, or herbs in Vṛndāvana, because the *gopīs* trample them and bless them with the dust of their lotus feet."

(*Bhajana-rahasya*, Chapter 6)

13. Do the gopis who have attained perfection in bhāva have any desire for material enjoyment or liberation?

"Among all persons on earth, these cowherd women alone have actually perfected their embodied lives, for they have achieved the perfection of unalloyed love for Lord Govinda. Their pure love is hankered after by those who fear material existence, by great sages, and by ourselves as well. For one who has tasted the narrations of the infinite Lord, what is the use of taking birth as a high-class *brāhmaṇa*, or even as Lord Brahmā himself?"

(*Bhajana-rahasya*, Chapter 6)

14. In which subject do the devotees who have attained bhāva show their attachment?

"Persons who have attained *bhāva* always manifest desire to hear, chant, and remember the transcendental qualities of the Lord."

(*Caitanya-śikṣāmṛta* 5/2)

51

Paramārtha

1. What is paramārtha or the ultimate goal of life?

"Anything other than pure devotional service to the Lord cannot be called *paramārtha* or the ultimate goal of life."

(*Sajjana-toṣaṇī* 10/9)

2. Are the vows of devotional service useless?

"Cultivating the limbs of devotional service are not useless endeavors."

(*Sajjana-toṣaṇī* 10/9)

3. What are the five best limbs of devotional service?

"Worshiping the Deity, relishing the purport of *Śrīmad-Bhāgavatam* with advanced devotees, associating with more advanced devotees who are affectionate and are in the same line as oneself, congregational chanting of the holy names, and residing in Mathurā. If we further summarize, then chanting the holy names and serving the Vaiṣṇavas are the topmost."

(*Sajjana-toṣaṇī* 11/6)

4. How many types of worship of Tulasī are there?

"Tulasī is auspicious in all respects. Simply by seeing, touching, remembering, praying to, bowing down before, hearing about, sowing, offering water, or simply by worshiping *tulasī*, there is always auspiciousness."

(*Sajjana-toṣaṇī* 11/6)

5. Among the service to the Lord's subordinates, which is the principal one?

"Serving Tulasī is the principal service among the service to the Lord's subordinates."

(*Sajjana-toṣaṇī* 11/6)

6. Under whose guidance should one circumambulate the abode of Śrī Gaurāṅga?

"I will happily visit with exalted devotees all those places where my beloved Lord Gaurāṅga enacted His pastimes."

(Song from *Śaraṇāgati*)

7. What should be the duty of a devotee if he gets his food and clothing but loses them?

"A devotee should not be agitated if food and clothing are not obtained or if they are obtained and then lost. He should peacefully remember Krishna."

(*Sajjana-toṣaṇī* 11/6)

8. In the course of practicing the best five limbs of devotional service, in which subject does a practitioner develop greed and what is the result of this?

"By offenselessly serving the Deities, relishing the purports of *Śrīmad-Bhāgavatam*, associating with senior devotees who are on the path of *rāga*, chanting the holy names of the Lord, and residing in Śri Mathura *mandala*, one achieves the mercy of the pure devotees. On the strength of such mercy, a practitioner of devotional service develops greed for the service of Krishna, who is the worshipable Lord of the residents of Braja. From such greed, *rāgānugā bhakti* under the guidance of the residents of Braja appears. It is transcendental to the Vedic consideration. While cultivating this devotional service, within a very short time, pure unalloyed devotional service becomes manifest. These are the confidential teachings of Śrīman Mahāprabhu."

(*Śrī Manaḥ-śikṣā*, Chapter 11)

52

Nine types of devotional service

1. How many types of cultivation of hearing are there?

"There are three types of cultivation of hearing: hearing about the scriptures, hearing about the holy names and topics of the Lord, and hearing about the devotion-filled discourses. Considering the science about the Absolute Truth, describing the pastimes of the Lord from *Śrīmad-Bhāgavatam*, discussing the characteristics of the Vaiṣṇavas, and hearing about the ancient history of the families of Vaiṣṇavas, are counted in the category of 'hearing the scriptures.' These are to be understood from hearing about the conclusive statements based on the *Vedānta* written by great personalities after carefully rejecting inconclusive non-Vaiṣṇavas statements."

(*Caitanya-śikṣāmṛta* 3/2)

2. What happens if one hears the topics of and conclusion about Hari?

"By hearing about the topics and science of Hari one automatically cultivates knowledge of the scriptures."

(*Jaiva Dharma*, Chapter 8)

3. By hearing the topics of Hari does one worship the Lord and become detached from material enjoyments?

"By hearing the topics of Hari both cultivation of spiritual science and detachment from material enjoyment are done."

(*Tattva-sutra* 34)

4. What are the different stages of hearing?

"There are two stages of hearing. The first stage is hearing about the qualities of Krishna from the mouths of the saintly persons, before one's faith develops. By such hearing one certainly develops faith. When one's faith is awakened one develops a strong desire to hear about the names, forms, qualities and pastimes of Krishna. The second stage is hearing Krishna's holy names, etc., from the mouths of the spiritual master and the Vaiṣṇavas."

(*Jaiva Dharma*, Chapter 19)

5. Does hearing during the time of sādhana helps the hearing when one attains perfection?

"The hearing in the perfectional stage appears while hearing from the mouths of the spiritual master and the Vaiṣṇavas during the time of *sādhana*."

(*Jaiva Dharma*, Chapter 19)

6. What are the gradual platforms beginning from śravana daśā to sampatti daśā?

"Hearing about the Absolute Truth from the mouth of the spiritual master is called '*śravana daśā*'. When a practitioner accepts those instructions in truth, it is called ' *varana daśā.*' When he cultivates that mood with blissful remembrance, it is called '*smaraṇa daśā*.' When he is able to properly bring that mood within himself, it is called ' *āpana* or *prāpti daśā*.' And when one separates himself from the temporary material existence and obtains his own desired constitutional form, it is called '*sampatti daśā*.'"

(*Harināma-cintāmani*)

7. How many types of cultivation of chanting are there?

"Cultivation of *kīrtana* or chanting is extremely sublime. Reciting the scriptures, glorifying the Lord's names and qualities, offering prayers, making humble appeals, and chanting the holy names softly, are the five kinds of cultivation of *kīrtana*. Glorification of the Lord's holy names and qualities are done through discourses, explanations, and singing. Appealing is of three types: prayers, humility and hankering."

(*Caitanya-śikṣāmṛta* 3/2)

8. Among all the limbs of devotional service, which one is the best?

"It has been described that *kīrtana* or chanting is the best among all the limbs of devotional service. "

(*Jaiva Dharma*, Chapter 19)

9. Why kīrtana or chanting is the best?

"Among the three limbs of devotional service namely hearing, chanting and remembering, chanting is the best of all; because hearing and remembering are included in the chanting."

(*Jaiva Dharma*, Chapter19)

10. Why kīrtana is beneficial to all?

"The principle of *kīrtana* invites, as the future church of the world, all classes of men without distinction of caste or clan to the highest cultivation of the spirit. This church, it appears, will extend all over the world and take the place of all sectarian churches, which exclude outsiders from the precincts of the mosque, church or the temple."

(*Caitanya Mahāprabhu: His Life & Precepts*)

11. How should one practice remembrance or smaraṇa of the Lord?

"Remembering Lord Krishna's names, forms, qualities and pastimes is called *smaraṇa. Smaraṇa* is of five kinds. A little bit of thinking or searching is called *smaraṇa*; abstracting the mind from the previous subject matter and engaging it in preliminary remembrance is called *dhāranā*; particularly thinking about the Lord's forms, etc., is called *dhyāna*; constant and uninterrupted *dhyāna* is called *dhruvānusmṛti*, and the manifestation of the object of *dhyāna* is called *samādhi*."

(*Jaiva Dharma*, Chapter 19)

12. What is the best type of atonement?

"There is no superior atonement in this world than to remember Lord Viṣṇu."

(*Harināma-cintāmani*)

13. What is the difference between smaraṇa and dhyāna?

"The difference between *smaraṇa* and *dhyāna* is that in *smaraṇa* the holy names, *mantras*, forms, qualities and pastimes manifest to some extent. In *dhyāna* the forms, the qualities, and the pastimes of the Lord are properly remembered. Prolonging the duration of *dhyāna* is called *dhāranā*. When *dhyāna* is matured it is called *nididhāsana*. Therefore *dhāranā* and *nididhāsana* are included in *dhyāna*."

(*Caitanya-śikṣāmṛta* 3/2)

14. How many kinds of smṛtis are there and what are their names?

"There are two kinds of *smṛtis* or remembrance: remembrance of the holy names and remembrance of the *mantras*. Chanting a prescribed numbers of holy names on a *tulasī* bead is called remembrance, and remembrance of the *mantras* while keeping track with one's fingers is called remembrance of the *mantras*."

(*Caitanya-śikṣāmṛta* 3/2)

15. How can one revive the aṣṭakāla service to the Supreme Lord?

"One should remember *Śikṣāṣṭaka* and practice *smaraṇa* and *kīrtana* accordingly, then gradually *aṣṭakāla* service will be awakened in the heart. At that time all unwanted contaminations, including religiosity, economic development, sense gratification, and liberation will appear insignificant, and one will achieve the treasure of love.

(*Bhajana-rahasya*, Chapter 1)

16. What is pādasevana and which limbs of devotional service are included in it?

"Serving the lotus feet of the Lord is the fourth limb of devotional service. One should serve the lotus feet of the Lord along with hearing, chanting and remembering. In the course of serving the lotus feet of the Lord it is extremely necessary for one to consider himself a beggar and an unqualified person. One should also realize his worshipable Lord as eternal, full of knowledge and bliss. Looking at the face of the Lord, touching the Lord, circumambulating the abode of the Lord, visiting the holy places, temples, Ganges, Jagannātha Purī, Dvārakā and Navadvīpa as well as following the Lord's procession are included in *pādasevana*. While describing the sixty-four limbs of devotional service Śrī Rūpa Gosvāmi has elaborated on these points clearly. Serving *tulasī* and the devotees are also included in this limb."

(*Jaiva Dharma* –Ch-19)

17. What is the necessity for worshiping the Deity?

"Although chanting the Lord's holy names awards all perfection, in order to lead a devotional life, worship of the Deity is required."

(*Bhajana-rahasya*)

18. What should one do if he has developed special faith in the worship of the Lord?

"There are many considerations regarding the worship of the Lord. After engaging in hearing, chanting and remembering, if one still possesses some attachment for the worship of the Lord then he should take shelter of the lotus feet of a spiritual master, take initiation from him and engage in the worship of the Lord."

(*Jaiva Dharma*, Chapter 19)

19. What is the harm if one does not take initiation before engaging in Deity worship and what are other considerations that are found on the path of worship?

"Since the hearts of the conditioned souls are polluted due to sinful activities, in order to purify such hearts, worship of the Deities with proper *mantras* have been prescribed in the *śāstras*. Taking initiation is required for the materialistic persons. In the *kṛṣṇa-mantra* there is no need of any consideration. Taking initiation into the *kṛṣṇa-mantra* is most auspicious for the living entities. Among all *mantras* in this world, the *kṛṣṇa-mantra* is the best and is the most powerful. As soon as a qualified person accepts initiation from a bonafide spiritual master he attains spiritual strength. The spiritual master instructs his inquisitive disciple in the process of worshiping the Deity. In brief it is to be understood that *Śrī Krishna Janmāstami*, performing *kārttika* vows, observing *ekādaśī* and bathing in the month of January are included in the process of *arcana*. It is very important to note regarding the worship of Krishna that it is extremely necessary to worship the devotees of Krishna along with the worship of Krishna."

(*Jaiva Dharma*, Chapter 19)

20. How many types of arcana are there, and which worshiper did Śrīman Mahāprabhu respect more?

"Śrīmurti worshipers are divided into two classes: the ideal and the physical. Those of the physical school are entitled from their circumstances of life and state of the mind to establish temple institutions. Those who are by circumstances and position entitled to worship the Śrīmurti in mind have, with due deference to the temple-institutions, a tendency to worship usually by *śravaṇa* and *kīrtana*, and their church is universal and is independent of caste and color. Mahāprabhu prefers this latter class and shows their worship in His *Śikṣāstaka*."

(*Caitanya Mahāprabhu: His Life & Precepts*)

20. What is the duty of a worshiper who is endowed with the knowledge of his relationship with the Lord?

"If one wants to worship the Deity form of the Lord with full knowledge of his relationship with the Lord, then he should simultaneously worship Lord Krishna and His devotees."

(*Jaiva Dharma*, Chapter 8)

21. What is the gradual process of worship?

"First one should worship one's spiritual master by offering him *āsana* (sitting place), *pādya* (water for washing his feet), *argya* (certain ingredients), *snāniya* (water for taking bath), *vastra* (clothes), and *ābharaṇa* (decorations). Thereafter one should take his permission to engage in the worship of Śrī Rādhā and Krishna. After worshiping Śrī Rādhā Krishna, one should first offer Their remnants to the spiritual master and then to other Vaiṣṇavas and the demigods. One should also offer the Lord's remnants to one's forefathers."

(*Harināma-cintāmani*)

21. Is it necessary to worship the demigods apart from Lord Viṣṇu?

"By worshiping Lord Viṣṇu all the demigods are automatically worshiped, therefore, there is no need to worship the demigods separately."

(*Harināma-cintāmani*)

24. Which propensity is prominent among the unalloyed devotees?

"There are two kinds of propensities in the cultivation of devotional service: the propensity for worshiping, and the propensity for hearing, remembering etc. Even though both are reasonable still the propensity for hearing, chanting and remembering is more prominent among the unalloyed devotees. Many great personalities perform up to some extent the act of remembrance in the course of chanting the holy names, and up to some extent the act of chanting the holy names loudly. The special benefit of loud *kīrtana* is that the processes of hearing, chanting and remembering are simultaneously carried out."

(*Harināma-cintāmani*)

25. What is vandana or offering prayers to the Lord and how many kinds of vandanas are there?

"*Vandana* is the sixth limb of devotional service. Although *vandana* is included within *pādasevana* and *kīrtana* it has been described as a separate limb of devotional service. Offering obeisances is also *vandana*. This offering of obeisance are of two kinds: offering obeisances with one part of the body, and offering obeisances with eight parts of the body. Offering obeisances with one hand, offering obeisances with once body fully covered, offering obeisances to the Lord from the front, from the back or from the left side of the Lord as well as offering obeisances to the Lord inside the Deity room are considered to be offenses."

(*Jaiva Dharma*, Chapter 19)

26. What are the principles of dāsya?

"'I am an eternal servant of Krishna' —this conviction is called *dāsya*. Worship in the mood of *dāsya* is best. Offering obeisances, offering prayers, offering all one's activities, performing worship, remembering and hearing the topics of the Lord are included within *dāsya*."

(*Jaiva Dharma*, Chapter 19)

27. How many kinds of sākhya are there?

"The symptom of friendship with a desire to benefit Krishna is called *sākhya*. There are two kinds of *sākhya*: *vaidha-sākhya* and *rāga-sākhya*. At this juncture we have to accept only *vaidha-sākhya*. The friendship which is found in the worship of the Deity form of the Lord is called *vaidha-sākhya*."

(*Jaiva Dharma*, Chapter 19)

28. What is the symptom of ātma-nivedana?

"To surrender everything to Krishna is called *atma-nivedana*. The symptom of *atma-nivedana* is to become free from any personal endeavor and to dovetail all endeavors for the pleasure of Krishna, just as a soldout cow does not endeavor for her own maintenance. One should also remain subordinate to the will of Krishna and surrender one's own independence to Krishna."

(*Jaiva Dharma*, Chapter 19)

53

One's Constitutional Propensities

1. What is one's constitutional and temporary propensities, and how is one's nature determined?

"The eternal nature of an object is its constitutional propensity. The nature of an object arises from its constitution. When an object is created by the will of Krishna, a nature is also created as the eternal companion of that object. This nature is the eternal propensity of that object. Later on, when due to some reason or some different association that object undergoes some changes, then its nature also changes or becomes perverted. After a while when this perverted nature becomes stronger it appears as the constitutional propensity. This perverted nature is not the constitutional propensity of the living entities. The perverted nature occupies the position of the constitutional propensity and passes as the constitutional propensity. For example, water is an object, liquidness is its nature; incidentally if the water becomes ice then hardness becomes its nature and acts like its constitutional nature. Actually this perverted nature is not eternal, but is temporary. Because it appears from some cause and when that cause is removed it disappears. But the constitutional propensity of a living entity is eternal. Even when it is perverted it remains dormant within. In due course of time, it will certainly manifest. The nature of the object is its eternal constitutional propensity, and the perverted nature of the object is its temporary propensity.

(*Jaiva Dharma*, Chapter 1)

2. What is the eternal constitutional propensity of the living entities?

"Krishna is the infinite supreme spirit, and the living entities are the fragmental part and parcels of that supreme spirit. In spiritual qualities they both are identical, but according to the difference in their perfection and imperfection their nature certainly becomes different. Krishna is the eternal Lord of the living entities and the living entities are His eternal servants, this is natural. Krishna is all attractive, and the living entities are attracted. Krishna is the Supreme Personality of Godhead, and the living entities are controlled by Him. Krishna is the seer, and the living entities are seen. Krishna is complete, and the living entities are poor and insignificant, Krishna is omnipotent, and the living entities are powerless. Therefore eternal subordination or service to Krishna is the living entities eternal nature or the constitutional duties.

The constitutional duty of a living entity is to love God, the living entity is not a product of matter rather he is transcendental to matter. Consciousness is its constitution, to love God is its nature. Service to Krishna is that pure love of God. Therefore, the constitutional duty of a living entity is to love Krishna by engaging in His service.

(*Jaiva Dharma*, Chapter 1)

3. Why is Vaiṣṇava dharma the eternal religious principles?

"The pure Vaiṣṇava *dharma* that is found in *Śrīmad-Bhāgavatam* is the eternal constitutional *dharma* of the living entities. All religious principles which have been preached throughout the world can be divided into three categories. These are eternal religious principles, occasional religious principles, and temporary religious principles. Those religious principles in which there is no discussion about God and the eternity of the spirit soul is denied are called temporary religious principles. Those religious principles which accept the eternity of God and the spirit soul but preach that one can attain the favor of God only through temporary methods are called occasional religious principles. Those religious principles which teach the attainment of the service of Krishna through pure love are called eternal religious principles. Even though these eternal religious principles appear differently according to different country, caste, and language, yet they are one and the most relishable. The Vaiṣṇava religion, which is widely spread throughout India, is the ideal of eternal religious principles. Moreover great personalities and exalted devotees have accepted that the religious principles taught by our most beloved Lord Gaura Hari, the son of Śacī, as the pure Vaiṣṇava religion."

(*Jaiva Dharma*, Chapter 2)

4. Which religious principles are the purest of all?

"That religion is the purest, which gives you the purest idea of God. The absolute religion requires an absolute conception."

(The *Bhagavat*: *Its Philosophy*, *Its Ethics and Its Theology*)

5. Which religious principle is worth being called the actual religious principle?

"That religious principle whose ultimate goal is pure love of God is the actual religious principle."

(*Caitanya-śikṣāmṛta* 1/1)

6. Are religious principles one?

"The religious principles of the human beings can never be many. That religious principle which is eternal for all human beings can never become different due to time, place, and circumstances. In fact, an eternal religious principle is one without a second."

(*Śrī Manaḥ-śikṣā*, Chapter 1)

7. Is the eternal religious principle one or many?

"The eternal religious principle is one. Every living entity has an eternal religious principle, and it is called Vaiṣṇava *dharma*. This *dharma* cannot be changed due to differences in language, country or caste. Many people address this *dharma* of the living entities in various names, but they cannot create any separate *dharma*. Rather the minute spirit soul's loving propensity towards the supreme spirit is its eternal constitutional propensity or *jaiva dharma*. Since the living entities have got different nature, their constitutional propensity also appears to be of different shapes and perversion. That is why the pure state of the living entities has been addressed as Vaiṣṇava *dharma*. Other religious systems are pure in proportion to the possession of Vaiṣṇava *dharma*."

(*Jaiva Dharma*, Chapter 2)

8. What is pure Vaiṣṇavas Dharma?

"Two separate *dharma* are passing on in this world in the name of Vaiṣṇava *dharma*: One is pure Vaiṣṇava *dharma* and the other one is perverted Vaiṣṇava *dharma*. Even though pure Vaiṣṇava *dharma* is one in truth, according to different *rāsas* it has been categorized as four: Vaiṣṇava *dharma* in the mood of *dāsya*, Vaiṣṇava *dharma* in the mood of *sākhya*, Vaiṣṇava *dharma* in the mood of *vātsalya*, and Vaiṣṇava *dharma* in the mood of *mādhurya*. Actually pure Vaiṣṇava *dharma* is one and without a second. Another name of this *dharma* is *nitya dharma* or *para dharma*. The following statement from the Veda "*jajjnāte sarvaṁ vijnātaṁ bhavati*" or (by knowing which everything becomes known) aims at pure Vaiṣṇava *dharma*."

(*Jaiva Dharma*, Chapter 4)

9. Why only Bhāgavata dharma is eternal dharma?

"Due to spiritual propensity all fortunate souls have a natural taste in the science of pure devotional service to the Lord. Their worship of the Supreme Lord is neither part of fruitive activities nor mental speculation. But it is pure devotional service. Such worship is called pure Vaiṣṇava *dharma*. It is stated in *Śrīmad-Bhāgavatam* 1/2/11 as follows:

vadanti tat tattva vidas tattvaṁ yaj jñānam advayam
brahmeti paramātmeti bhagavān iti śabdyate

"Learned transcendentalists who know the Absolute Truth call this nondual substance Brahman, Paramātmā or Bhagavān."

The Absolute Truth which includes Brahman and Paramātmā is the ultimate goal of all truths. The Absolute Truth is *viṣṇu-tattva* and all pure spirit souls are His servants, the pure propensity of the spirit soul is called devotional service. Devotional service to Hari alone is known as *suddha vaiṣṇava dharma, nitya dharma, jaiva dharma, bhāgavata dharma, paramārtha dharma* or *para dharma*. All religious principles that have arise from the principle of Brahman and Paramātmā are simply occasional religious principles. There is also a cause behind the cultivation of impersonal Brahman, therefore it is also occasional and not eternal. The followers of impersonal Brahman consider material bondage as the cause of their conditional state and thus they take shelter of occasional religious principles in the form of searching after impersonal Brahman. Therefore cultivation of impersonal Brahman is not eternal. Even those living entities who follow the principles of *paramātmā dharma* with a desire to attain pleasure derived from *samādhi*, also make the subtle material enjoyment as the criteria and thus follow the path of occasional religious principles. Therefore cultivation of *paramātmā dharma* is also not eternal. Only pure *bhāgavata dharma* is eternal."

(*Jaiva Dharma*, Chapter 4)

10. Why religious principles are many?

"Why religious principles have become many? The answer is that in pure state the living entities have only one type of *dharma*. After becoming conditioned the *dharma* of the living entities have become two fold namely materially designated *dharma* and pure *dharma*. Pure religious principle can never change at any circumstances. But according to time, place, and person, and due to a difference in the nature of the materially designated

living entities, the materially designated *dharma* has naturally become separate. This materially designated *dharma* gets various shapes and names in various countries. The more the living entities become purified the more their *dharma* becomes free from material designations. On the pure spiritual platform all living entities have one eternal *dharma*."
(*Śrī Manaḥ-śikṣā*, Chapter 1)

11. Why the existence of the spirit soul and Supersoul can not be established through arguments and reasoning and what is proved by direct perception?

"Since the truth is never lost, it only remains hidden. The eternity of the spirit soul and the existence of Brahman cannot be established through logical arguments, because arguments have no access to the subject matter that is beyond material universe. Direct self perception is the only establisher of such truths. By direct perception or spontaneous *samādhi* the saintly persons constantly realize the eternal abode of Vaikuntha and service to Krishna."
(*Śrī Krishna Saṁhita* 9/5)

12. What is the religion of the soul?

"It would indeed be the height of error to conceive that all the opposite qualities of matter, space and time are in spirit. Hence we must look to some other attributes for spirit. Love and wisdom are certainly spiritual attributes which are not opposite qualities of matter. Man must be wise and love God. This is the religion of the soul."
(*The Temple of Jagannāth at Purī*)

13. Is the religion of the soul sectarian?

"We do not profess to belong to any of the sects of religion under the sun, because we believe the Absolute Faith, founded upon instinctive love of God, natural in human souls."
(*The Temple of Jagannāth at Purī*)

14. Why is the ultimate goal of the religion of the soul beyond the realization of the mental speculators and ordinary righteous people?

"Bhakti (love) is thus perceived in the very first development of the man in the shape of mind, then in the shape of soul and lastly in the shape of will. These shapes do not destroy each other but beautifully harmonize themselves into a pure construction of what we call the spiritual man or the *ekanta* of Vaiṣṇavas Literature. But there is another sublime truth behind this fact which is revealed to a few that are prepared for it. We mean the spiritual conversion of the soul into a woman. It is in that sublime and lofty state in which the soul can taste the sweetness of an indissoluble marriage with God of love. The fifth or the highest of Vaiṣṇavas development is what we call *madhura-rāsa*, and on this alone the most beautiful portion of the Vaiṣṇava Literature so ably expatiates. This phase of human life, mysterious as it is, is not attainable by all, nay, we should say, by any but God's own. It is so very beyond the reach of common men that the rationalists and even the ordinary theists cannot understand it. Nay, they go so far as to sneer at it as somewhat unnatural."

('To Love God', (*Journal of Tajpur* 25th August 1871))

15. How is love of God the eternal religion of the soul and how is it beneficial to all?

"The essence of the soul is wisdom and its action is to love the Absolute. The absolute condition of man is his absolute relation to the Deity in pure love. Love then alone is the religion of the soul and consequently of the whole man."

('To Love God', (*Journal of Tajpur* 25th August 1871)

16. What are the ordinary principles of devotional service?

"You must love God with all thy strength and with all thy will. You are wrong in concluding that you will lose your active existence, rather you will get it the more. Work for God and work to God, proceeding from no interested views but from a holy free will (which is above the strength of man but identifying itself with pure love). This description is of *bhakti* in general."

('To Love God', (*Journal of Tajpur* 25th August 1871))

17. What is Pratyag-gati and Parāg-gati of the living entities?

"When a soul sits in the chariot of the mind and chases the sense objects through the gates of the senses, this is called *parāg-gati*. When this current again flows towards the soul's own abode, it is called *pratyag-gati*. With a desire to convert material attachment into spiritual attachment, all the spiritual emotions are mixed with material emotions for giving up *parāg-gati* and practicing *pratyag-gati*. The *pratyag-dharma* of being greedy to eat palatable foods is to eat *mahāprasāda*. The *pratyag-dharma* of the eyes is to see holy places and the beautiful form of the Lord. The *pratyag-dharma* of the ears is to hear devotional songs and the pastimes of Hari. The *pratyag-dharma* of the nose has been exemplified by the four Kumāras when they smelled the *tulasī* and sandalwood that was offered to the feet of the Lord. The *pratyag-dharma* of associating with the opposite sex through marriage for the prosperity of a Vaiṣṇava family was exemplified by Manu, Janaka, Jayadeva, and Pipāji. The *pratyag-dharma* of festivals is seen in the festivals celebrating the pastimes of Lord Hari. These human characteristics filled with emotions of *pratyag-dharma* are seen in the lives of pure swanlike personalities.

(*Śrī Krishna-saṁhitā* 10/11)

18. Is there any difference between the attachment for material objects and the attachment for the Supreme Lord?

"Attachment is present whether the repository is for the Lord or for something mundane. The only difference is its repository. When attachment is turned towards Vaikuṇṭha, then no attachment for the material world remains; one only accepts what is required for maintenance of the body. When the objects that are thus accepted become transcendental, then all attachments become spiritualized.

(*Śrī Krishna-saṁhitā* 10/2)

54

Surrendering

1. What is the eternal perfect religion of the living entities?

"Surrendering and subordination to the Supreme Lord is the eternal perfect religion of the living entities."

(*Sajjana-toṣaṇī* 10/9)

2. How can one attain pure devotional service?

"Aiming at the ultimate instruction of surrender given in *Bhagavad-gītā*, if one accepts all object of the senses as the remnants of the Supreme Lord, and engages in the service of the Supreme Lord giving up karma and *jñāna*, then he can attain pure devotional service."

(*Sajjana-toṣaṇī* 10/9)

3. What is the root of pure Bhajana?

"No one can attain the mercy of Krishna simply by studying the scriptures or hearing their conclusions. To give up endeavor for karma and *jñāna* and become fully surrendered to the Supreme Lord is the root of pure *bhajana*. As a result of this, one achieves the ultimate goal of life which is love of Krishna."

(*Sajjana-toṣaṇī* 11/7)

4. Is there any meaning to the life of a person who is devoid of surrendering?

"Without surrender the lives of living entities are useless. All living entities should worship Krishna with full surrender."

(*Sajjana-toṣaṇī* 11/6)

5. What is the ornament of a practitioner of devotional service?

"The entire life of a practitioner of devotional service should be decorated with surrendering."

(*Sajjana-toṣaṇī* 11/6)

6. What is the method for giving up name and fame?

"The Vaiṣṇava spiritual masters have given me the name Bhaktivinoda. But because I have no true devotion, for me this name is only a disease. To cure myself of this disease, I take shelter of the Vaiṣṇavas' feet.

(*Song from Gītā Mālā*)

7. What is the fate of a person who is overwhelmed with temporary material happiness and distress?

"Any woman who wishes to always keep her temporary relationship with husband or son will find that she cannot. When the fruit of her karma is ripe, the son will perish. Even if the son sits on her lap, she has no power to protect him. Thinking happiness and suffering come from material relationships, the soul falls far from Lord Krishna's feet and falls into a lower life. Therefore, please stop your grief! Dive into the bliss of the holy name."

All these words fulfill the desires of Bhaktivinoda.

(*Song from Gītā Mālā*)

8. What is the prayer of a fully surrendered pure devotee?

"I will behave equally with everyone, not try to demand respect from other's. I will always try to give respect to other's. In this way I will constantly remain absorbed in the thought of Krishna through the process of Krishna *sankīrtana*."

(*Kalyāna Kalpataru*, Song 6)

9. Do the Vaiṣṇavas feel any external ordinary distress?

"The external distress of the Vaiṣṇavas is not actual distress as it is foreign to them. But it is temporary and passes off blissfully in course of time."

(*Sajjana-toṣaṇī* 10/2)

10. How many types of surrender are there?

"Surrender is of six kinds:

1. Accept things which are favorable.
2. Reject things which are unfavorable.
3. To maintain the conviction that Krishna will certainly protect me.
4. To maintain the mentality that Krishna alone is my sustainer.
5. Offering everything to the Lord.
6. Humility.

Each of these six types of surrender are further divided into three categories. These are bodily, mental and verbal."

(*Sajjana-toṣaṇī* 4/9)

11. In what kind of behaviors are the fully surrendered devotees situated?

"One should accept only which is favorable for devotional service and reject only which is unfavorable for devotional service. One should have firm conviction that there is no protector for me other than Lord Krishna. One should also have full faith that Krishna will certainly maintain me. One should offer everything to Krishna and spend his life with sincere humility."

(*Bhajana-rahasya*, Chapter 3)

12. In which subject should a fully surrendered soul have determination and detachment?

"I will reject with firm determination, whatever is unfavorable in the path of my worship to the Lord. While worshiping the Lord, I will give up my body when the proper time comes."

(*Kalyāna Kalpataru*, Song 6)

13. Does a surrendered devotee think about his own maintenance?

"I will never think of my own maintenance, rather I will remain absorbed in love of God. O Lord! Bhaktivinod has accepted You as his sole maintainer."

(*Śaraṇāgati*)

14. Being surcharged with love of God, how does a pure devotee see the Lord's relationship with himself and this world?

"O Lord Hari! You are the father of the universe. You are the mother of the universe. You are the beloved Lord and the son. You are the well-wisher, the friend, the spiritual master, the husband and the desire tree. I am only Your eternal servant."

(*Gītā Mālā*, Song 26)

15. What is the hope of the living entities who are submerged in the material ocean?

"O Lord! When I was submerged in the material ocean, I called you pathetically to please deliver me. At that time You came forward to protect me. Realizing You as the pivot for my deliverance, I saw a ray of hope."

(*Gītā Mālā*, Song 10)

16. What is the result if one goes against or in favor of Krishna's will?

"Whatever Krishna desires is auspicious for everyone. One should give up one's own independence and destroys all problems. Krishna gives, Krishna takes away, and Krishna maintains everyone. Krishna protects, Krishna kills by His own sweet will. Whoever desires to oppose Krishna's will, never becomes successful but simply suffers."

(*Gītā Mālā*, Song 3)

17. How should one accept Krishna as the only maintainer so that one can achieve love of Krishna?

"I am an eternal spirit soul, a servant of Krishna. There is no protector or maintainer for me other than Krishna. I am the most fallen and poor. If I spend my life enjoying the fruits of my previous karma but at the same time hearing and chanting the holy names of Krishna, then I will certainly attain the Lord's mercy. If I remain with this conviction then I can attain love of Krishna."

(Purport of *Bṛhat-bhāgavatāmṛta*)

18. How is it desirable for a devotee to depend on the mercy of Krishna?

"'Either today or in one hundred years, or in some lifetime, Krishna will certainly bestow His mercy on me. I will take shelter at His lotus feet with firm determination and never leave Him.' Such attitude and patience is a must for a practitioner of devotional service."

(*Sajjana-toṣaṇī* 11/5)

19. What is ātma-nivedana or fully surrendering to Krishna?

"To possess the mentality that I do not belong to myself but to Krishna is the symptom of fully surrendering to Krishna."

(*Sajjana-toṣaṇī* 4/9)

20. Does a fully surrendered devotee remember his past history?

"O Lord! After attaining Your blissful service, I have forgotten all my previous histories. I belong to You and You belong to me. So what is the use of anything else."

(Song from *Śaraṇāgati*)

21. How does a surrendered servant of Krishna accept the happiness and distress born out of service to Krishna?

"All the distresses born in the course of Your service are also the source of my pleasure. Happiness and distress born from Your service are the supreme wealth, and they destroy the unhappiness of nescience."

(Song from *Śaraṇāgati*)

22. While living in the family of Krishna does a surrendered soul desire material enjoyment?

"I take a respite from material enjoyments and become fearless of material existence. I will constantly serve You and not desire to enjoy the fruits of my karma. I will remain attached to Your lotus feet and constantly endeavor to please You."

(Song from *Śaraṇāgati*)

23. What kind of humility does a practitioner who is engaged in the chanting of the holy names display before an exalted Vaiṣṇava?

"I do not find the strength to carry on alone the *saṅkīrtana* of the holy name of Hari. Please bless me by giving me just one drop of faith with which to obtain the great treasure of the holy name of Krishna. Krishna is Yours. You have the power to give Him to me. I am simply running behind you as a beggar shouting,"Krishna! Krishna!"

(Song from *Śaraṇāgati*)

24. How should a practitioner, who desires to chant the holy names of the Lord, pray to his spiritual master?

"Gurudeva, give this servant just one drop of mercy. I am lower than a blade of grass. Give me all help. Give me strength. Let me be as you are, without desires or aspirations. I offer you all respects, for thus I may have the energy to offer respect to everyone properly. Then, by chanting the holy name in great ecstasy, all my offenses will cease.

(Song from *Śaraṇāgati*)

25. Does an unalloyed devotee ever give up the lotus feet of Krishna?

"It is not possible for one who has no other desire to give up Your lotus feet. O Lord! Such a person spends his life taking shelter at Your lotus feet, and Your lotus feet are the cause of his fearlessness."

(*Gītā Mālā*, Song 11)

26. How should one worship Krishna until death?

"As long as one possesses this material body one should remain attached to Krishna and accept Him as one's wealth, friend and life. One should consider the relationship to one's brother, friend, husband and children which are related to one's own body as temporary."

(*Gītā Mālā*, Song 2)

27. Does a sincere worshiper of Hari ever consider himself a guru?

"I will consider myself as Your servant and give up the pride of being a guru. I will honor without duplicity, remnants of dust from Your lotus feet, and drink water that has washed Your lotus feet."

(*Kalyāna Kalpataru*, Song 8)

28. To whom does the Absolute Truth manifest?

"The *Bhagavat* teaches us that God gives us truth when we earnestly seek for it. Truth is eternal and unexhausted. The soul receives a revelation when it is anxious for it."

(*The Bhagabat*: *Its Philosophy*, *Its Ethics* & *Its Theology*)

29. Does a fully surrendered devotee ever proudly consider himself the doer?

"O Lord! If You search after my qualifications You will find none, for Your mercy is my life and soul. If you do not bestow Your mercy then I will simply cry and no longer remain alive."

(Song from *Śaraṇāgati*)

30. Whose shelter should a living entity who is lost in the dense forest of material existence take?

"The four directions are fully covered with thick dark clouds in the form of foolishness. Upon that, the rain of material miseries are constantly being showered. Seeing such a situation I am frightened and I have lost my way. O Lord Acyuta! Due to my foolishness I have fallen in the grip of misfortune and I am suffering in the ocean of material existence. I have no guide to show me the real path and thus I am almost dying. Therefore, O Lord! I pray to You with my heart and soul."

(*Gītā Mālā*, Song 18)

31. How does a pure devotee pray for Krishna's mercy?

"O Lord! I am the most wretched person, and You are the most merciful. Therefore I have a right to receive Your mercy. The more one is fallen the more You display Your mercy to him. Therefore I am the suitable candidate for Your mercy."

(*Gītā Mālā*, Song 19)

32. What kind of eagerness does an exalted devotee display in order to attain the qualification for chanting the Lord's name?

"If I do not expect any respect for myself but always give respect to other's then You will award me the qualification to chant Your holy names. O Lord! I grab Your lotus feet without duplicity, and fall on the ground with great humility."

(*Kalyāna Kalpataru*, Song 8)

32. When does an exalted Vaiṣṇavas bestow mercy upon the living entities?

"When will I be so fortunate that the Vaiṣṇavas will consider me as their own servant? I will sing the transcendental qualities of Śrī Krishna in Vrṇdavana, and be intoxicated in drinking the beverage of the nectar from the lotus feet of the spiritual master. The fruitive workers, the mental speculators, and persons who are envious of and adverse to Krishna will reject this beggar with hatred. The smārtas who are attached to ritualistic ceremonies will conclude that this person is devoid of proper behaviors and therefore extremely restless. Persons who are proud of their material knowledge, as well as the impersonalists, will give up my association considering me a madman. The most pious Vaiṣṇava will mercifully embrace me seeing me devoid of bad association."

(*Kalyāna Kalpataru*, Song –2)

55

Chanting The Holy Names Of The Lord

1. Which qualifications should a chanter of the holy names of Hari possess?

"One should have the following symptoms in order to constantly chant the holy names of Hari: humility, freedom from envy, compassion, freedom from false pride, and respect for everyone."

(Commentary on *Śikṣāstaka*, Verse 3)

2. How does Harikīrtana become effective in the material world?

"One who has developed faith should first take shelter of a bonafide spiritual master and hear about the spiritual truth from him. Thereafter he should engage in chanting and glorifying whatever he has heard from his spiritual master. And thus the processes of destroying Māyā in the form of self-realization take place. In this way *harikīrtana* becomes effective in the material world."

(Commentary on *Śikṣāstaka*, Verse 1)

3. What is the purpose of sankīrtana?

"The endeavor of *sankīrtana* is to call out the holy names of the Lord with heartiest feelings."

(*Sajjana-toṣaṇī* 10/9)

4. By following which process are one's obstacles removed and does one's cultivation of the holy names becomes constant?

"At first one should chant the holy names for a short time in a solitary place with undivided attention. Gradually by increasing the prescribed numbers of the holy names, one will attain perpetuity in the cultivation of chanting, and all one's obstacles will certainly diminish."

(*Harināma-cintāmani)*

5. Which process should a practitioner who is full of anarthas follow, in the course of chanting the holy names?

"Everyday a person should give up the disturbance caused by material enjoyment, and chant with love for a while in a solitary place. Gradually he should try to increase the duration of this process. Finally a wonderful mood will be awakened in him and will remain all the time."

(*Jaiva Dharma*, Chapter 40)

6. What is the meaning of 'constant chanting of the holy names'?

"Except during the time of sleep, to always chant the holy names of the Lord during taking care of the bodily activities, and at all other times, is called 'constant chanting of the holy names.'"

(*Jaiva Dharma*, Chapter 23)

7. How should one chant the holy names of Hari in the association of tulasī?

"Tulasī is very dear to Hari. Therefore by chanting in her association one feels the spiritual strength of the holy names. While chanting the holy names, one should consider that there is no difference between Lord Krishna and His holy names."

(*Jaiva Dharma*, Chapter 23)

8. Is it beneficial to chant more rounds without any feeling and eagerness?

"One should try hard to constantly chant the holy names of Krishna clearly and lovingly rather than trying to increase the number of rounds."

(*Harināma-cintāmani*)

9. Which religion in this world will be the goal of all religion?

"In their matured stage all religions of this world will end up in one religion in the form of *nāma-sankīrtana.* We feel this to be a certain fact."

(*Sajjana-toṣaṇī* 4/3)

10. At what time during the period of Śrī Bhaktivinoda Ṭhākura was nāma-sankīrtana first preached in Calcutta? How can hari-kīrtana be performed in a pure way?

"Once upon a time the leaders of Śrī Gaurāṅga Samāja decided to perform *sankīrtana* . Being induced by such thought and with the help of the citizens of Calcutta they performed the first *nāma-sankīrtana* on the appearance day of Śrī Mahāprabhu at Bidon Street, Calcutta. According to the opinion of many elderly persons, such a *sankīrtana* festival never took place in Calcutta before. Everyone including the atheists and the devotees joined in this congregational chanting of the Lord's holy names. Such a tumultuous *sankīrtana* should be performed in all countries on the appearance day of Śrī Mahāprabhu. Due to this *sankīrtana* festival the citizens became attached to *kīrtana*. What to speak of this, people gave up all other engagements and formed *kīrtana* groups in every village, and spent lavishly for this purpose. It was very pleasing that the citizens of Calcutta who hailed from different states of India joined in the *nāma-kīrtana*. Particularly people from the Western part of India who have never heard Mahāprabhu's name also became intoxicated by chanting the names of Nityānanda-Gaurāṅga in the course of their participation in *harināma-kīrtana*. Many shopkeepers and commission agents of Bada Bazār who belong to the Western part of India participated in the *nagara-kīrtana* by spending huge amounts of money and labor. The residents of each village of Calcutta performed *kīrtana* in their respective villages with pomp.

On the appearance day of Śrī Mahāprabhu we were engaged in holding a grand festival at Śrī Navadvīpa Mayāpura, which is the birth place of Mahāprabhu and *harināma*. After a few days we came to Calcutta and perfomed this *harināma-sankīrtana*. It appeared that the religious principles which were extinct in Calcutta are now, by the mercy of Mahāprabhu becoming prominent. This is because *hari-kīrtana* which is the essence of all religion is being performed here. But in spite of these encouraging activities, Mahāprabhu has not distributed love of God, which is the most confidential mystery, in this metropolitan city. In order to reveal Himself the Lord has given sufficient encouragement to all kinds of people. Even He gave them the strength to give up material happiness. Still He has not opened the door of pure love and devotion. He has induced people to chant the holy names but He has not given them the propensity to follow in the footsteps of the *mahājanas* even today.

We saw many people performing *kīrtana* with *mṛdaṅga* and *karatāla* giving up their leather shoes, yet we did not find any *tulasī* beads on their neck. If even some people do have t*ulasī* beads they are new one's. This creates some doubts. Many people have not decorated their bodies with twelve marks of *tilaka*. In order to hear *kīrtana* in the *mahājanas*' way, we went to Neemtala Ghat one day, Jodā Sanko another day, and Jhāmā Pukura on yet another day, but we could not find any such things. We were extremely pained to hear *kīrtana* performed by Nyādās, Bāhuls and other unauthorized people in the tune of cinemas songs. But our pain was somewhat diminished by hearing the eternal names of Hari, Krishna and Rāma uttered by them in the course of their singing. Those who possess love and devotion in their hearts love to hear *kīrtana* in the old and ancient tune. They do not like to hear or sing useless topics. They sing and hear the pure holy names of Hari in the old tune. Due to lack of good association, the residents of this metropolitan city do not easily realize the characteristics of pure devotional service. Therefore they follow their own concocted process. Anyhow our Śrī Gaurāṅga is most merciful. Since He has mercifully allowed the residents of Calcutta to perform *kīrtana*, we hope that gradually He will reveal pure devotional service in their hearts.

Some people say that the residents of Calcutta have started this process of *kīrtana* in order to avoid the dreaded diseases like plague. There is no doubt that those who are against this *kīrtana* are certainly enemies of the country. We have a proposal for them. They can perform *sankīrtana* but they must do so on occasions. It is better that they perform *hari-kīrtana* on occasions such as Purnima, Ekādasī, Gaura Purnimā, Janmāstami, Month of Kārttika, Month of Baisaka, the days when the Lord is taken out on a procession, and on days when the sun enters a particular zodiac signs. May the residents of Calcutta increase our happiness by performing *kīrtana* with *mṛdaṅga* and *karatāla* in a pure Vaiṣṇava way following the footsteps of the *mahājanas*. Śrī Gaurāṅga is Jagatguru. Therefore He will certainly award them their desired result.

(*Sajjana-toṣaṇī* 11/3)

11. What does a chanter of the holy names beg?

"Accompany us and chant the names of Rādhā And Krishna. This is our only appeal. Śrī Bhaktivinoda says, 'whenever I chant the holy names all dangers go away.'"

(*Gitāvali*)

56

The Reflection on the Chanting of the Holy Names

1. What is the benefit of nāmābhāsa?

"In *nāmābhāsa* or reflective chanting of the holy name of the Lord, all one's sinful reactions are destroyed. When all one's sinful reactions and *anarthas* are destroyed, then the pure holy name dances on the tongue of the devotees. Then pure holy names award such a person love of Krishna."

(*Harināma-cintāmani*)

2. Are the holy names uttered by the māyāvādis actual holy names?

"Holy names uttered by the māyāvādis are not holy names; but simply perverted reflection of the holy names. Therefore in spite of chanting such names the *māyāvādis* are affected by the faults of *nāmāparādha*."

(*Sajjana-toṣaṇī* 5/12)

3. What is the difference between perverted and shadow nāmābhāsa?

"Words such as *nāmābhāsa, vaiṣnavābhāsa, śraddhābhāsa, bhavābhāsa, ratyābhāsa, premābhāsa* and *muktyābhāsa* are found in many places in the scriptures. A nice meaning of the word *nāmābhāsa* is given everywhere and it is explained as follows: 'the *ābhāsa* is of two kinds, actual reflection and perverted reflection.' In the actual reflection, the effulgence of an object manifest in a contracted form. In the perverted reflection the perversion of the actual form appears in a different shape. It is like the light reflected in the water. As long as the sun-like holy name remains covered by the clouds and storm in the form of the living entities' ignorance and *anarthas*, an insignificant and contracted light of the sun is visible. In such state *nāmābhāsa* produces great auspicious results in this world. When this effulgent holy name becomes reflected from the lake of *māyāvāda*, it is called perverted reflected *nāmābhāsa*. Such *nāmābhāsa* is one of the principal *nāmāparādha*; hence it cannot be called *nāmābhāsa*. Only shadow *nāmābhāsa* is actual *nāmābhāsa*. It is divided into four categories. Glorification of *nāmābhāsa* by condemning the abominable reflected *nāmābhāsa* is found in all the scriptures. Shadow *nāmābhāsa* is caused by *anarthas* born of ignorance. Reflected *nāmābhāsa* is born from shrewd and polluted knowledge, and thus it has been ascertained as an impediment on the path of devotional service. Although a person who is as good as a Vaiṣṇava may not be called a Vaiṣṇava, but since he is free from the contamination of *māyāvāda* he can be respected as a *kaniṣṭha adhikari* devotees. By the influence of good association, such a person will soon achieve auspiciousness and the pure devotees will shower their blessings on him considering him an ignorant friend. They will not ignore him like they do to the envious *māyāvādis*. They will enhance his propensity for deity worship with ordinary faith and award him the devotional service mixed with the knowledge of his relationship with the Lord that is suitable for the service of the Lord and His devotees. But if he has an inseparable belief in *māyāvāda*, then the pure devotees will certainly ignore him."

(*Harināma-cintāmani*)

4. Can one chant the pure names of God as long as one has anartha?

"The clouds of *anartha* consisting of material desires, weakness of the heart, and committing offenses, cover the sun-like holy names. When the rays of the sun-like holy names are thus covered then the subdued illumination is called *nāmābhāsa*. This *nāmābhāsa* obstructs the appearance of the self-illuminated holy names of Krishna."

(*Harināma-cintāmani*)

5. Why nāmābhāsa is more beneficial than all kinds of pious activities?

"*Nāmābhāsa* is counted as one of the principal kinds of piety of the living entities. *Nāmābhāsa* awards superior fruits than all types of pious activities like following religious principles, observing vows and practicing yoga."

(*Harināma-cintāmani*)

6. What is the result of nāmābhāsa?

"It is stated in the *śāstras* that in Kali-yuga one can attain the spiritual abodes of Vaikuntha simply by the influence of *nāmābhāsa*."

(*Harināma-cintāmani*)

7. How many types of nāmābhāsa are there and what are the differences between them?

"If the holy names of the Lord are chanted with *sanket*, *parihāsa*, *stobha* and *helā*, then it is called *nāmābhāsa*. Therefore *nāmābhāsa* is of four types. *Stobha* is less offensive than *helā*, *parihāsa* is less offensive than *stobha*, and *sanket* is less offensive than *parihāsa*."

(*Harināma-cintāmani*)

8. When does nāmābhāsa ceases?

"Until a person achieves the knowledge of his relationship with the Lord, he continues to be in the association of *nāmābhāsa*."

(*Harināma-cintāmani*)

9. How many kinds of ābhāsa or reflections are there?

"There are two kinds of reflections of the sun-like holy names: shadow reflection and perverted reflection. Learned scholars always use the terms like *bhāktyābhāsa*, *bhāvābhāsa*, *nāmābhāsa* and *vaiṣṇavabhāsa*. All kinds of *ābhāsas* or reflections are of two categories — shadow and perverted."

(*Jaiva Dharma*, Chapter 20)

10. Who is a vaiṣṇava-prāya or as good as a Vaiṣṇava?

"The meaning of the word *vaiṣṇava-prāya* is that a person decorates himself like a Vaiṣṇava with *tulasī* beads, *tilaka* and so on, but actually he is not a real or pure Vaiṣṇava."

(*Jaiva Dharma*, Chapter 25)

11. When does nāmābhāsa turns into nāmāparādha and what is the result of this?

"The absence of chanting the pure name is called *nāmābhāsa*. This *nāmābhāsa* is addressed as *nāmābhāsa* in some stage and as *nāmāparādha* in other stage. When due to ignorance, in other words when due to the four defects, the pure holy name is chanted impurely, it is *nāmābhāsa*. When due to the association of *mayāvāda*, due to duplicity, due to desire of liberation, and due to material desires the pure holy name is chanted impurely, it is called *nāmāparādha*. If ten kinds of *nāmāparādha* that I have already explained to you is committed with simplicity and ignorance then they are known as *nāmābhāsa*. The point is that as long as *nāmābhāsa* is untouched by the symptoms of *nāmāparādha* there is an opportunity for the pure holy names to appear by destroying *nāmābhāsa*. However if *nāmābhāsa* is affected by the symptoms of *nāmāparādha* then the pure holy names of the Lord do not appear. In such a situation there is no alternative for achieving auspiciousness other than eradicating the offenses against the holy names by the prescribed process."

(*Jaiva Dharma*, Chapter 25)

12. What is the example of sanket nāmābhāsa?

"At the time of his death Ajāmila called his own son by the name Nārāyaṇa. Since Nārāyaṇa is the another name of Krishna, Ajāmila attained the result of chanting the Lord's names with *sanket*."

(*Jaiva Dharma*, Chapter 25)

13. What is the example of stobha nāmābhāsa?

"Suppose an exalted Vaiṣṇava is chanting the holy names of Hari, and at that time an atheist comes there and says, 'O your Lord Hari will do everything for you.' This is the example of *stobha nāmābhāsa*. Even that atheist can attain liberation by doing so. This is the natural strength of the holy names."

(*Jaiva Dharma*, Chapter 25)

14. How does one practice nāmābhāsa in 'helā'?

"If one cunningly neglects the chanting of the holy names then it is a *nāmāparādha*, but if one neglects the chanting of the holy name out of ignorance then it is called *nāmābhāsa*."

(*Jaiva Dharma*, Chapter 25)

15. What does one achieve by nāmābhāsa?

"Material enjoyments, liberation and all types of mystic perfections are achieved by *nāmābhāsa*. However the ultimate goal of life in the form of love of Krishna cannot be attained by *nāmābhāsa*."

(*Jaiva Dharma*, Chapter 25)

57

Offenses Against the Chanting of the Holy Names

1. How grave is the importance of nāmāparādha?

"As the holy names of the Lord are the highest object, so *nāmāparādha* is also more serious than all other kinds of sinful activities and offenses. All kinds of sinful activities and offenses are destroyed by taking shelter of the holy names of the Lord, but *nāmāparādha* does not go away so easily."
(*Jaiva Dharma*, Chapter 24)

2. Can nāmāparādha be compared with any sinful activity?

"If the five kinds of sinful activities are multiplied by ten million times, still it can not be compared with *nāmāparādha.*"
(*Jaiva Dharma*, Chapter 25)

3. Can one gain anything by making a show of chanting the holy names without giving up the offenses?

"Without realizing the difference between *nāma* and *nāmābhāsa* many people think that the holy names consist of only the alphabets, therefore assume that by chanting the holy names without faith, one can attain perfection. To substantiate their claim, they put forth the history of Ajāmila and various scriptural injunctions. It has been described before that the holy name is fully transcendental. Therefore it can not be accepted by the blunt material senses. In such a case unless one takes shelter of the holy names offenselessly there is no possibility of achieving any fruit from chanting the holy names. The result of uttering the holy names by the faithless persons is that later on they can chant the holy names faithfully. Therefore those who misinterpret the glories of the holy names and advertise the holy names as a limb of fruitive activities by considering the holy name as mundane sound vibration, are extremely materialistic and are offenders at the feet of the holy names."
(*Harināma-cintāmani*)

4. Is it not a nāmāparādha to unlawfully initiate a woman, in order to take advantage of her association, on the strength of chanting the holy names?

"Once upon a time a Vaiṣṇava *sannyāsi* became attracted to a beautiful young woman. Being induced by his sinful propensity he finally decided as follows: 'Since I always chant the holy names I can make that woman my disciple by giving her *harināma* initiation and then I can accept service from her. In the process whatever sinful activities will be committed, that will certainly be destroyed by the holy names chanted by both of us. The woman will also get an opportunity to become a Vaiṣṇavī. The association of a Vaiṣṇava is very rare; moreover I will learn many things about the ecstatic love of the *gopīs* from her association. Where can I get such an association?' Thinking in this way the Vaiṣṇava *sannyāsi* made that woman a Vaiṣṇavī and enjoyed her service. This is example of ultimate *nāmāparādha*."

(*Sajjana-toṣaṇī* 8/9)

5. What is the reason behind the holy names not bearing fruit immediately?

"If the all powerful rain of holy names fall on the hard stones like the body, house, wealth, followers and greed, then it does not bear fruit immediately. These obstacles are divided into two classes namely small obstacles and big obstacles. When there are small obstacles in the course of chanting the holy names, such chanting of holy name becomes *nāmābhāsa*. They award result very late. If there are big obstacles while chanting the holy names then such chanting becomes *nāmāparādha*. Without incessant chanting of the holy names, these offenses do not go away."

(*Jaiva Dharma*, Chapter 24)

6. What is the symptom of a person who is devoid of unalloyed devotional service?

"The following are the symptoms of a person devoid of pure devotional service: engaging in the condemned activities such as disregarding the pure Vaiṣṇavas, associating with nondevotees, in other words illicit association with women and materialists, disregarding the spiritual master, blaspheming the devotional literatures, considering the Lord and His holy names to be different, considering the holy names to be equal to pious activities, lack of faith in the chanting of the holy names due to possessing the mentality of 'I and Mine,' and committing sinful activities on the strength of the holy names.

(*Sajjana-toṣaṇī* 6/7)

7. What are the ten kinds of nāmāparādhas?

"The ten kinds of *nāmāparādhas* are as follows:

1. Blaspheming the devotees who have taken shelter of the holy names. It is also an offense to neglect them, thinking that they know only the science of the holy names and do not know anything about *jñāna-yoga*, etc.

2. Considering the demigods to be independent. Krishna is the Supreme Personality of Godhead and the Lord of lords. All the demigods and demigoddesses are His servants and maidservants. Simply by worshiping Krishna all the demigods are automatically worshiped. Without having such a faith if one considers Krishna as one God, Shiva as another god and thus imagine many independent gods then it is an offense.

3. Disobeying the spiritual master. If one thinks that the spiritual master is expert only in the science of the holy names but does not know anything about other types of *sādhana* then it is an offense. Actually one who has attained the science of the holy names which is the ultimate goal of all pious activities, there is nothing left for him to be attained or known.

4. Blaspheming the Vedic literatures. The Vedic literatures have glorified the holy names in various ways. It is an offense to maintain a hostile attitude and faithlessness in the statements of the Vedas glorifying holy names.

5. Giving some interpretation on the holy names. It is an offense to think that the holy names like Rāma, Krishna and Hari are all imaginary, and as such the Lord has no names, form, quality or activity.

6. Committing sinful activities on the strength of the holy names. It is a grave offense to think that, 'by chanting all my sinful reactions will be destroyed or by chanting gradually my heart will be purified and I will no longer have any taste for committing sinful activities, therefore, for the time being let me commit some sinful activities for my own sake.' Such a mentality of committing sinful activities on the strength of the holy names is an offense.

7. Considering the holy names as equal to the pious activities. It is an offense to not take shelter of the holy names by thinking that the chanting of the holy name is a pious activity like following religious principles, observing vows and undergoing austerities, therefore thinking that by taking shelter of any of the pious activities one can become purified.

8. Remaining inattentive while chanting the holy names. It is an offense to not pay attention while chanting the holy names, in other words to become indifference and lazy towards chanting the holy name. To become indifference means to think of various material enjoyments during the time of chanting, to not have a taste for chanting and to repeatedly check out

the ending point of the chanting bead to make sure when will the round be finished. It is also an offense to chant the holy names under the influence of cheating propensity as well as for name and fame.

9. Instructing a faithless person about the glories of the holy names. First one should preach the glories of the holy names to a foolish faithless person. When he develops sufficient faith in the holy names then he should be awarded Holy names—Mantra initiation. It is a grievous offense to initiate an unqualified person for the sake of money.

10. Maintaining the mentality of 'I and mine.' It is an offense to engage in the chanting of the holy names while maintaining excessive attachment for material enjoyments even after understanding the glories of the holy names.

If one gives up these ten kinds of *nāmāparādha* and engages in hearing and chanting the holy names of Krishna then he certainly achieves love of God which is the goal of chanting the holy names."

(*Sajjana-toṣaṇī* 11/7)

8. What is the definition of first the nāmāparādha?

"The first *nāmāparādha* is to blaspheme those saintly persons who have taken complete shelter of the holy names and have given up all pious activities, cultivation of knowledge, and practice of yoga. The holy names of Hari can not tolerate the blasphemy of His devotees who are engaged in spreading the actual glories of the holy names. By accepting the devotees who are attached to chanting the holy names as the topmost, and by chanting the holy names in their association while giving up blaspheming, then one can quickly attain the mercy of the holy names."

(*Jaiva Dharma*, Chapter 24)

9. How many types of the second nāmāparādha are there?

"There are two types of the second *nāmāparādha*. The first type is to consider the names, qualities etc., of Sadāśiva the foremost demigod, and Lord Vishnu to be different is an offense. The purport is that if one imagines Sadāśiva as an independent god and Lord Viṣṇu as an independent God, then one falls in the category of accepting many gods. As a result one's unalloyed devotional service to Krishna becomes obstructed. Krishna is the Lord of lords, and the lordships of all the demigods headed by Śiva is dependent on Krishna. In other words those demigods have no separate independence or power. By chanting the holy name with such a conviction one does not commit any offense. The second type is to consider the names, forms, qualities and pastimes of the Lord to be different from the eternally perfected body of the Lord. Therefore one should accept the forms of Krishna, the names of Krishna, the qualities of Krishna, and the pastimes of Krishna to be spiritual and nondifferent from each other. With such a mentality one should chant the holy names of Krishna, otherwise one commits *nāmāparādha*. It is prescribed that one should engage in chanting the holy names of Krishna after achieving this knowledge."

(*Jaiva Dharma*, Chapter 24)

10. What is the symptom of disobeying the spiritual master, which is the third offense?

"Those who consider that the spiritual master, who awards the holy names, is conversant with the scriptures dealing only with the holy names but is inferior to the spiritual master who is well acquainted with Vedanta and philosophical literature, are certainly offenders at the feet of the holy names. Actually there is no superior spiritual master to the one who knows science of the holy names. To consider such a spiritual master as insignificant is an offense."

(*Jaiva Dharma*, Chapter 24)

11. How should one treat his spiritual master?

"One should not think his spiritual master to be an ordinary human being, rather one should respect him as an associate of Krishna filled with the energy of Krishna. To consider the spiritual master as Krishna is also a philosophy of the impersonalists. It is not the philosophy of the pure Vaiṣṇavas.

(*Harināma-cintāmani*)

12. What is the fourth Nāmāparādha?

"The glories of the holy names are found in all the Vedas and *Upaniṣads*; therefore it is an offense to blaspheme such Vedic literatures. Due to misfortune many persons respect other instructions of the Vedic literature and neglect the instructions of the Vedas which glorify the holy names. This is their offense at the feet of the holy names. Due to this offense they do not develop a taste for chanting the holy names of the Lord."

(*Jaiva Dharma*, Chapter 24)

13. What is giving some interpretation on the holy names of the Lord?

"Those who say that the statements of the Vedas, the revealed scriptures and the *Purānas* which are indicative of the glories of the holy name are exaggeration, they go to hell forever."

(*Jaiva Dharma*, Chapter 24)

14. What does it mean by giving some interpretation on the holy name?

"This means that whatever the *śāstras* have glorified regarding the chanting of the holy name are not factual rather they have done so in order to draw everyone's attention towards the holy name. To think like this an offense and as a result those who think like this do not develop any taste for chanting. You should engage in chanting the holy names of Hari by keeping full faith in the words of the *śāstras*. You should not associate with those who give interpretation on the holy names of the Lord; what to speak of this if you suddenly meet such person you should take bath immediately with your clothes on. This is the teaching of Śrī Gaurāṅga."

(*Jaiva Dharma*, Chapter 24)

15. What is the result if one thinks that the glories of the holy names of Hari is imaginary?

"It is an offense to consider the Lord's holy names as imagination. The impersonalists and the materialists think that the Supreme Absolute Truth is impersonal and devoid of names, forms, etc. Those who conclude that His holy names such as Rāma and Krishna have been imagined by the sages, for the sake of formality, are offenders at the feet of the holy names."

(*Jaiva Dharma*, Chapter 24)

16. What is the definition of 'committing sinful activities on the strength of chanting the holy name'?

"Those who engage in committing sinful activities on the strength of chanting the holy names are offenders at the feet of the holy names. The sinful activities which are committed on the strength of the holy names cannot be counteracted by the process of *yama*, *niyama* and so on, because since it is counted as one of the *nāmāparādhas*, it will only be counteracted by the prescribed process for counteracting the offenses against the holy names."

(*Jaiva Dharma*, Chapter 24)

17. What does it mean by counteracting the sinful reactions with chanting of the holy names?

"Those who conclude that 'let us commit sinful activities and also chant the holy names of Hari and thus after debit and credit there will be no balance of sinful reactions left' and thus commit fresh sinful activities after taking shelter of the holy names, are cheaters and offenders at the feet of the holy names."

(*Sajjana-toṣaṇī* 8/9)

18. What makes one commit sinful activities on the strength of chanting the holy names?

"Since there are some offenses already existing in a person his chanting of the holy names becomes *nāmābhāsa* and not pure chanting. Due to *nāmābhāsa*, previous sinful reactions are eradicated, and the taste for fresh sinful activities does not develop. Whatever sinful reactions that is left over from the previously committed sinful activities also gradually becomes destroyed by the strength of *nāmābhāsa*. If a person seldom commits any sinful activities, they also becomes nullified by *nāmābhāsa*. But if a person who has taken shelter of the holy names thinks that, since all sinful reactions are destroyed by chanting the holy names of the Lord, then if I commit any sinful activities that will also get destroyed by the process of chanting, then his chanting of the holy name becomes an offense because he is committing sinful activities on the strength of the holy names."

(*Jaiva Dharma*, Chapter 24)

19. What is the offense of considering the chanting of holy names to be equal to pious activities?

"Because *harināma* is the *sādhana*, process for achieving the goal of life, and *sadhya*, perfection of goal of life, *harināma* can not be compared with other pious activities. Those who consider the holy names as nondifferent from pious activities, are offenders at the feet of the holy names."

(*Jaiva Dharma*, Chapter 24)

20. What is the main cause of not having attachment for chanting the holy names?

"If even one gives up all offenses against the holy names, if he is inattentive while chanting he can never develop attachment for chanting."

(*Sajjana-toṣaṇī* 11/1)

21. How many kinds of inattention to chanting the holy names of the Lord are there?

"O Lord! All *anarthas* are produced from not paying attention to the chanting of the holy names. The exalted devotees have understood this inattention as indifference, laziness and restlessness."

(*Harināma-cintāmani*)

22. What is the symptom of a restless chanter?

"Those who are afflicted with restlessness try to finish up their prescribed rounds of chanting as soon as possible. One should remain extremely careful not to commit such an offense while chanting."

(*Harināma-cintāmani*)

23. Why paying no attention to 'chanting the holy names' is the source of all offenses?

"O reservoir of all transcendental qualities ! If one chants the holy names of the Lord but his attention is somewhere else, how can he achieve any benefit? If even such a person chants one hundred thousand holy names of the Lord, still a drop of mellows of ecstatic love will not be attained. O Lord! This is the definition of paying no attention while chanting the holy names. This offense is deeply rooted in the hearts of the materialists.

(*Harināma-cintāmani*)

24. By which process can laziness be destroyed?

"The characteristic of a saintly person is that he does not waste any time. By seeing such a character one will certainly hanker after it. One will think, 'Alas! When will I become fortunate enough to chant, sing, and remember the holy names of the Lord like this saintly person?' Such an enthusiasm in the mind of a lazy person will destroy his laziness by the remembrance of Krishna."

(*Harināma-cintāmani*)

25. Why does one become indifferent to chanting of the holy names?

"If desire for accumulating wealth, enjoying the association of women, the sensing of victory and defeat, aspiring for name and fame and cheating other's fill one's heart that one will naturally become indifference to chanting the Lord's holy names."

(*Harināma-cintāmani*)

26. What is the fault of instructing the faithless persons about the glories of the holy names?

"To instruct about the holy names of Hari to those who are faithless, who are averse to the service of the Supreme Lord and who are devoid of a taste for hearing the holy names of Hari, is an offense against the holy names."

(*Jaiva Dharma*, Chapter 24)

27. What kind of offense is maintaining the mentality of 'I and mine'?

"Those who are intoxicated by the mentality that I am such and such in this material world and this wealth and followers are mine and who seldom hear the glories of the holy names from the mouths of the saintly persons on account of flickering faith or knowledge and so do not display any love for the holy names, are offenders at the feet of the holy names."

(*Jaiva Dharma*, Chapter 24)

28. What is the cause behind an initiated devotees falling from the path of devotional service?

"Even after being initiated a majority of the materialistic persons fall down from the path of devotional service due to their mentality of 'I and mine.' "

(*Harināma-cintāmani*)

29. What is the method for removing the mentality of 'I and mine'?

"One should search for devotees who have given up material enjoyments and possessiveness, and who worship the lotus feet of Krishna by engaging in chanting of His holy names, and associate with them. By serving such devotees one will gradually be able to give up the waves of material enjoyments and develop faith in the chanting of the holy names. In this way one's mentality of 'I and mine' will be destroyed and one will cross the ocean of material existence."

(*Harināma-cintāmani*)

30. What is the goal of the offenders at the feet of the holy names?

"Whatever fruits an offender of the holy names desires while chanting, the holy names certainly awards them to him. But the holy name never awards him the fruit of love of God. One also enjoys the fruits of *nāmāparādha* simultaneously."

(*Jaiva Dharma*, Chapter 25)

31. What is the process for counteracting Nāmāparādha?

"If one commits offenses against the Deity worship, the holy names can counteract them. The *nāmāparādhas* are counteracted only by chanting the holy names of Hari. Constant chanting of the holy names awards all perfections."

(*Bhajana-rahasya*)

58

Compassion Towards Living Entities

1. What is the highest kind of welfare activities?

"Exhibiting compassion towards living entities is of three kinds. Display of compassion in regard to the gross body of the living entities is counted among pious activities. Distributing free food to the hungry people, distributing free medicine to the diseased persons, distributing free water to the thirsty people and distributing clothes to persons who are afflicted with cold are all born from the compassion in regard to the body. Giving free education is born from the compassion in regard to the mind of the living entities. But the highest kind of compassion is in regard to the soul of the living entities. From such compassionate propensity, the eagerness for delivering the fallen souls from the miseries of material existence by awarding them the devotional service to Krishna is produced."

(*Sajjana-toṣaṇī* 9/9)

2. The phrase jive dayā or showing compassion apply to which living entities?

"It is to be understood that *jive dayā* refers to only the conditioned souls. Moreover among the conditioned souls those who have achieved inclination towards Krishna should be treated as friends and not as candidates for compassion. Therefore only those who are foolish or ignorant among the conditioned souls are to be showed mercy."

(*Sajjana-toṣaṇī* 4/8)

3. What is the difference between welfare activities of the karmīs, jñānis and bhaktas?

"The followers of *karma-kāṇḍa* do not endeavor to give eternal benefits to living entities, they consider that exhibition of compassion in regard to one's body and mind is most auspicious. The followers of *jñāna-kāṇḍa* consider the exhibition of compassion in regard to the mind as more beneficial. But the pure devotees of the Lord give eternal benefit to the living entities by preaching devotional service to them."

(*Sajjana-toṣaṇī* 9/9)

4. What is the example of a Vaiṣṇava's display of compassion to living entities?

"Until a living entity's good fortune is awakened, his propensity for serving Krishna does not arise. To help the living entities in this cause is the only proof of a Vaiṣṇava's compassion towards living entities."

(*Sajjana-toṣaṇī* 4/8)

5. How does a Vaiṣṇava show compassion to living entities?

"The main activity of a Vaiṣṇava is to make living entities inclined towards serving Lord Krishna. Whenever curing of disease or satisfying hunger of the gross body becomes the main object, it is to be understood that there is a lack of Vaiṣṇavisṁ there, because by such activities the living entities get only temporary relief and not eternal relief. But whenever such activities are directed to help the living entities inclination towards Krishna the Vaiṣṇavas take pleasure in them."

(*Sajjana-toṣaṇī* 4/8)

6. How should one conduct oneself as a devotee?

"Teach your saintly characteristics to other's. You are engaged in good activities, that is alright, but the living entities of the material world who are just like your brothers, are becoming degraded due to sinful activities. Your duty is to manifest saintly qualities and induce other's to follow."

(*Sajjana-toṣaṇī* 5/10)

7. Which materialists are fit for receiving the Vaiṣṇava's mercy?

"The devotees should display mercy towards the nonduplicitous materialists."

(*Bhāgavatārka Maṛicimālā* 15/126)

8. What kind of preaching makes a Vaiṣṇava happy?

"A Vaiṣṇava becomes particularly happy when he sees that by his preaching the topics of Krishna, even one living entity has taken to the service of Krishna."

(*Sajjana-toṣaṇī* 4/8)

8. Is there any difference between jive dayā and the basis of devotional service to Krishna?

"Compassion cannot be separated from *rāga* or attachment, there is no difference between *jive dayā* and the basis of devotional service to Krishna."

(*Śrī Krishna-saṁhitā* 8/18)

10. How does a Vaiṣṇava show his mercy, and why is it the topmost?

"On the spiritual platform there is only friendship, and on the conditional state there is friendship, compassion and negligence according to persons. These are the identification of eternal constitutional compassion. When the compassion for the conditioned soul is in its stage as a bud it is confined to one's own body. When this bud is little bit blossomed it applies to one's family members; when it is further blossomed it applies to one's own caste; when it is more blossomed it applies to one's own countrymen. When it is further blossomed it applies to all humanity, and when it is fully blossomed it applies to all living entities. In English this is called patriotism and philanthropy . The Vaiṣṇavas cannot remain confined to all these narrow mindedness. Their mood is to show compassion to all living entities regardless of their caste, creed, nationality, as well as mental and physical condition."

(*Caitanya-śikṣāmṛta* 3/3)

59

Developing Taste for Chanting the Holy Names

1. Can one develop taste for chanting if he does not possess any piety born of devotional service?

"A person who does not have piety born of devotional service can never achieve any faith in the science of devotional service. Among all the limbs of devotional service chanting the holy names is the topmost. Therefore one can not develop a taste for chanting if he lacks piety. "

(*Harināma-cintāmani*)

2. Is there any necessity for performing eternal and occasional activities if one has developed a taste for chanting the holy names of Hari?

"When one develops a taste for cultivating the chanting of the holy names in the association of the saintly person, then one no longer needs to perform any kind of pious activities. Chanting of holy names is a complete spiritual cultivation. Pious activities such as chanting Vedic *mantras* and offering prayers are simply support of the above mentioned principle activity of chanting the holy names; they are never complete in themselves."

(*Jaiva Dharma*, Chapter 3)

3. How and when does one develop a taste for chanting the holy names?

"If I sing Your holy name aloud every day with warm affection, then as sugarcandy taken medicinally destroys the very disease which make it bitter taste, so your holy name, O Lord Hari, will cure my spiritual disease and allow me to gradually taste Your sweetness. How great is my misfortune that I feel no appreciation for your holy name, O merciful Lord! In such a lamentable state how will I be freed from committing the ten offenses to the holy name? If I sing Your name every day, gradually by Your mercy the ten offenses will disappear, taste for Your holy name will grow within me, and then I shall relish the intoxicating wine of the holy name."

(*Śaraṇāgati*)

60

Service to the Vaiṣṇavas

1. Should a person who is aspiring for Krishna's mercy not consider the differences among the Vaiṣṇavas?

"I will recognise the Vaiṣṇavas as they are according to their qualification and offer my respect to them. Then I will certainly achieve their mercy which is the secret of all perfection."

(*Kalyāna Kalpataru*, Song 7)

2. Can one achieve the result of serving a devotee by mistakenly serving a nondevotee as a devotee?

"Do not think that if we serve the nondevotee by considering them as devotees, we will achieve the result of serving the devotees."

(*Sajjana-toṣaṇī* 5/5)

3. Are serving the living entities and the Vaiṣṇavas the same?

"If one serves all living entities by considering them as Vaiṣṇavas one get only the result of serving the living entities. However it can not be called 'the service to the Vaiṣṇavas who are attached to the chanting of the holy names,' as prescribed by Śrīman Mahāprabhu."

(*Sajjana-toṣaṇī* 6/1)

4. Can one achieve the result of Vaiṣṇava sevā by feeding the pseudo Vaiṣṇavas who are greedy after opulent food, wealth, and disciples?

"The present custom in the holy places is extremely harmful. There one person goes out and invites one hundred Vaiṣṇavas for lunch. After receiving such invitation the Vaiṣṇavas immediately give up their respective duties and decorate themselves with *tilaka*, etc. They then began to manifest symptoms of devotional service thinking today we will get sufficient *puris* and *mālpoyās* as well as some *dakṣinas*. In his book *Śrī Bhakti-rasāmṛta-sindhu* Śrī Rūpa Goswāmī has not accepted these activities as devotional service. Therefore if these activities are not devotional service then the performers of such activities can not be accepted as Vaiṣṇavas."

(*Sajjana-toṣaṇī* 6/1)

5. Is feeding the descendants of the Supreme Lord Vaiṣṇava seva and is there any need to respect Vaiṣṇavas spiritual status while serving them?

"Nowadays the system in the holy places is that when someone wishes to serve Vaiṣṇavas, he invites one of the descendants of the Lord (like Nityānanda-vaṁsa or Advaita-vaṁsa), cooks various opulent foodstuff, then invites some people as Vaiṣṇavas and feeds them. We cannot accept such activities as Vaiṣṇava *sevā*. In the service of the Vaiṣṇavas there is no need to respect the spiritual status of a Vaiṣṇava. The differences in the degree of devotional service, determines the superiority and inferiority of the Vaiṣṇavas."

(*Sajjana-toṣaṇī* 6/1)

6. With what kind of consideration and carefulness should one serve a Vaiṣṇava?

"One should consider the Vaiṣṇava sevā as an eternal occupational duty. But with a desire to gain name and fame, one should not serve an invited Vaiṣṇava with food and donation and then engage in activities hostile to devotional service."

(*Sajjana-toṣaṇī* 6/1)

7. Is giving dakṣina after feeding a Vaiṣṇava part of karma-kāṇḍa?

"Giving *dakṣina* to a Vaiṣṇava after feeding him is certainly a part of *karma-kāṇḍa*. There is no system of giving *dakṣina* to a Vaiṣṇava. Giving *dakṣina* to a Vaiṣṇava has been created from the system of giving *dakṣina* to the *brāhmanas* after feeding them. This system should certainly be rejected."

(*Sajjana-toṣaṇī* 6/1)

8. What kind of Vaiṣṇava should one satisfy?

"O devotees! Glorify the Vaiṣṇavas who are attached to chanting the holy names of Hari in all respects. But do not degrade the Vaiṣṇava *sevā* into the level of *karma-kāṇḍa* by giving donations to the Vaiṣṇava after feeding them. It is not the opinion of the Lord to invite some renounce Vaiṣṇavas and feed them."

(*Sajjana-toṣaṇī* 6/1)

9. How should one feed a pure Vaiṣṇava and an ordinary guest?

"If you have to feed a professional teacher who is afflicted with hunger you should do so, according to the rule of serving the guests. There is no need to show special love to him. You can serve him with care but not with love. However you should feed the pure Vaiṣṇavas with love and affection and if required, you should accept their remnants with love and respect."

(*Sajjana-toṣaṇī* 11/11)

10. Is giving alms to a sannyāsi and serving a Vaiṣṇava guest the same?

"An uninvited renounce Vaiṣṇava is called a guest Vaiṣṇava. If incidentally any such Vaiṣṇava comes to our house we should serve them. This will amount to householder's Vaiṣṇava *sevā*. By inviting too many *sannyāsis* it becomes difficult to properly take care of them. And as a result offense is committed. As soon as a Vaiṣṇava is invited he is no longer a guest. Giving alms to a sannyāsi cannot be called Vaiṣṇava *sevā*."

(*Sajjana-toṣaṇī* 6/1)

11. What is the difference between serving the guest and serving the Vaiṣṇavas, and which one of them should a Vaiṣṇava householder do?

"The difference between *atithi sevā* and Vaiṣṇava *sevā* is that, *atithi sevā* is the religious principles of the householders and Vaiṣṇava *sevā* is the religious principle of the Vaiṣṇavas. A Vaiṣṇava householder must perform *atithi sevā*; because, since he is a householder he should serve the guest and since he is a Vaiṣṇava he should serve the Vaiṣṇavas."

(*Sajjana-toṣaṇī* 8/2)

12. What is proper Vaiṣṇava sevā?

"Nowadays a practice is going on in the name of 'festival.' Many people are thinking this to be a Vaiṣṇava *sevā*. Actually without serving the pure Vaiṣṇavas one can not get the result of serving the Vaiṣṇavas. If even the numbers of pure Vaiṣṇavas are very few, still one can attain the result of Vaiṣṇava *sevā* only by serving pure Vaiṣṇavas."

(*Sajjana-toṣaṇī* 4/5)

13. What procedure should one follow when a Vaiṣṇava arrives or departs?

"If one hears that a Vaiṣṇava is coming one should go forward and welcome him, and when a Vaiṣṇava leaves one should follow him up to some distance."

(*Sajjana-toṣaṇī* 7/3)

61

Iṣṭagoṣṭhi or Vaiṣṇava Counseling

1. What is Iṣṭagoṣṭhi?

"Without the association of pure devotees there cannot be an *iṣṭagoṣṭhi*. The word *iṣṭa* means desired subject matter and the word *goṣṭhi* means an assembly. The assembly of the pure devotees has been described as *iṣṭagoṣṭhi* by combining the above mentioned two words."

(*Sajjana-toṣaṇī* 10/12)

2. How many kinds of Iṣṭagoṣṭhis of the pure devotees are there?

"*Iṣṭagoṣṭhi* is of two kinds, following and preaching. At the time of following, the pure devotees recite *Śrīmad-Bhāgavatam*, hear, and chant the holy names of Hari. At the time of preaching they propagate the science of the Absolute Truth, the living entities, the science of the transcendental mellows, and glories of the holy names according to the qualification of the audience."

(*Sajjana-toṣaṇī* 10/12)

3. What is Krishna kathā-goṣṭhi?

"When two devotees meet together and discuss the topics of Krishna it is called Krishna *kathā-goṣṭhi*."

(*Sajjana-toṣaṇī* 10/11)

4. What is the difference between ordinary talk and iṣṭagoṣṭhi?

"What to speak of awarding happiness, ordinary talk causes extremely unhappiness, however, in *iṣṭagoṣṭhi* such a thing never takes place."

(*Sajjana-toṣaṇī* 10/11)

5. Why the assembly of pure devotees is very rare?

"Pure devotees are very rare in this world. Therefore it is very difficult to find more than four or five such devotees in an assembly or *iṣṭagoṣṭhī*"

(*Sajjana-toṣaṇī* 10/11)

6. What are the different stages of Śrīmad Gaurāṅga Samāj?

"A gathering of all types of people is called Śrīmad Gaurāṅga Samāj. A gathering of devotees is called Vaiṣṇava *samāj* or Vaiṣṇava *iṣṭagoṣṭhi*. A meeting of two pure devotees is called Krishna *kathā-goṣṭhi*. And the existence of one pure devotee is called solitary *bhajana* of chanting the holy names."

(*Sajjana-toṣaṇī* 10/11)

62

Preaching

1. Who are attached to preaching, and who are attached to both following and preaching?

"The *bhajanānandi* devotees or those who take pleasure in performing *bhajana* in a solitary place are attached to following the codes of conduct. The *goṣṭhānandi* devotees or those who take pleasure in performing *bhajana* in the association of other devotees are always attached to preaching. Among *goṣṭhānandi*s, some of them are attached to following the codes of conduct and preaching. Remembering the Lord is the primary code of conduct for the loving devotees, and chanting the holy names of the Lord is their preaching."

(*Caitanya-śikṣāmṛta* 6/3)

2. Are the religious principles preached by Mahāprabhu not fit to be preached?

"Mahāprabhu has entrusted everyone the responsibility of preaching Vaiṣṇava *dharma*."

(*Jaiva Dharma*, Chapter 8)

3. What procedure should one follow while preaching?

"One should transform an unqualified person into a qualified person and then instruct about the holy names. Whenever possible, one should avoid speaking in such a way that it puts obstacles in the act of preaching."

(*Jaiva Dharma*, Chapter 8)

4. What recommendation did Śrīmad Bhaktivinoda Ṭhākura gave to vigorously preach the order of Śrīman Mahāprabhu?

"Preach the chanting of the holy names of Krishna and the teachings of Śrī Gaurāṅga in every town and village. Take *Śrī Caitanya-caritāmṛta* in your hands, go door to door, and preach the Lord's holy names and the teachings of Śrīman Mahāprabhu. As Mahāprabhu ordered Śrī Nityānanda and Śrī Haridāsa to travel and preach His messages, similarly being servants of Śrī Gaurāṅga, you should engage proper candidates to travel and preach the teachings of Mahāprabhu. Preaching cannot be done by unqualified persons. In our opinion you should immediately set up a Vaiṣṇava school. After educating some selfless well-behaved persons in the teachings of Mahāprabhu in that school, send them to every town and village to preach His message.

(*Sajjana-toṣaṇī* 11/3)

5. What have the previous Vaiṣṇavas and the Goswāmīs done to protect and preach Vaiṣṇava dharma?

"Some of the previous Vaiṣṇavas and the Goswāmīs have illuminated the entire world with the light of pure eternal Vaiṣṇava *dharma* by writing devotional literatures, by writing songs, by preaching the religious principles and chanting the holy names of Hari, and by their pure characteristics and sublime Vaiṣṇavism. Since the entire world has now plunged into darkness in the form of various irreligious principles due to the influence of Kali, Mahāprabhu is attracting the minds of many persons, and empowering many devotees to preach His own teachings, to distribute love of God, and to preach actual Vaiṣṇava etiquettes."

(*Sajjana-toṣaṇī* 2/1)

6. In order to protect Śrī Caitanya's pure religious principles, what is our duty towards persons who find faults in His instructions?

"It is our duty to remove those harmful insects who have entered into the flower of pure religious principles followed and instructed by Śrī Mahāprabhu. It is not that such insects are only plundering the fragrance of the flower of religious principles; but they are trying to finish the flower by gradually eating it away. The seed of pure instructions that Mahāprabhu Caitanyadeva, Prabhu Nityānanda and His son Prabhu Vīrachandra, showed in order to establish the society of Vaiśnava has in some places become fruitless due to falling into some barren land, and in some places produced unwanted weeds due to falling into uncultured land."

(*Sajjana-toṣaṇī* 2/4)

7. What should be done to reestablish the principles of Vaiṣṇava dharma?

"In order to deliver Vaiṣṇava *dharma* from mire, one must try to remove all oppressions from it."
(*Sajjana-toṣaṇī* 2/7)

8. How much should one tolerate in order to destroy evil philosophy?
"If evil philosophies exist in your country then you should try to correct them. If even this causes a confrontation with cheaters and cunning people, still you should fight them for the sake of Śrīman Mahāprabhu."
(*Sajjana-toṣaṇī* 4/6)

9. Should one expose the characters of those who are opposed to pure devotional service while preaching?
"Many activities which are illegal and hostile to devotional service are widely being performed in the name of devotional service. Unless those activities are clearly exposed, there cannot be any victory of preaching pure devotional service."
(*Sajjana-toṣaṇī* 2/4)

10. Why is it necessary to write the pastimes of Śrī Caitanya in all languages of the world?
"It is extremely necessary to write Śrī Caitanya's pastimes in all languages of the world. Within a very short time the name of Mahāprabhu will be spread all over the world, and He will become the only worshipable Lord of everyone."
(*Sajjana-toṣaṇī* 4/3)

11. How should the preachers propagate the teachings of Mahāprabhu?
"The preachers should propagate the teachings of Mahāprabhu simply out of love. They should neither expect any salary nor any reward. It is not possible to preach pure religious principle without pure devotees. That is why, even though hired people of other religious groups try to preach their religion, they hardly achieve any result."
(*Caitanya-śikṣāmṛta* 1/2)

12. How did Śrīman Mahāprabhu and His associates preach the holy names of Hari?

"After accepting *sannyāsa* Śrīmad Godrumachandra who is the most merciful incarnation and the purifier of Kali-yuga, preached the holy names of Hari all over the world. While residing at Jagannātha Purī the Lord personally distributed love of Krishna to the residents of Orissa and South India. He ordered Śrīmad Nityānanda Prabhu and Śrī Advaita Prabhu to preach the holy names of Krishna and reveal the science of the Absolute Truth in Bengal. He sent Śrīmad Rūpa and Sanātana Goswami's to the Western part of India to preach the glories of holy name and pure devotional service. Being ordered by Śrīman Mahāprabhu, Śrī Rūpa Goswami lived in Vṛndāvana and preached the glories of the holy names and pure devotional service. Today I will sing before you the eight verses glorifying the holy names composed by Śrī Rūpa Goswami who was the *ācārya* of the mellows of the holy names. Kindly hear them and realize these glories of the holy names of Hari."

(*Vaiṣṇava Siddhānta Mālā*, Song 5)

13. Who is the inaugurator of nāma-haṭṭa and what are His instructions?

nadīyā-godrume nityānanda mahājana
patiyāche nāma-haṭṭa jīvera kāraṇa
(śraddhāvān jan he, śraddhāvān jan he)
prabhura ājñāy, bhāi, māgi ei bhikṣā
bolo 'kṛṣṇa,' bhajo kṛṣṇa, koro kṛṣṇa-śikṣā
aparādha-śūnya ho'ye loho kṛṣṇa-nām
kṛṣṇa mātā, kṛṣṇa pitā, kṛṣṇa dhana-prān
kṛṣṇaera saṁsāra koro chāḍi' anācār
jīve doyā, kṛṣṇa-nām-sarva-dharma-sār

"In the land of Nadīyā, on the island of Godruma, the magnanimous Lord Nityānanda has opened up the Marketplace of the Holy Name, meant for the deliverance of all fallen souls.

O faithful persons! O faithful persons! O brothers! By the order of Lord Gaurāṅga, I beg this one request: Chant Krishna! Worship Krishna! Follow Krishna's instructions!

Being careful to remain free of offenses, just take the holy name of Krishna. Krishna is your mother, Krishna is your father, and Krishna is the treasure of your life.

Giving up all improper behavior, carry on your worldly duties only in relation to Krishna. The showing of compassion to all fallen souls

by loudly chanting the holy name of Krishna is the essence of all forms of religion. "

(*Vaiṣṇava Siddhānta Mālā*, Song 6)

15. What were the duties of the principle mahājanas, workers, and guards of nāma-haṭṭa and how did pure patrolling perform?

"Śrī Mahāprabhu displayed His mercy towards the living entities who are tortured by Kali-yuga by ordering Śrī Nityānanda Prabhu to preach the holy name home to home. Therefore Śrī Nityānanda Prabhu is certainly the *mūla-mahājana* or the chief proprietor of the *nāma-haṭṭa* located at Godruma. Even though all the employees of the *nāma-haṭṭa* are qualified for performing *ājñā-ṭahal*, the 'Patrol According to the Lord's Order,' still the great *mahāśayas*, who are like patrolling watchmen, are especially empowered to render these duties in an entirely selfless manner. Above all the rest, Prabhu Nityānanda and patrolman Haridāsa Ṭhākura have each exhibited the glories of this post in their own unique ways. If one goes out on patrol with hopes of simply collecting money and rice, then that is not the pure form of *ājñā-ṭahal*.

The *mahāśaya* on patrol plays his *karatāls* and calls out,'O faithful persons! I do not wish to beg from you any worldly thing or mundane favor. The only alms I beg is that all of you honor the order of the Lord by chanting the name of Krishna, worshiping Krishna, and teaching other's about Krishna. Just invoke the true name of Krishna. Specifically, by giving up *nāmābhāsa* (a hint of the name due to offenses) please chant the purely spiritual holy name of the Lord.'

O faithful persons! To give up *nāmābhāsa* and sing the pure holy names is certainly the true welfare of the living entities . Please worship Lord Krishna by chanting *kṛṣṇa-nāma.* Perform *bhajana* by engaging in *śravaṇa*, *kīrtana*, *smaraṇa*, *sevana*, *archana*, *vandana*, *dāsya*, *sakhya*, and *ātma-nivedana.* Execute that *bhajana* either on the path of *vidhi-mārga* or *rāga-mārga*, according to your specific qualification.

O faithful persons! Remaining free from the ten offenses, just worship Lord Krishna. Only Krishna is the living entities' mother, father, offspring, wealth, husband, and life-treasure. The living entities are the spiritual ray, Krishna is the spiritual sun, and the material world is the living entities prison. Truly the pastimes of Krishna, which lie beyond the material realm, are your factual riches to be sought.

O faithful persons! You have turned away from Krishna and thus suffered the experience of so-called happiness and distress in the realm of material world. This situation is not befitting you.

All the following things come under the heading of unfavorable actions, performed either by oneself or by society: theft, speaking lies, cheating, and hostility, lust, inflicting bodily harm, duplicitous politics, and so forth. Abandoning all these, just resort to pious means and spend your life in Krishna's world. The ultimate statement is this: showing mercy to all living beings, living a pure lifestyle, just chant the holy name of Krishna. There is no difference whatsoever between *kṛṣṇa-nāma* and Lord Krishna Himself. By the mercy of the holy name, Krishna in the form of His names, forms, attributes and pastimes will personally reveal Himself to the vision of the eyes of your spiritual body. Truly in a few days your spiritual consciousness will be awakened and you will remain floating in the ocean of eternally sweet *kṛṣṇa-prema.*

(*Vaiṣṇava Siddhānta Mālā*, Song 6, purport)

16. What kind of enthusiasm and happiness did Śrīla Jagannātha dāsa Bābāji Mahārāja and Śrīmad Bhaktivinoda Thākur display in preaching the program of nāma-haṭṭa?

"We were present in the village of Āmlājoḍā on 28th Phālgun. After staying up whole night on account of Ekādaśī, the next morning, all the devotees of the village went out for *nagara-saṅkirtana* with great pomp. Keeping the most worshipable Śrīla Jagannātha dāsa Bābāji Mahārāja in front, everyone reached Prapannāśrama. The symptoms of ecstatic love that Bābāji Mahārāja began to exhibit at the time of *kīrtana,* is beyond description. Even though he was more than hundred years old at that time, yet he wonderfully sang, cried and rolled on the ground like a lion. It was an unprecedented scenery the way he sang as follows—'What wonderful holy names has Lord Nityānanda brought. He is distributing the holy names in exchange of only one's faith. Although my most merciful Nityānanda was hit on the head by Jagāi, still He distributed love of God to everyone.' On seeing the symptoms of Bābāji Mahārāja's ecstatic love everyone became filled with bliss of *kīrtana,* displayed the symptoms of ecstatic love such as shedding of tears, standing of the hairs on end, and danced for a long time with ecstasy. After a while when *kīrtana* came to an end, he briefly delivered a lecture on *nāma-haṭṭa.* With great pleasure Bābāji mahārāja ordered the activities of Prapannāśrama to be carried out from that day onwards. According to the order of Bābāji Mahārāja, the person in charge of nāmahatta program completed the formality of inaugurating Prapannāśrama on that day.

It is customary in all countries, that the head of the local administration is invited as the chief guest whenever a school or a hospital is inaugurated.

The most worshipable Śrīla Jagannātha dāsa Bābāji Mahārāja was invited as the chief guest during the inauguration of Prapannāśrama and it was completely reasonable. Wherever Prapannāśrama is established such a procedure should be followed."

(*Sajjana-toṣaṇī* 4/2)

63

Singing About the Mellows of Ecstatic Love

1. What is correct procedure for singing about the pastimes of Lord Krishna?

"One should first sing about the pastimes of Gauracandra. It is the custom among the devotees that they do not sing about the pastimes of Krishna without first singing about the pastimes of Gauracandra."

(*Sajjana-toṣaṇī* 2/6)

2. What kind of music should a practitioner of devotional service hear?

"A practitioner of devotional service should hear only those songs and music which do not satisfy one's senses only, but by describing the pastimes of the Lord help him cultivate devotional service. One should carefully give up hearing ordinary music and songs which simply increase one's attachment for material objects and sense gratification."

(*Caitanya-śikṣāmṛta* 3/2)

3. When did singing with the musical instruments start among the Gauḍīya Vaiṣṇavas?

"Singing with musical instrument started only from the time of Śrinivāsa Ācārya. Śrinivāsa Ācārya, Śrī Narottama dāsa, and Śrī Śyāmānanda Prabhu resided for sometime as the students of Śrī Jīva Goswami in Vṛndāvana,. By the approval of Śrī Jīva Goswami these three started the process of performing *kīrtana* accompanied by musical instruments. All the three were expert in the science of music. Moreover they were proficient in Indian classical music of Delhi. They were intimate friends of each other and had one goal of life."

(*Sajjana-toṣaṇī* 6/2)

4. How did the process of singing songs in ' manoharasāhī, 'garāṇahāti,' and 'reṇetī' ways, come into existence?

"Śrīnivāsa Ācārya illuminated the province of Katwa through his preaching. His area fell under the jurisdiction of manoharasāhī sub-division. Therefore the process of singing inaugurated by him is called '*manoharasāhī.*' Śrī Narottama dāsa was a resident of Kheturī village which fell under the jurisdiction of '*garāṇahāti*' sub-division in the district of Rājashāhī, Bangladesh. That is why the process of singing inaugurated by him is called '*garāṇahāt.*' Śrī Śhyāmānanda Prabhu belongs to the district of Midnapur. The process of singing inaugurated by him is called '*reṇetī.*' In order to encourage all these three *ācāryas* of singing songs, Śrī Jīva Goswami awarded Śrīnivāsa the title 'Ācārya,' Śrī Narottama dāsa the title 'Thakur,' and Śrī Śyāmānanda the title 'Prabhu.'

(*Sajjana-toṣaṇī* 6/2)

5. Why is it improper for persons who are ignorant about the mellows of devotional service to add alphabets or words in the songs of the mahājanas?

"There is neither any overlapping of *rāsas* nor any contradiction in the words of the *mahājanas*. Therefore if persons or singers who are ignorant about about the mellows of devotional service add anything to them then it certainly becomes *rāsābhāsa* or overlapping of *rāsas* and opposed to the Vaiṣṇava conclusion."

(*Sajjana-toṣaṇī* 6/2)

6. What is the value of the professional singers of rāsa kīrtana? Should the Vaiṣṇavas hear those kīrtana?

"Professional singers of *rāsa kīrtanas* are called *rasika* in the name only. In fact they are devoid of any knowledge regarding *rāsa* and are averse to Vaiṣṇava conclusions. Their songs are full of different musical modes and tunes, but their *kīrtana* is not fit to be heard by the Vaiṣṇavas. They add so much to the original *mahājana* songs in order to please the assembled women and foolish people. Such people are full of pride because they get money and praise from foolish audience."

(*Sajjana-toṣaṇī* 6/2)

7. What is the strict instruction of Śrī Bhaktivinoda Ṭhākura regarding rāsa kīrtana by the unqualified people?

"The majority of the people of this world are perverted. They love artificial fun. They fulfill their whims in the name of actual *bhajana*. As long as this bad practice is not checked, the gravity of conjugal *rāsa* will not be realized. O devotees! Do not hear *rāsa kīrtana* in the assembly of selfish singers and foolish ambitious audience. Forget about attending any assembly of *śrāddha* ceremony and make sure that such a system does not exist inside a Vaiṣṇava *āśrama*. Where all kinds of qualified persons are present, chanting of the holy names, praying and singing only about *dāsya rāsa* should be done. Where only unalloyed pure *rasika* Vaiṣṇava are present, hearing of *rāsa kīrtana* is allowed, and while hearing *rāsa kīrtana*, one should try to realize one's mode of *bhajana* befitting his own constitutional position. If, as a result of this, the process of professional singing itself vanishes, it will be beneficial to the Vaiṣṇavas. It is an act of Kali to let the artificial *rāsa kīrtana* go on anywhere and everywhere just for the sake of money and some sense gratification."

(*Sajjana-toṣaṇī* 6/2)

8. What goal does the materialist attain by hearing the topics of the transcendental pastimes?

"Those who glorify the happiness of the gross body and are ignorant of the variegatedness of spiritual happiness, should not glance over, think about, or discuss the transcendental pastimes of the Lord. Because, by doing so, they will either blaspheme such activities as obscene, thinking such descriptions of the Lord's pastimes to be born of flesh and skin, or eagerly accept them in the mood of the *sahajiyās* and thus fall down."

(*Caitanya-śikṣāmṛta* 7/7)

64

Activities that are Unfavorable to Devotional Service

1. Is there any determination required to accept items favorable for devotional service and reject items unfavorable for devotional service?

"It is extremely necessary for a practitioner of devotional service to possess utmost care and determination while accepting things favorable for devotional service and rejecting things unfavorable for devotional service. Materialistic persons often face many things that are detrimental to the worship of the Lord, but with special care and determination, they should give them up otherwise they create impediments in the paths of their *sādhana* and cause delay in achieving the ultimate goal of life."

(*Sajjana-toṣaṇī* 11/5)

2. What is rejecting things which are unfavorable to devotional service?

"I will not eat anything other than the remnants of the Lord and His devotees. I will not see anything other than temples and places connected with the Lord and His devotees. I will not hear anything other than the topic concerning the Lord and His devotees. I will not engage my body in any activities devoid of any relationship with the Lord and His devotees. I will not meditate, consider, or relish anything other than the subject matter related to the Lord and His devotees, and I will not sing or read any other songs or literature other than those related to the Lord or His devotees." These resolutions are called rejecting things that are unfavorable to devotional service."

(*Sajjana-toṣaṇī* 4/9)

3. What is the promise of a devotee who gives up items which unfavorable to devotional service?

"Oh Lord! I will not associate with those who are averse to Your devotional service. I will not see the face of persons who oppose Śrī Gaurāṅga."

(Song from *Śaraṇāgati*)

4. What kind of association should be given up?

I"t should be understood that wherever activities opposed to devotional service are performed, there is no question of pure devotional service there, and as such one must give up such association."

(*Sajjana-toṣaṇī* 6/7)

5. What is the method of ascertaining bad or good association?

"The pious and sinful persons who are averse to the Lord both cause bad association. Even sinful persons who are inclined towards God should be considered good association."

(*Sajjana-toṣaṇī* 10/11)

6. Whose association is called good association?

"One should always carefully give up the association of godless people who are proud of their wealth, knowledge, high birth and so on, and one should associate with those people who are inclined towards Krishna. Four types of persons are inclined towards Krishna. They are:

1. Devotees who depend on fruitive activities and religious principles
2. Matured yogis who are indifferent to fruitive activities and religious principles.
3. Immature yogis and the imitators of all the above three.
4. Devotees who are sincere and non-duplicitous are certainly better association."

(Commentary on *Bhajanāmṛtaṁ*)

7. What is the result of associating with sinful persons and saintly persons?

"The result of associating with sinful persons is material existence. Association with saintly persons keeps one aloof from associating with sinful persons."

(*Sajjana-toṣaṇī* 15/2)

8. Are the materialists and the impersonalists devotees of Krishna?

"Both materialists and impersonalists are devoid of devotion to Krishna and their lives are useless."

(Song from *Śaraṇāgati*)

9. Who is more abominable among the impersonalists and materialist?

"Among the two, the materialist is still better. One should never aspire for the association of the impersonalist."

(Song from *Śaraṇāgati*)

10. In ordinary dealings how long should a devotee associate with a materialist?

"One should not associate with persons who are averse to the Lord's service. One will have to meet such people in his ordinary dealings, but one should deal with them only until the work is finished. After the work is finished one should not deal with them."

(*Sajjana-toṣaṇī* 11/6)

11. What kind of mentality makes association?

"Giving charity to a materialist or accepting charity from one, if done out of love, becomes *asatsaṅga.* When a materialist approaches you, whatever is required to be done should be done only out of duty. One should not speak confidentially with a materialist. Generally there is some love involved in confidential speaking, therefore it is association. While meeting a materialistic friend, one should speak only what is extremely necessary. At that time it is better not to exhibit heartfelt love."

(*Sajjana-toṣaṇī* 11/11)

12. Is intimate brotherhood with godless people not condemnable?

"Sitting together in an assembly, crossing the river together on a boat, taking bath together in a bathing *ghāt,* or buying or selling things together in the market is not called 'association'. To deal intimately with someone as a brother is called 'association.' One should never associate in this way with godless people."

(*Caitanya-śikṣāmṛta* 3/3)

13. What harm do the six enemies which are unfavorable for devotional service cause to a practitioner of devotional service?

"The six enemies: lust, anger, greed, illusion, pride and envy, constantly appear in the mind of the human beings and create all kinds of disturbances. These six enemies engage the mind in the following temporary material activities; the urge of speech in the form of creating anxiety through words, the urge of mind in the form of mental speculation, the urge of anger in the form using harsh language, the urge of the tongue in the form of relishing four kinds of food such as sweet, sour, salt and bitter, the urge of the stomach in the form of eating palatable foodstuffs, and the urge of the of genital in the form of enjoying the association of men and women. As of result of these six enemies, pure cultivation of devotional service does not take place in the heart."

(Commentary on *Upadeśāmṛta*)

14. Is the happiness derived from eating, sleeping, mating and defending eternal or temporary?

"The sensual pleasure derived from associating with women, eating palatable food stuffs, taking bath, applying sandalwood paste and chewing betel nuts is extremely temporary. As soon as one indulges in these activities one begins to feel distress. The characters of the drunkards, and the women hunters are the prime examples of these. What eternal happiness is there in enjoying the atmosphere of Nandankānana in heaven, enjoying the dancing of the Apsarās such as Urvaśī and Menakā, or drinking the *soma-rāsa*? Such sense pleasures are simply products of imagination."

(*Tattva-sutra* 27)

15. Why attachment for material assets is obstacle on the path of devotional service? How can it be destroyed?

"People in general have spontaneous attachment for house, household paraphernalia, clothes, ornaments, wealth, wife, children's health, their own health, eatables, trees, and animals. Many people are addicted to bad habits like smoking, chewing pan, eating fish and meat, and drinking alcohol, thus, their practice of spiritual life is obstructed. Due to attachment for eating fish and meat, they fail to respect the Lord's remnants. And due to attachment to these bad habits, relish for studying devotional scriptures, hearing and chanting the Lord's names, and remaining in the temples for considerable time, is obstructed. One should carefully give up attachment for these material attachments. If one does not carefully give up these things then he cannot get happiness from his devotional service. Attachment for these things is easily destroyed by the association of devotees. One should try to destroy these petty attachments by fully engaging in devotional service. By observing vows approved in devotional service, those attachments are vanquished."

(*Sajjana-toṣaṇī* 11/11)

16. What is association with the eatables, and what are the prescriptions for giving up or minimizing partaking of eatables?

"There are two types of eatables—those which sustain one's life and those which gratify one's senses. Eating grains and drinking are life sustaining. Fish, meat, pan, intoxicants, and smoking are all for gratifying the senses. According to the prescribed needs of one's bodily condition, one must try as far as possible to reduce the acceptance of life sustaining eatables. There is no prescription for acceptance of sense gratifying items; the only prescription is to reject them. One of the limbs of a vrata is to diminish one's propensity for enjoyment. On days of vows, unless one totally gives up sense gratifying items, it is not vow. If one thinks,"Today somehow or other I will renounce, but tomorrow I will enjoy profusely," then the purpose of the vow will not be successful. The reason is that vows have been prescribed to give up the association of such items by gradual practice."

(*Sajjana-toṣaṇī* 11/11)

17. Who is not fit to be seen? Whose association is desirable?

"One should never see the face of a cruel person who is an offender at the feet of spiritual master. One should always associate with those who are firmly fixed at the feet of the spiritual master and the Vaiṣṇavas."

(*Sajjana-toṣaṇī* 7/4)

18. What is the behavior of an exalted devotee towards an offender of a Vaiṣṇava?

"The character of a Vaiṣṇava is always pure. I envy that person who blasphemes such a Vaiṣṇava. Śrī Bhaktivinoda Ṭhākura does not converse with such a person but rather remains silent."

(*Kalyāna Kalpataru* Song 7)

19. How should a surrendered soul deal with a person who is opposed to devotional service?

"You should always keep me at your doorstep and maintain me. I will not allow persons who are averse to devotional service to come in rather I will keep them away on the other side of the fence."
(Song from *Śaraṇāgati*)

20. Should one give up sincerity for truth for the sake of people?
"A Vaiṣṇava should not agree with various opinions at various places for the sake of people."
(*Sajjana-toṣaṇī* 11/12)

21. With whom should a Vaiṣṇava not live? If the materialists put on the garbs of a Vaiṣṇava, is their association desirable?
"One should never live with a person who proudly considers his body as self. If even the cheating materialists put on the garbs of a Vaiṣṇava one should not live with them."
(*Sajjana-toṣaṇī* 7/4)

22. Why attachment for material education is detrimental to devotional service?
Oh Lord! All material education is simply the influence of Māyā and it put obstacles on the path of Your worship. It creates attachment for this temporary material world and makes an ass of a living entity.
(Song from *Śaraṇāgati*)

23. How should one accept and reject education that is favorable to devotional service and unfavorable to devotional service?
"One should kick out all education that put impediments in the path of one's devotional service. Goddess Sarasvatī, who is the personification of devotional service to Krishna, represents spiritual education. She is the treasury of Śrī Bhaktivinoda Ṭhākura."
(*Kalyāna Kalpataru* Song 10)

24. Does an intelligent person postpone his Hari-bhajana till the old age?
"An intelligent person never says; 'I will worship Hari at the end of my life, now let me enjoy material happiness.' Because this material body is fallible at any moment."
(*Kalyāna Kalpataru* Song 8)

25. What is the prescription for a devotees livelihood? What is the harm if one accumulates too much or too little?

"Don't endeavor for palatable foodstuffs and fine clothes. Accept the sanctified *bhāgavata-prasāda* that is easily obtainable. This is the devotee's lifestyle. Whatever is required, take only that. Taking more or less will not yield auspicious results. If a devotee takes or accumulates more than necessary, his spiritual life will be lost due to his being controlled by material mellows. If he does not properly accumulate, then the body, which is his means of worship, will not be protected."

(*Sajjana-toṣaṇī* 10/9.)

26. Why is blaspheming the demigods unfavorable to devotional service?

"It is prohibited to disrespect the demigods. One should duly worship them and beg for their blessings to attain devotional service to Krishna. One should not disrespect any living entity. One should also respect the deity forms of various gods worshiped in various countries. Because by doing so persons of the lower level can graduate to the platform of devotional service. By disrespecting such gods, one's false ego increases, one's humility diminishes, and one's heart no longer remains fit to become the abode of devotional service."

(*Caitanya-śikṣāmṛta* 3/3)

27. Which association of so-called Vaiṣṇavas should be given up?

"The association of the following pseudo Vaiṣṇavas must be given up;

1. Those who put on the garbs of a Vaiṣṇava out of cunningness.
2. Those who identify themselves as the followers of the Vaiṣṇava *ācāryas* just to make impression among the impersonalists.
3. Those who identify themselves as Vaiṣṇavas because of greed for money, fame or any other enjoyment."

(*Caitanya-śikṣāmṛta* 3/2)

28. Should one associate with the Māyāvādīs?

"One should never associate with Māyāvādīs who proudly consider themselves as liberated souls."

(*Śrī Bhāgvatārka Marīchimālā* 14/47)

29. If symptoms of ecstatic love are found in a Māyāvādī, should he be considered a Vaiṣṇava?

"The eight symptoms of ecstatic love displayed by a Māyāvādī are of no use."

(*Sajjana-toṣaṇī* 5/12)

30. How should one deal with persons who are averse to devotional service?

"Oh Lord! Awarding material enjoyment and liberation is a trick of Your illusory energy. They cheat the living entities and create havoc on the path of Your devotional service. However they are good at bewildering the materialists. Śrī Bhaktivinoda Ṭhākura offers his obeisance to them from a distance and accepts the lotus feet of the devotees as his life and soul."

(Song from *Śaraṇāgati*)

31. If some activities are detrimental to devotional service and need the support of many persons, what should one do?

"If an activity cannot be performed without the help of many persons, yet there is no easy way of obtaining such a help, then it is better not to endeavor for such a works. It will simply create disturbances in the path of one's worship. If huge enterprises like building *maṭhas*, *āśramas*, temples and assembly halls are difficult to carry out by the above mentioned method then one should not try for it."

(*Caitanya-śikṣāmṛta* 3/3)

32. Can a practitioner of devotional service drink wine?

"What to speak of wine, opium, hemp and charas, a Vaiṣṇava should not even consume tobacco. Consuming such intoxicants is against the injunctions of the Vaiṣṇava literatures. By smoking tobacco a person becomes addicted to, and controlled by it; He even dares to commit sinful activities."

(*Caitanya-śikṣāmṛta* 3/3)

33. Why greed for palatable foodstuffs and wine as well as attachment for sinful and pious activities are unfavorable for devotional service?

"If one has greed for nice foodstuffs, drinks, sleeping, smoking, and drinking wine, then one's devotion diminishes. Greed for wine, wealth, and women is most contrary to devotional principles. Those who have a desire for attaining pure devotional service should carefully give up such things. Whether for auspicious things or sinful things, greed for anything not related to Krishna is most despicable. Greed only in relation to Krishna is the cause of all auspiciousness."

(*Sajjana-toṣaṇī* 10/11)

34. Can one compromise with the teachings of Śrī Caitanya just to please the mind of the materialists?

"If one tries to satisfy the materialistic people one will gradually face many *anarthas* and one will float in the continuous waves of Māyāvāda. One can accept the faultless support of the materialists in order to preach devotional service to Śrī Gaurāṅga. But it is extremely unlawful to compromise with the teachings of Śrī Caitanya just to please their mind."

(*Sajjana-toṣaṇī* 11/3)

35. Is hankering of the tongue hostile to the devotional service?

"It is extremely difficult to attain Krishna for those who are simply busy to satisfy their tongue."

(*Sajjana-toṣaṇī* 11/5)

36. Which items fall in the category of gambling? Are they unfavorable devotional service?

"Wherever games are being played with nonliving things that is the place of gambling. Playing cards, chess, dice, checker, and so on, fall in the category of gambling. The modern day lottery is also called gambling. If we discuss the histories of King Nala, Yudhiṣṭhira, Duryodhana and Śhakuni then we can see that in order to accumulate wealth by cheating and stealing at the place of gambling, fierce quarrel and ruination have been resulted. Even today the places of gambling are destroying many persons religiosity, economic development, sense gratification and liberation. Those who engage in the acts of gambling certainly becomes lazy and quarrelsome. They cannot perform any religious duties or pious activities."

(*Sajjana-toṣaṇī* 51)

37. Is taming birds or animals unfavorable to devotional service?

"One should not become attached to taming birds or animals."

(*Śrī Bhāgvatārka Marīchimālā* 14/37)

38. What is envy? Are envy and love opposed to each other?

"To become happy on seeing other's distress and to become distressed on seeing other's happiness is called envy. Envy and love are contradictory. Wherever there is envy there is no question of love and wherever there is love there is no question of envy."
(*Sajjana-toṣaṇī* 4/6)

39. Why envy is the leader of all enemies?
"Lust, anger, greed, illusion and pride are included within envy. Lust is included in anger; Lust and anger are included in greed; Lust, anger and greed are included in illusion; Lust, anger, greed and illusion are included in pride and lust, anger, greed, illusion and pride are included in envy."
(*Sajjana-toṣaṇī* 4/7)

40. Why Vaiṣṇava dharma is non-envious religion?
"Vaiṣṇava *dharma* which consists of compassion for the fallen souls, eagerness in chanting the Lord's holy names and serving the Vaiṣṇavas, stands in one side and envy stands on the other side."
(*Sajjana-toṣaṇī* 4/7)

41. What is the living entities' liberation and bondage?
"Non-enviousness is the living entities liberation and enviousness is the living entities bondage."
(*Sajjana-toṣaṇī* 4/7)

42. Can an envious person become compassionate towards the living entities, become faithful to the Vaiṣṇavas and become lower than the straw in the street?
"A person who feels distresses on seeing other's happiness can never show compassion to the living entities. He cannot worship the Supreme Lord with a simple mind. Due to his perverted nature he maintains hatred and enviousness towards the Vaiṣṇavas. It is to be understood that a person who is devoid of envy has actually understood the purport of the verse beginning with '*tṛnādapi.*'"
(*Sajjana-toṣaṇī* 4/7)

43. Can a cheater become a pious man?

"One cannot become pious unless he gives up cheating propensity and execute religious duties. By committing sinful activities on the pretext of religion, such a person becomes a cheater." (*Sajjana-toṣaṇī* 8/9)

44. Can a devotee of the Lord afford to spend his time desiring for material happiness?

"There is no more time left to neglect the spiritual cultivation while remaining absorbed in bodily happiness and to engage in activities hostile to pure devotional service."
(*Sajjana-toṣaṇī* -9/12)

45. What is the prayer of a pure devotee?

"Oh Lord! I do not want any benediction in which there is no happiness of serving Your lotus feet."
(Song from *Śaraṇāgati*)

46. Are the arguments of the followers of nyāyā and vaiśeṣika fruitful?

"All the arguments of the followers of *nyāyā* and *vaiśeṣika* are simply godless quarrels. They do not yield any result other than wasting the mind's strength and increasing one's restlessness."
(*Sajjana-toṣaṇī* 10/10)

47. Should a devotee display a spirit of argument while discussing the topics of the Lord?

"While discussing topics of the Lord and His devotees, the practicing devotee should always be careful to avoid useless arguments."
(*Sajjana-toṣaṇī* 10/10)

48. Why can't one understand the pastimes of Śrī Caitanya through dry argument?

"The transcendental pastimes of Śrī Caitanya are a like deep ocean, whereas the process of mundane logic is troublesome, like the sheath covering the banana flower. Whoever wants to cross the ocean of material existence by logic and argument will simply toil in vain. He will receive nothing."
(*Navadvīpa Mahātmya*, Chapter 2)

49. Why the mentality of finding faults in other's should be given up?

"Faultfinding arises only from imposing one's own bad habits on other's. This should be given up in all respects."

(*Sajjana-toṣaṇī* 10/10)

50. Why talking about other's is unfavorable for devotional service?

"Talking without reason about other people is extremely adverse to devotional service. Many people talk about other's to establish their own reputation. Being envious, some people are accustomed to discuss other's' character. The minds of those who are busy in such topics can never be fixed on the lotus feet of Krishna. Talking about other's should be rejected in all respects. But in the practice of devotional service there are many favorable topics that are faultless, even though they are about other's."

(*Sajjana-toṣaṇī* 10/10)

51. Is reading worldly newspaper unfavorable for devotional service?

"In newspapers there is so much useless talk. For the practicing devotee to read newspapers is a great loss. But if there are topics about pure devotees described in the newspaper, then that can be read."

(*Sajjana-toṣaṇī* 10/10)

52. Can a person who indulges in useless talk with other materialistic persons or who reads worldly novel become a follower of Śrī Rūpa?

"After finishing their meal, mundane people normally smoke and engage in useless talk with other godless people. It is certainly difficult for them to become followers of Śrīla Rūpa Goswami. Reading novels is the same. But if one gets a novel with a story like that of Purañjana in the *Śrīmad-Bhāgavatam*, then reading that is not an impediment, rather it is beneficial."

(*Sajjana-toṣaṇī* 10/10)

53. Can a householder or a sannyāsi indulge in hearing and speaking worldly topics?

"Worldly talk is completely rejected by renounced devotees. Householders may accept some worldly talk that is favorable to devotional service."

(*Sajjana-toṣaṇī* 10/10)

54. What is the principal rule? Is there any harm if at the time of advancement one gives up the previous rule and adopts the next rule?

"Forgetting Krishna is never allowed. All other prohibitions mentioned in the *śāstras* have arisen from this main prohibition. Keeping this main prescription in mind while advancing, the practitioner should give up his attachment for the prescriptions of the previous level and accept the prescriptions of the next level. Otherwise he will be guilty of *niyamāgraha*, and weak in reaching the next level."

(*Sajjana-toṣaṇī* 10/10)

55. Should one associate with one's wife, if she is unfavorable to devotional service?

"If one's wife is an impediment in the discharge of devotional service, then one should carefully give up her association. We should consider the behavior of the great Vaiṣṇava *ācārya*, Śrīmad Rāmānujācārya, in this connection."

(*Sajjana-toṣaṇī* 10/11)

56. Is it an impediment for a householder's devotional service to collect more than he requires?

"If a householder collects more than his requirement, then this is an impediment in his devotional service and in his achieving the Lord's mercy."

(*Sajjana-toṣaṇī* 10/9)

57. Is it unfavorable for a householder's devotional service to become overwhelmed with grief?

"Householders lament if they lose their wife, children, etc. But a practitioner of devotional service should not maintain this lamentation very long. They should quickly give up their lamentation and engage in the cultivation of Krishna consciousness."

(*Sajjana-toṣaṇī* 11/6)

58. Why should a practitioner of devotional service give up lamentation and anger?

"A practicing Vaiṣṇava should give up all urges like lamentation and anger; otherwise, there will be obstacles in his constant remembrance of Krishna."

(*Sajjana-toṣaṇī* 11/6)

59. What harm do lamentation and illusion cause?

'If one's heart becomes filled with lamentation and grief then Krishna does not manifest in that heart."

(*Śrī Bhāgavatārka Marīchimālā* 15/90

60. What is the harm if the numbers of the Vaiṣṇava sannyāsīs increase?

"It is natural that the numbers of the Vaiṣṇava *sannyāsīs* are to be less; if it increases it will become the cause of disturbance."

(*Sajjana-toṣaṇī* 4/2)

61. Is it proper for a renunciate to lament if he lacks any material object?

"A renunciate should not lament if he does not possess a quilt, a water pot, or other alms, or if these things are stolen by man or animal."

(*Sajjana-toṣaṇī*)

62. Is any association with women for a renunciate approved?

"For a renunciate, there cannot be any type of talking or touching a woman, otherwise his practice of devotional service will be completely spoiled. Association with such a deviated person should be totally rejected."

(*Sajjana-toṣaṇī* 11/6)

63. What are the most prohibition for a renunciate?

"All topics regarding one's family and children are worldly topics. Such topics should not be heard of, or spoken of, by a renunciate. It is also prohibited for a renunciate to eat palatable foodstuffs and wear opulent dresses."

(Commentary on *Caitanya Caritāmṛta*, Antya 6/236, 237)

64. Which prayāsa or endeavors are unfavorable to devotional service?

"*Jnānaprayāsa*, *karmaprayāsa*, *yogaprayāsa*, *muktiprayāsa*, as well as over endeavoring for material enjoyment, worldly achievements, and association with materialistic people are all hostile principles for one who has taken shelter of the holy name. These different forms of *prayāsa* ruin one's devotional service."

(*Sajjana-toṣaṇī* 10/9)

65. Is it favorable for devotional service for a devotee to accept anyone as the spiritual master?

"The more one's greed for receiving a bonafide spiritual master increases the better it is. One should not accept anyone and everyone as his spiritual master just to fulfill this greed."

(*Sajjana-toṣaṇī* 2/1)

66. What harm does it cause to devotional service if an unqualified spiritual master and an unqualified disciple do not give each other's association?

"The relationship between a spiritual master and a disciple is eternal. As long as their qualification continues, their relationship will not break. If the spiritual master becomes fallen then the disciple has no choice but to reject him, and if the disciple becomes fallen then the spiritual master should reject him. If they fail to do so then both of them will fall down."

(*Harināma-cintāmani*)

67. For what reasons can one reject his initiating spiritual master?

"It is a fact that the initiating spiritual master cannot be rejected, but due to two following reasons, he can be rejected. The first reason is that if a disciple did not test his spiritual master's credentials at the time of accepting him as his spiritual master, then he cannot obtain any benefit from him. In such a case he should reject his spiritual master. The second reason is that at the time of accepting a spiritual master the spiritual master was a Vaiṣṇava, and the knower of the truth, but later on due to bad association he may become a *māyāvādī* or envious to the Vaiṣṇavas. In such a case also one should reject his spiritual master."

(*Jaiva Dharma*, Chapter 20)

68. Who are ass-like people and cheaters? Why are they unfavorable to devotional service?

"Those who do not understand their qualification but accept the instruction of a bogus guru and engage in the process of worship meant for exalted devotees are cheated ass-like people. And those who have understood their ineligibility, yet with a goal to accumulate money and prestige, still follow the process of worship meant for exalted devotees are called cheaters. Until this cheating in the name of religion is destroyed, one's attachment to Krishna will not awaken. Such people deceive the entire world by making a show of sectarian formalities and pseudo renunciation."

(*Śrī Krishna-saṁhitā*, Chapter 8/16)

69. What is the harm if one gives up the path of regulative principles before achieving its maturity?

"Many weak-hearted people give up the path of regulative principles and enter the path of attachment. When they are unable to realize the souls' spiritual attachment, they behave like Vṛṣabhāsura [Ariṣṭāsura, the bull] by cultivating perverted material attachment. They will be killed by the prowess of Krishna."

(*Śrī Krishna-saṁhitā*, Chapter 8/21)

70. Are services in the mood of Mathurā, Dvārakā and Vraja impediments on the path of devotional service?

"Those who want to happily serve Krishna in the pure mood of Vraja, should carefully destroy the above-mentioned eighteen obstacles. Those who are on the path of *jñāna* should give up the offenses found in the realm of Mathurā, and those who are on the path of fruitive activities should give the offenses found in Dvārakā. But devotees should give up the obstacles that pollute the mood of Vraja and be absorbed in love for Krishna."

(*Śrī Krishna-saṁhitā*, Chapter 8/30-31)

71. If activities like dhyāna are not favorable for awakening love of God do they create any anartha?

"During *dhyāna*, *dhāraṇā*, and *samādhi*, if even material thoughts are removed, if *prema* is not awakened, the living entity loses his individuality. If the understanding, 'I am Brahman' does not awaken pure love, then that results in destruction of his existence."

(*Prema-pradīpa* Second Ray)

72. What ettiquette should one follow towards his spiritual master, the Vaiṣnavas and the Supreme Lord?

"One should never sleep with one's legs stretching towards the house of his spiritual master, the Vaiṣnavas and the Supreme Lord."

(*Sajjana-toṣaṇī* 7/3)

73. How should one deal with those who consider the glories of the holy names as exaggeration?

"One should not see the face of those who give interpritation on the holy names. If by chance one happens to meet with such people, then one should immediately take bath in the Ganges with his clothes on. If the Ganges is not available, then he should take bath in other pure water. If even that is not available then one should purify himself by taking bath in the mind."

(*Harināma-cintāmani*)

74. Should pure Vaiṣnavas participate in the saṅkīrtana performed by the offenders at the feet of the holy names?

"The Vaiṣnavas should not participate in the *saṅkīrtana* performed by the offenders at the feet of the holy names."

(*Jaiva Dharma*, Chapter 24)

75. Are musical instruments used in saṅkīrtana for the sake of sense gratification unfavorable to devotional service?

"Apart from ancient musical intruments such as *mṛdanga* and *karatāla*, if modern and foreign musical intruments are introduced in the *kīrtana* it certainly makes the *kīrtana* very attractive, but irregularity in the process of devotional service comes up. Nowadays we are so much overwhelmed by using foreign items that we even try to introduce such items into the process of our *bhajana*."

(*Sajjana-toṣaṇī* 11/3)

76. Why does an increase in the number of immature renunciates pose a threat to society?

"It is certainly an anxiety if the numbers of the pesudo renunciates increase, because it is to be understood that there is an evil plan by Kali behind this. The character of genuine Vaiṣṇava renunciate must be pure and faultless."

(*Sajjana-toṣaṇī* 5/10)

77. Is it proper for a renunciate Vaiṣṇava to accumulate?

"The renunciate Vaiṣṇavas must not accumulate at all."

(*Sajjana-toṣaṇī* 10/9)

78. Should a renunciate Vaiṣṇava build maṭha or āśrama?

"A renunciate Vaiṣṇava should not endeavor for building *maṭha* or *āśrama*, for this will entangle him in worldly matters."

(*Sajjana-toṣaṇī* 11/12)

79. Is begging alms by a renunciate, favorable to devotional service?

"A renunciate should neither beg food from a materialist nor invite other renunciates for lunch for the sake of money."

(*Sajjana-toṣaṇī* 11/12)

80. Should a renunciate sees a king, a materialist or a woman?

"A renunciate should not see a king, a materialist or a woman."

(*Sajjana-toṣaṇī* 11/12)

81. Should a renunciate live in his own village?

"A *sannyāsī* or a renunciate should not live in his village with his family members."

(*Sajjana-toṣaṇī* 11/12)

82. Why is it prohibitive for a renunciate to converse with women?

"Conversing with women is the cause of fall down of Vaiṣṇava *sannyāsīs*."

(*Gaurāṅga Smarana Mangala*, Stotra 62)

83. What is the fate of those who immaturely follow the path of attachment by following instructions of bogus gurus?

"Bogus gurus who did not consider their disciples' qualification for the path of attachment and thus instructed many Śakaṭa-like people to accept service in the mood of *mañjarīs* and *sakhīs* committed offenses by disrespecting confidential subject matters and thus fall down. Those who worship according to such instructions also gradually fell away from spiritual life, because they do not attain the symptoms of deep attachment for those topics. Yet they may still be delivered by the association of pure devotees by receiving proper instructions."

(*Śrī Krishna-saṁhitā*, Chapter 8/150

84. What is the root of all sinful activities?

"Being unable able to tolerate other's' progress is called envy. This is the root of all sinful activities."

(*Caitanya-śikṣāmṛta* 2/5)

85. What is women debauchery?

"Debauchery of women is a grave sin."

(*Caitanya-śikṣāmṛta* 2/5)

86. What should debauchery for name and fame be called?

"Due to debauchery for name and fame all one's activities become extremely selfish. Therefore one should give up debauchery."

(*Caitanya-śikṣāmṛta* 2/5)

87. Is it approved by the śāstras to leave home because of being agitated with mundane, peace or disturbance?

"Many householders give up their family life and home due to feeling distressed at home or due to some other disturbance; this is a sin."

(*Caitanya-śikṣāmṛta* 2/5)

88. What are the different names of sin?

"According to its gravity and lightness, the sin is addressed in various names such as '*pāpa*,' '*pātaka*,' '*ati-pātaka*' and '*mahā-pātaka*.'"

(*Caitanya-śikṣāmṛta* 2/5)

89. Is laziness abominable?

"Laziness is counted among sinful activities. To become free from laziness is the duty of every pious person."

(*Caitanya-śikṣāmṛta* 2/5)

65

Desiring Material Objects

1. Is there any limit to material desires? Do they award any peace?

"There is no limit to material desires. In fact, the paths of material desires are filled with the thorns of dissatisfaction. The more you want to advance, the more you have material desires. Desires are neither killed nor discriminate between temporary or permanent objects."

(*Kalyāna Kalpataru*, Song 2)

2. Is there any aim of pleasing Lord Viṣṇu in the materialists worship of goddess Annpurnā?

"Those materialists, who, with a desire of getting abundance of rice in their future lives worship goddess Annapurnā, only with a false resolution of 'love for Lord Viṣṇu."

(Conclusion, *Caitanya-śikṣāmṛta* 8)

3. How many kinds of godless persons are there?

"There are six kinds of godless persons:

1. Those who are unfaithful to God and are devoid of moralities.
2. Those who are moral yet unfaithful to God.
3. Those who are God-fearing but think that He is under the control of morality.
4. Those who speak lie or are proud.
5. Impersonalists.
6. Those who believe in many gods."

(*Caitanya-śikṣāmṛta* 3/3)

4. What is the life of an immoral godless person?

"Those who are immoral and Godless, are attached to sinful activities and non-activity. Without moralities one becomes whimsical."
(*Caitanya-śikṣāmṛta* 3/3)

5. Is the character of a moral Godless person trustworthy?

"Where is the guarantee that if opportunity arrives, a moral Godless person will not sacrifice his morality for his self-interest? Just by analyzing his character this fact can be confirmed, and one will realize the insignificance of the philosophy."
(*Caitanya-śikṣāmṛta* 3/3)

6. Are God-fearing karmīs devotees?

"The third kinds of Godless persons are addressed as 'God-fearing *karmīs*. They are divided into two categories. The first categories of God-fearing *karmīs* are those who consider the gratefulness to God as their principle duty, but do not accept the existence of God. It is also their belief that one should imagine a God and offer Him obeisance with faith, and when one's good character, which is the result of morality, awaken, there is no harm in giving up faith in God. The second category of God-fearing *karmīs* believe that by worshiping God in the form of chanting His names and offering Him prayers, his heart will be purified; and when his heart thus becomes purified, he obtains the knowledge of the impersonal Brahman. At such time, he becomes inactive. According to this philosophy, relationship between God and the living entities is temporary and not eternal."
(*Caitanya-śikṣāmṛta* 3/3)

7. How many kinds of liars are there?

"Liars are counted as the forth category of Godless persons. They are divided into two namely, the hypocrites and the cheated."
(*Caitanya-śikṣāmṛta* 3/3)

8. What is the nature of the hypocrites and what is the fate of those who intimate them?

"By cheating everyone, the hypocrites clear the path of irreligion. Many foolish people become cheated by following them. Ultimately, such foolish people become averse to God. The hypocrites externally display symptoms of putting on transcendental Vaiṣṇava signs, chanting the holy names constantly, showing detachment for the worldly objects, and speaking sweet words; but internally maintain strong desires for accumulating gold and women."

(*Caitanya-śikṣāmṛta* 3/3)

9. Is there any end to material desires?

"Abandoning the position of Lord Brahma, you will constantly think how to obtain the position of Lord Siva. After obtaining the position of Lord Siva, you will want to be one with the Brahman, as is normally desired by the followers of Śaṅkarācārya. Therefore, try to destroy the chain of material desires and keep them away from your heart. Take shelter of the lotus feet of Śrī Caitanya and always reside at Santipura in the mood of a beggar."

(*Kalyāna Kalpataru*, Song 2)

10. Is there any place for material desires in pure devotional service?

"There cannot be any desire other than making advancement in the path of one's spiritual life, in pure devotional service. To serve Krishna, there cannot be any objects like Brahman and Paramātmā, other than the object of worship, Krishna. There cannot be any tinge of performance of fruitive activities and cultivation of impersonal knowledge."

(Commentary on *Caitanya Caritāmṛta* Madhya-līlā 19/168)

66

Fruitive Activities

1. What is karma?

"Karma is nothing but selfish activities. Karmis do not exclusively search for the mercy of Krishna. Although they respect Krishna, their main purpose is to attain some kind of happiness."

(*Sajjana-toṣaṇī* 11/11)

2. Is there any direct spiritual cultivation in the performance of pious activities, even though such activities may aim at Lord Viṣṇu?

"Even though pious activities like the performance of sacrifice are executed while accepting the supremacy of Lord Viṣṇu, and the master of all sacrifices, yet there is no direct spiritual cultivation in the performance of such pious activities."

(*Harināma-cintāmani*)

3. What is the unseen or the result of one's previous deeds?

"A *jīva* gets his nature in accordance to the impressions created from previous births and accordingly, his activity can have a beginning. This is called"the unseen" or the result of one's previous deeds. His natural impulse is formed according to the nature of the deeds done by him in the previous lives."

(*Brahma-saṁhitā* 5/23)

4. How is the contamination caused by karma and jñāna purified?

"When one offers the fruit of karma for the pleasure of the Lord, then one's performance of karma becomes purified. When one becomes attached to the service of the Lord, then one's renunciation becomes purified. When one realizes himself as the servant of the Supreme Lord, then one's knowledge becomes purified."

(Commentary on *Bṛhat-Bhāgavtāmṛta*)

5. Is the fortune of the theistic persons undecided?

"Unlike the atheistic persons, the fortune of the theistic persons is not undecided. The fortune of the living entities is decided according to their respective Karma."

(*Śrī Manaḥ-śikṣā*, Chapter 8)

6. What right do persons have in the performance of karma?

"Whatever activity a living entity performs, he always remains the original doer. By supporting in the performance of that activity, the material nature becomes the secondary doer and by awarding the fruit of such activities, the Supreme Lord becomes the associate doers. Since the living entities have fallen into nescience out of their own will, their original doer-ship never ceases. Whatever activities the living entities perform after entering into nescience are called 'fortune' when those activities are about to bear fruit."

(*Śrī Manaḥ-śikṣā*, Chapter 8)

7. Why is karma beginningless?

"To forget that I am an eternal servant of Krishna is called nescience. This nescience has not started from within the material time factor rather the root of karma of the living entities grew from the marginal juncture. Therefore, one cannot trace out the origin of karma within the material time factor. Therefore karma is said to be beginning-less."

(*Jaiva Dharma*, Chapter 16)

8. What is the difference between devotional service and activities adverse to the Lord?

"If anyone performs karma in order to achieve the mercy of Krishna, then that karma is called *bhakti*. The karma that yields mundane results or mundane knowledge is adverse to the Lord."

(*Sajjana-toṣaṇī* 11/11)

9. When does karma transform into devotional service?

"Before changing its own form, karma goes through three different stages; the stage of desirelessness, the stage of offering the fruits of karma to the Lord, and the stage of performing karma on behalf of the Lord. When these three stages are surpassed then karma transform into devotional service."

(*Śrī Manaḥ-śikṣā*, Chapter 10)

10. Are karma and jñāna pieties that award devotional service?

"Knowledge and renunciation mostly keep the living entities engrossed in the knowledge of undivided Brahman. The knowledge of impersonal Brahman often deceives the living entities from the lotus feet of the Lord. That is why they cannot be faithfully accepted as piety that awards devotional service."

(*Jaiva Dharma*, Chapter 17)

11. Which process has been ascertained by the Vedic literature as safe for attaining the Supreme Lord?

"Vedic literature and the *Purānas* have mentioned at various places about various processes for attaining the Supreme Lord. In some places, they described the process of *karma-kānda* in the form of bumblebee and mammon. In some places, the process of yoga in the form of python; and in some places, the process of *bhakti* that easily avails one the pot of hidden treasury. Therefore Vedic literatures have concluded that one can attain Krishna only by devotional service and not by karma, *jñāna* and yoga."

(Commentary on *Caitanya Caritāmṛta,* Madhya-lila 20/135)

12. Is karmī a servant of the Supreme Lord?

"Those who are entangled in karma, with aim of achieving happiness, consider karma as all in all, and consider the Supreme Lord as 'part of karma.' The fruit of their karma is certainly not eternal. Their consistency is not faultless. They have no inclination for cultivating Krishna consciousness; rather dependence on the rules and regulations is prominent in their lives. Such people are called *karmī*."

(*Caitanya-śikṣāmṛta*, Chapter 8)

13. Can karma be destroyed by karma? What is perfection of karma?

"If the cause of a disease is used as the cure for that disease, then such a disease will never be cured. The process of *karma-kānda* itself is the cause of the living entities' material disease. It will never bear the fruits of destroying the living entities material existence, whether the activities are performed without material desires, or their fruits are offered to the Lord. If one can first accept karma as the only means of his livelihood but later dovetail it with devotional service, then there is a possibility of the karma being destroyed. If one accepts only that karma which is suitable for pleasing the Lord, then all his activities become transform into *bhakti-yoga*. It is the intention of all the *śāstras* to induce everyone to engage in devotional service to Krishna, and according to the teachings of the Lord, constantly sing and remember the holy names, forms, qualities, and the pastimes of Krishna."

(*Śrī Manaḥ-śikṣā*, Chapter 10)

14. What is the difference between a karmī's worship of Krishna and a devotee's worship of Krishna?

"The *sādhana bhakti* practiced by the Vaiṣṇavas is meant to awakened their *prema bhakti*. However, when nondevotees practice *sādhana bhakti* their goal is either material enjoyment or liberation. There maybe no difference in the practice of *sādhana bhakti* of the two, but there are certainly differences in their intentions. By worshiping Krishna, the *karmīs* may eventually achieve the result of purification of heart from the desire for liberation, as well freedom from desires for material enjoyment. By worshiping Krishna, the devotees become attached to the holy names of Krishna. By observing the vow of Ekādaśī, the *karmīs* counteract their sinful reactions, whereas by observing the vow of Ekādaśī, the devotees increase their devotion to Lord Hari. Just see how much difference is there between the two."

(*Jaiva Dharma*, Chapter 5) mlechha

15. What is the difference between a godless family and a Vaiṣṇava family?

"The only difference between a godless family and a Vaiṣṇava family is the intention. There is no difference in their appearance. The godless persons get married, earn money, build house, beget children and perform all activities in the name of justice; but their intention is that by all their activities, they want to increase the happiness of the world and their own. Even though the Vaiṣṇavas perform all activities just like the godless people, they do not grab the fruit of their activities, rather they engage in the service of the Supreme Lord. Ultimately, the Vaiṣṇavas attain satisfaction. The godless people become controlled by lust and anger and thus loose their peace of mind, due to the desire for material enjoyment and liberation."

(*Caitanya-śikṣāmṛta* 3/2)

16. When does one commit the nāmāparādha of blaspheming the devotees?

"Offenses at the feet of *sadhus* is due to being proud of one's karma and *jñāna*. The offense in chanting in the form of blaspheming devotees, enters the heart of the nondevotee and takes up residence there."

(*Sajjana-toṣaṇī* 11/11)

17. Are sin and piety constitutional activities of the soul?

"Both sin and piety is relative, not constitutional. The activity or a desire that relatively help a soul attain his constitutional position is called piety. The opposite is called sin."

(*Śrī Krishna-saṁhitā*, Chapter 10/2)

18. For whom is the system of marriage beneficial?

"Those who are very attached to material objects should associate with women through marriage, as this is piety for such persons."

(*Śrī Krishna-saṁhitā*, Chapter 10/3)

19. What is the irrelevant fruit of traveling to the holy places?

"By visiting holy places people become quite purified. Although associating with saintly persons is the ultimate goal of visiting the holy places, people who visit holy places consider themselves purified. Because by visiting holy places their sinful propensities get destroyed."

(*Caitanya-śikṣāmṛta* 2/2)

20. What is constitutional and temporary piety?

"Justice, compassion, truthfulness, purity, religiousness and love are called constitutional piety. They are called so, because they always remain with the living entities like their ornaments. In the conditional state these pieties become somewhat gross and are called *punya* or pious activities. Apart from that, all other pieties are temporary, because they have arisen due to the living entities' contact with matter. In the perfected stage however both constitutional and temporary pieties have no existence."

(*Caitanya-śikṣāmṛta* 2/23)

21. Is there any desire for sin or piety in the hearts of Krishna's devotees?

"Since devotional service to Krishna is one's constitutional position, when one cultivates this service, then nescience, which is the root cause of relative situations in the form of sin and piety, is gradually fried and abolished. Although the desire to engage in sinful activity may suddenly manifest like a fried kai fish, it is quickly subdued by the process of devotional service."

(*Śrī Krishna-saṁhitā*, Chapter 10/2)

22. How many types of atonement are there? What is the result of each atonement?

"There are three types of atonement—atonement through karma, atonement through *jñāna*, and atonement through *bhakti*. Remembering Krishna is the atonement through *bhakti*. Therefore, devotional service is atonement through *bhakti*. There is no need for devotees to separately endeavor for atonement. Atonement in *jñāna* is through repentance. By atonement through *jñāna*, one's sins and seeds of sin, or desires, are destroyed, but nescience is not destroyed without *bhakti*. By atonement through karma, such as *candrāyaṇa* (a kind of expiatory penance), one's sins are checked, but the seeds of sinful desires and nescience, the root cause of sins and the desire to sin, remains. One must understand this science of atonement with careful consideration."

(*Śrī Krishna-saṁhitā*, Chapter 10/2)

23. Why are the whimsical persons, who give up the principles of varnāśrama dharma, fit for atonement?

"By associating with *mlecchas*, those who give up the practice of *varnāśrama dharma* and also act whimsically like the *mlecchas*, fall down as a result of opposing the proper proper code of conduct."

(*Caitanya-śikṣāmṛta* 2/5)

24. What is the cause of being born as an outcast?

"The cause of being born as an outcast is one's fructified karma. It can be destroyed by chanting the holy names of the Lord."

(*Jaiva Dharma*, Chapter 6)

25. How do the seeds of sinful activities become destroyed?

"Among the methods of purifying the mind, remembering Lord Vishnu is the principal one. The arrangement of atonement is meant for purifying the sinful mind. By undergoing the atonement such as *cāndrāyana*, which fall under the category of *karma-kānda*, the sinful activities leave the sinner; but the root of sinful activities that is the desire to commit sin does not go away. By undergoing the atonement in the form of repentance which fall under the category of *jñāna-kānda*, desires for committing sinful activities become destroyed. However the seed of sinful activities in the form aversion to the Lord is destroyed only by the remembrance of Lord Hari."

(*Caitanya-śikṣāmṛta* 2/2)

26. How many types of impurities are there and what are the differences between them?

"Impurity is of two types; mental and physical. Mental and physical impurities are further divided into three categories namely; impurities born of place, impurities born of time, and impurities born of person. If one goes to an impure country one becomes affected. The impurity of a place is caused by the sinful activities committed by the inhabitants of that place. That is why in the religious scriptures it is described that if one goes or lives in a *mleccha* country, one becomes affected by the impurities of that country. However, there is no prohibition in going to the *mleccha* country for the sake of acquiring knowledge about those countries, delivering those countries from the hands of miscreants through war or any other means, and for the sake of preaching religious principles. Going to the *mleccha* countries just to acquire insignificant education, learn religious teachings or live with the inhabitants of those countries, certainly hamper the prestige of the Āryans. Whoever is affected by this is fit for atonement."

(*Caitanya-śikṣāmṛta* 2/5)

27. What is the impurity of the mind?

"Illusion and envy make the mind impure. It is extremely necessary to remove them."

(*Caitanya-śikṣāmṛta* 2/5)

67

Empiric Knowledge

1. What is the definition of jñāna?

"*Jñāna* is also a particular form of karma in the mode of goodness." (Commentary on *Bhagavad-gītā* 3/2)

2. What kind of knowledge and renunciation is acceptable to the devotees?

"Knowledge and renunciation are not counted among the limbs of devotional service, because they make the heart hard like a rock. But devotional service is smooth and sublime, therefore knowledge and renunciation which arise from devotional service should be accepted."

(*Jaiva Dharma*, Chapter 20)

3. Can one attain pure knowledge as long as one is inquisitive?

"Material knowledge consists of all physical knowledge. The original knowledge is called transcendental knowledge. Transcendental knowledge when perverted, becomes material knowledge. The twenty-four material truth put forth by Sānkhya philosophy is entirely material knowledge. When this knowledge is refined through *samādhi* it awakens transcendental knowledge. This transcendental knowledge is scientific. As long as one is inquisitive, one is still under the clutch of ignorance. Destruction of ignorance and the awaken of scientific transcendental knowledge takes place simultaneously. After receiving this knowledge, when one relishes it then that is called devotional service. Therefore there difference between scientific transcendental knowledge and devotional service."

(*Sajjana-toṣaṇī* 11/10)

4. What kind of jñāna is condemned by the Vaiṣṇavas?

"The knowledge which is often condemned by the Vaiṣṇavas is not pure knowledge. They condemn that material knowledge, by which the materialists try to ascertain the inconceivable Absolute Truth. If it is said to a thief that human beings are nonsense, this does not mean that all human beings are nonsense but certainly the thieves are."

(*Sajjana-toṣaṇī* 11/10)

5. What kind of jñāna is condemned by the devotional literatures?

"Considering loving devotional service and pure knowledge has equal, impure knowledge has been condemned in the devotional literatures. Pure knowledge is never referred to as *Jñāna* Kānda."

(*Caitanya-śikṣāmṛta* 5/3)

6. What is pratyag and parag-caitanya?

"*Caitanya* is of two kinds—*pratyag* and *parag*. When Vaiṣṇavas are absorbed in *prema*, at that time *pratyag-caitanya*, or internal knowledge, arises. When one's absorption in *prema* is broken, he then comes to his external senses and *parag-caitany*a arises. *Parag-caitanya* is not *cit*, but a shadow of *cit*."

(*Prema-pradīpa* Ninth Ray.)

7. Are the pastimes of the Supreme Lord measurable by human knowledge?

"Human knowledge is most insignificant. If one tries to measure the prowess and pastimes of the Supreme Lord, then one will certainly fall into illusion."

(*Sajjana-toṣaṇī* 8/4)

8. What is the difference between the knowledge of the impersonal Brahman and the Supreme Lord?

"Knowledge of the impersonal Brahman is just a branch of knowledge of the Supreme Lord."

(*Caitanya-śikṣāmṛta* 5/3)

9. Where does kaivalya or merging into the Brahman exist?

"*Kaivalya* or merging into the Brahman constitutes the line of demarcation between the world of limitation and the transcendental world."

(*Brahma-saṁhitā* 5/34)

10. What is the fate of those who follow the system jñāna-kānda?

"The followers of *jñāna-kānda*, who are entangled in the conception of merging into the existence of Brahman, practice false renunciation in order to destroy their individuality. They neither achieve anything in this life nor in the next. They simply waste their life while contemplating on some indirect thoughts.

(*Caitanya-śikṣāmṛta*, Chapter 8)

11. What is the danger in trying to go to Goloka through jñāna or yoga?

"There are ten tridents in ten directions that prevent and disappoint those who are aspiring for an entrance into Goloka through meditations without the grace of Krishna. Self-conceited people who try to reach this region through the paths of yoga (meditation) and *jñāna* (empiric knowledge) are baffled in their attempts, being pierced by the ten tridents."

(*Brahma-saṁhitā* 5/5)

12. Who are demigods and demons? What is the difference between their goal of life and the process to achieve it?

"The devotees of the Supreme Lord are the demigods and those who are envious of the Supreme Lord are the demons. Just as there is always, a principle of opposition between the demigods and the demons, similarly there is also a principle of opposition between their *sādhana* and *sādhya*. The *sādhana* of the demons is to torture the devotees and to kill cows and *brāhmanas* and their *sādhya* is to attain liberation. The *sādhana* of the devotees is devotional service and their *sādhya* is love of God. Those who endeavor to achieve that liberation necessarily take shelter of dishonest *sādhana* in the form of cultivating impersonal knowledge like the nondevotees ."

(Commentary on *Bṛhat-Bhāgavatamṛta*)

68

Mystic Yoga and Observing Vows

1. Is yoga not an unbroken process?

"Yoga is one not two. Yoga is a particular path for spiritual cultivation. The first stage of yoga is desireless karma or *karma-yoga*; when it is mixed with knowledge and renunciation it becomes known as *jñāna* yoga which is the second stage. When *jñāna* is mixed with the meditation in the form of remembering the Lord, it is called *astāṅga-yoga*, which is the third stage of yoga. When it is mixed with love for the Supreme Lord, it becomes Bhakti yoga. The entire process which consists of various stages is called Yoga."

(Commentary on *Bhagavad-gītā* 6/47)

2. When are karma, jñāna, and yoga capable of awarding secondary fruit?

"If karma, *jñāna* and yoga and their respective processes do not aim at devotional service they cannot award any kinds of fruit to their followers. If devotional service to Krishna becomes their ultimate goal, then only are they able to award some secondary fruits."

(*Caitanya-śikṣāmṛta* 1/6)

3. In which scriptures is haṭha-yoga described?

"*Haṭha-yoga* is described in the *śākta* and *śaiva tantras* as well as the scriptures written from those *tantras*, like *Haṭha-yoga dīpikā* and *Yoga-cintāmaṇi.*

(*Prema-pradīpa* Ray 3)

4. What is the difference between Rāja-yoga and Haṭha-yoga?

"The yoga practiced by philosophers and Puranic scholars is called *rājayoga*. Yoga prescribed by the *tantric paṇḍitas* is called *haṭha-yoga*."

(*Prema-pradīpa*, Ray 3)

5. Why is path of yoga fearful and path of devotional service fearless?

"*Yama, niyama, āsana, prāṇāyāma, pratyāhāra, dhyāna, dhāraṇā,* and *samādhi*—these are *aṣṭāṅga-yoga*. It is true that by these practices, one may achieve peace, but sometimes in the process, one may be overwhelmed by lust and greed. Then instead of attaining peace, one may enjoy some yogic opulence for sometime before ultimately falling. However, in the devotional service of Lord Krishna, there is no fear of irrelevant fruits, for the servants of Krishna certainly attain peace.'"

(*Prema-pradīpa*, Ray 2)

6. Where is the danger in haṭha-yoga?

"If someone practices *haṭha-yoga* in this way, he can do many wonderful feats. By seeing the results, one can believe this. By practicing *mudrās*, so many kinds of powers are acquired that the practitioner cannot make further progress."

(*Prema-pradīpa*, Ray 3)

7. What is the fate of a practitioner of yoga who tries to separate his attachment for Vaikuntha from his life?

"Thought and practice like *dhyāna, pratyāhāra,* and *dhāraṇā* are advised for attaining the end result of awakening one's spiritual attachment. And many people practice these. But they don't sufficiently discuss how to attain spiritual attachment. That is why yogis often become captivated by yogic opulence and ultimately fail to attain spiritual attachment. On the other hand, Vaiṣṇava practices are superior.

"You see, any *sādhana* is just a special activity. One may develop attachment to whatever activities are required to be performed in human life, and one may only think and labor hard while endeavoring to achieve the Absolute Truth. Are those who work in this way, able to quickly awaken spiritual attachment? If the *sādhaka* keeps his attempts to develop spiritual attachment as a separate activity in his life, then he will be pulled by material attachment on the one hand and spiritual consciousness on the other.

(*Prema-pradīpa*, Ray 4)

8. What are the limbs of rāja-yoga?

"*Samādhi* is the main process of *rāja-yoga*. In order to attain *samādhi* one first practices *yama*, then *niyama*, then *āsana*, then *prāṇāyāma*, then

pratyāhāra, then *dhyāna*, and then *dhāraṇā*. One must practice these processes.
(*Prema-pradīpa*, Ray 5)

9. How does one attain samādhi through rāja-yoga?
"In the state of *samādhi* in *rāja-yoga*, truth beyond material nature is realized. In that state, one can taste unalloyed love. That subject cannot be described by words."
(*Prema-pradīpa*, Ray 5)

10. What is the process followed by the ascetics? How many kinds of yoga processes are there?
"With great distress the ascetics want to loosen the knots of their karma. The ascetics practice Vedic *pancāgni-vidyā*, *nididhyāsana* and Vedic yoga. Yoga such as *astānga-yoga*, *ṣaranga-yoga*, *dattatreyī-yoga*, and *gorakṣanārthi-yoga* have been proposed in the *śāstras*. Among them *haṭha-yoga* mentioned in the *tantras* and *rāja-yoga* propounded by Patañjali have been widely accepted in the world."
(*Caitanya-śikṣāmṛta*, Chapter 8)

11. What is the difference between yoga and the path of devotional service?
"The main difference between yoga and devotional service is this: in the strict practice of yoga, when one attains *samādhi* by giving up false designations, he attains his constitutional position—that is, *prema* is awakened. There is fear, however, that in the long process of giving up false designations the *sādhaka* may become captivated by insignificant byproducts and fall down before attaining the ultimate goal. On the other hand, in devotional service there is only discussion of *prema*. Devotional service is simply the cultivation of the science of love of God. When all activities are meant for cultivating the ultimate result, there is no fear of useless results. The means are the end, and the end is the means."
(*Prema-pradīpa*, Ray 2)

12. What does one gain by achieving perfection in the practice of yoga?
"The domination over material nature attained in the practice of yoga is only a temporary result. In that position, the ultimate result may be far off and time and again impediments are observed. In the path of yoga, there are

hindrances at every step. First, at the time of practicing *yama* and *niyama*, religiosity is awakened, and as a result of attaining this insignificant result one becomes known as religious, even though no attempt has been made to achieve *prema*."

(*Prema-pradīpa*, Ray 2)

13. When do one's sensual endeavors diminish?

"The path of devotional service is to cultivate love of the Absolute Truth. The more the attachment for such cultivation of love increases the more the endeavor of the senses diminishes."

(*Prema-pradīpa*, Ray 2)

14. What is the purpose of observing vows and fasting?

"Taking bath in the morning, circumambulating, offering obeisances are exercise related to bodily vows. Due to the imbalance of any of the bodily elements, one falls sick. In order to check such sicknesses, vows like fasting on the tenth day of both the waning and waxing moon, fasting on the full moon, and fasting on Mondays have been prescribed. Therefore it is beneficial to either completely fast, or makes changes in the routine of eating, etc., on those particular days and engages the mind in thinking of the Supreme Lord with controlled senses."

(*Caitanya-śikṣāmṛta* 2/2)

15. What is the aim of observing the month long vow?

"The month long vow consists of the twenty-four Ekādaśīs and the six other appearance days including Janmāṣṭhami. The only aim of observing such vows is spiritual cultivation."

(*Caitanya-śikṣāmṛta* 2/2)

16. What is the gradual procedure for attaining renunciation?

"By following the body related vows of Cāturmāsya, the full moon day and every tenth day of the waning and the waxing moon, one becomes habituated in the process of renunciation. First, one should gradually give up desire for eating, sleeping and so on. Thereafter one should give up desire for all happiness and practice renunciation by accepting only those material enjoyments which are required to maintain his body and soul together. When this method is completed then one attains the platform of renunciation."

(*Caitanya-śikṣāmṛta* 2/2)

69

False Renunciation

1. What harm does false renunciation cause to a practitioner of devotional service? What is the benefit of giving up false renunciation?

"*Markata vairāgya* or false renunciation is a major weakness of the heart. By carefully giving it up one gains strength in the path of one's *bhajana*. Then all kinds of enemies of the living entities such as duplicity, the cheating propensity and desire for name and fame become defeated. In this way the living entities attain pure devotional service and thereby make their lives successful."

(*Sajjana-toṣaṇī* 8/10)

2. Should a renunciate watch cinema or a theatre?

"There is no doubt that a renunciate who watches women and their acting in a cinema hall or in a drama theatre also behaves like a false renunciate. The renunciate who indulges in hearing and watching plays and dramas is certainly at fault."

(*Sajjana-toṣaṇī* 8/10)

3. Can one formally accept the dress of a renunciate before reaching the platform of bhāva?

"Just by identifying oneself as a renunciate does not make one renunciate. If one has not automatically developed detachment from sense gratification as a result of awakening of his *bhāva*, it is illegal to accept the dress of a renunciate."

(*Caitanya-śikṣāmṛta* 5/2

4. Is it proper to take sannyāsa in an immature stage when the desire for associating with women is still present in one's heart?

"If propensity for associating with women is present in any corner of one's heart, then he should not take *sannyāsa*. Stay at home, try to give up false renunciation and make progress in the spiritual life by relishing the chanting of the holy names of Krishna. There is no need to take *sannyāsa* in a hurry and in an improper time."

(*Sajjana-toṣaṇī* 8/10)

5. Whose acting of renunciation is prone to transform into false renunciation?

"If a householder leaves his family life before developing strong natural detachment, then his renunciation is prone to transform into false renunciation."

(*Sajjana-toṣaṇī* 8/10)

6. What is the symptom of a false renunciate?

"Thinking of sense gratification within the heart, secretly enjoying the company of women, and externally putting on the signs of a renunciate like *kaupina* and *chādara* are the symptoms of a false renunciate."

(Commentary on *Caitanya Caritāmṛta* Madhya 16/238)

7. Who is a false renunciate?

"A renunciate who intimately converses with women is a false renunciate."

(*Harināma-cintāmani*)

8. Can only a sannyāsi become a false renunciate? What is the householder's false renunciation?

"There are two kinds of false renunciates; the householder's false renunciation and the *sannyāsi*'s false renunciation. Among the householder, those who are unnecessarily eager to leave home are outrageous."

(*Sajjana-toṣaṇī* 8/10)

9. Can one become free from sense gratification just by wearing the dress of a renunciate?

"Simply by wearing the dress of a renunciate does not make a devotee free from sense gratification, because renunciates often collect and save objects for sense enjoyment. On the other hand, many persons resemble sense enjoyers but utilize everything in the worship of Lord Hari in the mood of detachment."

(*Sajjana-toṣaṇī* 10/11)

10. What is the harm if one gives up the gradual path due to the desire for liberation?

"If one gives up the gradual path due to the desire for liberation, then false renunciation overpowers the living entities, and makes them abominable."

(*Caitanya-śikṣāmṛta* 1/7)

11. Who are unsteady renunciates?

"Those who take *sannyāsa* by being induced by temporary detachment born from quarrel, distress, lack of wealth, disease and accident, in the process of getting married, are unsteady renunciates. Their detachment does not last long; very soon they become pseudo renunciates."

(*Caitanya-śikṣāmṛta* 5/2)

12. Who are conventional renunciates?

"Those who become controlled by intoxication and thus become useless in the society, try to practice exhibiting the symptoms of devotional service to Hari under the control of intoxication and try to execute loving devotional service under the shelter of material attachment, they are called conventional renunciates even though they put on the signs of a renunciate."

(*Caitanya-śikṣāmṛta* 5/2)

13. Who is a disgrace to the Vaiṣṇava dharma, and what is the cause of disturbance in the society?

"One who accepts the signs of a renunciate, before he actually becomes detached, is certainly the cause of disturbance in the society, and is a disgrace to the Vaiṣṇava *dharma*."

(*Sajjana-toṣaṇī* 2/7)

14. Who are responsible for creating doubt in the minds of the people about the character of the renounced saintly persons?

"It is extremely necessary for the *bābājis* in the renounced order of life to give up greed for women, wealth, palatable food and material happiness. Since some renounced saintly persons have these possessions, people of the world develop a doubt in the character of the renounced saintly persons."

(*Sajjana-toṣaṇī* 2/7)

15. Is the custom of keeping maidservants by the bābājis, who live in the cottage, approved by the Vaiṣṇava dharma?

"It is extremely inauspicious for *bābājis* who live in cottages to keep maidservants. In some cottages, the daughter of a *bābāji* from his previous *āśrama* lives as a maidservant. A real renunciate never lives in a cottage where nothing works without women. To intimately enjoy the association of the opposite sex, on the pretext of serving the Supreme Lord and the saintly persons, becomes the goal of all such activities."

(*Sajjana-toṣaṇī* 2/7)

16. Can one get any result simply by subduing material attachments?

"It is not that subjugating material attachment awakens one's spiritual attachment. Many people take shelter of renunciation just to subjugate material attachment, but they do not try to increase their spiritual attachment. This ends in misfortune.

(*Prema-pradīpa*, Ray 4)

17. Is there any use of renunciation if there is no spiritual goal?

"Although by the process of *pratyāhāra* one achieves control of the senses, if *prema* is lacking this is called dry or insignificant renunciation. The reason is that for attaining the ultimate goal, enjoyment and renunciation give equal results. Useless renunciation simply makes one stonehearted."

(*Prema-pradīpa*, Ray 2)

18. When is one qualified to leave home?

"When a person's propensity becomes totally introspective, then only he becomes qualified to leave home. If he leaves home before that, then there is a danger of his falling down."

(*Jaiva Dharma*, Chapter 7)

70

Association with Women

1. What is 'association with opposite sex'?

"A man's attachment for a woman and a woman's attachment for a man is called 'association with opposite sex.' By chanting the holy names of Krishna while giving up that attachment, a householder can achieve ultimate goal of life."

(*Jaiva Dharma*, Chapter 25)

2. Is association with women detrimental to devotional service?

"When there is no marital relationship and one converses with a woman with evil intentions, then this is *strīsaṅga*. That is sinful and detrimental to devotional service."

(*Sajjana-toṣaṇī* 10/11)

3. What should a person who desires to attain pure devotional service give up?

"Those who desire to attain pure devotional service should totally give up the association of nondevotees and women."

(*Sajjana-toṣaṇī* 11/11)

4. What is the purpose of marriage? Who are engaged in animalistic activities? What is the mentality of a person who is attached to spiritual life?

"Those who possess a material body made of flesh and blood are always inclined to associate with women. To minimize this inclination, the marriage ceremony is recommended. Those who wish to get free from the codes of marriage are almost like animals. But those who have crossed beyond the rules of this natural inclination by the association of devotees and the strength of their service, and have thus attained attraction for spiritual subject matters, for them associating with the opposite sex is very insignificant."

(*Sajjana-toṣaṇī* 11/5)

5. Who are actually 'stri-sangis'?

"Those who are attached to associating with women are called '*stri-sangis.*' The materialists who are fond of gold and women, the Sahajiyās, Bāuls, Sāins and other so-called religious minded people who are greedy after women as well as the women -oving tāntrics are all examples of *stri-sangis*. The main point is that those males who are attached to females are all said to be *stri-sangis*. The Vaiṣṇavas, by all means, should give up the company of such *stri-sangis*. This is the order of Śrī Caitanya Mahāprabhu."

(*Sajjana-toṣaṇī* 11/6)

6. Is a Vaiṣṇava householder licentious?

"A Vaiṣṇava, whether a householder or a renunciate, is desirous of transcendental happiness. A householder Vaiṣṇava always works together with his wife for the purpose of achieving transcendental happiness. Although engaged in all kinds of work in this way, he never becomes licentious. In this way, he remains free from women's association throughout his life. He totally gives up illicit intimate speaking with women and the mundane licentious mood in licit association with his wife."

(*Sajjana-toṣaṇī* 11/11)

7. Is it good to become licentious?

"One should never become licentious for it ruins everything."

(*Caitanya-śikṣāmṛta* 2/5)

8. Is associating with his wife a limb of devotional service for a householder?

"For a householder associating with his wife is not a limb of devotional service. Therefore it has been accepted as sinless as long as one uses it to maintain his family life."

(*Sajjana-toṣaṇī* 4/6)

9. How should women devotees give up bad association?

"It is essential for women devotees to give up the association of their nondevotee husbands. It is very difficult to consider the nondevotees as husband. This illusory enjoyer acts like a bull and proudly considers himself as the husband."

(*Śrī Bhāgvatārka Marīchi-mālā* 14/36)

10. What is the harm if a tinge of material conception enters into the worship of Hari?

"According to pure Vaiṣṇava philosophy the male practitioners of devotional service should worship Hari in a separate away from the group of the female practitioners of devotional service, and the female practitioners of devotional service should not allow the male practitioners to come near them. Worship of Hari is fully spiritual activity; a little bit of material conception can spoil everything."

(*Sajjana-toṣaṇī* 4/6)

11. Whose association is most detrimental to devotional service?

"Associating with those who are fond of women is most detrimental to devotional service."

(*Harināma-cintāmani*)

12. What is the atonement for a renunciate who purposely sees a woman?

"If a Vaiṣṇava who is in the renounced order of life deliberately sees a woman, then he should atone by drowning himself in the waters of the Ganges in Triveni in order to become purified in his future lives."

71

The Desire for Material Fame

1. What is the main purpose behind artificially displaying symptoms of ecstatic love such as shedding of tears and standing the bodily hairs on end?

"You have practiced shedding tears, jumping and rolling on the ground. You often fall on the ground unconscious. This is however purely a drama to deceive people. In this way you spread bad association and ultimately get gold and women."

2. What is most difficult to give up even though one is able to give up almost everything?

"Although one can give up almost everything, but it is very difficult to give up *pratiṣṭhāśā* or desire for name and fame."

(*Bhajana-rahasya*, Chapter 2)

3. What is the purpose behind a cheater's imitation of the behavior of the great personalities? Does endeavor for imitation last long?

"Those who are cheaters try to hide their own nature and attain name and fame by imitating the nature of the great personalities. But such imitation does not last long. Their own natures certainly get exposed within a few days."

4. Is verbal humility the proof of giving up desire for fame?

"Until we can give up desire for fame, we cannot claim to be Vaiṣṇavas, verbal humility alone will not do. I often say, 'I am not even qualified to become a servant of the servant of the Vaiṣṇavas. But I think that by hearing this the audience will respect me as a pure Vaiṣṇava.' Alas! the desire for fame does not want to leave us."

(*Sajjana-toṣaṇī* 8/3)

5. In which anartha do the peace-loving people fall into, even after giving up family life?

"The peace loving people give up family life and accept renounced order of life because they think that the householders are more prone to desire for name and fame. But at that stage their desire for name and fame becomes even stronger."

(*Sajjana-toṣaṇī* 8/3)

6. Why is the endeavor for attaining fame most abominable?

"The endeavor for attaining fame is most abominable among all endeavors. Although it is abominable it becomes unavoidable for many people."

(*Sajjana-toṣaṇī* 10/9)

7. What means do the cheaters adopt in order to achieve fame?

"In order to achieve the spiritual master's appreciation, respect from the devotees and ordinary people, praise by holding grand festival, and in order to get their work done, many people take to cheating propensity and artificially display the symptoms of ecstatic love such as dancing, perspiring, shedding tears of love, rolling on the ground and shivering. But actually they do not possess any symptoms of ecstatic love within their hearts."

(*Caitanya-śikṣāmṛta* 5/4)

8. Why is it improper to proudly identify oneself as a 'Vaiṣṇava'

"If I think that 'I am a Vaiṣṇava' then I can not become *amānī* or not expecting any respect for myself. The desire for material fame will then pollute my heart and I will go to hell."

(*Kalyāna Kalpataru*, Song 8)

72

Cheating Propensity

1. What is kutīnātī and what is its result?

"The phrase *kutīnātī* has two words *kutī* and *nātī*. Persons who have a mania for cleanliness always find *ku* or bad in everything. In other words they take bath in a pond and since there is a place for passing stool next to that pond they always think bad about the pond and spend their whole day in discussing about this. They cannot discuss any good subject matters. Mania for cleanliness is an example of *kutīnātī*. Those who are affected by this cannot think of any place in the whole world as pure, cannot think any time as auspicious and cannot accept any persons as a pure Vaiṣṇava. When they see any activity of a pure devotee, which is opposed to the principles of the *smārthas*, they immediately disassociate with such a pure devotee by considering him a nonVaiṣṇava. This is an example of *nātī* or negation. To not accept the remnants of the deity form of the Lord installed by the devotees from lower caste is also an example of *kutīnātī*. As long as kutīnātī is prominent in one, he cannot achieve any happiness from eating any foodstuffs. *Kutīnātī* is one kind of mental disease; as long as one is influenced by this it is very difficult to achieve devotional service to Krishna. For a person who is influenced by *kutīnātī* it is extremely difficult to serve and associate with the Vaiṣṇavas."

(*Sajjana-toṣaṇī* 6/3)

2. Which obstacles in the path of devotional service did Śrīmān Mahāprabhu count among kutīnātī?

"In the course of Śrīman Mahāprabhu's instructions regarding giving up of *kutīnātī*, He has enlisted activities like committing sinful activities, violence towards the living entities and desire for material fame which are detrimental to devotional service as *kutīnātī*."

(*Sajjana-toṣaṇī* 6/3)

3. How did Mahāprabhu explain the word 'kutīnātī'?

"Mahāprabhu explained the meaning of the word '*kutīnātī*' by the words '*ei bhāla ei manda*' or 'this is good and this is bad.'

(*Sajjana-toṣaṇī* 6/7)

4. How do people who are affected by kutīnātī become offenders to the holy names and the Vaiṣṇavas?

"Due to their pride for caste and beauty, people who are affected by *kutīnātī* do not have firm faith in the remnants of the Lord's foodstuffs, in the water that has washed the feet of the Vaiṣṇavas, and in the dust from the feet of the Vaiṣṇavas. Therefore, they are always offenders at the feet of the holy names and the Vaiṣṇavas. It is impossible for such people to chant the holy names of the Lord. There are some people who hate the pure Vaiṣṇavas when those Vaiṣṇavas are in distress. But Mahāprabhu has said, 'O Sanātana! The Vaiṣṇavas do not hate you because you have scabies in your body.'"

(*Sajjana-toṣaṇī* 6/3)

5. What kind of affection is cheating?

"Whenever the affection is applied only to the body it is nothing but cheating."

6. Why are the cheaters eager to worship the demigods and demigoddesses?

"With a desire to receive palatable foodstuffs particularly the goat flesh, many cheaters worship the imaginary demigods and goddesses while displaying symptoms of ecstatic love. In this way they become the example of possessing pseudo-love of God."

(*Caitanya-śikṣāmṛta* 5/4)

7. Are people who simply carry the burden of the scriptures not croocked?

paramārtha-vicārai 'smin bāhya-doṣa-vicārataḥ
na kadācid dhata-śraddhaḥ sāragrāhī janor bhavet

We have discussed the Absolute Truth in this book, so please excuse any grammar or language defects. Swanlike persons should not waste any time in this way. Those who criticize such external defects while studying this book will obstruct its main purpose—accepting the essence of the Absolute Truth—and are not eligible to study this book. Arguments born of childish education are despicable in serious subject matters."

(*Śrī Krishna-saṁhitā* 10/19)

8. What is the definition of pseudo-love of God?

"The pseudo-love of God appears to be like the play of a drama, and it results only in sense gratification. Therefore, O mind, always give up sensual pleasures, which are full of offenses."

(*Kalyāna Kalpataru*, Song 19)

9. When does devotional service become ineffective?

"When devotional service is performed with a desire to attain wealth, followers, and so on, then it is far away from pure devotional service, and as such it is not a limb of devotional service."

(*Jaiva Dharma*, Chapter 20)

73

Violence to the Living Entities

1. What is the way of removing the sinful mentality of committing violence to the animals?

"'*mā himsyāt sarvāni būtāni.* One should not commit any violence to any living entity.' By this statement of the Veda, violence to the animals has been prohibited. Until human beings give up slaughtering animals, enjoying the association with women, drinking wine, and becoming situated in the mode of passion, they may, in order to diminish such propensities, associate with women through marriage, kill animals in the sacrifice, and drink wine in particular circumstances. By doing so when their propensities are diminished, they will gradually become relieved from such activities. This is the purport of the Vedas. To kill animals is not the instruction of the Vedas."

(*Jaiva Dharma*, Chapter 10)

2. What is violence? Which violence must be given up?

"Persons who are attached to sinful activities generally become envious and violent to other living entities. Violence is a heinous sin. It is the duty of everyone to give up violence. Violence to human beings is the gravest sin. The gravity of violence depends on the degree of glories that person possess to whom the violence is caused. Violence to the *brāhmanas*, to one's own relatives, to woman, to the Vaiṣṇavas and to the spiritual master are extremely sinful. Violence to the animal is also not an ordinary sin. Killing of animals by selfish greedy people is the result of the human beings abominable animalistic propensities. Unless human beings refrain from killing animals, their nature will not improve.

(*Caitanya-śikṣāmṛta* 2/5)

3. Why is violence to the living entities detrimental to devo-

tional service?

"If one wants to eat the flesh of another living entity then he has to kill that living entity. Therefore any activity that encourages violence to the living entities is detrimental to devotional service."

(*Sajjana-toṣaṇī* 9/9)

4. Should a devotee of Hari maintain propensity for violence?

"Violence to other living entities is the root of all sinful activities; therefore, it is graver than the sin. Those who are fortunate enough to engage in devotional service to Krishna naturally do not have any propensity for violence."

(*Sajjana-toṣaṇī* 9/8)

5. Which activities are favorable for devotional service, and which activities are unfavorable for devotional service?

"Those activities which aim at benefiting other's are favorable for devotional service and those activities which aim at causing violence to other's are opposed to devotional service."

(*Sajjana-toṣaṇī* 9/8)

6. How many kinds of violence are there? How should one utilize attachment and envy?

"There are three kinds of violence; namely violence to the human beings, violence to the animals, and violence of the demigods. Violence is born from hatred. To become attracted to any object of enjoyment is called attachment, and to become detached from any object of enjoyment is called hatred. Proper attachment has been counted among piety. Improper attachment is called licentiousness. Hatred is just the opposite to the principle of attachment. Proper hatred is also counted among piety. But improper hatred is the root of violence and envy."

(*Caitanya-śikṣāmṛta* 2/5)

7. Is violence to the animals a religious principle for the human being?

"The arrangement for killing animals in the sacrifices that has been prescribed in the Vedic literatures is simply meant for gradually diminishing people's animalistic propensity. Actually violence to the animals is the nature of the animals not the human beings."

(*Caitanya-śikṣāmṛta* 2/5)

8. How many types of cruelty are there and what is their result?

"There are two types of cruelty. They are cruelty against the human beings and cruelty against the animals. Cruelty against man and woman causes great disturbance in the world. As a result, compassion leaves the world and irreligiousness in the form of cruelty become prominent in the world."

(*Caitanya-śikṣāmṛta* 2/5)

9. Is cruelty against the animals be given up?

"There is an arrangement for inflicting cruelty towards the animals in the modern insignificant religious principles. However, this arrangement is bringing bad name to its founder. The heart of a kindhearted person becomes shattered when they see how materialistic people give trouble to the bulls and horses that pull carts. One should give up such cruelty toward the animals."

(*Caitanya-śikṣāmṛta* 2/5)

74
Committing Offences

1. Is it an offense to unknowingly engage in bad association?

"Even if you associate with nondevotees unknowingly you commit an offense against devotional service."

(*Sajjana-toṣaṇī* 5/5)

2. Why offense is most grave?

"If one disregards and disrespects the Vaiṣṇavas he commits an offense. The sinful reactions are nullified simply by undergoing ordinary atonement; but offense is not nullified so easily. The sin is committed by both gross and subtle bodies. An offense degrades one's self-realization. Therefore, those who desire to worship the Supreme Lord must remain careful from committing any offense."

(*Sajjana-toṣaṇī* 5/2)

3. What is an offense?

"When sinful activities are committed against the saintly persons and the Supreme Lord, it is called offense. Offense is most grave and therefore must be given up by all means."

(*Caitanya-śikṣāmṛta* 2/5)

4. Is it possible to attain kṛṣṇa-prema if one commits offenses?

"One who does not attain love of God after worshiping Krishna birth after birth has certainly committed heaps of offenses. For only by chanting Krishna's name without offenses can one attains *kṛṣṇa-prema*."

(*Navadvīpa Mahātmya*, Chapter 1)

5. Who are offenders at the feet of Bhakti Devī?

"Being induced by propensities that are detrimental to devotional service like envy, hatred, pride or desire for fame, those who criticize other's, are offenders at the feet of Bhakti Devī."

(*Sajjana-toṣaṇī* 10/10)

6. How do the madhyama adhikārīs commit offenses against the Vaiṣṇavas?

"The counting of pure Vaiṣṇavas begins with *madhyama adhikārīs* because their goal of life is to serve the pure Vaiṣṇavas. If *madhyama adhikārīs* give up the considerations of Vaiṣṇava and non-Vaiṣṇava, then they commit an offense against the Vaiṣṇavas."

(*Harināma-cintāmani*)

7. What is more offensive than a Vaiṣṇava aparādha?

"For a living entity there is no offense graver than an offense committed against the Vaiṣṇavas."

(*Sajjana-toṣaṇī* 2/6)

8. Where is the test of persons who consider that the Vaiṣṇavas belong to a particular caste?

"Those who become averse to accepting the remnants of a pure Vaiṣṇava by considering him to be belonging to a particular caste are cheaters and as such they cannot be counted as Vaiṣṇavas. Those who are proud of their own caste, accepting remnants during the festivals, is their real test."

(*Prema-pradīpa*, Ray 7)

9. Why is it improper to consider that the Vaiṣṇavas belong to a particular caste?

"If you are really afraid of cheating your own self, then you should not consider that the Vaiṣṇavas belong to a particular caste."

(*Sajjana-toṣaṇī* 9/9)

10. Does criticizing faults of a Vaiṣṇava results in blasphemy of a Vaiṣṇava?

"One who criticizes a Vaiṣṇava's caste, a Vaiṣṇava who unknowingly commits an offense, a Vaiṣṇava's almost destroyed faults, and a Vaiṣṇava's sinful behavior prior to his surrender, is certainly a blasphemer of a

Vaiṣṇava. Such a person will never develop a taste for chanting the Lord's holy names. A pure Vaiṣṇava is he who has taken shelter of pure devotional service. The above-mentioned four types of faults may be occasionally found in him; but there is no possibility of having any other faults in him."

(*Harināma-cintāmani*)

11. What is the easiest way to achieve devotional service?

"One should give up the mentality of considering the Vaiṣṇavas as belonging to a particular caste and then he should take the dust from the feet of a devotee who is fully engaged in chanting the Lord's holy names, and respectfully smear it all over his body."

(*Harināma-cintāmani*)

12. Is it a sevāparādha to offer obeisance to anyone inside the temple?

"One should not offer obeisance to any one other than the Supreme Lord inside the temple. However one must offer obeisances to one's spiritual master inside the temple."

(*Harināma-cintāmani*)

13. What is the definition of a Krishna conscious family?

"In a Krishna conscious family, there is no cheating. There is only simplicity. Therefore there is no question of any offense."

(*Jaiva Dharma*, Chapter 7)

14. To whom should a pious householder give alms?

"By giving alms to the illegitimate professional beggars the householders commit an offense. As a result they gradually fall down. During the revolution of the society, this sinful practice must be checked. Then the condition of the pious householder will improve, the distress of the beggars will be destroyed and the general advancement of the society will take place. '*Apātre dīyate dānaṁ tat dānaṁ tāmasaṁ viduḥ.* 'giving charity to an unqualified person is an act in the mode of ignorance.' Following this statement of the Supreme Lord one should give charity only to the qualified candidates."

(*Sajjana-toṣaṇī* 6/3)

15. Is it not an offense to hear or sing publicly about the conjugal pastimes of Śrī Rādhā Krishna?

"To sing and hear about Śrī Rādhā Krishna's conjugal pastimes are the principal and eternal mode of worship of the Lord. However, to sing about these pastimes before ordinary people is improper and offensive. '*āpana bhajana kathā nā kahibe yath tathā* 'one should not disclose one's own process of devotional service to anyone.' If one is to follow this instruction of the *ācārya* then it becomes an offense to hear the recitation of Krishna's conjugal pastimes from the mouths of the professional singers."

(*Sajjana-toṣaṇī* 6/2)

16. Is it not an offense to blaspheme a Vaiṣṇava by finding in him some behaviors opposed to the scriptures?

"If there happens to be some uncivilized activities in a Vaiṣṇava according to his karma, it is an offense to consider such activities as uncivilized. Even though there might be some particular improper conducts in a Vaiṣṇava that are opposed to the *smṛti* literature, still he should be consider saintly otherwise one will commit an offense against the chanting of the holy names."

(*Sajjana-toṣaṇī* 6/7)

17. Who are responsible for committing offenses against the service of the Lord?

"Offenses against the Lord's service are committed in regard to the service of the Lord's deity form. There are some offenses to be avoided by those who worship the deities. There are some offenses to be avoided by those who install the deities. There are some offenses to be avoided by those who go to see the deity form of the Lord. And there are some offenses to be avoided by all."

(*Harināma-cintāmani*)

18. What are the thirty-two offenses against the service to the Lord?

"1. One should not enter the temple of the Deity in a car or palanquin or with shoes on the feet.

2. One should not fail to observe the various festivals for the pleasure of the Supreme Personality of Godhead, such as Janmāṣṭamī and Ratha-yātrā.

3. One should not avoid bowing down before the Deity.

4. One should not enter the temple to worship the Lord without having washed one's hands and feet after eating.

5. One should not enter the temple in a contaminated state.

6. One should not bow down on one hand.

7. One should not circumambulate in front of Śrī Krishna.

8. One should not spread his legs before the Deity.

9. One should not sit before the Deity holding the ankles, elbows or knees with one's hands.

10. One should not lie down before the Deity of Krishna.

11. One should not accept *prasāda* before the Deity.

12. One should never speak a lie before the Deity.

13. One should not talk very loudly before the Deity.

14. One should not talk with other's before the Deity.

15. One should not cry or howl before the Deity.

16. One should not quarrel or fight before the Deity.

17. One should not chastise anyone before the Deity.

18. One should not be charitable to beggars before the Deity.

19. One should not speak very harshly to other's before the Deity.

20. One should not wear a fur blanket before the Deity.

21. One should not eulogize or praise anyone else before the Deity.

22. One should not speak any ill names before the Deity.

23. One should not pass air before the Deity.

24. One should not fail to worship the Deity according to one's means.

25. One should not eat anything, which is not offered first to Krishna.

26. One should not fail to offer fresh fruit and grains to Krishna, according to the season.

27. After food has been cooked, no one should be offered any foodstuff unless it is first offered to the Deity.

28. One should not sit with his back toward the Deity.

29. One should not offer obeisances silently to the spiritual master, or in other words, one should recite aloud the prayers to the spiritual master while offering obeisances.

(30) One should not fail to offer some praise in the presence of the spiritual master.

(31) One should not praise himself before the spiritual master.

(32) One should not deride the demigods before the Deity.

These *sevāparādhas* have been described in the *Purānas*."

(*Harināma-cintāmani*)

19. What are the different kinds of offenses and what are their symptoms?

"Although offenses are of many kinds, they are mainly divided into three categories; *vaiṣnavāparādha, sevāparādha* and *nāmāparādha*. In the *Skanda Purāṇa* the six *vaiṣnavāparādhas* are listed as follows; 'to kill a Vaiṣṇava, to blaspheme a Vaiṣṇava, to hate a Vaiṣṇava, to not offer respect to a Vaiṣṇava, to display anger to a Vaiṣṇava and to not feel happy on seeing a Vaiṣṇava. By committing these offenses one certainly falls down. No practitioner of devotional service should commit these offenses. The *sevāparādhas* are considered in regard to the deity worship. There are ten types of *nāmāparādhas*."

(*Sajjana-toṣaṇī* 11/7)

20. Why professional recitation of Śrīmad-Bhāgavatam is rejected?

"Give up this business (of professional recitation) immediately. You are supposed to be greedy for drinking the mellows of ecstatic love. So do not commit any offense against the mellows of ecstatic love. According to *Taittiriya Upaniṣad* 2/7 '*raso vai saḥ*' Krishna is nondifferent from the mellows of ecstatic love. There are many types of professions described in the *śāstras* for maintaining one's livelihood. You should take up those. Do not earn money by reciting *Śrīmad-Bhāgavatam* to ordinary people. If you find qualified audience then recite *Śrīmad-Bhāgavatam* with great ecstasy without accepting any salary or fee."

(*Jaiva Dharma*, Chapter 28)

21. Are the sellers of harināma not offenders?

"There are many other ways of earning one's livelihood, and one should maintain his life by following them. To earn money by selling *harināma* and to consider this money as a means of one's livelihood is extremely improper and opposed to devotional service. It is impossible for both who sell *harināma* and who purchase it to attain love of God which is the fruits of chanting *harināma*. In fact by doing so, such people simply accumulate sin. Money is not the price for *harināma*. Faith is the only price for *harināma*. Therefore, it is the duty of everyone to faithfully chant and hear the holy names of Hari."

(*Sajjana-toṣaṇī* 8/8)

22. What are the symptoms, activities and fate of those who commit offense against the abode of the Lord?

"With a desire to fulfill their own self-interest, and due to envy, some people are creating obstacles in the path of improving the standard of Śrī Māyāpura. On seeing the prosperity of the *dhāma* these people have become hopeless nowadays. Being controlled by intense envy a few of them have even begun to publish articles against the *dhāma* in some small magazines. There is no doubt that Mahāprabhu will soon destroy them. The amazing factor is that from a long time some people has been engaged in accumulating money and enjoying the association of women while hiding the actual glories of Śrī Māyāpura. As soon as the glories of Māyāpura began to manifest, these disciples of Kali began to conceal the glories of Māyāpura in various forms and tactics. But both the Supreme Lord and the eternal truth are unconquerable. For the last two years, these disciples of Kali have been very embarrassed. The society of devotees no longer trusts them. Therefore, they are making fools of themselves. What a game plan of Kali! They are trying to prove no-moon as full-moon and get away with it. But suddenly people have understood their game plan and they are laughing at them. Now everyone has understood that Śrīdhāma Māyāpura is the crest jewel of the entire Navadvīpa."

(*Sajjana-toṣaṇī* 8/1)

75

Blaspheming the Vaiṣṇavas

1. What should one do if one happens to hear the blasphemy of a pure Vaiṣṇava? How should one deal with a so-called guru who indulges in blasphemy of the Vaiṣṇavas?

"Devotees who are engaged in regulative devotional service should neither approve nor support the blasphemy of the Supreme Lord or the devotees. If such blasphemy is taking place in an assembly, then if one is able, one should immediately protest. If protest does not yield any result, then one should remain like a deaf and not pay any attention to such blasphemy. If one is unable to do even that, then he should immediately leave that place. If one hears blasphemy of the Vaiṣṇavas even from the mouth of his spiritual master then one should humbly caution him. If such a spiritual master is still extremely envious to the Vaiṣṇavas, then one should give him up and take initiation from a qualified spiritual master."

(*Caitanya-śikṣāmṛta* 3-4)

2. What is the disadvantage of hearing blasphemy of the Vaiṣṇavas?

"A practitioner of devotional service should never hear blasphemy of Lord Krishna and the blasphemy of the Vaiṣṇavas. Wherever such activities are taking place he should leave that place. One who is weak-hearted hears blasphemy of Krishna and the Vaiṣṇavas for the sake of other's, and thus gradually falls from the platform of devotional service."

(*Sajjana-toṣaṇī* 11/6)

3. Why blasphemy of the devotees is the most grave among all offenses?

"It is a great offense to blaspheme a devotee who has taken shelter of the Lord's holy names and who has given up the process of karma,

Dharma, *jñāna* and yoga. Because the holy names of Harī cannot tolerate the blasphemy of those who are spreading the glories of the holy names all over the world. If one gives up blaspheming the devotees who are engaged in chanting the holy names and chants the holy names in their association by considering them as 'the topmost devotees' then he will soon attain the mercy of the holy names."

(*Jaiva Dharma*, Chapter 24)

4. What is the result of blasphemy of the Vaiṣṇavas?

"One should resolve to respect the Vaiṣṇavas and give up the association of the non-Vaiṣṇavas. The glories of the holy name will never manifest in the hearts of those who blaspheme the Vaiṣṇava devotees."

(*Sajjana-toṣaṇī* 5/5)

5. What are the six types of Vaiṣṇava aparādha and what the result?

"A foolish person who blasphemes a pure devotee goes to hell along with his forefathers. Any person who kills a Vaiṣṇava, who blasphemes a Vaiṣṇava, who hates a Vaiṣṇava, who does not offer obeisances to a Vaiṣṇava when he meets one, and who feels unhappy on seeing Vaiṣṇava certainly goes to hell."

(*Sajjana-toṣaṇī* 5/2)

6. What is the result of hearing blasphemy of the Vaiṣṇavas?

"A person, who does not immediately leave that place where the Supreme Lord or the Vaiṣṇavas are being criticized, loses all his piety and degrades himself."

(*Sajjana-toṣaṇī* 5/2)

7. Can a pure Vaiṣṇava become the object of blasphemy?

"If one is found to be inclined towards sinful activities, then he cannot be counted amongst the Vaiṣṇavas. Even the neophyte Vaiṣṇavas has no taste for sin or piety. A pure Vaiṣṇava is faultless, therefore, he is above blasphemy. One who blasphemes such a Vaiṣṇava simply attributes false accusation on himself."

(*Sajjana-toṣaṇī* 5/2)

8. Which topics do the envious miscreants discuss, in the course of their blasphemy of the Vaiṣṇava?

"There are three topics with which the envious sinful people can criticize. The faults of a devotee before the awakening of his Krishna consciousness becomes the subject matter for their discussion. As soon as devotional service to the Lord is awakened, all his faults are eradicated. The process of eradication takes some time. During this period, those envious miscreants criticize the devotee for his left over sins. The third subject of their discussion is that, although a pure Vaiṣṇava has no desire for committing any sin yet sometimes by chance, he may commit a sin. However, such a fault does not last long in a Vaiṣṇava. Nevertheless the envious sinful people criticize such a Vaiṣṇava and fall into the pit of formidable Vaiṣnava *aparādha*."

(*Sajjana-toṣaṇī* 5/2)

9. How should one become careful while discussing the characteristics of a Vaiṣṇava?

"One should never discuss about the faults of a Vaiṣṇava prior to his awakening of Krishna consciousness unless it is done with a good purpose. One should never blaspheme a Vaiṣṇava by discussing his left over faults after awakening of his Krishna consciousness."

(*Sajjana-toṣaṇī* 5/3)

10. Should the old, suddenly committed or almost destroyed faults of a Vaiṣṇava be discussed without a good purpose?

"The almost natural sinful activities that accompany a person from before he awakens his Krishna consciousness gradually diminish by the strength of devotional service and soon get exhausted. By discussing those faults of a Vaiṣṇava without a good purpose, one commits the offense of blasphemy of the Vaiṣṇavas. In spite of seeing some accidental fault one should not blaspheme a Vaiṣṇava."

(*Sajjana-toṣaṇī* 5/5)

11. By criticizing which faults of a Vaiṣṇava, does one commit Vaiṣnava aparādha?

"By criticizing a Vaiṣṇava's accidentally committed sinful activities, without a good intention, one commits the offense of blaspheming a Vaiṣṇava. The main point is that if one attributes false accusations on a Vaiṣṇava and criticize his above mentioned three faults then such a person commits an offense against the chanting of the holy names. As a result pure name of God does not manifest in his heart. Unless the pure name of God manifests in one's heart one cannot become a Vaiṣṇava."

(*Sajjana-toṣaṇī* 5/5)

12. Is criticizing other's without good purpose desirable?

"Discussing about other's faults with a good purpose has not been condemned in the *śāstras*. There are three kinds of good purposes; if by discussing about a person's faults that person is benefited in anyway, then such a discussion is auspicious. If discussing a person's sinful activities brings about auspiciousness to the world, then it is counted as a pious activity."

(*Sajjana-toṣaṇī* 5/5)

13. Is it an offense against the Vaiṣṇavas to criticize the characteristics of the nondevotees in order to reveal the glories of the Vaiṣṇavas?

"When a spiritual master is requested by his disciple to ascertain a Vaiṣṇava, the spiritual master, with a desire to benefit his disciple and the world, ascertains the Vaiṣṇava by declaring the sinful people as non-Vaiṣṇavas. To give up the association of the sinful hypocrites with a desire to take shelter at the feet of Vaiṣṇavas does not result in blasphemy of the Vaiṣṇavas or offending the Vaiṣṇavas."

(*Sajjana-toṣaṇī* 5/5)

76

Mental Speculation

1. Why is the meditation of the conditional souls mental speculation?

"Meditation is the function of the mind. Until the mind is purified and spiritualized meditation can never become spiritual."

(*Jaiva Dharma*, Chapter 4)

2. What is the conception of the mental speculators regarding the soul, the material world and liberation?

"Some people guess that the soul was first born in this gross world in the form of a human being. The Supreme Lord has created this material world with the desire that the living entities would gradually advance by following religious principles. Some people say that this material world will become a happy place, like heaven, through human intelligence. Yet, there are other's who have decided that at the end of the body, they will achieve liberation in the form of *nirvāṇa*. All these conclusions are as useless as blind people ascertaining the shape of an elephant. Swanlike people do not enter into this type of useless argument, because no one can come to the proper conclusion by human intelligence."

(Introduction of *Krishna-saṁhitā*)

3. Is mundane selflessness not a figment of imagination?

"The existence of selflessness is impossible. Von Halbach wrote a book called 'the system of nature' in 1770. In fact, in the book, he has specifically said, 'there is no selflessness in the material world at all; we call the art of becoming happy by other's happiness religion.' We also find that the word selflessness is as useless as the flower in the sky. To achieve happiness without any difficulty is the goal of selflessness. People think that if other's respect them as selfless persons then they will get their job done easily. Are motherly affection, brotherly affection, friendly affection and love between man and woman selfless? If there were no personal happiness in these acts, no one would have done those. Some people even give up their lives, in order to attain personal happiness."

(*Tattva Viveka* 1/9-12)

4. Is it reasonable to accept a separate existence of the Satan?

"Instead of imagining a strange matter like 'Satan' one should carefully try to understand the science of the nescience."

(*Jaiva Dharma*, Chapter 11)

77

Impersonal Philosophy

1. Who are Māyāvādīs?

"Those who accept all spiritual objects as illusion, consider Brahman as beyond illusion, consider the supreme controller as affected by illusion, and consider the bodies of all the Lord's incarnations as illusion. They say that the functions of Māyā are present in the constitution of the living entities. In other words the false egos of the living entities are created by Māyā. There ore when the living entities are liberated there is no such state for them as pure living entities. They also teach that after liberation the living entities become one with Brahman."

(Commentary on *Caitanya Caritāmṛta* Ādi 7/29)

2. Is impersonalism the universal opinion of the Vedas? Where is the birthplace of impersonalism?

"The philosophy called 'impersonalism' has been current since a long time. This is a partial opinion of the Vedas. Although many scholars have preached the philosophy of impersonalism outside India, there is no doubt that this philosophy was spread throughout the world from India. A few scholars came to India with Alexander and carefully learnt this philosophy. These scholars then partially preached about this philosophy in their respective books and respective countries."

(*Tattva-sutra* 30)

3. Why are Māyāvādīs more condemned than the Buddhists?

"Since Lord Buddha opposed Vedic injunction, Vedic Aryans criticized him as an atheist. But, Māyāvādīs propagation of atheism under the shelter of the Vedas is more dangerous than Buddhism because an enemy in the guise of a friend is more dangerous than an enemy."

(Commentary on *Caitanya Caritāmṛta* Madhya 6/168)

4. Are the commentaries of the Māyāvādīs not opposed to the codes of Vyāsadeva?

"Factually, the devotional service of the Lord is described in the *Vedānta-sūtra*, but the Māyāvādī philosophers prepared a commentary known as *Śārīraka-bhāṣya*, in which the transcendental form of the Lord is denied. The Māyāvādī philosophers think that the living entity is identical with the Supreme Soul, Brahman. Their commentaries on the *Vedānta-sūtra* are completely opposed to the principle of devotional service."

(Commentary on *Caitanya Caritāmṛta* Madhya 6/169)

5. Can the existence of the living entities be illusory?

"The living entities are eternally spiritual; they are not subjected to any bondage or distress. They suffer miseries due to their misconception of identifying the body as the self. Considering the rope as snake and oyster as silver are the two Vedic examples, Māyāvādīs mistakenly consider the very existence of the living entities as illusory. When a living entity, by the mercy of a bona fide spiritual master, understands that these two examples have not been said in regard to the existence of the living entities rather they have been said in regard to considering the gross and subtle bodies as self, then he actually finds the real path."

(*Caitanya-śikṣāmṛta* 1/6)

6. How are the Māyāvādīs offenders at the feet of Krishna?

"A Māyāvādī is naturally an offender to Krishna, Because he says that the form of Krishna, the name of Krishna, and the pastimes of Krishna are all material. The word 'material' means illusory or product of matter. According to the opinion of the Māyāvādīs, the Absolute Truth is formless and without variegatedness. To get the work done the Absolute Truth takes shelter of illusion and accepts various material forms like Rāma or Krishna. The name of the Absolute Truth is Brahman or Paramātmā or Caitanya, the consciousness forms like Rāma or Krishna are products of matter, the names like Rāma or Krishna are material sound vibration and the pastimes of Rāma and Krishna are also mundane. But the difference between the living entities and Rāma or Krishna is that the living entities are forced to accept material bodies as a result of their Karma. But Caitanya or consciousness accepts a material body out of His own sweet will to fulfill His mission in this world and then gives up His material body again out of His own sweet will. Therefore the names, forms, and pastimes of Rāma or Krishna are certainly material. As long as a practitioner does not attain knowledge, he should worship personalities like Rāma or Krishna. After attaining knowledge he no longer needs to chant or meditate on material names and forms of Rāma, Krishna, etc, rather he should only chant Brahman, Paramātmā or Caitanya. Therefore, the Māyāvādīs consider the forms of Rāma and Krishna to be more abominable than the Absolute Truth. That is why the Māyāvādīs are the greatest offenders at the feet of Krishna."

(*Sajjana-toṣaṇī* 5/12)

7. Is Māyāvādī's glorification of Krishna an offense against the chanting of the holy names?

"Māyāvādī's glorification to Krishna in the course of their *sādhana* is also an offense. Pure devotees should not approve their activities like chanting Krishna's names because in their association one will simply commit *nāmāparādha*. Even though Māyāvādīs display various symptoms of ecstatic love such as shedding of tears or standing of hair on end, these symptoms are not genuine. These are simply a shadow of reflection of transformation of ecstatic love. Hence these are offenses."

8. Why Māyāvādī commentaries and philosophy should not be heard by the devotee?

"Even though someone firmly fixed in devotion to Krishna's service might not be deviated by hearing the Māyāvāda *bhāṣya*, that *bhāṣya* is nevertheless full of impersonal words and ideas — such as Brahman— which represent knowledge but which are impersonal. The Māyāvādīs say that the world created by Māyā is false and that actually there is no living entity but only one spiritual effulgence. They further say that God is imaginary, that people think of God only because of ignorance, and that when the Supreme Absolute Truth is befooled by the external energy, Māyā, He becomes a *jīva*, or living entity. Upon hearing all these nonsensical ideas from the nondevotee, a devotee is greatly afflicted, as if his heart and soul were broken.

(Commentary on *Caitanya Caritāmṛta* Antya 2/98-99)

9. Where is the origin of godlessness and impersonalism?

"Nescience results in adoration of matter, and too much knowledge results in atheism and monism. Adoration of matter has two forms; positive adoration is to accept material characteristics as knowledge of the Supreme Lord, and negative adoration is to accept material characteristics as the Supreme. Those who engage in positive adoration accept and worship a material image as the Supreme. Those who engage in negative worship accept the negative features of material characteristics as Brahman. Such people conclude that the Supreme is impersonal, without form, without activity, and without senses."

(*Śrī Krishna-saṁhitā* Conclusion)

10. What is the result of dry argument and too much knowledge?

"Therefore acceptance of the gross form of the Supreme as well as acceptance of the impersonal form are both products of nescience and are always contradictory. When reasoning overcomes knowledge and becomes established as argument, then one does not accept the soul as eternal. In this situation the philosophy of atheism is born. When knowledge comes under the subordination of reasoning and gives up its nature, then one aspires for merging. This aspiration is born from too much knowledge and does not benefit the living entity."

(*Śrī Krishna-saṁhitā* Conclusion)

11. Is the philosophy of theosophy another form of impersonalism?

"The philosophy of theosophy preached in the countries like America is also impersonalism. Whatever the proud scholars preach, the less intelligent people naturally accept. In our country, many proud scholars like Dattātraya, Astāvakra, and Sankara, who were fond of arguments, preached this philosophy from time to time in different shapes. Nowadays, all philosophies other than Vaiṣṇava philosophy are subordinate to that philosophy."

(*Caitanya-śikṣāmṛta* 5/3)

12. Are atheism and merging into the existence of Brahman unhealthy symptoms of consciousness?

"After becoming civilized, when a living entity cultivates various knowledge, then he, through his false arguments, covers his faith up to some extent and thereby either accepts atheism or merging into the existence of Brahman. It is to be understood that this clumsy faith is the symptom of an undeveloped weak consciousness."

(*Caitanya-śikṣāmṛta* 1/1)

13. Can too much knowledge or the philosophy of nondifference, equate proper reasoning?

"Even by proper reasoning, too much knowledge cannot be beneficial. We will now give four considerations in this regard:

1. If merging with the Supreme Brahman were the living entities' ultimate goal, then we would have to imagine that the Lord out of cruelty, has created the living entities. If we accept Māyā as the sole creator in order to verify Brahman as faultless, then we are bound to accept an independent truth that is separate from Brahman.

2. When a soul merges with Brahman, neither is benefited.

3. In the eternal pastimes of the Absolute Truth, there is no need for the souls to merge in Brahman.

4. If one does not fully accept the quality of variegatedness, which is the manifestation of the Lord's energies, then there is no possibility of existence, knowledge, or happiness, and as a result, the Supreme Brahman is considered impersonal and without basis. One may even develop doubts about the existence of Brahman. But, if one accepts the quality of variegatedness as eternal, then the soul cannot merge with Brahman.

(*Śrī Krishna-saṁhitā* Conclusion)

78

Idol Worship

1. Is it possible to give up deity worship in the course of worshiping the Supreme Lord?

"It is a fact that the Supreme Lord has no material form; but His *Sat-cid-ānanda*

Spiritual form is certainly accepted. The full manifestation of the Supreme Lord is not possible in a conditioned soul, therefore whatever form of the Supreme Lord is meditated upon by the human beings, will certainly be incomplete and thus, idol worshiping. Idolatry can be easily rejected by words but in the process of worshiping the Supreme Lord, it is inevitable."

(*Tattva-sutra* 35)

2. Has the spiritual form of God been denied in the Muslim literatures?

"Śrī Gaurāṅga had instructed Chānd Kāzi that only material form of God has been denied in the Koran; pure spiritual form, however, has not been denied. According to his own qualification, the prophet has seen that transcendental blissful form. Other forms of transcendental mellows of the Supreme Lord were covered."

(*Jaiva Dharma*, Chapter 6)

3. Who are the first class idol worshipers?

"Uncivilized tribes, the worshipers of fire god, Jove and people of Greece who worship planets like Saturn are the frontline idol worshipers."

(*Caitanya-śikṣāmṛta* 5/3)

4. Who are the second-class idol worshipers?

"Those who, after scrutinizingly studying material knowledge, accept with reasoning an impersonal image opposed to all material qualities as 'God'; they are the second class of idol worshipers."
(*Caitanya-śikṣāmṛta* 5/3)

5. Who are the third-class of idol worshipers?

"Those whose ultimate goal is to merge into the existence of the Lord and who imagine that the worship of the qualitative forms of Lord Viṣṇu, Śiva, Durgā, Ganeśa and Surya is the process to achieve that goal are counted amongst the third-class idol worshipers. They do not accept the eternal form of God. So they worship some imaginary form of God. Nowadays these people are known as 'five god worshipers'."
(*Caitanya-śikṣāmṛta* 5/3)

6. Who are the forth-class of idol worshipers?

"The yogis who meditate on the concocted form of Viṣṇu are the fourth-class of idol worshipers."
(*Caitanya-śikṣāmṛta* 5/3)

7. Who are the fifth-class of idol worshipers?

"Those who worship living entities as"God" are the fifth-class of idol worshipers."
(*Caitanya-śikṣāmṛta* 5/3)

8. What is the difference between worshiping the spiritual form of the Supreme Lord and idol worship?

"There is a great difference between serving the Deity of the Lord and worshiping idols. Deity worship is an indicator of the Absolute Truth, because by this process one attains the Absolute Truth. Idol worship, however, means to accept a material form or formlessness as the Absolute Truth, in other words, to accept a material form as the Supreme Lord."
(*Śrī Krishna-saṁhitā* 6/12)

79

The Philosophy of Synthesis

1. Is a person who disregards the path of the mahājanas not a cheater?

"You have concluded that the authorized *sampradāyas* are faulty and so you have become very eager to purify yourself. You did not accept *tilaka* and *tulasī* beads. You gave up the trouble of taking initiation and invented your own new system of religion.

(*Kalyāna Kalpataru*, Song 67

2. What do the harmonizers gossip? How were the 'modern day Gaurāngas' chastised?

"The same person who was a follower of Vaiṣṇavism four hundred years ago has now changed his mind and preached a new philosophy which harmonizes all religious systems. They thought this would be a universal religion. They further said that if one follows a particular type of religion one could not pursue universal love. By merging all religious systems, universal love for all living entities can be awakened. Last year Śrīman Mahāprabhu has punished them completely. Some of them were removed all together from this planet. And the rest engaged in quarreling among themselves and finally took up their respective professions. Only one or two are still trying to pose as Gaurāṅga, but being unable to get any attention from the civilized society they are finally taking shelter of the cobblers. What a pastime of Mahāprabhu! However Kali raises his head, Mahāprabhu smashes all his attempts by hitting a stick on his head."

(*Sajjana-toṣaṇī* 8/1)

3. Who are the real paramahaṁsas and what are their behaviors?

"Those who have divine eyes consider them equipoised yogis, and those who are less-intelligent, or third-grade people, consider them as attached to material enjoyment. Some people may occasionally even consider them averse to the Lord. A swanlike person can identify another swanlike brother who possesses all the appropriate symptoms, whether he is from the same country or not. Although their dress, language, worship, Deity, and behavior may appear different, they should freely address each other as brother. These types of people are called paramahaṁsas, and *Śrīmad-Bhāgavatam* is the scripture that is meant for such paramahaṁsas."

(*Śrī Krishna-saṁhitā*, Introduction)

4. Why are there different behavior and different sādhanas?

"According to one's nature one accepts his worshipable Lord, suitable *śāstras* and like-minded associates. According to the logic '*samaśilā bhajanati vai*' or 'one associates with like-minded persons' various worshipable Lord's, various *sādhana*s, various associates and various behavior naturally come into existence in the world. The worshipable lord is one without a second."

(*Sajjana-toṣaṇī* 11/3)

5. Is neutrality a principle of devotional service? Can it help manifest one's faith in the Absolute Truth?

"Without developing faith in the eternal Absolute Truth a living entity can never achieve any benefit. If everything is good in this world then what is bad? If, whatever one does is good, then where is the distinction between good and bad? Then puffed rice and sugar candy becomes one and the same. If there is no need for a living entity to perform any *sādhana*, then what is the difference between a debauchee who is attached to the prostitutes, and a paramahaṁsa who is completely free from such desires? Then truth and illusion becomes one. Therefore, faith in the Absolute Truth is supremely beneficial whereas attachment for temporary object is abominable. Maintaining neutrality for everything cannot be called good. Rather one should take side of the good and reject the neutrality."

(*Sajjana-toṣaṇī* 2/6)

80

Civilization

1. What is the meaning of the word 'sabhyatā' or civilization?

The meaning of the word *sabhyatā* is to become qualified to sit in a *sabhā* or an assembly. That is plain gentlemanliness.

(*Jaiva Dharma*, Chapter 9)

2. What is the definition of modern civilization?

"The process for covering internal evil is the definition of modern civilization."

(*Jaiva Dharma*, Chapter 9)

3. How do the cunning people protect their civilization?

"The prestige of cunning people's civilization is protected by their useless arguments and physical strength."

(*Jaiva Dharma*, Chapter 9)

4. Is it proper to lose the treasury of devotional service for the sake of insignificant civilization?

"I used to laugh within my mind seeing the signs of devotional service, as I thought them to be utterly madness. What happened to that civilization which I considered as the topmost and in trying to praise that civilization, I lost the most valuable touchstone.

(*Kalyāna Kalpataru*, Song 2)

5. Is the civilization of Kali yuga not a sinful act?

"If civilization means to simply wear attractive clothes, then the prostitutes are more civilized than you. Wine and flesh are naturally impure; therefore, civilization that grows by eating such things is certainly sinful. The modern state of civilization is certainly the civilization of the age of Kali."

(*Jaiva Dharma*, Chapter 9)

81

Politics

1. Is present administration not favorable to the worship of Hari?

"May our present empress Śrīmati Queen Victoria continue to freely rule over India without any anxiety. May we continue to relish and preach the pure Vaiṣṇava religion without any anxiety under her administration."

(*Sajjana-toṣaṇī* 4/1)

2. How can the friendship between the Englishmen and Indians remain intact?

"Friendship between the Englishmen and the Indians is natural. The English people are Āryans and the Indians are also Āryans, therefore relationship between them is that of brother. Where is that natural brotherly affection? Because the Englishmen have become our ruler, why should the natural propensity be lost? In relationship, the Indians are elder brothers and the Englishmen are younger brothers. When the younger brother becomes matured and competent and takes the responsibility of the family, the elder brother at that time is old and therefore weak. Therefore, he lovingly accepts the subordination of his younger brother. What is wrong with this? When we were young, we also displayed our authority over other castes. Now, due to old age, we are incapable. Therefore, what could be more pleasing than spending our lives under the care our younger brothers? What could be more fortunate than blessing our younger brothers and relishing the nectar from the ever-blissful lotus feet of Hari constantly? The younger brothers will always protect us from all kinds of disturbances. We no longer have to undergo miseries in the battlefield. We will sit at home and chant the holy names of Hari. If, while working hard for the family, the younger brothers sometimes become dissatisfied and display anger, then we, as elder brothers, will tolerate it and make them happy by our sweet words and affectionate dealings. In this way, we will command their respect. We will not fail to commit monetary help to the best of our ability to our younger brothers if they ever require such help in the course of fulfilling their familial duties. We will follow the same procedure for showing affection a well-to-do pious householder would show to his younger brother. We will never display any opposition. O my national brothers! This is my advice to you. Please act in this way."

(*Sajjana-toṣaṇī* 2/5)

3. Is it possible to attain peace and prosperity in human life if there is enmity between the Indians and the Englishmen?

"I appeal to both the Englishmen, who are endowed with good qualities and power and my fellow Indians. O brothers! Give up enmity; there is no profit form enmity. If you give up aversion then my well-known Shānti devī or the goddess of peace will award you happiness. Everyone is hankering after happiness; obtain happiness in the shelter of goddess of peace. Originally, all human beings are brothers. The Supreme Personality of Godhead does not become pleased by your mutual aversion to each other. You all are spirit souls. We all are always afflicted by various miseries, accidents, and scarcities. If we maintain universal brotherhood we can decrease our miseries up to some extent. But mutual co-operation, fulfillment of the scarcities and by joint effort natural calamities can be taken care of. If we oppose each other in such a situation then there is no hope for mitigating the miseries. The happiness leaves the world forever. Therefore O brothers! Give up envy, hatred and false ego and love each other."

(*Sajjana-toṣaṇī* 2/5)

4. Can the former glory of the Indians be protected, even if they refrain from war?

"Even though, due to old age, the Indians retired from activities like war they nevertheless lived happily by acting like instructors of other castes."

(*Caitanya-śikṣāmṛta* 2/3)

5. What kind of war is approved by the religious scriptures?

All wars to expand one's Kingdom are unlawful and harmful to the world. No war other than extremely legitimate war has been recommended in the religious scriptures."

(*Sajjana-toṣaṇī* 2/5)

82

Sociology

1. Why is the system of varnāśrama appreciated?

"In order to maintain social order, the Āryans divided society into four castes and four social orders. If the social system is protected, then good association and discussion nourish people's spiritual lives. Therefore, the *varṇāśrama* system should be accepted in all respects. By this arrangement, there is a possibility of gradually attaining love for Krishna. The main purpose for this arrangement is the cultivation of spiritual life, or love for Krishna."

(*Śrī Krishna-saṁhitā*, Chapter 5/9)

2. Is there a possibility of any auspiciousness if a conditioned soul transgresses the principles of varṇāśrama?

"Those who have sufficiently studied sociology certainly conclude that the system of *varṇāśrama* is the topmost social system. If one is situated in the principle of *varṇāśrama*, then his nature cannot be lost. Rather one can receive huge opportunity and advantage to cultivate Krishna consciousness. *Varṇāśrama dharma* is the society of the Vaiṣṇavas in their conditional stage."

(*Sajjana-toṣaṇī* 2/7)

3. Can there be any civilized society without the principles of varṇāśrama?

"Mercantile communities of Europe love to do business and they prosper from business. Those whose nature is like that of the *kṣatriyas*, pickup the military lines or activities of the army, and those whose nature is like that of *sudras* engage in ordinary services. Actually, unless some extent of *varṇāśrama dharma* is followed, a society cannot run. Superior or inferior status and nature is tested in the act of marriage based on *varṇāśrama* principles. Even though the principles of *varṇāśrama dharma* have been established up to some extent in the societies of Europe, they have not taken full shape scientifically."

(*Caitanya-śikṣāmṛta* 2/3)

4. What kind of sociology is followed before the excellent improvement of the varṇāśrama system?

"As until the ships were invented through scientific process, voyages used to be conducted by simple boats made through unscientific process. In the same way, until the system of *varṇāśrama* was fully implemented in a country, an unscientific state of previous existence continued to run the society. This unscientific state of previous existence has become the director of the societies in Europe and everywhere except India.

(*Caitanya-śikṣāmṛta* 2/3)

5. What is the difference between a Vaiṣṇava society and a non-Vaiṣṇava society?

"The difference between a Vaiṣṇava society and a non-Vaiṣṇava society is that the ultimate goal of the Vaiṣṇava society is love of God and the goal of the non-Vaiṣṇava society is selfish lust. Those who are situated in the ordinary society consider the nourishment of the body, sense gratification, following worldly moralities, discovering object that enhance their sense gratification by cultivating material knowledge, and the activities of temporarily stopping the material miseries, and the societies ultimate goal. Among them, some praise the happiness after death, some praise the heavenly enjoyment, and some praise the state of merging into the existence of the Lord. The living entities who are situated in the Vaiṣṇava society utilize nourishment of the body, sense gratification, following worldly moralities, science, and rejection of material happiness as means to favorably cultivate Krishna consciousness. The shape of both Vaiṣṇava society and non-Vaiṣṇava society is one, but its characteristics are different."

(*Sajjana-toṣaṇī* 2/7)

6. By following which rules, can the varṇāśrama system of India be revived?

"In order to revive the principles of *varṇāśrama* the following few rules have to be reintroduced:

1. No one's caste should be ascertained simply by birth.

2. A person's caste should be determined according to the nature he develops in the association of the children and by the accumulation of knowledge.

3. At the time of ascertaining a person's caste one should, along with that person's nature and taste, consider the caste of his parents.

4. After a person become matured, in other words, when he becomes fifteen years old, the family priest, the landlord, the parents, and a few selfless educated people of the village should sit together and determine his caste.

5. Which caste should a matured person belongs? Such a question should never arise. Rather the question should be raised whether that matured person is qualified to retain his father's caste or not.

6. If it is found that a person is qualified to retain his caste then appropriate *saṁskāra* or purificatory rituals should be performed. If it is seen that he is qualified for a higher caste then his *saṁskāra* should be performed accordingly. If it is found that, he is qualified for a caste lower than that of his father, then he should be given two more years.

7. After this additional two years, he should be examined again and his caste should be ascertained.

8. Every village should have a committee consisting of landlords and the scholars to protect the rules and regulations of the society.

9. The support of the king has to be taken in order to keep these activities going. The king is actually the protector of the principle of *varnāśrama.*

10. According to one's caste, one's marriage and other activities should be carried out

(*Sajjana-toṣaṇī* 2/7)

7. How many types of societies are there? Can the living entities ever remain out of society?

"Some people think that social people cannot be called Vaiṣṇavas; this is a misconception. Actually, the society is divided into three; namely the society of the materialists, the society of the those who desire liberation, and the society of the liberated souls. The living entities can never become unsocial, sociability is their nature. Even when the living entities are free from matter, a pure society of devotees is inevitable. Therefore whether a living entity lives in the forest or lives at home or lives in Vaikuṇṭha, he is always a social creature. The difference between the Vaiṣṇavas and ordinary living entities is that the Vaiṣṇavas live in a Vaiṣṇava society and the ordinary living entities live in a ordinary society. The conclusion now is that there is no difference between Vaiṣṇava religion and Vaiṣṇava society.

(*Sajjana-toṣaṇī* 2/7

8. What kind of social etiquette is beneficial for India? Is it proper to take up the activity of reforming the society in haste?

"There is danger in both sides. On one side, the insect of prejudice is eating away our society; if we simply keep quiet, we will certainly invite inauspiciousness. Our social strength, heroism and good fortune are gradually diminishing. Those same descendants of the Āryans by whose influence the entire world remained shaking for a long time have now become lower than the *mlecchas* and gradually becoming even more degraded. Those who have good hearts are lamenting while discussing these topics. Those who do not have good hearts are living without any anxiety and are gradually becoming degraded. If we glance on the other side, we find various dangers. If we give up the system of *varṇāśrama* and establish a new society then we can no longer be called Āryans because a scientific society ceases to remain. For example, societies like Buddhism, Jainism, local Christianity and Brāhmo Samāja who are devoid of the principles of *varṇāśrama* never prospered in the land of India. Buddhism and Jainism remained hidden in the caves. The local Christianity only remained in the possession of the *mlecchas*. Brāhmo Samāja became locked in the cottage. None of them could lead a life of independence. What happened to the *tantras* of the Buddhist? What happened to the newly-formed rules and regulations. They were all useless. They will never be of any use in India, which is the abode of the science. If we suddenly begin to reform the society and try to establish the principles of *varnāśrama* then there will be a big chaos. We can see darkness in all directions."

(*Sajjana-toṣaṇī* 2/7)

83

The Rights of the Living Entities

1. What is the root of a devotee's qualification?

"The mercy of Krishna and His devotees is the agent for purifying the senses. Out of compassion, the *sādhus* give this mercy to the devotees by their association. Proper qualification cannot be attained by following the paths of *jñāna*, karma, or yoga. Only by the strength of devotional faith and association with devotees is material illusion conquered."

(*Navadvīpa-bhāva-taranga*, Verse 5)

2. When does a living entity become qualified to see the abode of the Lord?

"The moment the senses are released from the network of material illusion, the eyes will see the splendor of the spiritual *dhâma*."

(*Navadvīpa-bhāva-taranga*, Verse 6)

3. Are material senses eligible for serving the abode of the Lord?

"By attaining proper qualification, the senses of the living entities can taste the spiritual nectar of these *dhâmas*. Those with unqualified material senses repeatedly deride these places as insignificant matter, and cannot taste that sweet nectar."

(*Navadvīpa-bhāva-taranga*, Verse-4)

4. Is it proper to glorify the transcendental pastimes of the Lord without considering the qualification of the audience?

The unfortunate people do not understand the essential meaning of *rāsa-līlā* just as a pig does not understand the importance of a garland of pearls. Desiring welfare for the unqualified persons, I have thus completed my glorification of the Lord. Considering that the time was appropriate."

(*Kalyāna Kalpataru*)

5. Who is qualified to attain the Lord's mercy?

"The advancement made through material education and intelligence is not spiritual advancement. The spiritual advancement is achieved simply by progressive pure mood. Even a most foolish person can attain ample mercy of the Supreme Lord, and a most learned scholar, on account of his godlessness can become animalistic and unqualified to attain the Lord's mercy. Therefore, in the attainment of the Lord's mercy, education, wealth, strength, beauty and expertise in material activities do not play any role. On one hand greatly learned scholars and powerful people are gradually running towards hell because of their pride, and on the other hand, most foolish and weak people are attaining great peace of mind by engaging in devotional service to the Supreme Lord."

(*Śrī Manaḥ-śikṣā*, Verse 5)

6. Are the characteristics of the devotees fit for nondevotees discussion?

"For those, who have no devotion, to discuss the characteristics of devotees like Śrī Haridāsa Ṭhākura is simply a mere mockery. Non-devotee's discussion of the devotee's characteristics is as useless as the reading by a blind man or hearing songs by a deaf man."

(*Sajjana-toṣaṇī* 8/4)

7. Which brāhmanas are qualified for which Vedas?

"Ordinary *brāhmanas* are qualified for the *karma-kānd*a section of the Vedas, and the spiritual *brāhmanas* are qualified for the Vedas that deal with the Absolute Truth."

(*Jaiva Dharma*, Chapter 6)

8. Which path should a living entity follow until his spiritual propensities are awakened?

"Until a living entities spiritual propensity is awakened, he has no alternative other than engaging in religiosity, economic development and sense gratification."

(*Sajjana-toṣaṇī* 11/11)

9. In which āśrama do the ladies generally belong?

"The ladies should not accept any *āśrama* other than the *gṛhasta āśrama* and in particular cases the *vānaprastha āśrama*. If any extraordinarily powerful woman becomes successful by accepting the *brahmacārī* or *sannyāsa āśramas* with the help of her education, religiosity and ability, still it is not a prescription for ordinary women whose faith, body and intelligence are shaky, soft and immature."

(*Caitanya-śikṣāmṛta* 2/4)

10. What arrangements are safe regarding the male and female practitioner's place of worship?

"Male and female embodied souls should always live separately. Women's place of worship should be separate and men's place of worship should be separate; otherwise, if they are together, mundane distaste based on material male and female relationships will gradually overcome those who have entered into the science of *rāsa*. Then in order to save their character they distort the meanings of the *śāstras* and end up in blaspheming the exalted Vaiṣṇavas."

(*Sajjana-toṣaṇī* 10/6)

84

Giving up Bad Association

1. Why doesn't one achieve any result even after performing thousands of sādhanas?

"If one is influenced by bad association, he can never achieve any good result even after performing thousands of *sādhanas*."

(*Sajjana-toṣaṇī* 4/5)

2. What are the characteristics of the cheaters? Do the devotees expose them in public for the benefit of themselves and other's?

"Those who are averse to the association and conversation of the Vaiṣṇavas; their polluted internal devotional service to Viṣṇu is certainly an external ornament. Absence of desire for associating with the devotees is their symptom. One should test the disguised devotees with these symptoms. People think that they should serve such Vaiṣṇavas. But that is a mistake. There are many genuine Vaiṣṇavas, and one should try to associate with and serve them. It is not that those who are intelligent, sincere and pure devotees only remain indifferent to the pseudo-affection of such so-called devotees but they establish pure devotional service in this world by exposing their deceit to the world. It is the duty of everyone to associate with such pure devotees who are expert in destroying deceitfulness and begin to relish the love of God. This is a well known fact."

(Commentary on *Bhajanāmṛtam*)

3. Why association with nondevotees is totally fit to be rejected?

"People who have faith in fruitive rituals are not devotees. Therefore, they are nondevotees . If anyone performs karma in order to achieve the mercy of Krishna, then that karma is called *bhakti*. That karma which yields mundane results or mundane knowledge is adverse to the Lord. *Karmīs* do not exclusively search for the mercy of Krishna. Although they respect Krishna, their main purpose is to attain some kind of happiness.

Karma is nothing but selfish activities, therefore, *karmīs* are also called nondevotees. Yogis sometimes search for liberation, the fruit of *jñāna*, and sometimes they search for *vibhūti*, or opulence, the fruit of karma. Hence, they too, are called nondevotees. Due to lack of full surrender, worshipers of the demigods are also called nondevotees. Those who are attached to discussing dry logic are also adverse to the Lord. And what to speak of those who conclude that the Lord is only a figment of the imagination. Those who are attached to sense gratification and thus have no opportunity to remember the Lord are also counted among the nondevotees. If one associates with these nondevotees, then in a very short time, one's intelligence is polluted and one's heart is overcome by their propensities. If anyone desires to attain pure devotional service, then he should carefully give up the association of nondevotees."

(*Sajjana-toṣaṇī* 11/11)

4. Do the proud jñānis accept devotional service to Krishna?

"Those who are not subordinate to the Lord are called nondevotees . The *jñānī*s are never subordinate to the Lord. They think that they can become one with the Lord on the strength of their knowledge. They think, '*Jñāna* is the topmost object; the Lord cannot keep one who attains *jñāna* under His control; the Lord became Supreme by the strength of this *jñāna*, and I too will become Supreme.' Therefore, all the endeavors of the *jñānī*s are to become independent of the Lord. They also think 'the Lord's power does not act on one who achieves liberation in the form of merging with the Lord, which is attained by *jñāna*.' This is the attempt of the *jñānī*s! The *jñānī*s and mundane scholars do not depend on the mercy of the Lord. They try to achieve everything on the strength of their knowledge and reasoning. They do not care for the Lord's mercy. Therefore, *jñānī*s are nondevotees. Although some *jñānī*s accept devotional service as their process of *sādhana*, at the time of perfection they discard it."

(*Sajjana-toṣaṇī* 11/11)

5. What kind of guru is fit to be rejected?

"At the time of accepting a spiritual master one should test whether he is expert in the science of transcendental sound vibration and the Absolute Truth. Such a spiritual master is certainly capable of imparting instructions about all spiritual topics. Although an initiating spiritual master is non-rejectable; but he too can be rejected by two reasons. The first is that when a disciple accepted a spiritual master, if he did not test whether his spiritual master was a Vaiṣṇava and fully conversant with the science of the Absolute

Truth, then such a spiritual master is useless for him and so he must give him up. There are many scriptural evidences of this. The second reason is that at the time of accepting a spiritual master, the spiritual master was a Vaiṣṇava and fully conversant with the science of the Absolute Truth, but later on due to bad association he has become a Māyāvādī and envious to the Vaiṣṇavas. Such a spiritual master must also be rejected."

(*Jaiva Dharma*, Chapter 20)

6. Is an unauthorized spiritual master not fit to be rejected?

"One who does not know the path of attachment yet instructs other's in this path or who knows that path and instructs his disciples without considering their qualification is a bogus guru and must be given up."

(*Śrī Krishna-saṁhitā* 8/14)

85

Activities Favorable to Devotional Service

1. What is the resolution of the devotees regarding items favorable for devotional service?

"I will surely execute with utmost care those activities favorable to Your pure devotional service. I will feel fondness for those things in this world which are conducive to devotional service, and with my senses I will engage them in Your service."

(*Śaraṇāgati*)

2. What is most favorable for devotional service?

"Dust from the lotus feet of pure devotees is conducive to devotional service, while service to the Vaiṣṇavas is itself the supreme perfection, and the root of the tender creeper of divine love."

(*Śaraṇāgati*)

3. What is the conception of an exalted devotee about things that are favorable for devotional service?

"Goloka Vṛndāvana appears in my home whenever I see the worship and service of Lord Hari going on there. Upon seeing the Ganges, which is a river of nectar emanating from the lotus feet of the Lord, my happiness knows no bounds."

(*Śaraṇāgati*)

4. What is the consideration of favorable and unfavorable āśrama in the worship of Supreme Lord?

"There is no hard and fast rule for a devotee who has taken complete shelter of the holy names, to either live at home, or live in the forest. Because, if the house is more favorable for cultivation of the holy names, then it is better than the renounced order of life. Moreover, it is the duty of a Vaiṣṇava to give up his house if it is unfavorable to the cultivation of his chanting the holy names."

(*Harināma-cintāmani*)

5. What is the conception of those who engage in chanting the holy names regarding items favorable and unfavorable for devotional service?

"Persons who are engaged in chanting the holy names should not do anything other than that which is favorable for his devotional service. He should give up all *nāmāparādhas*, in other words he should give up everything that are unfavorable for his devotional service. He should also maintain without deviation that Lord Krishna alone is his protector or sustainer."

(*Sajjana-toṣaṇī* 11/6)

6. Why is honoring tulasī leaves, sandalwood pulp, etc., that have already been offered to the Lord favorable to devotional service?

"Smelling of items like *tulasī* destroys the urge of smelling strong agitating scent. Attachment for aromatic substance leads to many dangers in this world. By smearing their bodies with perfumes, foolish people invite many *anarthas* such as debauchery and laziness. In order to control this urge, if one first offer the sweet smelling *tulasī* leaves and sandalwood paste to the Lord, and then honor then, then he can simultaneously control his senses and cultivate spiritual consciousness."

(*Tattva-sutra* 35)

7. Are the objects of material enjoyment favorable to devotional service?

"It is not a fact that all objects of material enjoyment are hostile to the living entities. Only attachment and detachment for the objects of material enjoyment are great enemies of the living entities. Therefore, one should control one attachment and detachment at the time of accepting objects of material enjoyment. Then despite one's accepting objects of material enjoyment, one will not become entangled."

(Commentary on *Bhagavad-gītā* 3/34)

8. Why discussing of the Absolute Truth is favorable for strengthening one's devotional service? What is the definition

of persons who are indifferent to discussing about the Absolute Truth?

"Just as it is essential for the devotees to give up dry knowledge, false renunciation, and useless argument, in the same way they should also engage in discussing about the Absolute Truth, and attribute pure attachment in the spiritual objects. It is to be understood that those who disregard the discussion about the Absolute Truth due to their excessive attachment, are either extremely liberated or extremely conditioned."

(*Tattva-sutra* 4)

9. What kind of family life is favorable for the householder's devotional service? Is offering of oblations to the forefathers, according to the rules and regulations of the smārthas, favorable to devotional service?

"When the *śrāddha* ceremony of the forefathers arrives, a householder devotee should first offer foodstuffs to Krishna, and then offer that remnants to his forefathers, to the *brāhmanas* and to the Vaiṣṇavas. In this way, a householder can make his family life favorable for devotional service. If devotional service is mixed in the performance of *smārtha* rituals, then the reactions of those rituals are nullified."

(*Jaiva Dharma*, Chapter 7)

10. Does a surrendered devotee performed śrāddha ceremony according to karma-kānda? Which prescription is favorable for his devotional service?

"There is no recommendation for the surrendered devotees to perform *śrāddha* ceremony according the *karma-kānda* in order to repay the debts to their forefathers. It is recommended that such devotees should first worship the Supreme Lord and then after offering the remnants of the Lord to their forefathers, they should honor the Lord's remnants along with their family members."

(*Jaiva Dharma*, Chapter 10)

11. Is marring a girl of another caste and giving up the principles of four varṇas favorable for a Vaiṣṇava householder's devotional service?

"If a Vaiṣṇava householder is an Āryan or if he follows the principles of four *varṇas*, then his marriage should be arranged with a girl from the same caste. Because, even though the principles of *varṇāśrama* are temporary, they are nevertheless beneficial for him. It is not a fact that by rejecting the principles of four *varṇas*, one can become a Vaiṣṇava. A Vaiṣṇava should only do that which is favorable for his devotional service."

(*Jaiva Dharma*, Chapter 6)

12. What is the proper profession of the renunciates and the householders?

"For the renunciates, begging alms from door to door, and for the householders professions that are approved by the rules and regulation of their respective *varṇas* and *āśrama*, are the proper professions."

(Commentary on *Upadeśāmṛta*, Verse 3)

13. Is becoming vegetarian favorable for devotional service to Hari? Why simply becoming vegetarian does not yield any result?

"By eating foodstuffs that are in the mode of goodness, one's existence becomes purified. The word existence means the body and the mind. Even if one's existence is purified, but his behavior is not in the mode of goodness then his purified state of existence gradually degrades. By the word behavior, all other activities except eating are revered. Giving up the association of human, truthfulness, simplicity, nonviolence as well as controlling the mind and the senses are all included with in the category of behavior. Even though a human beings eating and behavior are in the mode of goodness, yet unless he regularly cultivates Krishna consciousness, how can his human nature be improved? If anyone wants to personally see the results of eating foodstuffs in the mode of goodness, then he should try eating *sāttvik* food, engage in *sāttvik* behavior, and cultivation. One will certainly achieve results. However if there is any discrepancy in this endeavor it will certainly affect the result. In order to attain the qualification to behave or to cultivate, one first need to eat the foodstuffs in the mode of goodness."

(*Sajjana-toṣaṇī* 2/8)

14. How do the devotee's activities based on the principles of varṇāśrama become favorable for his devotional service?

"A devotee who desires to properly pass his life still accepts his duties according to *varṇāśrama*, as those duties are favorable to devotional service and counted as part of devotional service. All these activities are no longer called karma. In these activities, the *svaniṣṭha* devotees, or devotees addicted to their own line of devotion, bring karma and its results within the realm of devotional service. The *pariniṣṭhita* devotees, or devotees fully addicted to devotional service, perform pious activities that are not contrary to devotional principles only to attract people. The devotees who are *nirapekṣa*, or neutral, accept activities favorable for devotional service without caring for popular approval."

(*Sajjana-toṣaṇī* 10/9)

15. What kind of karma is recommended in the Bhagavad-gītā?

"Another name of karma is to maintain one's livelihood. Lord Krishna has instructed to the transcendentalists in the *Bhagavad-gītā* that they should engage only in those activities which are favorable to devotional service and give up those activities which are unfavorable to devotional service."

(*Caitanya-śikṣāmṛta* 2/2)

16. What is the difference between the activities of the devotees and the karmīs?

"You make as much advancement as you can in the field of science, art, industry and worldly morality; we have no objection with that, because it will help in the cultivation of devotional service in many ways. We are not renunciates, we are devotees. We only say that let all activities be performed in the spirit of Krishna consciousness. May the activities never be induced by one's self interest which is the irrelevant fruit of all karma. Let all the activities be performed with the aim of making advancement in the path of the devotional service to the Lord. As far as the activities are concern, there is no difference between your life and my life. The only difference is that you engage in the activities as the matter of duty, and I engage in the activities in the mood of serving the Supreme Lord. May my endeavor for karma be destroyed at some stage due to dissatisfaction. This is exactly similar to your retire from karma at some stage. You uselessly retire from your activities, and I retire from activities only to be engaged in devotional service to the Supreme Lord. For you this material world is a field of activity, for me it is a field for cultivating Krishna consciousness. I consider all your activities hostile because you engage in activities for the sake of engaging in the activities. You do not act for the pleasure of the Supreme Lord. You are a *karmī* but I am a devotee."

(Conclusion of *Caitanya-śikṣāmṛta*)

17. Why is forgiveness glorious?

"Because forgiveness is favorable to devotional service."

(*Śrī Bhāgavatārka Maricimālā* 15/91)

18. What kind of faith is favorable for devotional service?

"A Vaiṣṇava must maintain firm faith that the Supreme Lord is his only protector."

(*Śrī Bhāgavatārka Maricimālā* 15/93)

19. Why poverty is helpful for a devotee's execution of devotional service to Hari and giving up bad association?

"On should not consider poverty as a distress. The Supreme Lord has said that to whom I show my favor I gradually take away all his wealth. Because, then his artificial friends will consider him a distressed person and reject him. In this way, his bad association will automatically be removed."

(*Śrī Bhāgavatārka Maricimālā* 15/99)

20. What is the benefit of observing vows regarding Lord Hari?

"By observing vows such as Janmāṣṭhami, Ekādaśī and Kārttika one's devotional service is increased."

(*Śrī Bhāgavatārka Maricimālā* 15/74)

21. What is enthusiasm?

"To cultivate Krishna consciousness with utmost care is called enthusiasm."

(Commentary on *Upadeṣāmṛta*, Verse 3)

22. Why enthusiasm is favorable for devotional service?

"If one has enthusiasm in the beginning of devotional service, and that enthusiasm does not become cold, then one will never become apathetic, lazy, or distracted in chanting the holy names. Therefore, enthusiasm is the only support for all types of devotional service. By enthusiastically performing devotional service one can very quickly give up *aniṣṭhitā* service and attain *niṣṭhā*."

(*Sajjana-toṣaṇī* 11/1)

23. Is enthusiasm without faith effective?

"The word *śraddhā* certainly means faith, but enthusiasm is the life of *śraddhā*. Faith without enthusiasm is meaningless. Many people think they have faith in God, but because they have no enthusiasm, their faith has no meaning."

(*Sajjana-toṣaṇī* 11/1)

24. What is the means of the conditioned soul's advancement?

"By attaining piety that helps one in his devotional service through the mercy of the devotees, the *mahājanas*, and Lord Krishna, the conditioned soul attain auspiciousness."

(*Sajjana-toṣaṇī* 11/4)

25. Can useless talks be favorable to devotional service?

"The practitioners of devotional service should not speak unnecessarily. If you do have to speak unnecessarily, better to keep quiet. Besides topics regarding Krishna, all other topics are unnecessary. But to speak about the subjects favorable to devotional service is not unnecessary."

(*Sajjana-toṣaṇī* 11/5)

26. What is patience? Can the six urges be made favorable to devotional service?

"To subdue the six urges is called *dhairya*. As long as one has a material body these propensities cannot be totally uprooted, but by properly engaging them in their appropriate subjects they no longer remain faulty."

(*Sajjana-toṣaṇī* 11/5)

27. What kind of patience is favorable for devotional service to Hari?

"Being impatient due to prolonged *sādhana*, some people fall from the path to the ultimate goal; therefore a practicing devotee who desires to achieve his goal attains that result only when he becomes patient." Krishna must be merciful to me either today or after one hundred years or in some other birth. I will take shelter of His lotus feet with determination and never leave." This type of *dhairya*, patience, is most desirable for the practitioners of devotional service."

(*Sajjana-toṣaṇī* 11/5)

28. What kind of food is favorable for devotional service?

"One should fill his belly with whatever is easily available. By offering Krishna foods in the mode of goodness and honoring them as *prasāda*, the tongue is satisfied and service to Krishna is cultivated."
(*Sajjana-toṣaṇī* 11/5)

29. How can ordinary and spiritual dealings became favorable for devotional service?

"It is certainly auspicious to dovetail all our ordinary and spiritual endeavors for the service of the Supreme Lord."
(*Sajjana-toṣaṇī* 11/6)

30. Why accepting sense gratification only as much as required to keep the body and soul together is favorable to devotional service?

"At every stage of life one should accept only as much wealth as needed for the practice of devotional service. By desiring more than needed, *bhakti* will disappear. If wealth is not accepted according to one's need, however, then the practice of devotional service will be hampered."
(*Sajjana-toṣaṇī* 11/6)

31. What kind of family life is favorable to devotional service? What is Krishna conscious family life?

"Marriage is for the establishment of Krishna's family; producing children is for increasing Krishna's servants; offering oblations to the forefathers is for the satisfaction of Krishna's servants; feasting is for the gratification of Krishna's living entities—all these activities should be dovetailed in the favorable service of Krishna. Then one will not fall into the grip of unfavorable fruitive activities. The body, house, and everything else belongs to Krishna—thinking in this way one should protect the body, the house, and the community. This is called Krishna's family."
(*Sajjana-toṣaṇī* 11/6)

32. What is the necessity for observing Vaiṣṇava vows and associating with devotees?

"It is extremely necessary for them to associate with *sādhus* in order to give up the attachment for prejudices. They must follow all vows meant for Vaiṣṇavas in order to give up the attachment for material objects. One should not be negligent in these practices. One should follow these instructions with great care and respect. If one does not follow carefully, then cheating in the form of duplicity renders the whole endeavor useless. For those who do not have respect in this regard, attaining devotion to Śrī Hari becomes very rare, even after hearing for many births."

(*Sajjana-toṣaṇī* 11/11)

33. Why observing the vow of cāturmāsya favorable to devotional service?

"First by practicing vows for three days, then by practicing for one month, then by practicing for four months (Cāturmāsya)—in this way gradually one should completely uproot the attachment for sense gratifying items and leave them forever."

(*Sajjana-toṣaṇī* 11/11)

34. Under which consideration should one live at home or leave home?

"If the home is favorable for a devotee's devotional service, then he should not leave. It is his duty to remain a *gṛhastha* with detachment. But when the home becomes unfavorable for his service, he then becomes eligible to leave home. At that time, the detachment he develops for his house through his devotional service is accepted. For this reason, Śrīvasa Paṇḍita did not leave home. For this reason, Svarūpa Dāmodara took *sannyāsa*. All genuine devotees have remained either at home or in the forest due to this consideration. Whoever has left home due to this consideration is called a genuine renunciate."

(*Sajjana-toṣaṇī* 11/12)

35. How should a householder Vaiṣṇava earn his livelihood?

"According to his own occupation a householder Vaiṣṇava should earn wealth for the maintenance of his livelihood. He should not accumulate wealth through any unfair means."

(*Sajjana-toṣaṇī* 11/12)

36. What is proper occupation?

"To know this one should see the behavior of Śrī Caitanya Mahāprabhu's followers."

(*Sajjana-toṣaṇī* 11/12)

37. How does one's material bondage becomes exhausted?

"If one accepts only those items which are favorable for his devotional service to Krishna, then he will automatically cultivate Krishna consciousness and his material bondage becomes exhausted.

(*Sajjana-toṣaṇī* 4/9)

38. How can one engage his eyes in spiritual cultivation?

"If one wants to make his eyes favorable to devotional service, then he must see the deities of the Supreme Lord, see the Vaiṣṇavas, see the beauty of those places where the Supreme Lord had performed His pastimes, and see the dioramas that depict the Lord's pastimes. The main point is that one should see the Lord's relationship in the object of one's vision."

(*Sajjana-toṣaṇī* 4/9)

39. How does one cultivate devotional service with one's ears?

"In order to make one's ears favorable to devotional service, one must take a vow of only hearing the topics of Hari, hearing the topics of the devotees, and hearing the subject matters related to Hari."

(*Sajjana-toṣaṇī* 4/9)

40. What is the process for making the nose favorable to devotional service?

"To make one's nose favorable to devotional service, one must take a vow of only smelling *tulasī* leaves, flowers, sandalwood pulp and other fragrant objects that have already been offered to Krishna. All objects of one's smell should be connected with Krishna."

(*Sajjana-toṣaṇī* 4/9)

41. How can one make his tongue favorable to devotional service?

"Honoring the remnants of Krishna and the devotees is the only process for making one's tongue favorable to devotional service. One should not honor the Lord's remnant in the spirit of enjoyment; rather he should remember the pleasure of his beloved Lord Śrī Krishna. If one takes *prasāda* in the spirit of enjoyment, one will miss the feelings of the Lord's grace."

(*Sajjana-toṣaṇī* 4/9)

42. How should one make his body favorable for devotional service?

"To make one's body favorable to devotional service one should utilize his entire body in the service of the Supreme Lord and the Vaiṣṇavas."
(*Sajjana-toṣaṇī* 4/9)

43. Is accepting spiritual names and titles favorable to devotional service?

"We find the practice of awarding spiritual names and titles such as 'Ratnabāhu' 'Kavikarṇapura' and 'Premanidhi' during the manifested pastimes of Śrīman Mahāprabhu. Later devotees have also been accepting names and titles like '*Bhāgavatbhuṣana*' '*Gītā bhuṣana*' and so on.
(*Sajjana-toṣaṇī* 4/1)

44. What is the mentality of an exalted personality regarding favorable and unfavorable objects of devotional service?

"The mental state of a great personality regarding things that are favorable for devotional service is as soft as flowers. As soon as a great personality sees any item, paraphernalia, time, candidate or place that is favorable to devotional service, his heart melts. When a great personality sees any item, paraphernalia, time, candidate or place that is unfavorable to devotional service, his heart becomes as hard as thunderbolt. He never accepts these things."
(*Sajjana-toṣaṇī* 4/11)

45. How can conversations, songs, or poetries, be favorable to devotional service?

"If one can relate ordinary talks, songs, and poetries, with Krishna, then one will achieve perfection in converting them as favorable to devotional service."
(*Sajjana-toṣaṇī* 4/9)

46. Is discussing about other's at the time of giving instruction regarding devotional service to Hari unfavorable for devotional service?

"When a guru enlightens his disciple on some topic, then unless he occasionally talks about other's, his instruction may not be clear. When previous *mahājanas* talked about other's in this way, there is merit in such talk, not fault."
(*Sajjana-toṣaṇī* 10/10)

47. Is prajalpa, which is favorable to devotional service harmful?

"All the *mahājanas* have respected the *prajalpa* that enhance one's devotional service to Hari."

(*Sajjana-toṣaṇī* 10/10)

48. What are the purposes for which discussing about other's is not faulty?

"Discussing about other's faults with a good purpose has not been condemned in the scripture. There are three kinds of good purposes. If by talking about the sinful activities of a person, that person is benefited, then such a discussion is auspicious. If such a discussion amount to benefit of the world, then it is counted among the pious activities. And if such a discussion gives one benefit, then it is also auspicious not a fault."

(*Sajjana-toṣaṇī* 5/5)

49. How can one transform ordinary activities into devotional service?

"Since maintaining one's life is not possible without action, one must work to maintain his life. If such activities are done in the mood of enjoyment, then one's qualification as a human is lost and he becomes like an animal. Therefore if one can transform all his bodily activities into activities favorable to the devotional service of the Lord, then that is bhakti-yoga."

(*Sajjana-toṣaṇī* 10/9)

50. Is accepting sense objects amount to atyāhāra or too much eating?

"The purport is that if one accepts sense objects in the spirit of enjoyment, that is *atyāhāra*. But if sense objects are accepted as the Lord's mercy and only as far as required and favorable for devotional service, then it is not *atyāhāra*."

(*Sajjana-toṣaṇī* 10/9)

51. How should a person who is fully surrendered to Krishna spend his life?

"I will perform all my bodily activities out of habit just to keep my body and soul together. I will become attached to all those activities which are favorable for the worship of Krishna."

(*Kalyāna Kalpataru*, Song 4)

86

Five Types of Saṁskāras or Purificatory Processes

1. What is the use of undergoing purificatory process?

"A living entity who has already undergone purificatory process becomes more purified when he is tested by his spiritual master. When one is thus purified then the spiritual master decorates his body with the marks of Vishnu *cakras* and makes an arrangement so that the disciple continues to put on these marks without fail till the end of his life."

(*Sajjana-toṣaṇī* 2/1)

2. What is the purpose of the process of deity worship?

"The process of deity worship to cultivate Krishna consciousness by engaging in touching, seeing, hearing about, smelling, relishing, thinking and meditating are called *yāga* or the process of deity worship. These activities are specially recommended in the worship of Śālagrāma *śilā*. The process of deity worship is called *vaiṣṇava-yāga*. As long as one remains within this material world one must engage in many activities in order to maintain his life. Therefore, it is recommended that an initiated person should offer all activities for the pleasure of the Supreme Lord through proper rules and regulations. By instructing about this process of deity worship, the merciful spiritual master certainly delivers his disciples from the ocean of material existence."

(*Sajjana-toṣaṇī* 2/1)

3. What is the necessity for decorating one's forehead with the marks of tilaka?

"The meaning of putting *tilaka* is to go upwards or make advancement in spiritual life. After becoming purified through purificatory process, a living entity accepts proper renunciation from his family life. But until he decorates his body with the marks of *tilaka*, he does not get any result from undergoing purificatory process. All his miseries, all his renunciation, all his resolution of abandoning material happiness, and all his controlling the senses goes in vain if he does not endeavor to make further advancement in his spiritual life. Marking the body with the *tilaka* means decorating the temple of Lord Hari. In other words to fully take shelter of the *Sac-cid-ānanda* Lord, one needs to put on *tilaka* all over his body. These markings, apart from the body, have a bearing on the mind, and on the soul. To become attached to the Supreme Lord by becoming detached to the material world is called purification and inclination towards the lord. These two ornaments are extremely necessary for the conditioned souls. A body without the marks of *tilaka* is a dead body; if one sees such a body, he should purify himself by taking bath in the ocean of repentance. The mind of a person who does not decorate with the marks of *tilaka* simply wanders in insignificant maters, becomes attached to insignificant object and engages in discussing insignificant topics. O service inclined living entities! Do not waste your time. Mark your mind, body and self with the marks of *tilaka* and proceed towards the abode of the Vaiṣṇavas. The essential characteristic of a person who does not decorate his body with the marks of *tilaka* gets lost. Therefore one must decorate his body with the marks of *tilaka*."

(*Sajjana-toṣaṇī* 2/1)

4. What did Śrīmān Mahāprabhu teach by enacting the pastime of accepting initiation?

"By accepting initiation from Śrīmad Iśvara Purī, who was the crest jewel among the Parivrājakācāryas in the Mādhva *sampradāya*, Śrīman Mahāprabhu has taught all living entities about the necessity of taking shelter at the lotus feet of the devotees and the spiritual master."

(Commentary on *Śikṣāstaka*, Verse 8)

5. Is the rule of accepting initiation, fit to be rejected by ordinary practitioners?

"It is not the duty of materialistic persons to renounce the process of initiation because a few great souls like Jaḍa Bharata did not take initiation. Initiation is a constitutional injunction for every birth of the living entity. If initiation is not seen in the life of a perfected soul, it should not be taken as an example. General rules are not changed because something happens to a particular person in a special situation. Śrī Dhruva Mahārāja went to Dhruvaloka in his material body; seeing that, should one waste time hoping for the same? The general rule is a living entity gives up his material body and goes to Vaikuṇṭha in his spiritual body. General rules should be accepted by people in general. Whenever and whatever is desired by the Lord, who is full of inconceivable potencies, that only happens. Therefore we should never transgress the general rules."

(*Sajjana-toṣaṇī* 11/6)

6. When does a spiritual master award devotional name to his disciple?

"When a spiritual master gives initiation to his disciple, he also mercifully gives him a name indicating the relationship with devotional service to Hari."

(*Sajjana-toṣaṇī* 2/1)

87

Spiritual Varṇāśrama

1. Is it proper to confine a Vaiṣṇava within the rules of varṇāśrama?

"Considering that there is no difference between a Vaiṣṇava and an ordinary person many people inquire about a Vaiṣṇava's caste and try to establish a Vaiṣṇava as belonging to one of the four *varṇas*. This endeavor is extremely detrimental to Vaiṣṇava principle and an act of the ordinary social people."

(*Sajjana-toṣaṇī* 11/10)

2. Is the illegal system of varṇāśrama not the reason for the Indian Āryans' downfall?

"Alas! The Āryans of India are the administrators and the spiritual masters of all other castes. It is not a fact that their degradation has been caused by their old age; but it has come due to the illegal system of *varṇāśrama*. If the Supreme Personality of Godhead who is the controller of all the living entities, all rules and regulations, and who is capable of re-establishing auspiciousness in the place of inauspiciousness, desires, then some empowered personality will again reestablish the actual system of *varṇāśrama*."

(*Caitanya-śikṣāmṛta* 2/3)

3. Under whose rule the social etiquettes reached its peak?

"Every kind-hearted and responsible person will accept that the social etiquettes reached its peak at the hands of the sages."

(*Caitanya-śikṣāmṛta* 2/1)

4. Is it proper to destroy the principles of varnāśrama?

"The Principles of *varṇāśrama* are the life and soul of the social human beings. If the system of the *varṇāśrama* is destroyed, then the scientific society of the human beings will be destroyed and they will be cursed by the old saying, 'become a mouse again' and thus lead an illegal life like the wayward mleechas. It is not the intention of those who are devoted to the welfare of one's native land to destroy the principles of *varṇāśrama.* It is the duty of everyone to remove the contamination that has entered into the principles of *varṇāśrama.*"

(*Sajjana-toṣaṇī* 2/7)

5. Which qualities do not make one a brāhmaṇa?

"A person who does not possess peacefulness, self control, austerity, cleanliness, satisfaction, tolerance, forgiveness, simplicity, knowledge, compassion, truthfulness and devotion to the Supreme Lord can not be called a *brāhmaṇa.*"

(*Sajjana-toṣaṇī* 4/6)

6. What kind of āśrama should a devotee who desires to attain love of God accept?

"Whether one who is desirous of attaining love of God belongs to *gṛhaṣṭha āśrama, vānapraśtha āśrama*, or *sannyāsa āśrama*, he should accept any *āśrama* that is favorable for cultivating love of God, and he should give up any *āśrama* that is unfavorable for cultivating love of God."

(*Caitanya-śikṣāmṛta* 6/4)

7. What is kṣetra-sannyāsa or vānaprastha?

"When one takes *kṣetra-sannyāsa,* he leaves his household life and goes to a place of pilgrimage devoted to Lord Viṣṇu. Such places include Puruṣottama (Jagannātha Purī), Navadvīpa-dhāma and Mathurā-dhāma. The *kṣetra-sannyāsī* lives in these places alone or with his family. *Kṣetra-sannyāsa* is to be considered the preferable *vānaprastha* situation in this Age of Kali."

(Commentary on *Caitanya Caritāmṛta,* Madhya 16/130)

8. Is it proper for a householder to accept the dress of a sannyāsī? What is the fate of such cross-āśrama people?

"Among the householder Vaiṣṇavas, many shave their heads, wear *brāhmaṇa* underwear and live at their own house as *bābājīs.* What can be more an *anartha* than this? What is the need of such illegal changing of *āśrama*? If they are really detached, then let them take proper dress of a renunciate. But if they are not detached then what is the use of accepting such artificial external signs? By doing so, they are disgracing the Vaiṣṇava religion to the people of the world. But they will certainly suffer the consequences in their next lives."

(*Sajjana-toṣaṇī* 2/7)

9. Can one advance in spiritual life, if he does not accept any discrimination in the caste system?

"When it is seen that caste is simply based on worldly discrimination, then the defects that the Brahmos point out in judging caste is simply extraneous."

(*Prema-pradīpa*, Ray 7)

10. Since when did the destruction of the system of varṇāśrama begin in India?

"The principles of *varṇāśrama* had been purely followed in India for a long time. Thereafter in due course of time, when sage Jāmadagni who was a *kṣatriya*, and his son Paraśurama, were illegally converted into *brāhmanas*, they then, according to the characteristics opposed to their own nature and selfishness broke peace among the *brāhmanas* and *kṣatriyas*. The seed of quarrel that was planted among the *brāhmanas* and *kṣatriyas* as a result of this resulted in ascertaining one's *varṇas* according to one's own birth. In due course of time when this unnatural rule was included in the literature of the Manu, etc., the *kṣatriyas*, being hopeless of attaining higher *varṇa*, began to create means to ruin the *brāhmaṇa* by inventing the system of religion known as Buddhism. It is a fact that every action has an equal and opposite reaction. That is why determination of *varṇas* according to one's birth became prominent."

(*Caitanya-śikṣāmṛta* 2/3)

11. What are the reasons behind the advent of Buddhism and Jainism?

"By composing selfish religious literatures, the so-called *brāhmanas* began to cheat people. Being unable to fight any more the so-called *kṣatriyas* became bereft of their kingdom and thus they eventually began to preach the philosophy of Buddhism. The so-called *vaiśyas* began to preach the philosophies like Jainism and as a result, India lost a great deal of business. The so-called *sūdras*, being unable to engage in their natural activities, became plunderers. The study of Vedic literatures gradually diminished. Taking advantage of the situation, the kings of the *mleccha* countries attacked and conquered India."

(*Caitanya-śikṣāmṛta* 2/3)

12. What is reason behind the degradation of varṇāśrama system in India?

"Incidentally for the time being, since one's *varṇas* is been determined by one's birth the system of *varṇāśrama* has been degraded in India."

(*Sajjana-toṣaṇī* 2/3)

13. Is spiritual life dependent on varṇāśrama?

"The system of *varṇāśrama* or caste system is going on for the sake of maintaining social etiquettes. There is no tinge of spiritual cultivation in it. Spiritual cultivation is always based on the individual."

(*Sajjana-toṣaṇī* 9/9)

14. For what is reason the existence of Indian Āryans still not lost?

"At one time, the Romans and the Greeks were more powerful and courageous than the present day Europeans. What is their condition now? Being bereft of the symptoms of their own caste, they have become completely different by accepting the symptoms and principles of modern castes. What to speak of this, they no longer feel proud of the prowess displayed by their national heroes. Despite being older than the Romans and Greeks, our native Āryans feel proud of their ancient heroes. Why? Because the system of *varṇāśrama* was prominent, their symptoms of caste did not deteriorate. Rana, who was killed by the *mlecchas*, proudly considered himself a descendant of Lord Rāmachandra."

(*Caitanya-śikṣāmṛta* 2/3)

15. What is the purpose of accepting tridanda sannyāsa?

"In order to control their bodies, minds and speech the *sannyāsīs* accept *tridanda*. Śankarācharya had accepted *ekadanda sannyāsa*."

(Commentary on *Caitanya Caritāmṛta* Madhya 5/143)

16. Is there any use of ascertaining a varṇa according to one's occupation? What is the purpose of varṇāśrama dharma?

"The nature of human beings is developed by their birth, association and education. If one does not accept his *varṇa* according to his nature, he cannot achieve perfection in his life. Although there are many types of nature, but they are mainly divided into four categories. Those who are inclined towards the Supreme Lord and who cultivate spiritual knowledge are *brāhmanas*. Those whose natural propensities are fighting and administration are *kṣatriyas*. Those who engage in farming, trading and protecting animals are *vaiṣyas*, and those whose nature is to simply work for the above three *varṇas* are *śūdras*. By worshiping Lord Vishnu after properly maintaining his life while remaining situated in the principles of *varṇāśrama*, the nature of the human beings becomes advanced. If one acts contrary to this, one's nature becomes degraded. Therefore religious life is the root of the human beings advancement."

(Commentary on *Caitanya Caritāmṛta* Madhya 8/58)

17. Is any one other than an incarnation of the Supreme Lord able to protect the principles of varṇāśrama?

"The cause of My (Lord Krishna's) appearance is that I am fully independent and by My sweet will I incarnate. Whenever there is a decline in religious principles and an increase in irreligiosity, I appear by My sweet will. My rules and regulations by which I maintain the functions of material creations are beginningless, but in due course of time when these rules become perverted due to some indefinite reason, then the principles of irreligiosity become prominent. No one other than Me is able to remove such a discrepancy. Therefore, I appear in this material world through My internal potency and stop the decline of religious principles. It is not a fact that I only appear in the land of Bhārat or India; I appear among the demigods and the animals according to the need by My sweet will. Therefore, do not think that I do not appear in the country of the *mleccha* and *antajas*. If there is any decline of religious principles even among such *mleccha* and *antajas*, then I incarnate as an empowered incarnation and protect their religion. But since the occupational duties based on the principles of *varṇāśrama* are properly performed in India, I take more care in reestablishing the religious principles of My subject. Therefore, all My transcendental incarnations such as *yugāvatāras*, *aṁśāvatāras*, are found only in India. Where there is no system of *varṇāśrama*, *karma-yoga*, *jñāna-yoga* or *bhakti-yoga* cannot be properly executed. But whatever little devotional service that is found among the *antajas*, know it for certain that it is a sudden development made possible by the mercy of the devotees."

(Commentary on *Bhagavad-gītā* 4/7)

18. What is the difference between Brahmanism and Vaiṣṇavism?

"Brahmanism is a stage or qualification of a Vaiṣṇava and Vaiṣṇavism is the fruit of Brahmanism."

(*Sajjana-toṣaṇī* 4/6)

19. If one is attached to the principles of varṇāśrama, can he make progress in spiritual life?

"Due to being firmly attached to the principles of *varṇāśrama* many followers of *varṇāśrama dharma* become extremely indifference to the achievement of *bhāva* and *prema*. As a result their gradual progress in the path of spiritual life becomes sufficiently hampered."

(*Caitanya-śikṣāmṛta* 3/1)

20. Why have all the incarnations of the Supreme Lord appeared only in India?

"Therefore all My transcendental incarnations such as *yugāvatāras*, *aṁśāvatāras* are found only in India. Where there is no system of *varṇāśrama*, *karma-yoga*, *jñāna-yoga* or *bhakti-yoga* cannot be properly executed."

(Commentary on *Bhagavad-gītā* 4/7)

21. What kind of dealings is proper between a brāhmaṇa and a Vaiṣṇava?

"No one can become a Vaiṣṇava by disregarding the position of the *brāhmanas* and a *brāhmaṇa* can never become successful by disregarding the position of the Vaiṣṇavas."

(*Sajjana-toṣaṇī* 4/6)

22. How many kinds of brāhmanas are there? What is the stage prior to Vaiṣṇavism?

"There are two kinds of *brāhmanas* namely ordinary *brāhmanas* and spiritual *brāhmanas*. Ordinary brahmanism is based on the caste and spiritual brahmanism is based on qualities. Unless one becomes the spiritual *brāhmaṇa* he can not become a Vaiṣṇava."

(*Sajjana-toṣaṇī* 4/6)

23. What kind of prestige do the caste brāhmanas and the spiritual brāhmanas deserve?

"There are two kinds of *brāhmanas*. Those who are *brāhmaṇa* by nature, and those who are *brāhmaṇa* by caste. The *brāhmanas* by nature are almost Vaiṣṇavas. Therefore their respectability is approved by all. The caste *brāhmanas* deserve ordinary respect."

(*Jaiva Dharma*, Chapter 6)

24. When are the social, mental and spiritual inauspiciousness destroyed?

"Until the principles of *varṇāśrama* are refined and properly established the social, mental and spiritual inauspiciousness will continue to trouble us. There is no doubt that the Supreme Lord who is the source of all auspiciousness will certainly bestow his mercy one day."

(*Sajjana-toṣaṇī* 2/7)

25. Is it approved by the sāstras to identify a person as brāhmaṇa just by his caste?

"By birth no one is an actual *brāhmaṇa* or a *sūdra*. By birth, one only gets a worldly designation. If the sons of the *brāhmanas* are devoid of brāhminical qualifications such as spiritual knowledge, peacefulness, self control, then according to their qualities and activities they can be called *kṣatriyas*, *vaiṣyas* or *sūdras*. This is clearly accepted by Manu himself."

(*Tattva-sutra* 44)

26. Do the rules and regulations of varṇāśrama affect one's devotional service to Hari?

"The Vaiṣṇavas are not busy in establishing their own reputation in the four *varṇas* and four *āśrama*. The Vaiṣṇava is not embarrassed if his actions violate the rules and regulations of the *varṇāśrama* system, because the only purpose of all his activities is to increase his devotion towards the Supreme Lord. It does not matter whether a Vaiṣṇava is a *brāhmaṇa*, *mleccha*, or *caṇḍāla*. Whether he is a householder or a renunciate, he has no honor or dishonor. If a Vaiṣṇava goes to hell or heaven for the sake of devotional service to the Lord, it is the same thing."

(*Sajjana-toṣaṇī* 11/10)

88

Vaiṣṇava Etiquette

1. Which symptoms of devotees should one associate with?

"It is the eternal duty of Vaiṣṇavas to develop the symptoms of love by associating with and serving devotees, while remaining indifferent to external formalities."

(*Śrī Krishna-saṁhitā* 8/17)

2. What is the duty of every Vaiṣṇava? Can one create detachment by his own endeavor?

"One should not find faults with Vaiṣṇavas if even they were previously engaged in sinful activities, if they still have some sins left, or if they accidentally commit some sins. Without a good purpose, one should not criticize about other's sins. One should display appropriate mercy on all living entities. One should consider himself a fallen soul and expect no respect for himself while giving respects to everyone. The householder Vaiṣṇavas should remain unattached to material objects and accept only those material enjoyments, which purely related to Krishna. In this way they should cultivate the mellows of chanting the Lord's holy names. When taste for Krishna will increase, the taste for sense gratification will automatically be destroyed. In such a situation, a mood of spontaneous detachment will automatically arise. However this mood cannot be awakened artificially."

(*Śrī Manaḥ-śikṣā*, Verse 10)

3. How should one glorify the qualities of the Vaiṣṇavas?

"Birth, sleeping and laziness of the Vaiṣṇavas are undisclosable. One should not speak to any one about these if one happens to see them. One should quickly stop finding faults of the Vaiṣṇavas and start glorifying their qualities."

(*Sajjana-toṣaṇī* 7/3)

4. How should one sit in front of Lord Vishnu or the Vaiṣṇavas?

"One should not sit before Lord Vishnu or the Vaiṣṇavas with stretching of the legs."

(*Sajjana-toṣaṇī* 7/3)

5. Is it right to either glorify oneself or criticize other's in front of the Vaiṣṇavas?

"One should neither glorify oneself nor criticize other's before the Vaiṣṇavas."

(*Sajjana-toṣaṇī* 7/4)

6. Should a practitioner consider himself as equal to other Vaiṣṇavas?

"A practitioner of devotional service should not consider himself as equal to other Vaiṣṇavas."

(*Sajjana-toṣaṇī* 7/4)

7. Is it proper to associate with hypocrites and Māyāvādīs on the pretext of displaying compassion to them?

"Those who are induced by the desire for name and fame or by the desire for sense gratification and liberation, take shelter of cheating propensity, and either become hypocrites and woman hunters to take shelter of personal philosophy and thus become offenders or envious. The devotees should carefully avoid such association and should never indulge in their association. On the pretext of displaying compassion to them many people associate with them and eventually fall down.

(*Sajjana-toṣaṇī* 11/6)

8. Is it right to associate with those who are attached to materialists?

"There are some people who themselves are not so materialists but they take pleasure in associating with materialists. Their association should also be given up."

(*Sajjana-toṣaṇī* 10/11)

9. In whose house can a householder Vaiṣṇava take prasādam?

"A Vaiṣṇava householder can take *prasādam* and drinks at the house of a pious and well behaved householder. He should be extremely careful about taking *prasādam* at the house of the nondevotees and sinful people."

(*Sajjana-toṣaṇī* 11/11)

10. Should one remember the difference between begging door-to-door or gross begging?

"One should always remember the difference between begging door to door or gross begging."

(*Sajjana-toṣaṇī* 11/11)

11. Is there any hope for attaining devotional service to Krishna if one does not give up bad association?

"There is no hope for attaining devotional service to Krishna unless one gives up bad association."

(*Sajjana-toṣaṇī* 11/11)

12. What is the main etiquette of a Vaiṣṇava?

"To give up bad association is the principal etiquette of a Vaiṣṇavas. There are two kinds of bad association: woman hunters and nondevotees . For woman devotee associating with a male is to be considered a bad association. Illicit association with woman and being henpecked are both bad association."

(*Harināma-cintāmani*)

13. What should one specifically think of, on an each Ekādaśī?

"On each Ekādaśī, one should think, how much advancement I have made since the last Ekādaśī? If one finds that he has not made any advancement or rather he has degraded then one should think bad association as the cause of this, and thus he should endeavor to give up that association."

(*Sajjana-toṣaṇī* 4/5)

14. How is Vaiṣṇava etiquette protected?

"Unless one gives up bad association, one can not become situated in the platform of Vaiṣṇava etiquette. There are two kinds of bad association, namely those who are overly attached to women and those who devoid of devotional service to Krishna."

(*Sajjana-toṣaṇī* 4/5)

15. How should Vaiṣṇavas be respected?

"If an *uttama adhikārī* is a householder and a *madhyama adhikārī* is a *sannyāsi*, the *madhyama adhikārī sannyāsi* should offer obeisances to the *uttama adhikārī* Vaiṣṇava."

(*Jaiva Dharma*, Chapter 8)

16. What are the characteristics of a renunciate?

"The first characteristic of a renunciate is that he is completely devoid of desire for associating with woman. He is compassionate to all living entities. He considers money as insignificant. He accumulates his livelihood only when he needs. He has pure attachment for Krishna. He gives up associating with the materialists. He is equal to honor and dishonor. He is reluctant to take up a huge enterprises, and he is neither attached nor detached in life and death."

(*Jaiva Dharma*, Chapter 7)

89

Proper Renunciation

1. How can one practice yukta-vairāgya?

"It is the duty of everyone to bring their minds under control by offering some token sense gratification exactly like controlling a horse with a morsel of grass. This is called *yukta-vairāgya* or proper renunciation. By this process one can make advancement in the path of spiritual life."

(*Caitanya-śikṣāmṛta* 6/5)

2. What is actual renunciation?

"When one's genuine detachment is awakened one should cultivate renunciation befitting the *sannyāsa āśrama* or one should gradually diminish his familial activities by becoming more and more inclined towards the service of the Supreme Lord. This is called actual renunciation."

(*Caitanya-śikṣāmṛta* 2/5)

3. In proportion to what does one's spiritual knowledge and renunciation increases?

"Pure knowledge and pure renunciation must increase in proportion to one's advancement in devotional service."

(*Caitanya-śikṣāmṛta* 1/7)

4. What is the purport of accepting material enjoyment only as much as necessary?

"The purport of the instruction 'accept material enjoyment only as much necessary' is that one should not accept material enjoyment for sense gratification, rather one should accept material enjoyment only as much as needed to establish one's relationship with Lord Krishna."

(*Caitanya-śikṣāmṛta* 1/7)

5. How do spiritual knowledge, renunciation and devotional service help a spirit soul?

"Knowledge regarding one's relationship with the Supreme Lord and detachment for material objects automatically develop in a person who engages in devotional service. Wherever they are not developed, it is to be understood that there is an absence of devotional service. Therefore, it should be called pseudo devotional service. Through renunciation, a spirit soul attains satisfaction. Through knowledge regarding one's relationship with the Supreme Lord, a spirit soul attains nourishment, and through devotional service, a spirit soul attains mitigation of his hunger."

(*Śrī Bhāgavatārka Marīci-Mālā* 15/117)

6. What type of mentality is in the topmost platform of yukta-vairāgya?

"One should take care of the body knowing that it is favorable for achieving perfection in Krishna consciousness. Without a body, one cannot worship Krishna. Therefore, even though one takes special care in protecting his body which is favorable for cultivation of devotional service, he considers all objects related to its body that are unfavorable for the cultivation of devotional service as insignificant. This type of mentality is in the topmost platform of *yukta-vairāgya*."

(*Śrī Bhāgavatārka Marīci-Mālā* 17/21)

90
Humility

1. What mentality should a devotee maintain?

"A devotee should always maintain humility within his heart."

(*Śrī Bhāgavatārka Marīchi Mālā*)

2. What kind of devotional activity is humility?

"I am a servant of Krishna, I am poor, I do not possess anything. Krishna is my all in all. Such a mentality is humility. "

(*Jaiva Dharma*, Chapter 8)

3. What type of devotional service helps in direct cultivation of Krishna consciousness?

"When one's humility is strong one certainly attains Krishna's mercy. As a result, debauchery, profit, adoration, and distinction are immediately destroyed. This helps one in direct cultivation of Krishna consciousness. This process is naturally confidential, and one must learn it from a bona fide spiritual master."

(*Caitanya-śikṣāmṛta* 6/6)

4. How is actual humility expressed?

"I am a pure spirit soul. Due to my previous misdeeds, I am suffering various material miseries. I am a proper candidate for punishment. Even though I am an eternal servant of Krishna, due to my forgetfulness of His lotus feet, I am entrapped in the wheel of karma and thus I have to suffer so much misery. Therefore, who is more unfortunate than I am? I am the most fallen, wretched and poor person."

(*Sajjana-toṣaṇī* 4/9)

5. Does a humble devotee feel proud of his own strength?

"I have not performed any pious activities and I have no spiritual knowledge. I have no devotion for Lord Krishna. Please tell me how I can attain the shelter of Your lotus feet. Your mercy is my only hope. It is the conclusion of the Vedas that Your mercy is causeless.

(*Kalyāna Kalpataru*, Prārthanā, Song 2)

6. Is humble prayer of a pure devotee spontaneous?

"This ocean is full of fearful crocodiles in the form of material sense objects. The waves of lusty desires always agitate me. I cannot tolerate the urge of prejudice, which is like the forceful wind. My mind is very restless because I do not see any sailor."

(*Kalyāna Kalpataru*, Prārthanā, Song 3)

7. What kind of humble prayer should a pure devotee offer to the Goswamis headed by Śrī Rūpa and Sanātana?

"When will Śrī Rupa Goswami bestow mercy on me and deliver me by imparting the principles of true renunciation. When will Śrī Sanātana Goswami, out of compassion, remove my attachment for sense gratification and offer me at the lotus feet of Śrī Nityānanda Prabhu? When will Śrī Jīva Goswami extinguish the blazing fire of my arguments by pouring water of scriptural conclusions? My heart is constantly burning."

(*Kalyāna Kalpataru*, Prārthanā, Song 4)

8. How should one who desires his own benefit offer nonduplicitous humble prayer to the Vaiṣṇavas?

"As soon as I will see a Vaiṣṇava, I will hang a cloth on my neck and with folded hands taking a straw in my mouth, I will stand before him without duplicity.

I will relate my miserable conditions to him while crying and begging for respite from the fire of material existence.

((*Kalyāna Kalpataru*, Prārthanā, Song 1)

91

Tolerance

1. What is the duty of a person who is tolerant?

"If anyone blasphemes you, you should tolerate it. Do not insult anyone. Taking shelter of this material body, you should not envy anyone. There is no doubt that lust is a place for Kali. Becoming lusty for the service of Krishna is transcendental. Another name of which is love of God. Desire for sense gratification is mundane. That is the place for Kali. One must give it up."

(*Sajjana-toṣaṇī* 15/2)

2. Is it part of one's occupational duty to display intolerance for other processes?

"Those who blaspheme, hate, or envy other processes, are certainly ignorant and foolish. They are not as concerned about their own goal of life as they are concerned about indulging in useless arguments."

(*Caitanya-śikṣāmṛta* 1/1)

3. Can the devotees with material desires become tolerant?

"Those whose devotional service is motivated cannot conquer anger. It is not possible to conquer anger by intelligence alone. In a very short time attachment for sense enjoyment overcomes the function of the intelligence and gives anger a place in its kingdom."

(*Sajjana-toṣaṇī* 11/5)

4. How should a devotee who chants the holy names be tolerant?

"One should become more tolerant than a tree. One should give up envy and maintain proper respect for everyone."

(*Śikṣāstaka* 3)

5. What kind of compassion is indicated by the phrase 'more tolerant than a tree'?

"By the phrase more tolerant than a tree; it is indicated that even though a tree is cut it does not protest, rather it helps other's by its shadow, fruits and flowers. Similarly, the devotees of Krishna should show greater compassion than a tree by helping everyone including the friends and enemies. Such compassion is the ornament of the nonenvious devotees who chant the holy names."

(*Śikṣāstaka* 3)

6. Can an impatient person engage in the worship of Hari?

"For the practitioner of devotional service, *dhairya*, patience, is extremely necessary. Those who possess the quality of *dhairya* are called *dhīra*, sober. Due to lack of this quality, men become restless. Those who are impatient cannot do any work. By the quality of *dhairya*, a practitioner controls first himself and then the whole world."

(*Sajjana-toṣaṇī* 11/5)

92

Not Expecting Any Respect From Others

1. How can one become amānī or free from desire for achieving respect?

"One should not proudly consider I am a *brāhmaṇa*, I am rich, I am a learned scholar in the scriptures, I am a Vaiṣṇava or I am a *sannyāsi*. Even if other's offer me any respect, I will not proudly expect any respect from them nor will I desire other's adoration. I will think myself as a poor, fallen, wretched and lower than the straw in the street."

(*Jaiva Dharma*, Chapter 8)

2. How should a person who chants Krishna's names become humble?

"I will give up false ego and consider myself lower than a straw in the street, a fallen and an insignificant beggar."

(*Śikṣāstaka* 3)

3. How can one make himself an amānī?

"One can make oneself an *amānī* by thinking himself a fallen soul and offering due respects to other's."

(*Śrī Manaḥ-śikṣā* 10)

4. What should an embodied soul think of himself?

"This material body is simply a prison house. The spirit soul has a temporary relationship with this body. Therefore as long as one is destined to live in this body one should consider himself lower than the straw in the street."

(*Tattva-sutra* 23)

5. Is it not proper for a conditioned soul to become lower than the straw in the street?

To become humbler than a blade of grass is not unjustified, but for a conditioned soul to take shelter of false identification is certainly improper. This is the actual meaning of being humbler than a blade of grass.

Śikṣāstaka 3.

6. What is the purport of the word 'amānī'

The word *amānī* indicates the third symptom of the *sādhaka* engaged in the performance of *kīrtana*, namely, that he is freed from false ego. All egotism arising from yogic powers, material opulence, wealth, beauty, high birth, social status, strength, prestige, and high position associated with the gross and subtle body of the living entity who is bound by the illusory energy, is false and opposed to one's real identity. To be freed from such false designations is to be devoid of false ego.

One who, in spite of possessing all these qualifications, is further ornamented with the qualities of tolerance and freedom from false ego is most competent to chant the holy name. Such a pure *sādhaka-bhakta*, completely renouncing the pride of being a *brāhmaṇa* householder, or the egotism of being a *sannyāsī* or ascetic in the renounced order of life, fixes his mind exclusively on the lotus feet of Śrī Krishna and engages constantly in *śrī-kṛṣṇa-nāma-saṅkīrtana*

Śikṣāstaka 3

93

Giving Respect to Everyone

1. What is the meaning of the word 'mānada' or offering respect to everyone?

"The meaning of the word *mānada* is to offer due respect to all living entities. Realizing that all living entities are servants of Krishna, one should never become envious or hate them. One should please everyone by sweet words and welfare activities."

(*Śikṣāstaka* 3)

2. What does it mean by offering due respect?

"The Vaiṣṇavas alone are worthy of respect. If the son of a Vaiṣṇava becomes a pure Vaiṣṇava then his respect will depend on the proportion of his devotional service. And if the son of a Vaiṣṇava is only an ordinary human being then he should be counted as an ordinary human being and should not be counted or respected as a Vaiṣṇava. A Vaiṣṇava must be offered respect appropriate for a Vaiṣṇava and one who is not a Vaiṣṇava should be respected as an ordinary human being. Unless one offers respects to other's one does not develop the qualification to chant the holy names of Hari."

(*Jaiva Dharma*, Chapter 8)

3. Is it not contrary to the principle of mānada to consider oneself an exalted guru?

"If I consider myself the topmost and thus distribute my remnants to other's then I will be heavily burdened by pride. Therefore I will constantly remain a servant of the Vaiṣṇavas and not accept anyone's worship."

(*Kalyāna Kalpataru*, Song 8)

94

Unalloyed Surrender To The Holy Names

1. What is the conviction of an unalloyed devotee?

"'Krishna is my only protector. Nothing else or none else can protect me.' This is the conviction of an unalloyed devotee."

(*Caitanya-śikṣāmṛta* 6/3)

2. What is the mood of a devotee who has taken shelter of the holy names, if he is faced with worldly distress?

"The mind of one who has taken shelter of the holy name is undisturbed, even if food and clothes are not easily obtained, or if they are obtained but then lost. Leaving behind all material attachments, he takes complete shelter of Govinda."

(*Śrī Bhajana-rahasya*, Chapter 4)

3. What is the difference between transcendental liberation and transcendental devotional service?

"There is no difference between transcendental liberation and transcendental devotional service at all. Rather those who make a distinction between them are to be understood that they have not understood either of them."

(*Tattva Sūtra* 19)

4. Which limbs of devotional service do the unalloyed devotees perform?

"The unalloyed devotees of Krishna are extremely attached to remembering Krishna and chanting the holy name of Krishna. Mostly they remain busy in executing these two limbs."

(*Sajjana-toṣaṇī* 10/6)

5. In which subjects should a devotee be eager to perform?

"One who desires to attain the result in chanting the holy names of Krishna, should be eager in three subjects: he should associate with devotees, he should live in a solitary place away from the nondevotees, and he should maintain determination. This is called *nirbandha*."

(*Harināma-cintāmani*)

6. What is the meaning of the word nirbandha?

"The word *nirbandha* means that a practitioner should chant sixteen names thirty-two syllables *mahāmantra* on a *tulasī* bead for one hundred and eight times. Chanting four rounds is called one *granṭha*. One should start with one *granṭha* and gradually increase the number to sixteen *granṭhas* or sixty-four rounds. That will make a prescribed numbers of one hundred thousand holy names. By gradually increasing the number of chanting the holy name to three hundred thousand times, one will spend his entire time simply in chanting the holy names. All previous *ācāryas* have attained perfection by following this order of the Lord."

(*Harināma-cintāmani*)

7. Should there be a gap between the chanting of the holy names?

"The chanting of the holy names must be constant. One should be careful that at the time of chanting the holy names no other sensual activities create obstacles."

(Śrī Bhāgavatārka Marīci-Mālā 13/15)

8. What kind of mentality should a practitioner have at the time of chanting?

"'At the time of chanting the holy names may this desire arise in my heart. As the baby birds who can not fly desire to see their mother, as the hungry calves intensely wait for drinking their mothers milk, and as a wife becomes morose while meditating on her husband who is away in a foreign country, similarly O Lord !let my mind also become extremely eager for Your *darśana*.'"

(*Śrī Bhāgavatārka Marīci-Mālā* 13/16)

9. Should a person who has taken shelter of the holy names need to undergo atonement based on karma and jñāna?

"Those who have fully taken shelter of the holy names have no need to undergo atonement based on karma and *jñāna*."

(*Śrī Bhāgavatārka Marīci-Mālā* 13/17)

10. What are the characteristics of a person who has taken complete shelter of the holy names?

"By misusing the six propensities of the heart such as lust, anger, greed, illusion, pride and envy one commits sin. One who has taken complete shelter of the holy names does not commit any sin. He engages his lust for discussing the topics of Krishna and maintaining Vaiṣṇava family based on the service to Krishna. He never engages in sinful activities like enjoying other's wife, accumulating more money than required, desiring name and fame, cheating and stealing. He engages his anger against those who are envious of Krishna and the Vaiṣṇavas. In this way, he remains aloof from the association of the materialists. He avoids subduing and torturing other's. Then his anger transforms into tolerance like a tree. He engages his greed for relishing the mellows of ecstatic love for Krishna, and thereby he does not even bother to eat palatable foodstuffs, wear opulent clothes, enjoy beautiful women and accumulate unlimited wealth. He engages his illusion in the transcendental mellows and thus becomes bewildered by the beauty of Krishna's pastimes and Vaiṣṇavas' characteristics. Wealth, followers and material happiness do not enamor him. He does not get involved in impersonalism, or atheism and false argument that are caused by bewilderment from improper conclusions. By engaging his pride in the service of Krishna, he gives up pride of high birth, wealth, beauty, education, followers and bodily strength. He totally gives up self-esteeme of being envious and violent to other's. By regulating one's life in this way one cannot have any opportunity for committing any sin. Rather his propensities for sinful activities become totally uprooted. But sometimes there may be some sinful activity committed accidentally which is nullified without atonement."

(*Sajjana-toṣaṇī* 8/9)

11. Do the so-called devotees who take shelter of duplicity attain love of God?

"As a patient attains the result of medication even without knowing its power similarly one who chants the holy name of the Lord without knowing the strength of the holy name easily achieves the result of chanting the holy name. If persons who are affected by prejudices and fault of interpretation take shelter of duplicity, the holy names reserve the right to award them result according to their duplicity. The holy names never award them supreme fruit of love of God."

(*Śrī Bhāgavatārka Marīcī-Mālā* 13/24)

12. What is real Braja-vāsa or residing in Braja?

"To live in a solitary place with transcendental emotion is called Braja-vāsa. One should chant the holy names of the Lord with a prescribed number of rounds and engage in the service of the Lord twenty-four hours a day. One should engage in favorable service to the Supreme Lord in such a way that it does not create any impediment in the maintenance of his livelihood."

(*Jaiva Dharma*, Chapter 40)

95

Rāgātmika Bhakti

1. What is rāgātmika bhakti?

"The materialists' natural attraction for material enjoyment is called *rāga* or attachment. As the eyes become agitated by seeing beautiful objects similarly the hearts of the materialists remain fully absorbed in material enjoyment. When Lord Krishna becomes the object of one's attachment it is called *rāga bhakti*. Śrī Rūpa Goswami has said that *rāga* means full absorption in one's worshipable Lord. When devotional service to Krishna is executed through such *rāga* it is called *rāgātmika bhakti*. In brief, the loving intense thirst for Krishna is called *rāgātmika bhakti*. Intense greed for Krishna's pastimes acts in *rāgātmika bhakti*."

(*Jaiva Dharma*, Chapter 21)

2. Where is the existence of rāgātmika bhakti?

"The devotional service executed by the Brajavāsīs with intense attachment is the topmost form of devotional service. Such devotional service is not found anywhere else. Devotional service performed under the guidance of the Brajavāsīs is called *rāgānugā bhakti*.

The service propensity with natural absorption attributed to one's worshipable Lord is called *rāga*. When the devotional service to Krishna is executed with intense greed, it is called *rāgātmika*. This *rāgātmika bhakti* is present in its full form among the Brajavāsīs. Devotional service performed under the subordination of such *rāgātmika bhakti* is *rāgānugā bhakti*."

(Commentary on *Caitanya Caritāmṛta* Madhya 22/145, 146, 150)

96

Rāgānugā Bhakti

1. Who is a qualified candidate for rāgānugā bhakti?

"As regulative faith awards one the qualification to perform *vaidhi bhakti*, similarly faith with intense greed awards one the qualification to perform *rāgānugā bhakti*. According to their respective relationship to the Lord *rāgātmika bhakti* is prominent among the Brajavāsīs. One who is greedy for attaining the same mood which the Brajavāsīs have for Krishna, is a qualified candidate for *rāgānugā bhakti*."

(*Jaiva Dharma*, Chapter 21)

2. How many types of sādhanas are there and what are the processes?

"There are nine types of *sādhana bhakti* described in the *Śrīmad-Bhāgavatam* they are hearing, chanting, remembering, serving the lotus feet, worshiping, offering prayers, offering service as a menial servant, friendship and surrendering everything to the Lord. Śrī Rūpa Gosvāmīpāda has further divided these nine processes into sixty-four limbs of devotional service. The point of consideration here is that *sādhana bhakti* is of two kinds namely, *vaidhi* and *rāgānugā*. Among the two *vaidhi bhakti* is of nine kinds. *Rāgānugā sādhana bhakti* is mainly performed through one's mind under the subordination of the residents of Braja."

(*Jaiva Dharma*, Chapter 4)

3. What is the natural propensity of a spirit soul?

"As the natural propensity of the magnet is to attract iron, as the quality of the heat is liquidness, as the strength of fire is to burn, as the propensity of the mind is to think, feel and will, and as the characteristics of the objects is to be engaged in their respective usage, similarly the natural propensity of the spirit soul is to become attached to the Supreme Lord. In the liberated state this propensity is pure and fully manifested; but in the conditional state it is perverted."

(*Tattva-sutra* 17)

4. What is the difference between attachment for material objects and attachment for spiritual objects?

"Embodied souls attachment for material objects is the perverted reflection of their attachment of spiritual objects. When this propensity is completely purified and devoid of any material designation it is called spiritual attachment, but when it is materially contaminated and covered with material designation it is the perverted reflection of the spiritual attachment."

(*Tattva-sutra* 17)

5. What are the names and functions of attachment when it is materially designated?

"Attachment is the same propensity, but acquires different names according to different designations. When one is attached to wealth it is called greed, when one is attached to the beauty of woman it is called debauchery, when it is displayed on distressed people it is called compassion, when it is applied to brothers and sisters it is called affection, when it is applied to helpful people it is called gratefulness, when it is designated with kindness it is called love, and when it is designated with hatred it is called envy. In this way, one single propensity transforms into various propensities and manifests itself. Pluralism is its characteristic. This attachment remains with the liberated souls in its pure uncontaminated state. It is not that this attachment remains confined in only one state, but it increases unlimitedly and takes various shapes. This is its beauty."

(*Tattva-sutra* 17)

6. Who are actual worshipers of the Supreme Lord?

"Those who engage in the worship of the Supreme Lord under the compulsion of fear, ambition and sense of duty, their worship is not so pure. Those who engage in the worship of the Supreme Lord in the path of attachment are certainly the actual worshipers of the Supreme Lord."

(*Caitanya-śikṣāmṛta* 1/1)

7. Who is eligible for rāgānuga bhakti?

"One who has not realized the science of *rāga* and who desires to worship the Lord under the rules and regulations of this scriptures, he is eligible for *vaidhi bhakti*. One who does not wish to be controlled by the rules and regulations of the scriptures at the time of worshiping Hari and who has developed natural attachment for the worship of the Hari, he alone is eligible for rāgānuga *bhakti*."

(*Jaiva Dharma*, Chapter 4)

8. What is anxiety based on rāga?

"O my mind! For a long time I have yearned to see Your lotus feet. Will this difficult-to-attain desire be fulfilled in this birth? This thought overwhelms my heart."

(Gītā Māla, Song 32)

9. What is the root of rāgānugā bhakti?

"The taste for engaging in the service of the Lord by following the foot steps of the Brajavāsīs is the root of *rāgānugā bhakti*."

(*Āmnāya-sutra* 116)

10. Why is it necessary to possess the knowledge regarding the rāsas while performing bhajana under the guidance of Śrī Rūpa?

"One who wishes to understand the truth of Śrīla Rūpa Goswami's teachings must understand the *rāsas*. The spiritual blissful *rāsas* are the complete treasury of the Supreme Lord and all other truths are subordinate to this."

(Gītā Māla, Song 6)

11. What is the difference between vaidhi and rāgānugā bhakti?

"*Vaidhī bhakti* is a slow process and *rāgānugā bhakti* is a fast process. By following *rāgānugā bhakti* one quickly attains the stage of *rāsa*. One who has a taste for performing devotional service in the path of attachment certainly becomes a follower of Śrī Rūpa Goswami ."

(Gītā Māla, Song 5)

12. How many types of spiritual cultivation do the practitioners of rāgānugā bhakti engage in?

It is the duty of everyone to follow these seven categories of cultivation. But all the descriptions are not to be performed by everyone, because there is a need to consider one's qualification.

1. Spiritual cultivation —

(1) *Prīti* and (2) realization of *sambandha*, *abhidheya*, and *prayojana*.

2. Mental cultivation —

(1) Rememberance, (2) thinking, (3) meditation, (4) concentrated meditation, (5) *samādhi*, (6) consideration on the science of *sambandha*, (7) repentance, (8) *yama* (truthfulness, refraining from theft, giving up bad association, intelligence, not accumulating more than necessary, religiosity, celibacy, refraining from unnecessary talk, steadiness, forgiveness, and fearlessness), and (9) purification of the heart.

3. Bodily cultivation —

(1) Niyamas Cleanliness, *japa*, austerity, sacrifice, faith, hospitality, worship, pilgrimage, welfare work, satisfaction, proper behavior, and serving the spiritual master. (2) serving other's, (3) seeing and touching the devotees and the *Śrīmad-Bhāgavatam*, (4) praying, (5) hearing, (6) engaging the senses in devotional service, (7) transformations of ecstatic love, and (8) developing the mood of servitude to the Lord.

4. Cultivation of speech

Chanting hymns, (2) studying, (3) *kīrtana*, (4) teaching, (5) praying, and (6) preaching.

5. Cultivation of one's relationship —

(1) *śānta*, (2) *dāsya*, (3) *sakhya*, (4) *vātsalya*, and (5) *kānta*. There are two types of relationships—with the Lord and with the Lord's associates.

6. Social cultivation —

(1) *Varṇa*—*brāhmaṇa*, *kṣatriya*, *vaiśya*, and *śūdra*—their occupations and positions are divided according to people's nature, (2)*āśrama*—*gṛhastha*, *brahmācārya*, *vānaprastha*, and *sannyāsa*—divided according to peoples' social situation, (3) assemblies, (4) general festivals, and (5) activities like sacrifice.

7. Cultivation of sense objects —

The following sense objects help one in the development of Krishna consciousness. (1) The objects for the eyes are the Deity, the temple, the scriptures, the holy places, spiritual dramas, and spiritual festivals; (2) the objects for the ears are the scriptures, songs, lectures, and conversations; (3) the objects for the nose are *tulasī*, flowers, sandalwood, and other fragrant items offered to the Lord; (4) the objects for the tongue are *kīrtana* and taking a vow to accept only the palatable foodstuffs and drinks that were offered to the Lord; (5) the objects for the touch are the air of holy places, pure water, the body of a Vaiṣṇava, the soft bed offered to Krishna, and association with a chaste woman in order to propagate a God-centered family; (6) the times like Hari-vāsara (Ekādaśī) and festive days; and (7) the places like Vṛndāvana, Navadvīpa, Jagannātha Purī, and Naimiṣāraṇya.

(Conclusion to *Krishna-saṁhitā*)

13. What is the rāgānugā devotees procedure for serving Krishna?

"Those who have developed a greed for engaging in *rāgātmika bhakti* should, according to the activities of the residents of Braja, externally serve as a *sādhaka* and internally served as a perfected devotee."

(Commentary to *Caitanya Caritāmṛta* Madhya-22/154.

14. What should be the mood, process, endeavor for realizing the Lord's pastime, behavior, and service to the worshipable Lord, of those who engage in rāgānugā bhakti?

"One should engage in the Lord's service in the same way it is described in the book *Vilāpa Kusumānjali*. One should behave with each other in the same way it is described in the book *Braja-vilāsa-stotra*. One should endeavor to realize the Lord's pastime in the same way it is described in the prayers offered by Viśākha and Nanda. One should perceive these pastimes within the eight-fold pastimes of the Lord. One should engage one's mind in the pastimes of Krishna in the same process it is described in the book *Manaḥ-śikṣā* and one should strengthen one's mood revealed in the book *Svaniyama dvādasakaṁ*."

(*Jaiva Dharma*, Chapter 39)

97

The Teachings of Śrī Caitanya

1. What is the importance of Śrīman Mahāprabhu teachings? How can one adopt His teachings?

"The teachings of Śrī Caitanya Mahāprabhu are confidential and scientific. They are incomprehensible if one does not study them with special attention. Nowadays many people read novels while relaxing after lunch. The teachings of Śrī Caitanya Mahāprabhu should not be read like that. These teachings are the confidential purport of the Vedas and *Vedānta*. If one slowly and faithfully studies these teachings with special attention in the association of the devotees, one can understand the purport of these teachings."

(*Śrī Manaḥ-śikṣā*, Verse 1)

2. In which forms have the essence of Śrī Caitanya Mahāprabhu teachings been manifested?

"The direct instructions of Śrī Gauracandra are that the Vedic literatures are the only evidence and they establish the following nine auxiliary evidences.

1. Lord Hari is one without a second.
2. He is always vested with infinite power.
3. He is ocean of *rāsa*.
4. The spirit soul is His part and partial.
5. Certain souls are engrossed by His illusory energy.
6. Certain souls are liberated from the grasp of His illusory energy.
7. All spiritual and material worlds are simultaneously one and different from Hari.
8. Bhakti is the only means for attaining the ultimate goal of life.
9. Love of Krishna is the ultimate goal of life.

(*Śrī Gaurāṅga Smaraṇa Mangala*, Stotra 75)

3. Why Śrī Caitanya Mahāprabhu has condemned Bhakti-siddhānta-viruddha and rāsābhāsa?

"*Bhakti-siddhānta-viruddha* refers to that which is against the principle of unity in diversity, philosophically known as acintya-bhedābheda—simultaneous oneness and difference—whereas *rāsābhāsa* is something that may appear to be a transcendental mellow but actually is not. Those who are pure Vaiṣṇavas should avoid both these things opposed to devotional service. These misconceptions practically parallel the Māyāvāda philosophy. If one indulges in Māyāvāda philosophy, he gradually falls down from the platform of devotional service. By overlapping mellows (*rāsābhāsa*) one eventually becomes a *prākṛta-sahajiyā* and takes everything to be very easy. One may also become a member of the *bāula* community and gradually become attracted to material activities. Śrī Caitanya Mahāprabhu has therefore advised us to avoid *bhakti-siddhānta-viruddha* and *rāsābhāsa*. In this way, the devotee can remain pure and free from fall-downs. Everyone should try to remain aloof from *bhakti-siddhānta-viruddha* and *rāsābhāsa*."

(Commentary on *Caitanya Caritāmṛta,* Madhya 10/113)

4. Does Mahāprabhu approve any immorality?

"Mahāprabhu tells us that a man should earn money in a right way and sincere dealings with other's and their masters, but should not immorally gain it. When Gopinatha Patanayaka, one of the brothers of Ramananda Raya was being punished by the Raja of Orissa for immoral gains, Śrī Caitanya warned all who attended upon Him to be moral in their worldly dealings."

(*Chaitanya Mahāprabhu's Life & Precepts*)

5. Through His own behavior, what did Mahāprabhu teach regarding the duty of a householder?

"In His own early life, He has taught the *grhasthas* to give all sorts of help to the needy and the helpless, and has shown that it is necessary, for one who has power to do it to help the education of the people specially the *brāhmanas* who are expected to study the higher subjects of human knowledge."

(*Chaitanya Mahāprabhu's Life & Precepts*)

6. Is there any fault in the behavior, preaching and teachings of Śrī Caitanyadeva?

"Śrī Caitanya as a teacher has taught man both by precepts and by His holy life. There is scarcely a spot in His life, which may be made the subject of criticism. His *sannyāsa*, His severity to Junior Haridāsa, and such like other acts have been questioned as wrong by certain persons, but as far as we understand, we think as all other independent men would think, that those men have been led by a hasty conclusion or party spirit."

(*Chaitanya Mahāprabhu's Life & Precepts*)

7. What Śrīman Mahāprabhu has accepted as the commentary of Vedānta? And what are His teachings in this regard?

"Śrī Caitanya Mahāprabhu has said that *pranava* or *Oṁ* is the transcendental sound vibration. The purport of this sound vibration is vividly described in the *Upaniṣads*. The teachings of the *Upaniṣads* are completely approved in the *sūtras* of Vyāsadeva. *Śrīmad-Bhāgavatam* is the commentary on the *sūtras* of Vyāsadeva. In the first sutra of Vyāsadeva '*janmādi asya yataḥ* ' the teaching of *parināma vāda* has been taught. In the Vedic *mantra* '*yato vā imāni bhutāni*' the same principle is taught and in *Śrīmad-Bhāgavatam* also the same principle is taught. Fearing that in the philosophy of *parināma vāda* the supreme Brahman become transformed, Sankarācārya established his own philosophy called *vivartavāda*. Actually *brahmavivarta* is the root of all misconceptions and *parināma vāda* is the pure spiritual truth approved by all the scripture."

(*Caitanya-śikṣāmṛta* 1/5)

8. What is the essence of Śrīmān Mahāprabhu teachings?

"The essence of Śrīmān Mahāprabhu teachings is that love of Krishna is the living entities eternal constitutional propensity. The living entities can never be eternally separated from this propensity. But due to the forgetfulness of Krishna, the living entities are bewildered by the illusory energy of the Lord and thereby became attached to material objects, and their constitutional propensity has gradually become lost. It has almost become dormant within the core of their hearts. This is the cause of living entities suffering in the material existence. If out of good fortune the living entities remember that, 'I am an eternal servant of Krishna' then their dormant propensity will be revived and they will certainly regain their spiritual health."

(*Caitanya-śikṣāmṛta*)

9. What is the ultimate instruction of Śrīmān Mahāprabhu?

"*Śrīmad-Bhāgavatam* has declared that those who faithfully hear or glorify the transcendental pastimes of Braja, will certainly achieve love of god in the form of pure devotional service, and they will attain liberation from their mundane heart ailments."

(*Caitanya-śikṣāmṛta* 1/3)

98

Instructions to the Living Entities

1. What is the primary instruction of Ṭhākura Bhaktivinoda to the human beings?

"The human form of life is very rare. And even one day should not be misused."

(*Sajjana-toṣaṇī* 4/6)

2. How did Śrī Bhaktivinoda Ṭhākura instructs one to lead a religious life?

"There is no superior wealth in this material world than religious principles. This material body is temporary. Today it is alive, tomorrow it may be dead. Our most merciful Lord has kindly given this world the holy names and the treasury of love of God. One should accept them from a bona fide spiritual master and the Vaiṣṇavas. *Śrīmad-Bhāgavatam* and *Śrī Caitanya-caritāmṛta* are the two invaluable jewels in this world. One should discuss them with utmost care. There is no need to advertised oneself as a learned man. One should distribute the wealth of devotional service to all living entities. One should lead a pious life and earn one's livelihood through pious means and thus maintain himself and his dependents. But one should never forget the holy names of Krishna."

(*Autobiography of Śrī Bhaktivinoda Ṭhākura*)

3. Is a devotee of Krishna afraid of plague?

"Becoming afraid of plague is certainly not Vaiṣṇava etiquette. Just consider, O brothers! What can plague do to you? What can it harm you by taking away your useless life. If you want your own benefit then take a lesson from this plague. If you are attacked by plague tomorrow then you will be no more, where all your happiness and wealth will go then just imagine. Therefore, without wasting your time uselessly you should constantly and sincerely chant the holy names of Hari with devotion. Then millions of plague can not create any harm to you."

(*Sajjana-toṣaṇī* 10/2)

4. Which ideal did Śrī Bhaktivinoda Ṭhākura instructed those who are distressed on seeing other's distress to follow?

"Offer your respect to all living entities in this world. Always endeavor to mitigate the distress of all living entities. Always try to remain by the side of other living entities and benefit them. But at the same time never forget the supreme characteristics and most essential instructions of Śrī Gaurāṅga."

(*Sajjana-toṣaṇī* 11/3)

5. When does a living entity's birth in this material world become successful?

"A person who has accepted Krishna as his eternal son, there is no need for him to lament and as such all his temporary attachment becomes destroyed. In order to worship Krishna you have come to this material world, therefore always contemplate on the eternal science of Absolute Truth."

(*Gita Mālā*, Song 2)

6. What duty has been prescribed for a traveler on the path of spiritual life?

"After completing my family responsibilities I will go to Vṛndāvana. Now I am trying hard to repay the three types of debts." One should not maintain such a desire, because under the influence of such ill-desire, one will ultimately give up his body. Then one will not be able to serve the lotus feet of Krishna, the friend of the poor. If you want auspiciousness, then always chant the holy names of Lord Krishna. It is useless to argue whether you live at home or in the forest."

(*Kalyāna Kalpataru*, Song 3)

7. What is Śrī Bhaktivinoda Ṭhākura's prescription about the topmost duty of the temporary human life?

"You do not have many more days to live; whatever days are left is also full of obstacles. Therefore O brothers! Continue to drink the mellows of *Śrīmad-Bhāgavatam* with special attention and care."

(*Sajjana-toṣaṇī* 20/3)

8. What is Śrī Bhaktivinoda Ṭhākura's instruction regarding the pride for caste?

"O brother mind! You remain as a *brāhmaṇa* with your social prestige, but do not insult the Vaiṣṇavas. As such, an intelligent ginger trader never quarrels over the ship."

(*Kalyāna Kalpataru*, Song 9)

9. What is Śrī Bhaktivinoda Ṭhākura's instruction towards the pseudo-renunciates and those who desire material fame?

"You are a servant of Śrī Caitanya and you should desire devotional service to Hari. What is the use of various symptoms of *āśrama* life? Please reject material honor and reside in Śāntipura. Your only assets are the mercy of the devotees."

(*Kalyāna Kalpataru*, Song 13)

10. What is Śrī Bhaktivinoda Ṭhākura's instruction to those who are attached to matter?

A living entity is constitutionally pure. So O brother! Why are you being illusioned in this material world again and again? Please consider once that the spirit soul is like the flow of nectar and immortal."

(*Kalyāna Kalpataru*, Song 1)

11. What is Śrī Bhaktivinoda Ṭhākura's instruction to those who identify themselves as Vaiṣṇavas?

"There is no need for the introduction of the Vaiṣṇavas. Never proceed for accumulating material opulence. Śrī Bhaktivinod Ṭhākura requests that you always sing loudly the transcendental qualities of Śrī Rādhā and Krishna."

(*Kalyāna Kalpataru*, Song 13)

12. What is Śrī Bhaktivinoda Ṭhākura's advice to the proud people who neglect the path of the mahājanas?

"Because many cheaters artificially put on *tilaka*, beads and take initiation, therefore, you have developed detachment for them. You find faults in the path of the *mahājanas* and you become very angry. As a result, you give up attachment towards this path. Now see, O brother mind ! You grabbed ashes instead of gold and you have wasted this life and the life after your death. Everyone is calling you a cheater. Moreover, you have not achieved devotional service. So what will happen after your death?"

(*Kalyāna Kalpataru*, Song 17)

13. What is Śrī Bhaktivinoda Ṭhākura's instruction to the so-called exalted devotees?

"O my mind ! What else will I tell you? You are talking about love of God, but actually you have rejected gold and tied an empty knot in your cloth."

(*Kalyāna Kalpataru*, Song 18)

14. What is Śrī Bhaktivinoda Ṭhākura's warning to the demoniac people?

"From the discussion of historical incidences, you know very well that there were so many sinful demons whose goal was to gratify their senses. They engaged in various sinful activities and finally met with death. At the time of death, they lost all their hopes and were burnt by the fire of repentance. They spent their lives like the animals, such as dogs and hogs, and never cared for spiritual life."

(*Kalyāna Kalpataru*, Song 1)

15. What is Śrī Bhaktivinoda Ṭhākura's instruction to those who uselessly carry the burden of family life?

"I work hard like an ass, but I do not know for whom am I doing so much, yet my illusion is not removed. My days are spent in useless activities, and nights in sleeping; still I do not realize that death is sitting just next to me. I eat palatable foodstuff, see beautiful things, and wear nice clothes without any anxiety. I never think that any day I will have to give up this body."

(*Kalyāna Kalpataru*, Song 4)

16. What is Śrī Bhaktivinoda Ṭhākura's warning to those who consider the body as self?

"My body will lie down in the crematorium and birds and insects will enjoy it.

The dogs and jackals will happily enjoy a feast with my body. Such is the destination of a body. Yet worldly opulence and friends are all devoted to it."

(*Kalyāna Kalpataru*, Song 4)

17. What is Śrī Bhaktivinoda Ṭhākura's instruction to those who desire to attain eternal happiness, regarding subjects favorable and unfavorable for devotional service?

"O living entities, if you want to experience the flow of eternal bliss constantly then please take shelter of the lotus feet of the spiritual master. Give up all types of dry worships, such as meditating on the impersonal Brahman, and always cultivate attachment for the Supreme Lord. The abode of Vṛndāvana is full of flowers where *Śrī Rāsa-līlā* pastimes are enacted. You are a pure spirit soul. The pride of being the enjoyer is extremely weak in Vṛndāvana. You are intimately related to Śrī Rādhikā as an eternal companion. You are meant to experience the spiritual ecstasy. Enjoying the illusory material objects is the cause of your downfall."

(*Kalyāna Kalpataru*, Song 2)

18. What is Śrī Bhaktivinoda Ṭhākura's instruction to the lazy people?

"O brother, death is certain. It may come today or after a hundred years. Therefore, do not remain free from anxiety. Please worship the lotus feet of Śrī Krishna as soon as possible because there is no guarantee for life."

(*Kalyāna Kalpataru*, Song 2)

19. What is Śrī Bhaktivinoda Ṭhākura's instruction regarding the constitutional propensity and hope of the practitioners?

"For thee thy Sire on High has kept
A store of bliss above.
To end of time, thou art Oh! His
Who wants but purest love."

(*Saragrahi Vaiṣṇava*)

20. Who gives the living entities information about immortality when they are unable to solve the mystery of life?

"Man's life to him a problem dark!
A screen both left and right!
No soul hath come to tell us what
Exists beyond our sight!
But then a voice, how deep and soft,
Within ourselves is left:—
Man! Man! Thou art immortal soul!
Thee Death can never melt!"

(*Saragrahi Vaiṣṇava*)

21. How Śrī Bhaktivinoda Ṭhākura wanted the travelers on the path of spiritual life to be determined?

"Maintain thy post in spirit world
As firmly as you can,
Let never matter pushes thee down,
O stand heroic man!"

(*Saragrahi Vaiṣṇava*)

22. What is Śrī Bhaktivinoda Ṭhākura's instruction to the reader's of Śrī Caitanya Caritāmṛta?

"As one should carefully study *Vedānta* and literatures which deal with transcendental mellows from a bona fide spiritual master, similarly this great literature *Śrī Caitanya-caritāmṛta* should be read like that."

(*Sajjana-toṣaṇī* 3/11)

23. What is Śrī Bhaktivinoda Ṭhākura's warning to the readers of transcendental literatures?

"Whenever you read a literature you should read it completely otherwise you will fail to abstract the actual meaning and ultimately become a logician."

(*Caitanya-śikṣāmṛta* 3/3)

24. What is Śrī Bhaktivinoda Ṭhākura's instruction to those who are fond of reading mundane literature?

"Do not remain confined simply in the discussion of a literature, you should approach the saintly persons and Vaiṣṇavas and understand from them the actual distinction between *sādhana bhakti*, *bhāva bhakti* and *prema bhakti*. Vaiṣṇavism is not a science confined with in the literature. By the word *nirgrantha* the spiritual master and the Vaiṣṇavas have been defined as beyond the literature. Therefore the science of Vaiṣṇavism is a mystery?"

(*Sajjana-toṣaṇī* 6/2)

25. Which process did Śrī Bhaktivinoda Ṭhākura prescribe to the practitioners who are afraid of Kali?

"Always remember that this is Kali-yuga. In order to create impediment in one's cultivation of devotional service, Kali invents many sinful means. Kali has no control over whatever you do according to the characteristics and instructions of Mahāprabhu."

(*Sajjana-toṣaṇī* 6/1)

26. How much determined and tolerant should a practitioner be?

"If someone pushes you, if someone insults you, if a sinful person cheats you, if some one becomes envious of you, if some one chastises you, if someone arrests you, if someone steals your wealth, if someone spits on you, if someone passes urine on your body, and if foolish people frighten you in many ways, still you should be determined to achieve your goal of life, and must deliver your mind from sinful subject matter with the help of your devotion filled intelligence."

(*Śrī Bhāgavatārka Marīci Māla)*

27. What kind of assurance did Śrī Bhaktivinoda Ṭhākura give to the non-duplicitous devotees of the Lord?

"There is no doubt that soon by the mercy of the most merciful Mahāprabhu, all social inauspiciousness will be destroyed. There is need to worry anymore if you take shelter of the lotus feet of Mahāprabhu without duplicity."

(*Sajjana-toṣaṇī* 2/7)

28. How has Śrī Bhaktivinoda Ṭhākura invited the people of the whole world to see the pastimes of Śrī Caitanya, and attain love of Krishna?

"Why I, the most unfortunate fallen soul did not take birth at the time when Śrī Gauracandra inundated the entire world including the highest mountains with the flood of love of God? Therefore, I was unable to relish those waves of love of God.

Why I did not take birth at that time to serve the lotus feet of Śrī Caitanya? Why I did not become the servant of Śrī Rūpa and Sanātana. Why I did not carry the water pot of Raghunātha? Why I did not wander about with Rāmānanda Rāya around Chakratirtha? Why I did not see the deliverance of Śārvabhauma Bhaṭṭacārya? When Prakāśānanda Sarasvati the leader of the *sannyāsis* of Kāśī attained spiritual bliss in the form of devotional service to the Lord, why I did not take birth then to relish that devotion filled nectarean waves of the Lord's arguments with Prakāśānanda. Even though such a coveted desire is rare still if I would have taken birth as a mundane logician in the family of a *brāhmaṇa* at that time then Śrī Krishna Caitanya, the friend of all living entities, would have punished me with His sharp arrow like words and accepted an atheist like me as His servant. Then He would have entrusted me to Harīdāsa Ṭhākura to be rectified by the chanting of the holy names. Alas! If I could have constantly seen with my spiritual eyes the Lord sitting in the midst of the

Vaiṣṇavas and delivering all living entities who are burned by the fire of material existence through distributing the nectar of the holy name. How much would the associates of the Lord become ecstatic when the Lord would raise his hands and after awakening all living entities from the lap of illusion, say, 'Take this remedy for material disease, drink the mellows of ecstatic love and become immortal.' As a result, countless human beings who are afraid of demon-like material enjoyment would have begged for His shelter. Then the Lord would have embraced them out of love and happily awarded them the love of Krishna. Thus, the material disease of the living entities would have been cured. I am a servant of Śrī Caitanya and am fallen in the material ocean. The Lord is my only guide and protector. According to His order I am inviting all of you to chant the holy names of Harī. O living entities! O friends! Give up *karma-kānda*, *tarka-kānda* and *brahma-kānda*. Come and take the love of God distributed by Śrī Caitanya to your full satisfaction. Then your disappointment will be destroyed. Your contaminated state of conditional life will be vanquished, and you will regain your original constitutional position. You will then attain peace, which is your constitutional characteristic. You will relish the ecstatic love of Krishna unlimitedly."

(Servants of the Vaiṣṇavas, *Kedārnātha Sacīdānanda Premālankāra*) 27th February 1870. *Sajjana-toṣaṇī* 19/2.

99

Various Topics

1. What is the basis of a living entities gradual advancement?

"If the living entities can remain fixed in their respective positions, then they can make gradual advancement and if they fall from their positions they become degraded."

(*Sajjana-toṣaṇī* 10/6)

2. Can one arouse other's faith in devotional service without he himself chanting and preaching the holy name?

"Until desires opposed to devotional service are destroyed no amount of good instructions can affect a person's life. The instructions will simply hit the ears and come back. They will never reach the heart. Therefore, whatever principle of devotional service you preach, whatever topics of devotional service you discuss, they will not yield any result because the listeners are unqualified due to the fault of their karma. Therefore, your discourses and discussions will not produce any result. My order to all of you is that you should constantly sing the glories of the holy names for the benefit of the living entities. As a result of hearing the holy names, the living entities will accumulate piety and develop faith in the glories of the holy names. Then by the mercy of the holy names, they will develop non-duplicitous faith in devotional service in this lifetime or in the next."

(*Sajjana-toṣaṇī* 15/1)

3. What is beauty, happiness, distress, learning, foolishness, the actual path, wrong path, heaven, hell, home, rich, poor, a miser, the controller and the controlled?

"The qualities such as detachment are called beauty. Absence of happiness and distress is called happiness. Lack of sense gratification is called distress. The power of discrimination between bondage and liberation is called learning. A person who thinks I am this body is a fool. The orders of Krishna are the actual path. Bewilderment in the heart is the wrong path. Development of qualities in the mode of goodness is heaven. Development of a body in the mode of ignorance is hell. Krishna alone is the friend and the spiritual master. Human body is the home. A person enriched with good qualities is rich. An dissatisfied person is poor. A person whose senses are uncontrolled is a miser. A person who is transcendental to material qualities is the controller and a person who associates with material qualities is the controlled."

(*Śrī Bhāgavatārka Maricī Mālā* 1/44 – 47)

4. Is one's luck responsible for his good and bad result?

"As long as one goes through a bad time he never meets with success. When good times arrive for him he meets with all success."

(*Autobiography of Śrī Bhaktivinoda Ṭhākura*)

5. What is the meaning of the phrase 'soon ripe' (precocious)

"Nowadays there is one disease that as soon as tender boys learn to write A,B,C they begin to instruct like a teacher. This is called 'soon ripe' (precocious)."

(*Sajjana-toṣaṇī* 6/4)

6. What is the symptom of a modern scholar?

"Simply to attack ancient way of life has nowadays become the symptom of a scholar."

(*Sajjana-toṣaṇī* 4/2)

7. What is the difference between word jugglery and learning? Which one does the young generations prefer?

"Word jugglery and learning are two separate things. The scholars of the western countries are more into word jugglery than learning. However, the authors of India are highly learned scholars and less into word jugglery. The young generations are more in favor of word jugglery than learning."

(*Sajjana-toṣaṇī* 4/4)

8. Is it proper to define one's age as the proof of one's qualification?

"Only age cannot be accepted as the proof of one's qualification. Many old people crawl within their minds. There are many people who are sufficiently aged, who have no teeth, who have gray hair yet they dye their hair, artificially set silver teeth and enjoy sense gratification like young men. When such old people could not become detached then the age can not be the root cause of one's detachment."

(*Sajjana-toṣaṇī* 8/10)

9. What are dhāraṇā, anubhuti and yukti?

"As soon as the object of the senses meet the senses a reflection of the object of the senses goes to the heart through the door of the senses. There an internal sense carefully preserves that reflection. This propensity is called *dhāraṇā*. Later on when the propensity of the internal sense interacts with that preserved reflection one attains feelings of imaginary objects. This is called *anubhuti*. Thereafter the internal sense spreads its sovereignty over those imaginary objects and indulges in the conception of good and bad. This concept is called *yukti*. If one scrutinizingly study this process one will find that the entire process is sensory ."

(*Tattva-sutra* 16)

10. What is pure reasoning and mixed reasoning?

"There are two kinds of reasoning namely pure reasoning and mixed reasoning. A pure spirit soul's spiritual cultivation is called pure reasoning. It is faultless and the constitutional characteristic of a spirit soul. The materially perverted constitutional characteristic of a spirit soul who is conditioned by matter is called mixed reasoning. Mixed reasoning is of two kinds; reasoning mixed with karma and reasoning mixed with *jñāna*. Another name of which is *tarka* or argument. This is most condemnable."

(*Tattva* Viveka 1/18)

11. Is it reasonable for the mundane scholars to become proud as the judge of the spiritual truth?

"As immature doctors promise to cure physical disease by administering heavy doses of medicine similarly our modern mundane scholars, in order to conclude the confidential truth regarding the human life, use insignificant mundane methods. Disregarding the faults born from imperfect senses they rely heavily on material education which is as illusory as a dream and try to make research in all subject matters."

(*Sajjana-toṣaṇī* 7/7)

12. For what reason even thoughtful people were unable to understand the actual purport of Śrīmad-Bhāgavatam?

"Men of brilliant thoughts have passed by the work (the Bhagavat) in quest of truth and philosophy, but the prejudice which they imbibed from its useless readers and their conduct prevented them from making a candid investigation."

(*The Bhagavat: Its Philosophy; Its Ethics and its Theology*)

13. What kind of mentality should one maintain while studying the scripture?

"In fact, most readers are mere repositories of facts and statements made by other people. But this is not study. The student is to read the facts with a view to create, and not with the object of fruitless retention. Students like satellites should reflect whatever light they receive from authors and not imprison the facts and thoughts just as the Magistrates imprison the convicts in the jail!"

(The Bhagavat: Its Philosophy; Its Ethics and its Theology)

14. Why are the words of the mahājanas confidential and when can one realize them?

"The expressions of all great men are nice but somewhat mysterious-when understood, they bring the truth nearest to the heart, otherwise they remain mere letters that "kill." The reason of the mystery is that men, advanced in their inward approach to Deity, are in the habit of receiving revelations which are but mysteries to those that are behind them."

('To Love God, *Journal of Tajpur*, 25 August 1871)

15. Does material world give any hint of the spiritual world?

"The outward appearance of nature is nothing more than a sure index of its spiritual face. Matter is the dictionary of spirit and material pictures are but the shadows of the spiritual affairs which our material eye carries back to our spiritual perception."

(*The Bhagavat: Its Philosophy; Its Ethics and its Theology*)

16. Is there any difference in the process of worship by learned scholars and fools, even though they have equal rights in the religious principle preached by Śrī Caitanya.?

"The religion preached by Mahāprabhu is universal and not exclusive. The most learned and the most ignorant are both entitled to embrace it. The learned people will accept it with knowledge of *sambandha tattva* as explained in the categories. The ignorant have the same privilege by simply uttering the name of the Deity and mixing with the pure Vaiṣṇavas."

(*Caitanya Mahāprabhu: His Life and Precepts*)

17. Is it possible to explain about spiritual variegatedness in words?

"Spiritual variegatedness is not a subject matter for consideration, rather it is a subject matter for realization. Those whose hearts are filled with such wonderful realizations, only refer to them as transcendental truth but cannot understand what it is."

(*Sajjana-toṣaṇī* 6/2)

18. Are prayers offered by the self-realized mahājanas, and the demigods headed by Brahmā, comprehensible for less qualified people?

"The *mahājanas*, during the attainment of self-realization, and the demigods head by Brahmā, during the realization of the Supreme Lord's mercy, offer prayers in glorification of the Lord according to their respective realizations. These prayers are generally in condensed form and they appear to the less qualified people as incomprehensible. There is no need for the devotees to worry about it."

(*Jaiva Dharma*, Chapter 40)

19. Why are ordinary people unable to understand the subtle difference between transcendental and metaphysical?

"People often fail to understand the subtle difference between transcendental and metaphysical. Absence of knowledge regarding the transcendental objects is the cause of this."

(*Autobiography of Śrī Bhaktivinoda Ṭhākura*)

20. What is the definition of triśul or trident?

"The three modes of material nature and the three divisions of material time are the definitions of trident."

(*Brahma Saṁhitā* 5/5)

21. What is seeing Krishna's artistry within this material world?

"Seeing Krishna's artistry within the world is called seeing Krishna's picture. This material world is the reflected shadow of spiritual variegatedness. Whoever has realized this is said to have seen Krishna's picture."

(*Śrī Krishna-saṁhitā* 9/17)

22. Who is the supreme director of all creations?

"If creations take place by matter or dry consciousness, there would be no varieties in them. Can wonderful activities like the inconceivable relationship between the senses and the object of the senses, the arrangement of ingredients according to the requirement of the body, the arrangement of the human being's residence through the division of the earth with land and water, the beautification of the solar system by dividing the duties of the stars and planets, the ascertainment of good or bad times by establishing the rules of the seasons, and the fulfillment of the conditional state's requirements by the bodily limbs of the human beings, be the acts of dry consciousness? Unless one accepts that these are simply parts of the Supreme Lord's pastimes one cannot come to a satisfactory conclusion."

(*Tattva-sutra* 6)

23. Is trust in God not a normal characteristic for the humankind?

"Trust in God is a general propensity of the human beings. Although uncivilized tribes eat animal flesh and live like animals yet they worship the sun, moon, huge mountains, rivers, and trees as their suppliers and controllers."

(*Caitanya-śikṣāmṛta* 1/1)

24. Is little bit of Vaiṣṇava principles not found in the religious system that nourish devotional service?

"Some degree of Vaiṣṇava principles will be found in every religion that nourish devotional service."

(*Sajjana-toṣaṇī* 2/6)

25. What is the difference between the Vaiṣṇavas and the Hindus?

"Staunch atheists like Cārvāka was also a Hindu, but not a Vaiṣṇava. We are Vaiṣṇava Hindus not simply Hindus. In other words, our society is Hindu, but our religion is Vaiṣṇava. In the same way worshipable personalities like Haridāsa Ṭhākura was not a Hindu, but a Vaiṣṇava worshipable by all. According to the purport of the Vedic literatures, Śrīmān Mahāprabhu has instructed that people of all castes are eligible for Vaiṣṇava *dharma*."

(*Sajjana-toṣaṇī* 2/10-11)

26. What kind of intelligence is required to understand the science of Vaiṣṇavism?

"Subtle discrimination is extremely important for Vaiṣṇavas. Those who invent social distinctions and preach the unbreakable principles of Vaiṣṇavism while breaking them to suit their needs are said to possess gross discrimination."

(*Śrī Krishna-saṁhitā* 8/20)

27. What is the fate of those who, in spite of following Vaiṣṇava religion, but entangled in the conception of regulative principles?

"Vaiṣṇava principles are so unlimitedly exalted that those who simply remain entangled in the regulative process without endeavoring to understand the science of attachment are comparable to ordinary fruitive workers."

(*Śrī Krishna-saṁhitā* 8/20)

28. What is the goal and the process described by the śāstras?

"There are two kinds of subject matters described in the *śāstras*; the subject matter which is the ultimate purpose of the scripture is called the goal, and the subject matter by which the goal is pointed out is called the process."

(Commentary on *Bhagavad-gītā* 2/45)

29. Should the devotees who follow regulative devotional service and who follow rāgānuga devotional service transgress their respective status?

"If a follower of regulative devotional service tries to instruct a follower of *rāgānugā* devotional service, then he will never achieve any good result and his position will be like a blacksmith trying to make yogurt. Just as if a *rāgānugā* devotee blasphemes any regulative principles followed by a

regulative devotee is improper, similarly if a neophyte tries to instruct a *rāgānugā* devotee then it becomes an unauthorized interference."
(*Sajjana-toṣaṇī* 4/1)

30. What is Śrī Bhaktivinoda Ṭhākura's instruction and appeal for preaching the glories of the songs written by the exalted Vaiṣṇavas?

"We humbly request Ravindra Bābu and Śrīśa Bābu to carefully publish a scientific history of Vaiṣṇava *kīrtana* or songs and thus please the entire Vaiṣṇava community. In that book all aspects of the song such as melody and other musical notes should be provided. They should also include the biography of the *ācāryas* who wrote songs in *renetī*, *garānahātī* and *manoharasāhī* languages and as far as possible they should also put the time and descriptions of the later *mahājanas*."
(*Sajjana-toṣaṇī* 2/9)

31. What is the future impediment or the three faults facing Śrīmad Gaurāṅga Samāja?

"If the followers of Śrīmad Gaurāṅga Samāja are not very careful about selfishness, name, fame, and duplicity, this *samāja* will not last long. Any big activity that takes place in the land of Bengal soon becomes spoiled by the above mentioned three faults."
(*Sajjana-toṣaṇī* 10/11)

32. Is it easy to oppose the truth under the shelter of lie? Is there any gain for the liars' enthusiasm?

"It is not easy to oppose the truth. Those who determined to oppose the truth soon fall prey to the time even while remaining in the shelter of lie. Taking shelter of lie is extremely illusory. This material world is illusory. The more the truth regarding the Supreme Lord is manifest the more the illusion created by Māyā is destroyed. Moreover it has also been seen that whenever there is a prosperity of truth, illusion comes forward and try to create havoc in order to oppose the truth; this is also the will of the Supreme Lord. Unless there is an opposition, actual truth is difficult to be established. Just as the necessity of light is not felt if there is no darkness, similarly people who are under the shelter of illusion, and enthusiastic persons who are under the shelter of truth relish victory and happiness when they are in direct opposition."
(*Sajjana-toṣaṇī* 8/1)

33. How do you substantiate that the Āryans of India should never eat meat, fish etc.?

"Nowadays a strong misconception has deeply rooted in the hearts of the people that unless they eat fish and meat their body and senses will not remain healthy for a long time. This misconception is the result of the foreign doctors advice, urge of the people who love eating meat and fish and various inherited prejudices. Especially people who are fully controlled by their senses and are extremely greedy take advantage of this idea and try to arouse the propensity for eating meat and fish of the younger generation of India. As a result the Aryan descendants of the holy land of India are giving up their traditional food and by taking pleasure in eating foreign foods they are gradually becoming weak and powerless."

(*Sajjana-toṣaṇī* 2/8)

34. Is self-interest not natural?

"That which is natural is one's self-interest; because the word nature refers to one's own interest. Self interest is natural; selflessness is extremely unnatural."

(*Tattva Viveka* 1/9/12)

35. Is the instruction for giving up sense gratification not imaginary?

"As soon as the living entity gives up sense enjoyment, he leaves his body. Therefore, giving up sense enjoyment is only a figment of the imagination; it can never be applied in practice."

(*Sajjana-toṣaṇī* 10/9)

36. How should one deal, if one has to disobey the unreasonable instruction of the spiritual master?

"It is not that one should follow the unreasonable instruction of his spiritual master. At the same time, one should not express his hatred towards the spiritual master by using harsh words and behaving in an insulting manner. One should try to check his spiritual master from imparting unreasonable instruction by one's sweet words, humility, and by humbly reminding about his conduct and instruction in an appropriate time."

(*Caitanya-śikṣāmṛta* 2/2)

37. Can love between man and woman remain forever either in gross and subtle form?

"The relationship between man and woman is based on the body. When the body is finished, where will that love be reposed? One living entity is male and the other is female—but I do not feel this state remains eternal; for the difference between man and woman is based on the body, not on the soul. Therefore, the love between man and woman can remain only until death. If, like the Vedāntists, we accept transmigration and residence in heavenly planets, and believe that the satisfaction of that sincere love is revived in that state, still loving relationships between man and woman cannot exist in the completely liberated state."

(*Prema-pradīpa*, Ray 9)

38. What is the root and purpose of moral science? How many kinds of worldly moralities are there.

"The subject of moral science is to mainly deal with the root of happiness and distress. Happiness refers to the mind's indulgence in favorable activities and distress refers to the minds hatred towards unfavorable activities. The entire purpose of moral science is to uplift the standard of one's happiness and to diminish one's hatred. There are many kinds of moralities such as politics, penal code, law of trade, utilitarianism, division of labor, rules of health, socialism, rule of life and training and development of feelings. Only knowledge of morality does not contain any knowledge of the spiritual world or of the supreme controller. Some people accept the moral knowledge as transcendental knowledge and call it positivism. But since the human beings possess much superior propensity than this they do not become satisfied simply by moral knowledge. In moral knowledge there is a little bit of religiosity and irreligiosity, piety, and sin, as well as there is bodily, mental and social results prescribed for the human beings. But after death nothing remains except one's own fame or infamy."

(*Caitanya-śikṣāmṛta* 5/3)

39. Is it reasonable to create a quarrel in the foreign countries just to establish the philosophy of one's own spiritual master?

"Even for the sake of firm faith if one accepts that the teachings of of the *ācāryas* of his own country are better than the teachings of the *ācāryas* of all other countries, one should not preach such a quarrelsome and controversial doctrine. No auspiciousness is resulted from this."

(*Caitanya-śikṣāmṛta* 1/1)

40. Where is the āśrama of sage Gautama? What did Śrī Bhaktivinoda Ṭhākura do to develop this place?

"The *āśrama* of sage Gautama is in Godana. It is here that Ahalyā became stone. Because it is Gautama's *āśrama*, it is necessarily the birth place of logic. With a desire to develop this place and to open a school for the study of the logic I arranged a meeting at Chhāprā and delivered a discourse entitled Gautama Speech."

(*Autobiography of Śrī Bhaktivinoda Ṭhākura*)

41. How ecstatic did Śrī Bhaktivinoda Ṭhākura feel when he saw Śrī Vṛndāvana?

"I had a conversation with King Rādhākānta in Vṛndāvana. He was very pleased to see me. He was reading *Garga Saṁhitā* at that time. After seeing the temples of Vṛndāvana I was greatly satisfied."

(*Autobiography of Śrī Bhaktivinoda Ṭhākura*)

42. How was Śrī Bhaktivinoda Ṭhākura's visit to Jagannāth Purī?

"I expressed a desire to visit Jagannāth Purī. With a desire to go to Jagannāth Purī, I took *Śrīmad-Bhāgavatam* and *Śrī Caitanya-caritāmṛta* with me and went to Calcutta. It took me four days from Calcutta to reach Jagannāth Purī. On the way I spent one night at Bhadrak, one night at Baleshvara and one night at Cuttack."

(*Autobiography of Śrī Bhaktivinoda Ṭhākura*)

43. What did Śrī Bhaktivinoda Ṭhākura see in Bhuvaneshwara and in Khandagiri?

"I arrived in Bhuvaneshwara. There I met with my Panda (guide) Gopīnātha Miśra along with a few more Pandas from Purī. In the afternoon, I visited Khandagiri. Khandagiri is a place where the Buddhist lived. The caves in the mountainous range of Khandagiri look beautiful."

(*Autobiography of Śrī Bhaktivinoda Ṭhākura*)

44. When did Śrī Bhaktivinoda Ṭhākura visit Braja Mandala? Which places did he see, which devotees did he meet and which activities did he perform there?

"I went to Vṛndāvana in the month of Śrāvaṇa (July) in 1881. Rādhāmohan Bābu took me to a place called Kālākunja. I associated with many saintly persons in Braja for a few days. I used to receive palatable *prasāda* from Lālābābu's *kunja*. I saw Govindaji, Gopīnātha and Madana Mohana. I had a verbal argument at the house of Gopīnātha over donation. I honored *prasāda* at the *kunja* of Rūpadāsa Bābāji. In his *kunja* I found a book written by Nimbārkācārya which consists of ten verses. Thereafter I heard the discourse of Nīlamani Goswami while remaining incognito. It was here that I met Śrī Jagannāth dāsa Bābāji for the first time. I took a palanquin and went to Rādhākunda and Govardhana to take *darśana*. Then I returned to Vṛndāvana and again went out to see different temples. From Vṛndāvana I went to Lucknow via Mathurā. There I stayed at the house of prince Sarvādhikāri and visited the entire city in his care. From Lucknow I went to Ayodhya via Faizabād. Out of fear for the *pandas*, I returned to Faizabād before it was dark and stayed at the house of one Bengali gentleman. On the next day, I took bath at Gopratā *ghāt*. On that same day, I departed for Kāśī. At Kāśī I stayed at the house of Tinubābu."

(*Autobiography of Śrī Bhaktivinoda Ṭhākura*)

45. When did Śrī Bhaktivinoda Ṭhākura visit Śrī Rāmpur, Memari and Kulina Grām?

"I lived at Śrī Rāmpur. Rādhika, Kamal and Bimala studied here. In 1885, myself, Rādhika, Kamal, Bimal and Prabhu went to Memari and Kulina Grām. Thereafter we went to Saptagrām."

(*Autobiography of Śrī Bhaktivinoda Ṭhākura*)

46. When did Śrī Bhaktivinoda Ṭhākura go to Baghnapada, Kalna, Jannagar, Pyariganj, Denur, Indrarkapur, Kakshashali, Purbasthali, Kuliya-Navadvip and Amlajoda?

"I went to Baghnapada on 26th March 1890 and stayed in a tent. There I visited a school and got some judicial work done. I saw the deity of Baladeva and took *prasāda* here. On 30th march, I returned to Kalna. On 31st March I went to Parulgrām via Jannagar. Thereafter on 9th April I visited Pyariganj and saw the place of Nakula Bramachāri. On 23rd April I went to Kaigrām. On 25th I visited Denur and saw Vṛndāvana dāsa Ṭhākura's place. 18th May I visited Godruma. From there I went on foot with Kamala to Indrarkapur. From there we crossed and went to Kakshashali. From here, I went to Purbasthali via Chupi and had my lunch in the Police station. On the next day, I walked down to Kuliya-Navadvip and took *darśana* of Jagannāth dāsa Bābāji in his *bhajana kutir*. On 17th June I again went to Burdwan. On 18th October afternoon, I went to Amlajoda. I gave discourse at Amlajoda and Gopālpur.

(*Autobiography of Śrī Bhaktivinoda Ṭhākura*)

47. Which forests of Vṛndāvana did Śrī Bhaktivinoda Ṭhākura visit?

"On 27th Fālgun (March) 1892. I started for Vṛndāvana along with Bhakti Bṛṅga Mahāśaya. On the same day, we reached Āmlājoḍā. With great care, we took Mahendrabābu on a palanquin and brought him to the house of Kṣetrabābu. We observed the vow of Ekādaśī with Śrīla Jagannāth dāsa Bābājī Mahāśaya.' Next day we inagurated a Prapannāśrama there. 29th Fālgun we arrived at Gidhaur. From there we went to Umānāth's house at Allahabad on 1st Caitra. 6th Caitra we moved from Allahabad to Etawa. 8th Caitra Hathras. I lost my puse and money here. 9th Caitra Śrī Vṛndāvana. 11th Caitra, I first went to Vilvavana then to Bhāndirvan. I spend that night at Māṅṭh. 12th Caitra Mānsarovar. 13th and 14th Caitra Śrī Vṛndāvana. 15th Caitra Mathurā. 16th I visited Gokula. 17th Madhuvan, Muhulī village, Kṛṣṇakunda, Tālavana, Baladevakunda, Kumudvana, Śāntanu Kunda and Bahulāvana. 18th I went to Rādhā Kunda. On 20th Caitra I returned to Śrī Vṛndāvana in a horse cart."

(*Autobiography of Śrī Bhaktivinoda Ṭhākura*)

48. How are the loving symptoms between the supreme consciousness and the minute consciousness?

"The minute conscious living entities are spontaneously attracted to the supreme conscious Personality of Godhead just like iron is attracted by magnet."

(*Dutta Kaustubha*)

100

Words of Blessing

1. What blessings did Śrī Bhaktivinoda Ṭhākura shower on New Year's Day?

"O New Year, all glories to you! Pay special attention for the development of Śrī Māyāpura. Publish all devotional literatures. Satisfy the people of the world by distributing the holy names of the Lord. Guide the living entities in such a way that they take to chanting the holy names of the Lord while cultivating pure devotional service."

(*Sajjana-toṣaṇī* 6/1)

2. What Śrī Bhaktivinoda Ṭhākura's advice to the jñānīs?

"O brothers! March ahead. Penetrate the realm of transcendental effulgence and enter into the spiritual abode of Supreme Lord. There you can meet with the supreme Brahman and His pastimes face to face. Then you will actually relish the uninterrupted spiritual bliss, and not degrade the condition of yourself like a piece of dry wood."

(*Caitanya-śikṣāmṛta* 6/3)

3. What is Śrī Bhaktivinoda Ṭhākura's order to all living entities?

"O brothers! Let the detachment remain effective concerning material enjoyments, but throw it from your heart when it comes to the service of the Supreme Lord. Cultivate the eternal pastimes of the Supreme Lord and become close to the Supreme Personality of Godhead. Attain *bhāva bhakti* through the help of *sādhana bhakti* and then by the help of *bhāva bhakti* attain the transcendental state of *prema bhakti*. Surpass the relative forms like the controller, or the Supersoul, and attain the original eternal form of the Supreme Lord with love and devotion."

(*Sajjana-toṣaṇī* 2/6)

PRAYOJANA

101

Goal of Life

1. What is prayojana, the ultimate goal of life?

Who am I? What is this material world? Who is God? What is our relationship with one another? The answers to these four questions are known as *sambandha-jñāna*, knowledge of our relationship with the Lord. What is the duty of a person who has attained this knowledge? Having received such knowledge, we then perform our prescribed duties to achieve the goal of life. This is known as *abhidheya*, the process we must follow to achieve the goal. The result we attain by performing our duties is called *prayojana*, the ultimate goal of life.

(Commentary on *Caitanya Caritāmṛta* Ādi 7.146)

2. What is real prayojana?

Happiness is the goal of life, but material sense gratification, the desire for mundane happiness, is not eternal happiness. Real happiness is spiritual. Such happiness is the ultimate goal of life. There is no happiness in liberation; liberation is only the cessation of distress. By understanding that *prayojana* is eternal happiness, we nourish our *sambandha-jnana* and strengthen and purify our excecution of *abhidheya.*

(*Śrī Bhāgavatārka-marīci-mālā* 17/2)

3. What is the most prayojana?

Learned scholars have concluded that love of God is the living entities' ultimate goal of life. For love, human beings are even willing to give up their lives. Love is nectar. When this love is applied to Krishna, it becomes extremely relishable; when it is applied to objects other than Krishna, it becomes abominable. Therefore love of God has been defined as the ultimate goal of all pious activities, such as worship, austerity, sacrifice, charity, yoga, cultivation of impersonal knowledge, and *samādhi*. Love of God is the living entities' most auspicious goal of life. It is attained by following the prescribed process given in scripture.

(*Śrī Bhāgavatārka-marīci-mālā* 17/22)

4. What is the difference between the desire to satisfy Krishna's senses and the desire to satisfy our own senses?

All desires arising from the mentality, 'I am a servant of Krishna,' are desires to satisfy Krishna's senses. Desires arising from the mentality, 'I am the enjoyer,' are desires to satisfy one's own senses.

(Commentary on *Caitanya Caritāmṛta* Adi 4.165-68)

5. What is the spirit soul's natural propensity?

The mood of separation from Krishna is the spirit soul's natural propensity.

(Commentary on *Caitanya Caritāmṛta* Adi 4.197)

6. What is the perfect stage of worship for those following Śrī Caitanya Mahāprabhu?

The perfect stage of worship for the followers of Śrī Caitanya's lotus feet is to internally see oneself in a *sakhī's* grove, dependent upon the maidservant there who assists Śrīmatī Rādhikā in Her constant service to Krishna, while constantly taking shelter of chanting the Lord's holy name.

(*Sajjana-toṣaṇī* 9/11)

102

Four Objectives of Life

1. Is bondage to fruitive activities destroyed by observing vows and fasts with a desire to achieve heavenly pleasure?

O my mind! I have wasted my time in the pit of fruitive activities. The knots of karma entangle me because I desired to enjoy heavenly pleasures. The network of karma is just like a spider's web. I voluntarily accepted bodily suffering by fasting and observing vows, but this was as useless as pouring ghee on ashes. Due to my faults, I am now entangled in the cycle of birth and death. Hence I cannot be delivered.

(*Kalyāṇa-kalpataru*, Song 3)

2. Are lust and love the same?

O brothers! There is no difference between lust and love as far as the symptoms are concerned. Still, lust cannot be called love. How will you benefit if you engage in lust and call it love?

(*Kalyāṇa-kalpataru*, Song 18)

3. Why is liberation, or merging into the Brahman effulgence suicidal?

We cannot achieve happiness through renunciation or cultivating knowledge. Renunciation and knowlege vanquish our material bondage and deliver liberation, but liberation does not bring happiness. Rather it brings ruination. Liberation is therefore extremely abominable. Just consider this: on one hand, liberation means we lose material enjoyment, yet do not achieve the highest benefit.

(*Navadvīpa-māhātmya* 7)

4. Why is merging into Brahman useless?

The impersonalist desires to merge the soul into the impersonal Brahman, but searching for liberation by merging into Brahman is a mistake.

It is the stealing of the self, because there is no happiness in that state. Neither the living entity nor the Lord gains anything from such merging.

(*Śrī Krishna-saṁhitā* 8.23)

5. Why isn't the liberation that comes from merging into Brahman praiseworthy?

How can the liberation of merging into the existence of Brahman be praiseworthy when even demons like Kaṁsa, who have been condemned by *śāstra* as killers of cows and *brāhmaṇa*s, attained this state?

(*Bṛhad-bhāgavatāmṛta*, purport)

6. Why is merging into the Supreme Lord's body more abominable than merging into the Brahman effulgence?

There are two kinds of merging, merging into the Brahman and merging into the Supreme Lord's body. According to the opinion of Māyāvādī Vedāntists, the living entity's ultimate goal is to merge into Brahman. According to Pataṇjali, in the liberated stage the living entity merges into the Supreme Lord's body. Of these two types of liberation, merging into the Supreme Lord's body is more abominable. When merging with the Brahman, we attain nonvariegatedness because we have cultivated impersonal knowledge, but when merging into the Lord's body after meditating on that personal body, we are more condemnable. This type of liberation only proves what a degraded mentality we possess. The Patanjali system describes the Lord's form as *kleśa-karma-vipākāśayair aparāmṛṣṭa puruṣa-viśeṣa īśvara*: 'the Supreme Personality of Godhead is a person who does not partake of a miserable material life.' The followers of the Pataṇjali system therefore accept the eternality of the Supreme Lord. They also say, *sa pūrveṣām api guru kālānavacc hedāt*: 'Such a person is always supreme and is not influenced by the element of time.' Yet according to them, *puruṣārtha-śūnyānāṁ pratiprasava kaivalyaṁ svarūpa-pratiṣṭhā vā citi-śaktir iti*. That is, they believe that in the perfectional stage, the *puruṣa* conception is vanquished. This yoga system is therefore abominable because its final conception is impersonal. The purport is that instead of attaining a substantial result due to substantial worship, such people attain an abominable result.

(Commentary on *Caitanya Caritāmṛta* Madhya 6.269)

7. Why is happiness derived from devotional service unlimitedly greater than happiness derived from merging into the Lord's existence?

Happiness derived from merging into the Lord's existence is always insignificant and abominable, but the happiness derived from devotional service is wonderful and full of variety, because Śrī Hari's ecstatic pastimes are full of sweetness. These two kinds of happiness are always opposed to one another. Those who have not relished the happiness of devotional service find the topic about which happiness is superior worth debating.

(*Bṛhad-bhāgavatāmṛta*, purport)

103

Sthāyi-bhāva or Rati

1. What is sthāyi-bhāva ?

Sthāyi-bhāva brings all other *bhāva*s under its control and governs them. When a person's attachment for Krishna becomes stronger and is mixed with undeviated affection, it transforms into *sthāyi-bhāva*. When *sthāyi-bhāva* is mixed with the necessary ingredients, it is called *rāsa*. Although this attachment has crossed its determined limit and has reached the platform of *prema*, still it should be called attachment. *Prema* is unlimited and is not always identified only as attachment. Sometimes *prema* becomes manifest when it conquers the highest ingredients of *rāsa*. Attachment, *rati*, should therefore be accepted as *sthāyi-bhāva*.

(*Caitanya-śikṣāmṛta* 7/1)

2. What is rati? How many types of rati are there?

Rati is the preliminary stage of *prema*, and *prema* is the mature stage of *rati*. *Prema* is just like the sun whereas *rati* (*bhāva*) is the sun's ray. When our *rati* is awakened, we slowly exhibit the symptoms of ecstatic transformation. Although *rati* appears within the mind of the conditioned souls, it is fully spiritual. Despite being self-manifest, it appears like an object and function of the mind. There are two types of *rati*. One arises by the mercy of Krishna or His devotees and the other from *sādhana*. *Rati* arising from *sādhana* is found most often in this world. *Rati* arising from mercy is rarely found. The *rati* that arises from *sādhana* is further divided into two: *vaidhi-sādhana-rati* and *rāgānugā-sādhana-rati*.

(*Manaḥ-śikṣā*, Chapter 11)

3. What are temporary and eternal rati?

Rati (affection) for the material body is burned at the crematorium along with the body. It does not remain with us permanently. *Rati* experienced in dealings between men and women in this world is insignificant, because the body's pleasure is finished with the body. The living entities are spirit souls; they have eternal bodies. In the eternal body every living entity is *strī*, enjoyed, and Śrī Kṛṣṇacandra is the only *puruṣa*, enjoyer. The material body's demands should be reduced and those of the eternal body increased. As a woman's *rati* rushes powerfully toward a man, the transcendental *rati* of the eternal *strī's* body rushes toward Śrī Krishna. The heart's lust for sense objects is called temporary *rati*, and the spiritual body's natural lust for Krishna is our eternal *rati*.

(*Prema-pradīpa*, Ray 7)

4. Where does the bhāva appearing in the hearts of those who have no concept of rāsa come from?

People have no concept of *rāsa*. Lacking knowledge, they discuss *rāsa*, considering it meditation, trance, worship, glorification, or prayer. Whenever a worshiper absorbs himself in the activities of worship or prayer, a flash of *bhāva* appears in his heart like lightning and moves his mind. It also awakens symptoms such as horripilation. He feels at that time that if such *bhāva* can remain within him eternally, he will no longer have to suffer. O brother! What is that *bhāva*? Is it of the nature of matter or thought? Is it the opposite of matter? You will never find such *bhāva* even if you search the entire world. Even the most subtle material objects — electricity and magnetism — do not possess it. You will not find this *bhāva* even after scrutinizing all material thoughts, what to speak of those thoughts that are considered the opposite of matter. Where did such *bhāva* come from? Consider deeply and you will find that this *bhāva* appeared from the living entity's perfect existence.

(*Caitanya-Śikṣāmṛta*, Part 2, 7/2)

5. Is rati a conditional function of the mind?

Rati is a natural propensity. It has no cause. It becomes agitated as soon as it sees its object. *Rati* is the seed of *prema*— and as such, should be sprouted by the watering process of hearing and chanting.

(*Prema-pradīpa* 7)

6. What is the symptom of a person who has attained rati?

In its preliminary stage, unblossomed *prema* is full of bliss. At that time it is called *rati*. This *rati* is first realized in *śānta-rāsa*. When we develop *rati*, everything other than Krishna appears insignificant.

(*Manaḥ-śikṣā*, Chapter 11)

7. How does sthāyi-bhāva or rati gradually transform into rāsa?

The more our *anarthas* are destroyed, the more we surpass higher levels like *niṣṭhā*, *ruci*, and *āsakti* and gradually approach *bhāva*. When *bhāva* or *rati* becomes permanent and mixes with various ingredients, it becomes *rāsa*.

(*Sajjana-toṣaṇī* 10/10)

8. How do those practicing devotional service see themselves after attaining bhāva?

On the platform of *bhāva*, a person does not identify himself with his material body. Rather, he predominantly identifies himself with his spiritual body.

(*Harināma-cintāmaṇi*)

9. Does rati bring fearlessness?

Possessing mystic opulence and material enjoyment both cause fear, but developing our *rati* in the abode of Vṛndāvana brings no fear.

(*Kalyāṇa-kalpataru*, Song 1)

10. How can someone develop pure rati in this life without practicing sādhana?

Someone may not have practiced *sādhana*, yet he may develop pure *rati*. In such a case, we can understand that for some reason the progress of his previous devotional service was checked. When the obstacle was removed, his devotional service bore fruit.

(*Manaḥ-śikṣā*, Chapter 11)

11. If we see a discrepancy in the behavior of a person who has developed rati, should we disregard him?

Even if we find a discrepancy in the behavior of a person who has developed *rati*, we should know that that person is still glorious. No one should be envious of him. Actually a person who has developed *rati* is faultless. Some small act may appear contradictory to the regulative principles, but such a glorious person should not be blamed for that. These things appear faulty only in the eyes of neophytes attached to regulative principles.

(*Manaḥ-śikṣā*, Chapter 11)

12. Is it possible for those desiring liberation or material enjoyment to develop rati?

It is rare to develop *rati*. The symptons of *rati* that are found in those desiring liberation or material enjoyment are simply *rati*'s reflections. There are two types of such reflections, perverted and shadow. When seeing either of these reflections, the ignorant think them genuine *rati*.

(*Manaḥ-śikṣā*, Text 11)

13. Māyāvādīs or those who synthesize matter and spirit exhibit the external transformations of love. Are these exhibitions real transformations of love born of transcendental realization?

If an indifferent *bābājī* develops *bhāva*, his life is glorious, but if he artificially displays the symptoms of *bhāva* for some purpose, we can understand that his symptoms are not real but reflective. Śrī Rūpa Goswami, who was an *ācārya* of pure love of God, said, "*Rati* has two types of reflections, perverted and shadow. All the symptoms of *rati* are found in its reflections, and foolish people become wonderstruck when they see them. Only those who actually relish *rati* can recognize true *rati* from its reflection."

(*Sajjana-toṣaṇī* 2/6)

14. What result do we achieve when we reach bhāva by practicing sādhana-bhakti?

When a devotional practitioner attains *bhāva*, his eyes are anointed with love of God by Krishna's mercy. Then he is able to see the Lord face to face.

(*Brahma-saṁhitā* 5/38)

15. How does śānta-rati manifest?

The living entity's pure *rati* becomes perverted because of his extremely long association with matter. When the living entity is free of *anartha*s, he is reinstated in his original position. On that platform a devotee becomes peaceful. This is called the platform of *śānta-rati*.

(*Caitanya-śikṣāmṛta* 7/1)

16. Who is the object and who is the subject of śānta-rati?

One is *śānta*, peaceful, when he is confident that the worshipable object is not indistinguishable but personal. The *rati* developed by such a peaceful worshiper is called *śānta- rati*. The peaceful living entities are the subject of *śānta-rati*, and the personal God is the object of that *rati*. Living entities on the platform of *śānta-rati* are devoid of the mundane mentality.

Their mode of worship gives them spiritual happiness. They give up material enjoyment because they are situated in that happiness. Thus Krishna appears to them as Paramātmā, or as the partial personal manifestation of Brahman, and becomes the object of their worship.

(*Caitanya-śikṣāmṛta* 7/3)

17. When does dāsya-rati manifest?

When unalloyed affection is mixed with *rati*, it is called *dāsya-rati* . In *dāsya-rati*, a living entity establishes his relationship with the Supreme Lord by considering the Lord the master and himself the eternal servant. *Dāsya-rati* is of two types: *dāsya-rati* based on awe and reverence and *dāsya-rati* based on affection. In the first form, the living entity thinks himself favored, and in the latter form, he thinks himself cared for. The Lord's servants take shelter of *dāsya-rati* based on awe and reverence, while the Lord's sons take shelter of *dāsya- rati* based on affection.

(*Caitanya-śikṣāmṛta* 7/1)

18. What is the nature of dāsya-rati?

When *dāsya-rati* is saturated with affection, it becomes *prema*, love of God. Therefore, on the platform of *dāsya*, the symptoms of both *rati* and *prema* are present as *sthāyi-bhāva*. On this platform, affection and attachment are also present to some extent.

(*Caitanya-śikṣāmṛta* 7/1)

19. What is love of God in awe and reverence?

Persons who proudly identifies themselves as Krishna's servants find that their love for Nanda's son develops with awe and reverence. When mature, this love is called love with awe and reverence. In this *rāsa*, both Krishna and His servants are *ālambana*, the shelter.

(*Jaiva Dharma*, Chapter 29)

20. What is sthāyi-bhāva in sakhya-rati?

In *sakhya-rāsa* the *sthāyi-bhāva* is *praṇaya* (with love). *Rati* and *prema* are included in that *bhāva*. The awe and reverence, as well as the affection, that is present in *dāsya* becomes mature and transforms into firm faith on the platform of *sakhya*.

(*Caitanya-śikṣāmṛta* 7/1)

21. How is vātsalya-rati superior to sakhya-rati?

In *vātsalya-rāsa*, firm faith matures and transforms into compassion.

(*Caitanya-śikṣāmṛta* 7/1)

22. To what extent does the sthāyi -bhāva of śṛṇgāra-rāsa mature?

The *sthāyi-bhāva* of *śṛṇgāra-rāsa* gradually passes through *prema, praṇaya,* and affection, then reaches the platform of attachment or *rāga. Bhāva* and *mahābhāva* are awakened in this *rāsa.*

(*Caitanya-śikṣāmṛta* 7/1)

23. Where do the transformations of ecstatic love (horripilation, etc.) come from in those who desire liberation?

The standing of the hairs on end of those who worship the Lord to attain liberation is simply a reflection of *rati*. A sudden reflection of unexpected joy and astonishment may appear in the hearts of those whose hearts are cold. All transformations born from this reflection are illusory.

(*Caitanya-śikṣāmṛta* 7/1)

104

Mellows of Devotional Service

1. What is the awakening of rāsa?

Rāsa is awakened when a living entity establishes his eternal relationship with the Lord.

(*Caitanya-śikṣāmṛta* 7/1)

2. Is the science of rāsa mundane?

The science of *rāsa* is fully transcendental. It has no tinge of material relationship, such as the material nature of relationships between men and women. It is entirely spiritual.

(*Sajjana-toṣaṇī* 5/3)

3. What is the proper ground to awaken rāsa?

Rāsa is cultivated only in the spiritual body of the living entity, never in the material body.

(*Caitanya-śikṣāmṛta* 7/1)

4. How many kinds of rāsa are there and what are their origins?

Rāsa is of three kinds: Vaikuṇṭha *rāsa*, heavenly *rāsa*, and worldly *rāsa*. Worldly *rāsa* is of six types. It is found in sugarcane, dates, and so on. Heavenly *rāsa* is found in emotional feelings. Because of this *rāsa*, some living entities consider themselves enjoyers and other's enjoyed. Vaikuṇṭha *rāsa* is found only in pure spirit souls.

(*Prema-pradīpa*, Ray 8)

5. What is the difference between Vaikuṇṭha rāsa, heavenly rāsa, and worldly rāsa?

When there is an abundance of *rāsa* in the soul, its waves may touch the mind. Those waves cross over the mind and pervade the *sādhaka*'s body. Then there is reciprocation between *rāsa* and the *sādhaka*. In spiritual *rāsa*, Śrī Kṛṣṇacandra is the only hero. The one spiritual *rāsa* is transformed and reflected as heavenly mental *rāsa*. Then it is further reflected as worldly *rāsa*. The rules, process, and nature of the three types of *rāsa* are therefore of one kind. Spiritual *rāsa* is the life of the Vaiṣṇavas. The other two are extremely detestable and irrelevant if they do not bring one to the platform of spiritual *rāsa*. People who are influenced by base, low propensities are enchanted by heavenly and worldly *rāsa*. Vaiṣṇavas carefully renounce them and desire only spiritual *rāsa*.

(*Prema-pradīpa*, Ray 8)

6. What is the difference between bhāva and rāsa?

Bhāva is like a painting and *rāsa* is like a canvas that contains many paintings. Unless the *bhāvas* that conjointly give rise to *rāsa* are described, *rāsa* cannot be explained. *Rāsa* is attained when all the *bhāva*s combine.

(*Prema-pradīpa*, Ray 8)

7. What is the speciality of Mādhavendra Purī's line, who was the root of transcendental conjugal rāsa?

Uncontaminated devotees who depend strictly on *Vedānta* philosophy are divided into four *sampradāyas* or transcendental parties. Of the four *sampradāyas*, Mādhavendra Purī accepted the Śrī Madhvācārya-sampradāya. Thus he took initiation according to that *parampara*. From Madhavacarya down to Laksmipati, Mādhavendra Purī's spiritual master, no one realized devotional service in conjugal love. Mādhavendra Purī first introduced the Madhvācārya-sampradāya to the concept of conjugal love, and Śrī Caitanya Mahāprabhu further revealed this conclusion. He toured South India and met the *Tattva-vādīs*, who supposedly belonged to the Madhvācārya-sampradāya.

When Śrī Krishna left Vṛndāvana and accepted the kingdom of Mathurā, Śrīmatī Rādhārāṇī, out of Her ecstasy of separation, expressed how Krishna can be loved in that mood. Worship in separation is considered the topmost level of devotional service by the Gauḍīya-Madhva-sampradāya. According to this concept, the devotee thinks himself poor and neglected by the Lord. Thus he addresses the Lord, as Mādhavendra Purī did, as *dīna-dayārdra nātha*, the supremely merciful Personality of Godhead. Such ecstatic feeling is the highest form of devotional service. Because Krishna had gone to Mathurā, Śrīmatī Rādhārāṇī was very much affected and expressed Herself thus: "My dear Lord, because of separation from You, My mind has become overly agitated. Now tell Me, what can I do? I am poor and You are merciful, so kindly have compassion upon

Me and let Me know when I shall see You." Śrī Caitanya Mahāprabhu was always expressing the ecstatic emotions Śrīmatī Rādhārāṇī exhibited when She saw Uddhava in Vṛndāvana. Similar feelings, experienced by Mādhavendra Purī, are expressed in this verse:

ayi dīna-dayārdra nātha he
mathurā-nātha kadāvalokyase
hṛdayaṁ tvad-aloka-kātaraṁ
dayita bhrāmyati kiṁ karomy aham

"O My Lord! O most merciful spiritual master! O master of Mathura! When shall I see you again? Because of My not seeing You, My agitated heart has become unsteady. O most beloved one, what shall I do now?"

Therefore Vaiṣṇavas in Gauḍīya-Madhva-sampradāya say that the ecstatic feelings experienced by Śrī Caitanya Mahāprabhu during His appearance came in line from Śrī Mādhavendra Purī through Īśvara Purī. All the devotees in the Gauḍīya-Madhva-sampradāya accept these principles of devotional service.

(Commentary on *Caitanya-caritamṛta* Madhya 4/197)

8. Are dry renunciants and sense enjoyers eligible for transcendental mādhurya-rāsa?

Mādhurya-rāsa is unsuitable for persons who follow the path of dry renunciation. Persons who are attached to material enjoyment are also disqualified from entering into the mystery of *mādhurya-rāsa.*

(*Caitanya-śikṣāmṛta* 7/7)

9. Who are the real authorities on transcendental rāsa?

Only those who are detached from material sense gratification and have attained love of God are qualified to relish *rāsa.* The endeavor to relish *rāsa* by persons who have not yet developed pure *rati* or attained detachment from matter is completely useless. If they try to do so, they will engage in sinful activities by accepting *rāsa* as *sādhana.*

(*Caitanya-śikṣāmṛta* 7/1)

10. Can rāsa be taught by just anyone?

Rasa is not a limb of *sādhana.* If anyone says, "Come, I will teach you *rāsa,*" he is certainly a cheater and a fool.

(*Caitanya-śikṣāmṛta* 7/1)

11. Is the science of rāsa a subject for jñāna or knowledge?

Rasa is not a subject for *jñana* of knowledge but a subject to be relished. Relishing *rāsa*, the ultimate goal of life, does not take place until we are finished with the two basic functions of knowledge, inquiry and collection.

(*Caitanya-śikṣāmṛta* 7/1)

12. Can we understand the science of rāsa through reason and argument?

We cannot realize the science of *rāsa* through argument. What to speak of spiritual *rāsa*, we cannot even understand mundane *rāsa* through reason and argument.

(*Caitanya-śikṣāmṛta* 7/1)

13. Can a living entity become the hero or object of rāsa?

The devotees' duty is to serve Krishna in *mādhurya-rāsa*, following in the *gopīs*' footsteps. One who imitates Krishna and tries to become the hero of *rāsa* will certainly go to hell. Hypocrites, cheaters, and duplicitous persons commit such an offense.

(*Caitanya-śikṣāmṛta* 7/7)

14. What is the progressive limit of spiritual rāsa and the limit of its reflection?

Rasa is eternal, unbroken, inconceivable, and full of ecstasy. From the platform of pure *rati*, *rāsa* progressively advances to the platform of *mahābhāva*. When pure *rati* is diverted, it perverts to mundane illusion.

(*Caitanya-śikṣāmṛta* 7/1)

15. What is an example of rāsa? What is aversion to rāsa?

Worship is an example of *rāsa*. Material activities or nonmaterial, impersonal thoughts are never considered worship. They are always dry and averse to *rāsa*.

(*Caitanya-śikṣāmṛta* 7/1)

16. Where is rāsa found?

If we regard the Absolute Truth as impersonal, there is no question of experiencing *rāsa*. Then the Vedic statements such as *raso vai sah*, "The Supreme Lord is the reservoir of all pleasure," become meaningless. The impersonal concept is unpalatable because in it there is a total absence of happiness. The more the personal concept manifests, the more *rāsa* increases.

(*Caitanya-śikṣāmṛta* 7/7 and *Jaiva Dharma*, Chapter 31)

17. What is transcendental parakīya-rāsa?

The wonderful *rāsa* that arises when the hero and heroine meet out of spontaneous attachment, although they are yet unknown to one another, is called *parakīya-rāsa*. The more we are inclined toward self-satisfaction, the more *rāsa* dries up. The more we are inclined toward the Lord's pastimes, the more *rāsa* increases. Where Krishna is the only hero, there is no question of *parakīya-rāsa* being improper.

(*Caitanya-śikṣāmṛta* 7/7)

18. Why is transcendental parakīya-rāsa most relishable?

The damsels of Gokula, even though they are eternal energies of Krishna, relish pastimes in Goloka. The *parakīya-rāsa* they relish is topmost. To bring that topmost *rāsa* into this world, Lord Krishna brought His Goloka consorts to Gokula. Where is the fault in His action? He is not a mundane hero; He acts for the living entities' benefit. Otherwise, how could the living entities become qualified to achieve the topmost *rāsa* of relishing the supreme *mādhurya-rāsa*?

(*Caitanya-śikṣāmṛta* 7/7)[1]

---

1 To shed more light on the Goloka and Gokula pastimes being non-different and eternal, here are more passages from Śrī *Caitanya-siksamrta*:

"Amongst millions of liberated souls, to find a devotee of the Lord is very rare. Even the devotee interested in the majestic aspect of the Lord cannot see Goloka. They attain service to the majestic form of the Lord in Vaikuṇṭha, after getting liberation. Amongst those who worship Krishna in the rāsa of Vraja, only those to whom Krishna bestows mercy are able to see Goloka. By the mercy of Krishna the *vastu siddha bhakta* is brought to Goloka. Those who are *svarupa siddhas* remain in this world with the identity of a *gopī*. Those who are covered by the mode of ignorance, see only the material world, even when performing their worship. Those covered by the mode of passion can see a little better. Those devotees in *sattva* mode realize a reflection of Goloka when they see the earthy Gokula. The devotees beyond the modes of nature very quickly obtain a body of a *gopī* in Goloka, the spiritual world, by the mercy of Krishna. Goloka becomes realized to the extent of the removal of Māyā. Yasodā's giving birth, Krishna's birth in the prison, the marriage of eternal *gopīs* with Abhimanyu and other's which gives rise to the mood of *parakīya* appear to be very material in the earthly Vraja. But these events all occur by the influence of Yogamaya with specific spiritual intentions behind them. They are not false, but are the perfect replica of Goloka. But they appear material in Vraja due to the material vision of the seer.

19. Why is Vraja's parakīya-rāsa transcendental and not improper?

Worldly marriage does not exist in the Vraja pastimes. When the Lord of Goloka brings His supreme *parakīya-rāsa* into Gokula in this material world, the damsels of Gokula cannot be accused of the improper conduct of mundane paramour love?

(*Caitanya-śikṣāmṛta* 7/7)

20. Why is transcendental parakīya-rāsa pure?

According to the opinions of Śrī Rūpa and Śrī Sanātana, the pastimes that took place in Gokula in this world are fully present in Goloka. Therefore, the *parakīya-rāsa* in Goloka must be present in an inconceivably pure state. The pastimes arranged by *yogamāyā* are pure. The mood of *parakīya* is created by yogamāyā and it is certainly pure.

(*Brahma-saṁhitā* 5.37)

21. Which rāsa is extremely rare?

The *rāsa* in *sakhya-rati* is not fully blossomed. Therefore, from time immemorial, the *gopīs* have shown a natural inclination for *parakīya-rāsa*. Lord Krishna accepts the mood of a paramour in accordance with the *gopīs*' feelings and performs the *rāsa-līlā* with the support of His dearmost flute.

(*Brahma-saṁhitā* 5.37)

22. Is it possible while meditating on the Lord's transcendental pastimes to see Goloka in Gokula?

The pastimes beginning from the killing of Pūtanā to the killing of Kaṁsa are in the category of the Lord's demon- killing pastimes. These pastimes are manifest in Gokula and are present only as feelings in the transcendental abode of Goloka. They do not exist there. While relishing

---

In Goloka those same events are eternally present in the form of beliefs, which nourish the *rāsas*. Those who are aspirants for service of the eightfold pastimes by taking the form of *gopīs* must take support of earthly Vraja. According to the amount of mercy from Krishna, they obtain purity in their service.

"Will Vraja pastimes continue during the final devastation? At that time all the pastimes remain in Goloka. Through practice during eight times of the day, a person realizes the eternal nature of the daily pastimes of Krishna. During the duration of universes, the Vraja pastimes rotate from one universe to another. At the time of final devastation, the pastimes remain in Goloka. Though Krishna may disappear from the earth, Vraja and Mathura do not disappear, but remain for the benefit of the devotee's performing *sadhana*."

the Lord's pastimes, a pure *rasika* devotee in Gokula can see the Goloka pastimes.

(*Caitanya-śikṣāmṛta* 7/7)

23. Is it possible to enter the great rāsa ocean while following rules and regulation?

If we merely follow rules and regulations while cultivating Krishna consciousness, we cannot enter the great ocean of *rāsa*.

(*Caitanya-śikṣāmṛta* 7/7)

24. What is the difference in rasika feelings between the inhabitants of Goloka and the inhabitants of Gokula?

Vaikuṇṭha-*rāsa* is based on the principle of majesty. Therefore, in Vaikuṇṭha, there is no *rāsa* of parental affection toward the source of all *avatāras*. In Goloka, however, the seat of all superexcellent deliciousness, there is only the original sentimental assumption of parental *rāsa*. There, Nanda and Yaśodā are visibly present, but there is no real birth. Thus the assumed sentiment of Nanda and Yaśodā's parental affection has no foundation in the actual sense of giving birth to Krishna. Still, they maintain a parental ego toward Krishna (*jayati jana-nivāso devakī-janma-vāda*, etc.). For the perfection of *rāsa*, that sentiment is eternal.

Similarly in the *rāsa* of amorous love, if the corresponding sentiments of concubinage and paramourship are merely eternal assumptions, there is no blame in them; they do not go against the scripture. When those transcendental entities of Goloka become manifest in Gokula Vṛndāvana, then those two sentiments become somewhat more palpable to the mundane view in the phenomenal world and there comes to be this much difference: In the parental *rāsa*, Nanda and Yaśodā's sentiments appear much more "earthy" because they appear to give birth to Krishna, and in the amorous *rāsa*, the corresponding sentiments of concubinage in the *gopīs* appear more "earthy" because they appear to be married to Abhimanyu, Govardhana, and other cowherd men. In reality, there is no such thing as the *gopīs* being married to husbands or associating with husbands either in Goloka or Gokula.

(*Brahma-saṁhitā* 5.37)

25. How adulterous is rāsa among followers of unauthorized sects?

Unauthorize *sampradayas* take shelter of mundane *rāsa* on the pretext of manifesting spiritual *rāsa* . They are completely misguided.

(*Caitanya-śikṣāmṛta* 7/1)

26. How do we determine which living entities belong to which rāsa?

A living entity's *rāsa* is determined according to his confidential taste. When a practitioner's faith awakens and he gradually attains taste, then he begins to love his own *rāsa*. After determining his taste, his spiritual master teaches him his particular process of *bhajana*.

(*Caitanya-śikṣāmṛta* 6/5)

27. Who is the object and who are the followers of śānta- rāsa?

Śānta-rāsa is first among all *rāsas*. *Śānta-rati* is the *sthāyi-bhāva* of this *rāsa*. The happiness found in merging into the impersonal Brahman and the yogī's self-satisfaction are extremely insignificant in relation to this type of happiness. Spiritual happiness is so much more confidential. Realization of the Lord's personal form is the cause of this happiness.

The object of *śānta-rāsa* is the four-handed Nārāyaṇa. This form of the Lord possesses transcendental qualities like opulence and greatness. Persons who are peaceful and are situated in neutrality are the shelter of *śānta-rati*. The *ātmārāmas*, the self-satisfied, and the ascetics who have firm faith in the Absolute Truth, follow *śānta-rāsa*. The four great personalities, Sanaka, Sanandana, Sanat-kumāra, and Sanātana are the principal *ātmārāmas*. They wander about as celibates. In the beginning they were attached to the to the impersonal Brahman, but becoming attracted by the Lord's sweet transcendental form, they began to worship that spiritual form.

Although the ascetics have been able to renounce material enjoyment by practicing *yukta-vairagya*, they have not yet vanquished their desire for liberation. Such people enter *śānta-rāsa*.

(*Jaiva Dharma*, Chapter 29)

28. What are the characteristics of a śānta-bhakta? What are the vibhāva and anubhāva of śānta-rati?

The devotees in the *śānta* mood have not developed intense affection for Krishna. Affection is a natural mood based on our constitutional position.Therefore the *rati* of a *śānta-bhakta* is always pure. Lord Hari is eternal, blissful, unchangeable, compassionate, and full of knowledge, full of all opulence, the Supersoul, the Supreme Brahman, the giver of liberation, and the crest jewel among the *ātmārāmas*. He is the object of *śānta-rati*. The living entities under this *rati's* shelter are either ātmārāmas or ascetics.

This *rāsa*'s *sthāyi-bhāva* is to meet a personality named Mukunda, who is self-illuminated, fully spiritual, completely devoid of material qualities, and beyond the reach of sense perception. The activities that stimulate *śānta-rāsa* are hearing the principal *Upaniṣads*, associating with renunciants, introspection, contemplating truth, cultivating spiritual knowledge, seeing the Lord's universal form, associating with the learned, and discussing the *Brahma-sūtras* and *Upaniṣads* with like-minded persons.

The *anubhāvas* of *śānta-rāsa* are remaining silent, staring at the tip of the nose, behaving like a mendicant, looking only to a distance of five feet while walking, displaying the mudrā of knowledge by touching the tip of the thumb with the tip of the index finger, not being envious of those who are envious of the Supreme Lord, not exhibiting sufficient respect to the devotees; longing for perfection in the form of relief from material existence, glorifying liberation while living free of attachment within the gross and subtle bodies, and remaining impartial, devoid of false ego, and without a sense of proprietorship.

The devotees in *śānta-rāsa* exhibit all the transformations of ecstatic love except *pralaya*, but because they do not identify with their bodies, such ecstatic transformations are exhibited only in the form of smoke (*dhūmāyita*). Sometimes they are illuminated (*jvalita*), but never brightly illuminated (*dīpta*). Sometimes *vyabhicārī-* and *sañcārī-bhāvas* such as desire, emotion, patience, happiness, argumentativeness, remembrance, enthusiasm, and indifference are found in *śānta-rāsa*. Being decorated with such characteristics, *śānta-rāsa* is considered one of the *rāsas*.

(*Caitanya-śikṣāmṛta* 7/3)

29. When do the mellows of loving devotional service manifest?

Śānta-rāsa is not found in the description of the Vraja pastimes because it is not aimed at a particular form of the Lord. Rather, it is devoid of affection. By immense good fortune, a living entity develops affection for the Lord's transcendental form. As soon as this affection is born, pure *rati* is nourished and becomes *prema*. Then the mellows of loving devotional service manifest.

(*Caitanya-śikṣāmṛta* 7/1)

30. What is śānta-rāsa according to Vaiṣṇava literature?

"You must love God with all thy heart. Your heart now runs to things other than God, but you must make your feelings run to loving God as you would train a horse to run in a particular way." This is one of the four principles of worship, or what is called *śānta-rāsa*, in Vaiṣṇava literature.

(To Love God, *Journal of Tajpur,* August 25, 1871)

31. What is the difference between the mellows of loving devotional service and dāsya-rāsa?

Many people call the mellows of loving devotional service *dāsya-rāsa*, but the mellows of loving devotional service are twofold: loving devotional service with awe and reverence, and loving devotional service with affection. The mellows of loving devotional service with awe and reverence are known as *dāsya-rāsa*. Loving devotional service with affection is called *prīti-bhakti-rāsa*, not *dāsya-rāsa*.

(*Caitanya-śikṣāmṛta* 7/4)

32. What is dāsya-rāsa?

You must love God with all your mind. When you perceive, conceive, remember, imagine, and reason, you must not allow yourself to be a dry thinker; you must love. Love alone can soften the intellect's dryness. You must develop the intellect on all good and holy things by means of harmony, love of truth, and spiritual beauty. This is the second phase of Vaiṣṇava development and is called *dāsya-rāsa*.

("To Love God," *Journal of Tajpur,* August 25, 1871)

33. How far does dāsya-rāsa advance?

Dāsya-rāsa advances up to *rāga*, surpassing *prema* and *sneha.*

(*Caitanya-śikṣāmṛta* 7/4)

34. What is viśrambha?

Firm faith, devoid of pain, is called *viśrambha.* It has been explained as faith without awe and reverence.*[2]

(*Caitanya-śikṣāmṛta* 7/5)

35. What is praṇaya?

Despite possessing the quality of awe and reverence, when *rati* remains aloof from the touch of awe and reverence, it is called *praṇaya.*

(*Caitanya-śikṣāmṛta* 7/5)

36. What are the progressive stages of praṇaya?

Praṇaya gradually surpasses the stages of *prema* and *sneha* and reaches *rāga* in *sakhya-rāsa.*

(*Caitanya-śikṣāmṛta* 7/5)

---

2 *Strong faith in Krishna without the obstacle of awe reverence is called *viśrambha* or familiarity.

37. Is there separation between Śrī Krishna and the residents of Vraja?

According to the Lord's manifest pastimes, separation is described in relation to *sakhya-rāsa*, but actually there is never any separation between Śrī Krishna and the residents of Vraja.

(*Caitanya-śikṣāmṛta* 7/5)

38. What are the characteristics of vātsalya-rāsa?

When there is a lack of confidence in Krishna, *prīti-rāsa* is not nourished. In such an instance, *sakhya-rāsa* disappears. But there is no harm if this lack of confidence occurs in *vātsalya-rāsa*. It is a special quality of *vātsalya-rāsa*.

(*Caitanya-śikṣāmṛta* 7/6)

39. What are the characteristics of Baladeva, Yudhiṣṭhira, and Āhuka's respective *rāsas*?

Baladeva's *sakhya* mood is mixed with *vātsalya*. Yudhiṣṭhira's *vātsalya* mood is mixed with *dāsya* and *sakhya*. Āhuka's *dāsya* mood is mixed with *vātsalya*. The elderly cowherd men's *vātsalya* mood is mixed with *sakhya*. Nakula, Sahadeva, and Nārada's *sakhya* mood is mixed with *dāsya*. Śiva, Garuḍa, and Uddhava's *dāsya* mood is mixed with *sakhya*. A similar mixture of moods is found in Krishna's grandsons, such as Aniruddha and other's Other devotees also possess mixed moods.

(*Caitanya-śikṣāmṛta* 7/6)

40. What is the sakhya-rāsa of the Vaiṣṇavas?

You must love God with all thy soul. You must perceive yourself in spiritual communication with the Deity and receive holy revelations in your most sublime hours of worship. This is called the *sakhya-rāsa* of the Vaiṣṇavas: the soul approaching the Deity in holy and fearless service.

("To Love God," *Journal of Tajpur*, August 25, 1871)

41. Why is mādhurya-rāsa topmost and worship of the Lord under Śrī Rūpa's guidance most relishable?

Among the five principal *rāsas*, *mādhurya-rāsa* is topmost. I glorify this *rāsa* with all my heart. All the characteristics of the other *rāsas* are present in *mādhurya-rāsa*. All the secondary *rāsas*, which are categorized into *vyabhicārī-bhāvas*, nourish *mādhurya-rāsa*. Anyone who worships the Lord under Śrī Rūpa's guidance attains *mādhurya-rāsa*.

(*Gītāmālā*)

42. How are the secondary rāsas relishable in the mellows of devotional service to Krishna?

There are seven secondary *rāsas* in Krishna's devotional service. They are relishable because they nourish Śrī Krishna's pastimes. The seven secondary *rāsas*, which include laughter, are within the *vyabhicārī-* and *sañcārī-bhāva*s. Appearing at appropriate times as the waves of the transcendental mellows, they nourish and increase the beauty of the *prema* ocean. Being unable to realize the transcendental position of the science of *rāsa*, one may have the following doubt: laughter, astonishment, and enthusiasm are accepted as part of auspicious *rāsa*, but how can fear, anger, hatred, and lamentation be part of *rāsa*, which is fearless, calm, and free from grief? I am afraid that by accepting them, we are making *rāsa* mundane, a product of matter. The answer is this: ecstatic *rāsa* is variegated, yet it is full of bliss and not at all distasteful.

(*Caitanya-śikṣāmṛta* 7/1)

43. What are the root, cause, function, and support of rāsa?

Sthayi-bhāva is the root of *rāsa*, *vibhāva* is its cause, and both *anubhāva* and *sāttvika-bhāva* are its function. *Sañcārī-* and *vyabhicārī-bhāva*s support *rāsa*. *Vibhāva*, *anubhāva*, and *sāttvika-* and *vyabhicārī-bhāva*s make *sthāyi-bhāva* most relishable.

(*Caitanya-śikṣāmṛta* 7/1)

44. What is rāsābhāsa and what are its characteristics?

When *rāsa* is incomplete and devoid of a limb, it is called *rāsābhāsa*. *Rasābhāsa* is divided into three categories according to *uttama*, *madhyama*, and *kaniṣṭha*: *uparāsa*, *anurāsa*, and *aparāsa*.

(*Jaiva Dharma*, Chapter 30)

45. What is the symptom of rāsābhāsa?

Rasābhāsa makes *rāsa* unpalatable; just as a salt and sour preparation mixed with a sweet drink is unpalatable. A contradiction of *rāsa* is called *rāsābhāsa*.

(*Jaiva Dharma*, Chapter 30)

46. What causes uparāsa?

Uparāsa can occur to any of the twelve *rāsas* with the help of *sthāyi-bhāva*, *vibhāva*, and *anubhāva*. *Uparāsa* is caused by aversion to *sthāyi-bhāva*, *vibhāva*, and *anubhāva*.

(*Jaiva Dharma*, Chapter 30)

47. What is anurāsa and what are some examples of it?

Rāsa without a direct relationship with Krishna is called *anurāsa.* The cowherd boys laughing upon seeing the dance of the kakkhati birds and Nārada's wonder upon seeing the parrots discussing *Vedānta* in the trees of Bhāṇḍīravana are examples of *anurāsa.* In *anurāsa* Krishna is seen in the distance not directly.

(*Jaiva Dharma*, Chapter 30)

48. What is uparāsa and what ia an example of it?

If Krishna or His opponents become the objects of laughter, then this laughter is called *aparāsa.* An example of *aparāsa* is Jarāsandha laughing repeatedly upon seeing Krishna running away.

(*Jaiva Dharma*, Chapter 30)

49. Who are the friends and enemies of the rāsas beginning with śānta?

The friends of *śānta-rāsa* are *dāsya, bībhatsa, dharmavīra,* and *adbhuta-rāsa. Adbhuta-rāsa* is also a friend of *dāsya, sakhya, vātsalya,* and *mādhurya-rāsa.* The enemies of *śānta-rāsa* are *mādhurya, yuddhavīra, raudra,* and *bhayānaka-rāsa.*

The friends of *dāsya-rāsa* are *bībhatsa, śānta, dharmavīra,* and *dānavīra-rāsa.* The enemies of *dāsya-rāsa* are *mādhurya, yuddhavīra,* and *raudra-rāsa.*

The friends of *sakhya-rāsa* are *mādhurya, hāsya,* and *yuddhavīra-rāsa.* The enemies of *sakhya-rāsa* are *vātsalya, bībhatsa, raudra,* and *bhayānaka-rāsa.*

The friends of *vātsalya-rāsa* are *hāsya, karuṇa,* and *bhayabhedaka-rāsa.* The enemies of *vātsalya-rāsa* are *mādhurya, yuddhavīra, dāsya,* and *raudra-rāsa.*

The friends of *mādhurya-rāsa* are *hāsya* and *sakhya-rāsa.* The enemies of *mādhurya-rāsa* are *vātsalya, bībhatsa, śānta-* raudra, and *bhayānaka-rāsa.*

The friends of *hāsya-rāsa* are *bībhatsa, mādhurya,* and vātsaya-*rāsa.* The enemies of *hāsya-rāsa* are *karuṇa* and *bhayānaka-rāsa.*

The friends of *adbhuta-rāsa* are *vīra, śānta, dāsya, sakhya, vātsalya,* and *mādhurya.* The enemies of *adbhuta-rāsa* are *hāsya, sakhya, dāsya,* raudra, and *bībhatsa-rāsa.*

The friend of *vīra-rāsa* is *adbhuta-rāsa.* The enemy of *vīra-rāsa* is *bhayānaka-rāsa.* According to some opinions, *santa-rāsa* is also an enemy of *vira rāsa*

The friends of *karuna-rāsa* are *raudra* and *vatsalya rāsa*. The enemies of *karuna-rāsa* are *vira*, *hasya*, *madhurya*, and *adbhuta rāsa*.

The friends of *raudra-rāsa* are *karuṇa* and *vīra-rāsa*. The enemies of *raudra-rāsa* are *hāsya*, *śṛṅgāra*, and *bhayānaka- rāsa*.

The friends of *bhayānaka-rāsa* are *bībhatsa* and *karuṇa- rāsa*. The enemies of *bhayānaka-rāsa* are *vīra*, *śṛṅgāra*, *hāsya*, and *raudra-rāsa*.

The friends of *bībhatsa-rāsa* are *śānta*, *hāsya*, and *dāsya-rāsa*. The enemies of *bībhatsa-rāsa* are *śṛṅgāra* and *sakhya- rāsa*.

All other *rāsas* are neutral.

(*Jaiva Dharma*, Chapter 30)

50. Please explain the mystery of the gopīs becoming the wives of other men?

The Vraja *gopīs* never have sexual relationships with their so-called husbands. Their husbands are only illusory incarnations of the conjugal mood. The marriages are also illusory. The *gopīs* do not have husbands, but their mood of being the wives of other's is eternally present. If this mood were not present, how would they be able to manifest the wonderful play of being afraid or prohibited by their husbands, of obstacles and aversion? Unless we develop such a mood, we cannot become damsels of Vraja, as proven by the example of Lakṣmī.

(*Jaiva Dharma*, Chapter 32)

51. Why don't we consider the rāsa of Śrī Krishna's transcendental pastimes vulgar?

Moral persons naturally hate mundane *rāsa*. If we hate the thought of transcendental *rāsa*, we are certainly prejudiced. Controlled by such prejudice, unfortunate people hate transcendental *rāsa* in Krishna's *līlā* wherein the Lord associates with spirit souls who possess spiritual bodies. Thus such unfortunate people cheat themselves and gain nothing.

(*Manaḥ-śikṣā*, Verse 5)

52. How do devotees under the shelter of parakīya-rāsa respect rules and regulations?

When a married woman becomes overwhelmed by the beauty of another man and secretly becomes attached to him, she outwardly respects her husband even more to avoid arousing his suspicion. Similarly, Krishna's lovers take shelter of *parakīya-rāsa* by internally cultivating attachment while externally following the regulative principles.

(*Śrī Krishna-saṁhitā* 8/10)

53. What is the history of the development of transcendental rāsa in the Eastern and Western countries?

If we were to study the history of the five *rāsas*, clearly we would find that *śānta-rāsa* was visible in India's beginning days. Transcendentalists like Sanaka, Sanātana, Sananda, Sanat-kumāra, Nārada, and Mahādeva, who were not satisfied by performing sacrifices with material ingredients, became detached from this world and situated in transcendence. They realized *śānta-rāsa.*

Much later, Hanumān, the leader of the monkeys, manifested *dāsya-rāsa. Dāsya-rāsa* gradually expanded to the northwest and appeared in the great personality, Moses. Long after Hanumān's time, Uddhava and Arjuna became qualified authorities of *sakhya-rāsa.* They preached this *rāsa* throughout the world. Gradually this *rāsa* expanded to the Arabian countries and touched the heart of Mohammed, the knower of religious principles.

Vātsalya-rāsa manifested throughout India in different forms and at different times. Among the different forms, *vatsalya* mixed with opulence crossed India and appeared in the great personality, Jesus Christ, who was a preacher of religious principles.

Madhurya-rāsa first shown brightly in Vraja. This *rāsa* rarely enters the hearts of conditioned souls because it tends to remain with qualified, pure living entities. Navadvīpa-candra Śrī Śacīkumāra, preached this secret *rāsa* along with His followers. This *rāsa* has not yet gone beyond India. A short while ago, a scholar from England named Newman realized something about this *rāsa* and wrote a book about it.

The people of Europe and America are not satisfied with *vātsalya-rāsa* mixed with opulence, as preached by Jesus Christ. I hope that by the Lord's grace they will soon become attached to the intoxicating nectar of *mādhurya-rāsa.* We can see that any *rāsa* that appears in India eventually spreads to the Western countries. *Mādhurya-rāsa* will therefore soon be preached throughout the world. Just as the sun first rises in India and gradually spreads its light to the Western countries, similarly the matchless shining of spiritual truth first appears in India and gradually spreads to the Western countries.

(Introduction to *Śrī Krishna-saṁhitā*)

54. What is the difference between the ācāryas' preaching of mādhurya-rāsa before and after Śrī Caitanyadeva's advent?

Ācāryas such as Viṣṇusvāmī, Nimbāditya, and Rāmānuja preached *mādhurya-rāsa* long before Mahāprabhu's advent. Śrī Mādhavendra Purī, the *parama-gurudeva* of Mahāprabhu, first established preaching *mādhurya-rāsa*'s scientific basis and Śrī Īśvara Purī improved upon his work. Śrī Mahāprabhu then displayed the ultimate perfection of this *rāsa*. Although poets like Jayadeva and Vidyāpati scientifically relished this *rāsa*, it was not popular during their time. What to speak of Jayadeva, *Śrīmad-Bhāgavatam* itself is the complete storehouse of *mādhurya-rāsa* Still no one before Mahāprabhu opened the gate of that storehouse and allowed the ordinary people to drink of the nectarean love of God.

(*Sajjana-toṣaṇī* 2/9)

55. Are the mellows of ecstatic love subject matter for arguement?

The mellows of love of God are just like an ocean of milk. If one pours cow dung and cow urine in the form of arguments into milk, the whole pot becomes tasteless.

(*Jaiva Dharma*, Chapter 34)

56. What is the characteristic of vipralambha-rāsa?

Vipralambha means separation. When dyeing an already colored cloth, the color of the cloth intensifies. Similarly, through separation, the desire for conjugal enjoyment intensifies. Without *vipralambha*, the conjugal pastimes cannot be nourished.

(*Jaiva Dharma*, Chapter 37)

57. In what rāsa does the mood of female arise in the living entity's spiritual body?

The eternally pure body of the living entity is fully spiritual. There is no difference between male or female in that body. The living entity's spiritual body is full of pure, independent desires. According to each soul's mood, the pure body manifests either as a male or a female. In *śānta-rāsa*, however, the mood is neither male nor female. In *dāsya-* and *sakhya-rāsa*, the mood is male. In *mātri-vātsalya*, the mood is female, and in *pitri-vātsalya*, male. In the brightly shining *mādhurya-rāsa*, the mood of all pure living entities is female. All these devotees serve Krishna, the only supreme enjoyer.

(*Caitanya-śikṣāmṛta* 6/5)

58. Is mundane rāsa eternal and factual?

Mundane *rāsa*, which is preached by mundane literature, is the perverted reflection of supreme, transcendental *rāsa*. It is not eternal. It is a shadow of the original *rāsa*, a mirage in the desert.

(*Gitāmala*, Song 6)

59. What causes transcendental mellows to develop or decrease?

Life cannot be sustained without *rāsa*. Material life is full of material *rāsa*. In a devotee's life, spiritual *rāsa* appears momentarily like a flash of electricity. By the mercy of a bona fide spiritual master and on the strength of *sādhu-saṅga*, this mood gradually increases and fully blossoms. Due to a lack of *sādhu-saṅga* and hearing atheistic and impersonal instruction, undeveloped *rāsa* gradually decreases and is finally lost. This is a most unfortunate state.

(*Caitanya-śikṣāmṛta* 7/2)

60. What is the preliminary stage of vātsalya-rāsa as Jesus Christ preached it?

Jesus said, "You must love man as thy brother." This understanding is the fourth phase of love, which is a feeling that all men are brothers with God as their common father. It is *vātsalya-rāsa* in its first stage of development.

("To Love God," *Journal of Tajpur*, August 25, 1871)

61. What is the difference in rāsa between the Nimbārka and Gauḍīya sampradāyas? Why is the bhajana the Gauḍīya Vaiṣṇavas perform the best?

The Nimbārka line has not accepted the mood of *parakīya- āsa*. Rather, they perform *bhajana* in the mood of *svakīya-rāsa*. In the Gauḍīya line, *parakīya-rāsa* is topmost. The sweetness of *parakīya-rāsa* is greater than the sweetness of *svakīya-rāsa*.

(*Sajjana-toṣaṇī* Vol.7)

62. Why did Śrī Jīva Goswami sometimes give instructions on *svakīya-bhajana*? Was he himself a follower of that rāsa?

Śrī Jīva Goswami did not perform *bhajana* in the mood of *svakīya-rāsa*, but he saw that few devotees in Vraja were inclined to it. Therefore he gave instructions according to the different tastes of his various disciples. His commentary, *Locana Rocanī*, states this clearly.

(*Jaiva Dharma*, Chapter 69)

63. How does Bhaktivinoda Ṭhākura describe parakīya-rāsa as topmost?

Transcendental pastimes are like mysterious jewels. *Parakīya-madhura-rāsa* is the Kaustubha gem among such jewels.

(*Caitanya-śikṣāmṛta* 7/7)

64. Do the devotees experience separation in the Lord's unmanifest pastimes due to His going to a distant place?

The Lord's pastimes are of two types, unmanifest and manifest. The separation experienced in *vipralambha-rāsa* pertains only to the Lord's manifest pastimes. Actually, there is no separation between Śrī Krishna and the Vraja *gopīs*. *Mathurā-māhātmya* states that Lord Krishna enjoys His pastimes in Vraja in the company of the cowherd boys and girls. The word *kriḍati*, "plays," is in the present tense, so we can understand that Krishna's Vṛndāvana pastimes are eternal. Even if Krishna goes to a distant place, there is no separation in the Krishna's unmanifest pastimes in Goloka Vṛndāvana. There, enjoyment is eternal.

(*Jaiva Dharma*, Chapter 38)

105

Love of God

1. How is prema defined?

Dṛḍha mamatāśayātmikā prīti prema means,"When *prīti* is firm and mixed with affection, it is called *prema.*"

(*Āmnāya Sūtra* 87)

2. How does prema gradually develop? How are prema-sneha-māna and praṇaya defined?

Rati has the power to surpass everything. Therefore, it is called *samarthā.* It also has the power to make us forget everything. When *rati* intensifies and is unaffected by opposing moods, it is known as *prema.* Gradually manifesting its own sweetness, *prema* transforms into *sneha, māna, praṇaya, rāga, anurāga,* and *bhāva.* When *prema* matures and possesses the power of illumination, it melts the heart and is called *sneha.*

Sneha is of two types, butterlike and honeylike. *Sneha* with intense affection is like butter. *Sneha* in the form of possessiveness is like honey.

Rati is also of two types, "I belong to Him," and, "He is mine." The mood of "I belong to Him," is the butterlike *sneha* of Cāndravalī. The mood of "He is Mine," is the honeylike *sneha* of Srī Rādhā. When sneha matures and manifests symptons like inability and arrogance, it called *māna.*

Māna is of two kinds, *udātta* and *lalita.* When *mana* becomes more intenseand the lover and the beloved are considered one, it is called *pranaya.* When *pranaya* matures, both the extreme happiness and the miseries experienced through the relationship are called *rāga,* which appears in two types, *nīlimā* and *raktimā.*

The forty-one types of *bhāva* are *sthāyi-mādhurya-bhāva,* thirty-three *vyabhicārī-bhāva*s, and seven secondary *bhāva*s. The *rāga* that gives ever-newer pleasures to the lover is called *anurāga.* Fully controlled varieties of *prema* and the desire to take birth among inanimate beings are symptomatic of *anurāga*. *Anurāga* manifests Krishna in the mood of separation. The variegatedness of love of God contains the mood of separation.*[3]

(*Caitanya-śikṣāmṛta* 7/7)

3. What is the definition and function of prīti?

Prīti is the personification of spiritual pastimes. It always gives unlimited pleasure to Krishna, who is eternally full of knowledge and bliss. Because of *prīti*'s nature, Krishna enjoys the wonderful mellow of ecstatic love. Krishna's holy names are the manifestation of Krishna's all-attractive feature. His form as Śyāmasundara is the embodiment of complete spiritual bliss and is full of nectarian love. Krishna, the love of the *gopīs*, is always complete with His unlimited auspicious qualities. He eternally enjoys the mellows of the transcendental pastimes. By meditating on the Lord's holy names, forms, qualities, and pastimes, the living entity associates directly with his beloved Lord, Śrī Krishna.

(*Manaḥ-śikṣā*, Verse 11)

4. What is the ultimate goal of life?

According to the teachings of Śrīman Mahāprabhu, love of God is the ultimate goal of life. Love of God is twofold, love of God born from *bhāva* and love of God born from mercy. Love of God born from *bhāva* is divided into two: *vaidhī* and *rāgānugā*. Love of God born from mercy is very rare, whereas love of God born from *bhāva* is common.

(*Manaḥ-śikṣā*, Verse 11)

5. What is the difference between unalloyed love of God and love of God in awe and reverence?

Love of God is divided into two classes, unalloyed love of God and love of God in awe and reverence. By cultivating *rāgānugā-bhakti*, we

---

3 Śrīla Bhaktisiddhānta Sarasvatī Ṭhākura quotes Rūpa Goswami as follows: "The loving propensity of the *āśraya* (devotee) toward the *viṣaya* (Lord) becomes so ecstatic that even after enjoying the company of the beloved, the devotee feels that his enjoyment is insufficient. At such a time, the lover sees the beloved in different ways. Such a development of ecstasy is called *anurāga*. When *anurāga* reaches its highest limit and becomes perceivable in the body, it is called *bhāva*. When the bodily symptoms are not very distinct, however, the emotional state is still called a*nurāga*, not *bhāva*. When *bhāva* ecstasy is intensified, it is called *mahābhāva*. The symptoms of *mahābhāva* are visible only in the bodies of eternal associates like the *gopīs*."

(Commentary on *Caitanya Caritāmṛta* Madhya 6.13 BBT)

awaken unalloyed love of God. Those practicing *vaidhī-bhakti* attain love of God mixed with opulence. They obtain liberation, such as possessing the same opulence as the Lord.

(*Manaḥ-śikṣā*, Verse 11)

6. What are the symptoms and impediments of prema?

The absence of satisfaction is a symptom of love of God. Love of God is the ultimate fruit of devotional service. Liberation and so forth are devotion's irrelevant fruits. Since self-satisfaction is an impediment to love of God, saintly persons consider it loathsome.

(*Bṛhad-bhāgavatāmṛta*, Purport)

7. What is the prayer of one who loves Krishna?

With my body, mind, and speech, may my love for the reddish lotus feet of Śrī Caitanya Mahāprabhu increase day by day. Let me have unflinching love for the pure Vaiṣṇavas. Let me have love for the ocean of the Lord's transcendental qualities. Let me have love for the service of Krishna and the Vaiṣṇavas. Let me have love for chanting Krishna's holy name. Let me love those persons who have taken shelter of the Lord and who are inclined to worship Him. Let me also love myself, who am inclined toward Kṛṣna, so that I may attain devotion to Him.

(Commentary on *Bhajanāmṛtam*)

8. What is the most important object of life?

Pure devotees of Krishna are the *mahājanas* or great personalities. Love for them is desirable. We are the field into which the seed of love is to be sown. Try to capture love of God within your heart. Krishna alone is the only wealth in this world. The Vaiṣṇavas are dear to Him. Love of God is the most important object of life. There is nothing greater than this.

(Commentary on *Bhajanāmṛtam*)

9. What branch among the innumerable branches of the Vedas is dear to Gaurasundara? What is the goal of that branch?

The Vedic literature has thousands of branches. Among them, only one is dear to the Lord. That branch is devotional service to Krishna. Love of God is the fruit of that branch. There is nothing better than love of God in the material world. Love of God is the only desirable object.

(Commentary on *Bhajanāmṛtam*)

10. What is Mahāprabhu's weapon?

Love of God is the Lord's only weapon. If that weapon is put to use, all obstacles will be destroyed and everyone will be happy; the living entities will no longer suffer the pangs of material existence.

(Commentary on *Bhajanāmṛtam*)

11. If love of God is the eternally perfect object, why does attachment develop for objects not related to Krishna?

Just as a childless father does not develop affection for a child, an unmarried woman does not realize affection for a husband, a benefited person does not express gratitude to his benefactor due to ignorance, those foolish people who are attached to objects not related to Krishna cannot understand love of God.

(*Tattva-sūtra* 4)

12. Which is greater, love or liberation? How does a devotee who has attained love of God live?

There is nothing greater than love of God for a living entity. Liberation is temporary, and, when compared to love of God, insignificant. Among the many irrelevant fruits of love of God, liberation is only one. If love of God awakens while we are still connected with matter, we will find that we no longer appreciate our connection with matter. Those who have attained love of God are devoid of material association and full in Krishna consciousness. Glowworms hide when the sun rises. Similarly, the rules and regulations hide when love of God awakens. For a loving devotee, this material world appears as Vaikuṇṭha.

(*Caitanya-śikṣāmṛta* 6/1)

13. What are the irrelevant and principal fruits of devotional service?

As soon as a living entity becomes free from material contamination by the strength of devotional service, he attains liberation. But liberation is an irrelevant fruit of service, not the principal fruit. Pure love of Krishna is the principal fruit of *sādhana-bhakti*, and it can be achieved by liberated souls.

(*Sajjana-toṣaṇī* 10/11)

14. What is the difference between loving oneself and loving other's?

Universal love, or love between people, is simply a transformation of loving oneself. Love between spirit souls is the only ideal love.

(*Sajjana-toṣaṇī* 8/9)

15. Is it possible to awaken love of God without the association of saintly persons?

Love of God is the supremely pure medium for exchanging spiritual reciprocation. Only the hearts of saintly persons are qualified and prone to accept this medium. Nondevotional hearts distract from it. Unless we associate with saintly persons, this medium will not enter our heart. Just as attraction and repulsion are opposites in magnetism, so association with *sādhus* and nondevotees are opposites. Their association pushes us in opposite directions. Therefore, if we wish to attain love of God, we should associate with saintly persons.

(*Harināma-cintāmaṇi*)

16. What is the difference between love of Krishna and love of humanity?

Pure love of God is the root of all varieties of love. Uncivilized living entities experience pure love in a materially perverted state. A Western moralist named Comte instructed his followers to become a little selfless and to endeavor for universal love. Śrī Mahāprabhu taught everyone to cultivate pure transcendental love of God. Comte, a materialist, tried to expand the materially perverted form of pure love instead. The living entity finds no benefit in following Comte; his teachings instruct us to give up our iron shackles for gold one's. To relish pure love of God, Mahāprabhu taught the living entities about Śrī Rādhā-Krishna's pastimes.

(*Sajjana-toṣaṇī* 2/9)

17. What is the inconceivable influence of love of Krishna?

Love of Krishna is such that it transforms happiness into distress and distress into happiness.

(*Jaiva Dharma*, Chapter 39)

18. What are the eternal rāsalīlā pastimes of Krishna? What is the nature of pure love?

A giant object attracts a tiny object. The sun, a gigantic object, attracts other planets and satellites toward it, but to remain apart from the sun, the planets and satellites move in a circle. Moreover, the speed and attraction between the planets keeps them in orbit. As we understand things in this perverted world, we should understand things in the spiritual world. The transcendental personality, who enjoys His pastimes in Vṛndāvana, is the sun of the spiritual world; the living entities are His associates. Lord Krishna attracts the living entities on the principle of love. Because of their independent nature, the living entities try to remain apart from Him. Still, the attraction forcefully pulls the living entities and brings them toward Krishna. Although the tiny living entities are defeated, they circle around the sun, Krishna. This is Krishna's eternal *rāsalīlā*. The companions who belong to His internal potency are particularly close to Him, and the companions who have attained perfection through *sādhana* are a little distant. Krishna's transcendental pastimes have the nature of pure love.

(*Sajjana-toṣaṇī* 8/9)

19. What are the primary symptons of pure love?

According to its natural tendency, iron is attracted toward a magnet when it enters the magnified field. Similarly, the minute spirit souls display their natural inclination toward Krishna, the supreme consciousness, when they are fully Krishna conscious. This inclination toward Krishna is the primary symptom of pure love.

(*Manaḥ-śikṣā*, Verse 11)

20. What is the difference between love of God and love for material objects?

The difference between love for matter and love for Krishna is seen when the loving propensity transcends matter and becomes purely inclined toward Krishna. When that propensity is deviated toward material enjoyment, it is love for matter or attachment for material objects.

(*Manaḥ-śikṣā*, Verse 11)

21. Is conjugal rāsa enjoyable for the living entities in the material world?

According to Mahāprabhu, the living entities who have taken birth in the material world should relish the mood of separation, *vipralambha-rāsa.*

(Commentary on *Śikṣāṣṭaka*)

22. Do the devotees who relish the mellows of devotional service respect anything other than the happiness of chanting Krishna's holy name?

yoga-śruty-upapatti-nirjana-vana-dhyānādhva-sambhāvita-svārājyaṁ pratipadya *nirbhayam amī muktā bhavantu dvijā asmākaṁ tu kadamba-kuñja-kuhara-pronmīlad-indīvara-śreṇī-śyāmala-dhāma-nāma juṣatāṁ janmāstu lakṣāvadhi.*

"Let the twice-born enter the fearless kingdom of yoga, Vedic study, and solitary meditation in the forest. Let them become liberated in that way. As for us, we will spend hundreds of thousands of births chanting the holy name of Lord Krishna, whose splendid dark complexion and yellow garments are like a host of blue lotus flowers blooming in a grove of yellow- flower-bearing *kadamba* trees."

This verse was spoken by Śrīmad Īśvara Purī, a dear disciple of Śrīmad Mādhavendra Purī. In this verse he states that for devotees who can relish the mellows of devotional service, the happiness of liberation is insignificant. Instead, we derive our happiness from chanting the Lord's holy names, because such happiness is much more intense than the happiness of liberation.

There are eight types of yoga, beginning with sitting postures, breathing excercises, and so on. Study of the Vedas in this verse refers to the knowledge of impersonal Brahman contained in the *Upaniṣads*. Residing in a solitary place means practicing *vānapraṣtha*. Devotees who are devoid of pride in their *varṇāśrama* status and who are satisfied by chanting Krishna's holy name do not care if they have to accept millions of births.

23. What is the difference between residing in Vṛndāvana in the self-realized state and in the perfected state?

Lord Krishna is present in the spiritual abode of Vṛndāvana as the fresh Cupid. The materialistic poets describe "Cupid" as extremely mundane. Their explanations are full of abominable, lusty topics, and their poems refer only to the attraction of material flesh for material flesh. Being conditioned by Māyā and identifying the body as the self, the living entities have become subordinate to lust.

When a living entity understands his relationship with Krishna, he resides in the transcendental abode. This state is twofold. When we are self-realized but our contact with matter has not yet being destroyed, spiritual truth is revealed to some extent and we reside in Vṛndāvana. This state is called *svarūpa-siddhi*. When our relationship with the gross and subtle bodies is completely destroyed by Krishna's will, we actually reside in Vṛndāvana. This stage is called *vastu-siddhi*.*[4]

---

4 Śrīla Bhaktivinoda Ṭhākura considers the *brahma-bhūta* stage in two divisions—*svarūpa-gata* and *vastu-gata*. One who has understood Krishna in truth but is still maintaining some material connection is known to be situated in his *svarūpa*, his original consciousness. When that original consciousness is completely spiritual, it is called Krishna consciousness. One who lives in such con-

sciousness is actually living in Vṛndāvana. He may live anywhere; material location doesn't matter. When by the grace of Krishna one thus advances, he becomes completely uncontaminated by the material body and mind and at that time factually lives in Vṛndāvana. That stage is called *vastu-gata.*

One should execute his spiritual activities in the svarūpa-gata stage of consciousness. He should also chant the *cinmayī gāyatrī*, the spiritual *mantras*; *oṁ namo bhagavate vāsudevāya* or *klīṁ kṛṣṇāya govindāya gopījana-vallabhāya svāhā*, and *klīṁ kāma-devāya vidmahe puṣpa-bāṇāya dhīmahi tan no 'naṅgaḥ pracodayāt*. These are the *kāma-gāyatrī* or *kāma-bīja mantras*. One should be initiated by a bona fide spiritual master and worship Krishna with these transcendental *mantras*.

As explained by Kṛṣṇadāsa Kavirāja Goswami in the previous verse and the current verse:

vṛndāvane 'aprākṛta navīna madana'
kāma-gāyatrī kāma-bīje yāṅra upāsana
purusa yoṣit kibā sthāvara-jangama
sarva-cittakarsaka sākṣāt manmatha madana

A person who is properly purified and initiated by the spiritual master worships the Supreme Personality of Godhead, Krishna, by chanting this *mantra*, the *kāma-gāyatrī* with the *kāma-bīja*. As the *Bhagavad-gītā* (18.65) confirms, one should engage in transcendental worship in order to be fit for being attracted by Krishna, the all-attractive:

man-manā bhāva mad-bhakto
mad-yājī māṁ namaskuru
mām evaiṣyasi satyaṁ te
pratijāne priyo 'si me

"Always think of Me and become My devotee. Worship Me and offer your homage unto Me. Thus you will come to Me without fail. I promise you this because you are My very dear friend."

Since every living entity is part and parcel of Krishna, Krishna is naturally attractive. Due to the material covering, one's attraction for Krishna is checked. One is not usually attracted by Krishna in the material world, but as soon as one is liberated from material conditioning, he is naturally attracted. Therefore it is said in this verse, *sarva-cittākarṣaka*: "Everyone is naturally attracted by Krishna," This attraction is within everyone's heart, and when the heart is cleansed, that attraction is manifested.

(Śrīla Bhaktivedanta Swami Prabhupāda's commentary on *Caitanya Caritāmṛta* Madhya 8.139)

In *svarūpa-siddhi*, we must practice *sādhana*. At that time, we continue to worship Krishna by chanting the spiritual *kāma-gāyatrī* and *kāma-bīja mantras*. The all-attractive Krishna, who can enchant even Cupid, attracts everyone—men, women, and all other animate and inanimate beings.

(Commentary on *Caitanya Caritāmṛta* Madhya 8/137–138)

24. What is the ultimate goal of life. What is the first stage of pure devotional service?

Loving devotional service is the ultimate goal of life. In its first stage, pure devotional service appears as *śānta-bhakti*. At this stage there are no feelings of affection toward Krishna.

(Commentary on *Caitanya Caritāmṛta* Madhya 8/68)

25. Why is ecstatic love of Krishna the crest jewel of all happiness?

In pursuit of happiness, living entities in the material world follow various processes such as logic and mystic yoga. Some kings, seeking happiness, wage war with one another; other people in search of happiness renounce the material world and go to the forest. Others run after the women and wealth, while other's study arts and sciences. In pursuit of happiness, some people reject happiness and learn to tolerate life's miseries, while other's simply drown themselves in the ocean.

Raising His lotus hands in the air, Lord Nityānanda exclaims:

"Come, living entities! Give up the troubles of karma and *jñāna*. Since you are endeavoring for happiness, I will give you happiness without asking anything in exchange. In this happiness I will give you, there will be no trouble, loss, or pain. Just chant the name of Gaurāṅga and dance without anxiety. There's nothing equal to the happiness I am offering. That happiness is pure, eternal ecstasy, beyond all illusion!"

(*Navadvīpa-māhātmya*, Chapter 1)

26. Are a pure soul's ecstatic transformations (such as praṇaya or mahābhāva) transformations of material nescience?

jīvasya nitya-siddhasya sarvam etad anāmayam
vikārāś cid-gatā śaśvat kadāpi no jaḍānvitām

Some people say that unless there is oneness between the *ātmā* and the Paramātmā, there will be no *praṇaya* in spiritual affairs. They add that *mahābhāva* is a false acceptance of material feelings as spiritual. Regarding these impure opinions, we say that the living entity's different emotions arising from *praṇaya* are not transformations of material nescience. Rather, they are spiritual emotions.

vaikuṇṭhe śuddha-cid-dhāmni vilāsā nirvikārakā
ānandābdhi-taraṅgās te sadā doṣa-vivarjitā

"The pastimes in the pure spiritual abode of Vaikuṇṭha are faultless and are like waves in the ocean of bliss The word *vikara*, transformation cannot be applied to these pastimes."
(*Śrī Krishna-samhita*, Chapter 1/11-12)

27. Where is the temple of love situated?

The temple of *kṛṣṇa-prema* is situated on the highest peak of Goloka Vṛndāvana. To reach that peak, we must first cross the fourteen planetary systems of *karma-kāṇḍa*, the Virajā River, and the Brahmaloka of *jñāna-kāṇḍa*. Then we must rise above Vaikuṇṭha. By gradually giving up attachment to karma and *jñāna*, we become eligible for *bhakti*. After crossing the various stages of *bhakti*, we reach the temple door of *prema*.
(*Sajjana-toṣaṇī* 10/10)

28. How did Śrī Bhaktivinoda Ṭhākura instruct those who have attained love of God about progress on the devotional path?

O devotees of Krishna! You have surpassed the fourteen gross planetary systems in the material world and attained *bhāva* by following regulative devotional service. Now try to cross the four subtle layers of Hari-*dhāma*, which are situated above the fourteen planetary systems. Then penetrate the two pure layers of the Virajā, Brahma-*dhāma* and Vaikuṇṭha. Thus you will reach the border of Goloka Vṛndāvana. There are five brightly shining layers in Goloka: *śānta*, *dāsya*, *sakhya*, *vātsalya*, and *mādhurya*. After reaching *mādhurya*, take the eternally perfect spiritual body of a *gopī* and enter among the associates of Śrīmatī Lalitā in Śrīmatī Rādhikā's group. By Śrī Rūpa-mañjarī's mercy, enhance the *sthāyi-bhāva* in your own heart with the help of pure, transcendental *vibhāva* and the *sāttvika* and *vyabhicārī-bhāva*s. If you are attracted both to chanting the holy names and to someone who understands transcendental mellows, you can easily obtain the treasury of love to the point of *mahābhāva.* In this way, you should make your life successful. After considering your present qualification and becoming detached from your material body, you should earn the highest qualification of constantly drinking the nectar of the holy names.

(*Caitanya-śikṣāmṛta* 7/7)

29. What is the difference between those who have attained love of God and those who are fully enriched with love of God?

Love of God is the living entity's ultimate goal. When *bhāva* is fully mature, it is called *prema.* When a living entity makes further advancement and becomes inclined toward Krishna, he gradually attains the temple of love of God. There are thus two stages to love of God; the stage where the devotees have attained love of God and the stage where the devotees are fully absorbed in ecstatic love. Those who have reached the latter stage have nothing more to achieve, because their love for Krishna is uninterrupted. In the former stage, we are simply unalloyed devotees of Krishna; full surrender is our general symptom.

(*Caitanya-śikṣāmṛta* 6/3)

30. Who are prema-rūḍha-bhaktas — devotees fully absorbed in love of God?

While aiming for love of God, swanlike personalities quickly achieve their desired result. They are on the platform of love of God. Very soon, such devotees become devotees fully absorbed in love of God and are called *prema-rūḍha-paramahaṁsas*, *sahaja-paramahaṁsas*, or spontaneous *paramahaṁsas.*

(*Caitanya-śikṣāmṛta* 6/4)

31. Can the symptoms of love be found anywhere other than in a pure soul? Is there any pure love in this material world? Where did the attraction and movement for matter come from?

Both the supreme consciousness and the minute consciousness possess the symptoms of love. Pure love cannot exist anywhere except in a soul. The perverted reflection of pure love is found in the material world, a shadow of the spiritual world. Pure love cannot therefore be found in any material object in this visible material world. Attraction and movement which are perverted forms of pure love, are found here. Because of that perverted nature, all atoms are attracted to one another and are transformed into gross objects. Moveover, being attracted to one another, gross objects come closer to one another.

(*Sajjana-toṣaṇī* 8/9)

32. What is prema-*v*ilāsa-vivarta, inebriety or confusion in the enjoyment of love?

There are two moods in the enjoyment of love. They are the mood of direct enjoyment and the mood of separation. Without the mood of separation, the mood of direct enjoyment does not become inspired. Disconnection is called separation, and it causes inebriety and confusion in love of God. During separation, the devotee still enjoys, but direct enjoyment is absent because of intense love. When Rāmānanda Rāya sang a song he had composed, Mahāprabhu became overwhelmed by ecstasy and immediately covered Rāmānanda's mouth with His own hands. The song contained the words Rādhārāṇī spoke while She was separated from Krishna. This proves that even while experiencing separation, the devotee can still enjoy.

(Commentary on *Caitanya Caritāmṛta* Madhya 8.193)

33. What is enjoyment like during separation?

Just as there is enjoyment during loving pastimes, there is enjoyment during separation. In the mood of separation, one becomes particularly confused. The devotee might mistake a *tamāla* tree for Krishna just as we might mistake a rope for a snake. This confusion comes because of *mahābhāva*, and it brings pleasure.

(Commentary on *Caitanya Caritāmṛta* Madhya 8.194)

106

Samādhi or Trance

1. What are the various stages of natural samādhi?

When a spirit soul practices natural *samādhi*, he progressively realizes the following subjects: (1) himself, (2) the insignificance of the self, (3) the supreme shelter, (4) the relationship between the shelter and the sheltered, (5) the beauty of the qualities, activities, and form of the shelter, (6) the relationships among the sheltered, (7) the abode of the shelter and the sheltered, (8) the absolute time factor, (9) the various moods of the sheltered, (10) the eternal pastimes between the shelter and the sheltered, (11) the energies of the shelter, (12) the advancement and degradation of the sheltered by the energies of the shelter, (13) the illusion of the degraded sheltered, (14) the cultivation of devotional service for restoration of the degraded sheltered, and (15) the degraded sheltered regaining their constitutional position through devotional service. These fifteen subjects, as well as other inconceivable truths, are realized in *samādhi*.

(*Śrī Krishna-saṁhitā*, Chapter 9/5)

2. What is the difference between the jnani's artficial samādhi and the Vaiṣṇava's absolute samādhi?

There are two types of *samādhi*; artificial and absolute. Devotees accept natural *samādhi* as absolute and fabricated *samādhi* as artificial regardless of how the *jnanis* define the two states. Because the soul is spiritual, we naturally possess the qualities of self-knowledge and the knowledge of other objects. Self-knowledge means we can understand ourselves. The quality of knowing other objects allows us to understand them. Since such qualities are constitutional to the living entity, why should we doubt that natural *samādhi* is absolute? A living entity does not need to take shelter of another instrument in order to understand the supreme object. This *samādhi* is faultless.

(*Śrī Krishna-saṁhitā*, Chapter 9/2)

3. How does the conclusion of devotional service manifest in the ācāryas' hearts?

samudra-śoṣaṇaṁ reṇor yathā na ghaṭate kvacit
tathā me tattva-nirdeśo mūḍhasya kṣudra-cetasa
kintu me hādaye ko 'pi puruṣa śyāmasundara
sphuran samādiśat kāryam etat tattva-nirūpaṇam

Just as a particle of dust cannot absorb the ocean, a foolish person like me cannot understand truth. Although a living entity is never able to understand truth with his small intelligence, a blackish Personality with a form of pure consciousness has appeared in my heart and engaged me in the work of understanding truth. For this reason I have boldly taken up this work.

(*Śrī Krishna-saṁhitā*, Chapter 1/2–3)

107

Self-Realization and the Achievement of Perfection

1. How many types of liberation are there for devotees and what are their characteristics?

There are two kinds of liberation for devotees, *svarūpa-mukti* and *vastu-mukti*. Liberation personified begins to serve those who, by the strength of devotional service, have realized their constitutional position in the material world. This state is called *svarūpa-mukti*. When by the mercy of Krishna such devotees give up their bodies, they attain *vastu-mukti*, ultimate liberation.

(*Manaḥ-śikṣā*, Verse 8)

2. When do we achieve āpana-daśā and svarūpa-siddhi?

A devotee reaches *āpana-daśā* when he gradually remembers the Lord's holy name, meditates on the Lord's form, qualities, and pastimes, and absorbs himself in the mellows of Krishna by entering into the Lord's pastimes. In this state he meditates on Krishna's eternal pastimes twenty-four hours a day. When the devotee is fully absorbed in this state, he attains *svarūpa-siddhi*.

(*Caitanya-siksamrta* 6/4)

3. When do we feel happy to serve Śrī Rādhā Krishna, and when will the Lord's transcendental pastimes manifest in our heart?

In the state of *āpana-daśā*, from time to time a devotee resides in Vraja in his constitutional position. There is great pleasure in serving Rādhā-Krishna when we are situated on this level of self-realization. What to speak of such pleasures, we will often see the abode of Vraja and remain there in our constitutional position, relishing the Lord's transcendental pastimes.

(*Harināma-cintāmaṇi*)

4. After crossing āsakti, when do we attain self-realization?

Even though we surpass *āsakti*, we will remain in contact with matter as long as we possess a subtle body. However, by Krishna's mercy, the subtle body can be quickly destroyed. Contact with matter is an impediment. As long as this impediment is present, a living entity will not attain *vastu-siddhi*, ultimate perfection. As soon as we attain *prema*, however, our constitutional position will awaken and we will become eligible to achieve *rāsa*.

(*Caitanya-śikṣāmṛta* 7/1)

5. What is svarūpa-siddhi? What is its relationship with sambandha, abhidheya, and prayojana?

Realization of the Absolute Truth is called *svarūpa-siddhi*. Another name of this is *sambandha-jñāna*, knowledge of our relationship with the Lord. When knowledge of our relationship with the Lord awakens, we begin to practice *abhidheya* and cultivate love of God. Then, we can attain *prayojana*, love of God itself.

(*Caitanya-śikṣāmṛta* 6/4)

6.What state do we attain when we become perfect in devotional service?

There are two kinds of perfection in devotional service, *svarūpa-siddhi* and *vastu-siddhi*. When we are situated in *svarūpa-siddhi*, we see Goloka in Gokula. When we are situated in *vastu-siddhi*, we see Gokula in Goloka.

(*Brahma-saṁhitā* 5/2)

7. What is the ultimate goal of karma?

The goal of karma is to become free from fruitive activities; any other goals presented regarding karma have been spoken only to create a taste for fruitive activities.

(Śrī *Bhāgavatārka-marīci-mālā* 124)

8. What is vastu-siddhi?

By Krishna's mercy, when we attain a spiritual body after giving up our material body and become an associate in the Lord's Vraja pastimes, we will have achieved *vastu-siddhi*. This is the ultimate goal of chanting the Lord's holy names.

(*Caitanya-śikṣāmṛta* 6/4)

9. What is the meaning of the phrase, "entering into the Lord's eternal pastimes"?

While performing *bhajana*, we will see Krishna face to face and, by the sudden desire of the Lord, our gross and subtle bodies will be vanquished. As soon as our material body, which is composed of five gross material elements, is destroyed, our subtle body (mind, intelligence, and false ego) will also be destroyed. At that time, our pure spiritual body will manifest, and we will begin to serve their Lordships Rādhā and Krishna in the spiritual abode. This is called "entering into the Lord's eternal pastimes."

(*Harināma-cintāmaṇi*)

10. Is it possible to reside in the material world after attaining vastu-siddhi?

When we attain *vastu-siddhi*, we can no longer stay in the material world. A devotee then lives only in the transcendental world.

(Śrī *Bhāgavatārka-marīci-mālā* 17/24)

11. What does a mahā-bhāgavata realize when he attains perfection?

When will I beg food from the house of dogeaters and eat? When will I drink water from the Ganges? When will I roll on the ground in the forests near the bank of the Ganges while singing Krishna's names?

(*Gītāmālā*, Song 1)

12. How does a loving devotee feel separation from Śrī Rādhā, who is his life and soul?

If I give up Śrī Rādhikā's lotus feet for even a moment, I fall unconscious. For Rādhikā's sake I am prepared to die hundreds of times. I have no problem tolerating such distress.

(*Gītāmālā*, Song 10)

13. What is the mentality of a servant of Śrī Rādhā?

I cannot tolerate Śrī Rādhikā's distress, caused by Her separation from Krishna. My only happiness is to see Rādhā and Krishna together. To accomplish this, I can even give up my life.

(*Gītāmālā*, Song 10)

14. What does Śrī Bhaktivinoda say regarding partiality to Śrī Rādhikā?

Let anyone give up the side of Rādhā and live as they want. Always remaining partial to Rādhikā, I will never look at the face of such people.
((*Gītāmālā*, Song 9)

15. What is the symptom of svārasiki-siddhi?

The supremely chaste and restless gopis of Vraja are the treasury of *svārasiki-siddhi*. The meditation of yogis and the knowledge of impersonalists cannot reach that stage. On such a platform, one can directly see the Lord during His midday pastimes. O servants of the lotus feet of Rādhā! Please engage me in appropriate service to Śrī Rādhā according to the moment's need.
(*Gītāmālā*, Song 6)

16. What does those who follow in the footsteps of Śrī Rupa desire as their perfection?

When will this maidservant achieve perfection and live on the banks of Śrī Rādhā-kuṇḍa, giving up her previous memories and constantly serving the lotus feet of Śrī Rādhā and Krishna?
(*Gītāmālā*, Song 8)

17. What are the characteristics of those who serve Śrī Rādhā?

You are a maidservant of Rādhikā. Therefore, you should not independently serve Krishna without Her permission. Even though you display equal affection toward both Rādhā and Krishna, you should endeavor more for the loving service of Rādhikā than for the loving service of Krishna. This is called *sevā*. Your service is to serve Śrī Rādhā twenty-four hours a day.
(*Jaiva Dharma*, Chapter 39)

18. What does it mean to take birth in the house of a cowherd of Vraja?

Some Vaiṣṇava authors have explained that *svarūpa-siddhi* means to take birth in the house of a cowherd in Vraja even before the practitioner completes his *sadhana*. This is correct. Thus a Vaiṣṇava attains second birth before *vastu-siddhi*. The devotee's attainment of a *gopi* form is the complete attainment of his pure second birth, *apana dāsa*. When a practitioner's body which is made of material qualities is destroyed, then he progresses from *svarūpa-siddhi* and achieves *vastu-siddhi*.
(*Caitanya-śikṣāmṛta* 6/5)

19. How much respect does a pure devotee give to the Lord's abode and the service of the Lord's devotees?

When will I offer my respectful obeisances at the feet of the residents of the *dhāma* and beg their mercy? When will I wander like a mendicant after smearing the dust from the feet of the Vaiṣṇavas on my body?

(*Gītāmālā*, Song 1)

20. Does a pure devotee differentiate between Gaura- maṇḍala and Vraja-maṇḍala?

When will I attain service to Śrī Rādhā? When will I stop making a distinction between Gaura-maṇḍala and Vraja-maṇḍala and thus become a resident of Vraja? At that time, the *dhāma*'s actual form will manifest before my eyes and I will become Śrī Rādhā's maidservant.

(*Gītāmālā*, Song 1)

108

Benedictions for the Whole World

1. How will the world truly be benefited? Is Śrī Bhaktivinoda Ṭhākura's heartiest desire to benefit the entire world beyond understanding?

We are completely indifferent to the advancement and deterioration of our material situation, but we are naturally busy for the advancement of the living entity's spiritual life. We are even ready to throw the happiness of our life in the water to benefit our brothers. The primary engagement of Vaiṣṇavas is to deliver their fallen brothers from the well of material existence. The more the Vaiṣṇava's family expands, the more the atheist's family diminishes. This is the natural law of the universe. Let the love and devotion of all living entities flow toward the unlimited Supreme Lord. Let Vaiṣṇava principles, which are the source of happiness, gradually spread from one end of the universe to the other. Let the hearts of those who are averse to the Lord melt with love of God. By the Lord's mercy, the association of devotees, and the influence of devotional service, let third-class people become first-class and take shelter of pure ecstatic love. Let the exalted *madhyama-adhikaris* renounce their doubts and their cultivation of knowledge and establish themselves in the science of love. Let the whole universe echo with the sound of the congregational chanting of the holy names of Hari.

(*Śrī Krishna-samhita*, introduction)

2. Did Śrīla Ṭhākura Bhaktivinoda have a strong desire to preach the holy names of Hari all over the world and to thus fulfill Śrī Caitanya Mahāprabhu's mission?

Alas! When will that day come when the fortunate people of England, France, Russia, and America constantly and congregationally chant the names of Hari and glorify the names of Śrī Caitanya Mahāprabhu, holding flags, *mṛdaṅgas*, and *karatālas* in their hands? Alas! When will that day come when the white Western devotees stretch up their hands and, while chanting "Jaya Śrī Śacīnandana *kī jaya*," embrace the devotees of our country as brothers? When will that day come when they say, "O Vaiṣṇava brothers! We have taken shelter of the lotus feet of Śrī Caitanyadeva, who is the ocean of love. Now please embrace us!" When will that day come when pure transcendental love for the Vaiṣṇavas is the only occupation of all living entities and, as the rivers mix into the ocean, all insignificant religions mix into the unlimited Vaiṣṇava religion?

(*Sajjana-toṣaṇi* 4/3)

3. Did Śrīla Ṭhākura Bhaktivinoda appeal to all Vaiṣṇavas and saintly persons to preach Mahāprabhu's saṅkīrtana-dharma all over the world?

O pure devotees! Vaiṣṇava-dharma, preached by Śrī Gaurāṅga, is the supreme treasury of all living entities. The religious principles that are being preached with pomp in every country are incomplete and full of faults. When those religious principles diminish and hide inside their fort, supreme religious principles will come forward and be spread all over the world. That happiest moment has arrived! Now everyone should encourage the preaching of Śrī Nama Hatta with determination. All the hawkers, the devotees of Gaurāṅga, should carry the merchandise of the pure holy names on their heads. They should preach in India and the rest of the world about the purifying holy names of Hari and the topics of our beloved Śrī Gaurāṅga.

(*Viṣṇupriyā Pallī Magazine*)

4. How did Śrī Ṭhākura Bhaktivinoda start preaching through Śrī Nāma Haṭṭa and how did he desire its future success?

The preaching work of *Śrī Nāma Haṭṭa* has begun. Godrūma which is one of the nine island of Navadvīpa, is the ideal and original place of *Nāma Haṭṭa*. At that place, a few Vaiṣṇavas who are attached to the chanting of the holy names of Hari are arranging the preaching work of *Nāma Haṭṭa*. Those who are preaching the Lord's holy names by establishing an *āśrama* in a remote village or in the city are the shopkeepers of the holy names. Those who are preaching the holy names village to village, carrying the merchandise of the holy names on their heads, are the hawkers of the holy names. In a brochure about Godrūma, names of a few servants of *Nāma Haṭṭa* have been published. Perhaps Śrīmad Gaurāṅga Prabhu, Who delivered the entire universe, desires to award the pure holy names to the people of the whole world. We hope that within a short time, Vaiṣṇava-

dharma, preached by Śrīman Mahāprabhu, will purify the sinful Western countries.

(*Viṣṇupriyā Pallī Magazine*)

5. What prediction was made by a mahājana to indicate that the Hari's holy names would be glorified all over the world?

Those who selflessly preach the Lord's holy names will be worshipable everywhere. There is no doubt that the spiritual effulgence of the pure holy names will soon dissipate the darkness of false arguement. We hope that very soon the *Nāma Haṭṭa* program will expand in a huge way. The positions and titles that have entered into the Śrī Gaurāṅga Sampradaya will soon be destroyed, and ultimately the victory flag of the pure holy names will continue to soar in the Eastern and Western countries.

(*Viṣṇupriyā Pallī Magazine*)

6. What is the sign that Śrī Caitanya's mission will spread all over the world in the near future?

The Vaiṣṇavas will be glad to hear that a Muslim from the District of Noyakhali took shelter of Vaiṣṇava-dharma after careful consideration. On the strength of great piety, that saintly person has attained such a reward. I hope that by the mercy of Śrī Mahāprabhu all Muslims and *mlecchas* will soon accept this pure Vaiṣṇava religion. There is no doubt that the use of *mṛdaṅgas*, *karatālas*, and *kīrtana* melodies are forcefully entering other religions, and soon Śrī Caitanya's mission will spread all over the world.

(*Sajjana-toṣaṇī* 2/9)

7. Is there any indication that Śrīman Mahāprabhu's prediction will soon become successful?

The signs that the unique supreme religious principle, congregational chanting of Hari's holy names, will soon be preached all over the world are seen everywhere. Christians have started to relish chanting the holy names accompanied by *mṛdaṅgas* and *karatālas* . Soon they will take Śrī Caitanyadeva's *mṛdaṅgas* and *karatālas* to countries like England. They will realize that Śrī Krishna is the Supreme Brahman, the greatest of all. The Lord's holy names are unlimitedly glorious, and simply by the Vaiṣṇavas' mercy we make spiritual advancement. The Christians will sing, "The two brothers Gaura and Nitāi have come. By seeing Them, the eyes become fully satisfied." They will dance, accompanied by *mṛdaṅgas* and *karatālas*. Moreover, Christians who are striving for liberation are also establishing the supremacy of *sankīrtana* in some way or other.

After seeing all these signs, we hope that the time has come for everyone to follow Śrī Caitanya Mahāprabhu's order. Although *kīrtana* has not manifest in other *sampradāyas* in a completely pure state, there is no doubt that within a short time, Śrīman Mahāprabhu's prediction will bear fruit. Nothing becomes pure immediately. In the beginning, *kīrtana* appears with contamination, then gradually becomes completely pure.

(*Sajjana-toṣaṇī* 4/3)

8. In what religion is pure brotherhood possible?

Singing the transcendental qualities of the Supreme Lord and establishing brotherhood with everyone based on love for God is the pure religious principle. Gradually, when the offensive portions of the established religions are destroyed, there will no be no more differences in the *bhajana* performed by the various *sampradāyas* nor any quarrel between them. Then as brothers, the people of all *varṇas*, castes, and countries will spontaneously chant the holy names of the Supreme Lord together. At that time, no one will hate anyone or consider other's dogeaters, nor will anyone be overwhelmed by the pride of high birth. The living entities will not forget the principle of natural brotherhood.

Taking a pitcher filled with the mellows of love of God, Haridāsa will then pour nectar into Śrīvāsa's mouth, and Śrīvāsa, after smearing the dust from Haridāsa's feet on his body, will spontaneously dance while chanting, "O Caitanya! O Nityānanda."

(*Sajjana-toṣaṇī* 4/3)

9. How did Śrī Bhaktivinoda pray to the Supreme Lord for the welfare of the entire world?

O God! Reveal Thy most valuable truths to all so that "Your own" may not be numbered among the fanatics and the crazed and the whole of mankind may be accepted as "Your own."

('To Love God,' *Journal of Tajpur*, August 25, 1871)

10. How does the Supreme Lord call the devotees who hav attained love of God?

I have carefully saved this storehouse of *rāsa* for you. You alone are qualified for this. Do not worry or lament, because you have attained immortality. You have broken all shackles for Me. I can never repay the debt of your love.

(*Caitanya-śikṣāmṛta*, Conclusion)

The Literary Works of Ṭhākura Bhaktivinoda

1849 *Ulā-caṇḍī-māhātmya*, Bengali verses composed at the tender age of 11 years old, glorifying the deity of goddess Ulā-caṇḍī in Ulā, Birnagar, the town of his birth.

1850 *Hari-kathā*, a poem in Bengali.

1850 *Līlā-kīrtana*, a poem in Bengali.

1851 *Śumbha-Niśumbha-Yuddha*, Bengali verses about the famous ancient battle between Goddess Durgā and two demons.

1855 Articles; Contributions of articles to various regional and national periodicals and magazines commenced from this year.

1857 Poriade Part One - A poem in classical English about the wanderings of Porus, who fought Alexander the Great in the pre-Christian era.

1858 Poriade Part Two - The second of what was planned to be a twelve-part series, but which was never completed. Still, these two volumes constitute an epic composition.

1860 Maṭhs of Orissa; English prose narratives about the various temples, monasteries and holy shrines in Orissa which were visited on pilgrimage by Ṭhākura Bhaktivinoda.

1863 *Vijana-grāma*, Bhaktivinoda's description of his affectionate return to the beautiful village of Ulā (his birthplace).

1863 *Sannyāsī*, an intricately detailed story of the adventures of a young *sannyāsī* traveling throughout ancient India and abroad. The narrative is naturally full of important spiritual lessons.

1863 Our Wants; An essay in English prose.

1866 Speech on Gautama; A lecture in English about Gautama Muni and the philosophy of *nyāya* (logic)

1868 *Sac-cid-ānanda-premālaṅkara*, a poem in Bengali on the glories of Śrī Caitanya Mahāprabhu.

1869 *The Bhāgavat: Its Philosophy, Its Ethics, and Its Theology*

1870 *Garbha-stotra-vyākhā* (Purport of the *Garbha-stotra*), or *Sambandha-tattva-candrikā* (A Moonbeam of the Truth of Eternal Relationship). A commentary in Bengali prose on the *Garbha-stotra* (Prayers by the Demigods to Śrī Krishna in the Womb) from the second chapter of the tenth canto of *Śrīmad-Bhāgavatam*.

1871 Ṭhākura Haridāsa, ten English verses about the disappearance of Nāmācārya Śrīla Haridāsa Ṭhākura, which are engraved in marble on the *samādhi* tomb of Haridās by the seashore at Jagannātha Purī.

1871 The Temple of Jagannātha at Purī; an English prose essay describing the history of the establishment of the great temple in Purī, Orissa.

1871 The Personality of Godhead, an essay in English prose.

1871 *Sāragrāhī Vaiṣṇava*, a 22-verse English poem describing the mood of a devotee who knows how to remain aloof from gross worldly attractions while extracting the essence of Krishna consciousness everywhere and in everything.

1871 A Beacon Light; English prose.

1871 To Love God; A short English article describing *bhakti* (love) as the religion of the soul.

1871 The Attibaris of Orissa; a long letter in English to the editors of the "Progress," exposing a questionable sect of pseudo-Vaiṣṇavas popular in Orissa.

1872 *Vedāntādhikaraṇa-mālā*, a compilation of Sanskrit verses on *Vedānta* philosophy, with Bhaktivinoda's own Bengali translations and explanations.

1873 *Datta-kaustubha*, 104 Sanskrit verses on Vaiṣṇava philosophy composed by Ṭhākura Bhaktivinoda, including his own Sanskrit prose commentary.

1878 *Datta-vaṁśa-mālā*, Sanskrit verses giving a genealogical description of the Datta family of Bali Samaj. Since he was born Kedarnath Datta, this is a chronicle of Bhaktivinoda's own family tree.

1878 *Bauddha-vijaya-kāvyam*, Sanskrit verses soundly defeating the atheistic philosophy of Buddhism, point for point.

1880 *Śrī Krishna-saṁhitā*, an amazing and revolutionary treatise on the science of Lord Krishna, His pastimes and His devotees. The book contains an 83 - page introduction in which Ṭhākura Bhaktivinoda discusses the philosophy and development of Indian religion from a historical and geographical platform. In the actual *Saṁhitā* portion of the book, he has composed 281 Sanskrit verses and divided them into ten chapters which deal with descriptions of the spiritual world, the multifarious energies of the Lord, His incarnations, astonishing aspects of His pastimes, descriptions of how Lord Krishna removes specific demonic obstacles in order for His devotees to attain the mood of Vraja, and a detailed analysis of the character of one who has attained Krishna's association, etc. Accompanying the Sanskrit verses are Bhaktivinoda's Bengali prose translations and explanations. At the end of the book, the Ṭhākura gives a 50-page conclusion in which religious philosophy is discussed in terms of the principles of *sambandha, abhideya* and *prayojana.*

1881 *Kalyāṇa Kalpa-taru,* a Vaiṣṇava Bengali songbook describing a desire-tree that Bhaktivinoda had brought directly from the spiritual world

1881 *Sajjana-toṣaṇī,* this was a monthly Vaiṣṇava periodical in the Bengali language which Bhaktivinoda began to edit and publish commencing from the year 1881 and continuing for 17 volumes.

1883 Review of the Sanskrit book; "*Nitya-rūpa-saṁsthāpanam*" (Proof of the Lord's Eternal Form). The book was composed in Sanskrit by Bhaktivinoda's contemporary named Paṇḍit Upendra Mohan Goswāmī Nyāya-ratna.

1885 *Viśva-vaiṣṇava-kalpa-tavi,* a small booklet published in order to acquaint the public with the functions and aims of a spiritual society he personally organized in Calcutta, called the Śrī Viśva Vaiṣṇava Sabhā (The Association of Universal Vaiṣṇavas).

1886 *Śrīmad Bhagavad-gītā,* published and edited by Śrīla Bhaktivinoda with the Sanskrit commentary of Śrīla Viśvanātha Cakravartī Ṭhākura entitled *Sārārtha-varṣiṇī.* The book contains an elaborate introduction in Bengali, and for each Sanskrit verse of the *Gītā,* he composed his own Bengali translation-commentary entitled *Rasika-rañjana.*

1886 *Śrī Caitanya-śiksāmṛta,* a philosophical work in Bengali prose which is meant to show exactly how the teachings of Lord Caitanya are to be applied in the modern world. This includes the perfectly nonenvious bridging of the gaps between all the world's major religions. These nectarean teachings, based on Lord Caitanya's instructions to Rūpa and Sanātana Goswāmī as found in the *Caitanya Caritāmṛta,* are just like a shower of pure nectar, and therefore the book is divided into eight showers, each of these being subdivided into downpours. The eight showers are listed as follows:

(1) Ascertainment of the Topmost Religion
(2) Secondary Duties, or Religious Activities
(3) Primary Duties, or Regulative Devotional Service
(4) Discussions on Spontaneous Devotional Service

(5) Discussions on Ecstatic Devotional Service
(6) Discussions on Devotional Service in Pure Love of God
(7) Discussions on Transcendental Mellow
(8) Conclusion.

1886 *Sanmodana-bhāṣyam*, a comprehensive Sanskrit commentary on Śrī Caitanya Mahāprabhu's 8 verses of instruction named *Śikṣāṣṭaka*.

1886 *Bhajana-darpaṇa-bhāṣya*, a Sanskrit commentary on Śrīla Raghunātha dāsa Goswāmī's 12-verse Sanskrit prayer entitled *Manaḥ-śikṣā* (Instructions to the Mind).

1886 *Daśopaniṣad-cūrṇikā*, a book of Bengali prose containing essential information gleaned from the 10 principle *Upaniṣads*.

1886 *Bhāvāvalī*, Sanskrit verses on the subject of *rāsa* written by different Vaiṣṇava *ācāryas* of the highest order, compiled by Ṭhākura Bhaktivinoda and published along with his own Bengali song translations.

1886 *Prema-pradīpa*, a philosophical Vaiṣṇava novel written in Bengali prose.

1886 *Śrī Viṣṇu-sahasra-nāma-stotram*, this prayer was published by the Ṭhākura along with the Sanskrit commentary of Śrīla Baladeva Vidyābhūṣaṇa entitled *Nāmārtha-sudhā*.

1887 *Śrī Krishna-vijaya*, a famous Bengali verse epic on the pastimes of Śrī Krishna, written in the early 1470's by Mālādhara Vasu (Guṇarāj Khān.) This book, written in a simple folk style, was not only renowned for being the first volume of Bengali literature ever published, but was one of Śrī Caitanya Mahāprabhu's favorite books. Edited and published by Ṭhākura Bhaktivinoda with his own introduction in Bengali.

1887 *Śrī Caitanyopaniṣad* (part of the *Atharva* Veda). An *Upaniṣadic* treatise in Sanskrit dealing with Śrī Krishna's appearance as the great preacher of love of Godhead, Śrī Caitanya Mahāprabhu. Published and edited by Ṭhākura Bhaktivinoda with his own Sanskrit commentary called *Śrī Caitanya-caraṇāmṛta* (The Nectar of the Lotus Feet of Lord Caitanya), and Madhusūdana dāsa's Bengali translation of the original Sanskrit verses called *Amṛta-bindu* (A Drop of Nectar).

1888 *Vaiṣṇava-siddhānta-mālā*, Bengali prose work that gives a crystallization of all the basic tenets of Gauḍīya Vaiṣṇava philosophy.

1890 *Āmnāya-sūtram*, a classical Sanskrit composition based on the *Upaniṣads*, presented in the traditional style as 130 aphorisms, plus a short commentary on each aphorism in Sanskrit, quoted from various ancient scriptures. Bhaktivinoda also gives his own Bengali translation called the *Laghu-bhāṣya* (Brief Explanation). This book helps the aspirants in easily engaging their lives in devotional practices by presenting very simple statements of transcendental truths. The 130 aphorisms are divided into 16 extremely condensed and irrefutable chapters.

1890 *Śrī Navadvīpa-dhāma-māhātmyam*, 18 chapters of Bengali verse in which Bhaktivinoda describes the complete tour of the nine islands of Navadvīpa that was traversed by Lord Nityānanda. Taking the young Śrīla Jīva Goswami along, Lord Nityānanda Prabhu points out all the different places of pilgrimage and tells the stories behind those sacred sites.

1890 *Śrī Navadvīpa-dhāma-māhātmyam*, (Pramāṇa-khaṇḍa), (The Canto Describing the Scriptural References). Five chapters of amazing quotes from many different Vedic scriptures, *Purāṇas* and Saṁhitās that glorify the holy land of Navadvīpa. The Sanskrit verses are accompanied by Bhaktivinoda's Bengali prose translations.

1890 *Siddhānta-darpaṇam*, a philosophical Sanskrit work by Śrīla Baladeva Vidyā-bhūṣaṇa, edited and published by Ṭhākura Bhaktivinoda with his own Bengali prose translations.

1891 *Śrīmad Bhagavad-Gītā*, edited and published by Ṭhākura Bhaktivinoda with Śrīla Baladeva Vidyābhūṣaṇa's Sanskrit commentary called *Gītā-bhūṣaṇa*, and his own Bengali translation-commentary called *Vidvad-rañjana* (That Which Pleases the Wise).

1891 *Śrī Godruma Kalpatavi*, a collection of Bhaktivinoda's Bengali essays describing his program of *nāma-haṭṭa*, or the Marketplace of the Holy Name.

1892 *Śrī Hari-nāma*, the second chapter of *Vaiṣṇava-siddhānta-mālā*, excerpted and published in pamphlet form.

1892 *Śrī Nāma*, the third chapter of *Vaiṣṇava-siddhānta-mālā*, excerpted and published in pamphlet form, also used by Bhaktivinoda for distribution during his public *nāma-haṭṭa* programs.

1892 *Śrī Nāma-tattva-śikṣāṣṭaka*, the fourth chapter of *Vaiṣṇava-siddhānta-mālā*.

1892 *Śrī Nāma-mahimā*, the fifth chapter of *Vaiṣṇava-siddhānta-mālā*.

1892 *Śrī Nāma-pracāra*, the sixth chapter of *Vaiṣṇava-siddhānta-mālā*.

1892 *Śrīman Mahāprabhur Śikṣā*, a book written by Bhaktivinoda in eleven chapters. In the first chapter, he summarizes Śrī Caitanya's philosophy in ten points (*daśa mūla*). Then the following ten chapters fully explain each point individually. All philosophical conclusions are supported with profuse scriptural quotations in Sanskrit, which are accompanied by Bengali prose translations and explanations.

1893 *Tattva Viveka* or *Sac-cid-ānandānubhūti*, in this book, Ṭhākura Bhaktivinoda discusses the different precepts of the great Vaiṣṇava *ācāryas* as compared to the ideas of other famous philosophers, both Oriental and Western. He mentions the Greek philosophers Leucippus, Democritus,

Plato and Aristotle; Diderot and Lamettrie of France; Lucretius of Italy; Von Holbach of Germany; Yangchoo of China; Carvaka of India; and Englishmen Mill, Lewis, Paine, Carlyle, Bentham, Combe, and so on. The book is composed of 48 Sanskrit verses, each with an exhaustive Bengali commentary. The First Realization, of 33 verses, is entitled "Realization of Eternity", and the Second Realization, of 15 verses, is entitled "Realization of Eternal Consciouṣṇess."

1893 *Śoka-śātana*, a small booklet of 13 Bengali songs, which Bhaktivinoda composed between 1888 and 1890. These songs were meant to be sung by the general public, as they describe an ecstatic pastime in Lord Caitanya's life, an incident giving expression to important teachings of transcendental truths.

1893 *Śaraṇāgati*, a Bengali songbook of 50 ecstatic songs about the process of purely devoted surrender unto the lotus feet of Lord Krishna

1893 *Gītāvalī*, a Bengali songbook of 70 rapturous songs which are meant to be sung regularly by devotees.

1893 *Gīta-mālā*, a Bengali songbook of 80 nectarean songs arranged in five chapters.

1893 *Baula-saṅgīta*, a collection of 12 songs in Bengali verse.

1893 *Dālālera Gīta*, a song in Bengali verse that describes how Lord Nityānanda has opened up The Marketplace of the Holy Name at Surabhi-kuñja, which was Bhaktivinoda's headquarters on the island of Godruma in Navadvīpa.

1893 *Nāma Bhajana*, a small booklet in English prose on the divine name of Śrī Krishna

1893 *Jaiva Dharma*, a philosophical Vaiṣṇava novel written in Bengali prose.

1893 *Tattva-sūtram*, composed in 50 concise Sanskrit aphorisms divided into 5 chapters. Bhaktivinoda gives a Sanskrit commentary on each verse, plus an elaborate Bengali commentary. The five divisions are:

(1) The Truth of the Lord and His Creation

(2) The Truth of His Conscious Portions (Souls)

(3) The Truth of His Temporary Portion (The Material World)

(4) The Truth of the Relationship Between the Lord and His Creation

(5) The Truth Regarding Devotional Principles.

1894 *Vedārka-dīdhiti*, a Sanskrit commentary on the famous *Īśopaniṣad* found in the *Vājasaneya Saṁhitā* portion of the *Śukla Yajur Veda*. This commentary by Bhaktivinoda Ṭhākura was published along with the Sanskrit explanation of Śrīla Baladeva Vidyābhūṣaṇa called *Īśopaniṣad-bhāṣyam* (An Explanation of *Īśopaniṣad*). Also included were the notes of Bhaktivinoda's friend, Śrīyukta Śyāmalāla Goswami Siddhānta Vācaspati, entitled *Īśopaniṣad-bhāṣya-rahasya-vivṛti* (The Purport of the Inner Secrets of the Explanation of *Īśopaniṣad*), plus Śyāmalāl Goswāmī's Bengali clarification of the *Īśopaniṣad* called *Siddhāntānuvāda* (Translation of the Truth).

1894 *Tattva-muktāvalī* or *Māyāvāda-śata-dūṣiṇī*, 119 Sanskrit verses composed by Śrīpād Madhvācārya which refute the impersonal Advaita *Vedānta* philosophy that was spread all over India by Śaṅkarācārya. Ṭhākura Bhaktivinoda had it published with his own Bengali prose translations for each verse.

1895 *Amṛta-pravāha-bhāṣya*, a Bengali commentary on Kṛṣṇadāsa Kavirāja Goswami's *Śrī Caitanya-caritāmṛta*.

1895 *Hari-bhakti-kalpa-latikā*, a Sanskrit work on pure devotion by an unknown Vaiṣṇava author. Edited and published by Ṭhākura Bhaktivinoda with the Sanskrit text only.

1895 *Shodaśa Grantha*, a collection of sixteen small Sanskrit works written by Śrī Vallabhācārya, a prominent *ācārya* who lived during Lord Caitanya's time. Original Sanskrit text edited and published by Ṭhākura Bhaktivinoda.

1895 *Śrī Gaurāṅga-stava-kalpataru*, a twelve-verse poem in Sanskrit from Śrīla Raghunātha dāsa Goswami's *Stavāvalī*. Sanskrit text edited and published by Ṭhākura Bhaktivinoda.

1895 *Manaḥ-santoṣaṇī*, a Bengali verse translation of a Sanskrit work called *Śrī Krishna Caitanyodayāvalī* by Pradyumna Miśra, a close relative of Śrī Caitanya Mahāprabhu. The author of this translation, Śrī Jagajjīvan Miśra, is the eighth descendant of Pradyumna Miśra, the older brother of Śrī Caitanya's father Jagannātha Miśra. Bengali text edited and published by Ṭhākura Bhaktivinoda.

1895 *Mukunda-mālā Stotram*, a devotional Sanskrit work from South India by one of the twelve Alvars, King Kulaśekhara, edited and published by Ṭhākura Bhaktivinoda.

1895 *Śrī Lakṣmī-carita*, a short work in Bengali verse by Śrī Mālādhara Vasu (Guṇarāja Khān), the renowned author of *Śrī Krishna-vijaya* (the first Bengali book). Original text edited and published by Ṭhākura Bhaktivinoda.

1895 *Bāla-Krishna-sahasra-nāma*, *Gopāla-sahasra-nāma*, *Kṛṣṇāṣṭottara-śata-nāma*, *Rādhikā-sahasra-nāma*, four different *nāma-stotras* excerpted from the *Nārada-pañcarātra*. Edited and published by Ṭhākura Bhaktivinoda with the Sanskrit text only.

1895 *Śrīman-Mahāprabhor-aṣṭa-kālīya-līlā-smaraṇa-maṅgala-stotram*, an 11-verse Sanskrit poem on the pastimes of Śrī Caitanya by an unknown Vaiṣṇava author, edited and published by Ṭhākura Bhaktivinoda.

1896 *Śrī Gaurāṅga-līlā-smaraṇa-maṅgala-stotram,* 104 original Sanskrit verses giving a condensed description of all the most important pastimes and teachings of Śrī Caitanya Mahāprabhu that are found in *Śrī Caitanya-bhāgavata* and *Śrī Caitanya-caritāmṛta.* Bhaktivinoda included in the beginning of the book, a famous 47-page introduction in English prose entitled, *Śrī Caitanya Mahāprabhu: His Life and Precepts.* This introduction summarizes the contents of the book's Sanskrit verses. Accompanying the Sanskrit verses is a Sanskrit commentary entitled *Vikāśinī Ṭīkā*) by the renowned Paṇḍita of Navadvīpa, Mahā-mahopādhyāya Śitikaṇṭha Vācaspati.

1896 *Śrī Rāmānuja-upadeśa,* Sanskrit verses explaining the philosophy of Rāmānujācārya, with Ṭhākura Bhaktivinoda's own Bengali translation.

1896 *Artha-pañcaka,* Ṭhākura Bhaktivinoda's explanatory notes in Bengali on Śrī Pillai Lokācārya's famous book of the same name, in which five principal points of Rāmānuja's philosophy are explained at length.

1896 *Sva-likhita Jīvanī,* this book is a 200-page Bengali prose letter which Bhaktivinoda wrote to his son, Lalita Prasāda Datta, in response to a request for details of his father's personal life.

1897 *Brahma-saṁhitā,* this book was edited and published by Ṭhākura Bhaktivinoda with the original Sanskrit verses, Śrīla Jīva Goswāmī's Sanskrit commentary, and Bhaktivinoda's own Bengali introduction, Bengali prose translations and Bengali commentary called *Prakaśini.*

1898 *Śrī Krishna Karṇāmṛta,* a famous Sanskrit book of ecstatic prayers and revelations of Krishna conscious moods and pastimes written by Śrī Bilvamaṅgala Ṭhākura (Līlāśuka). Published and edited by Bhaktivinoda with the original Sanskrit verses, the Sanskrit commentary by Caitanya dāsa Goswāmī (the older brother of Kavi Karṇapur) called *Bāla-bodhinī Ṭīkā,* and Bhaktivinoda's own introduction, final summary and Bengali prose translations of the verses.

1898 *Pīyūṣa-varṣiṇī-vṛtti,* Bengali commentary on Śrīla Rūpa Goswāmī's *Upadeśāmṛta*

1898 *Śrīmad Bhagavad-Gītā,* this edition was published by Ṭhākura Bhaktivinoda with the Sanskrit commentary *Dvaita-bhāṣyam* (Explanation of Supreme Duality) by Śrīpāda Madhvācārya.

1898 *Śrī Goloka-māhātmyam,* part two of Sanātana Goswami's *Bṛhad-bhāgavatāmṛta,* edited and published by Ṭhākura Bhaktivinoda with the original Sanskrit text and his own Bengali translations of the verses.

1899 The Hindu Idols, a thirty-two page English letter written to the Tract Society of Calcutta.

1899 *Śrī Bhajanāmṛta,* a treatise on pure devotion to the Supreme Lord written in Sanskrit prose by Śrīla Narahari Sarakāra Ṭhākura, a contemporary and intimate associate of Śrī Caitanya Mahāprabhu. Edited and published by Ṭhākura Bhaktivinoda with his own Bengali translation.

1899 *Śrī Navadvīpa-bhāva-taraṅga*, 168 Bengali verses describing the different transcendental places in the 32-square mile area of Navadvīpa, as seen through the perfected devotional eyes of a God-realized soul. In this book Ṭhākura Bhaktivinoda does not see the land of Navadvīpa as a mundane historical place of this world but sees it as the *īśodyāna* or transcendental garden of the Supreme Lord.

1900 *Harināma-cintāmaṇi*, divided into 15 chapters and composed in Bengali verse form, this book is an account of Śrīla Haridāsa Ṭhākura's teachings on the holy name. It is actually a conversation between Lord Caitanya and Haridāsa—the Lord asks questions about the glories of the holy name, and Haridāsa gives extensive answers.

1901 *Śrīmad Bhāgavatārka-marīci-mālā*, in this book Ṭhākura Bhaktivinoda has taken a selection of the most important verses of *Śrīmad-Bhāgavatam* and arranged them in 20 chapters, called 'rays.' Each Sanskrit verse is accompanied by a Bengali prose translation and explanation by Bhaktivinoda. The Bhāgavatam is compared to the brilliant sun, and therefore each particular chapter or ray of *Bhāgavata* sunlight expounds upon three major divisions of *Bhāgavata* philosophy of *sambandha*, *abhidheya*, and *prayojana*.

1901 *Padma Purāṇa*, edited and published by Ṭhākura Bhaktivinoda with the complete 55,000-verse Sanskrit text only.

1901 *Saṅkalpa-kalpadruma*, a book of 104 Sanskrit verses on the divine pastimes of Śrī Śrī Rādhā-Krishna originally composed by Śrīla Viśvanātha Cakravartī Ṭhākura. Edited and published by Ṭhākura Bhaktivinoda with his own Bengali prose translations.

1902 *Bhajana-rahasya*, Compiled by Ṭhākura Bhaktivinoda as a supplement to his *Harināma-cintāmaṇi*. This *Bhajana-rahasya* is arranged in eight chapters, and the chanting of each chapter is to be observed during each three hour period of the twenty-four hour day. Each chapter corresponds to one verse of Śrī Caitanya's *Śikṣāṣṭaka*, and explains one of the eight levels of advancement in the gradual development of Krishna-*bhajana*, from primary *śraddhā* to ultimate *prema*, as is enunciated by Śrīla Rūpa Goswāmī in his *Bhakti-rasāmṛta-sindhu*. All the chapters are filled with scriptural citations in Sanskrit, uniquely explaining the philosophy of *Krishna-bhajana* and its practice. Each Sanskrit verse is accompanied by the Ṭhākura's own Bengali translation in verse.

1904 *Sat-kriyā-sāra-dīpika* with the appendix *Saṁskāra-dīpikā*, a small Sanskrit work by Śrīla Gopāla Bhaṭṭa Goswāmī, extracted from the *Hari-bhakti-vilāsa*, on the philosophy and ritualistic practice of Vedic *saṁskāra* ceremonies for Gauḍīya Vaiṣṇava householders. It also contains the ritualistic codes and institutes for Gauḍīya Vaiṣṇava mendicants. Edited and published by Ṭhākura Bhaktivinoda with his own Bengali prose translation.

1906 *Prema-vivarta*, a book by Jagadānanda Paṇḍit in Bengali verse on Śrī Caitanya's philosophy of divine love and the holy name. Edited and published by Ṭhākura Bhaktivinoda

1907 *Sva-niyama-dvādaśakam*, twelve verses of self-imposed vows. This is the last literary work of Bhaktivinoda Ṭhākura, composed shortly before he shut himself up in his beach-front cottage at Jagannātha Purī. Although the Sanskrit verses and Bengali prose translations were completed by Bhaktivinoda, he never finished a Bengali prose commentary on this last work.

The following works of Bhaktivinoda Ṭhākura do not have specific dates of publication:

Navadvīpa-śatakam, this is an ecstatic book composed by Śrī Prabodhānanda Sarasvatī, one of Lord Caitanya's direct disciples. Ṭhākura Bhaktivinoda translated this composition into simple Bengali verses for easy reading by devotees, and published it without the original Sanskrit verses as a small pocket-sized booklet.

Daśa-mūla-niryāsa, a Bengali prose essay which explains a single Sanskrit verse composed by Bhaktivinoda. This verse summarizes Lord Caitanya's philosophy as having ten root principles. Then in the essay the Ṭhākura elaborately explains the essence of the essence of each point.

Śrī Viṣṇu Priyā O Ānanda Bazār Patrikā, a monthly Vaiṣṇava journal in Bengali edited by Bhaktivinoda and published by his friend Shishir Kumara Ghosh.

Baladeva Vidyā-bhūṣaṇa-carita, written by Bhaktivinoda in Bengali prose, this is a well-researched biography of Śrīla Baladeva Vidyābhūṣaṇa.

Vedānta-sūtra, this classic Vedic philosophy book, written by Śrīla Vyāsadeva, was published by Bhaktivinoda's friend, Śrī Śyāmalāl Goswami, along with the *Govinda-bhāṣya* of Baladeva Vidyābhūṣaṇa, and the explanatory notes of Bhaktivinoda Ṭhākura.

Made in the USA
Coppell, TX
26 December 2021

70015488R00371